Global Issues

Global Issues

2008 EDITION

CQ PRESS

A Division of Congressional Quarterly Inc. Washington, D.C.

SELECTIONS FROM **CQ RESEARCHER**

CQ Press
2300 N Street, NW, Suite 800
Washington, DC 20037

Phone: 202-729-1900; toll-free, 1-866-4CQ-PRESS (1-866-427-7737)

Web: www.cqpress.com

Cover design: Kimberly Glyder

♾ The paper used in this publication exceeds the requirements of the American National Standard for Information Sciences—Permanence of Paper for Printed Library Materials, ANSI Z39.48-1992.

Printed and bound in the United States of America

11   10   09   08   07   1   2   3   4   5

A CQ Press College Division Publication

Director	Brenda Carter
Acquisitions editor	Charisse Kiino
Marketing manager	Christopher O'Brien
Production editor	Allyson Rudolph
Compositor	Olu Davis
Managing editor	Stephen Pazdan
Electronic production manager	Paul Pressau
Print and design manager	Margot Ziperman
Sales manager	Chris Campbell

ISBN: 978-0-87289-465-5
ISSN: 1559-8047

Contents

ENERGY AND THE ENVIRONMENT

DEMOCRATIZATION

Annotated Contents

T he sixteen *CQ Researcher* reports reprinted in this book have been reproduced essentially as they appeared when first published. In the few cases in which important new developments have since occurred, updates are provided in the following overviews highlighting the principal issues examined.

CONFLICT, SECURITY AND TERRORISM

Rethinking Foreign Policy

President George W. Bush has instituted several fundamental changes in U.S. foreign policy, notably opting for unilateral action instead of multilateral initiatives and espousing a doctrine of preventive or preemptive war to ward off potential threats. Many Americans applauded the fortified U.S. policies in the immediate aftermath of the September 11, 2001, terrorist attacks and in the early days of the war in Iraq. With the war now in its fifth year, however, a growing number of foreign-policy experts are saying the Bush doctrines have hurt rather than helped to advance U.S. interests around the world. They want the United States to rely more on allies and multilateral institutions, discard the preventive war doctrine and be more realistic in promoting democracy abroad. Administration supporters, however, hope the president's strategy in Iraq ultimately will bring about a military and political success that will help vindicate his policies.

Anti-Americanism

"We are all Americans," a banner headline in *Le Monde* declared after the terrorist attacks on September 11, 2001. But the warm embrace from France and the rest of the global community was short-lived. The U.S. invasion of Iraq has unleashed a torrent of anger at the United States. Often directed at President Bush and his policies, it takes aim at everything from the abuses at Abu Ghraib prison to the mounting death toll in Iraq to U.S. policies on climate change. Before the war, anti-Americanism had seemed the province of leftists who demonized capitalism, or those who resented the United States' unrelenting cultural influence — what some call the McGlobalization of the world. Now, resentment of the United States seems epidemic, especially in the Muslim world but also in Europe, Asia and Latin America. In European intellectual circles it has even become a badge of honor. Ironically, while anti-Americanism simmers, people seeking economic opportunity continue to emigrate to the United States.

Nuclear Proliferation

Since the United States dropped atomic bombs on Hiroshima and Nagasaki some 60 years ago, the threat of nuclear war has been a dominant and troubling factor in world politics. For more than half the 20th century, the United States and the Soviet Union faced each other with vast nuclear arsenals, but the end of the Cold War brought hope that nuclear weapons finally had become irrelevant. Instead, concern has grown as other nation-states have turned to nuclear weapons for their security in an increasingly dangerous world, including feuding Pakistan and India; meanwhile, Iran and North Korea threaten to build their own nuclear weapons. Perhaps the biggest emerging danger is not from nation-states at all but from suicidal terrorists carrying nuclear weapons in backpacks. New preventive technologies and tighter regulations provide hope. But many proliferation experts say it's a race against time.

World Peacekeeping

After the United Nations rose from the ashes of the Holocaust, the world's collective vow "Never again" seemed ironclad and irrevocable. As part of its effort to prevent future wars and genocides, the U.N. began to station peacekeepers around the globe, beginning in 1948 in Jerusalem. But the peacekeeping missions have had limited success. Now, prompted by the horror of the killings in Rwanda and Darfur, and before that in Bosnia, the world body has adopted a controversial new concept — the Responsibility to Protect — designed to stop future catastrophes. Known as R2P, it holds that the world community has a moral duty to halt genocide, even inside a sovereign country. But detractors call R2P legal imperialism, and even its defenders admit that the rhetoric has not yet translated into meaningful aid for Darfur. Meanwhile, other international alliances, including NATO and the European and African unions, have stepped up to provide military muscle to keep the peace in other hotspots.

Radical Islam in Europe

The recent spate of foiled terrorist plots by Muslim extremists in Great Britain, Germany and Denmark is a grim reminder that radical Islam continues to pose a serious threat to public safety in Europe. Some experts warn that Europe could export its brand of terrorism to the United States, since many of Europe's 15 million Muslims carry European passports that give them easy access to this country. European capitals like London have provided a haven for radical terrorists to organize, some critics say, because countries like Britain have failed to integrate Muslims successfully into mainstream society. But other experts blame international terrorist networks, which recruit from a small minority of estranged European Muslims. Others argue that in fighting terrorism at home, countries like France have gone too far in curbing Muslims' civil liberties. Concerned that their secular Western values are under threat from conservative Muslims, some European countries are considering limiting immigration and requiring new citizens to adopt the national language and beliefs.

HUMAN RIGHTS

Torture Debate

Countries around the globe — including the United States — are using coercive interrogation techniques in the fight against terrorism that critics say amount to torture. Despite international laws banning the practice, authoritarian nations have long abused prisoners and dissidents, and a handful of democracies have used torture in recent decades against what they considered imminent threats. Republican presidential candidates say they would authorize torture to prevent impending terrorist attacks. U.S. soldiers in Iraq say they would torture suspects to save the lives of their comrades. Human rights advocates worry that the use of torture by the United States is legitimizing its use globally and destroying America's moral authority to speak out against regimes that abuse prisoners in far worse ways. U.S. officials credit "enhanced interrogation" methods with averting terrorist attacks. But many experts say information gained by torture is unreliable.

Ending Poverty in Africa

In 2005, President Bush and the other seven leaders of the world's leading industrial powers — the G-8 — agreed to double their global anti-poverty aid to $50 billion a year by 2010, with half the funding going to Africa. Some development experts say massive and well-targeted spending can wipe out the worst effects of poverty in Africa — the world's poorest continent — in just a few decades. Western governments and major philanthropic organizations have stepped up their pledges in recent years, but the governments have not always come through. Meanwhile, some wonder whether any amount of aid can wipe out poverty in Africa; among them are some Africans, who warn that corruption, rampant HIV/AIDS, drought, malaria, lack of infrastructure and civil conflict remain major obstacles to fighting poverty. Indeed, projections show that sub-Saharan Africa will remain far from meeting anti-poverty goals set by the U.N. by its target date of 2015.

ENERGY AND THE ENVIRONMENT

Energy Nationalism

A world thirsting for imported oil and gas is seeking new supplies in Central Asia and Africa, where many nations have nationalized their energy resources. In a dramatic reversal from 30 years ago, government-owned or controlled petroleum companies today control 77 percent of the world's 1.1 trillion barrels of oil reserves. While the emergence of these rising petrostates has helped diversify the world's energy sources, many are considered oil "hot spots" — vulnerable to disruption from international terrorists or domestic dissidents. In addition, many of the petrostates are blending politics and energy into a new energy nationalism, rewriting the rules of the world's energy markets and restricting international oil corporations' operations. Russia's confrontational energy policies alarm its neighbors, and critics say a booming China is combing the world for access to oil and gas resources without concern for suppliers' corruption or human rights violations. Many also worry that growing competition for dwindling oil supplies will lead to greater risks of international conflict.

Curbing Climate Change

The scientific consensus on global warming is sobering: It's real, it's happening now and carbon-dioxide emissions caused by the burning of fossil fuels are almost certainly responsible. Predicting what the exact effects will be on humanity and the planet's living resources is trickier, but a growing body of evidence suggests they will be profound. The international community generally, and the European Union in particular, take the threat very seriously, and most wealthy industrial nations have adopted mandatory limits on carbon emissions under the 2005 Kyoto Protocol. The United States — the world's largest carbon emitter — has refused to sign the protocol or adopt mandatory limits, and is seen by other nations as obstructing progress on the issue. Kyoto expires in 2012, and world governments are working on a successor agreement. Many experts say the effort will fail without active U.S. leadership and the participation of major developing-world polluters such as China and India, with potentially dire consequences.

Ecotourism

In the booming global travel business, ecotourism is among the fastest-growing segments. Costa Rica and Belize have built national identities around their celebrated environmental allure, while parts of the world once all but inaccessible — from Antarctica to the Galapagos Islands to Mount Everest — are now featured in travel guides, just like Manhattan, Rome and other less exotic destinations. Advocates see ecotourism as a powerful yet environmentally benign tool for sustainable economic development in even the poorest nations. But as the trend expands, critics see threats to the very flora and fauna tourists flock to visit. Moreover, traditional subsistence cultures may be obliterated by the ecotourism onslaught, replaced by service jobs that pay native peoples poverty wages. Meanwhile, tour promoters are using the increasingly popular "green" label to lure visitors to places unable to withstand large numbers of tourists.

DEMOCRATIZATION

Cuba's Future
Cuba is poised at the brink of change. After more than 45 years in power, Fidel Castro, now 80, has relinquished power to his brother Raúl. But with the old communist firebrand still making an occasional taped TV appearance and publishing political commentaries — and probably operating behind the scenes as well — the real post-Fidel era likely will have to await his death. The former Soviet ally has been a thorn in the sides of successive U.S. administrations, and during the 1962 Cuban missile crisis brought the world to the brink of atomic war. Now Washington worries whether Castro's death could provoke instability in Cuba, leading to a mass exodus toward Florida's nearby shores. Cuban-Americans, meanwhile, are debating what role to play if they are allowed free access to the island. And U.S. businesses are wondering if warmer relations with Cuba could finally end the long-running U.S. trade embargo — allowing unfettered access to 11 million Cuban consumers.

Afghanistan on the Brink
Three years ago, the Bush administration could still claim democracy was taking hold in Afghanistan and that the country was on the road to economic recovery. Today, Afghanistan is dangerously close to sliding back into lawlessness and chaos as more than 50,000 NATO and U.S.-led coalition troops battle an insurgent Taliban movement and a still-robust al Qaeda. A recent spike in civilian deaths, caused by terrorist suicide bombers and stepped-up air attacks by NATO and allied forces, also threatens to turn a war-weary population against the Western troops and the shaky, new Afghan government. President Hamid Karzai's authority barely extends beyond Kabul, and the country's only successful economic sector is its burgeoning drug trade. Afghan

women have seen their newfound rights shrink as Islamic fundamentalism elbows its way back into the courts and social system. Meanwhile, neighboring Pakistan has been unable or unwilling to prevent the Taliban and al Qaeda from using its mountainous border areas as a safe haven. Some Afghans and international experts believe recovery is still possible — but they say time is of the essence.

INTERNATIONAL POLITICAL ECONOMY

The New Europe
After the fall of the Berlin Wall, the former Eastern bloc began emerging from its communist past, with 10 Central and Eastern European countries joining the European Union (EU) since 2004. The EU-10, as they are called, have embraced a bold new course in foreign policy, focusing solidly on the West with their allegiances resolutely bound up with the EU and NATO. Democracy has gained a foothold in the so-called New Europe, and the region's enthusiastic adoption of free-market policies has spurred faster growth. But it has had its dark side too: large-scale westward emigration has robbed their economies of many of their best and brightest and strained relations with their new European partners. In addition, former Soviet satellites in the region also harbor growing apprehension about estranged "Big Brother" Russia's intentions under its increasingly authoritarian president Vladimir Putin.

India Rising
India's stars appear to have aligned. Four consecutive years of impressive growth have silenced doubts about the sustainability of India's economic boom, and its rising international stature is reflected in a recent historic deal with the United States, giving India access to nuclear power technology without having to relinquish its nuclear weapons. Experts say if India stays on its current path it could be a global power by mid-century. Yet India remains exceedingly poor. Per capita income is less than half of China's, and a quarter of the more than 1 billion Indians live below the poverty line. Government pledges to extend the benefits of growth to all are hampered by corruption and red tape. So, while the world's second-most-populous country and largest democracy is headed in the right direction, it still has a long way to go.

Emerging China

In just two decades, low-paid Chinese workers and a modernization-obsessed leadership have transformed China into one of the world's biggest economies. China produces two-thirds of the world's copiers, microwave ovens and DVD players, plus vast amounts of its clothing, shoes and toys. China's 10 percent growth rate over the past 30 years is the fastest economic acceleration in world history. Average incomes have quadrupled, and 400 million people were lifted out of extreme poverty. China's $2.7 trillion economic output — already the world's 4th largest — is expected to triple in 15 years, overtaking the United States by 2039. Critics say the communist nation owes much of its success to unfair trade practices and abysmal labor conditions for Chinese workers. In any case, China's leaders are intent on maintaining growth. High unemployment, continuing widespread poverty and growing social unrest create unstoppable demand for the economy to keep expanding.

Fair Trade Labeling

The number of products sold with fair trade labels is growing rapidly in Europe and the United States. Big chains like Wal-Mart, Dunkin' Donuts, Starbucks and McDonald's have begun offering fair trade coffee and other items. Fair trade brands hope to raise their profile by targeting consumers who care about the environment, health and fair-labor standards. Fair trade supporters say small farmers in the developing world benefit by receiving a guaranteed fair price, while the environment gets a break from intensive industrial farming. But critics say consumers pay too much and that fair trade's guarantee of a good return — no matter what the market price — sends the wrong economic signal to farmers. When the price of a global commodity like coffee tumbles in response to oversupply, overcompensated fair trade farmers will remain in an uneconomic sector long after they should have switched to some other crop or livelihood, free-market economists argue.

Preface

In this pivotal era of international policymaking, scholars, students, practitioners and journalists seek answers to such critical questions as "Did the United States desert Afghanistan for Iraq?" "Is the Nuclear Non-Proliferation Treaty obsolete?" and "Will reducing greenhouse gases harm the global economy?" Students must first understand the facts and contexts of these and other global issues if they are to analyze and articulate well-reasoned positions on them.

The 2008 edition of *Global Issues* provides comprehensive and unbiased coverage of today's most pressing global problems. This edition is a compilation of sixteen recent reports from *CQ Researcher,* a weekly policy brief that unpacks difficult concepts and provides balanced coverage of competing perspectives. Each article analyzes past, present and possible future political maneuvering, is designed to promote in-depth discussion and further research and helps readers formulate their own positions on crucial international issues.

This collection is organized into five subject areas that span a range of important international policy concerns: conflict, security and terrorism; human rights; energy and the environment; democratization; and international political economy. Thirteen of these reports are new to this edition; three others — "Rethinking Foreign Policy," "Ending Poverty in Africa" and "Emerging China" — have been updated to incorporate new material.

Global Issues is a valuable supplement for courses on world affairs in political science, geography, economics and sociology. Citizens, journalists and business and government leaders also turn to it to become better informed on key issues, actors and policy positions.

CQ RESEARCHER

CQ Researcher was founded in 1923 as *Editorial Research Reports* and was sold primarily to newspapers as a research tool. The magazine was renamed and redesigned in 1991 as *CQ Researcher*. Today, students are its primary audience. While still used by hundreds of journalists and newspapers, many of which reprint portions of the reports, *Researcher*'s main subscribers are now high school, college and public libraries. In 2002, *Researcher* won the American Bar Association's coveted Silver Gavel Award for magazine excellence for a series of nine reports on civil liberties and other legal issues.

Researcher staff writers — all highly experienced journalists — sometimes compare the experience of writing a *Researcher* report to drafting a college term paper. Indeed, there are many similarities. Each report is as long as many term papers — about 11,000 words — and is written by one person without any significant outside help. One of the key differences is that the writers interview leading experts, scholars and government officials for each issue.

Like students, staff writers begin the creative process by choosing a topic. Working with *Researcher*'s editors, the writer identifies a controversial subject that has important public policy implications. After a topic is selected, the writer embarks on one to two weeks of intense research. Newspaper and magazine articles are clipped or downloaded, books are ordered and information is gathered from a wide variety of sources, including interest groups, universities and the government. Once the writers are well informed, they develop a detailed outline and begin the interview process. Each report requires a minimum of ten to fifteen interviews with academics, officials, lobbyists and people working in the field. Only after all interviews are completed does the writing begin.

CHAPTER FORMAT

Each issue of *CQ Researcher*, and therefore each selection in this book, is structured in the same way. A selection begins with a number of key issue questions, such as "Should the United States scale back efforts to export democracy to the Middle East and elsewhere?" and "Can India match China's economic growth?" This section is the core of each selection. The questions raised are often highly controversial and usually the object of much argument among scholars and practitioners. Hence, the answers provided are never conclusive, but rather expose readers to the range of opinion within the field.

Following those issue questions is the "Background" section, which provides a history of the issue being examined. This retrospective includes important legislative and executive actions and court decisions to inform readers on how current policy evolved.

Next, the "Current Situation" section examines important contemporary policy issues, legislation under consideration and action being taken. Each selection ends with an "Outlook" section that gives a sense of what new regulations, court rulings and possible policy initiatives might be put into place in the next five to ten years.

Each report contains features that augment the main text: sidebars that examine issues related to the topic, a pro/con debate by two outside experts, a chronology of key dates and events and an annotated bibliography that details the major sources used by the writer.

ACKNOWLEDGMENTS

We wish to thank many people for helping to make this collection a reality. Thomas J. Colin, managing editor of *CQ Researcher,* gave us his enthusiastic support and cooperation as we developed this edition. He and his talented staff of editors and writers have amassed a first-class collection of *Researcher* articles, and we are fortunate to have access to this rich cache. We also thankfully acknowledge the advice and feedback from current readers and are gratified by their satisfaction with the book.

Some readers may be learning about *CQ Researcher* for the first time. We expect that many readers will want regular access to this excellent weekly research tool. For subscription information or a no-obligation free trial of *Researcher,* please contact CQ Press at www.cqpress.com or toll-free at 1-866-4CQ-PRESS (1-866-427-7737).

We hope that you will be pleased with the 2008 edition of *Global Issues.* We welcome your feedback and suggestions for future editions. Please direct comments to Charisse Kiino, Chief Acquisitions Editor, College Division, CQ Press, 2300 N Street, NW, Suite 800, Washington, DC 20037; or send e-mail to *ckiino@cqpress.com.*

—The Editors of CQ Press

Contributors

Thomas J. Colin, managing editor of *CQ Researcher*, has been a magazine and newspaper journalist for more than 30 years. Before joining Congressional Quarterly in 1991, he was a reporter and editor at the *Miami Herald* and *National Geographic* and editor in chief of *Historic Preservation*. He holds a bachelor's degree in English from the College of William and Mary and in journalism from the University of Missouri.

Brian Beary, a freelance journalist based in Washington, D.C., specializes in EU-U.S. affairs and is the U.S. correspondent for *Europolitics,* the EU affairs daily newspaper. Originally from Dublin, Ireland, he worked in the European Parliament for Irish MEP Pat "The Cope" Gallagher in 2000 and at the EU Commission's "Eurobarometer" unit on public opinion analysis. A fluent French speaker, he appears regularly as a guest international relations expert on various television and radio programs. Apart from his work for Congressional Quarterly, Beary also writes for *European Parliament* magazine and the *Irish Examiner* daily newspaper.

Peter Behr recently retired from the *Washington Post,* where he was the principal reporter on energy issues and served as business editor from 1987 to 1992. A former Nieman Fellow at Harvard College, Behr worked at the Woodrow Wilson Center for Scholars and is working on a book about the history of the U.S. electric power grid.

Rachel S. Cox is a freelance writer in Washington, D.C. She has written for *Historic Preservation* magazine and other publications. She graduated in English from Harvard College.

Roland Flamini is a Washington-based correspondent who writes a foreign-affairs column for *CQ Weekly*. Fluent in six languages, he served as *Time* magazine's bureau chief in Rome, Bonn, Beirut, Jerusalem and the European Common Market and later served as international editor at United Press International.

Sarah Glazer specializes in health, education and social-policy issues. Her articles have appeared in the *New York Times,* the *Washington Post, Public Interest* and *Gender and Work,* a book of essays. Glazer covered energy legislation for the Environmental and Energy Study Conference and reported for United Press International. She holds a bachelor's degree in American history from the University of Chicago.

Alan Greenblatt is a staff writer for Congressional Quarterly's *Governing* magazine. He previously covered elections as well as military and agricultural policy for *CQ Weekly*. He was awarded the National Press Club's Sandy Hume Memorial Award for political reporting. He holds a bachelor's degree from San Francisco State University and a master's degree in English literature from the University of Virginia.

Kenneth Jost, associate editor of *CQ Researcher,* is the author of *The Supreme Court Yearbook* and editor of *The Supreme Court A to Z* (both from CQ Press). He was a member of the *CQ Researcher* team that won the 2002 American Bar Association Silver Gavel Award. He graduated from Harvard College and Georgetown University Law Center, where he is an adjunct professor.

Peter Katel is a veteran journalist who previously served as Latin America bureau chief for *Time* magazine, in Mexico City, and as a Miami-based correspondent for *Newsweek* and the *Miami Herald*'s *El Nuevo Herald*. He also worked as a reporter in New Mexico for 11 years and wrote for several nongovernmental organizations, including International Social Service and the World Bank. He has won several awards, including the Interamerican Press Association's Bartolomé Mitre Award. He is a graduate in university studies from the University of New Mexico.

Lee Michael Katz has been a senior diplomatic correspondent for *USA Today,* the International Editor of United Press International, and an independent policy journalist who has written lengthy articles on foreign policy, terrorism and national security. He has reported from more than 60 countries. He holds a master's degree from Columbia University and has traveled frequently with the U.S. secretary of state.

Samuel Loewenberg, now based in Berlin, is an award-winning freelance writer who has reported on global issues for the *New York Times,* the *Economist,* the *Washington Post* and *Newsweek,* among others. He covered the terrorist bombings in both Madrid and London as well as the anti-globalization movement in Brazil. He is a former Columbia University Knight-Bagehot Journalism Fellow.

Ken Moritsugu, based for two years in New Delhi as special correspondent for McClatchy Newspapers, is the new Asia-Pacific enterprise editor for the Associated Press in Bangkok. Until August 2004, he was the national economics correspondent for McClatchy's Washington Bureau. He previously was a staff reporter at the *St. Petersburg Times, The Japan Times* in Tokyo and *Newsday,* where he was part of a reporting team that won a Pulitzer Prize in 1996 for coverage of the crash of TWA Flight 800.

Seth Stern is a legal-affairs reporter at *CQ Weekly*. He has worked as a journalist since graduating from Harvard Law School in 2001, including as a reporter for *The Christian Science Monitor* in Boston. He received his undergraduate degree at Cornell University's School of Industrial and Labor Relations and a master's degree in public administration from Harvard's Kennedy School of Government. He is coauthoring a biography of Supreme Court Justice William J. Brennan Jr.

Colin Woodard is a journalist who writes for *The Christian Science Monitor* and the *Chronicle of Higher Education,* has reported from more than 40 foreign countries and six continents, and has lived for more than four years in Eastern Europe. He is the author of *Ocean's End: Travels through Endangered Seas,* a narrative nonfiction account of the deterioration of the world's oceans.

1

Rethinking Foreign Policy

Kenneth Jost and Alan Greenblatt

A soldier's boots and a flag-draped coffin dramatize the anti-war message at a rally and march on the National Mall on Jan. 27, 2007. Thousands of demonstrators in Washington and other cities urged Congress to end the Iraq war, which has claimed more than 3,000 U.S. troops and tens of thousands of Iraqi civilians.

update
4/24/09: 4,800 dead
730,000 wounded

From *CQ Researcher*,
February 2, 2007 (updated October 2007).

With U.S. casualties rising in Iraq and public approval of his policies falling at home, President Bush got a small bit of hopeful foreign policy news in January 2007 from an unexpected source. Iran's stridently anti-American president, Mahmoud Ahmadinejad, appeared to be losing the confidence of the country's supreme leader, Ayatollah Ali Khamenei, for courting confrontation with the United States over its nuclear weapons program. The semi-authoritative daily *Jomhouri-Eslami* — owned by Khamenei — pointedly admonished Ahmadinejad to leave nuclear matters to Khamenei and tweaked him for minimizing the U.N. Security Council's decision in December to impose trade sanctions against Iran for continuing its uranium-enrichment program. "The resolution is certainly harmful for the country," the newspaper said. [1]

Far from treating the signs of dissent in Tehran as encouraging, however, the State Department's spokesman on January 19 blandly repeated the United States' willingness to negotiate with Iran on the nuclear issue. Meanwhile, President Bush was stepping up pressure on Iran by dispatching additional ships off Iran's coast and lashing out at Iran in his State of the Union speech for supporting Shiite death squads in Iraq. Rumors that the Bush administration had decided to bomb Iran's nuclear facilities circulated throughout the rest of 2007.

The tough talk on Iran has pleased administration supporters. "It seems to me the U.S. will be taking a tougher line with Iran, one way or another," Lawrence Kudlow, the conservative CNBC talk show host, wrote on his blog "MoneyPolitic$." [2] On Capitol Hill, however, Democrats were openly critical and even some Republicans voiced concern. "This whole concept of moving against Iran is

Disapproval of U.S. Policies Is Widespread

Two-thirds of the more than 26,000 people surveyed in 25 countries — including the United States — think the U.S. presence in the Middle East provokes more violence than it prevents (top graph). Nearly three-quarters disapprove of U.S. policies toward Iraq (bottom).

What is your opinion on:

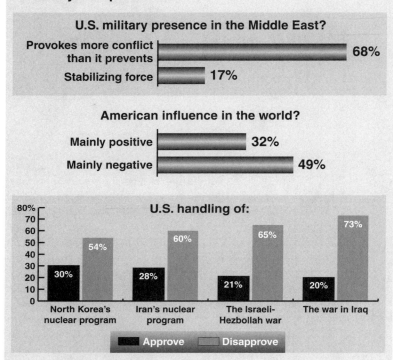

U.S. military presence in the Middle East?

Provokes more conflict than it prevents **68%**
Stabilizing force **17%**

American influence in the world?

Mainly positive **32%**
Mainly negative **49%**

U.S. handling of:

	North Korea's nuclear program	Iran's nuclear program	The Israeli-Hezbollah war	The war in Iraq
Approve	30%	28%	21%	20%
Disapprove	54%	60%	65%	73%

Source: The poll was conducted for BBC World Service by the international polling firm GlobeScan; 26,381 people in Asia, Africa, Europe, South America, the Middle East and the United States were interviewed between Nov. 3, 2006, and Jan. 9, 2007

bizarre," Senate Intelligence Committee Chairman Jay Rockefeller, D-W.Va., remarked. [3]

The emerging debate over Iran — and the full-blown debate over Iraq — are part of an even broader debate going on in foreign-policy circles over the past year. A growing number of experts representing diverse political and ideological backgrounds are saying U.S. foreign policy has gone fundamentally wrong under Bush and that a thoroughgoing change in approach is needed to regain support for U.S. foreign policy both at home and abroad.

Iraq necessarily forms part of the critique. "The focus on Iraq has diverted attention from a wide variety of domestic and global problems that have grown worse in the absence of U.S. attention and leadership," says Steven Hook, an associate professor at Ohio's Kent State University and lead author of a survey of U.S. foreign policy since World War II. [4] More broadly, critics charge Bush with repeatedly displaying an arrogant and unrealistic belief in U.S. power and a disdain for multilateral institutions and international traditions. They cite as examples Bush's rejection of some international treaties negotiated during the 1990s, his endorsement of "preventive war" as a national security strategy, and his self-proclaimed policy to export democracy to countries in the Middle East and elsewhere.

The result, these critics say, is a backlash of anti-Americanism around the world, even in countries closely allied with the United States. "U.S. policy in recent years has simply become too ambitious," says Anatol Lieven, a senior research fellow at the New America Foundation, a self-styled "radical centrist" think tank. "It's tried to do too much in too many directions simultaneously, and it's led to a very dangerous degree of over-stretching." A self-described progressive, Lieven joined with conservative foreign-policy expert John Hulsman to advocate what they call "ethical realism." As they wrote in a book-length manifesto in 2006, ethical realism avoids the pitfalls of either "hard-line realism" or "utopian morality" by recognizing the limits of U.S. power while supporting the moral purpose of U.S. foreign policy to spread freedom and democracy. [5]

Lieven and Hulsman, now a fellow at the German Council on Foreign Relations in Berlin, criticize in particular the so-called neoconservative school of foreign policy, which advocates the assertive use of American power — including military might — to promote peace, democracy, and economic freedom. "The neoconservatives are impatient with history," says Hulsman, formerly of the Heritage Foundation. "The idea that we can rush that along is arrogant and wrong."

A similar criticism of Bush-administration policy appears in the final report of a mammoth review of U.S. foreign policy completed in September 2006 under the auspices of Princeton University's prestigious Woodrow Wilson School of Public and International Affairs. U.S. efforts to "unilaterally transform the domestic politics of other states" have increased anti-Americanism abroad, discouraged cooperation with U.S. policies, and weakened the United States' global authority, write Professor John Ikenberry and Dean Anne-Marie Slaughter, co-directors of the review. [6]

Administration supporters and sympathetic observers reject the critique in its broad sweep and its particulars. "That's a cartoon version of either the president's policy or neo-conservatives," says Gary Schmitt, a senior fellow at the American Enterprise Institute (AEI) who served as executive director of the neoconservative Project for the New American Century from 1997 to 2005. "Neoconservatives aren't and the president isn't unaware of the difficulties" of implementing foreign-policy strategies. "The problem is not the American penchant for unilateralism," says Michael Mandelbaum, a professor at the Johns Hopkins School for Advanced and International Studies in Washington and author of the 2005 book *The Case for Goliath*. "It's the limited possibilities for multilateralism because other countries don't contribute anything. The problem is not that the Americans don't do too much, but other countries don't do enough."

Even though Bush has not abandoned any of his policies, some observers say they see signs of a shift — in tone and substance — in the president's second term in office. "The administration began to pull back and move

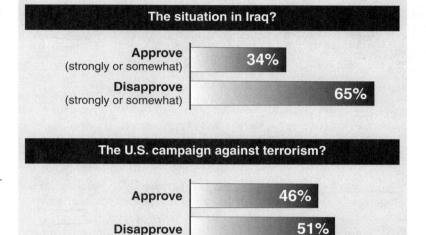

Most Americans Oppose Bush Iraq Policy

While 70 percent of Americans disapprove of the situation in Iraq, attitudes about the Bush administration's war on terrorism are more evenly divided.

Do you approve or disapprove of the way President Bush is handling:

The situation in Iraq?

Approve (strongly or somewhat) **34%**
Disapprove (strongly or somewhat) **65%**

The U.S. campaign against terrorism?

Approve **46%**
Disapprove **51%**

Source: This *Washington Post*-ABC News Poll was conducted by telephone on Sept. 4-7, 2007, among a random sample of 1,002 adults

toward a previous pattern with greater cooperation, a pullback from the use of force, and a pullback from 'regime change,' " says Jeffrey W. Legro, an associate professor at the University of Virginia and author of a 2007 book on international strategy. [7] "The White House has learned some bitter lessons about taking impulsive actions when it comes to military interventions and nation-building overseas," says Hook. "There is a more pragmatic sense now that the consequences of such interventions are profound, uncertain and of long-term duration."

As these debates continue, several questions are being considered:

Should the United States emphasize multilateral over unilateral initiatives in foreign policy?

President Bush entered office in 2001 with a marked shift away from the emphasis on multilateralism in U.S.

Secretary of State Condoleezza Rice meets with Egyptian President Hosni Mubarak in Cairo in October 2006. During a subsequent meeting in January 2007, Rice did not repeat past criticisms of Mubarak's regime, instead praising Egypt as part of the Middle East's "moderate mainstream."

foreign policy under his predecessors, Presidents Bill Clinton and George H. W. Bush, his father. Critics said the change was substantive as well, citing as examples Bush's early decisions to renounce the newly created International Criminal Court as well as the Kyoto Protocol on global climate change. [8] Bush followed a multilateral strategy in putting together the United Nations-authorized coalition to invade Afghanistan after the September 11, 2001, terrorist attacks. But two years later, he spurned the U.N. Security Council and two important European allies, Germany and France, with his decision to invade Iraq and oust Saddam Hussein.

With the Iraq war now nearing its fourth anniversary, a wide range of foreign-policy experts fault the administration for what they describe as a penchant for going it alone in world affairs. "This administration has lost the respect of the international community because it has failed to understand that American power is magnified and made more authoritative when it is exercised through institutions," says Princeton's Ikenberry. Up until the September 11 attacks, Bush was "the most isolationist president" since World War II, according to Charles Kupchan, a senior fellow at the Council on Foreign Relations and a professor of international relations at Georgetown University. Now, after having shifted to a more internationalist stance during the invasion of Afghanistan, Kupchan says, unilateralism appears to be

reemerging in administration rhetoric and policies. Administration supporters say the argument is overstated. "The notion that somehow the United States was going to act unilaterally in world affairs is a straw man," says James Carafano, a defense expert at the Heritage Foundation. "That was never the administration's strategy."

Instead, Carafano says, the Bush administration has tried to put together so-called coalitions of the willing — countries willing to join with the United States on a case-by-case basis. But he says the experience in Iraq shows the limitations of that approach and emphasizes instead the importance of more durable bilateral alliances. "It's ridiculous to call Iraq a unilateral action," Carafano explains. "We've got allies there." The important question, he continues, is "Who sticks with us?" — pointing as examples to Britain, Canada, and newer allies such as Poland. "The Poles want to have a long and enduring relationship with the United States, and they're stepping up to the plate." *[margin note: Update]*

Frederick W. Kagan, a military historian and resident scholar at AEI, says the critique essentially focuses on the administration's willingness to take action — as in Iraq — without U.N. approval. "The United States is not obliged to seek U.N. authorization before taking any action in the world at all," says Kagan. "We are not at the stage where any nation has ceded its sovereignty to that point."

For their part, "ethical realism" manifesto authors Lieven and Hulsman both emphasize the practical value of multilateral action in world affairs while acknowledging instances when the United States may have to act on its own. "There will be cases when America has to act alone, but the contrasting examples of Kosovo and Afghanistan on one hand and Iraq on the other show how infinitely preferable it is to act whenever you can with local allies," Lieven says. "You start at the multilateral level and — unlike the Bush administration — make good-faith efforts to get multilateral support," says Hulsman. "It's always good to start with that and see if you can get a good deal." Unilateral action is indicated, he says, only if the United States cannot get support from within or outside the affected region — "which will be, in practice, never."

Hulsman credits the administration with putting together an effective coalition in Afghanistan. And Lieven notes that the administration has pursued a multilateral approach in trying to get North Korea to renounce plans for a nuclear-weapons program.

[handwritten note: Update ▵ 1K]

Other experts also say the multilateralist critique of the administration has been overstated. "There's less difference than meets the eye" with the Clinton administration, according to Richard Betts, a professor and director of the Institute of War and Peace Studies at Columbia University in New York City. "It's more a distinction of style than of substance." But Ikenberry rejects those arguments. "They're deeply wrong," he says. "They don't appreciate the way in which America has signaled to the world that it does not respect institutions and rules that the rest of the world looks to as forms of governance."

However the past policies are characterized, a wide range of experts agree that the United States needs to pursue multilateral strategies more strenuously in the future. "It makes sense to have like-minded allies with us on board," says Karin von Hippel, co-director of the Post-Conflict Reconstruction Project at the Center for Strategic and International Studies in Washington. "When the United States works unilaterally, other countries see it as being arrogant." "There clearly needs to be more of a multilateral role as the limitations of U.S. power and leadership become apparent," says the University of Virginia's Legro.

Should the United States discard President Bush's doctrine of preventive war?

One year after the September 11 terrorist attacks, in September 2002, President Bush formally set out a new "national security strategy" that explicitly declared the United States' intention to act "preemptively" when necessary "to prevent or forestall hostile acts by our adversaries." With the rise of private terrorist groups, the White House document explained, the United States would sometimes need to take "anticipatory action to defend ourselves, even if uncertainty remains as to the time and place of the enemy's attack." [9] Bush depicted the idea of "preemptive action" as having a long historical pedigree. And the AEI's Schmitt likens the doctrine to President John F. Kennedy's decision to institute a naval blockade of Cuba during the 1962 missile crisis and President Clinton's plans (which ultimately were never acted on) in the early 1990s for a possible strike against North Korean nuclear sites. "It's something that one has to keep in one's toolbox of statecraft, but it's not something that one does easily or often," says Schmitt.

Most foreign-policy experts, however, read the document then — and still do today — as setting out a new

American soldiers patrol outside Kabul, Afghanistan, in December 2006. Following the Sept. 11, 2001, attacks, President George W. Bush rallied international support for a U.S.-led invasion of Afghanistan to root out al Qaeda and the Taliban. More recently, however, Secretary of State Rice found little support among U.S. allies for sending more troops back to Afghanistan to put down a Taliban insurgency.

"preventive war" doctrine that goes beyond an accepted doctrine of preemptive action against an imminent threat. And with that understanding a wide range of foreign-policy experts view the doctrine as ill-advised, contrary to international law, and — if followed by other countries — inimical to U.S. foreign-policy interests. "The United States has strayed from the international community only to find out that the real problems facing the United States, including global terrorism, cannot be solved in isolation and that the United States — even with all of its strength — cannot go it alone," says Kent State's Hook.

Johns Hopkins Professor Mandelbaum calls the administration's argument "serious" though "not compelling." "The logic is that since terrorists cannot be deterred, you have to strike them whenever you can," Mandelbaum explains. "Second, nuclear weapons change the calculus of international law in that the mere possession of nuclear weapons can be a great strategic setback." Therefore, if you wait for a rogue state to get nuclear weapons, it may be too late. "There's something to be said for that argument, but I don't think it has any chance of establishing itself," Mandelbaum continues. "Partly because it violates international law too sharply.

World Faces Many Cross-Border Challenges

Five years after the Sept. 11, 2001, terrorist attacks on the United States, the world "seems a more menacing place than ever," according to the Princeton Project on National Security. Here are some of the challenges confronting U.S. foreign policy:

- Americans and Iraqis are dying daily in an Iraqi conflict that some say is moving toward all-out civil war.

- Iran is seeking nuclear weapons, threatening to plunge the Middle East into chaos.

- Al Qaeda and its associated terrorist networks remain a potent threat while other terrorist sponsors, such as Hezbollah, are growing.

- Russia, riding high on rising oil prices, is seeking to reclaim its sphere of influence.

- North Korea is producing nuclear weapons and flexing its military muscle, as South Korea grows increasingly anti-American.

- Sino-Japanese relations are extremely tense; China is building relations with the rest of Asia and Africa in ways that exclude the United States.

- Populist Venezuelan President Hugo Chavez is fomenting a continent-wide anti-U.S. coalition in Latin America.

- Africa remains riven by conflict, poverty and disease.

- Global pandemics, such as avian flu, could threaten millions across continents.

- Climate change could trigger security consequences ranging from natural disasters to a fierce scramble for territory.

- U.S. budget deficits could undermine American global leadership and increase the risks of international financial crises.

Source: G. John Ikenberry and Anne-Marie Slaughter, "Forging a World of Liberty Under Law: U.S. National Security in the 21st Century," Princeton Project on National Security, September 2006

Lieven. "This notion that Iran or North Korea will suddenly fire a nuclear missile at Israel or the United States is absolutely crazy," because Iran and North Korea know they "would simply cease to exist the next day."

In their report, Princeton Professors Ikenberry and Slaughter call for updating the deterrence doctrine by announcing in advance that in the event of nuclear terrorism, the United States would hold the source of the nuclear weapons or material responsible. They also call preventive strikes "a necessary tool in fighting terror networks" but caution that any such actions should be "proportionate and based on intelligence that adheres to strict standards."

A preventive strike against a country should be "very rare," used "only as a last resort," and authorized by a multilateral institution like the United Nations Security Council or a broadly representative body such as NATO, Ikenberry and Slaughter argue. "If we can't convince even our most trusted allies that our course and policy is wise, then we are going to fail in the longer-term endeavor," Ikenberry explains.

Iraq casts a cloud over the preventive-war doctrine, but the Heritage Foundation's Carafano maintains that the conflict is being waged on a different ground: enforcement of the terms of the peace treaty that ended the first Gulf War in 1991. "We agreed to stop combat if Saddam Hussein agreed to do certain things," Carafano says. "He never did those things." Under those circumstances, he says, resuming combat operations is "traditional international law." Other foreign-policy experts view the administration's rationale differently. "The emphasis on preventive war in Iraq was a departure," says Betts at Columbia. "We've

Partly because the other potential cases — North Korea and Iran — don't lend themselves to it. And partly because Iraq has gone badly."

Hulsman and Lieven are firmer in rejecting the Bush doctrine. "Fighting wars of choice is antithetical to ethical realism," says Hulsman. "You might need those troops somewhere else." "In general, the international tradition [of deterrence] works well enough," says

done that before, but it was never in the mainstream of U.S. foreign policy."

Whatever the rationale for the war, experts across the ideological spectrum agree that the Iraq experience makes a future "preventive war" less likely but not out of the question. The doctrine "is down but not out," says Kupchan at the Council on Foreign Relations. "There will be much greater reluctance to implement that policy after Iraq." "It's probable that the outcome in Iraq will have a cushioning effect on U.S. action the way that failure in Vietnam did for a while," Betts says. But, he adds, "I don't think the outcome in Iraq will turn people off to the idea that we should use preventive action when warranted."

Should the United States scale back efforts to export democracy to the Middle East and elsewhere?

Since the eve of the Iraq war, President Bush has repeatedly advocated promoting democracy not only in Iraq but also throughout the Middle East. With Iraq's fledgling democracy beset by sectarian violence, however, U.S. policy appears to be deemphasizing the goal in the rest of the region. Secretary of State Condoleezza Rice visited Egypt in January 2007 without repeating her past criticisms of President Hosni Mubarak's autocratic regime. Instead, she praised Egypt as part of the "moderate mainstream" in the Middle East. [10] As Rice visited Egypt in fall 2007 in preparation for a Middle East peace conference the Bush administration was planning to host in November, she was criticized in some quarters for seeming to ignore Egypt's human rights violations. "I think the American government does give Egypt leeway to deal with the domestic opposition so long as Egypt supports the American foreign policy in the region," said Mustapha Kamel el-Sayyid, a political science professor at the American University in Cairo. [11] But at a news conference, Rice said that she had raised concerns with Egypt's leaders about the arrests of journalists and opposition leader Ayman Nour. [12]

Foreign-policy experts across the ideological spectrum agree the Bush administration's rhetoric raised unrealistic and unachievable expectations about exporting democracy to the Middle East and by analogy to the rest of the world. "History shows that promoting democracy is a long-term process and one that cannot be easily exported from one country to another," says Hook at Kent State. "Democracy can be imported, but it can't be exported," says Mandelbaum, who published a book

Going Nuclear?

North Korean leader Kim Jong Il has held six-power talks with the United States, China, Japan, Russia, and South Korea, leading to an October 2007 agreement to disclose and disable its nuclear weapons program in exchange for economic assistance.

about democratization in August 2007. "Democracy is more than just elections," he continues. "It's a whole set of institutions and practices. You can't just install them. It has to be homegrown over time." [13] "Exporting democracy is really the wrong term," says Carafano at the

Heritage Foundation. "There is no such thing as nation-building. Democracy really only takes root when it comes from below."

Advocates of democracy promotion cite the post-World War II reconstruction of Germany and Japan as evidence that U.S. assistance can be instrumental in fostering the establishment of stable democracies. Neoconservatives also point to the U.S. invasions of Grenada and Panama during the 1980s as successful efforts to install governments with democratic forms. In more recent history, however, Hulsman and Lieven cite less auspicious examples of trying to establish democratic governments as well as uncertain consequences of democratization in terms of support for U.S. policies. "Haiti, Somalia, Bosnia, Kosovo, Afghanistan, and now Iraq," Hulsman says, listing countries where the United States has intervened since the 1990s. "What have we done in these examples? I keep wondering how many more times we're going to invade Haiti in my lifetime." "Show me a success," echoes Lieven. He also points to recent examples in the Middle East — such as the Hamas victory in Palestinian elections in 2006 — to caution against expecting fledgling democracies to adopt pro-American policies. "In many countries, the early growth of democracy is intimately tied up with nationalism."

"There are times when you promote democracy, and it turns out to be problematic," the AEI's Schmitt concedes. "But on the whole the general trend is one of optimism and of strategic value." Liberal advocates of democracy promotion also view overall U.S. efforts positively. "There are many places around the world where U.S. support for democracy has been beneficial," says Thomas Carothers, director of the Democracy and Rule of Law Project at the Carnegie Endowment for International Peace. He lists Eastern Europe and South Africa among other examples. "Iraq has given democracy promotion a bad name in the United States and around the world," Carothers acknowledges. Within the United States, he notes, a poll by the German Marshall Fund found that a plurality of Americans — 48 percent to 45 percent — reject the goal of helping to establish democracy in other countries. [14] Meanwhile, the administration's expansive rhetoric has increased the perception around the world of hypocrisy in U.S. foreign policy, he adds. "Their deeds do not match their words."

Critics of the administration's policies question what they see as an after-the-fact adoption of democracy promotion as a goal of the Iraq war. "The war was in the first instance about security, about weapons of mass destruction, and about a belief that toppling Saddam Hussein could pacify the Middle East," says Kupchan of the Council on Foreign Relations. "It turned into a war for democracy once the original justifications for the war had evaporated."

Whatever the original goals, many experts say the Iraq experience makes similar U.S. adventures unlikely for the foreseeable future. "It sets back exporting democracy at the point of a gun, which is not a bad thing," says Columbia's Betts. "We're going to be a lot more careful of reforming nasty regimes by marching in and tossing them out."

Other experts, however, expect public support for democratization initiatives to return. "It may be that the United States reverts to a more evolutionary approach to democratization, which focuses on economic assistance and political support for civil society and domestic groups that would enable them to create their own solutions to problems," says Hook. "There's a robust consensus that encouraging the development of democracy is a very good thing," says the University of Virginia's Legro. "Using force to encourage democracy is where things fall apart."

BACKGROUND

America Ascendant

The United States began asserting itself on the world stage early in its history and moved toward global preeminence in the two world wars of the twentieth century. After World War II, the United States helped establish an array of multilateral and international institutions aimed at preventing future wars and promoting economic stability. It also adopted a policy of "containment" aimed at using diplomatic, economic, and military means short of war to counter the challenge of global communism from the Soviet Union and "Red China." The Vietnam War, the long and ultimately unsuccessful conflict in Southeast Asia, however, prompted a rethinking of U.S. goals and strategies abroad. [15]

President George Washington ended his presidency with a farewell address warning against foreign entanglements, but — as neoconservative foreign-affairs analyst Kagan argues in his book *Dangerous Nation* — the

United States was far from isolationist in the nineteenth century. The young republic invited the War of 1812 by confronting Great Britain over its blockade of U.S. shipping. A decade later, President James Monroe laid down his eponymous doctrine telling European powers to stay out of western hemispheric affairs. Kagan depicts westward expansion as a policy of conquest — sometimes peaceful, sometimes not — and the Spanish-American War as a humanitarian intervention of choice that turned the United States into an imperial power.

The United States fought in and won the two world wars in the twentieth century despite isolationist public opinion and pronouncements by leaders as both conflicts developed. President Woodrow Wilson campaigned in 1916 on keeping the United States out of the European conflict but asked Congress for a declaration of war barely six months later after German submarines continued to attack U.S. shipping. After the war, isolationist sentiment helped keep the United States out of the League of Nations and on the sidelines as war clouds formed again in Europe.

Like Wilson, President Franklin D. Roosevelt campaigned for reelection in 1940 on the strength of having kept the United States out of the European war. But he had already taken sides in 1939 by allowing Britain and France to buy arms from the United States and collaborating with Britain on the Lend-Lease program early in 1941. After the Japanese attack on Pearl Harbor on December 7, 1941 Roosevelt asked for a declaration of war and then led the country in an unprecedented military and economic mobilization. The war ended with Germany and Japan defeated, Europe and the Soviet Union ravaged, and the United States left standing as the strongest world power.

Before the war's end, the United States was already adopting a new, explicitly internationalist role in world affairs. It hosted the July 1944 conference at Bretton Woods, New Hampshire, that led to the creation of two largely U.S.-financed international lending institutions: the World Bank to help countries rebuild and the International Monetary Fund to help countries out of short-term currency crises. The United States again took the lead role in the international conference in San Francisco in 1945 that established the United Nations — with a charter giving the United States a permanent and powerful role in its enforcement arm, the Security Council.

Postwar hopes for international peace faded quickly with official and popular concern about an emerging conflict with the Soviet Union. George Kennan, then the U.S. ambassador to Moscow, presciently analyzed Soviet policies in a now-famous anonymously written memo in 1946 that called for the United States to counter the ideologically charged challenge with a policy of "long-term, patient, but firm and vigilant containment." [16] President Harry S Truman adopted that approach with such steps as aid to Greece and Turkey to defeat communist insurgencies, the Marshall Plan to rebuild Western Europe, and the Berlin airlift to counter the Soviets' blockade of the city's western sectors. Truman also led the United States into the Korean War, which his successor, Dwight D. Eisenhower, ended in 1953 with an uneasy cease-fire and a heavily fortified "demilitarized zone" between the communist North and the pro-Western South Korea.

Through the 1950s, the United States avoided direct military confrontations with either the Soviet Union or China, communist-ruled after the defeat of the U.S.-backed Nationalist government in 1949. In the 1960s, however, Presidents John F. Kennedy and Lyndon B. Johnson came to view the war between communist North Vietnam and the pro-Western South Vietnam as a critical test of the containment policy. The United States committed itself to South Vietnam's defense, but the U.S. troop buildup — eventually exceeding 500,000 soldiers — failed to repel a Vietcong invasion from the north. After four more years of war and with the pro-Western government still in power in Saigon, President Richard M. Nixon approved the 1973 treaty that ended the war with a cease-fire. Just two years later, however, a new invasion from the north toppled the Saigon government and unified Vietnam under a government communist in ideology and nationalist in sentiment.

America Conflicted

The United States conducted foreign policy from the 1970s on conflicted over the lessons to be drawn from the end of the Vietnam War. The "Vietnam War syndrome" introduced an explicit aversion to intervention abroad into many foreign policy debates but did not prevent Presidents Ronald Reagan or George H. W. Bush from sending U.S. troops into Grenada (1983), Panama (1989) and — most significantly — Kuwait (1991). In the 1990s President Clinton adopted "assertive multilateralism" as the watchword for U.S. foreign policy, but critics faulted the administration's actions in such trouble spots as Somalia, Rwanda, Haiti, and the former Yugoslavia as either ill-advised or ineffective or both.

CHRONOLOGY

Post-World War II *The Allies' victory is followed by Cold War with Soviet Union.*

1947-50 Truman administration lays foundation of "containment" policy to limit Soviet expansion with aid to Greece and Turkey, Marshall Plan to rebuild Europe and North Atlantic Treaty Organization (NATO) to guarantee security of Western Europe.

1950-53 Korean War ends with ceasefire, North and South Korea divided.

1961-73 U.S. support for South Vietnam against communist North Vietnam leads to major escalation after 1965; protracted war ends in 1973 with North and South divided.

1970s-1980s *End of Vietnam War brings recriminations at home, calls for retrenchment abroad.*

1975 Saigon falls to North Vietnam. . . . Helsinki Accords concede communist control of Eastern Europe in return for Soviets' recognition of human rights.

1978 President Jimmy Carter makes human rights a major objective of U.S. foreign policy.

1979-81 Iranian hostage crisis: U.S. Embassy personnel in Tehran held for 15 months, released as President Carter leaves White House.

1982 President Ronald Reagan labels Soviet Union "evil empire," vows to support democracy in communist countries.

1983 U.S. invasion of Grenada. . . . Bombing of Marine barracks in Lebanon kills 241 servicemen.

1989 President George H.W. Bush approves invasion of Panama to oust dictator Manuel Noriega.

1990s *Cold War ends; U.S. is sole superpower.*

1990-91 First Gulf War: First President Bush forges U.N.-sanctioned coalition to oust Iraq from Kuwait.

1993 President Bill Clinton withdraws U.S. troops from Somalia.

1995-96 U.S. helps broker Dayton Accords to end Bosnian war.

1998 U.S. embassies in Kenya, Tanzania bombed; attacks later linked to al Qaeda.

1999 Serbia halts war in Kosovo after NATO bombing campaign, approved by Clinton.

2000-Present *President George W. Bush declares "war on terror"; launches wars in Afghanistan, Iraq.*

2001 President Bush renounces International Criminal Court, Kyoto Protocol on climate change. . . . September 11 terrorist attacks leave nearly 3,000 Americans dead. . . . Bush declares "war on terror," launches U.S.-led invasion of Afghanistan with U.N. backing; Taliban ousted by November . . . pro-U.S. interim government installed in December.

2002 Bush labels Iran, Iraq, North Korea "axis of evil." . . . "National Security Strategy" says United States will act to "prevent or forestall" attacks by terrorists, other adversaries. . . . Congress grants Bush authority to use force in Iraq.

2003 Bush launches invasion of Iraq with U.S.-led coalition after failing to win U.N. backing. . . . Saddam Hussein ousted; United States occupies Iraq under "provisional authority."

2004-2005 United States transfers sovereignty to interim Iraqi government (June 2004) . . . Iraqi national elections (January 2005) . . . insurgency grows.

2006 Iran announces it has enriched small amount of uranium, adds to fears that it seeks nuclear weapons. . . . North Korea announces it has carried out first nuclear test. . . . Democrats regain control of Congress; growing opposition to war in Iraq seen as major factor. . . . Bipartisan commission calls for redeployment of U.S. troops in Iraq, diplomatic efforts to end conflict.

2007 Bush says he will send 21,500 more troops to Iraq to quell sectarian violence. . . . Democrats oppose plan, many Republicans voice doubts. . . . Congressional Democrats fail in repeated attempts to limit U.S. deployment in Iraq. . . . Bush raises the specter of World War III in discussing Iran's nuclear ambitions. . . . White House hosts a Middle East peace conference in Annapolis, Maryland.

In his brief presidency, Gerald R. Ford made a signal contribution to U.S. foreign policy by helping negotiate the Helsinki Accords, the 1975 pact that effectively accepted communist domination of Eastern Europe in return for the Soviet Union's agreement to recognize human rights in the region. President Jimmy Carter went further in stressing human rights as a keystone of U.S. foreign policy and helped negotiate an historic peace treaty between Egypt and Israel that represented the first recognition of the Jewish state by an Arab nation. But Carter's foreign policy accomplishments were lastingly overshadowed by the seizure of fifty-two U.S. embassy workers by Iranian militants in November 1979, a humiliating crisis that ended with their release on the day Carter left office in January 1981. After seeking to defuse Cold War tensions, Carter also ended his presidency with a more bellicose atmosphere after the Soviet invasion of Afghanistan in 1980.

Reagan came to office as an outspoken anti-communist and an unapologetic former hawk on the Vietnam War. He quickly moved to increase U.S. military spending and sharpen rhetorical attacks on the Soviet Union. On the pretext of protecting U.S. citizens, Reagan sent U.S. troops to oust a Marxist regime in the tiny Caribbean island of Grenada. He also defied congressional opposition to help fund the anti-communist rebels — known as contras — who were fighting the leftist government in Nicaragua. Reagan told a succession of Soviet leaders that the Vietnam War syndrome was a thing of the past. When a suicide bomber attacked the U.S. Marine barracks in Beirut in 1983, killing 283 servicemembers, however, U.S. peace-keeping troops were withdrawn from Lebanon, and military intervention abroad was denounced except when America's "vital interests" were at stake.

As Reagan maintained rhetorical pressure on the Soviet Union, the communist government was itself collapsing. Reagan's admirers say the U.S. defense buildup forced the Soviet Union into an unaffordable arms race that contributed to economic stagnation and the country's eventual dissolution. In posthumously published interviews, Ford was quoted as saying the recognition of human rights in the Helsinki Accords played a more important role. [17] Still others say reforms like the economic and political restructuring instituted by Mikhail S. Gorbachev beginning in the mid-1980s would have been adopted eventually without regard to U.S. policy. Whatever the causes, the combination of economic woes and pro-democracy protests in the satellite countries by 1991 brought down the communist empire and reduced the Soviet Union to the present-day Russian Federation.

In December 1989, during his first year in office, the first President Bush sent U.S. troops to Panama to assist a military coup in ousting President Manuel Noriega, who was facing indictment in the United States for drug trafficking. A year later, Bush responded to Saddam Hussein's August 1990 invasion of Kuwait by working in the United Nations to form a U.S.-led coalition to oust the Iraqi invaders. After a month-long bombing campaign, coalition ground forces moved in on February 24, 1991, and succeeded within 100 hours in liberating Kuwait with only 149 allied servicemembers killed. Bush made the controversial decision not to pursue the retreating enemy soldiers further into Iraq or try to remove Hussein from power.

Clinton inherited an Iraq policy that included U.S. and British enforcement of "no-fly zones" preventing Hussein's government from conducting air attacks on Kurdish areas in the north or on the predominantly Shiite southern region. Despite the United States' enhanced primacy in the post-Cold War era, Clinton also faced an array of vexing foreign policy challenges in trouble spots where U.S. interests were less than evidently vital and U.S. public opinion less than engaged. [18] Public reaction to the sight of a slain U.S. soldier being dragged through the streets of Mogadishu in 1993 led Clinton to pull U.S. troops out of a U.N. nation-building effort in Somalia. With public support lacking, Clinton stayed out of the humanitarian intervention during the Rwanda genocide. And he wavered on U.S. military intervention in the former Yugoslavia in the face of European and domestic inertia even though he had called for the United States to intervene during his 1992 campaign.

Meanwhile, al Qaeda had formed as a multinational, anti-American terrorist organization and carried out attacks on U.S. embassies in Kenya and Tanzania in 1998 and the U.S.S. *Cole* in October 2000. Clinton approved a missile strike aimed at bin Laden in 1999, but it was called off. He left office with plans written — but not acted upon — to retaliate for the *Cole* attack, which killed seventeen U.S. sailors and wounded thirty-nine others. [19]

America Challenged

The second President Bush entered the White House in January 2001 after having criticized Clinton's emphasis on multilateralism, humanitarian intervention, and

Is the Neoconservative Movement Dead?

That's not the point, say Robert and Frederick Kagan

Critics of the neoconservative movement are declaring it dead — a friendly-fire casualty of the Bush administration's failures in Iraq and elsewhere. But two of the people most closely identified with the movement say its views have been misrepresented and its influence on Bush's policies overstated. "I've always found it odd that people talk about a neoconservative vision of anything," says Frederick Kagan, a military historian and research fellow at the conservative American Enterprise Institute (AEI). "There is no cohesive neoconservative movement that gets together with regular congresses and decides what's the neoconservative line." Like his younger brother, author and think-tank fellow Robert Kagan says he does not even call himself a neoconservative. And he scoffs at what he calls "the absurd conspiracy theory" that a small group of "neocons" outside the government effectively hijacked U.S. foreign policy under Bush.

The picture of a well-organized movement dating from the 1960s and unified around a vision of a muscular U.S. foreign policy pursuing peace, democracy, and free markets may be overdrawn, experts and journalists sometimes concede. "Neoconservatives do not make up an organized bloc — much less a 'cabal,' as is sometimes alleged," *Vanity Fair* contributing editor David Rose writes. [1] But the view of Bush's foreign policy as shaped by neoconservatives in and out of government is widespread.

G. John Ikenberry, a professor at Princeton University's Woodrow Wilson School of International Affairs, accuses the neoconservative movement of a "radical" reorientation of U.S. foreign policy after the September 11, 2001, terrorist attacks that he says "squandered" the United States'

moral authority in the world. In their ideology-spanning book *Ethical Realism*, Anatol Lieven and John Hulsman credit neoconservatives with "tremendous success" in making democracy-promotion a central element of U.S. strategy in the Muslim world — but they call the policy a failure in Iraq and Mideast politics in general. [2]

As Robert Kagan explains, the original neoconservatives — literally, "new" conservatives — were one-time liberals and left-wingers who held on to hawkish anti-communist views during and immediately after the Vietnam War. Decades later, he says, the term has lost its original meaning. "I've never been on the left, and I don't consider myself a conservative," he says in a telephone interview from Brussels, where he writes a monthly column for the *Washington Post.* In Robert Kagan's view, the post-Cold War neoconservatives are successors to a continuous tradition — detailed in his history of nineteenth-century U.S. foreign policy — of seeking global influence in pursuit of liberal goals. "Neoconservatives did not come along and change American tradition," he says. [3]

In a "statement of principles" in 1997, the neoconservative Project for a New American Century (PNAC) argued that the United States should increase defense spending, "challenge regimes hostile to our values," and accept "America's unique role in preserving and extending an international order friendly to our security, our prosperity, and our principles." Signers included such future Bush administration officials as Vice President Dick Cheney, Defense Secretary Donald Rumsfeld and Undersecretary of Defense Paul Wolfowitz. [4] "We did a pretty good job of putting that strategic vision on the table," says Gary Schmitt, who served as executive director of PNAC from

Neoconservatives reflect a long American tradition, say Robert (left) and Frederick Kagan.

Carnegie Endowment (R. Kagan); American Enterprise Institute (F. Kagan)

1997 to 2005. Schmitt is now a fellow with AEI; PNAC — housed in the same building — is somewhat dormant.

Robert Kagan says neoconservatives supported President Bill Clinton's military interventions in Haiti, Somalia, Bosnia, and Kosovo against foreign-policy "realists" and Republican lawmakers who saw no vital U.S. interests at stake. "At the time we had more in tune with Clinton than with Republicans and conservatives," he says. Today, neoconservatives such as the Kagans and PNAC Founding Chairman William Kristol, editor of the *Weekly Standard*, are among the lonely voices supporting Bush's plan to send additional troops to Iraq. Many others are bailing out, however — as Rose devastatingly detailed in his *Vanity Fair* cover story in January. "The biggest industry" in Washington, Robert Kagan says, are people trying to explain away their previous support for the Iraq war.

Ikenberry, writing with the Iraq war still in its first year, saw the invasion as the neoconservatives' "crowning achievement" until it "turned into a costly misadventure." The policies, he wrote, were "unsustainable" at home and unacceptable abroad.

Neoconservatives' policy fails in Iraq and the Mideast, say Anatol Lieven and John Hulsman (right).

(c) Claudio Vazquez

Today he sees only further vindication: "The failure of the Bush administration is a ratification of the intellectual bankruptcy of the neoconservatives." Lieven, a self-described progressive, and the conservative Hulsman give neoconservatives credit for seeking to balance realism and morality and recognizing the role of "failed states" in fomenting Islamist extremism and anti-U.S. terrorism. But they say neoconservatives are too willing for the United States to go it alone in world affairs. "The neoconservative idea that we can act alone becomes a self-fulfilling prophecy," Hulsman says. Kagan calls it "absurd" to equate neoconservatism with unilateralism. Neoconservativism, he says, "is all about having allies and having democratic allies."

The continuing influence of neoconservatives was felt in the Bush administration's deliberations over possibly bombing Iran to hamper its nuclear program. Despite the blows to neo-

conservative ideas dealt by the Iraq war, it's possible that they will continue to play a leading role in the next Republican administration as well. Former New York mayor Rudy Giuliani solicited foreign policy advice from several leading neoconservatives during his presidential campaign. [5] Other foreign-policy experts see the neoconservatives' influence waning. "The neoconservatives' heyday is past," says Steven Hook, an associate professor at Kent State University in Ohio. But Charles Kupchan, a senior fellow with the Council on Foreign Relations and professor at Georgetown University, says they cannot be ignored as long as Bush remains in office. "There is no question that what was a unified and quite coherent movement has suffered a loss of influence and internal fragmentation," Kupchan says. "But they're still out there. They're still influential. As long as Bush is president, the neoconservatives' view of the world will remain influential within the administration."

For his part, Kagan goes further and says neoconservative views will be influential in the next administration — even if a Democrat wins the White House. "When the next administration is in office, we're going to have the same debate," he says, "but people will change sides." "Whoever is in the White House tends to favor the use of power" abroad, Kagan continues. "You can't tell me that Hillary Clinton won't get into the White House and want to meddle" in world affairs.

[1] David Rose, "Neo Culpa," *Vanity Fair*, January 2007, 82.

[2] G. John Ikenberry, "The End of the Neo-Conservative Movement," *Survival*, vol. 46, no. 1 (Spring 2004), 7-22; Anatol Lieven and John Hulsman, *Ethical Realism: A Vision for America's Role in the World* (New York: Random House, 2006), xiv-xv.

[3] Robert Kagan, *Dangerous Nation: America's Place in the World From Its Earliest Days to the Dawn of the Twentieth Century* (New York: Knopf, 2006).

[4] Project for a New American Century (www.newamericancentury.org/statementofprinciples.htm).

[5] Michael Hirsh, "Rudy Giuliani: Would You Buy a Used Hawk From This Man?," *Newsweek*, October 15, 2007, 36.

AP Photo/Elizabeth Dalziel

A military museum in Beijing displays wax models representing the Chinese Navy, Army and Air Force along with a Chinese missile and satellite model. The destruction of a Chinese weather satellite by a Chinese missile on Jan. 12 prompted the United States to reiterate its opposition to any militarization of space.

claimed he had put U.S. foreign policy "on sound footing," in part by "strengthening our relationships with our allies." Poll results two weeks later, however, showed that at least 73 percent of those surveyed in four European countries — Britain, France, Germany, and Italy — believed Bush made decisions "entirely on U.S. interests" without considering Europeans' views. [20]

The September 11 attacks brought a wave of pro-American sentiment throughout much of the world, including in many Arab and predominantly Muslim countries. While pushing broad anti-terrorism legislation through Congress, Bush also rallied international support in the U.N. Security Council for a U.S.-led invasion of Afghanistan to root out al Qaeda and oust its Taliban hosts. A U.S. and British bombing campaign in October set the stage for ground troops and opposition Northern Alliance forces to topple the Taliban by mid-November. An international conference in Bonn laid the framework for an interim government to take over in December, headed by the pro-American Hamid Karzai. He continues to lead the country after having won a presidential election in December 2004. [21]

With Afghanistan seemingly under control, Bush broadened the "war on terror" in his State of the Union message in January 2002 by linking terrorist groups with what he called an "axis of evil" — Iran, Iraq, and North Korea — aimed at destroying the United States. In September, the administration formally unveiled Bush's new doctrine in the thirty-three-page "National Security Strategy of the United States." [22] After promising to seek international support, the document declared, "we will not hesitate to act alone, if necessary, to exercise our right of self-defense by acting preemptively against such terrorists."

Many foreign-policy experts were critical. Harvard Professor Graham Allison, a leading expert on national-security strategy, said the doctrine amounted to "a devaluation of deterrence and containment, as if those were 20th-century ideas that are now outmoded." [23]

Meanwhile, Bush and his national security team had been not so quietly laying plans for a possible invasion of Iraq. [24] With midterm elections less than a month away, Bush won approval from Congress for a resolution authorizing the use of force against Iraq — with or without approval from the United Nations. At the United States' urging, the U.N. Security Council on Dec. 23 declared Iraq in "material breach" of past U.N. resolutions requiring, among other things, dismantling of any weapons of mass

nation-building. Bush successfully went through United Nations channels in the 2001 war against Afghanistan but invaded Iraq in 2003 without U.N. sanction. Over the next three years, popular support for Bush's policies on terrorism and Iraq fell as clear successes proved elusive. Meanwhile, U.S.-led efforts failed to deter Iran and North Korea from nuclear weapons programs — advanced in North Korea's case, less so in Iran.

Early in his presidency, Bush concentrated on domestic issues while bucking world opinion by refusing to join the International Criminal Court, renouncing the Kyoto Protocol and threatening to withdraw from the 1972 antiballistic missile treaty. In early August 2001, he

U.S. National Strategy Landmarks

The United States' "national security strategy" evolved from the Cold War policies of "containment" and "nuclear deterrence" aimed against the former Soviet Union to President George W. Bush's "preventive war" doctrine designed to forestall possible attacks by terrorists or other "adversaries."

1947 *Truman Doctrine* *Aims to contain communism through economic, military aid to Greece, Turkey.*

NSC 4/A [National Security Council] *Launches peacetime covert actions to counter Soviets' "psychological warfare."*

1950 *NSC-68* — *Calls for military buildup, shift to active containment to counter Soviets.*

1953 *NSC 162/2* — *Establishes "New Look" national security policy envisioning "massive retaliation" and optional use of nuclear weapons.*

1961 *NSAM 2 [National Security Action Memorandum]* — *Authorizes counterinsurgency "for use in situations short of limited war."*

1963 *"Assured Destruction" DPM [Draft Presidential Memorandum]* — *Calls for capacity to inflict "assured destruction" of Soviet government, military controls, population centers in event of first strike against U.S. nuclear forces — giving up emphasis on blocking Soviet ability to strike the U.S.*

1969 *Nixon Doctrine* — *Looks to treaty partners to assume primary responsibility for providing manpower for defense against aggression.*

1978 *PD-30 [Presidential Directive]* — *Makes promotion of human rights a "major objective" of U.S. foreign policy.*

1980 *PD-59* — *Calls for flexible use of nuclear weapons in case of aggression against U.S. interests.*

1982 *Reagan Doctrine* — *Uses overt and covert aid to anti-communist resistance to roll back Soviet-backed governments in Third World.*

1992 *Draft Defense Planning Guidance* — *Broaches plan to prevent emergence of rival superpower; later revised.*

1994 *NSSUS, "Engagement and Enlargement" [National Security Strategy of the United States]* — *Promises "engagement" throughout the world, efforts to promote "democratic enlargement."*

2002 *NSSUS, "Preemption"* — *Declares intention to act "preemptively" against terrorist groups, other adversaries, when necessary to "prevent or forestall" attacks, even if time and place are uncertain.*

Adapted from Richard K. Betts, "U.S. National Security Strategy: Lenses and Landmarks," Princeton Project on National Security, November 2004

---

destruction. U.S. efforts to get a second Security Council resolution authorizing an invasion foundered in the face of a promised veto from France and reluctance from Russia and other council members. Thwarted at the U.N., Bush on March 20 went ahead and — with a coalition said to include forty-eight other countries — launched the invasion that overthrew Hussein's government by mid-April.

Over the next three years, the administration's swaggering reaction to the Iraq military campaign — exemplified in Bush's famous declaration on May 1, 2003 that major combat operations were over — proved to be premature at best. Meanwhile, U.S. efforts to deter Iran and

North Korea from their apparent pursuit of nuclear weapons were proving unavailing. Iran announced in April 2006 that it had enriched a small amount of uranium — a critical step toward nuclear weapons. North Korea conducted a nuclear test in October 2006. The administration enlisted support from European countries and Russia on Iran and the East Asian powers of China, Japan, and South Korea on the North Korea issue.

By fall 2006, the administration's confident claims to be making progress in Iraq were failing to stem the growing discontent in Iraq, in Congress, in foreign policy circles, and among the general public. Two broad reviews were underway: one by a bipartisan commission headed by former Secretary of State James A. Baker III and former representative Lee H. Hamilton, D-Ind., the other by the administration itself. The results of both were held back until after the 2006 midterm elections. Opposition to U.S. policies in Iraq was widely seen as the primary factor in the Democrats' recapturing control of both houses of Congress for the first time in Bush's presidency.

Despite the changed political situation, Bush turned aside the Baker-Hamilton call for a redeployment of U.S. troops and diplomatic engagement with Iran and Syria. Instead, Bush used a nationwide address on January 10 to announce that he would send an additional 21,500 troops to Iraq to try to quell the sectarian violence in Baghdad and elsewhere.

CURRENT SITUATION

World of Troubles

Despite Washington's preoccupation with Iraq, China is suddenly bidding for renewed attention after a quiet but dramatic demonstration that it may have the capacity to destroy American spy satellites in space. A Chinese missile, launched in the early morning hours of January 12 Beijing time, destroyed a Chinese weather satellite scheduled to be retired. China gave no advance notice of the action and withheld any information about it for a week afterward.

Coming more than two decades after the United States and the former Soviet Union had stopped testing anti-satellite weapons, the Chinese move prompted a State Department spokesman to reiterate U.S. opposition to any militarization of space. Foreign-policy experts differed over China's possible motives, but Council on Foreign Relations analysts observed that the test showed China "can play with the big boys in space." [25] The Chinese test was a reminder as well that the United States faces a world of troubles beyond Iraq. China's surging economy and growing military give Beijing greater influence in East Asia than either the United States or Japan, while Russia is seeking to regain influence lost after the collapse of the Soviet Union. Columbia's Betts sees signs of "a re-emergence of great power conflict." Meanwhile, the Israeli-Palestinian conflict shows no signs of abating despite the U.S. efforts to restart a peace process. U.S. policies are unpopular in much of Europe. Venezuela's populist leader Hugo

Chavez is rallying an anti-U.S. coalition in South America. And Africa's daunting problems of poverty and disease dwarf any U.S. initiatives to combat them. In many ways, the array of problems makes the twenty-first century more difficult if not more dangerous than the Cold War's era of so-called mutually assured nuclear destruction. "In the 21st century, the game of American grand strategy is not a game of chess, but a Rubik's cube puzzle, where a lot of different pieces have to be put together," says Princeton's Ikenberry.

U.S. efforts to back North Korea and Iran away from a nuclear-weapons path reflect the administration's efforts to adapt strategies and tactics in differing geopolitical environments. In North Korea, the administration has channeled negotiations into six-power talks that include China, Japan, Russia and South Korea. In Iran, the administration deferred to diplomatic efforts by European allies but more recently stepped up U.S. pressure on Tehran — in part because of Iran's apparent support for Shiite forces in the sectarian fighting inside Iraq.

In October 2007, North Korea announced that it would offer information about all its nuclear programs and disable its main reactor complex by the end of the year in exchange for 950,000 metric tons of fuel oil or its equivalent in economic aid. [26] The Bush administration reaffirmed its willingness to remove North Korea from its list of state sponsors of terrorism if it made good on its promises, which would make the country eligible for further economic assistance. "It's the farthest we've gotten since the nuclear issue erupted 15 years ago," said Charles Armstrong, director of the Center for Korean Research at Columbia University. "No one said it was going to be easy, but it's an important first step." [27]

But the picture was much different regarding Iran's nuclear ambitions. The negotiating track there appears to be on hold in Iran as the United States combines economic pressure and gunboat diplomacy to gain Tehran's attention on both the nuclear and Iraq issues. Dissatisfied with the relatively weak economic sanctions voted by the U.N. Security Council in December 2006, U.S. officials are trying to pressure foreign governments and financial institutions to sever or cut back financial ties with Iran. A total of thirteen states have divested their pension funds from companies that do business in Iran. The Bush administration supports "sustained economic pressure" on Iran, but hasn't committed to backing divestment, out of concerns for allies with business ties to the country. [28]

Should Congress try to block President Bush's ability to send additional troops to Iraq?

YES
Sen. Edward M. Kennedy, D-Mass.
Member, Senate Armed Services Committee

Written for *CQ Researcher*, January 2007

For four long years, President Bush's assertion of unprecedented power has gone unchecked by Congress. For too long, the administration was allowed to operate in secrecy. Not just in Iraq, but also here at home — detentions in defiance of the Geneva Conventions, eavesdropping on people's telephone calls, reading their mail and reviewing their financial records, all without judicial authorization.

The president has made clear that he intends to move ahead with his misguided plan to escalate the war. That's the hallmark of his presidency — to go it alone and ignore contrary opinions. The American people spoke out against the war at the ballot box in November. Our generals opposed the escalation. They do not believe adding more American troops can end a civil war or encourage the transfer of responsibility to the Iraqis, but their warnings have gone unheeded. Now Congress is about to consider a non-binding resolution of no confidence in the president's reckless, last-ditch effort to salvage his strategy.

Passage of the non-binding resolution will send an important message about the need for a different course in Iraq, but it's only a first step. The president has made clear that he intends to ignore non-binding resolutions. If we disagree with the president's failed course, it will take stronger action to stop him. We cannot stand by as the president sends more of our sons and daughters into a civil war.

I've introduced legislation to prohibit the president from raising troop levels in Iraq unless he obtains specific new authorization from Congress. The initial authorization bears no relevance to the current hostilities in Iraq. There were no weapons of mass destruction and no alliance with al Qaeda, and Saddam Hussein is no more. The president should not be permitted to escalate our involvement unless Congress grants its approval.

For too long Congress has given President Bush a blank check to pursue his disastrous policy. He should not be permitted to take the desperate step of sending even more troops to die in the quagmire of civil war without convincing Congress why this escalation can succeed. As the constitutional scholars concluded in their recent letter to leaders of Congress: "Far from an invasion of presidential power, it would be an abdication of its own constitutional role if Congress were to fail to inquire, debate and legislate, as it sees fit, regarding the best way forward in Iraq."

We must not abdicate that responsibility any longer.

NO
Sen. Johnny Isakson, R-Ga.
Member, Senate Foreign Relations Committee

Written for *CQ Researcher*, January 2007

President Bush has proposed increasing the number of American troops to serve with Iraqi security forces in securing, holding and building in those areas of Baghdad engulfed in sectarian violence.

The president has laid out a clear and precise plan that absolutely requires the cooperation and support of the Iraqi people and the Iraqi military. I believe that the president's plan is the best opportunity — and quite frankly the last opportunity — for the Iraqi government to create a foundation for political reconciliation.

As the president said in his State of the Union address, "This is not the fight we entered in Iraq, but it is the fight we're in." The president also told Congress that, regardless of what mistakes may have been made, "Whatever you voted for, you did not vote for failure."

While the ultimate success of the president's plan depends on the Iraqis and their government living up to their responsibilities, the opportunity for them to do so depends on our help in securing Baghdad.

Our enemies and the enemies of the Iraqi people watch our actions and listen to our words. Our commander in chief has committed our armed forces to a plan, and the Iraqi government has committed to be a full partner. At such a critical time, when our country is committed to this major battle in the overall global war on terror, the words of Congress should not send a mixed message to our troops, the Iraqi people or our enemies.

While the situation in Iraq is grave, it would turn dire if we prematurely withdraw our forces and withdraw funding necessary to move Iraq forward. During two weeks of hearings, every expert witness — without exception — testified that if the United States retreats or redeploys its troops, there would be catastrophic loss of life, and the potential for a regional conflict in the Middle East would increase exponentially.

As I see it, we have two options: We can choose an opportunity for success or we can choose a recipe for disaster. Our brave men and women in uniform and the people of Iraq deserve to see a successful outcome, and our national security depends on it.

I remain committed to ensuring that the future holds this promise.

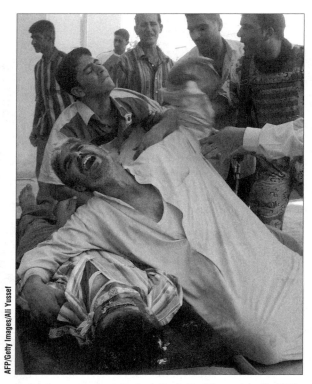

AFP/Getty Images/Ali Yussef

An Iraqi man mourns a dead relative in Baquba on July 12, 2006. At least 44,000 civilians have died since the U.S.-led invasion of Iraq in 2003, according to the Brookings Institution, and more than 3,000 American troops. The rising death toll has helped to turn U.S. public opinion against the war.

The United States in January 2007 dispatched a second aircraft-carrier strike group to the Persian Gulf and beefed up anti-missile defenses in two U.S. allies in the Gulf: Kuwait and Qatar. At the same time, officials confirmed that Bush had previously authorized U.S. troops inside Iraq to kill or capture Iranian operatives suspected of taking part in the sectarian violence. [29]

The tough moves against Iran appeared to recognize that — in contrast to economically strapped and diplomatically isolated North Korea — the United States was playing with a weak hand in dealing with Tehran. "Iran is riding a wave of Shiite resurgence, it has oil income, and it continues to have trade ties with European countries, China, and Russia," says Council on Foreign Relations fellow Kupchan. "Iran is holding a pretty good deck of cards." But the Bush administration refused to

let up on the rhetorical pressure. At an October 2007 press conference, Bush raised the specter of World War III if Iran manages to build nuclear weapons. "If you're interested in avoiding World War III, it seems like you ought to be interested in preventing them from having the knowledge necessary to make a nuclear weapon." The White House insisted that Bush was making a "rhetorical point" and not issuing a threat. [30]

Clash of Views

As the casualty count for U.S. and Iraqi troops and Iraqi civilians continues to rise, sectarian violence in Baghdad and elsewhere shows few signs of abating. The continuing bloodshed fuels growing domestic opposition to the U.S. role in Iraq, but President Bush has moved ahead with his plan to raise U.S. troop levels there in 2007, despite looming congressional action to go on record against the plan.

Bush presented the plan in his January 10 address as part of a coordinated strategy with the government of Iraqi Prime Minister Nouri al-Maliki to restore order in Baghdad. In fact, Maliki had actually urged a different plan on Bush in November. Maliki wanted U.S. forces to form a protective cordon around Baghdad while Shiite-led Iraqi security forces tried to quell the Sunni-Shiite conflict. Even in his address, however, Bush hinted at the tensions between the two governments by stressing Maliki's promise that his government would not allow "sectarian or political interference" with the efforts to end violence in Baghdad. "If the Iraqi government does not follow through on its promises," Bush said, "it will lose the support of the American people."

Bush passed over any mention of the recommendations to engage Iran and Syria in diplomatic efforts to restore order in Iraq. The administration would later reconsider this position. but at the time Bush blamed both countries for "allowing terrorists and insurgents to use their territory to move in and out of Iraq" and accused Iran of "providing material support for attacks on American troops." He promised to "seek out and destroy" networks providing weapons or training to "our enemies in Iraq."

Bush's plan drew virtually unanimous opposition from congressional Democrats, which was unabated after the president stood by his proposal in his State of the Union message. A few Republicans also expressed outright opposition, while several others voiced doubts. Opponents focused on two main themes: They doubted that the plan would succeed militarily or that Maliki would follow through with his political commitments. But congressional Democrats were unable to persuade a sufficient number of Republicans to break with the president to force major policy shifts regarding Iraq.

Three months after Bush announced his so-called surge plan to send additional numbers of troops to Iraq, Congress sent him a war spending bill that contained a requirement to start withdrawing troops by October 2007 at the latest. Bush vetoed the bill on May 1 and his veto was sustained the next day. Congress then approved a bill that deleted the withdrawal requirements, as well as provisions regarding troop readiness, which Bush signed. In July, Senate Democrats fell eight votes short of the sixty needed to overcome a GOP filibuster against an amendment that would have triggered a withdrawal of all but a limited set of U.S. forces from Iraq. The following month, the House passed a defense spending bill that contained provisions to prohibit permanent U.S. military bases in Iraq, as well as the use of torture. The White House threatened to veto the bill if it sought to restrict the president's war policies, so the Senate did not include the provisions in its version of the spending bill. The Senate also rejected, 28-68, an amendment by Russ Feingold, D-Wis., that would have barred the use of funds for Iraq combat operations after June 30, 2008. [31] In September, Senate Republicans blocked a proposal to lengthen the home leaves of U.S. troops fighting in Iraq and Afghanistan, which would have had the effect of limiting the pool of troops available for overseas combat. The move failed, in part, because Republican John W. Warner of Virginia, an influential former Armed Services Committee chairman, dropped his support for it at the last moment. [32]

Although Democrats drew heat from antiwar protesters for failing to change the course of the war, they blamed Republicans — including some who publicly criticized the war effort but declined to vote for substantive policy changes. "What was always missing, and continues to elude us, is the ten to twelve Republicans who will come over to our side and help us break the logjam," said Sen. Jack Reed, D-R.I. [33]

To Princeton's Lieven and Hulsman, Iraq provides a case study of the ethical-realism critique that U.S. foreign policy goes astray when it pursues overly ambitious goals with too little regard for obstacles and too little attention to the need for support from other countries. Iraq shows "the extreme difficulty of bringing about democracy in a deeply divided society and the difficulty of bringing about short-term economic development in a country with a weak government," says Lieven. "It also shows that even when an election is successful, it can be irrelevant to the purpose of nation-building." Now, Hulsman says, the United States must look to other countries in the region, including Iran and Syria, to achieve any acceptable outcome. "The only way to leave this very fragile state, the only way it stays unitary, is to get the consent of the regional players," he says. "Any construct we leave will fall apart unless they agree."

OUTLOOK

"Rebalancing" U.S. Policy?

From its earliest days, the United States has been a nation with big ambitions. The founding generations saw the American Revolution as an example for other subjugated peoples to follow. Later generations envisioned — and fulfilled — the nation's "manifest destiny" to reach from the Atlantic to the Pacific and beyond. Twentieth-century Americans saw a mission to "make the world safe for democracy."

Ambitions sometimes exceeded the reach. The United States did not annex Cuba or Nicaragua in the nineteenth century. The Senate turned away from the League of Nations and President Woodrow Wilson's internationalist vision after World War I. U.S. leaders talked about liberating the "enslaved peoples" of Eastern Europe during the Cold War but sent no help to Hungarians in 1956 or Czechoslovaks in 1968. The first President Bush left the Kurds and other Iraqi opponents of Saddam Hussein in the lurch after the first Gulf War.

Critics see a lesson that they say the current President Bush has failed to grasp: The United States can do only so much in world affairs. "There are opportunity costs in foreign policy," says Kent State Professor Hook. "The time, energy and resources devoted to one regional trouble spot divert time, energy and resources from other parts of the world."

Many critics of Bush's decision to raise troop levels in Iraq are using an analogy from the card game of blackjack to make their point — accusing him of a reckless decision to "double down," or double his bet in hopes of recouping his losses. Richard N. Haass, president of the Council on Foreign Relations and the State Department's director of policy planning in

Bush's first two years in the White House, makes the same point with an analogy from the world of business. By investing more in Iraq, Haass writes in an op-ed piece in *Financial Times*, Bush has failed to do what a prudent investor should do — "assess and rebalance" the U.S. foreign-policy portfolio. Beyond the likelihood that the troop increase will not bring success in Iraq, Haass says, the decision "limits the ability of the U.S. to focus on other matters, be they threats or opportunities. There are only so many troops, dollars and hours in the day to go round." [34]

Bush and other administration officials continue to profess optimism about Iraq. But Gen. David Petraeus, Bush's choice to be U.S. commander in Iraq, was temperate in predicting success when he appeared before the Senate Armed Services Committee on January 23, 2007. "There are no guarantees," he said. [35] In highly-publicized testimony before Congress in September 2007, Petraeus called for "a very substantial withdrawal" of U.S. forces — perhaps as many as 30,000 — but made clear his belief that the U.S. would have to keep tens of thousands of troops in Iraq for years to come.

The leading candidates seeking to succeed Bush on the Republican side have largely been supportive of his recent strategy on Iraq, arguing that the surge in troop levels has helped to stabilize the country. "They are making progress and we are winning on the ground," Arizona senator John McCain said at an August 2006 debate. "We must win, and we will not set a date for surrender as the Democrats want us to do." [36] Administration supporters believe the plan has a chance for success. "Victory in Iraq is still possible at an acceptable level of effort," the AEI's Kagan writes in a forty-seven-page report. [37] Critics, however, say the U.S. military is simply ill-equipped to bring order to Iraq. "The shock-and-awe approach to nation-building has proved to be fatally flawed," says Hook, referring to the administration's description of the initial military campaign.

Meanwhile, America's remaining twenty-five coalition partners, including Britain, are pulling troops out of Iraq. And Secretary of State Rice, meeting with NATO diplomats in Brussels early in 2007, found little support among U.S. allies for sending more troops to Afghanistan, where a Taliban insurgency continues to fester. "The good will that has greased the machine that is the transatlantic partnership is just not there," says conservative foreign-policy expert Hulsman.

Some experts expect a post-Iraq retreat from international ventures. "The appetite of the American public for the broad-ranging internationalism of Bush's first term is clearly drying up," says Kupchan, at the Council on Foreign Relations. Others are less certain about the impact. "I don't think it's likely that the United States is going to retreat into isolationism," says Betts, of Columbia's Institute of War and Peace Studies. "But if there's real failure in Iraq, there will be a marginal tilt toward greater caution."

Just as Democrats in Congress have been unable to change the course of the war, so have the party's presidential candidates strongly criticized the administration's handling of the war — without coming to any clear agreement as to how to end it. All the contenders have stated their desire to withdraw U.S. troops from the conflict, but at a New Hampshire debate in September 2007, none of the three leading candidates would pledge that combat troops would be withdrawn from the country by the end of his or her first term in early 2013.

Whatever the outcome in Iraq, says the New America Foundation's Lieven, American policymakers must recognize the need to be realistic in defining U.S. national interests abroad and more cautious in committing U.S. resources. "If your resources aren't unlimited, you've got to choose," he says, adding: "You should be cautious and prudent when it comes to the lives of your soldiers and the international prestige of your country." In the end, Schmitt, the AEI neoconservative, agrees. "Foreign policy is just made up of principles that have to be prudently applied," he says. "Sometimes you get it right, and sometimes you get it wrong."

Those ideas — that America must grow perhaps more cautious about asserting its power after Iraq — have helped to some extent frame the debate about whether the country should bomb Iran in order to disrupt its nuclear weapons program. Democrats have, for the most part, argued a cautious line, not wishing to hand an administration that they feel bungled the war in Iraq another "blank check" to attack Iran. "I have no intention of giving George Bush the authority to take the first step on a road to war with Iran," former North Carolina senator John Edwards said at the New Hampshire debate. "Because what I learned in my vote on Iraq is, you cannot give this president the authority and you can't even give him the first step in that authority, because he cannot be trusted." [38]

It is still unclear what course the West's long-running conflict with Iran over its nuclear ambitions will ultimately take. But it is clear that the GOP presidential hopefuls have sounded more belligerent on the issue than their Democratic counterparts. "Iran has to understand that not only is the military option on the table, it is in our hand," said former Massachusetts governor Mitt Romney. The next president, he said, must make it clear that "this is not just some far-flung idea . . . but instead we are poised and ready to act." [39]

NOTES

1. See Nazila Fathi and Michael Slackman, "Rebuke in Iran to Its President on Nuclear Role," *New York Times*, Jan. 19, 2007, p. A1.

2. http://Kudlowsmoneypolitics.blogspot.com, Jan. 10, 2007.

3. Quoted in Mark Mazzetti, "Leading Senator Assails President on Iran Stance," *New York Times*, Jan. 20, 2007, p. A1. See also John M. Donnelly, "Democrats Warn Bush on Iran, Syria," *CQ Today*, Jan. 12, 2007.

4. Steven W. Hook and John Spanier, *American Foreign Policy Since World War II*, 17th ed., (Washington D.C.: CQ Press, 2007).

5. Anatol Lieven and John Hulsman, *Ethical Realism: A Vision for America's Role in the World* (New York: Random House, 2006).

6. G. John Ikenberry and Anne-Marie Slaughter, "Forging a World of Liberty Under Law: U.S. National Security in the 21st Century," Princeton Project on National Security, Sept. 2006; www.wws.princeton.edu/ppns/.

7. Jeffrey W. Legro, *Rethinking the World: Great Power Strategies and International Order* (Ithaca, New York: Cornell University Press, 2005).

8. For background, see the following *CQ Researcher* reports: Kenneth Jost, "International Law," December 17, 2004, pp. 1049-1072; Mary H. Cooper, "Global Warming Treaty," Jan. 26, 2001, pp. 41-64; and Marcia Clemmitt, "Climate Change," Jan. 27, 2006, pp. 73-96.

9. White House, "The National Security Strategy of the United States," September 2002; www.whitehouse.gov/nsc/nss.html; cited in Hook and Spanier, American Foreign Policy, pp. 325-328. For background, see Mary H. Cooper, "New Defense Priorities," *CQ Researcher*, Sept. 13, 2002, pp. 721-744; and Adriel Bettelheim, "Presidential Power," *CQ Researcher*, Nov. 15, 2002, pp. 945-968.

10. See Jackson Diehl, "Rice's Rhetoric, in Full Retreat," *Washington Post*, Jan. 22, 2007, p. A18. For background, see Kenneth Jost and Benton Ives-Halperin, "Democracy in the Arab World," *CQ Researcher*, Jan. 30, 2004, pp. 73-100, and Peter Katel, "Middle East Tensions," *CQ Researcher*, Oct. 27, 2006, pp. 889-912.

11. Michael Slackman, "On Human Rights, U.S. Seems to Give Egypt a Pass," *New York Times*, Oct. 16, 2007, p. A4.

12. Steven Lee Myers, "Egypt Helps Bolster Prospect of Peace Talks," *New York Times*, Oct. 17, 2007, p. A12.

13. Michael Mandelbaum, *Democracy's Good Name: The Rise and the Risks of the World's Most Popular Form of Government* (New York: Public Affairs, 2007).

14. German Marshall Fund, "Transatlantic Trends 2006," 50; www.gmfus.org.

15. Background drawn from Robert Kagan, *Dangerous Nation: America's Place in the World from Its Earliest Days to the Dawn of the Twentieth Century* (New York: Knopf, 2006); Charles A. Kupchan, *The End of the American Era: U.S. Foreign Politics and the Geopolitics of the Twenty-First Century* (New York: Knopf, 2003); and Hook and Spanier, *American Foreign Policy*.

16. For excerpts, see Hook and Spanier, *American Foreign Policy*, pp. 39-40. The full text is reproduced in George F. Kennan, *American Diplomacy: 1900-1950* (Chicago, IL: University of Chicago Press, 1951), pp. 107-128.

17. The Associated Press, "Ford Once Called Carter a 'Disaster'; Ex-President Also Said Reagan Got Too Much Cold War Credit," Jan. 13, 2007.

18. For background, see Kenneth Jost, "Foreign Policy and Public Opinion," *CQ Researcher*, July 15, 1994, pp. 601-624.

19. For background, see Kenneth Jost, "Re-examining 9/11," *CQ Researcher*, June 4, 2004, pp. 493-516.

20. Bush quoted in Frank M. Bruni, "At 6 Months, Bush Says, He's Doing Pretty Well," *New York Times*,

August 4, 2001, A12; survey by the *International Herald Tribune*, Pew Research Center and Council on Foreign Relations reported in Adam Clymer, "Surveys Find European Publics Critical of Bush Policies," *New York Times*, Aug. 16, 2001, p. A12.

21. For background, see Kenneth Jost, "Rebuilding Afghanistan," *CQ Researcher*, Dec. 21, 2001, pp. 1041-1064.

22. Available at www.whitehouse.gov/nsc/nss.pdf.

23. Quoted in Sonni Effron and Carol J. Williams, "Plan Likely to Further Isolate U.S.," *Los Angeles Times*, Sept. 21, 2002, p. 1A.

24. For a compact overview through early 2006, see Hook and Spanier, *American Foreign Policy*, pp. 339-357. See also these *CQ Researcher* reports: David Masci, "Confronting Iraq," Oct. 4, 2002, pp. 793-816; David Masci, "Rebuilding Iraq," July 25, 2003, pp. 625-648; Pamela M. Prah, "War in Iraq," Oct. 21, 2005, pp. 881-908; and Peter Katel, "New Strategy in Iraq," Feb. 23, 2007.

25. Joanna Klonsky and Michael Moran, "China Ups Ante in Space," Council on Foreign Relations Daily Analysis, Jan. 19, 2007; www.cfr.org/publication/12454/china_ups_ante_in_space.html. The backgrounder provides links to news coverage and other resources. See also David E. Sanger and Joseph Kahn, "U.S. Officials Try to Interpret China's Silence Over Satellite," *New York Times*, Jan. 22, 2007, p. A3.

26. Helene Cooper, "North Koreans in Nuclear Pact," *New York Times*, Oct. 4, 2007, p. A1.

27. Bruce Wallace, "Relief, Mistrust at Korea Talks," *Los Angeles Times*, Oct. 4, 2007, p. A4.

28. Jonathan Alter, "Before We Bomb Iran...," *Newsweek*, Oct. 22, 2007, p. 45.

29. See Lionel Behner, "New Squeeze on Iran," Council on Foreign Relations Daily Analysis, Jan. 25, 2007; www.cfr.org/publication/12495/new_squeeze_on_iran.html?breadcrumb=/; Dafna Linzer, "Troops Authorized to Kill Iranian Operatives in Iraq," *Washington Post*, Jan. 26, 2007, p. A1.

30. Peter Baker, "Bush's War Rhetoric Reveals the Anxiety That Iran Commands," *Washington Post*, Oct. 19, 2007, p. A5.

31. Josh Rogin, "Senate Passes Defense Spending," *CQ Weekly*, Oct. 6, 2007.

32. Dana Milbank, "Standing on One Principle, Voting on Another," *Washington Post*, Sept. 20, 2007, p. A2.

33. David Nather, "Anti-War Movement Stuck in a Quagmire," *CQ Weekly*, Oct. 6, 2007.

34. Richard N. Haass, "America Needs to Rethink Its Portfolio," *Financial Times*, Jan. 17, 2007, p. 15.

35. See Peter Baker, "Defending Iraq War, Defiant Cheney Sees 'Enormous Successes,' " *Washington Post*, Jan. 25, 2007, p. A1; Michael R. Gordon, "General Says New Strategy in Iraq Can Work Over Time," *New York Times*, Jan. 24, 2007, p. A1.

36. Adam Nagourney and Michael Cooper, "In Debate, Republicans Make the Case for Staying in Iraq," *New York Times*, Aug. 6, 2007, p. A14.

37. Frederick W. Kagan, "Choosing Victory: A Plan for Success in Iraq," American Enterprise Institute, Jan. 2007 (www.aei.org).

38. Jeff Zeleny and Patrick Healy, "Candidates Hedge Bets on Iraq Withdrawal," *New York Times*, Sept. 27, 2007, p. A26.

39. Baker, "Defending Iraq War."

BIBLIOGRAPHY

Books

Harvey, Robert, *Global Disorder: America and the Threat of World Conflict*, Carroll & Graf, 2003.
A British journalist-author combines a comprehensive overview of post-9/11 world threats with a call for the United States to act as the "cornerstone" of world order while avoiding the risks of "unilateralism." Harvey is a columnist for the [London] *Daily Telegraph* and author of five other books on international relations. The book was published in paperback as *Global Disorder: How to Avoid a Fourth World War* (2004).

Kagan, Robert, *Dangerous Nation: America's Place in the World from Its Earliest Days to the Dawn of the Twentieth Century*, Knopf, 2006.
A neoconservative foreign-policy expert and *Washington Post* columnist argues that the United States has

played an assertive role in world affairs throughout its history. A planned second volume will cover 20th-century foreign policy. Includes detailed notes, 26-page bibliography.

Kupchan, Charles A., *The End of the American Era: U.S. Foreign Policy and the Geopolitics of the Twenty-first Century*, Knopf, 2002.
A senior fellow at the Council on Foreign Relations and a professor at Georgetown University synthesizes history and current events to argue that as the era of American primacy ends, the United States must work harder to cultivate a sense of "common interest" with emerging centers of power. Includes detailed notes, nine-page bibliography.

Lieven, Anatol, and John Hulsman, *Ethical Realism: A Vision for America's Role in the World*, Random House, 2006.
Coming from different political backgrounds, the authors argue that U.S. foreign policy must combine genuine morality with tough, practical common sense. Lieven is a senior fellow at the centrist New America Foundation; Hulsman, formerly with the conservative Heritage Foundation, is at the German Council on Foreign Relations.

Mandelbaum, Michael, *The Case for Goliath: How America Acts as the World's Government in the Twenty-First Century*, Pantheon, 2005.
A professor at the Johns Hopkins University's School of Advanced International Studies depicts the United States' role in world affairs not as an empire or a superpower but as the "world's government." Includes detailed notes.

Reports and Studies

Ikenberry, G. John, and Anne-Marie Slaughter (co-directors), *Forging a World of Liberty Under Law: U.S. National Security in the 21st Century: Final Report of the Princeton Project on National Security*, Woodrow Wilson School of Public and International Affairs, 2006; www.wws.princeton.edu/ppns/.
The report advances a series of proposals, including the creation of a global "Concert of Democracies," to strengthen security cooperation and promote creation of liberal democracy. Slaughter is dean and Ikenberry a professor at the Wilson School.

Books on Foreign Policy From CQ Press

CQ Press publishes a number of reference works on foreign policy, including:

American Foreign Policy Since World War II, 17th ed., by Steven W. Hook and John Spanier, provides a concise review of the conduct of American foreign policy. ***U.S. Foreign Policy: The Paradox of World Power***, by Steven W. Hook is a foundational book covering the process of foreign-policy formulation. ***Contemporary Cases in U.S. Foreign Policy: From Terrorism to Trade***, 2nd ed., edited by Ralph G. Carter, is a collection of 15 case studies with chapters on Iraq, North Korea and detainees' rights, among others.

In print and online, ***Political Handbook of the World 2007*** (2006) is a staple resource for in-depth political profiles on countries, territories and intergovernmental organizations. CQ Press also offers four regional political guides: ***Political Handbook of Asia 2007*** (2007); ***Political Handbook of Africa 2007*** (2006); ***Political Handbook of Europe 2007*** (2006); and ***Political Handbook of the Middle East 2006*** (2006).

For further in-depth analysis of the Middle East, ***The Middle East***, 10th ed., (11th ed. available July 2007) is considered a classic text among students, professors and researchers. Jacob Bercovitch and Judith Fretter's ***Regional Guide to International Conflict and Management from 1945 to 2003*** (2004) provides information on 340 conflicts since World War II. Bert Chapman's ***Researching National Security and Intelligence Policy*** (2004) is a useful guide for researchers seeking resources on national security policy. Bruce Maxwell's ***Terrorism: A Documentary History*** (2002) is a ready-reference featuring 100 entries from 1972 through 2002. ***World at Risk: A Global Issues Sourcebook*** (2002) arranges global issues in a convenient A-to-Z format, covering 30 topics from arms control to war crimes.

For More Information

American Enterprise Institute, 1150 17th St., N.W., Washington, DC 20036; (202) 862-5800; www.aei.org. Conservative public-policy organization dedicated to research and education.

Carnegie Endowment for International Peace, 1779 Massachusetts Ave., N.W., Washington, DC 20036; (202) 483-7600; www.ceip.org. Think tank advancing international cooperation and U.S. international engagement.

Center for Strategic and International Studies, 1800 K St., N.W., Washington, DC 20006; (202) 887-0200; www.csis.org. Promotes global security by providing insight and policy solutions to decision-makers.

Council on Foreign Relations, 58 East 68th St., New York, NY 10021; (212) 434-9400; www.cfr.org. Nonpartisan foreign-policy think tank.

Heritage Foundation, 214 Massachusetts Ave., N.E., Washington DC 20002; (202) 546-4400; www.heritage.org. Conservative policy-research institute.

New America Foundation, 1630 Connecticut Ave., N.W., 7th Floor, Washington, DC 20009; (202) 986-2700; www.newamerica.net. Dedicated to bringing new voices and ideas into foreign-policy discourse.

Princeton Project on National Security, Woodrow Wilson School of Public and International Affairs, Princeton University, 423G Robertson Hall, Princeton, NJ 08544-1013; (609) 258-2228; www.wws.princeton.edu/ppns/. Academic initiative for developing a long-term U.S. national security strategy.

Project for the New American Century, 1150 17th St., N.W., Suite 510, Washington, DC 20036; (202) 293-4893; www.newamericancentury.org. Neoconservative think tank promoting U.S. global leadership.

2

Anti-Americanism

Samuel Loewenberg

AFP Photo/Stephen Jaffe

President George W. Bush lands on the aircraft carrier *USS Abraham Lincoln* in May 2003 and declares the formal end to combat in Iraq. Many critics abroad blame Bush and the Iraq war — now entering its fifth year — for the decline in U.S. prestige.

From *CQ Researcher*, March 1, 2007.

S oon after the Sept. 11, 2001, terrorist attacks, the cover of *Newsweek* pictured a turbaned child holding a toy machine gun. The headline read: "The Politics of Rage: Why Do They Hate Us?" [1]

Since then, versions of that question — simultaneously plaintive and rhetorical — have been repeated throughout the U.S. media. The most common answer often reflected the views of Harvard scholar Samuel P. Huntington, who described an inevitable schism between Christianity and Islam in his seminal 1993 essay, "Clash of Civilizations." [2]

But America's critics are far more diverse, and their criticisms more differentiated, than can be explained away by a simple East vs. West conflict. Today not only radical Eastern Islamists but also more and more Latin Americans and former close allies in Europe are finding America and its policies reprehensible.

Some of the most outspoken voices come from Europe, where dismissive attitudes about the mixing bowl of people in the New World have long been a staple of intellectual preening. Since the 17th century, America has been depicted as a haven for uncouth debauchers, religious zealots and puffed-up nationalists. Only after World War II, when America emerged into a position of military and economic might, did it became an object of both desire and envy.

As the United States flexed its muscles over the subsequent decades, others began to perceive it as a threat to their own national sovereignty and identity. America was too big, too influential, too sure of its virtues. Protesters around the world began to attack all three facets of American influence — economic, political and cul-

America's Global Image Slips

Since the beginning of the Bush administration in 2001, favorable opinions of the United States have declined in many countries. In Great Britain — an ally in the war in Iraq — approval levels fell from 83 percent in 1999-2000 to 56 percent in 2006.

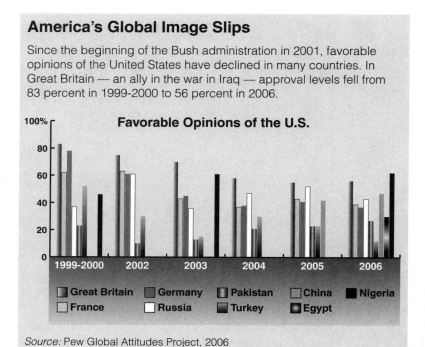

Favorable Opinions of the U.S.

Legend: Great Britain, France, Germany, Russia, Pakistan, Turkey, China, Egypt, Nigeria

Source: Pew Global Attitudes Project, 2006

• Moral: America is viewed as the purveyor of the death penalty and of religious fundamentalism, while Europe abolished the death penalty in favor of rehabilitation and adheres to an enlightened secularism;

• Social: America is viewed as the bastion of unbridled "predatory capitalism," as former German Chancellor Helmut Schmidt put it, while Europe is the home of the considerate welfare state; and

• Cultural: America is viewed as common, prudish and prurient, Europe as refined, savvy and wise. [6]

Those bleak assessments of the United States have played out in innumerable protests in recent years. When tens of thousands of leftist protesters from around the world gathered in Porto Alegre, Brazil, during the World Economic Forum in February 2002, they waved signs declaring "No blood for oil," and "Bush is #1 Terrorist." Raucous anti-globalization protests have followed the meetings of the World Trade Organization and the G8 from Doha to Davos to Seattle.

When 70,000 protesters gathered in Berlin's Alexanderplatz in March 2003, a banner proclaimed: "We Aren't Allowed to Compare Bush to Hitler. Too Bad!" [7]

When 2,000 Pakistanis in Islamabad rallied against Danish cartoons that had caricatured the Prophet Muhammad in 2006, they also shouted "Death to America!" and torched an effigy of President George W. Bush, as if Bush himself had commissioned the works. [8]

This was a long way from the moment after the 9/11 attacks, when the globe was in brief solidarity with the United States, as epitomized by the famous banner headline in the French newspaper *Le Monde*, "We are all Americans." [9]

Something had changed.

In just a few years, what once seemed to be a clash of two halves of the globe had metastasized into a clash between America and the rest of the world. These sentiments were not coming from isolated pockets of religious

tural. By the end of the Cold War, the United States was the only remaining superpower, and even more vulnerable to accusations of arrogance and bullying.

In 1999 this sole superpower was symbolically attacked on a much smaller — and non-lethal — scale than it was on Sept. 11, 2001, when French protesters dismantled a McDonald's restaurant in the town of Millau, turning farmer and union leader José Bové into an international hero. [3]

"Look," Bové said later, "cooking is culture. All over the world. Every nation, every region, has its own food cultures. Food and farming define people. We cannot let it all go, to be replaced with hamburgers. People will not let it happen." [4]

That act of cultural theater preceded many others, and by 2003, as the United States led the invasion into Iraq, America was regularly being pilloried as an international villain, damned for its military excursions and held up as a convenient target for all sorts of global discontent. [5]

The indictment against America, writes Andrei S. Markovits, a Romania-born professor of comparative European politics at the University of Michigan, "accuses America of being retrograde on three levels":

fundamentalists but from America's longstanding allies throughout the world. In Europe, anti-U.S. sentiment had reached record levels.

The Iraq invasion "did not create anti-Americanism but it increased it and gave it form," according to Professor Gérard Grunberg, deputy director of Sciences Po, a political institute in Paris. [10]

Many clearly think that negative attitudes toward the United States are now at an all-time high. "Anti-Americanism is deeper and broader now than at any time in modern history. It is most acute in the Muslim world, but it spans the globe," according to a recent survey by the Pew Research Center for People & the Press. [11] In another Pew poll, Europeans gave higher approval ratings to China than to the United States. [12]

Yet much of the anti-American hostility disguises the fact that many of the most vociferous European critics really don't know much about the USA. As British scholar Tony Judt, director of the Remarque Institute at New York University, points out, Europeans complain about their own governments' policies by saying they have been influenced by America. [13]

But on both sides of the Atlantic, says Judt, even in the supposed age of "globalization," there is a massive ignorance about the reality of politics, and of everyday life. "We don't actually understand each other any better than we did in the 1930s."

How did America go, in the eyes of many, from being the symbol of democracy, freedom and opportunity — an ideal to strive for — to an example to be avoided? Judt calls anti-Americanism the "master narrative" of the current age, in which declared opposition to the United States became a uniting factor for disparate critics of economic, cultural and foreign policies around the globe. In America they had found "a common target."

But these days, the overwhelming source of anti-American sentiment, not only in Europe but also throughout the world, is U.S. foreign policy, especially the Bush administration's pursuit of the war in Iraq.

Resentment of the policies and personalities in the Bush administration cannot be overstated. Even President Richard M. Nixon's transgressions were mostly identified as domestic problems (the Watergate scandal), while the Vietnam War was seen as part of larger Cold War politics and did not evoke the same strong anti-American sentiment as Iraq does today.

French activist and farmer José Bové has a following in Solomiac, France, after attempting to rip up a crop of genetically modified maize. Bové gained fame for destroying a French McDonald's restaurant in 1999.

AFP/Getty Images/Eric Cabanis

Although there certainly was European criticism about the American war in Vietnam, Americans did not hear about it on a daily basis, as they do with criticisms of the war in Iraq. Instant television reporting and the Internet bring the war as well as its critics into homes every hour. Now, says Judt, "Whatever catastrophes the Americans are involved in overseas are immediately visible, with no time lag."

Another foreign conflict strongly identified with the United States and a recurrent theme at anti-war protests around the globe is the Israeli-Palestinian stalemate. European and Middle Eastern criticism of U.S. support of Israel ranges from humanitarian concerns about Palestinian rights to demagoguery invoking a Jewish-American-capitalist conspiracy.

"This didn't come from nothing," says Markovits. In his new book, *Uncouth Nation: Why Europe Dislikes America*, he traces the origins of anti-American sentiment to the 19th century, when European elites feared the pugnacious, young country.

For Americans, it is easy to dismiss criticism of U.S. policies as simply an irrational ideology, Markovits writes. But the term "anti-Americanism" is misleading, he says, because it lumps together rational criticisms, whether one agrees with them or not, with a disembodied, ideological

AFP/Getty Images

Yankee mice Mickey and Minnie reign at Disneyland Paris during Disney's 100th anniversary. Despite protests against American cultural imports by French intellectuals, more people visit the Paris theme park than any other Disney attraction in the world.

ernment. This is particularly true when it comes to the view, shared by much of the globe, that the United States is too tightly connected to Israel.

As Beirut's *Daily Star* said after the United States deposed Saddam Hussein: "Having waged an 'illegitimate' war on Iraq that has stoked anti-American feelings around the world, challenged and ignored international law and the United Nations . . . the Bush administration is not about to 'offer Iraq on a golden platter to an opposition group or to the U.N. Security Council.'

"It will deny others a say in shaping post-war Iraq, and it won't withdraw its forces on request. . . . Israel, of course, will be an exception, and is the only U.S. partner whose participation in shaping post-war Iraq is 'guaranteed.' That is because Israel was the main reason for which the war was waged." [14]

Trying to sort out real criticisms of the United States from the political symbolism that makes up much anti-Americanism is a daunting task. But for America's many critics around the globe, the daily carnage in Iraq has confirmed that America, having found no weapons of mass destruction in Iraq, is now on a reckless crusade.

In the week after the Sept. 11, attacks, Bush declared, "this crusade, this war on terrorism, is going to take a while." [15] While the term "crusade" went largely unnoticed in the United States, it alarmed many around the world with its evocation of the ancient wars between Christianity and Islam.

As Americans seek to understand global criticism of the United States, here are some of the key issues being debated:

Is the United States the primary force behind globalization policies that harm other countries?

Before there was anti-Americanism there was anti-globalization. For many critics, they are mostly the same. [16]

Globalization is the umbrella term for the rapidly increasing social, technological, cultural and political integration of nation-states, corporations and organizations around the world.

Its supporters believe that globalization is a positive engine of commerce that brings increased standards of living, universal values, multiculturalism and technology to developing countries. Globalization's critics claim it is a slave to corporate interests, harms the environment and tramples human rights and the economic and ethical claims of the poor and working classes.

opposition to an idea of America, in which the country stands as a symbol for a variety of foreign, cultural and political discontents.

As Markovits notes, "Anti-Americanism is a particularly murky concept because it invariably merges antipathy toward what America does with what America is — or rather is projected to be in the eyes of its beholders." In contrast to classical stereotypes, which usually depict powerless minorities, the United States does, in fact, have great political, economic and cultural power. This makes it especially difficult to disentangle the perception from the reality. Critics of America assume that the expansion of this power, rather than a more benign exercise of it, is always the top priority of the American gov-

It's no surprise, then, that America has become the country most vilified by the anti-globalization movement. After all, U.S. brands like McDonald's, Marlboro and Nike are among the most recognized in the world.

Globalization does have its defenders, and at least one links the movement to an old socialist tradition in Europe. "Globalization simply means freedom of movement for goods and people," wrote the late French journalist and philosopher Jean-Francois Revel, "and it is hard to be violently hostile to that.

"But behind the opposition to globalization lies an older and more fundamental struggle against economic liberalization and its chief representative, the United States. Anti-globalism protests often feature an Uncle Sam in a stars-and-stripes costume as their supreme scapegoat."

Lashing out at America through targeting its products had roots in the Cold War. For example, some Eastern Bloc countries prohibited Coca-Cola but not Pepsi, because Coke was so strongly identified with the United States. But the movement reached its peak at the turn of the 21st century with global protests against the World Trade Organization, against the incursion of McDonald's and Starbucks and against acceptance of genetically modified foods from the United States. [17]

Championing the pure-food cause was Great Britain's Prince Charles. In 1999, after representatives of 20 African countries had published a statement denying that gene technologies would help farmers to produce the food they needed, Charles came to their defense: "Are we going to allow the industrialization of life itself, redesigning the natural world for the sake of convenience? Or should we be adopting a gentler, more considered approach, seeking always to work with the grain of nature?" [18]

Reluctance to accept American products and economic power has brought together critics from the left and the right. For both, "America represents the ideal of unfettered capitalism itself," says Fernando Vallespin, director of the Sociological Research Centre of Spain, a nonpartisan think tank in Madrid. "For those on the left, the concern is for labor exploitation. For those on the right, it is the loss of national sovereignty."

Resentment of the American economic model is particularly strong in Europe, which is currently confronting painful and unpopular adjustments to its own long-held social-welfare state model. Politicians, unions and disenfranchised workers in France, Italy and Spain say they do not want to adopt the "Anglo-Saxon" model,

a reference not to Germany or England but to the United States. Spaniards are vociferous critics of the American way of life, says Vallespin, "but on the other hand we are probably one of the most American in terms of our patterns of consumption."

Cost-cutting proposals that seem to erode Europe's time-honored cradle-to-grave welfare privileges — such as fees for seeing a doctor or reducing the meal allowances of factory workers — have been denounced as "American." But in truth, most policies are still far from American-style capitalism.

In Germany, American business interests are seen as a double threat. After a recent buying spree of distressed companies by hedge funds, most of them American, German Vice Chancellor Franz Muentefering said the funds "fall like a plague of locusts over our companies, devour everything, then fly on to the next one."

Muentefering's statement was widely scrutinized, with some critics suggesting that the image of locusts preying on German companies evoked sentiments that were not only anti-American but also anti-Semitic.

There is no doubt the United States has been leading the current charge to deregulate markets, but it is still wrong to blame it for the world's economic inequalities, says Charles Kupchan, a professor of international affairs at Georgetown University and the former director for European affairs at the National Security Council during the Clinton administration.

He points out that large corporations in nearly every European country have been globalizing. In fact, the precursor to modern globalization was not the commercial efforts of the United States but European imperialism of the past 500 years. A large part of that was the economic domination and exploitation of Latin America and Africa.

The remnants of Europe's imperialist past continue to earn big profits for European countries, with Spain holding powerful telecom and banking concessions in Latin America, and the French profiting off mining and agricultural interests in their former colonies in Africa. Yet, curiously, the focus of the anti-globalization debate continues to revolve around the United States.

"There is an unjustifiable equation between globalization and Americanization," says Kupchan.

At the same time, the U.S. government, under both the current Bush administration and the Clinton presidency, pushed often and hard on behalf of U.S. business interests.

Spanish Blame Bombing on War in Iraq

Spain's support of U.S. seen as critical factor

On the morning of March 11, 2004, a coordinated bomb attack on four rush-hour trains in Madrid killed 191 people and injured more than 1,700. Spain had lived through decades of terrorism from the Basque separatist group ETA, but these bombers were not seeking independence; they were attempting to intimidate the Spanish government. In February 2007, Spanish authorities put 29 men on trial for the bombings, claiming they belonged to a local cell of Islamic militants aligned with al Qaeda.

In sharp contrast to the American reaction after the Sept. 11, 2001, terrorist attacks, Spanish citizens did not view the assault as part of a war between Islam and the West. Instead, many turned their anger toward the United States and their own government, which had supported the U.S.-led invasion of Iraq.

"We didn't want to go to war, but we did because of [former Prime Minister José Maria] Aznar," said Miguel Barrios, a 45-year-old maintenance worker who was in one of the bombed trains. "They didn't pay attention to the anti-war movement." [1]

It became clear that in an effort to stay aligned with the interests of the United States, the world's sole superpower, the Spanish government had run against the will of its own people. In the wake of the railroad attacks that Spanish government was voted out. The new prime minister, José Luis Rodriguez Zapatero, withdrew Spain's 1,300 troops from Iraq within weeks, risking a rupture of the close alliance Spain had enjoyed with the U.S.

"Mr. Bush and Mr. Blair will reflect on our decision," said Zapatero. "You cannot justify a war with lies. It cannot be."

People felt the war in Iraq had never been Spain's business, said Miguel Bastenier, a columnist for El Pais, Spain's largest newspaper. "Aznar was doing what Bush wanted without any particular reason for Spain to be there.

"There was undoubtedly the feeling that Spain was being punished for its association with the aggressive policies of the United States," and that "their country had been targeted by Muslim terrorists because it was now seen as being allied with the Jewish state."

In 2002, when war in Iraq was still only imminent, millions of Spaniards had taken to the streets to protest the coming invasion; polls showed more than 80 percent opposed to supporting the United States.

"Bush wants to go into Iraq to get the oil," said Virgilio Salcedo, a 29-year-old computer programmer who came to

---

The most famous attempt, which failed spectacularly, was the U.S. attempt to open Britain to bioengineered foods. The lobbying attempt, led by former Clinton U.S. Trade Representative Mickey Kantor, ran up against deeply held British attitudes of reverence for pristine nature.

"These senior executives thought they could just walk in and buy [British officials] a glass of champagne and charm them," said Evie Soames, a British lobbyist who represented the U.S. company Monsanto, which was attempting to sell its genetically modified seeds in England for several years. [19]

More recent American lobbying efforts have borne fruit. In 2001 the European Union tried to impose a strict safety-testing regime on chemical manufacturers; the Bush administration mounted a massive lobbying campaign that mobilized American embassies across Europe and Asia. The final, much scaled-back, version of the testing regime will save U.S. chemical companies billions of dollars.

Perhaps the biggest global concern about U.S. economic interests has been the perception that the U.S.-led invasion of Iraq was driven by America's thirst for petroleum. Notably, the most ubiquitous slogan, "No blood for oil," popped up at protests in the United States and abroad during the first Persian Gulf War in 1991 as well as the current war.

In a scathing commentary about President Bush's belief that he is on a direct mission from God, Henry A. Giroux, a professor of communications at Canada's McMasters University, wrote: "Surrounded by born-again missionaries . . . Bush has relentlessly developed policies based less on social needs than on a highly personal and narrowly moral sense of divine purpose." [20]

the rally in Madrid with his parents. "Everybody knows that he doesn't want to help the people there."

"We think our president has sold out the country to the Americans," said Susanna Polo, a 30-year-old economist.

"Aznar is Bush's dog," added Raquel Hurtado, a 19-year-old economics student. [2]

Even for those most deeply affected by 9/11, like 53-year-old Rosalinda Arias, whose sister died in the World Trade Center attacks, U.S. motives were suspect. "It is all business. They want petroleum; they want to bring U.S. imperialism," said Arias, owner of a restaurant in Madrid.

For the many older people attending the rally, memories of the Franco dictatorship were still fresh, including America's support of the fascist regime in the 1930s. Now they had little faith in Bush administration claims that America was going to liberate Iraq.

"There are lots of dictatorships that have been backed by the USA," said Carlos Martin, a 67-year-old translator of Italian literature. "I can't imagine how the Iraqi people are feeling now. They were bombed in 1991, then they had 12 years of horrible sanctions, and now they are being bombed again. I can't imagine they will look at the Americans as liberators."

Some of the protesters' worst fears were realized as the U.S. Coalition Forces invaded and subdued Baghdad in 2003, then settled into the current quagmire.

But Spain did not seek revenge against the killing of 191 of its citizens. A 40-year-old teacher named Valeria Suarez

Getty Images/Ian Waldie

A tear rolls down a girl's cheek during a rally in Madrid following terrorist bombings in March 2004 that killed nearly 200 people. Her message: "Peace, not terrorism."

Marsa gave a softer voice to the public mood. "It is more important then ever to call for peace," she said. "The bombs reminded us of that urgency."

---

[1] The author covered the Madrid protests in 2002.

[2] Quoted in Samuel Loewenberg, "A Vote for Honesty," *The Nation*, March 18, 2004.

In the months before the invasion of Iraq in March 2003, *The Economist* summed up the anti-Bush sentiment: "Only one thing unsettles George Bush's critics more than the possibility that his foreign policy is secretly driven by greed. That is the possibility that it is secretly driven by God. . . . War for oil would merely be bad. War for God would be catastrophic." [21]

Is the United States threatening other cultures?

Any American who has traveled abroad for any length of time will be familiar with the following exchange: "Oh, you're American. I hate Americans." Or, the rhetorical litmus-test question: "What do you think of your president?" This, however, is soon followed by "I love New York" or "Have you ever been to Disneyland?"

For decades, America's most influential export has not been cars or televisions, but culture. This can be mass media like Hollywood movies and hip-hop music, fast-food restaurants that are often seen as crass and objectionable, or soft drinks such as Coca-Cola.

While these cultural products have long been embraced on a worldwide scale, they have also raised concerns that their appeal would diminish traditions and habits that other cultures hold dear. This love-hate relationship with American popular culture and consumerism was reflected in a 2005 Pew study that found "72 percent of French, 70 percent of Germans and 56 percent of Britons regard the spread of American culture negatively. In all of these countries, paradoxically, large majorities of respondents — especially young people — say they like American movies and other cultural exports." [22]

The University of Michigan's Markovits says resentment of U.S. culture has deep roots among European elites. "Many of the components of European anti-

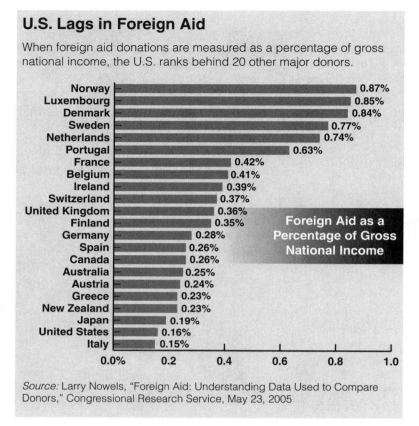

U.S. Lags in Foreign Aid

When foreign aid donations are measured as a percentage of gross national income, the U.S. ranks behind 20 other major donors.

Foreign Aid as a Percentage of Gross National Income

Country	Percentage
Norway	0.87%
Luxembourg	0.85%
Denmark	0.84%
Sweden	0.77%
Netherlands	0.74%
Portugal	0.63%
France	0.42%
Belgium	0.41%
Ireland	0.39%
Switzerland	0.37%
United Kingdom	0.36%
Finland	0.35%
Germany	0.28%
Spain	0.26%
Canada	0.26%
Australia	0.25%
Austria	0.24%
Greece	0.23%
New Zealand	0.23%
Japan	0.19%
United States	0.16%
Italy	0.15%

Source: Larry Nowels, "Foreign Aid: Understanding Data Used to Compare Donors," Congressional Research Service, May 23, 2005

Americanism have been alive and well in Europe's intellectual discourse since the late 18th century," he writes. "The tropes about Americans' alleged venality, mediocrity, uncouthness, lack of culture and above all inauthenticity have been integral and ubiquitous to European elite opinion for well over 200 years. All of these 'Americanizations' bemoan an alleged loss of purity and authenticity for Europeans at the hands of a threatening and unwelcome intruder who — to make matters worse — exhibits a flaring cultural inferiority." [23]

"The fear is that what's happening in America will happen in Europe, and that left to their own devices people will go to vulgar theme parks and shop at Wal-Mart," says Nick Cohen, a liberal British columnist. At its roots, this strain of anti-Americanism is a conservative ideology, he says. European elites were concerned that Americans had forsaken the church and the social hierarchy, according to Cohen, the author of a book reassessing European social liberals, *What's Left? How Liberals Lost Their Way.*

Nowhere is the ambivalence toward American culture more apparent than in France. When a Walt Disney theme park opened near Paris in 1994, French critics called it "a cultural Chernobyl." Yet today it rivals the Eiffel Tower as the country's most popular tourist destination. Without doubt, the biggest symbol of American cultural effrontery for the French is McDonald's. Yet the French are the biggest consumers of Big Macs in Europe. [24]

When France was making a national celebrity of farmer-activist Bové in 1999, the quality of McDonald's cheeseburgers was not the big issue; the enemy was the corporation. But food in France has deep and sentimental roots.

At a protest gathering on Bové's behalf, *The New York Times* interviewed a 16-year-old French lad who had come mostly for the carnival atmosphere. "But my father was a farmer," he said, "and I am here representing my family, too. We believe in what Mr. Bové believes in. We don't want the multinationals to tell us what to eat." [25]

In the 19th and early 20th centuries, when millions of Europeans sought their fortunes in the United States, American culture promised relief from the restrictions of European social hierarchies. "America was a hope, especially for the lower classes, in those times," says Detlev Claussen, a professor of social theory, cultural studies and sociology at Germany's Leibniz Hannover University. In the wake of World War I, Germans embraced American jazz, literature and art.

Nazi propaganda enthusiastically portrayed Americans as evil capitalists during World War II, but attitudes mellowed after the war when, despite the continued presence of the American military, the U.S. Marshall Plan helped rebuild Europe. Even in the 1960s and '70s, Germans were enthralled by American history and pop culture and established hundreds of re-enactment clubs that staged "Wild-West" shootouts and sympathetic portrayals of Indians.

The positive view of America began to change only in the Vietnam War era of the late 1960s, says Claussen. Even then, Germans made a distinction between disdain for American policies and adoration of cultural icons like Bob Dylan and the Rev. Martin Luther King Jr.

Now even those distinctions are eroding. The new anti-Americanism, Claussen says, stems from a sense of disappointment in the American utopia, tinged with envy of its political and economic power. Many Germans, he says, have simply given up on the idea of a virtuous America as a land of promise.

"When you can make no distinction between politics and culture, when you say, 'I don't like America, full stop,' that's real anti-Americanism," he says.

Is the "American Century" over?

On Feb. 7, 1941, in an editorial in *Life* magazine entitled "The American Century," media magnate Henry Luce advocated that the United States enter World War II and begin a global crusade on behalf of the values of freedom, opportunity, self-reliance and democracy. [26]

The concept of the "American Century," a potent ideal even before Luce's epochal essay, encompasses the modern history of American dominance, from the Spanish-American War to World War II, the Cold War and America's emergence as the world's only superpower in the 1990s.

These days, many are questioning whether the United States has squandered its position atop the global hierarchy. Rivals have emerged, even as the Soviet Union, once a contender, has dissolved. The European Union has been revitalized by the membership of new former Soviet-bloc countries. China and India, with their massive populations, are rapidly becoming developed countries. Perhaps the American "empire," like the Roman Empire and others before it, is already locked into inevitable decline.

Time recently devoted a cover story to China which concluded that, "in this century the relative power of the U.S. is going to decline, and that of China is going to rise. That cake was baked long ago." [27]

For the time being, however, the United States is the world's richest country and leading economy, with a gross domestic product (GDP) of $13 trillion. Its armed forces are stationed in 40 countries, its corporations and its charities operate throughout the globe and its technology arguably remains the most innovative. America is still a magnet for millions around the world, but its image has been badly tarnished by the Iraq War.

"There is a perception in the rest of the world that the U.S. is no longer capable of being the global leader that it once was," says Julia E. Sweig, director of Latin America studies at the Council on Foreign Relations and author of the 2006 book *Friendly Fire: Losing Friends and Making Enemies in the Anti-American Century.*

For many, that would be no great loss. No one likes the king of the hill for long. America (at least as a concept) is genuinely unpopular. A Pew survey found that "favorability ratings for the United States continue to trail those of other major countries. In Europe, as well as in predominantly Muslim countries, the U.S. is generally less popular than Germany, France, Japan and even China. In Western Europe, attitudes toward America remain considerably more negative than they were in 2002, prior to the Iraq War." [28]

"The tendency now is to view the U.S. as a threat to international stability," says Georgetown University's Kupchan.

Muslims in Southeast Asia, for example, no longer look up to the United States, says Farish A. Noor, a history professor at the Centre for Modern Oriental Studies in Berlin. "That's gone. It's completely erased now. An entirely new image of America has been constructed by the Islamists."

Of course, the damage to America's status did not begin with the invasion of Iraq. Still alive is the memory of the war in Vietnam, as well as America's Cold War support of totalitarian regimes, such as Augusto Pinochet's in Chile and Saddam Hussein's in Iraq (when Iraq was fighting Iran). In Latin America, many blamed the United States for encouraging the "dirty war" of the 1970s and '80s in Argentina and for supporting right-wing paramilitary squads in Nicaragua against the Marxist Sandinista junta.

At the same time, the United States cut back many "soft power" programs in cultural, economic and humanitarian aid in Latin America. Many of these were replaced with aggressive law-and-order programs that were part of the American government's war on drugs, and, after Sept. 11, the "war on terror."

And even before al Qaeda's 9/11 attacks, foreigners were critical of the U.S. rejection of global treaties, including the Kyoto Protocol for climate change, the creation of the International Criminal Court and rules for curbing biological weapons. Some of these treaties were actually rejected during the Clinton administration. The impression was strong that the United States would go it alone, because it thought it could.

It was at that point that many nations began to view the United States as "a delinquent international citizen." [29]

Some analysts wonder if the end of the American Century will begin in the Americas. Stepping into the hemispheric leadership vacuum, leftist President Hugo Chávez of Venezuela mocks President Bush as "the little gentleman" from the North and works at consolidating the region under his own oil-rich leadership.

American involvement in Latin America, long treated as a vast raw-material commodities mart by U.S. businesses, had already alienated many South and Central American countries, and, more recently, many Latin Americans have blamed U.S.-backed free-market economic policies for destabilizing their economies.

In 2005 Chávez even attempted to turn old-style American "soft power" on its head, offering and delivering 17 million gallons of heating oil to low-income families in New York and New England.

President Bush's March 2007 diplomatic swing through Latin American was intended to soothe feelings, but his administration's neglect, says Sweig, "has ripped off the Band-Aid that had covered up latent wounds for a long time."

As Bush was addressing an audience in Uruguay on March 10, Chávez led a counter rally in Argentina in which he called Bush a "political corpse." Alluding to the fact that he had previously called Bush "the devil" at the United Nations, Chávez bragged that, "He does not even smell of sulfur anymore; what [smells] is the scent of political death, and within a very short time it will become cosmic dust and disappear." [30]

In Muslim nations, the fiery rhetoric of the Bush administration's war on terror sparked a new depth of hostility. Among predominantly Islamic countries in Southeast Asia, which had previously looked on the U.S. as liberators, the Bush administration "squandered five decades of goodwill," says Noor. "So much of this has been personalized in Bush. He is like an icon of everything that is bad about the U.S."

Because of the war in Iraq and the festering Palestinian question, hatred for America on the Arab "street," as well as among Islamists, is raw and without nuance. But it is instructive to hear voices from a recent *New York Times* report about a new al Qaeda training camp for jihadists at a Palestinian refugee camp north of Beirut.

" 'The United States is oppressing a lot of people,' the group's deputy commander, Abu Sharif, said in a room strewn with Kalashnikovs. 'They are killing a lot of innocents, but one day they are getting paid back.'

" 'I was happy,' Hamad Mustaf Ayasin, 70, recalled in hearing last fall that his 35-year-old son, Ahmed, had died in Iraq fighting American troops near the Syrian border. 'The U.S. is against Muslims all over the world.'

"On the streets of the camp, one young man after another said dying in Iraq was no longer their only dream."

It was suicide.

" 'If I had the chance to do any kind of operation against anyone who is against Islam, inside or outside of the U.S., I would do the operation,' " said 18-year-old Mohamed. [31]

In England, *The Guardian* noted the continuing concern about the United States' use of its power during the months leading up to the invasion of Iraq. "Of course, enemies of the U.S. have shaken their fist at its 'imperialism' for decades," the paper editorialized. "They are doing it again now, as Washington wages a global 'war against terror' and braces itself for a campaign aimed at 'regime change' in a foreign, sovereign state.

"What is more surprising, and much newer, is that the notion of an American empire has suddenly become a live debate inside the U.S. And not just among Europhile liberals either, but across the range — from left to right." [32]

BACKGROUND

The Ungrateful Son

The story begins in Europe. The roots of antagonism toward the New World grew among the nations that first colonized it. America was the repository of the old world's disenfranchised and discontented, after all.

It was 18th-century British author Samuel Johnson who famously declared, "I am willing to love all mankind except an American." And another Briton, the 19th-century playwright George Bernard Shaw, quipped that "an asylum for the sane would be empty in America." Austria's Sigmund Freud, the father of psychoanalysis, was not enamored of the United States either. "A mistake," he called it, "a gigantic mistake." [33]

While some Americans might take pride in being loathed by European intellectuals, most have been mystified by, if not indifferent to the barbs. European anti-American feeling, argues the University of Michigan's Markovits, stems from the Europeans' sense that they have lost their own power and influence, and the subsequent search for a contemporary identity in a differently aligned global pecking order.

"Unlike elsewhere in the world," he said, "at least until very recently, America represented a particularly loaded concept and complex entity to Europeans precisely because it was, of course, a European creation."

The son, in other words, had rejected the father; America had "consciously defected from its European origins," Markovits says.

European conservatives and elites were miffed at America's rejection of the strictures of European class and religious hierarchies, the very things that people rebelled against when they emigrated to America.

One of the first Anti-American sentiments was the "degeneracy hypothesis," the belief that humidity and other atmospheric conditions in America created weak and morally inferior animals and human beings. The court philosopher to Frederick II of Prussia, Cornelius de Pauw, argued in 1768 about Americans that, "the weakest European could crush them with ease." [34]

As American industry rose in the late 19th century, the speed of American life became a major threat to European traditions of craftsmanship. "The breathless haste with which they work — the distinctive vice of the new world — is already beginning ferociously to infect old Europe and is spreading a spiritual emptiness over the continent," observed the German philosopher Friedrich Nietzsche. [35]

The notion that the mixing of races was bringing down the level of capability in Americans was another major thrust of anti-Americanism. Blacks and "low quality" immigrants, it was said in European salons, would lead to ultimate dissolution.

Arthur de Gobineau, a French social thinker, declared that America was creating the "greatest mediocrity in all fields: mediocrity of physical strength, mediocrity of beauty, mediocrity of intellectual capacities — we could almost say nothingness." [36]

After World War I, allies of the United States, France and Great Britain, found themselves massively in debt to the brash and newly powerful Americans, which generated resentment. These sentiments spread during the Great Depression. Sometimes the bias took on anti-Semitic overtones, including the widely held theory that the American government was ruled by a Jewish conspiracy. [37]

After World War II, the U.S. Marshall Plan helped rebuild Europe. Yet as American power grew while Europe licked its wounds, the United States became a scapegoat for an increasing sense of weakness among those nostalgic for their former empires. It was then that the global spread of American cultural, economic, and political power — rock 'n' roll, McDonald's and U.S. military bases — established the United States as a symbol of global authority, and one to be resisted.

Religious Differences

The staying power of American religiosity created another divide between Europe and the United States. Historian Huntington's "clash of civilizations" theory postulated that the big divide was between Christianity and Islam. But one of the deepest rifts between Europe and the United States centered on the relationship between religion and government.

Europeans had begun abandoning churchgoing in the 1950s and no longer felt that religion should play a role in political affairs. [38] But a large majority of Americans not only continued to go to church but also maintained the belief that religious tenets should provide moral direction to their elected leaders.

Many Europeans have been aghast at what they viewed as American religious fervor, particularly when it has seemed to influence government policy. "An American president who conducts Bible study at the White House and begins Cabinet sessions with a prayer may seem a curious anachronism to his European allies, but he is in tune with his constituents," write Judt and French scholar Denis Lacorne. [39]

Even in Spain, which has one of the most conservative religious establishments in Europe, American evangelicals' penchant for focusing on sexual issues does not resonate. In 2005, for example, a large majority of the Spanish population voted to legalize gay marriage, a key moral issue to some conservative American Christians.

Policies and traditions that regularly mix church and state in the United States — prayer in schools, God in the Pledge of Allegiance and the open displays of faith by President Bush — "were really shocking to the average Spaniard," says Charles Powell Solares, a deputy director

CHRONOLOGY

1700s–1800s *Europeans express disdain over U.S. independence.*

1768 Dutch philosopher Cornelius de Pauw describes America as "a Moronic Spirit" and the people "either degenerate or monstrous."

1776 English radical Thomas Day decries American hypocrisy: "If there be an object truly ridiculous in nature, it is an American patriot, signing resolutions of independency with the one hand, and with the other brandishing a whip over his affrighted slaves."

1842 British writer Charles Dickens lambastes oppressive Northern cities, Southern ignorance and Mississippi River pollution in *American Notes*.

1901–1980 *U.S. industrial power helps win world wars; Cold War begins.*

1919 Allies defeat Germany in World War I after U.S. enters war in 1917.

June 6, 1944 American forces lead invasion of Europe on D-Day; millions extend thanks to GIs.

August 1945 U.S. drops atomic bombs on Hiroshima and Nagasaki, forcing Japan to surrender. . . . Post-war U.S.-funded Marshall Plan provides development assistance to war-ravaged Europe.

1961 U.S. involvement in Vietnam begins, sparking anti-U.S. sentiment.

1967 Israel wins Six-Day War against Egypt, Jordan and Syria, begins occupation of West Bank and Gaza Strip. U.S. support for Israel feeds anti-Americanism.

1979 Shah overthrown in Iran. U.S. declared "The Great Satan."

1980s–1990s *Soviet Union collapses. U.S. involvement in Central America misfires. Resentment of world's sole superpower grows.*

1981 U.S.-trained Salvadoran soldiers massacre 800 women and children and elderly people in the country's

bloody civil war; U.S. blamed.

Nov. 9, 1989 Berlin Wall falls. Citizens of newly reunited German capital dance to American TV star David Hasselhoff's "Looking for Freedom."

1989 U.S. arrests former American ally Gen. Manuel Noriega of Panama for drug trafficking.

1999 Negotiations conclude for Kyoto global warming pact; U.S. signs but Congress refuses to ratify.

1999 Farmer José Bové destroys a McDonald's in southern France as a consumer protest. Protests are held against globalization, multinational corporations and U.S. products.

2000s *President George W. Bush begins a unilateralist foreign policy, alienating allies.*

Sept. 11, 2001 Terrorists hijack four airplanes and crash three into the World Trade Center and the Pentagon. . . . In October a worldwide, U.S.-led coalition invades Afghanistan.

2002 In France, Thierry Meyssan's bestseller *L'Effroyable Imposture* (*The Terrible Fraud*) alleges the U.S. was behind the Sept. 11 attacks. . . . Venezuelan strongman Hugo Chávez, temporarily toppled in an aborted coup, accuses Bush administration of backing the revolt. . . . American companies abroad are vandalized.

2003 Millions march in Europe to protest U.S-led invasion of Iraq.

2004 U.N. Secretary-General Kofi Annan calls Iraq invasion "illegal." . . . Abu Ghraib prison abuses shock the world. . . . Terrorists bomb Madrid trains.

2005 U.S. sends disaster aid to Indonesia and Pakistan, gaining goodwill. . . . Terrorists bomb London buses.

2006 British television airs a mock documentary about the imagined assassination of President Bush.

Feb. 10, 2007 Russian President Vladimir Putin denounces U.S. expansionism and military spending.

March 8, 2007 President Bush begins five-nation Latin American tour, sparking protests across the region.

at the Elcano Royal Institute, a think tank in Madrid. He says that 90 percent of Spaniards are in favor of a radical separation between church and state.

On the other hand, polls in Indonesia, Pakistan, Lebanon and Turkey reveal that the majority of people in Muslim countries believe the United States is secular and ungodly. [40]

Foreign Affairs Bully?

Muslims and Americans have not always been adversaries. The United States, after all, supported Islamists in Afghanistan in their fight against the Soviet Union in the 1980s, as well as Bosnian Muslims against Christian Orthodox Serbia in the 1990s.

Moreover, the United States maintains strong relationships with Saudi Arabia, Jordan and Egypt, and Muslim immigrants continue to flow into America — from Pakistan, Bangladesh, Afghanistan, India and even Iraq.

In Indonesia and Malaysia, home to some of the world's largest Muslim populations, anti-Americanism is a recent phenomenon. For most of the postwar 20th century, the United States was seen as an anti-colonial power because of its role in liberating those countries from Japan.

"It's not a coincidence that the Malaysian flag looks like the American flag," says Noor of Berlin's Centre for Modern Oriental Studies.

The advance of high-speed communications has been a key factor in the attitude shift in Southeast Asia. "New media, especially satellite television and the Internet, reinforce negative images of the U.S. through a flood of compelling, highly graphic images," said Steven Simon, a Middle East scholar at the Council on Foreign Relations. "Some of these images present the Muslims as victims; others as victors. All tend to frame events as segments of an ongoing drama between good and evil." [41]

This "us vs. them" dynamic had its genesis in Europe. "Many of these originated outside the Muslim world entirely," Simon told the House International Relations Committee. They were "introduced to the region by Nazi and Soviet propaganda in mid-20th century."

Most notoriously, the British-appointed mufti of Jerusalem, Haj Amin al-Husayni, made a pact with the German government in the 1930s and spread ill will throughout the region against the Western allies, including the United States. Great Britain, of course, was

Venezuelan President Hugo Chávez fulminates about the United States at Miraflores Palace, Caracas, in 2006. Chávez, who is attempting to form an alternative coalition of South American countries opposed to the United States, insults and belittles the American president at every opportunity.

already an object of scorn and resentment for its heavy-handed colonial administration of Muslim territory.

Simon also noted that after Britain pulled out of the Middle East in the 1940s and America began to vie for influence during the Cold War, the United States inherited the animosity that Muslim countries had against Britain, their former conquerors. "The substitution of American power in the region for British authority was bound to tar the U.S. with the imperialist brush," Simon said.

American Exceptionalism

Americans' self-image has been rooted in the certitude that their country is different — a beacon of personal, political and economic freedom in the world. This idea really came of age during World War II, when American industrial power, along with Soviet manpower, liberated Europe. Then the Yanks were cheered and admired, but some scholars believe that the roots of anti-American feelings by many Europeans stem from this U.S. "salvation."

A residue of that feeling remains in France, which truly had been liberated. Germany, however, had been the enemy, and even during the height of the Cold War in the 1960s and '70s, many West Germans deeply resented the presence of American military bases.

Even though the American army's airlift of supplies had saved West Berlin, few thought of the United States

At a Berlin Café, Musing About America

"We were hoping America would not elect Bush"

Prenzlauer Berg was once on the gritty side of town, in East Berlin, when Berlin was a divided city. The Berlin Wall was torn down nearly 20 years ago, and few signs of it remain.

Prenzlauer Berg is now fashionable, but there's still a certain working-class feel to it. On a rainy afternoon last February three friends met for coffee at the Wasser und Brot (Water and Bread), a barely decorated neighborhood café frequented mostly by local workmen, artists, students and retirees.

Baerel Boesking is a 45-year-old actress, originally from Lower Saxony; *Robert Lingnau*, 33, is a composer and writer. *Petra Lanthaler*, 30, is a psychologist. She came to Berlin four years ago from northern Italy.

They sipped tea and coffee and smoked, musing about the United States, George Bush and the future of relations with those increasingly alienating Americans:

Is America different from other countries?

ROBERT: America is very powerful so it has more impact on us than any other country. All of the oil stuff, all of the pollution, the politics.

BAERBEL: Since the student protests here in the 60s, many people still think of the United States as an imperialist, capitalist power. People think Americans are just super-ficial, and Bush has only made that worse. But I know that not all Americans are superficial, like [filmmaker] Michael Moore, for instance.

PETRA: I don't think the American people are superficial. As far as I know, there are also many people in the United States who are rebelling against Bush.

Did your impression of America change after Sept. 11?

ROBERT: I think that the American government in some way participated or co-arranged for 9/11, or at least they knew certain things in advance and didn't act to prevent it. They wanted to install the Patriot Act, so that the government could take more control over people's lives. With the terrorist threat, people let the Patriot Act go through. Meanwhile, Bush is cutting billions from Medicare but putting more and more money into the war in Iraq.

BAERBEL: I often hear things like this from my friends. Many of them have the opinion that this whole thing, 9/11, was self-done by the U.S. itself. These are really educated people, it's horrible. This is an unbelievable point of view, like people who believe that the landing on the moon was just a Hollywood production.

ROBERT: I have two degrees actually. I think the Americans landed on the moon, but I don't think the gov-

as having saved them from the Nazis or the Soviets, says Claussen, at Leibniz Hannover University, and West German politicians were loath to suggest that "America has liberated us."

Spain until recently was America's closest ally in continental Europe, but enmity toward the United States has existed since the 1950s, says Powell Solares, at Madrid's Elcano Royal Institute. Spain never viewed America as a liberator because the country was largely uninvolved with World War II. Instead, they tend to condemn the U.S. for supporting fascist Gen. Francisco Franco as part of its Cold War policy.

"And that means that Spaniards have never associated the U.S. with freedom and democracy," says Powell Solares, citing polls from the 1960s and '70s in which Spaniards viewed the United States as a bigger threat to world peace than the Soviet Union.

After the collapse of the Soviet Union in 1991 the former republics of the Soviet Union and its satellite nations emerged with more solidarity with the United States than most of the countries of Western Europe. Except for Great Britain, Eastern European nations have contributed more troops per capita to the Coalition Forces in the invasions of Afghanistan and Iraq. Several have allegedly allowed controversial secret CIA prisons on their soil.

When U.S. Secretary of Defense Donald Rumsfeld distinguished between the "Old Europe" and "New Europe" in 2003, he was paying homage to the willingness of the newly liberated nations to aid the United States, in contrast to the recalcitrance of Germany and

ernment did their best to prevent what happened. I don't think they wrote the script for what happened, but in a way they participated in order to get the Patriot Act through and for what came after.

PETRA: I don't want to believe that a government would do that. It's true that after 9/11 the U.S. took advantage of these fears of terrorism.

Anti-war demonstrators sometimes have signs comparing Bush to Hitler.

BAERBEL: Bush is not equal to Hitler. You can't compare somebody to Hitler.

ROBERT: You can compare Stalin to Hitler, but not Bush.

BAERBEL: You can compare Mao, this new guy in Korea and Saddam Hussein, but it is crazy to say that Bush is like Hitler.

BAERBEL: I was watching a television debate between Bush and [Sen. John] Kerry [D-Mass.], and Bush said that his role model was Jesus. He's got a long way to go. I don't think Jesus would have started a war with Iraq. I'm a Christian, too.

What do you think about American culture?

PETRA: The first words that come into my mind are big size. The shops are much bigger, the portions are much bigger, everything is bigger. People are bigger. But I know that's a really superficial answer because I've never actually been to America. I am impressed by their scientific research. They think much more globally than Europeans do.

ROBERT: They don't seem to think globally about pollution and global warming. For me, there are two things that constitute my everyday life: that's jazz music and Apple Macintosh. That's what I think of when I think about U.S. culture. Both native American art forms.

BAERBEL: I had an American boyfriend once. From Kansas.

Do you think relations between America and Europe will improve with a new president in 2008?

BAERBEL: Yes, if it's a Democrat. It's really good you have term limits in the United States. We had Helmut Kohl for 16 years.

ROBERT: But if Jeb Bush gets elected, this is like 16 years of Kohl.

PETRA: All of my friends, most everybody I knew, we were really hoping that America would not elect Bush for the second term. It was really disappointing.

ROBERT: My hope for the next president is that he didn't study at Yale and that he hasn't been a member of Skull and Bones [the exclusive secret society].

It was still raining and cold when the friends left the smoky warmth of the Wasser and Brod. It wasn't their anti-Americanism that stood out but how much they knew about America and American life. And it begged the question: Would Americans know half as much about Germany, even the name of the chancellor?

France — Old Europe. [42] French officials labeled the secretary's bluntness as "arrogance."

Anti-Americanism got only a short reprieve in the aftermath of the 9/11 attacks.

"Initially, there was a spontaneous outpouring of sympathy and support for the United States," Pew researchers found. "Even in some parts of the Middle East, hostility toward the U.S. appeared to soften a bit. But this reaction proved short-lived. Just a few months after the attacks, a Global Attitudes Project survey of opinion leaders around the world found that, outside Western Europe, there was a widespread sense that U.S. policies were a major cause of the attacks."

In Venezuela, President Chávez cynically suggested, "The hypothesis that is gaining strength . . . is that it was the same U.S. imperial power that planned and carried out this terrible terrorist attack or act against its own people and against citizens of all over the world. Why? To justify the aggressions that immediately were unleashed on Afghanistan, on Iraq." [43]

CURRENT SITUATION

Missteps and Failures

Because of their self-proclaimed virtues and their emphasis on human rights, Americans are often held to higher expectations on the world stage than are other nations. When they fail to perform to those standards, they are doubly condemned. Many who see U.S. foreign policy floundering are as disappointed as they are angry.

AFP/Getty Images/Rizwan Tabassum

Pakistani protesters burn the American flag and a mock Israeli flag to protest the Israeli attack on southern Lebanon in August 2006. Anti-American sentiment often ties the U.S. and Israel together as partners in the exploitation and humiliation of other countries.

Some of the criticisms of the United States — such as the allegations that the government was behind the 9/11 attacks — are so irrational that there is no way to answer them. But there are inescapable realities that will not go away.

America's credibility on human rights has been severely damaged by prisoner abuse at Abu Ghraib, the U.S.-run Baghdad prison for terrorism suspects, and alleged mistreatment at the Guantanamo Bay detention camp in Cuba, as well as by CIA renditions and secret detention camps in Eastern Europe. [44] Its reputation for competence has been trampled by revelations that Iraq's alleged weapons of mass destruction had been trumped up by an overeager White House yearning for battle. Most jarring of all is the bloodshed in Iraq that has claimed at least 34,000 Iraqis and more than 3,000 American troops. [45]

After the revelations at Abu Ghraib, Patrick Sabatier of the French newspaper *Liberation* wrote, "One can lose a war in places other than battlegrounds. The torture that took place in the Abu Ghraib prison is a major defeat for the U.S. The photographs fan the fires of anti-American hate in the Arab world. Elsewhere they trigger reactions of disgust, and take away from the coalition's small dose of moral legitimacy, gained by toppling Saddam's regime." [46]

Even Americans themselves no longer defend the U.S position in Iraq, Pew researchers found. "As to whether the removal of Saddam Hussein from power made the world a safer place," the survey said, "views are also lopsidedly negative. In no country surveyed, including the United States, does a majority think the Iraq leader's overthrow has increased global security." [47]

Another strike against the American war in Iraq is its duration — longer now than World War II. And the carnage can be seen daily on television. "If the war had had a quick or favorable ending, people would have forgotten about it. But it is in the news every day," says Vallespin, at the Sociological Research Centre of Spain.

Support for Israel

For many Americans and Europeans, Israel cannot be forsaken. It is a place of immense historical and spiritual importance, and was established to right grievous historic wrongs. This is felt not only by America's 3 million Jews but also by an overwhelming number of the country's Christians.

Muslim nations, however, and many other non-Muslim countries, see Israel as a regional bully propped up by the United States. Pew surveys found that many people "suspect the United States of deliberately targeting Muslim nations and using the war on terror to protect Israel," as well as to gain control of Middle East oil. [48]

Clear evidence of a biased relationship was seen in the fact that the United States announced a $10 billion military-aid package to Israel on the same day that the U.S. military began its assault on Iraq in 2003.

"To announce this package on the same day that Iraq is bombed is as stupid as it is arrogant," said Nabeel Ghanyoum, a military analyst in Syria. "This is effectively telling the Arab world, 'Look we are bombing Iraq as we please, and we are giving Israel as much financial aid [as] it wants.' " [49]

In his study of the links between anti-Israeli sentiment and anti-Americanism, the University of Michigan's Markovits found that the crucial link was made after the Israeli victory in the 1967 war, while America was embroiled in Vietnam.

"Israel became little more than an extension of American power to many, especially on Europe's political left," he wrote. "Israel was disliked, especially by the left, not so much because it was Jewish but because it was American. And as such it was powerful." [50]

A Good Neighbor?

There have been positive moments in the past few years. The Council on Foreign Relations' Simon says that there was an upsurge in America's standing in 2004, when it provided substantial aid in the wake of the devastating

Southeast Asian tsunami. The perception that this aid was "unconditional," he said, had a "sharply positive effect" on perceptions of the United States.

Noor at the Centre for Modern Oriental Studies in Berlin disagrees. He says he visited storm-damaged areas of Indonesia and Pakistan after the disaster and perceived even this seemingly altruistic venture was a public-relations disaster for the United States.

"They showed up on aircraft carriers and other warships," he says, "and the soldiers sent to help the victims were still wearing their combat fatigues from the Iraq War." It would have been far wiser to send civilian aid workers rather than the military, he says, who were regarded by many storm victims as emissaries of the imperial United States. "America is now seen [there] as something alien."

The Remarque Institute's Judt says that the U.S. government's disdain for international institutions has had a lasting negative effect, particularly among America's long-time allies. The Bush administration created an "in-your-face America," he says, that conveyed the message: "Not only do the things we do annoy you, but we don't care. We are going to do what we do, and you can take it or leave it."

For example, during his short stint as U.S. envoy to the United Nations, Ambassador John Bolton was criticized — and also praised — for his straight-from-the-shoulder diplomacy, including his disparagement of the United Nations itself. "The Secretariat building in New York has 38 stories," he famously once said. "If it lost 10 stories, it wouldn't make a bit of difference." [51] Bolton was blamed by some U.N. officials for quietly sabotaging the organization's reform initiative by stirring differences between poor and rich countries.

"He sometimes makes it very difficult to build bridges because he is a very honest and blunt person," said South Africa's ambassador, Dumisani Shadrack Kumalo, chairman of a coalition of developing nations. He said it sometimes appeared that "Ambassador Bolton wants to prove nothing works at the United Nations." [52] Bolton resigned in December 2006.

In addition, both Noor and Latin America expert Sweig at the Council on Foreign Relations say the U.S. reputation for generosity has been hurt by drastic cuts in foreign-assistance programs under the U.S. Agency for International Development (AID), as well as cuts in funds for libraries, scholarships and other cultural activities. Private giving by Americans remains the highest per

A female U.S. Army soldiers frisks a Kurdish woman at a checkpoint in Ramadi, Iraq, in October 2004. Several people had been killed in clashes between rebels and U.S. troops. The war in Iraq underlies much of the spiraling anti-American sentiment around the world today.

capita in the world, and American foreign-development aid is the highest in the developed world in pure dollar terms, but the level of aid sinks very low when measured as a percentage of GDP. [53]

Such aid programs in many cases were replaced by "War on Terrorism" initiatives, including a $300 million propaganda campaign from the Pentagon. The psychological-warfare operation included plans for placing pro-American messages in foreign media outlets without disclosing the U.S. government as the source. [54]

Alarmist rhetoric is a poor substitute for help, says Noor, because the United States no longer has people on the ground in Muslim countries who know the cultures and the languages. When they were in effect and fully funded, he says, U.S. aid programs were so successful that Islamist movements in those countries have mimicked them. "They borrowed the tactics of the Peace Corps."

Missed Opportunities

By linking Israel and the United States into a single, fearsome conspiracy, anti-American activists have created strange bedfellows: fundamentalist Muslims, socialists and Western pacifists. Left-leaning groups used to find common cause in socialist ideals. Now, "anti-Americanism is the glue that holds them together, and hatred of Israel is one aspect," said Emmanuele Ottolenghi, a research fellow at the Centre for Hebrew and Jewish studies at Oxford University in England. [55]

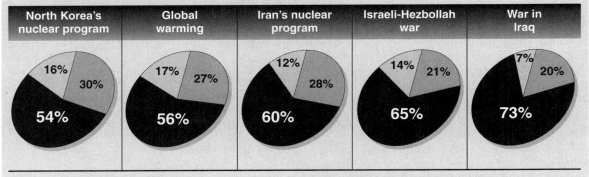

Disapproval of American Policies Is Widespread

More than half of the 26,000 people surveyed in 25 countries disapprove of the United States' role in several foreign-policy areas. Fifty-six percent disagree with the U.S. approach toward global warming, while nearly three-quarters are critical of the war in Iraq.

Do you agree or disagree with U.S. handling of:

North Korea's nuclear program	Global warming	Iran's nuclear program	Israeli-Hezbollah war	War in Iraq
16% / 30% / 54%	17% / 27% / 56%	12% / 28% / 60%	14% / 21% / 65%	7% / 20% / 73%

Approve   Disapprove   No opinion

Source: The poll was conducted for BBC World Service by the international polling firm GlobeScan; 26,381 people in Asia, Africa, Europe, South America, the Middle East and the United States were interviewed between Nov. 3, 2006, and Jan. 9, 2007

While America's close relationship with Israel was often questioned outside the United States, the U.S. role in opposing the Soviet Union during the Cold War more than outweighed it, says Georgetown University's Kupchan. Now, he says, the old bonds don't count for so much.

"The World War II generation is dying off; the reflexive support of the transatlantic partnership of that generation is disappearing. You have a new generation of Europeans for whom the United States is not the savior from the Nazis and the Soviets that it was for their parents," says Kupchan.

Meanwhile, even with a new U.S. presidential election nearing, fears remain strong in Europe about the actions of the Bush administration in its remaining months. Of particular concern is the possibility of a dangerous new U.S. offensive against Iran, which says it will continue developing nuclear energy.

"We think that the growing tensions between the two countries are made more dangerous by George Bush's detachment from the electorate: There's a real risk that he may strike at Iran before he leaves power," John Micklethwait, editor of *The Economist*, recently wrote. [56]

OUTLOOK

Lasting Damage?

When prosecutors in Munich decided in January to charge CIA counterterrorism operatives with kidnapping a German citizen, Khalid el-Masri, the newspaper *Sueddeutsche Zeitung* declared: "The great ally is not allowed to simply send its thugs out into Europe's streets." Indeed, Craig Whitlock reported, the decision "won widespread applause from German politicians and the public." [57]

In the wake of such incidents, many at home and abroad are asking how — and even if — the United States can repair its image and its relations with its allies. Some analysts believe that the coming new presidential administration, whether Republican or Democratic, can do it through diligent cooperation and outreach. Others say the damage is so severe that it would take decades.

"When Bush goes, assuming that there isn't a war with Iran, it will be possible for the next president to exercise damage control," says Remarque Institute Director Judt.

Sweig of the Council on Foreign Relations sees a longer road ahead. "It will be the work of a generation to turn this around," she says.

Will anti-Americanism wane after President Bush leaves office?

YES   Dr. Farish A. Noor
Professor of history, Centre for Modern Oriental Studies, Berlin

Written for *CQ Researcher*, March 2007

It is undeniable that the image of the United States of America has declined significantly in Southeast Asia during President George Bush's term. Over the past two years I have witnessed more than two-dozen anti-American demonstrations in Malaysia and Indonesia, where the issues ranged from Malaysia's protracted negotiations with the USA on the Free Trade Agreement to America's actions in Afghanistan and Iraq. At almost all of these demonstrations effigies of George Bush and Condoleeza Rice were paraded and sometimes set alight.

Historically America was seen as a liberator and savior in the Southeast Asian region, especially in its role against the Japanese imperial army during the Second World War and its efforts to prevent the Western European colonial powers (Britain, France and the Netherlands) from recolonizing their former colonies Malaya, Indonesia, Vietnam, Burma and the Philippines.

Admiration for America, the American way of life and American values was at its peak during the postcolonial developmental era of the 1960s to 1980s, when Southeast Asian countries sent tens of thousands of students to the U.S. for further education. The American economic model became the framework for the postcolonial economies of the region; and America was doubly thanked for helping to keep the region safe from communism.

Yet, America today is seen as the enemy of Islam, and for Muslim-majority countries like Malaysia, Indonesia and Brunei this poses new problems for bilateral relations. One major factor that has worsened the situation was the use of bellicose rhetoric by the Bush administration in its unilateral "war on terror," which was couched in terms of a "crusade." Subsequent actions and misjudgments (such as the invasion of Iraq without sufficient consultation with Muslim countries) and the deteriorating security condition in Iraq and Afghanistan have merely compounded the problem even more.

Much of the damage, however, is due to the unilateralist character of a Bush administration that was seen as cavalier, gung-ho and insensitive to Muslim concerns. Thanks in part to the over-reach and over-projection of the image of Bush in this campaign, however, much of the controversy surrounding the war on terror, the invasion of Afghanistan and Iraq, etc. has been associated with President Bush himself on a personal level.

There is every reason to believe that some of the anti-Americanism we see in Southeast Asia today will wane with a change of administration. But this also depends on whether the next U.S. government can bring the campaigns in Afghanistan and Iraq to a close with minimum loss of life.

NO   Manjeet Kripalani
Edward R. Murrow Press Fellow, Council on Foreign Relations; India Bureau Chief, Business Week

Written for *CQ Researcher*, March 2007

The favorability rating of the U.S. in the eyes of the world has fallen precipitously since the Iraq invasion, and continues to decline as the war wears on.

Will America ever recover its lost reputation? Perhaps, but it will take years. The perception of the U.S. is that of a power in descent, a nation spent in the ignominious and outmoded task of building Empire. The ideals and positive force that the U.S. represented have been discredited since 2003, given the fundamentalist fervor with which they have been pursued.

That's not the best option in an increasingly complex world. Getting a global consensus on crises like Darfur, trade imbalances, terrorism and Middle East peace in a world without the powerful moral authority of the U.S. will be more difficult. But it has created space for other leadership to step up to the task.

This ascendant world comprises powers like Russia, but more widely the countries of Asia — notably China, India and even Japan. As the beneficiary of past American ideals, Japan has developed goodwill over decades through aid, anti-war sensitivities and the potential to be the stable "America" in Asia.

China and India are both poor, developing countries — but much of today's world looks more like them than it does the U.S.-dominated developed world. Their experiences are being closely watched by their peers, with whom there are centuries-old cultural and historic ties.

In this new world order, the U.S.'s tarnished image really doesn't matter. America is still a powerful country, and these same ascendant nations are meshed with it economically and politically. China is in a tight economic embrace with America. Japan is still militarily protected by the U.S. and is its strongest, staunchest ally in Asia.

India, after years of hostile relations with the U.S., has turned pragmatic. Since 2001, America's popularity in India has been on the rise. That's because Indians, affected by terrorism for decades, view Washington as fighting their war for them. And despite domestic pressure, President Bush has continued to support the outsourcing of back-office jobs to India. The signing of the nuclear deal last December is surely good for U.S. business and Indian consumers. But its symbolism is far greater: Its confidence in India's non-proliferation record has ensured that democratic India will wholeheartedly embrace the U.S. economically, technologically and politically.

This ensures that in the future, no matter how much moral authority the U.S. loses, its wagon is hitched firmly to the stars of these ascendant nations — and vice versa.

Political theater plays out in Paris as orange-jump-suited Amnesty International protesters call on the United States to close the Guantanamo Bay, Cuba, prison camp.

Gerard Baker, U.S. editor for the *Times of London*, posits a more complex future. "Somewhere, deep down," he writes, "tucked away underneath their loathing for George Bush, in a secret place where the lights of smart dinner-party conversation and clever debating-society repartee never shine, the growing hordes of America-bashers must dread the moment he leaves office.

"When President Bush goes into the Texas sunset, and especially if he is replaced by an enlightened, world-embracing Democrat, their one excuse, their sole explanation for all human suffering in the world will disappear too. And they may just find that the world is not as simple as they thought it was." [58]

Critics agree that as long as the United States remains the world's greatest economic and military force, it will often be blamed for its negative impact on other countries, and seldom thanked for positive contributions. The inferiority complex that the University of Michigan's Markovits says drives Europe's brand of anti-Americanism will probably continue to fester until the EU can learn to assert itself in global affairs when humanitarian as well as military demands are compelling.

The Israeli-Palestinian conflict also will remain a problem and a source of agitation against U.S. policy, as long as Israel insists on occupying Palestinian land, America supports its right to do so and Palestinian politicians are unable to bring their angry streets to a compromise solution for statehood. The problem is multi-faceted.

But, as Powell Solares at Madrid's Elcano Royal Institute points out, much of the global public sees only one thing: "The perception that the main problem with the Arab-Israeli conflict is that the U.S. will always back Israel."

Iraq looms over all questions about the future. "The U.S. presence in Iraq will seriously impede American efforts to influence hearts and minds," Simon, the Middle East expert at the Council on Foreign Relations, told a House subcommittee last September. "Our occupation will reinforce regional images of the United States as both excessively violent and ineffectual." [59]

But what will follow the "American Century" in the near future if the United States has lost the trust of the world?

"It may be that the United States has not shown itself worthy or capable of ensuring the unity of a civilization whose laws have governed the world, at least for the last few centuries," writes Jean Daniel in *Le Nouvel Observateur* in Paris.

"But since a united Europe capable of taking over this mission hasn't yet emerged," Daniel continues, "all we can do is hope that the American people will wake up and rapidly call a halt to these crude interventionist utopias carelessly dredged out of the Theodore Roosevelt tradition. Utopias that, in the words of an American diplomat, have made George W. Bush and his brain trust 'lose their intelligence as they turned into ideologues.' " [60]

NOTES

1. See Fareed Zakaria, "The Politics of Rage: Why Do They Hate Us?" *Newsweek*, Sept. 24, 2001.

2. Samuel P. Huntington, "The Clash of Civilizations?" *Foreign Affairs*, summer 1993; www.foreignaffairs. org/19930601faessay5188/samuel-p-huntington/the-clash-of-civilizations.html.

3. James Keaten, "French Farmer José Bové Leads New McDonald's Protest," The Associated Press, Aug. 13, 2001; www.mcspotlight.org/media/press/mcds/theassociatedpr130801.html.

4. Quoted in David Morse, "Striking the Golden Arches: French Farmers Protest McDonald's Globalization," *The Ecologist*, Dec. 31, 2002, p. 2; www.socsci.uci.edu/~cohenp/food/frenchfarmers.pdf.

5. For background, see Mary H. Cooper, "Hating America," *CQ Researcher*, Nov. 23, 2001, pp. 969-992.

6. Andrei S. Markovits, "European Anti-Americanism (and Anti-Semitism): Ever Present Though Always Denied," Working Paper Series #108. Markovits is Karl W. Deutsch Collegiate Professor of Comparative Politics and German Studies at the University of Michigan.

7. Paul Hockenos, "Dispatch From Germany," *The Nation*, April 14, 2003; www.thenation.com/doc/20030414/hockenos.

8. "Pakistani Cartoon Protesters Chant Anti-American Slogans," FoxNews.com, Feb. 21, 2006; www.foxnews.com/story/0,2933,185503,00.html.

9. Jean-Marie Colombani, "We Are All Americans," *Le Monde*, Sept. 12, 2001.

10. Quoted in Denis Lacorne and Tony Judt, eds., *With Us or Against Us: Studies in Global Anti-Americanism* (2005).

11. "Global Opinion: The Spread of Anti-Americanism," Trends 2005, p. 106; Pew Research Center for People and the Press, Jan. 24, 2005; http://people-press.org/commentary/display.php3?AnalysisID=104.

12. "U.S. Image Up Slightly, But Still Negative American Character Gets Mixed Reviews," Pew Research Center for People and the Press, June 23, 2005; http://pew-global.org/reports/display.php?ReportID=247.

13. Lacorne and Judt, *op. cit.*

14. "War in Iraq: Winning the Peace," *The* [Beirut] *Daily Star*, April 6, 2006, from Worldpress.com; www.worldpress.org/Mideast/1041.cfm.

15. Peter Ford, "Europe Cringes at Bush 'Crusade' Against Terrorists," *The Christian Science Monitor*, Sept. 19, 2001.

16. For background, see Brian Hansen, "Globalization Backlash," *CQ Researcher*, Sept. 28, 2001, pp. 961-784.

17. For background, see Sarah Glazer, "Slow Food Movement," *CQ Researcher*, Jan. 26, 2007, pp. 73-96, and David Hosansky, "Food Safety," *CQ Researcher*, Nov. 1, 2002, pp. 897-920.

18. Quoted in *The Daily Mail*, June 1, 1999, BBC Online Network; http://news.bbc.co.uk/2/hi/uk_news/358291.stm.

19. Quoted in Sam Loewenberg, "Lobbying Euro-Style," *The National Journal*, Sept. 8, 2001.

20. Henry A. Giroux, "George Bush's Religious Crusade Against Democracy: Fundamentalism as Cultural Politics," *Dissident Voice*, Aug. 4, 2004; www.dissidentvoice.org/Aug04/Giroux0804.htm.

21. "God and American diplomacy," *The Economist*, Feb. 8, 2003.

22. Pew Research Center, *op. cit.*, Jan. 24, 2005.

23. Markovits, *op. cit.*

24. "Burger and fries à la française," *The Economist*, April 15, 2004.

25. Suzanne Daley, "French Turn Vandal Into Hero Against US." *The New York Times*, July 1, 2000.

26. Henry Luce, "The American Century," *Life*, Feb. 7, 1941.

27. Michael Elliott, "China Takes on the World," *Time*, Jan. 11, 2007.

28. "America's Image Slips, But Allies Share U.S. Concerns Over Iran, Hamas; No Global Warming Alarm in the U.S., China," Pew Research Center for People and the Press, June 13, 2006; http://pewglobal.org.

29. Lacorne and Judt, *op. cit.*

30. "Hugo Chávez: Latin America Rises Against the Empire," March 10, 2007, from audio transcript on TeleSUR; http://latinhacker.gnn.tv/blogs/22178/Hugo_Chavez_Latin_America_Rises_Against_the_Empire.

31. Souad Mekhennet and Michael Moss, "New Face of Jihad Vows Attacks," *The New York Times*, March 16, 2007.

32. "Rome AD . . . Rome DC?" *The Guardian*, Sept. 18, 2002; www.guardian.co.uk/usa/story/0,12271,794163,00.html.

33. Quoted in Judy Colp Rubin, "Is Bush Really Responsible for Anti-Americanism Around the World," Sept. 27, 2004, George Mason University's History Network; http://hnn.us/articles/7288.html.

34. Cornelius de Pauw, "Recherches philosophiques sur les Américains ou Mémoires interessants pour servir à l'histoire de l'espèce humaine," London, 1768.

35. Friedrich Nietzsche, *The Gay Science*, sec. 329 (1882).

36. Arthur Gobineau, (Count Joseph Arthur de Gobineau) and Adrian Collins [1853-55] 1983. *The Inequality of Human Races*, Second edition, reprint.

37. Barry Rubin and Judith Colp Rubin, *Hating America: A History* (2004).

38. Lacorne and Judt, *op. cit.*, p. 26.

39. *Ibid.*

40. Pew Research Center, *op. cit.*, June 23, 2005.

41. Testimony before House International Relations Committee, Sept. 14, 2006.

42. Quoted in "Outrage at 'Old Europe' Remarks," BBC Online, Jan. 23, 2003.

43. "Theory That U.S. Orchestrated Sept. 11 Attacks 'Not Absurd,'" The Associated Press, Sept. 12, 2001, www.breitbart.com/.

44. For background, see Peter Katel and Kenneth Jost, "Treatment of Detainees," *CQ Researcher*, Aug. 25, 2006, pp. 673-696.

45. For background, see Peter Katel, "New Strategy in Iraq," *CQ Researcher*, Feb. 23, 2007, pp. 169-192.

46. Patrick Sabatier, Liberation, Paris, Quoted in WorldPress.com, "Iraq Prisoner Abuse Draws International Media Outrage," May 12, 2004; www.worldpress.org/Mideast/1861.cfm.

47. Pew Research Center, *op. cit.*, June 23, 2005.

48. Pew Research Center, *op. cit.*, Jan. 24, 2005.

49. Firas Al-Atraqchi, "Disillusion, Anger on the Arab Street," *Dissident Voice Online*, March 21, 2007; www.dissidentvoice.org/Articles3/Atraqchi_ArabStreet.htm.

50. Markovits, *op. cit.*

51. Quoted in Anne Applebaum, "Defending Bolton," *The Washington Post*, March 9, 2005, p. A21.

52. Quoted in Peter Baker and Glenn Kessler, "U.N. Ambassador Bolton Won't Stay," *The Washington Post*, Dec. 6, 2006, p. A1.

53. "Review of the Development Cooperation Policies and Programmes of United States," Organization for Economic Cooperation and Development, 2006.

54. Matt Kelley, "Pentagon Rolls Out Stealth PR," *USA Today*, Dec. 14, 2005.

55. Glenn Frankel, "In Britain, War Concern Grows Into Resentment of U.S. Power; Anxiety Over Attack on Iraq Moves to Political Mainstream," *The Washington Post*, Jan. 26, 2003, p. A14.

56. John Micklethwait, "Letter to Readers," *The Economist*, Feb. 8, 2007.

57. Craig Whitlock, "In Another CIA Abduction, Germany Has an Uneasy Role," *The Washington Post*, Feb. 5, 2007, p. A11.

58. Gerard Baker, "When Bush Leaves Office," *Times of London*, TimesOnline, March 2, 2007.

59. Testimony before International Relations Subcommittee on the Middle East, Sept. 14, 2006.

60. Jean Daniel, "Our American 'Enemies,'" *La Nouvel Observateur*, Sept. 23, 2003, quoted on WorldPress.org.

BIBLIOGRAPHY

Books

Cohen, Nick, *What's Left? How Liberals Lost Their Way*, Fourth Estate, 2007.
A well-known liberal British columnist for *The Observer* and *The New Statesman* gives a scathing critique of anti-Americanism among the British Left, the anti-globalization movement and intellectuals who have become apologists for militant Islam.

Garton Ash, Timothy, *Free World: America, Europe and the Surprising Future of the West*, Random House, 2004.
In an engaging critique of anti-American sentiment, a former journalist who runs the European Studies Centre at Oxford University argues that in the post-Cold War world, America is the "other" against which Europeans try to define their own identity.

Joffe, Josef, *Uberpower: The Imperial Temptation of America*, W. W. Norton, 2006.
The editor and publisher of *Die Zeit*, a German weekly, and a fellow in international relations at the Hoover Institution, provides a European intellectual's insight into the envy at the heart of anti-Americanism and its parallels with classical anti-Semitism.

Katzenstein, Peter, and Robert Keohane, eds., *Anti-Americanisms in World Politics*, Cornell University Press, 2006.
Two international-relations scholars bring together the insights of historians, social scientists and political scientists.

Kohut, Andrew, and Bruce Stokes, *America Against the World: How We Are Different and Why We Are Disliked*, Times Books, 2006.
Kohut, director of the Pew Research Center for the People and the Press, and Stokes, international economics columnist for *National Journal*, provide a comprehensive survey of public opinions about America from around the world.

Kupchan, Charles, *The End of the American Era: U.S. Foreign Policy and the Geopolitics of the Twenty-first Century*, Vintage, 2003.
A former National Security Council staffer and a senior fellow at the Council on Relations argues that with the

rise of China and the European Union America can no longer afford to have a unilateralist foreign policy.

Lacorne, Denis, and Tony Judt, eds., *With Us or Against Us: Studies in Global Anti-Americanism,* **Palgrave Macmillan, 2005.**
Essays by 11 scholars analyze anti-American sentiment in Western and Eastern Europe, the Middle East and Asia.

Markovits, Andrei S., *Uncouth Nation: Why Europe Dislikes America,* **Princeton University Press, 2007.**
A professor of comparative politics and German studies at the University of Michigan, Ann Arbor, writes provocatively about the anti-Americanism in everyday European life.

Revel, Jean-Francois, *Anti-Americanism,* **Encounter Books, 2003.**
Revel, a leading French intellectual, castigates his countrymen for pointing their fingers at America when they should be dealing with their own current and historical problems.

Sweig, Julia, *Friendly Fire: Losing Friends and Making Enemies in the Anti-American Century,* **Public Affairs, 2006.**
The director of Latin American studies at the Council on Foreign Relations argues that American policies in Latin America, including sponsoring dictators and condoning human-rights violations, set the stage for the current animosity toward the U.S.

Articles

Judt, Tony, "Anti-Americans Abroad," *The New York Review of Books,* **May 2003.**
The director of the Remarque Institute at New York University examines the rage for new books in France attacking America.

Reports and Studies

"America's Image Slips, But Allies Share U.S. Concerns Over Iran, Hamas," Pew Research Center, 2006; http://pewglobal.org/reports/display.php?ReportID=252.
The latest poll by the Pew Global Attitudes Project finds that while anti-Americanism had dipped in 2005, it began rising again.

"Foreign Aid: An Introductory Overview of U.S. Programs and Policy," Congressional Research Service, Library of Congress, 2004; http://fpc.state.gov/documents/organization/31987.pdf.
This study of American foreign aid includes data on humanitarian, military and bilateral-development aid.

"Worldviews 2002," German Marshall Fund of the United States and The Chicago Council on Foreign Relations, 2002; www.worldviews.org.
A comprehensive survey of contrasting European and American public opinion following the Sept. 11 terrorist attacks finds that Europeans believed U.S. foreign policy contributed to the attacks.

For More Information

Centre for Modern Oriental Studies, Kirchweg 33, 14129 Berlin, Germany; +49-(0)-30-80307-0; www.zmo.de. German think tank conducting comparative and interdisciplinary studies of the Middle East, Africa, South and Southeast Asia.

Council on Foreign Relations, 58 E. 68th St., New York, NY 10065; (212) 434-9400; www.cfr.org. Promotes a better understanding of the foreign-policy choices facing the United States and other governments.

Elcano Royal Institute, Príncipe de Vergara, 51, 28006 Madrid, Spain; +34-91-781-6770; www.realinstituto-elcano.org. Non-partisan Spanish institution generating policy ideas in the interest of international peace.

Pew Global Attitudes Project, 1615 L St., N.W., Suite 700, Washington, DC 20036; (202) 419-4400; www.pewglobal.org. Assesses worldwide opinions on the current state of foreign affairs and other important issues.

USC Center on Public Diplomacy, USC Annenberg School, University of Southern California, 3502 Watt Way, Suite 103, Los Angeles, CA 90089-0281; (213) 821-2078; http://uscpublicdiplomacy.com. Studies the impact of government-sponsored programs as well as private activities on foreign policy and national security.

VOICES FROM ABROAD

Hugo Chávez

President, Venezuela
March 9, 2007

Bush in the Red

"The President of the United States of North America, George W. Bush, the little gentleman of the North, the political cadaver that is visiting South America, that little gentleman is the president of all the history of the United States, and in the history of the United States, he has the lowest level of approval in his own country. And if we add that to the level of approval that he has in the world, I would think he's in the red now — negative numbers."

Henry A. Giroux

University Professor, Canada
Aug. 4, 2004

Direct Mission from God

"Bush has relentlessly developed policies based less of social needs than on a highly personal and narrowly moral sense of divine purpose."

El Pais

Spain
April 27, 2002

We Are All Americans

"Years ago, we believed that the Americanization of the world was due to cultural influence. Now we know that it is because of a gene. The final phase of capitalism, of which the United States is decidedly in charge, has ceased to be a system of material production. It has become a civilization, and sooner or later all of us will be caught up in it, for better or worse."

Grand Ayatollah Mohammed Hussein Fadlallah

Lebanon
July 2004

Terrorism will increase by 100 percent

"American foreign policy has succeeded in spreading political, economic and security instability in the region without attaining any important goal. Even more, I find its occupation of Iraq and its absolute commitment to Israel has frozen the war against terrorism in the region and the whole world. . . . I believe that as long as the American policy is what it is in the region, terrorism shall increase by 100 percent."

Worldpress.Org

Czech Republic
May 7, 2006

"Freedom" Means Loss of Rights

"The United States exports 'freedom and democracy.' . . . Freedom, in the form of free trade agreements, is exported around the globe, which enables corporations to usurp national sovereignty and operate beyond the 'rule of law' with impunity in pursuit of greater market access. In the process, this forces 'target nations' to give up their rights over their domestic industries to multinational control and ownership."

Vladimir Putin

President, Russia
Feb. 2007

U.S. Policies Encourage Terrorism

"We are seeing a greater and greater disdain for the basic principles of international law. One country, the United States, has overstepped its national borders in every way. This is visible in the economic, political, cultural and educational policies it imposes on other nations. This force's dominance inevitably encourages a number of countries to acquire weapons of mass destruction. Moreover, threats such as terrorism have now taken on a global character."

The Times (London)

United Kingdom
Sept. 2006

Sept. 11 Attacks Changed America

"For some time after September 11, many U.S. critics distinguished between anti-Bush and anti-American sentiment. . . . After 2004, confronted with the reality that President Bush, Dick Cheney and Donald Rumsfeld really were the representative leaders of America, the rest of the world formed an alternative impression of the U.S. — that 9/11 had, in fact, induced a dramatic change in the psychology of the nation."

CBC News

Canada
Aug. 29, 2006

Reeking of Racism

"Canadian hatred for George W. Bush and his war on terrorism is massive. Bush-hatred is definitely anti-American. Anti-Americanism has always been tied up with the Canadian identity. Anti-Americanism is dangerous and reeks of racism."

Pavel Constantin, Romania

3

Nuclear Proliferation

Roland Flamini

President Mahmoud Ahmadinejad of Iran has agitated the world by threatening to wipe Israel off the map, while maintaining that Iran's nuclear program is only for peaceful energy purposes.

Getty Images/Salah Malkawi

From *CQ Researcher,*
January 1, 2007.

W ho is making bombs today in the world?" asks the slight, bearded man with the neat haircut. "Whom should one be afraid of? Who is destabilizing the world? They have even once used their nuclear weapons. Less than a month has passed from the anniversary of Hiroshima and Nagasaki. They should be ashamed of themselves for talking about trust. . . . It is they who must give answers, not us."

The speaker is Mahmoud Ahmadinejad, the Holocaust-denying president of Iran, which claims to be developing nuclear power only for peaceful purposes but has been accused of trying to build a nuclear arsenal. Deftly, the former political agitator is turning the tables on the United States, his primary accuser. If "they" can have bombs, he seems to say, why can't we? [1]

Although nuclear power in war has been unleashed only twice, against the two benighted Japanese cities in 1945, there have been several close calls, notably the 1962 Cuban Missile Crisis, which brought the Soviet Union and the United States to the brink of nuclear war.

The 1968 Nuclear Non-Proliferation Treaty (NPT) was intended to dissuade other countries from acquiring nuclear weapons, with the promise that the five nuclear-weapon states — the United States, the Soviet Union, China, France and Great Britain — would themselves disarm and share peaceful nuclear technology with those who didn't have it. The NPT prohibited non-nuclear-weapon states from developing nuclear weapons, and enjoined the nuclear states — the "haves" — to reduce and eventually eliminate their stockpiles. (*See sidebar, p. 60.*)

Instead, despite some reductions, the original five still have a combined arsenal powerful enough to destroy the world several times over.

The Roster of Nuclear Weapon States

The 1968 Nuclear Non-Proliferation Treaty (NPT) has been ratified by 188 nations. In the 60 years since the 1945 bombing of Japan, only four countries — India and Pakistan and probably Israel and North Korea — have developed nuclear weapons, joining the original "nuclear club" — the United States, the Soviet Union (Russia), China, England and France.

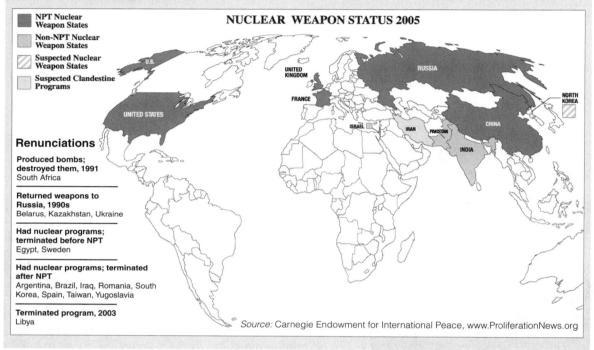

NUCLEAR WEAPON STATUS 2005

NPT Nuclear Weapon States

Non-NPT Nuclear Weapon States

Suspected Nuclear Weapon States

Suspected Clandestine Programs

Renunciations

Produced bombs; destroyed them, 1991
South Africa

Returned weapons to Russia, 1990s
Belarus, Kazakhstan, Ukraine

Had nuclear programs; terminated before NPT
Egypt, Sweden

Had nuclear programs; terminated after NPT
Argentina, Brazil, Iraq, Romania, South Korea, Spain, Taiwan, Yugoslavia

Terminated program, 2003
Libya

Source: Carnegie Endowment for International Peace, www.ProliferationNews.org

And, there are players in the shadows who do not share the trepidation and sense of awe toward nuclear weapons common to most established nation-states.

"If a nuclear bomb went off in Moscow or New York City or Jerusalem, any number of groups would claim they have another," said Sam Nunn, co-chairman and CEO of the Nuclear Threat Initiative and former chairman of the Senate Armed Services Committee.

Even if the weapon were crude, he said, fear and panic would be epidemic. "The psychological damage would be incalculable. It would be a slow, step-by-step process to regain confidence. And the question will be, Why didn't we take steps to prevent this? We will have a whole list of things we wish we'd done." [2]

In the euphoria that followed the collapse of the Soviet Union and the end of the Cold War, intentions were good. Swords were turned into plowshares with the joint U.S.-Russian "Megatons to Megawatts" project of converting highly enriched uranium from Russian warheads into fuel for commercial American nuclear reactors; more than 10,000 weapons were thus repurposed between 1993 and 2005.

But the world celebrated too soon. All nuclear weapons have not been destroyed or rendered obsolete, as was hoped. The "bomb" has spread, and to some dangerously unstable places.

India and Pakistan, who were not parties to the NPT, have developed weapons, mostly to deter each other. With the apparently full consent of the government in Islamabad, Pakistani nuclear scientist A. Q. Khan sold black market nuclear plans and materials to Libya, Iran and North Korea. (*See sidebar, p. 54.*)

Israel, also not part of the treaty, is assumed to have an arsenal, and North Korea, the only signatory to have resigned from the treaty, exploded a nuclear device underground last October. Iran now seems likely to follow suit, and the threat from terrorists with nuclear weapons heightens the danger to critical levels unseen since the Cuban crisis.

Moreover, tons of poorly guarded nuclear material stockpiled in the old Soviet Union make the prospect of mischief or error with stolen nuclear material as daunting as a big nuclear bomb.

In February 2007 North Korea agreed to halt its weapons program in exchange for shipments of fuel oil, but the word of Pyongyang has been notoriously untrustworthy.

Former West German Chancellor Helmut Schmidt presciently described the nuclear future after the breakup of the Soviet Union in 1991. "In a couple of decades you'll have to reckon with the fact that the knowledge of how to [build nuclear weapons] will have spread widely enough for terrorists to create nuclear weapons in their garages," he said. "Does the fact that I or my allies possess nuclear weapons deter that terrorist or, say, a little terrorist state? I have quite some experience with terrorists. No, it will not deter them." [3]

Indeed, in this first decade of the 21st century, the psychology of nuclear deterrence seems profoundly changed. "The international community seems almost to be sleepwalking down a path where states, after long living without nuclear arms, now feel compelled to reverse their logic, as if they felt that possession of weapons of mass destruction offers the best protection against being attacked," said U.N. Secretary-General Kofi Annan shortly before leaving his post last January. [4]

At the end of the Cold War, the United States and the Soviet Union had 60,000 nuclear weapons. Today, according to the Carnegie Endowment for International Peace, they have less than half that number. The United States has about 10,300 nuclear weapons, Russia some 16,000, France and China 350 each and the United Kingdom 200. Of the three nations who have weapons but have not signed the NPT, India has 90, Pakistan 80 and Israel perhaps 100. [5]

Global Nuclear Stockpiles

The U.S. and Russia still hold more than 95 percent of the world's nuclear weapons. The 1968 Nuclear Non-Proliferation Treaty stipulated that stockpiles must be gradually reduced to zero.

Total Nuclear Weapons

United States 10,300 · Russia 16,000 · China 350 · France 350 · United Kingdom 200 · Israel 100* · India 90 · Pakistan 80 · North Korea 3-10

* Estimate

Source: Carnegie Endowment for International Peace, 2007

On the credit side, several nations have given up their nuclear capabilities in recent years. South Africa destroyed already developed weapons. Belarus, Kazakhstan and Ukraine, with U.S. financial support, returned arsenals inherited from the old Soviet Union back to Russia. And Libya, Brazil, Sweden, Taiwan and Argentina halted ongoing programs.

Past confrontations between nuclear-powered nations have been both tense and strangely reassuring. During the Cold War, the Soviet Union and United States were locked in the nuclear stalemate known as mutual assured destruction (MAD).

But new regional tensions have flared, particularly in the Middle East and Asia. The rise of Islamic fundamentalism has deepened internal unrest in fragile nations and spawned a jihadist movement capable of striking terror anywhere, even inside the United States. In Asia, an emerging China and Kim Jong-Il's unpredictable North Korea have added to the unease.

Add to that mix President George W. Bush's self-appointed mission to convert the world to Western-style democracy, and it is small wonder nervous countries began looking more to nuclear weapons for security.

Iran's apparent nuclear ambitions, especially, have destabilized the Middle East for decades. Western suspi-

AFP/Getty Images/Sergei Supinsky

Worries of nuclear poison motivate Ukrainian activists, who picket with barrels of symbolic radioactive waste during a meeting of a Chernobyl conference in Kiev. The Chernobyl reactor disaster, which affected millions of people, marks its 20th anniversary in April.

cions of Iran's intentions grew out of its secrecy, its determination to enrich uranium and its efforts to be a dominant force in the region. President Ahmadinejad's repeated denials of his intentions are taken with a generous pinch of salt.

Iran argues it needs nuclear power for its burgeoning population and industrial sector. After Russia and Saudi Arabia, Iran has the world's richest oil and gas reserves. [6]

"There is an economic rationale to diversifying energy sources," says Mark Fitzpatrick, senior fellow for nonproliferation at the London-based International Institute for Strategic Studies. "But the strongest critical question for the Iranians is why they should want to enrich uranium, which is costly, when they can get it commercially. Very few countries enrich their own."

The standard Iranian answer is that they cannot trust the recognized international suppliers to deliver. "Well," says Fitzpatrick, "that's why the International Atomic Energy Agency (IAEA) is trying to establish an independent supply."

Concern about instability in the Middle East and the capriciousness of oil prices has more nations turning to

nuclear power, potentially putting bomb-making materials within terrorists' reach. According to the World Nuclear Association in London, 28 new reactors are under construction, 62 are planned, and 160 proposed, mostly in Asia. [7]

Not too far down the road, predicts an IAEA economist, "An increase to 5,000 reactors is well within the range of many longer-range studies. People are positioning themselves. There seems to be a race coming and nobody wants to be left out."

But if Shiite Iran acquires nuclear capability, can Sunni nations like Saudi Arabia and Egypt afford to do nothing, given the enmity between the two Muslim sects? In September 2006, Cairo announced plans to revive its once-active nuclear program, and Saudi Arabia reportedly is recruiting nuclear engineers for its own program.

Egyptian Mohamed ElBaradei, head of the IAEA, warns that if Pyongyang carries out further tests, "countries in the region will clearly re-think their reliance on the U.S. nuclear umbrella and shift the emphasis onto the possibility of having their own nuclear weapons."

Deterrence worked for the United States and the Soviet Union. But the spread of nuclear weapons to multiple hands can have an opposite effect on deterrence; clearly, the danger of an accidental nuclear confrontation increases in proportion to the number of "nuclear club" members.

In addition, says China's *People's Daily*, "The stark global reality today is that different nations are confronted with different security dilemmas." [8]

Do Ahmadinejad's aggressive calls to wipe out Israel, for example, mean that Iran will launch a nuclear attack on the Jewish state, even though Israel could probably still retaliate?

The question is a valid one, experts say, reflecting the dangerous, new jihadist wrinkle. As Noah Feldman, adjunct senior fellow at the Council on Foreign Relations, asked recently, "If leaders of Iran or some future leaders of a radicalized, nuclear Saudi Arabia shared the aspiration to martyrdom of so many young jihadists around the world, might they be prepared to attack Israel or the United States, even if the inevitable result were the martyrdom of their entire people? The answer depends on whether you consider Islam susceptible to the kind of apocalyptic thought that might lead whole peoples, rather than just individuals, into suicidal behavior." [9]

As nuclear-proliferation efforts continue, here are some of the questions being debated:

Is the Nuclear Non-Proliferation Treaty obsolete?

"Let's not abandon the Non-Proliferation Treaty but look at the regime and see how we can strengthen it," says the IAEA's ElBaradei. "Thirty years ago, it was based on the theory that no one could enrich uranium."

Kennette Benedict, executive director of the *Bulletin of the Atomic Scientists*, agrees. "The fundamentals of the treaty are right," she says. "New nuclear-weapons programs should be discouraged or prohibited; civilian nuclear-energy development should be made available; nuclear-weapons states should be encouraged to reduce their arsenals so nuclear disarmament is the end goal of the treaty, as it now states. As with all rules, implementation is everything, but until now we've actually done fairly well on the discouragement element."

India, Pakistan and Israel did not sign the treaty because "there is no provision in the NPT" for new members, says Olivia Bosch, an associate fellow on arms control at the Royal Institute for International Affairs in London. The treaty "still matters" and would be strengthened by a provision to accept new nuclear states, but "they don't want to reopen it for renegotiation" because other articles could be challenged.

Some analysts maintain that the NPT already effectively has been abandoned — if not when India, Pakistan and Israel became nuclear weapon states then surely when the Soviet Union and the United States recently agreed to supply India with nuclear technology, in direct violation of the 1968 treaty's intent.

The American argument was that India had "behaved well" and, unlike Pakistan, had not proliferated nuclear-weapon technology. But a Bush administration official admitted privately, "We made the Indian deal aware that it was not in the spirit of the NPT, but [was] in America's interests."

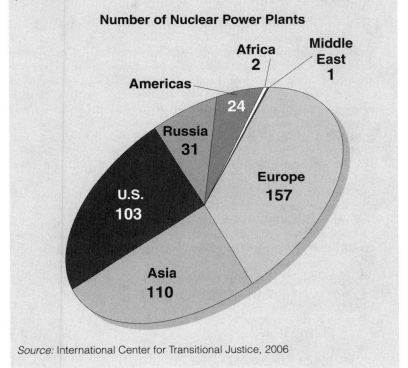

World's Nuclear Power Plants

Nuclear-power plants can be seen as part of the proliferation calculation, since they have the potential to be converted to weapons production.

Number of Nuclear Power Plants

Africa 2
Middle East 1
Americas
24
Russia 31
Europe 157
U.S. 103
Asia 110

Source: International Center for Transitional Justice, 2006

Critics of the NPT say the reluctance of the original five nuclear weapon states to fulfill their obligations under Article Six, which calls on them to disarm, has undermined the treaty's validity. James P. Thomas, a member of the U.S. Arms Control Commission, writes that current Bush administration plans to develop a new generation of tactical nuclear weapons when the United States should be dismantling its arsenal threatens to "disintegrate" the NPT. [10]

A 1995 U.N. conference that extended the NPT indefinitely ended the treaty's effectiveness as a disarmament tool "and gave way to a different, irrelevant, stillborn NPT," wrote Miguel Marin-Bosch, a senior Mexican diplomat specializing in disarmament. In a lengthy analysis of the treaty, Bosch maintained that the United States had waged an "intensive campaign" to ensure the indefinite, unconditional extension of the

A.Q. Khan's Black Market Nuclear Wal-Mart

Pakistan's chief scientist sold secrets

On Feb. 4, 2004, Abdul Qadeer Khan, Pakistan's chief nuclear scientist, went on national television and confessed that he had secretly sold nuclear designs and technology to other countries. "It pains me to realize in retrospect that my entire lifetime achievements providing foolproof national security to my country have been placed in serious jeopardy on account of my activities," Khan said.

The next day, President Pervez Musharraf announced that he had pardoned Khan, and, while declaring him placed under house arrest, called him "my hero" and said, "I revere him for his contribution to making the defense of the country impregnable." [1] Pakistanis were stunned. A.Q. Khan (as he is usually known) was a national hero who in the eyes of many had delivered their country from the threat of a nuclear attack by India by developing Pakistan's own strategic capability. [2]

India had tested a nuclear weapon in 1978. Under Khan's direction Pakistan was successful in producing its own nuclear response, carrying out six decisive tests in 1998.

But Khan's success had a dark side: Recognizing a major business opportunity, he also organized the largest known international nuclear black market ring. Robert L. Gallucci, a former top State Department nuclear proliferation expert, calls it "one of the greatest threats to international security of which I am aware." [3]

By his own admission, Khan had between 1989 and 2000 provided technology and expertise to Iran, Libya and North Korea. In a complex ongoing investigation, International Atomic Energy Agency (IAEA) officials have still not ruled out other possible customers.

Born in Bhopal, India, Khan migrated with his Muslim family to Pakistan when the two nations split in 1947. He trained as a metallurgist in Germany, and in December 1972 was hired by an Amsterdam-based engineering firm with links to a manufacturer of nuclear equipment with an enrichment facility in Almelo, the Netherlands.

By 1974, Khan had an office in that facility and became familiar with centrifuges and the enrichment process. But the story starts earlier, in 1971, as Khan watched Pakistan lose the war with India and vowed to help prevent another defeat from happening.

Three years later, as India tested its nuclear device, he offered Prime Minister Zulfikar Ali Bhutto his help in creating the world's first Islamic nuclear bomb. In 1975, when his Dutch employers discovered that Khan had stolen centrifuge blueprints he fled back to Pakistan. [4]

"The Pakistan-based network traded everything from blueprints for centrifuges that enrich uranium to weapons' designs and parts," according to a Council on Foreign Relations background briefing paper. "It also included a sophisticated transportation system to move the goods from the supplier to the buyer." [5]

Khan began transferring nuclear technology to the Iranians in 1989, even before Pakistan's own weapons had been fully developed. The help started with a centrifuge design and went on to hardware; the IAEA says Khan's assistance to Tehran continued until 1996, with the ruling ayatollahs paying millions of dollars for his expertise.

Starting in 1994 Khan was also involved in a technology trade with North Korea. The regime in Pyongyang exchanged its knowhow in nuclear-capable long-range missiles for Pakistani nuclear technology. One source says that Khan made 13 trips to North Korea to help with the design and equipping of uranium-enrichment facilities. [6]

Libya was to prove Khan's downfall. Western intelligence and the IAEA for some time had indications that the head of Pakistan's nuclear program was engaged in nuclear proliferation on a large scale. For example, IAEA inspectors in Iran discovered that some centrifuge components in Iranian reactors had originated in Pakistan and that the Iranian enrichment program resembled Pakistan's. [7]

A major breakthrough came in October 2003 when Italian authorities intercepted a German ship bound for Libya with thousands of parts for uranium centrifuges. They had been made in Malaysia from Khan's designs. [8]

The discovery is said to have "tipped the balance" for Libyan leader Muammar Qaddafi, "forcing him to agree in

NPT, and the non-nuclear weapon states "surrendered what little leverage the temporary nature of the NPT gave them," and got nothing in return. [11]

In the 1960s, non-proliferation was one of the few areas of agreement among the original five nuclear club members. Now, NPT critics say, as the "club" fails to make a more

December to disclose and dismantle his own nuclear program." [9] Qaddafi's decision put "a mother lode of information" in the hands of the IAEA investigators. Documents turned over by the Libyans included centrifuge designs and even precise blueprints for the design and construction of a half-ton nuclear bomb. [10] It was "the Libyans who blew up the Pakistanis," and who made the role of Khan's black market known, according to a *New Yorker* article by investigative journalist Seymour Hersh. [11]

While the nuclear black market goes back almost to the dawn of the nuclear age, Khan's approach broke new ground in scope and concept. Mohamed ElBaradei, head of the International Atomic Energy Agency, called it "the Wal-Mart of private-sector proliferation" because — as the CFR study states — Khan "created a centralized one-stop shop that offered technical advice, parts, and customer support." [12] Shipment of the Malaysia-produced centrifuges tended to be through a shipping company in Dubai, on the Persian Gulf.

A 2006 report by the Stockholm-based Weapons of Mass Destruction Commission charged that Khan's network could not have functioned "without the awareness of the Pakistani government." [13] This has long been the belief of intelligence sources and experts. Islamic fundamentalists in the Pakistani intelligence service, they say, provided help and protection.

Pakistani officials from Musharraf on down have consistently denied this. Moreover, a spokesman at the Pakistani embassy in Washington, Mohammed Akram Shaheedi, says there was no question of trying Khan because of his popularity: "It would have been difficult for the government to undertake an open trial," he says.

U.S. and British officials have complained publicly that efforts to learn which other countries Khan was in touch with prior to his discovery have been blocked by Pakistani authorities. But the consensus is that he has made the world more dangerous because some of the members of his wide organization could still do business. Already in 2004, ElBaradei was quoted as saying, "the information is now all over the place, and that's what makes it more dangerous than in the 1960s." And, says Gallucci, "Bad as it is with Iran, North Korea having nuclear-weapons material is much worse. The worst part is that they could transfer it to a non-state group." In other words, to terrorists. [14]

Abdul Qadeer Khan tossed the world of nuclear proliferation into consternation by admitting to passing nuclear designs and technology to Iran, Libya and North Korea in 2004.

[1] Khan's confession and presidential pardon are described in *Pervez Musharraf: In the Line of Fire* (2006).

[2] Interview with Anwar Iqbal, Pakistani poet and writer, Washington correspondent *Dawn* newspaper.

[3] Gallucci is dean of the Edmund K. Walsh School of Foreign Service at Georgetown University. For details of Khan's black market activities see, for example, www.globalsecurity.org/wmd/world/pakistan.

[4] The firm was Physics Dynamic Research. The company (also known as FDO) had business links to URENCO, a joint Dutch-German-British nuclear organization. Details of Khan's early career from Gordon Corera: *Shopping for Bombs: Nuclear Proliferation, Global Security, and the Rise and Fall of A.Q. Khan* (2006). Other sources, however, say it was Bhutto who approached Khan.

[5] Council on Foreign Relations backgrounder — "Nonproliferation: The Pakistan Connection," Feb 12, 2004.

[6] CFR backgrounder; also www.globalsecurity.org/; A.Q.Khan's Network; Corera, *op. cit.* Pakistan successfully test-fired a Ghauri missile in April 1998.

[7] Interviews with IAEA officials.

[8] "From Rogue Nuclear Programs, Web of Trails leads to Pakistan," *The New York Times*, Jan. 4, 2004, other reports.

[9] *Ibid.*

[10] Seymour M. Hersh, "The Deal," *The New Yorker*, March 8, 2004.

[11] *Ibid.*

[12] Council on Foreign Relations, Feb. 12, 2004.

[13] "Weapons of Terror," Swedish Weapons of Mass Destruction Commission, Stockholm, 2006.

[14] Quoted in *The New Yorker, op. cit.*

determined effort to disarm in the post-Cold War climate, that collective agreement is a fatal flaw in the treaty. "It gives a sense of cynicism" to the agreement, admits ElBaradei.

His predecessor, Hans Blix, who heads Sweden's Weapons of Mass Destruction Commission, recently expressed the same sentiment: "The moral authority of

AFP/Getty Images/STR

A defiant army rallies in Pyongyang's Kim Il-Sung Square last October, celebrating North Korea's underground nuclear-weapon test. Despite world pressure to desist, the reclusive regime has also fired warhead-capable rockets into the sea, spreading unease throughout Asia.

the 'have' states is undermined when they are easing their doctrines for the use of nuclear weapons rather than restricting them." [12]

The apparent credibility gap provides the justification to President Ahmadinejad to build the case for Iran's nuclear-enrichment program, whatever his real motives. "In our view," he said, "the legal system whereby a handful of countries force their will on the rest of the world is discriminatory and unstable.

"There are a number of countries that possess both nuclear energy and nuclear weapons. They use their atomic weapons to threaten other peoples. And it is these powers who say that they are worried about Iran deviating from the path of peaceful use of atomic energy." [13]

Charles D. Ferguson, a specialist in disarmament and weapons of mass destruction at the Council on Foreign Relations, says the NPT fails in a number of ways. "It is a discrimination treaty" limiting the nuclear-weapon states to those that had them by Jan. 1, 1967. This leaves India, Pakistan and Israel out in the cold. They are considered non-nuclear-weapon states in international law, yet actually possess nuclear weapons. It is also flawed in having "no time-bound commitment" for the nuclear states to disarm.

Another of the treaty's failures is "the lack of adequate enforcement mechanisms to ensure compliance," says Ferguson. The IAEA can make inspections, but its powers are limited, he notes. "The safer course is for nations to create an equitable system that would outlaw all nuclear weapons," he says.

Will nuclear deterrence work today?

Pakistani fighter planes protectively circled Islamabad in May 2002 as India and Pakistan confronted each other over the status of Kashmir. Nuclear war seemed imminent.

But Pakistani Gen. Mirza Aslam Beg stood defiant, seemingly untroubled by the potential horror of nuclear war. "We can make a first strike, and a second strike, or even a third," he said. When asked about the massive deaths such a tactic would cause, he was cavalier. "You can die crossing the street," he observed, "or you could die in a nuclear war. You've got to die some day anyway."

In India, Defense Minister George Fernandes seemed equally unmoved. "India can survive a nuclear attack," he told the *International Herald Tribune*, "but Pakistan cannot." [14]

Yogendra Narain, India's secretary of defense, rolled the drumbeat even faster in an interview with India's *Defence Outlook* magazine: "A surgical strike is the answer," he said, adding that if this failed to resolve things, "We must be prepared for total mutual destruction." [15]

Added Indian security analyst Brahma Chellaney, "India can hit any nook and corner of Pakistan and is fully prepared to call Pakistan's nuclear bluff." [16]

Ever since India and Pakistan tested nuclear weapons in 1998, the international community had worried over what would happen if these adolescent nuclear powers ever reached the point of irrational enmity. Would the prospect of mutual mass annihilation bring them back from the brink?

The pessimists pointed out that there were significant differences between India-Pakistan and the United States-Soviet Union. India and Pakistan shared a deep mutual hatred. And their nuclear arsenals were much smaller than those of the Cold War superpowers, so the threat of total mutual destruction seemed remote. At worst, major cities would be wiped out. [17]

Yet the peace held.

The widely held perception that nuclear deterrence averted a major conflict between the United States and the Soviet Union is not a universal truth. But the impact of something that did not happen is hard to assess accurately, and as a result there has long been a dispute among scholars over the exact role of deterrence in the Cold War.

Cold War nuclear deterrence depended on close communication between adversaries, and accurate information about their respective nuclear strengths. It was "a tight club of nuclear powers with interlocking interests and an appreciation for the brutal doctrine of 'mutually assured destruction,' " writes Bill Powell in *Time*. Today, he notes, that deadly but orderly pattern has been replaced by "an unpredictable host of potential bomb throwers," casting serious doubt on whether the same thinking can have either effect or validity. [18]

Whether it's "a Stalinist bomb out of North Korea, a Shiite bomb out of Iran, a Sunni bomb out of Pakistan, and down the road possibly out of Egypt and Saudi Arabia as well, and, of course, an al Qaeda bomb out of nowhere," the rules of the game have changed to a frightening random pattern, Powell continues.

Indeed, some observers see the current geopolitical situation as "a natural byproduct of a fragmented world in which countries no longer have to choose between the United States and the Soviet Union but can go separate ways and build independent alliances." [19]

Therese Delpech, director of strategic affairs at the French Atomic Energy Commission, worries that, "The new actors, such as Ahmadinejad or Kim (Jong-Il) are much more prone to act impulsively, [unlike] the United States and the Soviet Union." [20]

Paul Nitze, an adviser to President Ronald Reagan, once famously observed, "The deterrent effect of nuclear arms on [irrational] parties is questionable . . . rational thinking is necessary for deterrence to work." [21]

Graham Allison, a security adviser to former President Bill Clinton, however, believes that is no reason to abandon deterrence. "Deterrence is a concept that still works" he says, "but it needs three main components — clarity, capability and credibility."

In other words, a nation must make it clear exactly what kind of retaliatory strike a potential nuclear aggressor can expect; must be seen to have the weapons to carry out its threat; and must have a reputation of following through on its warnings. What could tempt a rogue state to use its nuclear weapons would not be a lack of rational thinking, Allison believes, but the conviction that the targeted country lacks the will to hit back.

The danger of a terrorist nuclear attack by a rogue group is an added complication, but Allison says even a terrorist bomb has a return address — the country that supplied the device. A recent British government white paper on deterrence warns, "Any state that we can hold responsible for assisting a nuclear attack on our vital interests can expect that this would lead to a proportionate response." [22]

President Bush aimed a similar warning at North Korea. The United States would hold Pyongyang "fully accountable" for any delivery of nuclear weapons to another state or "a non-state entity," he said last year.

As international-affairs scholar Derek D. Smith, author of *Deterring America: Rogue States and the Proliferation of Weapons of Mass Destruction*, observed, "If you can't deter the terrorist organizations, you'd better be sure to deter whoever is supplying them." [23]

Bush was not the first to zero in on the suppliers of weapons of mass destruction. During the Cuban Missile Crisis, President John F. Kennedy grimly warned Soviet Premier Nikita Khrushchev in Moscow: "It shall be the policy of this nation to regard any nuclear missile launched from Cuba against any nation in the Western Hemisphere as an attack on the United States, requiring a full retaliatory response against the Soviet Union." [24]

But Kim Jong-Il is considered less rational than Khrushchev, and Ahmadinejad, if his words reflect his beliefs, may choose martyrdom for the Islamic cause.

"Some analysts have argued that all countries should have nuclear weapons, so they could deter each other," says the Council on Foreign Relations' Ferguson. "But this situation could lead to disaster by increasing the likelihood of accidental use, or deliberate use if a national leader cannot be deterred."

Could terrorists get nuclear weapons?

Despite the spread of nuclear weapons, experts still consider a full-scale nuclear attack less likely than a small "suitcase" bomb or similar device, which could still kill thousands. In 1998, when al Qaeda leader Osama bin Laden was asked about his reported attempts to acquire chemical and nuclear weapons, he replied: "Acquiring such weapons for the defense of Muslims is a religious duty."

The fact that bin Laden apparently hasn't acquired them yet does not mean he and other terrorists are not trying. Nor, unfortunately, does it mean international preventive measures have successfully blocked their attempts. [25]

CHRONOLOGY

1940s *U.S. drops world's first atomic bombs.*

1945 Atomic bombing of Hiroshima (Aug. 6) and Nagasaki (Aug. 9).

1949 Soviet Union tests nuclear weapon.

1950s-1960s *U.S.-Soviet nuclear-arms race launches Cold War.*

1952 Great Britain tests nuclear weapon.

1957 U.N. establishes International Atomic Energy Agency (IAEA). . . . Soviet Union tests intercontinental ballistic missile (ICBM). . . . First U.S. ICBM goes operational.

1960 France tests first nuclear weapon.

1963 Partial Test Ban Treaty outlaws tests in the atmosphere, outer space and underwater.

1964 China tests first nuclear weapon.

1967 Israel acquires nuclear weapons.

July 1, 1968 Nuclear Non-Proliferation Treaty (NPT) is launched for signature.

1970s *U.S. and Soviet Union slow arms race.*

1971 Strategic Arms Limitation Treaty (SALT I) halts production of ICBM launchers and limits further production of submarine-launched missiles.

1974 India tests nuclear device.

1977 Soviets deploy SS-20 medium-range missiles targeting Europe.

1979 U.S. and Soviet Union sign SALT 2 treaty limiting strategic weapons.

1980s *President Ronald Reagan announces plans to develop a "Star Wars" nuclear defense system in space.*

1983 Reagan announces plans to create a ground- and space-based system to protect the United States from nuclear attack. . . . NATO deploys American Pershing II and ground-launched cruise missiles in response to the Soviet SS-20s.

1988 North Korea builds two nuclear weapons.

1990s-2000s *Attacks on New York and the Pentagon on Sept. 11, 2001, raise the specter of terrorist nuclear attacks. U.S. invades Iraq.*

December 1991 Soviet Union disbands, leaving behind thousands of poorly guarded nuclear weapons.

1994 Stolen nuclear material turns up in Czech Republic and Germany.

1995 The NPT is made permanent.

1996 Comprehensive Nuclear Test Ban Treaty is signed by 71 states on its first day, including the five original nuclear weapon states.

1998 Pakistan conducts six nuclear weapons tests.

2000 Iran is revealed to be constructing a large uranium-enrichment facility.

2002 Clandestine nuclear-weapons program disclosed in North Korea.

2004 Pakistani nuclear scientist A. Q. Khan admits to selling nuclear technology to Libya, North Korea, Iran.

2006 President George W. Bush and Russian President Vladimir Putin announce the Global Initiative to Combat Nuclear Terrorism at G-8 summit. . . . North Korea test fires seven missiles into the Sea of Japan in July, and conducts underground test on Oct. 9. . . . President Ahmadinejad denounces efforts to stop Iran's nuclear program.

2007 North Korea agrees to seal its main nuclear reactor in exchange for heating oil. . . . U.N. Security Council votes 15-0 on March 24 to ban all Iranian arms exports and freeze Iranian financial assets over Iran's refusal to stop enriching uranium. Iran responds by partially suspending cooperation with IAEA.

The Nuclear Threat Initiative warned in a recent study that "urgent actions are needed to prevent a nuclear 9/11." The private group was founded by entrepreneur Ted Turner and former Sen. Nunn and receives funding in part from financier Warren Buffett. The study warns, however, that, "A dangerous gap remains between the urgency of the threat of nuclear terrorism and the scope of the U.S. and world response." [26]

President Bush is among many who regard a terrorist nuclear attack on American soil as the single greatest threat to the United States. At the G-8 economic summit in St. Petersburg, Russia, in July 2006, he persuaded Russian President Vladimir Putin to join him in launching the Global Initiative to Combat Nuclear Terrorism. It requires countries to improve accounting, control and protection of nuclear and radioactive material, tighten security at nuclear facilities and prevent acts of terrorism.

"It is extremely important for us to synchronize our watches with you," Putin told Bush. Involving the Russians is considered the key to any improvement in global nuclear security because theft of nuclear fuel from Russia's often poorly guarded facilities is a widely recognized danger. [27]

Before its collapse in 1991 the Soviet Union had some 27,000 nuclear weapons. There are no confirmed reports of missing weapons or theft, but the former Soviet republics of Ukraine, Belarus and Kazakhstan still have stockpiles of weapons-grade uranium and plutonium, and a black market in nuclear material survives.

Despite the grim possibility, many experts say it is highly doubtful a terrorist group could manufacture the necessary fissile material by itself. First, it would have to steal the weapons-grade material or the weapon or acquire it from a rogue state. Since 1993 the IAEA has recorded roughly 630 incidents of trafficking nuclear and other radioactive material through its Illicit Trafficking Database, with 17 cases involving the most dangerous kinds of nuclear materials: plutonium 25 and HEU (highly enriched uranium).

But Fitzpatrick, of the International Institute for Strategic Studies, believes "neither Iran nor North Korea would give or sell nuclear weapons to terrorists as a decision of state." They would be afraid of retaliation, he explains, and in addition there would be no guarantee that the weapons would not be used against them.

Terrorists could get their hands on nuclear weapons, however, "if there is a breakdown in society," he says. "In the case of a second Iranian revolution — which is possible — some fundamentalists might get nuclear weapons and give them to terrorists, or become terrorists themselves."

Or, Fitzgerald says, a succession crisis in Saudi Arabia could fragment the government "and control over nuclear weapons, should the Saudis have acquired them, falls in the hands of Saudi elites who are sympathetic to Osama bin Laden, or at least to his ideas."

As for actions by North Korea, "we're not so sure because the decision-making process is more opaque," Fitzpatrick says.

"I would not say it's inevitable that there will be a nuclear terror act," says former Clinton security adviser Allison, "but I would say it is highly likely." Then why hasn't it happened already? "Why didn't 9/11 happen before 9/11?" he asks. "We were fortunate."

To discourage such an attack, nuclear fuel needs to be kept under tighter international controls — "locked up as tight as Fort Knox," as Allison puts it. "If they can't get the fissile material, they can't have a bomb."

An equally important deterrent, he says, is "the principle of accountability." That is, the supplying state must be made aware of the consequences. To ensure that "a return address" is traceable, the Los Alamos National Laboratory in New Mexico is developing a system for detecting the molecular fingerprint of nuclear material. "It's technically feasible, and the work is advancing quite successfully," Allison says.

Fitzpatrick cites other "purposeful steps" to limit the danger of a terrorist attack, such as "rolling back" Khan's black-market network, and more restrictive export controls for uranium by the Nuclear Suppliers Group, the 45 countries that strictly control their nuclear-fuel exports.

Also reportedly working well is the Proliferation Security Initiative proposed by President Bush in 2003, under which some 70 countries undertake to stop and search ships suspected of carrying banned weapons or technology in their territorial waters. Another initiative is U.N. Security Council Resolution 1540, passed in 2004, which requires all member nations to tighten their export-control regulations, ensure security of all nuclear materials and make breaches of the rules a criminal offense.

Also needed, says Allison, is a change of philosophy about nuclear weapons that would lead to a more rapid disarmament. A Martian looking down at Earth "would never realize that the Cold War is over," he says. "The arsenals look almost the same, except neither side means to threaten the other. It's a fantastic anachronism. It's just the dead hand of the past."

ide the Nuclear Non-Proliferation Treaty

Dealing with the "haves" and "have nots"

The landmark U.N. Nuclear Non-Proliferation Treaty (NPT) was essentially a bargain between the nuclear-weapon states — the "haves" — and the non-nuclear-weapon states — the "have nots." Its three aims were, and remain, to prohibit new nuclear weapons programs; to encourage civilian nuclear energy development; and to encourage nuclear-weapon states to reduce their arsenals to zero, or close to it. Opened for signature on July 1, 1968, and entered into force on March 5, 1970, it has so far been ratified by 188 sovereign states, including the original five "haves" — the United States, the former Soviet Union, Britain, China and France.

Pakistan and India, both of which have nuclear weapons, and Israel — also known to be a weapons state even though the Israelis have never publicly admitted it — have not signed the treaty. Iran was one of the early signatories (1968). North Korea signed the NPT in 1985 but withdrew — the only country so far to have done so.

In Article I of the agreement the "haves" undertook "not to transfer to any recipient whatsoever nuclear weapons or other explosive nuclear devices or control over such weapons or explosive devices directly, or indirectly," or to help the non-weapon states to acquire such weapons. [1]

In Article II, the "have nots" agreed "not to receive the transfer from any country whatsoever of nuclear weapons or other nuclear explosive devices," and "not to manufacture or otherwise acquire nuclear weapons." But Article IV confirms "the inalienable right" of all signatory states to develop, research, produce and use nuclear energy "for peaceful purposes without discrimination and in conformity with Articles I and II of this Treaty."

It has been said that by giving all states the right to develop their own nuclear power plants, the treaty in effect opens the way to proliferation since any nuclear reactor, if it has enough centrifuges, can enrich uranium to weapons level. On the other hand, the treaty drafters may have felt that Article VI would counterbalance this risk.

Article VI enshrines the heart of the bargain. In return for a commitment from the non-nuclear-weapon states not to develop weapons programs, the "haves" in effect promised to also become "have nots." They agreed "to pursue negotiations in good faith on effective measures relating to cessation of the nuclear arms race at an early date and to nuclear disarmament, and on a treaty or general and complete disarmament under strict and effective international control." In other words, they promised a nuclear-free world.

The treaty established a safeguards system under the responsibility of the International Atomic Energy Agency (IAEA), which was to verify compliance with the treaty through inspections.

Tucked away almost at the end of its 11 articles is the treaty's definition of a nuclear-weapon state as a country that detonated a nuclear weapon prior to Jan. 1, 1967. In 1970, that meant the United States, the Soviet Union and the United Kingdom. China and France were retroactively added to the group in 1992.

BACKGROUND

"Destroyer of Worlds"

Hitler desperately wanted an atomic bomb, but despite pressure on German scientists, he did not get it. Werner Heisenberg, the Nobel Prize-winning founder of quantum mechanics who headed one of the Nazi atomic weapon projects, would claim later that, troubled by his conscience, he had deliberately slowed down the work. [28]

Heisenberg's critics say he failed to make a bomb only because he had miscalculated the amount of uranium needed. Either way, Heisenberg's biographers agree his report to the authorities in July 1942 on the difficulties, expense and time required to acquire enough uranium convinced the Nazis to scuttle the project. [29]

The United States, of course, was at work on its own atomic bomb using enriched uranium. In 1942, the U.S. launched the top-secret Manhattan Project, with Italian nuclear physicist Enrico Fermi, Danish physicist Niels Bohr and American theoretical physicist J. Robert Oppenheimer, scientific director of the project.

Near the war's end, on July 16, 1945, the United States successfully tested its first atomic device at Alamogordo, N.M. Watching its famous mushroom cloud, Oppenheimer tersely remarked, "It worked."

Originally — and unusually for an international treaty — the NPT was supposed to run for 25 years. However, in 1995 it was extended indefinitely. At mandatory review conferences held every five years the treaty has invariably been criticized by the "have nots" as discriminatory by the "haves." They have claimed that nuclear-weapon states have not done enough to comply with Article VI and reduce their arsenals.

The final declaration of the 1975 conference, for example, expressed serious concern that the nuclear arms race had continued unabated and called for more effort on reduction. [2] The United States and the Soviet Union argued that the two agreements limiting offensive and defensive strategic weapons resulting from SALT I, the first stage of arms limitation talks, represented considerable progress in nuclear arms limitation.

The same complaints surfaced from non-nuclear-weapon countries in 1980, and again five years later. In 1990 their differences with the "haves" — particularly the United States — over a proposed comprehensive test ban treaty led to the conference closing without a final declaration. In 1995, a conference declaration stressed that with the Cold War consigned to history the time was right for arms reduction "to be fulfilled with determination." [3]

Despite the criticism, the 1995 conference decided in favor of extending the treaty indefinitely instead of for another 25-year period. As with all rules, implementation is everything, and the NPT has its defenders. "More countries have dismantled their nuclear weapons than have established such programs, and given that [President] John Kennedy believed in the 1950s that we would end up with 20 or 30 actual nuclear-weapon states by this time, we haven't done badly with nine," observes Kennette Benedict, executive director of the Bulletin of the Atomic Scientists.

Russia's Vladimir Putin and U.S. President George Bush meet at the G-8 Summit in St. Petersburg last summer, after setting up the Global Initiative to Combat Nuclear Terrorism, which seeks to safeguard stockpiles of nuclear materials.

Benedict concedes that the United States and the Soviet Union/Russia have made a good start on drawing down their respective nuclear arsenals — from a high of 60,000 in the 1970s to about 26,000 today. "But given the horrific destruction of these weapons, the goal of zero is still the right one," Benedict says. "And the political conditions — no more Cold War — would seem to set the stage for a realistic drawdown."

[1] The full text of the NPT and a list of the signatories can be found on the U.N. Web site, www.disarmament.un.org.

[2] For reports on the NPT Review Conferences 1975-1995 see www.reachingcriticalwill.org, Web site of the Women's International League for Peace and Freedom.

[3] See 1995 Conference Decision on www.disarmament.un.org: "Nuclear disarmament is substantially facilitated by the easing of international tension and the strengthening of trust between states which have prevailed following the end of the cold war."

Later, with chilling prescience, he described his colleagues' reactions: "We knew the world would not be the same. A few people laughed, a few people cried, most people were silent. I remembered the line from the Hindu scripture, the 'Bhagavad-Gita.' Vishnu is trying to persuade the prince that he should do his duty, and to impress him he takes on his multi-armed form and says, 'Now I am become Death, the Destroyer of Worlds.' I suppose we all thought that in one way or another." [30]

By then Germany had capitulated, but Japan was still fighting, and President Harry S Truman ordered an atomic bomb dropped on Hiroshima. The bomb was dropped on Aug. 6, virtually destroying the city and

killing some 140,000 people, mostly civilians. Three days later, a second bomb hit Nagasaki; 74,000 died. The Japanese, stunned, surrendered on Aug. 15.

Boston for Berlin?

The devastation of Hiroshima and Nagasaki shocked many of the Manhattan Project scientists, including Oppenheimer, who ended up lobbying for international arms control. When the Soviets acquired nuclear capability in 1949, Oppenheimer attempted to influence policy away from a heated arms race. [31]

But escalation was inevitable. In the 1950s, the Soviets had relatively few bombers that could reach the

Physicist J. Robert Oppenheimer, civilian director of the Manhattan Project, and Gen. Leslie R. Groves, military head of the project, at the testing grounds in New Mexico.

United States, while the far more numerous long-range U.S. aircraft, based around the world, could reach almost anywhere in the Soviet Union. The American nuclear arsenal was designed primarily to deter, and if necessary defeat, a Soviet attack on Europe, not on the United States.

The United Kingdom became the third nuclear power in 1952, followed by France in 1960 and China four years later.

The development of intercontinental ballistic missiles (ICBMs) during the 1960s put every corner of the globe — the United States included — within reach of nuclear attack. If the United States answered a Soviet attack on Europe, the Russians could hit the continental United States.

The nagging question was: Would the Russians believe that — as a commentator put it, "America was prepared to sacrifice Boston for Berlin?" [32]

On the Soviet side, as newly gained documents of the Warsaw Pact reveal, the Soviet Union had plans to invade Western Europe with Warsaw Pact partners. * The invasion would be an offensive thrust deep into enemy territory, not a defensive reaction, despite the probability of igniting a nuclear war. [33]

The Warsaw Pact postulated that the North Atlantic Treaty Organization (NATO) had weak defenses in Europe, that Soviet air defenses could destroy incoming NATO missiles before they landed, and that the Soviet Union would prevail because the West was less willing to suffer nuclear devastation. [34]

As the Cold War escalated in the 1960s, the United States and the Soviet Union trained nuclear missiles at each other. Particularly alarming to the Soviets were the U.S. weapons in nearby Turkey.

After the U.S.-led Bay of Pigs invasion failed to dislodge communist leader Fidel Castro from Cuba in 1962, the Soviets sent nuclear missiles to protect the island, citing the U.S. missiles in Turkey.

President Kennedy's showdown with Khrushchev over the missiles nearly plunged the world into nuclear war, but Khrushchev "blinked" first, dismantling the installations.

As former U.S. Secretary of State Henry Kissinger later observed, "America and its allies had an incentive to emphasize both the certainty and the ferocity of their reaction to challenge. Since deterrence can only be tested negatively, by events that did not take place, and since it is never possible to demonstrate why something has not occurred, it became especially difficult to assess whether the existing policy was the best possible policy or just a barely effective one." [35]

Whatever its shortcomings, nuclear deterrence remained a key factor in U.S.-Soviet strategic thinking for nearly three decades.

In the 1950s, the United States and other nations were building the first generation of nuclear reactors for peaceful use. But this technological breakthrough also made weapons-grade fuel more accessible. Israel was already secretly creating its "unconfirmed" arsenal to

---

* The Warsaw Pact, including communist Central and Eastern European states, was established in 1955 to counter the perceived threat from the NATO alliance.

ensure, as Israel Atomic Energy Commission Chairman Ernst David Bergmann said in 1952, "that we shall never again be led as lambs to the slaughter," referring to the Nazi Holocaust. [36]

In 1957, in a harbinger of problems to come, Iran launched a nuclear-energy program with U.S. help. "Petroleum is a noble material, much too valuable to be burned," Iran's ruler, Shah Mohammed Reza Pahlavi, remarked. "We envision producing, as soon as possible, 23,000 megawatts of electricity using nuclear power." [37]

In an attempt to stem the rising nuclear tide, the world's five nuclear nations — also the five veto-wielding members of the U.N. Security Council — launched the Nuclear Non-Proliferation Treaty in 1968. But there were problems from the beginning.

Iran, for example, had agreements with the United States and France to develop nuclear power, and Iranian nuclear engineers began training at MIT. But in the late 1970s the United States said it had learned the shah was secretly developing nuclear weapons.

Following the 1979 Islamic revolution and the shah's overthrow, the ruling ayatollahs suspended Iran's nuclear program. In 1985, however, Iran's foreign minister said Iran needed weapons of mass destruction to counter Israel, and Iran's nuclear efforts were restarted with secret help from North Korea and Pakistan's Khan.

Weapons Ban Elusive

From the 1970s until the end of the Cold War, alternate cycles of nuclear escalation and disarmament followed the ebb and flow of East-West tension. Two major multilateral initiatives stand out — the effort to ban the production of fissile material for nuclear weapons and an attempt to halt nuclear testing.

The accumulation of weapons continued through the Reagan era in the 1980s, when the United States decided

Tally of Nuclear Testing, 1945 to 1998

The first atomic test was held by the United States on July 16, 1945. Signatories to the 1963 Limited Test Ban Treaty pledged to stop atmospheric, underwater or in-space testing. France was last to halt atmospheric testing, in 1974. Underground tests by the major powers continued until 1996; India and Pakistan tested until 1998, and North Korea conducted an underground test in October 2006.

2,050 Tests (528 Atmospheric, 1,522 Underground)

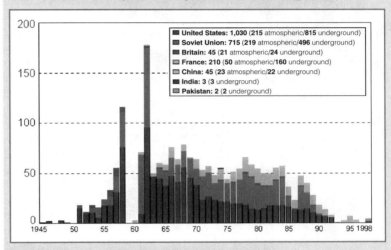

United States: 1,030 (215 atmospheric/815 underground)
Soviet Union: 715 (219 atmospheric/496 underground)
Britain: 45 (21 atmospheric/24 underground)
France: 210 (50 atmospheric/160 underground)
China: 45 (23 atmospheric/22 underground)
India: 3 (3 underground)
Pakistan: 2 (2 underground)

Source: Natural Resources Defense Council, 2002

to position intermediate-range, ground-launched cruise and Pershing II missiles in Western Europe to counter the Soviet SS-20 missile. The SS-20 was mobile, more accurate than its predecessors and capable of targeting Europe, the Middle East and North Africa.

In 1983, Washington made Moscow a "dual track" offer in which talks about removing the medium-range missiles were to be held at the same time that they were being deployed. After hesitating, the Soviets agreed to negotiate. Meanwhile, the U.S. plan to deploy cruise and Pershing missiles had drawn widespread public protests throughout Europe.

In Germany, the missile-deployment issue split the ruling Social Democratic Party and brought down Chancellor Helmut Schmidt's government. Eventually the United States and Russia agreed in the Intermediate Range Nuclear Forces Treaty (INF) to destroy their intermediate and short-range missiles, with attendant

AFP/Getty Images/Jung Yeon-Je

A South Korean activist in Seoul demonizes North Korea's Kim Jong-Il. North Korea has been virtually blackmailing the South, as well as Western powers, for economic help, by continuing to pursue nuclear weapons.

The SALT treaties led eventually to the START (Strategic Arms Reduction Treaty) talks. START I in 1991 and START II in 1993 (an agreement with the newly constituted Russia) limited the number of warheads to 6,000 for both sides, whether rocket-launched, fired from submarines or carried by bombers. [39]

Talks on a Comprehensive Nuclear Test Ban Treaty, after four decades of efforts, began in Geneva, Switzerland, in 1994. The treaty, which President Clinton signed on Sept. 24, 1996, expanded an existing ban on atmospheric testing to include underground tests, even for peaceful purposes.

Clinton called it "the longest-sought, hardest-fought prize in the history of arms control." The treaty allowed testing of non-radioactive explosives and would use an international network of monitors to ensure compliance. But the U.S. Senate stunned the world by soundly rejecting it in 1999.

Republican senators said the ban would leave the United States vulnerable and that the verification process would be difficult to implement. Sweden's Blix recently called on the U.S. Senate to ratify the treaty because, he said, "it would set in motion a good communal effort. If the United States ratifies it, then China might; if India does, Pakistan could, and so on." [40]

The Bush administration took a skeptical view of nuclear-arms treaties. It did not resubmit the 1996 Comprehensive Test Ban Treaty to the Senate for ratification. It also abrogated the 1972 U.S.-Soviet Anti-Ballistic Missile Treaty, which was meant to discourage the superpowers from building safeguards against each other's arsenals.

In December 2001, after the shock of the Sept. 11 terrorist attacks on New York City and the Pentagon, the administration called for research into new types of low-yield nuclear "bunker-busters" designed to penetrate deep underground — and for small-scale invasions against an entrenched enemy. [41]

CURRENT SITUATION

New Threats

Recent nuclear-related developments seriously threaten the fragile stability of two of the world's most volatile regions. North Korea's first underground nuclear test, on Oct. 9, 2006, "has produced an immense impact on

inspections. By the time the Pershings were removed from Germany, Italy and elsewhere they had still not functioned correctly in testing. [38]

Bilateral (U.S.-Soviet) disarmament negotiations resulted in two Strategic Arms Limitation Treaties (SALT I & II). In 1972, SALT I froze the number of strategic ballistic missile launchers at existing levels. It also allowed old intercontinental ballistic missiles (ICBMs) that were dismantled to be replaced by submarine-launched ballistic missiles. Salt II, negotiated between 1972 and 1979, sought to curtail the manufacture of strategic nuclear weapons.

Is a total ban on nuclear weapons possible today?

YES

Kennette Benedict
Executive Director, Bulletin of the Atomic Scientists

Written for *CQ Researcher*, January 2007

The chances of a total ban on nuclear weapons are certainly better than zero. Eliminating nuclear weapons is still like eliminating the institution of slavery to some people. But a *Wall Street Journal* essay in January by former Secretaries of State Henry Kissinger and George Shultz, former Secretary of Defense William Perry and former Armed Services Committee Chairman Sen. Sam Nunn, D-Ga., was one of several signs that some prominent people are rethinking the nuclear situation.

The *Journal* article called on President Bush to take the lead in reversing reliance on nuclear weapons as a step toward preventing further proliferation. It also called for ratification of the Comprehensive (Nuclear) Test Ban Treaty, taking nuclear weapons off high alert, further reducing the number of nuclear forces and halting the production of fissile materials.

While the authors didn't talk of prohibition, they did call for a world free of nuclear weapons.

In Washington, there is at least understanding that it doesn't make sense to be calling on others not to have nuclear weapons while at the same time continuing to have them. Prohibition would require the powers that have the weapons — and that really means the United States and Russia — to take seriously Article Four of the Nuclear Non-proliferation Treaty, which commits the nuclear states to nuclear disarmament.

That would be a beginning. At the height of the Cold War the combined number of weapons held by America and the Soviet Union was 60,000. Estimates are now down to 27,000 — so we're halfway there.

After the fall of the Berlin Wall, President George H.W. Bush made a significant start on dismantling America's nuclear arsenal. In Russia, thousands of missiles have been dismantled — the Russians can't afford to maintain the large arsenals they had in the past. People understand the danger to their own security of the spread of nuclear weapons, and the only way to protect ourselves is for nobody to have them.

It would take a pretty robust monitoring effort, but the International Atomic Energy Agency (IAEA) has shown that it can measure up to the task. We also would have to deal with the problem of enriched uranium being available for weapons, but there are ways to reduce and lock these materials away. And there would have to be security assurances, but isn't that what the United Nations was set up to do?

NO

Paolo Cotta-Ramusino
Professor of physics, University of Milan, Italy

Written for *CQ Researcher*, January 2007

There are two existing treaties that ban the production, stockpiling and use of weapons of mass destruction. One is the 1972 convention banning biological weapons, and the other is the chemical weapons ban of 1993. Would a similar measure outlawing nuclear weapons be possible?

The advantages of such a ban are obvious: an end to the danger that nuclear states might use their weapons, to the problem of proliferation — and to the discriminatory situation between the "have" states and those without nuclear weapons. Outlawing them would also brand the use of nuclear weapons as illegal and immoral.

But equally obvious are the problems connected with the transition to an effective prohibition. How to ensure that some states will not retain nuclear weapons in defiance of the convention? How to prevent states with nuclear capability for commercial development from making the relatively easy switch to weapons production?

In the present international situation the pace of nuclear disarmament should be stepped up. But as the numbers of remaining weapons decrease to very small levels, the process of reaching zero will become more complex and laborious. Then there's also the difficulty of putting in place a mechanism to prevent clandestine weapons production. At this point, if we are realists, we will have to say that total nuclear disarmament is a utopian concept that works better in peace demonstrations than in the world of "serious" international politics.

If the nuclear situation were stable, it would be different. But a state of affairs that includes nations that are "officially" nuclear, others that are de facto nuclear, still others that want to be nuclear, and those that could become nuclear if the necessity arose, is not a stable situation despite the last 50 years of "cold peace."

Much depends on the attitude of the United States and Russia. If nuclear disarmament moves swiftly, and if the emphasis on nuclear arms is eventually reduced, moving in the direction of zero, then international opinion will be more inclined not to condone nuclear proliferation, and the prestige of possessing nuclear weapons will become a thing of the past. But if the disarmament process were to slow down even further, and the emphasis on the nuclear component in defense were to increase even to a small degree, then the result will be the opposite.

Director General Mohamed ElBaradei of the International Atomic Energy Agency (IAEA) won the Nobel Peace Prize in 2005 for his work against nuclear proliferation.

peace and stability in the Korean peninsula and in northeast Asia," commented China's *People's Daily Online*, which tends to reflect official opinion in Beijing. [42]

Meanwhile, the growing likelihood that Shiite Iran will become nuclear power has become a matter of grave concern to Sunni powers such as Saudi Arabia and Egypt, to say nothing of Israel. The Jewish state sees itself as the No. 1 target of Iran, whose president threatens to wipe it off the map.

"Tehran is making a mockery of the international community's efforts to solve the crisis surrounding Iran's nuclear program," Shimon Peres, vice premier of Israel, said last year, noting, "The president of Iran should remember that Iran can also be wiped off the map." [43]

"North Korea's nuclear test alters the balance of power in northeast Asia," says Fitzpatrick, of London's Institute for Strategic Studies. "In every other field — economics, culture, diplomacy, technology, to name a few — the gap between the impoverished citizens of Kim Jong-Il's regime and their world-class southern kinsmen could hardly be greater. The north's aging conventional military capabilities have also fallen behind the south. But now North Korea boasts of possessing the ultimate equalizer" — a boast that has been confirmed by U.S. and other intelligence sources.

The IAEA's ElBaradei calls the Pyongyang test "the only trump card Kim Jong-Il had. He felt isolated, and he was threatening: 'We can do more harm unless you come and talk.' "

North Korea has been cut off from most of the outside world for decades, first under Kim Il-Sung, who transformed a Marxist regime into a personality-cult regime, and since his death in 1994 under his son. Soon after taking over, Kim had signed the so-called Agreed Framework with the Clinton administration: The United States and South Korea would supply light-water reactors and other nuclear energy technological aid in return for Pyongyang's commitment to halt its nuclear-weapons program.

Bureaucratic complications delayed delivery of the reactors, and they had not arrived when George W. Bush succeeded Clinton in the White House. Where the Clinton administration had offered North Korea a carrot, Bush preferred the stick, pulling out of negotiations with the North Koreans. The Agreed Framework was scrapped, and Bush labeled North Korea a member of the "Axis of Evil," along with Iran and Libya, for its human rights violations and efforts to develop nuclear weapons. Bush also labeled the diminutive Kim as the "Communist pygmy."

But Kim still wanted bilateral talks with Washington as the price for halting his nuclear program. Instead, the United States demanded six-party talks involving Pyongyang and South Korea, along with Russia, China and Japan. Talks began on Aug. 6, 2003, centering on variations of the original technology-for-renunciation offer, buttressed by the warning of action by the U.N. Security Council in the case of non-compliance.

The talks were suspended on Feb. 10, 2005, and resumed on July 25. Between sessions and walkouts, North Korea was rumored to be continuing enrichment efforts. But on Sept. 19 Pyongyang announced that it was scrapping its nuclear program and rejoining the NPT, and the United States gave the North Koreans assurances that it would not attack.

The arrangement quickly soured, however, over attempts at an accord. North Korea refused to shut off its nuclear operations until it received the promised light-water reactors; Washington said delivery would follow the shutdown. As the deal went up in smoke, the six-party talks reconvened for their fifth session on Nov. 11, 2005.

On July 17, 2006, after the North Koreans had test-fired seven long-range Taepodong 2 missiles, the U.N. Security Council voted unanimously to impose sanctions to prevent North Korea from importing missile parts and materials. But then came the Oct. 9 nuclear underground test, and on Oct. 14 the Security Council imposed financial and weapons sanctions. On Dec. 18, the stalled talks were back on track.

Fitzpatrick at the London-based International Institute for Strategic Studies argues that "it's questionable whether North Korea has the means of delivering a nuclear weapon." The bomb design would not fit on North Korea's Scud, Nodong or Taepodong missiles, he notes, and any plane or ship carrying the missile would be detected and taken out before reaching its target.

Moreover, a nuclear weapon fired over the 38th parallel into South Korea is unlikely because the "casualties and fallout would affect as many Koreans in the north as in the south," he says.

America's greatest concern is that "North Korea would sell or barter its nuclear weapons to another country or, God forbid, a terrorist group," Fitzpatrick adds. "North Korea's record of nuclear commerce, its financial crisis and its eagerness to sell missiles, weapons and illicit goods to any prospective buyer make the nightmare scenario a real possibility."

A breakthrough finally came in the six-nation negotiations on Feb. 13, 2007, when North Korea promised to shut down its nuclear facilities at Yongbyon. In exchange, the other nations agreed to unfreeze certain contested North Korean bank accounts and to provide Kim with 50,000 tons of fuel oil as a first-step incentive to ensure eventual abandonment of all nuclear weapons and research programs. The final payoff would be additional economic, energy and humanitarian assistance to the value of 1 million tons of fuel oil.

The deal requires that the North Koreans seal the main nuclear reactor within 60 days and allow the IAEA to inspect the facilities. But at least one of China's scientists expressed doubts. "What if North Korea doesn't show them to inspectors, if they say we've stopped this and shut down that, what if they say you have to trust us?" asked Liu Gongliang, a physicist at the Institute of Applied Physics and Computational Mathematics who has followed North Korea's nuclear program for the Chinese government. [44]

The Japanese reaction hinged largely on the simmering issue of whether or not North Korea would apologize and make reparations for abducting Japanese citizens decades ago. "We understand it marks the first concrete step by North Korea toward its nuclear dismantlement," Japanese Prime Minister Shinzo Abe said. "But our position that Japan cannot provide support without a resolution of the abduction issue is unchanged." [45]

At the end of February 2007, North Korea asked IAEA head ElBaradei to visit Pyongyang. U.N. Secretary-General Ban Ki-moon called the invitation a "good beginning," and added, "I hope sincerely that Iranian authorities should learn from the North Korean issue." [46]

The Iranian Conundrum

"We face no greater challenge from a single country than we do from Iran," President Bush declared in 2006. Yet Iran has so far tested no nuclear device, and experts believe it is not likely to be able to manufacture the bomb for another decade. [47] President Ahmadinejad insists Iran has no intention of making nuclear bombs at all. He says Iran is within its rights as an NPT signatory to develop a nuclear program for peaceful purposes, and that is what is happening.

But the Bush administration points out that Iran, a major oil producer, has no need for a nuclear-energy program anyway. Yet a leading Iranian journalist, Kianouche Amirie of the *Iran Times*, argues, "Why should immense oil and gas reserves bar a country from developing nuclear energy? Everyone knows that oil and gas reserves will be finally exhausted, even if they might last for years. Above all, nuclear technology is a modern branch of science, and Iranians are eager to learn it."

Nuclear technology maybe, but President Bush has said more than once that it would be "unacceptable" for Iran to have nuclear weapons. [48]

Concern for Israel and for the implications of a Shiite bomb in the Middle East largely drive Washington's opposition to the Iranian nuclear program. But foreign-policy experts believe that, like the North Koreans, the Iranians are at least partially trying to get America's attention.

"From Iran's perspective, the key is to normalize relations with the United States," says ElBaradei. "In all these situations [involving Iran and North Korea] negotiating is indispensable, and we should move away from the idea of dialogue as a reward" for disarmament. In other words, halting Tehran's nuclear program should not be considered a prerequisite for talking to the Iranians.

ElBaradei is not alone in thinking that Iran seeks to re-establish relations with the United States. The Bush administration itself believes that in refusing to talk directly to the Iranians, it is withholding a desired prize. Several leading Iranians, including former President Mohammed Khatami on his visit to the United States last summer, voiced similar sentiments.

One advantage to Iran from normalizing relations would be the restitution of over $10 billion in Iranian assets frozen by the United States following the 1979 revolution. But if Tehran's motivation is normalization, continued stalemate is likely. Direct, bilateral dealings with Iran remain anathema to President Bush.

As in its negotiations with North Korea, the United States is part of a group negotiation with Iran, along with Britain, France, Germany, Russia and China. The Western powers are focusing on persuading Tehran not to enrich its own uranium and not to develop nuclear weapons capability. The European governments began talks with Iran in October 2003, and at the Europeans' request, Iran stopped enriching uranium — the crux of the matter. Washington, after considerable hesitation, joined the talks in 2005, as did Moscow and Beijing.

The strategy was to offer Iran technical and financial incentives stiffened with warnings of U.N. action in the case of non-compliance. But Iran resumed its uranium enrichment in June 2006 at the Natanz reactor and two other locations.

An offer from Moscow to enrich uranium on Iran's behalf and then collect the spent fuel to remove suspicion that it could be converted for weapons use was turned down flat. In August 2006 the Iranians ignored a U.N.-imposed deadline to stop. The result: On Dec. 23, the U.N. Security Council voted to restrict Iran's imports of sensitive nuclear material and to freeze the assets of 22 Iranian officials and institutions connected with the nuclear program. [49]

Meanwhile, the debate about Iran's real intentions goes on in the international community with a growing tone of frustration. "The world is not against Iran going for nuclear power, but going for nuclear enrichment," says Blix. "They say they have a right, but that doesn't mean they must do it. Today, it's very much a prestige question and a pride question, and that should be taken into account."

French President Jacques Chirac let slip a comment that he quickly withdrew later, but it spoke volumes about the differences between French and U.S. policy toward Iran.

"[W]hat is dangerous about this situation is not the fact of having a nuclear bomb," he said. "Having one or perhaps a second bomb a little later, well, that's not very dangerous. But what is very dangerous is proliferation."

It would be an act of self-destruction, Chirac explained, for Iran to launch a bomb. "Where will it drop it, this bomb? On Israel?" he asked. "It would not have gone off 200 meters into the atmosphere before Tehran would be razed to the ground." [50]

U.S. reaction to the threats from Iran and North Korea is affecting U.S.-Russian relations and causing concern about a possible new arms race between the two former Cold War adversaries. Moscow has been infuriated by U.S. plans — announced on Feb. 22 — to deploy 10 missile interceptors in Poland and a missile radar in the Czech Republic by 2011 as part of America's new missile defense system. While Washington says the system is essential to dealing with rogue states, Moscow sees the move as an example of NATO's expansion into Eastern and Central Europe and the remilitarization of Europe. [51]

"Plans to expand certain elements of the anti-missile defense system to Europe cannot help but disturb us," said Russian President Putin in February during a speech in Munich, with U.S. Defense Secretary Robert Gates, sitting nearby. "Who needs the next step of what would be, in this case, an inevitable arms race?" [52]

Two senior Russian generals later said Moscow might withdraw from the intermediate-range nuclear arms control agreement. Meanwhile, the Putin government — flush with burgeoning oil and gas revenues — has just announced a massive new $190-billion arms-buying spree that would replace nearly half of Russia's military arsenal over the next eight years, including its submarine-launched ballistic missiles.

OUTLOOK

Twin Threats

The specter of nuclear theft from the remaining stockpiles of Cold War belligerents, especially in Russia, remains undiminished. Mini-powers India and Pakistan seem mutually deterred but could easily come to blows at the drop of an ethnic insult or a crisis in Kashmir.

Meanwhile, some analysts worry that if Pakistan's radical, pro-Taliban mullahs were to take power, the country's nuclear arsenal could fall into the hands of Islamic extremists. Pakistan's hard-line Islamist parties have grown in strength in recent years, despite President Pervez Musharraf's authoritarian, secular rule, and there have been repeated attempts on his life. [53] The military under Musharraf, who seized power in a military coup in 1999, has instituted elaborate security measures to protect the nation's nuclear arsenal, but the Bush administration has criticized Musharraf for not cracking down harder on a resurgent Taliban movement on the border between Pakistan and Afghanistan.

Israel will continue to contend with regimes that have threatened to annihilate it. Last August, *The Jerusalem Post* quoted a "senior source" as saying that Iran "flipped the world the bird" by not agreeing to stop enriching uranium. "The Iranians know the world will do nothing," he said. "This is similar to the world's attempts to appease Hitler in the 1930s — they are trying to feed the beast."

Israeli Foreign Minister Tzipi Livni warned that, "Every day that passes brings the Iranians closer to building a nuclear bomb. The world can't afford a nuclear Iran." [54]

Meanwhile, despite cries of hypocrisy from developing nations and non-proliferation advocates, the United States will continue to augment its nuclear arsenal. In March 2007 the National Nuclear Security Administration announced the selection of a design for Reliable Replacement Warheads, a new generation of nuclear warheads initially for submarine-launched missiles — the first new U.S. nuclear weapons in more than 20 years. [55]

Simultaneously, the U.S. will attempt to placate, through carrot-and-stick diplomacy, North Korea's Kim Jong-Il. Despite the February agreement that suspends North Korea's nuclear program, the book is hardly closed on their episodic threats to global stability. [56]

If a revanchist North Korea is allowed to continue to develop nuclear weapons, the reverberations would thun-

Anti-aircraft guns protect the Bushehr nuclear power plant in southern Iran, which is being built with Russian help. Iranians began their nuclear programs under the late shah in the 1950s.

der throughout the Pacific Rim. As a dominant economy in the Far East, Japan would have to make a grave decision about its own security. That decision in part depends on whether or not Tokyo feels Japan is still covered by the U.S. nuclear umbrella.

The prospect of a U.S. umbrella is met with a dark sense of irony in the Japanese cities that actually experienced nuclear devastation. "I feel great anger over North Korea's conducting of a nuclear test," said Tadatoshi Akiba, mayor of Hiroshima. [57]

The six-nation accord with North Korea was greeted by most of the world with a sense of relief and hope, but even those loyal to the Bush administration, pointing to the Hermit Kingdom's record of obfuscation and brinksmanship, say the White House may have been outfoxed again.

"It sends exactly the wrong signal to would-be proliferators around the world: If we hold out long enough, wear down the State Department negotiators, eventually you get rewarded," said John Bolton, chief of staff to President Bush and a former U.S. representative to the United Nations. [58]

It is possible that North Korea, a nation that has suffered poverty and starvation under the mismanagement of its xenophobic regime, may keep its promises this time. But any return to its weapons program could easily launch a new chapter of the nuclear arms race in Asia.

Some Arab commentators even fear that Iran's nuclear capability will be directed at them. Abd Al-Rahman Al-Rashed, director of Al-Arabiyya TV in

Dubai, argues that Iranian nuclear weapons would more likely target the Gulf countries than anyone else.

"It is inconceivable that Iran will drop the bomb on Syria and target Jordan or Egypt," he said. "It is incomprehensible that Iran will bomb Israel, which has a shield of missiles, tremendous firepower, and nuclear weapons and artillery sufficient to eradicate every city in Iran. In addition, any attack on Israel would mean the immediate, wide-scale destruction of the Palestinians. . . . This means that if this destructive weapon is used, the only option for a target is the Arab Gulf. . . . Fear will plunge the region into an arms race that will serve no one in the region — only the arms dealers in the West, and particularly in Russia." [59]

"What is our sin, and that of our children and our grandchildren, who must live [in the shadow] of concern about Iran?" added Qatari intellectual Abd Al-Hamid Al-Ansari, former dean of the Faculty of Shari'a and Law at Qatar University. "How can we be calm about Iran, when it still occupies the United Arab Republic's islands and has a problem with every country in the region?" [60]

Iran has reacted with typical bravado. Its government-owned *Abrar* newspaper reported last year that Iranians know that "American military strategists are considering rapid strikes on Iran's sites in order to prevent Iran from continuing its nuclear program. The fact of the matter is that at times the news published in Western publications is aimed at launching a psychological warfare against the Islamic system. Although it might seem easy for the Americans to start a war against Iran, they cannot predict its outcome." [61]

The Russians, who have heavily invested in Iran, are urging caution in the dispute over Tehran's nuclear ambitions. "At the current stages, it is important not to make guesses about what will happen, and even more important not to make threats," said Russian Foreign Minister Sergei Lavrov. [62]

Iran continues to roil international feathers. On March 24 the U.N. Security Council voted for new trade and financial sanctions against Iran, prompting a defiant Iran to announce it was suspending cooperation with the IAEA. Then, two days later, Russia and China urged Iran to accede to the U.N. demands, indicating new impatience on the part of two of Iran's closest allies. [63]

As the international nuclear community grows, the need for more international control becomes more urgent, and this issue is likely to dominate the coming years. "Sanctions don't work as a penalty," says IAEA chief ElBaradei. "They tend to put hard-line leaders in the driver's seat. Enrichment and re-processing must be put under multinational control."

He and others believe the answer lies in persuading countries to give up enriching their own uranium and obtaining the nuclear fuel they need ready-made, thus removing or limiting their ability to make weapons.

In September 2006, an IAEA meeting discussed the creation of multinational fuel banks where nations could watch one another and ensure that no country tried to divert some of the uranium for weapons. Russia has taken the lead in proposing to set up such a bank, selling the fuel internationally, and also collecting the spent fuel.

"The problem is to separate the enrichment capacity from the problem of deterrence," says ElBaradei. "A lot of countries enrich for security reasons, and we need to reassure them."

NOTES

1. Quoted in Niusha Bogharati, "Ahmadinejad Challenges Bush to a Debate at the U.N. General Assembly," Worldpress.org, Sept. 12, 2006; www.worldpress.org/Mideast/2489.cfm.

2. Quoted in Michael Crowley, "The Stuff Sam Nunn's Nightmares Are Made Of," *The New York Times Magazine*, Feb. 25, 2007; www.nytimes.com/2007/02/25/magazine/25Nunn.t.html?pagewanted=1.

3. Quoted in Disarmament and Peace Education, online, an arm of the Global Security Institution, February 2004; www.gsinstitute.org/dpe/quotes.html.

4. Quoted in Nov. 8, 2006, speech, Parliamentary Network for Nuclear Disarmament, Wellington, New Zealand; www.gsinstitute.org/pnnd/PNND%20update/PNNDupdate15.html.

5. Carnegie Endowment for International Peace, "Worldwide Nuclear Weapons Stockpiles," Oct. 1, 2005; www.carnegieendowment.org/npp/numbers/default.cfm.

6. Morteza Sabetghadam, Institute for International Energy Studies, Tehran, Helio International online, Sustainable Energy Watch 2005-2006, "Energy and Sustainable Development in Iran," p. 11; www.helio-international.org/reports/pdfs/Iran-EN.pdf.

7. World Nuclear Association online, "World Nuclear Power Reactors 2005-2007 and Uranium Requirements," Jan. 29, 2007; www.world-nuclear. org/info/reactors.

8. *People's Daily*, editorial, Beijing, Oct. 30, 2006.

9. Noah Feldman, "Islam, Terror, and the Second Nuclear Age," *The New York Times Magazine online*, Oct. 29, 2006; www.nytimes.com/2006/10/29/ magazine/29islam.html?pagewanted=5&ei=5070& en=e6f17de2b496f00d&ex=1172725200.

10. Martin D. Fleck and James P. Thomas, "U.S. Undermines Non-Nuclear Treaty," *Seattle Post-Intelligencer*, April 29, 2004. Fleck is executive director of Washington Physicians for Social Responsibility.

11. Miguel Marin-Bosch, "Nuclear Disarmament on the Eve of the Twenty-first Century: Is this as Good as it Gets?" *Disarmament Diplomacy*, Acronym Institute for Disarmament Policy, Issue 36, December 1999. Marin-Bosch was Mexico's representative at the U.N. Conference on Disarmament in Geneva.

12. Hans Blix, "Revive Disarmament," statement at the United Nations, 61st General Assembly, New York, Oct. 16, 2006; www.wmdcommission.org.

13. "We are Determined," *Der Spiegel online*, May 30, 2006; www.spiegel.de/international/spiegel/0,1518, 418660-2,00.html.

14. Quoted in Michael Richardson, "India and Pakistan are not 'imprudent' on nuclear option; Q&A/George Fernandes," *The International Herald Tribune*, June 3, 2002.

15. "A Surgical Strike Is The Answer: interview with Defense Secretary Yogendra Narain," *Defence Outlook* magazine, India, June 10, 2002, quoted in Pervez Hoodbhoy and Zia Mian, Nautilus Institute, ZNet online, "The India-Pakistan Conflict: The Failure of Nuclear Deterrence," Nov. 24, 2002; www.zmag.org/ content/showarticle.cfm?ItemID=2659.

16. Brahma Chellaney, "India Tests Nuclear-Capable Missile, Angers Pakistan," Agence France-Presse, Jan. 25, 2002.

17. Hoodbhoy and Mian, *op. cit.*

18. Bill Powell, "When Outlaws Get the Bomb," *Time*, Oct. 15, 2006; www.time.com/time/magazine/article/ 0,9171,1546300,00.html.

19. Dafna Linzer, "Optimism Turns to Anxiety on Curbing Nuclear Arms," *The Washington Post*, Nov. 3, 2006. p. A23.

20. Quoted in Powell, *op. cit.*

21. William Burr and Robert Wampler, "The Master of the Game: Paul H. Nitze and U.S. Cold War Strategy from Truman to Reagan," The National Security Archive, Oct. 27, 2004; www.gwu.edu/~ nsarchiv/NSAEBB/NSAEBB139/index.htm.

22. Quoted in Claire Taylor and Tim Youngs, "The Future of the British Nuclear Deterrent," Government White Paper, 2006, House of Commons Library, London, Nov. 3, 2006; www.parliament.uk/commons/lib/research/rp2006/ rp06-053.pdf. See also Bush's warning and Kennedy's famous statement, in Roland Flamini, "Corridors of Power," *World Politics Watch*, Jan. 20, 2007; www.worldpoliticswatch.com.

23. Derek D. Smith, *Deterring America: Rogue States and the Proliferation of Weapons of Mass Destruction* (2006).

24. Flamini, *op. cit.*

25. Phillip Watson and Roland Webster, "Bin Laden's Nuclear Threat," *London Times*, Oct. 26, 2001; see also "The Bomb in the Backyard," *Foreign Policy*, November/December 2006.

26. Matthew Bunn and Anthony Wier, "Preventing a Nuclear 9/11," *The Washington Post*, Sept. 12, 2004; reprinted online by Harvard University, www.ksg.harvard.edu/news/opeds/2004/bunn_wier _preventing_nuke_911_wash_post_091204.htm. Bunn and Weir are scholars with the Managing the Atom Project at Harvard University's Kennedy School of Government. See Crowley, *op. cit.*

27. Tom Raum, The Associated Press, "Bush, Putin Announce Anti-Terror Program," July 15, 2006, *Washington Post.com*; www.washingtonpost.com/ wp-dyn/content/article/2006/07/15/AR200607150 0371.html.

28. British playwright Michael Frayn adopted this controversial interpretation in his play "Copenhagen."

29. For a thorough discussion of Germany's attempts to build nuclear weapons, see Thomas Powers, *Heisenberg's War: The Secret History of the German Bomb* (2000).

30. Quoted in J. Robert Oppenheimer; www.atomic archive.com.

31. Kai Bird and Martin Sherwin, *American Prometheus, the Triumph and Tragedy of J. Robert Oppenheimer* (2005).

32. Quoted in Strobe Talbott, *Deadly Gambits: The Reagan Administration and the Stalemate in Nuclear Arms Control* (1985).

33. *Ibid.*

34. Voytech Mastny, "Planning for the Unplannable," Parallel History Project on Cooperative Security, International Relations and Security Network, Center for Security Studies, Swiss Federal Institute of Technology, Zurich, Feb. 6, 2007; www.php.isn. ethz.ch/collections/coll_warplan/introduction_mastny. cfm?navinfo=15365.

35. Henry Kissinger, *Diplomacy* (1995).

36. Quoted in Seymour M. Hersh, *The Samson Option. Israel's Nuclear Arsenal and American Foreign Policy* (1991).

37. Quoted in www.reference.com (nuclear program of Iran) and other sources. For oil reserves see *CIA World Fact Book*; www.cia.gov/cia/publication/factbook.

38. For a history of Pershing missiles see www.red-stone.army.mil/history/systems/pershing.

39. See *CQ Congress Collection*, "Test Ban Treaty, 1999-2000 Legislative Chronology."

40. U.N. press conference, Dec. 14, 2006; Weapons of Mass Destruction Commission, Stockholm; www.wmdcommission.org.

41. Mary H. Cooper, "Nuclear Proliferation and Terrorism," *CQ Researcher*, April 2, 2004, pp. 297-320.

42. "US Seeking Favorable Development of Korean Nuclear Issue," editorial, *People's Daily Online*, Oct. 30, 2006; http://english.people.com.cn/other/archive.html.

43. Quoted in Nathan Gutman, editorial, *The Jerusalem Post*, May 8, 2006.

44. The Associated Press, quoted in MSNBC online, Feb. 13, 2007; www.msnbc.msn.com/id/17130195.

45. *Ibid.*

46. Quoted in George Jahn, "IAEA chief: North Korea soliciting talks," *Seattle Post-Intelligencer online*, Feb. 13, 2007; http://seattlepi.nwsource.com/national/1104ap_koreas_nuclear.html.

47. Quoted in "Bush vows to end 'tyranny' in N. Korea, Iran in new security strategy," *Asian Political News*, March 20, 2006. The phrase is from a report prepared by the White House National Security Council in 2006 and has been repeated many times by President Bush, Secretary of State Condoleezza Rice and presidential spokesman Tony Snow.

48. For one example, see unsigned article in Fox News and The Associated Press, Fox News.com, "Bush: Iran with Nuclear Weapons is Unacceptable," Oct. 27, 2006; www.foxnews.com/story/0,2933,225864,00.html.

49. For a time-line on Iran's nuclear quest going back to 1957, see http://irannuclearwatch.blogspot.com.

50. Elaine Sciolino and Katrin Bennhold, "Chirac Muses on Iran, then Retreats," *International Herald-Tribune Europe*, Jan. 31, 2007; www.iht.com/articles/2007/01/31/news/france.php.

51. Peter Goodspeed, "Russia Embarks on $190b Military Spending Spree: Hawkish Stance: Plan Calls for Replacing 45% of Entire Arsenal," *National Post* (f/k/a *The Financial Post*) (Canada), March 8, 2007, p. A17.

52. Quoted in Daniel Dombey and Demetri Sevastopulo, "Intercept or Interfere? How Missile Defence Pits the Pentagon Against Allies," *Financial Times* (London, England) March 7, 2007, p. 13.

53. See Salman Masood and Talat Hussain, "Pakistani Links Military To Failed Plot To Kill Him," *The New York Times*, May 28, 2004, p. A12.

54. Herb Keinon, "Israel May 'Go It Alone' Against Iran," *Jerusalem Post online*, Aug. 24, 2006; www.jpost.com/servlet/Satellite?pagename=JPost%2FJPArticle%2FShowFull&cid=1154525933028.

55. William J. Broad, David E. Sanger, and Thom Shanker, "U.S. Selecting Hybrid Design for Warheads," *The New York Times*, Jan. 7, 2007.

56. Walter Pincus, "U.S. Selects Design for New Nuclear Warhead," *The Washington Post*, March 3, 2007, p. A8.

57. David Pilling, "Japan PM Calls Test a 'Serious Threat,'" *Financial Times*, London, online, Oct. 9, 2006; www.ft.com/cms/s/6818aaee-576b-11db-833b-0000779e2340.html.

58. Bill Gertz, "Bolton hits agreement as 'bad signal' to Iran," *Washington Times*, Feb. 14, 2007.

59. Abd Al-Rahman Al-Rashed, "For These Reasons, We Fear Iran," *Al-Sharq Al-Awsat*, London, online for "Regime Change Iran;" http://regimechangeiran. blogspot.com/2006_05_21_regimechangeiran_archive. html.

60. Quoted in H. Avraham, "Arab Media Reactions to Iran's Nuclear Project," in Middle East Media Research Institute, online, Washington, May 23, 2006; http://memri.org/bin/articles.cgi?Page=archives&Area =ia&ID=IA27706.

61. Unattributed quote from Iran's government-owned newspaper, *Abrar*, as reported in the *Iran Daily*, Feb. 16, 2006, and Worldpress.com, "Is the U.S. Planning to Attack Iran?," Feb. 21, 2006; www .worldpress.org/Mideast/2270.cfm.

62. Vladimir Isachenkov, The Associated Press, "Do Not Threaten Tehran, Lavrov Says," *Moscow Times.com*, Feb. 7, 2006; www.moscowtimes.ru/ stories/2006/02/07/012.html.

63. Vladimir Isachenkov, The Associated Press, "Russia, China Prod Iran to Heed the U.N.," *Chicago Tribune*, March 27, 2007, p. A8.

BIBLIOGRAPHY

Books

Corera, Gordon, *Shopping for Bombs: Nuclear Proliferation, Global Insecurity, and the Rise and Fall of the A.Q. Khan Network*, Oxford University Press, 2006.
A BBC correspondent tells the riveting, and chilling, story of how the "father" of Pakistan's nuclear bomb used a global black-market network to sell nuclear-weapons technology to Libya, North Korea and Iran.

Harvey, Robert, *Global Disorder: America and the Threat of World Conflict*, Carroll & Graf, 2003.
A British journalist-author combines a comprehensive overview of post-9/11 world threats with a call for the United States to act as the "cornerstone" of world order while avoiding the risks of "unilateralism." Harvey is a columnist for the [London] *Daily Telegraph* and author of five other books on international relations. The book was published in paper as *Global Disorder: How to Avoid a Fourth World War* (2004).

Kagan, Robert, *Dangerous Nation: America's Place in the World from Its Earliest Days to the Dawn of the Twentieth Century*, Knopf, 2006.
A neoconservative foreign-policy expert and *Washington Post* columnist argues that the United States has played an assertive role in world affairs throughout its history. A planned second volume will cover 20th-century foreign policy. Includes detailed notes, 26-page bibliography.

Kupchan, Charles A., *The End of the American Era: U.S. Foreign Policy and the Geopolitics of the Twenty-first Century*, Knopf, 2002.
A senior fellow at the Council on Foreign Relations and a professor at Georgetown University synthesizes history and current events to argue that as the era of American primacy ends, the United States must work harder to cultivate a sense of "common interest" with emerging centers of power. Includes detailed notes, nine-page bibliography.

Lieven, Anatol, and John Hulsman, *Ethical Realism: A Vision for America's Role in the World*, Random House, 2006.
Coming from different political backgrounds, the authors argue that U.S. foreign policy must combine genuine morality with tough, practical common sense. Lieven is a senior fellow at the centrist New America Foundation; Hulsman, formerly with the conservative Heritage Foundation, is at the German Council on Foreign Relations.

Mandelbaum, Michael, *The Case for Goliath: How America Acts as the World's Government in the Twenty-First Century*, Pantheon, 2005.
A professor at the Johns Hopkins University's School of Advanced International Studies depicts the United States' role in world affairs not as an empire or a superpower but as the "world's government." Includes detailed notes.

Articles

Broad, William J., David E. Sanger, and Thom Shanker, "U.S. Selecting Hybrid Design for Warheads," *The New York Times*, Jan. 7, 2007.
The Bush administration is expected to announce next week a major step forward in the building of the country's first new nuclear warhead in nearly two decades. The warheads will replace, not add to, aging weapons.

Crowley, Michael, "The Stuff Sam Nunn's Nightmares Are Made Of," *The New York Times Magazine*, Feb. 25, 2007, p. 50.
The former chairman of the Senate Armed Services Committee may have more influence over non-proliferation as the president and CEO of the Nuclear Threat Initiative.

Lederer, Edith M., "U.N. Treaty Prohibits Terrorists From Possessing Nuclear Material," *Toronto Star*, April 14, 2005, p. A12.
The General Assembly approved a global treaty that makes it a crime for would-be terrorists to possess nuclear weapons or radioactive material.

Pilling, David, "Japan PM calls test a "serious threat," *Financial Times*, London, online, Oct. 9, 2006; www.ft.com/cms/s/6818aaee-576b-11db-833b-0000779e2340.html.
North Korea's apparent nuclear test constitutes a "serious threat [that] would transform in a major way the security environment of North East Asia," Japanese Prime Minister Shinzo Abe said.

Sanger, David E., "U.S. and Russia Will Police Potential Nuclear Terrorists," *The New York Times*, July 15, 2006, p. A8.
Presidents Bush and Putin will announce a new global program to track potential nuclear terrorists and coordinate responses if terrorists ever obtain atomic weapons.

Reports and Studies

Ikenberry, G. John, and Anne-Marie Slaughter (co-directors), Forging a World of Liberty Under Law: U.S. National Security in the 21st Century: Final Report of the Princeton Project on National Security, Woodrow Wilson School of Public and International Affairs, 2006; www.wws.princeton.edu/ppns/.
The report advances a series of proposals, including the creation of a global "Concert of Democracies," to strengthen security cooperation and promote creation of liberal democracy. Slaughter is dean and Ikenberry a professor at the Wilson School.

For More Information

Bulletin of the Atomic Scientists, 6042 South Kimbark Ave., Chicago, IL 60637; (773) 702-2555; www.thebulletin.org. Nonprofit organization dedicated to security, science and survival since 1945.

Carnegie Endowment for International Peace, 1779 Massachusetts Ave., N.W., Washington, DC 20036; (202) 483-7600; www.ceip.org. Think tank advancing international cooperation and U.S. international engagement.

Center for Arms Control and Non-Proliferation, 322 4th St., N.E., Washington, DC 20002; (202) 546-0795; www.armscontrolcenter.org. Seeks the reduction of nuclear weapons as a significant tool of U.S. national security policy.

Council on Foreign Relations, 58 East 68th St., New York, NY 10065; (212) 434-9400; www.cfr.org. Independent, national membership organization and nonpartisan center for scholars providing up-to-date information about the world and U.S. foreign policy.

Federation of American Scientists, 1717 K St., N.W., Suite 209, Washington, DC 20036; (202) 546-3300; www.fas.org. Endorses the humanitarian use of science and technology.

Foreign Policy Association, 470 Park Avenue South, New York, NY 10016; (212) 481-8100; www.fpa.org. Nonprofit organization dedicated to inspiring the American public to learn more about the world; provides independent publications, programs and forums to increase public awareness of policy issues.

Foreign Policy Forum, 517 Third St., Annapolis, MD 21403; (410) 263-1139; www.foreignpolicyforum.com. A forum for critical analyses of U.S. foreign policy.

International Atomic Energy Agency, P.O. Box 100, Wagramer Strasse 5, A-1400 Vienna, Austria; (+431)-2600-0; www.iaea.org. Global center for cooperation on nuclear issues.

International Institute for Strategic Studies, 13-15 Arundel St., Temple Place, London WC2R 3DX, United Kingdom; +44-(0)-20-7379-7676; www.iiss.org. Think tank focusing on international security with emphasis on political-military conflict.

Israel Atomic Energy Commission, P.O. Box 7061, Tel Aviv 61070, Israel; +972-(3)-6462566; www.iaec.gov.il. Advises Israeli government on nuclear policy issues.

Nuclear Threat Initiative, 1747 Pennsylvania Ave., N.W., 7th Floor, Washington, DC 20006; (202) 296-4810; www.nti.org. Works to reduce threats from nuclear, biological and chemical weapons.

Weapons of Mass Destruction Commission, 103 39 Stockholm, Sweden; (+46)-8-543-56-112/123; www.wmdcommission.org. Works toward international cooperation for non-proliferation, arms control and disarmament.

World Nuclear Association, 22A St. James's Square, London SW1Y 4JH, United Kingdom; +44(0)20-7451-1520; www.world-nuclear.org. Global industrial organization that promotes the peaceful use of nuclear power as a sustainable energy resource.

VOICES FROM ABROAD

Yomiuri Shimbun

Japan
April 2, 2006

Don't criticize Japan — Our nuclear program is peaceful
   "Japan has . . . been singled out for operating a spent nuclear fuel reprocessing plant while not possessing nuclear weapons. Critics say there is no other nuclear weapons-free country in the world that operates such a facility. They are grossly mistaken. Japan's nuclear program is entirely aimed at serving peaceful purposes."

Xinhua News Agency

China
Dec. 9, 2006

Nuclear doublespeak by Western countries
   "While many blame [North Korea] and Iran for frustrating international efforts on nuclear non-proliferation, the double standards adopted by some Western countries on nuclear issues could also be said to add to the problem, for their stance has undermined the authority of the Nuclear Non-Proliferation Treaty."

Yashwant Sinha

Senior Leader, Bharatiya Janata Party, India
March 22, 2005

A blind eye on Pakistan?
   "The so-called international monitors are attacking Iran and Korea while they keep a blind eye on the nuclear proliferation activities of Pakistan."

Dawn

Pakistan
Oct. 10, 2006

American aid to Israel is hypocritical
   "The behavior of the Western powers, America especially, is not above board, because they themselves have contributed to nuclear proliferation by aiding Israel in its clandestine nuclear project."

The Jerusalem Post

Israel
Oct. 10, 2005

The entire edifice will collapse
   "If Iran, the foremost sponsor of terrorism in the world, is allowed to have nuclear weapons then the entire non-proliferation edifice will collapse, like a dam with one too many cracks."

The Globe and Mail

Toronto, Canada
Oct. 10, 2005

Much, much more to do
   "Despite all the talk about non-proliferation in the past few years, the international regime for controlling the spread of nuclear weapons is still woefully weak. Only the United States has made non-proliferation a real focus of its foreign policy. Others merely tag along"

Arab News

Jeddah, Saudi Arabia
Oct. 8, 2005

ElBaradei angers U.S.
   "As head of the U.N.'s nuclear watchdog, Mohamed ElBaradei has had a tough time, not simply in the agency's dealings with North Korea and Iran, but from the Americans, who opposed his reappointment. . . . His sin in Washington's eyes was that, as America prepared to invade Iraq, he said clearly he did not believe that Saddam's regime still had nuclear weaponry."

The Daily Telegraph

London, England
Oct. 8, 2005

Nuclear proliferation 'wishful thinking'
   "The award of the Nobel Peace Prize to the International Atomic Energy Agency and its Egyptian director general, Mohamed ElBaradei, is a classic case of wishful thinking. . . . For the past 15 years, the IAEA has proved inadequate to the task. . . . It is to the director general's credit that, before the invasion of Iraq in 2003, he resisted the fantasies of Tony Blair and George W. Bush about Saddam Hussein's weapons of mass destruction."

The Daily Star

Beirut, Lebanon
Aug. 10, 2005

Why deny Iran its rights?
   "The international community's reluctance to acknowledge Iran's rights to nuclear power is understandable, considering the fact that Iran hid its nuclear program from the world's eyes for nearly two decades. But if safeguards can now be established, it is unrealistic to deny Iran the rights that are extended to every other country in the global community."

Toronto Star/Patrick Corrigan

4

World Peacekeeping

Lee Michael Katz

A Polish soldier from the European Union Force supporting the U.N. mission in the Democratic Republic of the Congo participates in training for hostage-rescue operations at the EUFOR base in Kinshasa. A French helicopter hovers above.

AFP/Getty Images/Marco Longari

From *CQ Researcher,*
April 1, 2007.

As the United Nations marked Holocaust Commemoration Day this year, the world's failure to stop the deaths and devastation in Darfur made the occasion far more urgent than the usual calendar exercise.

New Secretary-General Ban Ki-moon had to deliver his remarks on videotape, pointedly noting he was on his way to Ethiopia for an African Union summit focusing on ending the carnage against black Africans in western Sudan. Just weeks after taking office, the head of the world body said he was strongly committed to this message: "We must apply the lessons of the Holocaust to today's world." [1]

Elderly Holocaust survivors in the audience served as visible witness before delegates of the international body that rose out of the ashes of World War II's Nazi evils. But it was clear that more than 60 years later, the lessons had not been fully learned.

"I still weep today" at the memories of those, including her father and brother, who were marched to the gas chambers at Auschwitz, said Simone Veil, a well-known French Holocaust survivor.

But she also pointed to slaughter that happened decades afterward and is still happening today. While those who survived hoped the pledge "Never Again" would ring true, Veil said, sadly their warnings were in vain. "After the massacres in Cambodia, it is Africa that is paying the highest price in genocidal terms," she said, in a call for action to stop the killings in Darfur. An estimated 200,000 have been killed, countless women raped and 2 million made homeless as armed Arab militia known as janjaweed prey on vulnerable villagers.

The laments about a lack of lifesaving action continue despite the fact that the United Nations has endorsed, at least in principle, a new concept to keeping the peace in the 21st century called the

Major Worldwide Peacekeeping Operations

The African Union, European Union Force, NATO and United Nations combine for 24 peacekeeping forces deployed around the world. The U.N. has 15 missions, with the most recent deployment being a police force in Timor-Leste in 2006.

Peacekeeping Missions

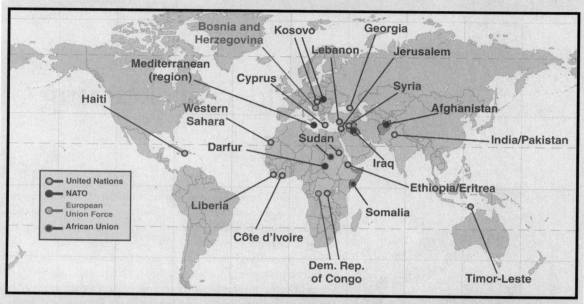

Sources: African Union, Delegation of the European Commission to the USA, NATO, United Nations Department of Peacekeeping Operations

Responsibility to Protect. At its heart is the fundamental notion that the world has a moral obligation to intervene against genocide.

This includes using military force if necessary, even when the deaths are taking place inside a sovereign nation as in the 1994 ethnic massacre in Rwanda. A reduced U.N. force in the African nation did not physically try to stop the slaughter by Hutus in Rwanda of 800,000 fellow Rwandans — mainly Tutsis but also moderate Hutus — in a matter of weeks. Traditionally, such intervention would be seen as off-limits inside a functioning state, especially a member of the United Nations.

So the notion of the Responsibility to Protect "is very significant because it removes an excuse to turn a blind eye to mass atrocities," says Lee Feinstein, a former U.S. diplomat and author of a 2007 Council on Foreign Relations report on R2P, as the concept is known. [2] Such

excuses went "unchallenged" until recently, he says. "If the U.N. is serious about this — and there are questions — this is a big deal." But a decade after Rwanda, the deaths, displacement and widespread rapes in Darfur have been ongoing even after the Responsibility to Protect was endorsed by the U.N. General Assembly in 2005 and in a Security Council resolution a year later.

"Darfur is another Rwanda," said Paul Rusesabagina, whose actions to save 1,268 refugees from genocide were made famous by the movie "Hotel Rwanda." [3] "Many people are dying every day. The world is still standing by watching," he said. "History keeps repeating itself — and without teaching us a lesson."

Secretary-General Ban must make the Responsibility to Protect his top priority if there is hope to stem mass killings in the future, Feinstein argues. That contradiction between the promise of the Responsibility to Protect and the situation in Darfur is what Ban faces in leading the world body.

Ban has cited Responsibility to Protect as at least one of his priorities, noting its unfulfilled promise. "We must take the first steps to move the Responsibility to Protect from word to deed," Ban declared. [4]

But, like his predecessors, Ban wields only moral authority as the leader of the world body. There is no standing U.N. army to back up his pronouncements. "He doesn't have troops to send," says the Secretary-General's spokeswoman Michele Montas. "What the Secretary-General can do besides an advocacy role is limited."

Though U.N. peacekeeping forces have taken on an increasingly aggressive posture in recent years, the U.N. system of relying on donated troops doesn't offer the speed or military capability for invading a country to force an end to murders. Nor is it likely countries that traditionally contribute troops would rush to put their soldiers in harm's way, notes Jean-Marie Guéhenno, U.N. Undersecretary General in charge of peacekeeping operations. "If they feel they are going to have to shoot their way in, it's no more peacekeeping. Sometimes, it may be necessary," Guéhenno says candidly in an interview, "but it will have to be done by other organizations."

NATO, possibly the African Union (with outside logistical help and equipment) and ad hoc "coalitions of the willing" nations are the likely global candidates for any truly muscular interventions to stop the slaughter of innocents.

But even for U.N. peacekeepers, fast-moving events can foster a combat atmosphere. Today's peacekeeping faces the dangers of unrest or battle from Latin America to Africa.

Such threats have spawned a new term that has taken root in 21st-century U.N. operations: "robust peacekeeping." Modern U.N. forces may have attack helicopters and Special Forces, "the type of military capabilities you would not have traditionally associated with peacekeeping operation," Guéhenno notes.

"We're not going to let an armed group unravel a peace agreement that benefits millions of people," he says. The peacekeeping chief sounds more like a general threatening overwhelming force rather than a diplomat cautious of its implications. "So we'll hit hard on those spoilers," he promises. Guéhenno cited Congo as an example, but there are others.

Peacekeeping forces today face rapidly changing situations. In Somalia, Ethiopian troops conducted a suc-

Ban Ki-moon, right, new secretary-general of the United Nations, gets a briefing in January 2007 at the United Nations Organization Mission in the Democratic Republic of the Congo in Kisangani, where he laid a wreath for fallen peacekeepers.

cessful invasion by New Year's 2007, well before peacekeepers could be deployed to stop the fighting. But attacks continued to rock Mogadishu, the capital, and emergency peacekeeping plans intensified.

In Lebanon last year, the deadly aftermath of Israel-Hezbollah battles brought the need for the U.N. to ramp up a large peacekeeping force extraordinarily quickly.

Guéhenno's U.N. peacekeeping department has its hands full as it is, trying to keep up with worldwide demand for troops, police and civilian advisors. Much like Microsoft dominates the computer world, the United Nations is by far the dominant brand in peacekeeping.

With more than 100,000 troops, police and civilian officials in 18 peace missions around the world, the United Nations has the largest amount of peacekeepers deployed since the organization's founding in 1945. That total could exceed 140,000 depending on the strength of any new missions in Somalia and Darfur. Former Secretary-General Kofi Annan warned before he left office: "U.N. peacekeeping is stretched as never before."

Traditionally, impoverished nations are major troop contributors, in part because the payments they receive help them economically. Bangladesh, Pakistan and India each had about 9,000-10,000 troops in U.N. peacekeeping forces in 2006. Jordan, Nepal, Ethiopia, Ghana Uruguay, Nigeria and South Africa were also major troop contributors. [5]

U.N. Provides Half of Peacekeeping Forces

With 82,751 personnel spread among 15 missions worldwide, the United Nations contributes over 50 percent of the world's peacekeeping forces.

Organization	Personnel	Missions	Nations Contributing Personnel
United Nations	82,751	15	114
NATO	55,000	5	37 (includes 11 NATO allies)
African Union	15,000	2	10
European Union Force	8,500	2	34 (includes 10 non-EU nations)
Organization for Security and Co-operation in Europe	3,500	19	56
Multinational Force & Observers	1,687	1	11

Sources: African Union, Delegation of the European Commission to the USA, Multinational Force & Observers, NATO, OSCE, United Nations Department of Peacekeeping Operations

Although peacekeeping advocates argue peacekeeping is a bargain compared to the cost of all-out war, peacekeeping on a global scale does not come cheap. The approved U.N. 2006-2007 budget is more than $5 billion.

Peacekeeping is paid for by a special assessment for U.N. members weighted on national wealth and permanent Security Council member status. The United States pays the largest share of peacekeeping costs: 27 percent (though congressional caps on payment have resulted in lower payments in recent years). [6] Other top contributors include Japan, Germany, the United Kingdom, France, Italy, China, Canada, Spain and South Korea. [7]

But peacekeeping operations often are hampered by having to run deeply into the red. In November 2006, peacekeeping arrears totaled $2.2 billion.

U.N. peacekeeping is also hobbled by the built-in logistical problem of having to cobble each mission together after Security Council authorization. Plans for standing U.N. military forces have never gotten off the ground. But U.N. police are starting to take "baby steps," starting with dozens of officers for a permanent force, says senior U.N. police official Antero Lopes.

In recent years, U.N. peacekeeping officials have made inroads to daunting logistical problems by maintaining pre-positioned materiel in staging area in Italy, notes former New Zealand Ambassador Colin Keating. But there is still a great need for equipment. "You can't just go down to Wal-Mart and buy a bunch of APCS" — armored personnel carriers, he says.

Other regional organizations involved in keeping the peace, with efforts ranging from armed intervention to watching over ballot boxes, include:

- **North Atlantic Treaty Organization (NATO):** The military alliance of 26 countries, including the United States, has 75,000 troops worldwide responsible for some of the more muscular interventions, such as the aftermath of the war in Afghanistan, where it has a force of 30,000.
- **African Union (AU):** Established in 2001, the 53-nation coalition has a 7,000-man force in Darfur, including many Rwandans. Another AU contingent of 8,000 has been in Mogadishu since March 6.
- **European Union (EU):** Its troops have taken over Bosnian peacekeeping with a force of 7,000. The EU's broader peacekeeping plans include creation of a long-discussed rapid-reaction force of 60,000. But EU foreign policy chief Javier Solana notes that despite those bold aims, the organization has been depending on a softer "mixture of civilian, military, economic, political and institution-building tools." [8]
- **Organization for Security and Co-operation in Europe (OSCE):** The 56-member group, working on a non-military level, has more than 3,000 OSCE officers in 19 locations from Albania to Uzbekistan. Their activities are aimed at encouraging political dialogue and supporting post-conflict resolution. [9]
- **Multinational Force and Observers (MFO):** It has about 1,700 troops from the United States and 10 other countries stationed on the Egyptian side of the Israeli-Sinai border.

As an abstract concept, global peacekeeping seems like a reasonable and virtuous response to global problems. Who better than neutral referees to keep fighters apart? Indeed, under the 1948 International Convention on the Prevention and Punishment of the Crime of Genocide, the United States and other participating countries are obliged "to prevent and punish" genocide. But forceful military intervention is clouded by questions that range from national sovereignty to international political will along with such practical issues as troop supply and logistics in remote corners of the world.

Increasingly, the Holocaust-related lesson seems to be the notion that the international community has a moral obligation — and indeed a right — to enter sovereign states to stop genocide and other human rights violations.

The Responsibility to Protect concept was detailed in a 2001 report by the International Commission on Intervention and State Sovereignty (ICISS), co-chaired by Algerian diplomat Mohamed Sahnoun and former Australian Foreign Minister Gareth Evans, now head of the non-governmental International Crisis Group, dedicated to stopping global conflict. "There is a growing recognition that the issue is not the 'right to intervene' of any State, but the 'Responsibility to Protect' of every State," the report said. [10]

By 2006, writes Evans in a forthcoming book, "the phrase 'Responsibility to Protect' was being routinely used, publicly and privately, by policymakers and commentators almost everywhere whenever the question was debated as to what the international community should do when faced with a state committing atrocities against its own people, or standing by allowing others to do so." [11]

More important, he points out, the concept was formally and unanimously adopted by the international community at the U.N. 60th Anniversary World Summit in September 2005. References to the Responsibility to Protect concept have also appeared in Security Council resolutions, including one calling for action in Darfur.

But R2P remains a sensitive concept, and the reference to U.N. military action in the 2005 World Summit document is very carefully couched: "We are prepared to take collective action, in a timely and decisive manner . . . on a case-by-case basis . . . as appropriate, should peaceful means be inadequate and national authorities are manifestly failing to protect their populations from genocide, war crimes, ethnic cleansing and crimes against humanity." [12]

An African Union peacekeeping soldier stands guard in the village of Kerkera in Darfur, a western province of Sudan, where government-sponsored troops and a militia of Arab horsemen known as "janjaweed" have been conducting a campaign of devastation against black tribes.

As a rule, national sovereignty has been a hallowed concept at the United Nations, and what countries did within their own borders was considered their own business.

"The traditional view of sovereignty, as enabling absolute control of everything internal and demanding immunity from external intervention, was much reinforced by the large increase in U.N. membership during the decolonization era," Evans said at Stanford University on Feb. 7, 2007. "The states that joined were all newly proud of their identity, conscious in many cases of their fragility and generally saw the non-intervention norm as one of their few defenses against threats and pressures from more powerful international actors seeking to promote their own economic and political interests."

Given that history, if nations back up the R2P endorsement at the U.N. with action, it will represent a dramatic shift in policy.

Will the new "Responsibility to Protect" doctrine actually translate into international protection for the people of Darfur? That question has yet to be answered.

Meanwhile, in the wake of the international community's discussion of new powerful action, here are some of the questions being asked about the future of global peacekeeping:

When Peacekeepers Prey Instead of Protect

U.N. seeking more women officers

The U.N. has been stung in recent years by reports that male peacekeeping soldiers have preyed on women — often girls under age 18 — in vulnerable populations. In Congo, U.N. officials admit that a "shockingly large" number of peacekeepers have bought sex from impoverished young girls, including illiterate orphans, for payments ranging from two eggs to $5.

What's more, some peacekeeping missions reportedly covered-up the abuse, as well as the children that have been born as their result. Between January 2004 and November 2006, 319 peacekeeping personnel worldwide were investigated for sexual misconduct, U.N. officials say, with 144 military and 17 police sent home and 18 civilians summarily dismissed. [1]

"I am especially troubled by instances in which United Nations peacekeepers are alleged to have sexually exploited minors and other vulnerable people, and I have enacted a policy of 'zero tolerance' towards such offences that applies to all personnel engaged in United Nations operations," Secretary-General Kofi Annan said in March 2005. He also instituted a mandatory training course for all peacekeeping candidates to address the issues.

"You get [these abuses] not just with peacekeepers but with soldiers in general, and it gets worse the further they are from home and the more destitute the local population," says Richard Reeve, a research fellow at Chatham House, a London-based think tank. "The UN will never get rid of the problem, but they are really dealing with it and putting changes into practice." [2]

Now the U.N. is sending women instead of men on certain U.N. troop and police peacekeeping missions. The first all-female police unit, from India, recently was sent to Liberia, where peacekeepers had been accused of trading food for sex with teenagers. [3] Cases of misconduct by women police are "almost non-existent," says Antero Lopes, a senior U.N. police official.

The head of the new unit, Commander Seema Dhundia, says its primary mission is to support the embryonic Liberia National Police (LNP), but that the presence of female troops will also raise awareness of and respect for women in Liberia, and in peacekeeping. "Seeing women in strong positions, I hope, will reduce the violence against women," she says. [4]

"We plead for nations to give us as many woman police officers as they can," says Lopes. Another advantage of the all-female unit in Liberia is that it is trained in crowd control, Lopes says, shattering a barrier in what had been seen as a male domain. "It is also a message to the local society that women can perform the same jobs as men."

The U.N. is aggressively trying to recruit more female peacekeepers, from civilian managers to foot soldiers to high-ranking officers. "Our predominantly male profile in peacekeeping undermines the credibility of our efforts to lead by example," Jean-Marie Guéhenno, head of the U.N. peacekeeping department, told the Security Council.

That message was not always heard. A decade ago, peacekeeping consultant Judith Stiehm, a professor of political science at Florida International University, was hired by the U.N. to write a pamphlet on the need for women in peacekeeping. Today she says it was a show effort. "I don't think they even really distributed it," Stiehm says. But pushed by the only female peacekeeping mission head, the issue eventually became U.N. policy.

Will the world support the Responsibility to Protect doctrine?

Judging by the inaction in Darfur in the face of highly publicized pleas from groups around world, the R2P is off to an inauspicious start. "Darfur is the first test of the Responsibility to Protect," says Feinstein, "and the world failed the test."

Echoes of the world's continuing failure to protect its citizens from mass murder reverberated off of the green marble podium in the cavernous U.N. General Assembly Hall this year. "It is a tragedy that the international community has not been able to stop new horrors in the years since the Holocaust," General Assembly President Sheikha Haya Al Khalifa of Bahrain stated. [13] "This makes it all the more important that we remember the lessons of the past so that we do not make the same mistakes in the future."

Yet the Responsibility to Protect concept faces a number of daunting challenges, from potential Third

Security Council Resolution 1325, passed in 2000, "urges the secretary-general" to expand the role of women in field operations, especially among military observers and police.

"The little blue pamphlet and the impetus behind it brought about this very important resolution," Stiehm says, "which is not being implemented, but it's on the books." In fact, "less than 2 per cent and 5 per cent of our military and police personnel, respectively, are women," Guéhenno told the Security Council.

Beyond the issue of sexual abuse, the role of women soldiers is important in nations where substantial contact between unrelated men and women is prohibited by religion or custom. "Military men just cannot deal with Arab women — that's so culturally taboo," Stiehm notes, but military women can gather information.

Because the United Nations' peacekeeping forces represent more than 100 countries, cultural variations make a big difference in both the prominence of women and what behavior is acceptable, according to Stiehm. "It is very uneven," she says and "dependant very much on who heads the mission."

Stiehm points to Yasushi Akashi, a Japanese U.N. official in the early 1990s. When confronted with charges of sexual abuse of young girls by troops in his Cambodian mission, "Akashi's reaction was, 'Boys will be boys,' " she says.

In another case, Stiehm recalls arguing with her boss over trying to prevent troops from having sex with underage women. "He didn't see anything wrong with it," she says.

The U.N. is now trying to short-circuit the different-cultures argument with a "Duty of Care" code that pointedly states: "These standards apply to all peacekeepers irrespective of local customs or laws, or the customs or laws of your own country."

Moreover, Stiehm says, "Peacekeepers have an obligation to do better."

Bebiche is one of hundreds of internally displaced persons forced to flee warfare in eastern Democratic Republic of Congo. Countless women and girls there have been brutalized by unprecedented sexual violence, and they have few options for existence but to pursue survival sex.

[1] "U.N. will enforce 'zero tolerance' policy against sexual abuse, peace-keeping official says." U.N. News Centre, Jan. 5, 2007. www.un.org/apps/news/storyAr.asp?NewsID=21169&Cr=sex&Cr1=abuse&Kw1=SExual+Exploitation&Kw2=&Kw3=

[2] Quoted in Tristan McConnell, "All female unit keeps peace in Liberia," *The Christian Science Monitor online*, March 21, 2005; http://news.yahoo.com/s/csm/20070321/ts_csm/ofemmeforce_1.

[3] Will Ross, "Liberia gets all-female peacekeeping force," BBC News, Jan. 31, 2007, http://news.bbc.co.uk/2/hi/africa/6316387.stm.

[4] *Ibid.*

World opposition to the appetite and physical ability of Western nations to intervene. Allan Rock, Canada's ambassador to the United Nations, who advanced the Responsibility to Protect resolution at the world body, said in 2001 that the doctrine was, "feared by many countries as a Trojan horse for the interveners of the world looking for justification for marching into other countries." [14]

Indeed, commented Hugo Chávez, president of Venezuela and nemesis of the United States, "This is very suspicious. Tomorrow or sometime in the future, someone in Washington will say that the Venezuelan people need to be protected from the tyrant Chávez, who is a threat. They are trying to legalize imperialism within the United Nations, and Venezuela cannot accept that." [15]

In Sudan, the shifting conditions of President Omar Hassan Ahmad al-Bashir to allow U.N. troops into Darfur has deterred them as of mid-April 2007.

AFP/Getty Images/Ermal Meta

A Swedish peacekeeper checks weapons seized in Kosovo. About 17,000 NATO-led peacekeepers in so-called KFOR missions are responsible for peace and security in the rebellious Albanian-dominated Serbian province. In 1999 NATO forces bombed the area to end ethnic cleansing by the Serbs.

Like Chávez, al-Bashir has said such a force would be tantamount to an invasion and warned that it could become a fertile ground for Islamic jihadists. Al Qaeda leader Osama bin Laden has already weighed in, urging resistance to any U.N. intervention in Sudan. [16]

And Libyan leader Muammar Qaddafi, far less of a pariah to the West than before, but still prone to inflammatory statements, told Sudanese officials last November, "Western countries and America are not busying themselves out of sympathy for the Sudanese people or for Africa but for oil and for the return of colonialism to the African continent. Reject any foreign intervention." [17]

With a lineup like that against U.N. deployment, cynics might say, there must be good reason to do so. In Darfur, however, the R2P doctrine has become bogged down by practical considerations: The geographical area to be protected is vast, and both the vulnerable population and predatory attackers are in close proximity.

But, says Chinua Akukwe, a Nigerian physician and former vice chairman of the Global Health Council, "The U.N. and its agencies must now think the unthinkable — how to bypass murderous governments in any part of the world and reach its suffering citizens in a timely fashion." [18]

Nicole Deller, program advisor for the pro-protection group Responsibility to Protect, says the careful wording of the R2P concept document has given pause to many countries. They remember the disastrous day when 18 Americans died in Mogadishu, Somalia in 1993 — memorialized in the book and movie "Black Hawk Down" — that gave both the United Nations and the United States a black eye. "A lot of that is still blowback from Somalia," she says.

But among African nations there appears an evolution of thinking about sovereignty. Ghana's representative to the United Nations, Nana Effah-Aptenteng, confirmed that change when he told a U.N. audience that African states "have an obligation to intervene in the affairs of another state when its people are at risk." [19]

This is further reflected in the AU Constitutive Act, which recognizes the role of African nations to intervene in cases of genocide. [20]

The Sudanese government, whose oil reserves have given them political and commercial leverage in resisting calls for an end to the slaughter, has reacted by changing the subject. When asked about his country facing possible international military action under The Responsibility to Protect for turning a blind eye to death and destruction in Darfur, Abdalmahmood Abdalhaleem, Sudan's U.N. ambassador, instead turns to resentment of the U.S. role in Iraq and Israel's actions in Lebanon last summer. "Why didn't they intervene when people in Iraq were slaughtered and people in Lebanon were bombarded and infrastructure destroyed?" he asks. "Why didn't they intervene there?"

The international community, either at the United Nations or elsewhere, is far from having a standard on when to intervene to stop violence or even genocide. But some attempts have been made to come up with questions that can help arrive at an answer. According to the International Commission on Intervention and State Sovereignty, five basic conditions are needed to trigger an intervention by U.N. or other multinational forces:

- **Seriousness of Harm** — Is the threatened harm to state or human security of a kind, and sufficiently clear and serious, to justify the use of military force? In the case of internal threats, does it involve genocide and other large-scale killing, "ethnic cleansing" or serious violations of international humanitarian law?
- **Proper Purpose** — Is the primary purpose of the proposed military action clearly to halt or avert the threat in question, whatever other motives may be in play?
- **Last Resort** — Has every nonmilitary option for meeting the threat in question been explored, with reasonable grounds for believing lesser measures will not succeed?
- **Proportional Means** — Are the scale, duration and intensity of the planned military action the minimum necessary to achieve the objective of protecting human life?
- **Balance of Consequences** — Is there a reasonable chance of the military action being successful . . . with the consequences of action unlikely to be worse than the consequences of inaction?

Certainly Darfur's miseries meet many of the conditions, but not all, Evans says. Questions remain whether all non-military options have been exhausted, and there are "hair-raisingly difficult" logistical concerns to consider as well as high potential for civilian injuries, Evans says.

Thus, the R2P is not necessarily a green light for unfettered military action, according to Feinstein and others. "This is not a question of sending in the Marines or even the blue helmets" of the United Nations, he says, pointing out that the doctrine is most effective in bringing international political pressure to bear before conditions lead to mass killings.

Are regional peacekeepers effective?

While the United Nations leads peacekeeping forces around the world, it does not maintain a standing armed force designed to initiate military interventions. When robust military operations are needed, the U.N. can authorize other actors to respond, such as better-equipped or more willing regional organizations such as

NATO, the European Union or the African Union, or a combination of those multinational forces. The R2P doctrine, in fact, specifies that U.N.-authorized military action be done "in cooperation with relevant regional organizations as appropriate."

"The U.N. culture is still very much against doing coercive types of operations," says French defense official Catherine Guicherd, on loan to the International Peace Academy in New York, "whereas the NATO culture goes very much in the other direction."

Two current regional operations — the NATO mission in Kosovo and the AU forces in Darfur — reflect the realities of such missions. NATO, working in its European backyard, has been largely effective. The AU, operating in a much larger area with fewer troops and less equipment and support, has been struggling.

At the beginning of 2007, there were 16,000 NATO troops from 36 mostly European nations stationed with the U.N. peacekeeping force in Kosovo, the Albanian-majority Serbian province seeking autonomy from Belgrade. There is a global alphabet of cooperation in Kosovo. The NATO "KFOR" forces coordinate closely with 2,700 personnel of the U.N. Interim Administration Mission — known as UNMIK — which in turn employs another 1,500 men and women from the EU and OSCE.

Two Israeli journalists who reported from Kosovo in 2002 described an atmosphere of tension and uncertainty and called the force of agencies "a massive and complex multinational presence signaling the commitment of the international community to restoring order and rebuilding civil institutions in this troubled region." [21]

But NATO's toughest deployment has been in Afghanistan, with about 32,000 troops contributing to what is called the International Security Assistance force (ISAF), which provides military support for the government of President Hamid Karzai. More than 100 peacekeepers died in Afghanistan in 2006. And 2007 brought more casualties.

"It's very bloody, much worse than NATO ever dreamed," says Edwin Smith, a professor of law and international relations at the University of Southern California and author of *The United Nations in a New World Order*.

"But this is a fundamental test of their ability to engage in peacekeeping and extraterritorial operations outside of their treaty-designated area," Smith continues. "If it turns out that they cannot play this function, then

CHRONOLOGY

1940s-1950s *Founding of U.N. promises peace in the postwar world. First peacekeeping missions are deployed.*

1945 United Nations is founded at the end of World War II "to save succeeding generations from the scourge of war."

1948 First U.N. mission goes to Jerusalem following Arab-Israeli War.

1949 U.N. observers monitor the struggle over Kashmir following the creation of India and Pakistan.

1950 Security Council approves a U.N. "police action" in Korea.

1956 United Nations Emergency Force is established during the Suez Crisis involving Egypt, Israel, Britain and France.

1960s *Death of U.N. secretary-general in Congo causes U.N. to avoid dangerous missions.*

1960 U.N. Secretary-General Dag Hammarskjold dies in an unexplained plane crash during a U.N. intervention in Congo by U.N. peacekeepers; the mission fails to bring democracy.

1964 U.N. peacekeepers are sent to keep peace between Greeks and Turks on divided Cyprus; the mission continues.

1970s *Cambodian genocide occurs unhindered.*

1974 U.N. Disengagement Force is sent to the Golan Heights after fighting stops between Israel and Syria.

1975 Dictator Pol Pot kills more than 1 million Cambodians. U.N. and other nations fail to act.

1978 U.N. monitors withdrawal of Israeli troops from Lebanon.

1980s *Cold War barrier to bold U.N. actions begins to crumble.*

1988 U.N. peacekeeping mission monitors ceasefire between Iran and Iraq.

1989 Fall of Berlin Wall symbolizes collapse of Soviet empire and Cold War paralysis blocking U.N. agreement.

1990s *Security Council confronts Iraq. Failures in Bosnia, Somalia, dampen enthusiasm to stop Rwanda killing.*

1990 Iraqi leader Saddam Hussein invades Kuwait and defies Security Council demand for withdrawal.

1991 U.N.-authorized and U.S.-led international coalition expels Iraq from Kuwait. . . . U.N. peacekeeping mission is sent to El Salvador.

1992 U.N. Protection Force fails to stop killings in Bosnian civil war.

1993 Ambitious U.N. peace operation fails to restore order in Somalia.

1994 U.N. peacekeepers are unable to stop the massacre of more than 800,000 Rwandans.

1995 U.N. peacekeepers in the Bosnian town of Srebrenica are disarmed and left helpless by Serb forces.

1999 NATO takes military action against Serbia.

2000s-Present *U.N. mounts successful peace-building mission in Liberia.*

2003 U.N. peacekeeping mission in Liberia begins to keep peace.

2005 U.N. General Assembly endorses Responsibility to Protect concept at World Summit.

2006 Security Council endorses Responsibility to Protect but intervention in killings in Darfur region is stalled by Sudan's government.

April 9, 2007 U.N. Secretary-General Ban Ki-moon calls for "a global partnership against genocide" and upgrades the post of U.N. Special Adviser for the Prevention of Genocide — currently held by Juan E. Méndez of Argentina — to a full-time position.

one wonders how do you justify NATO's continued existence?"

In Africa, European troops also may have to fight a psychological battle stemming from the colonial legacy. It is commonly held that many Africans resent non-African peacekeepers coming to enforce order. Perhaps a more pressing reason, observes Victoria K. Holt, a peacekeeping expert at the Stimson Center in Washington, is that a NATO or U.N. force under a powerful mandate "would be better equipped and thus, more effective and a challenge to what is happening on the ground."

The notoriously fickle government of Sudan has indicated it would be willing to accept only a hybrid AU-U.N. force. The U.N. should be limited to a "logistical and backstopping role," Ambassador Abdalhaleem says.

The AU can muster troops, but handling logistics and equipment in a huge and remote area such as Darfur is a major problem for even the best-equipped and trained forces. But the AU began 2007 with only 7,000 troops in Darfur, an area the size of France, and with limited equipment, according to Robert Collins, an Africa expert at the University of California-Santa Barbara, who has visited the war-torn nation over the past 50 years.

"They just don't have the helicopters," he says. "They don't have the big planes to fly in large amounts of supplies. They're just a bunch of guys out there with a couple of rifles trying to hold off a huge insurgency. It doesn't work."

Besides Darfur, the AU has sent peacekeepers to a few other African hotspots, in effect adopting the underpinnings of the Responsibility to Protect by moving to establish its own African Standby Force. Slated to be operational by 2010, the force would have an intelligence unit and a "Continental Early Warning System" to monitor situations that can potentially spark mass killings. The force would be capable of responding to a genocidal situation within two weeks. [22]

Whether such an African force will be able to live up to its optimistic intent poses another big question: Would it receive continuing outside financial help from the West?

African officials and experts report the biggest problem facing AU peacekeeping is funding, particularly in Sudan. "This is . . . one of the worst humanitarian disasters in the world, yet only five donors seem to be properly engaged," said Haroun Atallah, chief executive of Islamic Relief. "All rich countries must step up their sup-

port urgently if the disaster of Darfur isn't to turn into an even worse catastrophe." [23]

Should peace-building replace peace-keeping?

In the past, U.N. peacekeeping focused mainly on keeping warring nations apart while they negotiated a peace pact. Now, U.N. peacekeepers increasingly are being called in as part of complex cooperative efforts by regional military organizations, local military, civilians and police to rebuild failed governments.

Some say the shift is inevitable. More than military might is needed for successful peacekeeping, NATO Secretary-General Jaap de Hoop Scheffer noted last year. During a Security Council meeting to highlight cooperation between the United Nations and regional security organizations, he said he had learned "some important lessons," including the need for each organization to play to its strengths and weaknesses.

"NATO offers unparalleled military experience and capability," Scheffer said, "yet addressing a conflict requires a coordinated and coherent approach from the outset. Clearly defined responsibilities . . . are indispensable if we are to maximize our chances of success." [24]

So is post-conflict follow-through. The United Nations has set up a Peacebuilding Commission to follow up after conflicts have been quelled.

Because peacekeeping now often takes place inside nations rather than between them, the United Nations is typically charged not only with trying to keep the peace but also "with building up the basics of a state," notes Guéhenno. "That's why peacekeeping can never be the full answer. It has to be complemented by a serious peace-building efforts.

"Today, we have a completely different situation" from in the past, Guéhenno explains, referring to the world's growing number of so-called failed states. "You have a number of countries around the world that are challenged by internal divides. They don't have the capacity to maintain law and order."

But peacekeeping consultant Judith Stiehm, a professor of political science at Florida International University, sees a contradiction between peace-keeping and peace-building. "That's what gets them in trouble," she says. "You've got guys wearing military uniforms and their missions are very civilian. And once you add the mission of protection, you're not neutral anymore. Some people think of you as the enemy, and it muddies the waters. You can't have it both ways."

U.N. Police Face Difficult Challenges

Small problems can escalate quickly

In Timor-Leste (formerly East Timor), a country still raw from decades of fighting for independence, Antero Lopes knew that promptly dealing with a stolen chicken was crucial.

As acting police commissioner for the U.N. mission in the tiny East Asian nation in 2006, he discovered that in such a tense environment, overlooking even a petty crime like a marketplace theft could have serious consequences. "Friends and neighbors are brought in, many of them veterans of Timor's bloody struggles, and suddenly you have an inter-community problem with 200 people fighting 200 people," he say from U.N. headquarters in Manhattan, where he is now deputy director of U.N. Police Operations. [1]

United Nations police were sent to the former Portuguese colony last year to restore order in the fledgling state. Timor-Leste gained independence from Indonesia in 2002 following a long struggle, but an outbreak of death and violence that uprooted more than 150,000 people prompted the Timorese government to agree to temporarily turn over police operations to the U.N., which called it "the first ever such arrangement between a sovereign nation and the U.N." [2]

The U.N.'s Timorese role reflects how U.N. police have become "a critical component" of the institution's peacekeeping efforts, notes Victoria K. Holt, a senior associate at The Henry L. Stimson Center in Washington and co-director of its Future of Peace Operations program. The U.N. now recognizes "you just can't go from military to civilian society. You have to have something in between."

A critical role for police wasn't always a given, says Holt, author of *The Impossible Mandate? Military Preparedness, the Responsibility to Protect and Modern Peace Operations*. For much of the United Nations' nearly 60-year peacekeeping history, she says, the lack of a major police role was "one of the biggest gaps. They actually now have a whole police division that didn't exist a number of years ago."

The role and size of the U.N. police effort has grown dramatically in recent years. "Peace operations are increasingly using significant numbers of police to handle security tasks," according to the U.N.'s 2006 Annual Review of Global Peace Operations. Led by the United Nations, the number of police peacekeepers worldwide has tripled since 1998 to about 10,000.

Lopes says that although he is a university-trained police manager with experience ranging from anti-crime to SWAT teams, he is also accustomed to operating in environments without the "same legal framework" one finds in Europe.

Roland Paris, an associate professor of political science at Canada's University of Ottawa, sees inherent cultural flaws, including Western colonialism, in peace-building. "Peace-building operations seek to stabilize countries that have recently experienced civil wars," he wrote. "In pursuing this goal, however, international peace-builders have promulgated a particular vision of how states should organize themselves internally, based on the principles of liberal democracy and market-oriented economics.

"By reconstructing war-shattered states in accordance with this vision, peace-builders have effectively 'transmitted' standards of appropriate behavior from the Western-liberal core . . . to the failed states of the periphery. From this perspective, peace-building resembles an updated (and more benign) version of the *mission civilisatrice*, the colonial-era belief that the European imperial powers had a duty to 'civilize' dependent populations and territories." [25]

But despite an ongoing debate, one part of the formula for the near future seems set: The U.N. has increasingly relied on deploying police to help rebuild a society as part of its peacekeeping efforts around the globe. In fact, as "an interim solution," the global U.N. cops have become the actual police force of such nations as East Timor, Haiti and in Kosovo. "We provide a measure of law and order and security that creates the political window to build up a state," Guéhenno says.

U.N. police realize they are operating in a very different environment. "Now we are a significant pillar in helping the good-governance effort," says Lopes, deputy police advisor in the U.N. Department of Peacekeeping Operations, sounding like a bureaucrat as well as a sheriff.

He was deployed in Bosnia, for example, while the civil war still raged there in the 1990's. "If you really like these kinds of [policing] challenges," he notes, "you can get addicted."

Balkan violence may not be over, however. The U.N. mission in Kosovo — the Albanian-majority Serbian province seeking autonomy from Belgrade — is bracing for violence, with the disputed area's future set to be decided this year. Already, news of an impending Kosovo independence plan has triggered violent demonstrations. After U.N. police fired rubber bullets into a crowd of demonstrators in February, killing two people, the U.N. mission there pulled out. [3]

Outside of Kosovo (where the European Union plans to take over police responsibility), the major U.N. police presences are in Haiti and countries in Africa. In Africa, U.N. police missions are hampered by the African Union's lack of proper resources. "In many missions, we find even the lack of simple uniforms," Lopes says, not to mention operable radios, police cars or other basic police equipment.

In Sudan's troubled Darfur, any new police commitment would first focus on "stabilization" of the lawless situation, he says. However, he points out, while U.N. police must not compromise on basic law-enforcement tenets, they still must adapt to local customs in working with local authorities.

So Lopes finds it important to play the role of empathetic psychologist as well as tough global cop.

Protecting a Fledgling State

Just south of the Equator and north of Australia, Timor-Leste gained independence from Indonesia in 2002. In 2006, U.N. peacekeepers were redeployed to the fledgling state in absence of a local police force.

"This is an issue of local ownership," he says. "We must also read what is in their hearts and minds."

[1] U.N. News Service, December 2006.

[2] *Ibid.*

[3] The Associated Press, "Albanians protest UN Kosovo plan," *Taipei Times,* Feb. 12, 2007, p. 6.

The Portuguese-born Lopes, who has served as police commissioner for the U.N. mission in East Timor, calls such a heavy U.N. role "a revolution" in the way the United Nations intervenes in internal conflicts. "What we are actually doing is a mixture of peace-keeping and peace-building," he explains. "We are hoping that with good governance — promoting elections and democratized policing — problems will be reduced."

Now, Lopes says, "our role is really to restore the rule of law as opposed to the rule of might."

"It will increasingly be a necessary feature of peace operations," predicts activist Deller. "Just separating factions and establishing elections alone isn't a sustainable model."

But so far, the result in Timor-Leste (the former East Timor) has "been a real disappointment," Deller says. She cites the "re-emergence of conflict," with the U.N.

having to come back to try and restore security in the fledgling nation. (*See sidebar, p. 88.*)

Keating, the former New Zealand ambassador to the U.N., believes that without peace-building, "it's very easy to have all these peace-keeping missions out there like Band-Aids," masking deep wounds underneath. He cites the example of "insufficient stickability" in Haiti, where six different U.N. peace operations have sought to hold together the fractured nation since 1995. [26]

"You take your eye off the ball, and before you know it you're back where you started," Keating says.

The latest U.N. Stabilization Mission in Haiti began on June 1, 2004, with the mandate to provide a stable and secure environment, but some Haitian critics say the peacekeepers have behaved more like occupiers.

Alex Diceanu, a scholar at Canada's McMaster University, claims the Haiti operation "has become

U.N. Photo/Daniel Morel

Brazilian blue helmets of the United Nations' peacekeeping force in Haiti help Haitian police keep order in the capital, Port-au-Prince, after a fire that ravaged 50 stores in June 2004.

complicit in the oppression of Haiti's poor majority." For many Haitians, the operation has seemed more like "a foreign occupation force than a United Nations peace-keeping mission," he said. "The few journalists that have reported from these areas describe bustling streets that are quickly deserted as terrified residents hide from passing U.N. tanks." [27]

Armed battles are taking place in Haiti, where U.N. forces have taken casualties as they continue to battle heavily armed gangs for control of Haiti's notorious slums. Exasperated by an infamous warlord's hold on 300,000 people in a Port-au-Prince slum called *Cite Soleil*, U.N. troops took the offensive in February 2007. Almost one-tenth of the 9,000-man Haiti force took the battle to the streets, reclaiming control in a block-by-block battle. Thousand of shots were fired at the peacekeepers. [28]

U.N. troops and police are now willing to battle warlords to try and build a democratic political foundation in the impoverished Caribbean nation, Guéhenno says. "This notion of protection of civilians," he says, "that's a change between yesterday's peace-keeping and today's peace-keeping."

Impoverished Haiti is a tough case, but the United Nations can claim success in building democracy after civil wars in Liberia and Congo, Keating says, where mis-

sions are still ongoing. Finding a "sustainable solution" to get people to live together "ain't easy" for the United Nations, he adds. "They can make a huge difference, but it's a commitment involving many years" to rebuild civilian institutions.

Indeed, notes the legendary Sir Brian Urquhart, a former U.N. undersecretary-general and a leading pioneer in the development of international peacekeeping, "The challenges are far weightier than the U.N. peacekeeping system was ever designed for.

"It's a very ambitious thing," he says. "What they're really trying to do is take countries and put them back together again. That's a very difficult thing to do."

BACKGROUND

Late Arrival

The ancient Romans had a description for their effort to pacify their 3-million-square-mile empire: Pax Romana, the Roman Peace. It lasted for more than 200 years, enforced by the Roman legions. [29]

The Hanseatic League in the 13th and 14th centuries arguably was the first forerunner of modern peacekeeping. Without a standing army or police force, the German-based alliance of 100 northern towns stifled warfare, civic strife and crime within its domain, mostly by paying bribes. [30]

For French Emperor Napoleon Bonaparte, peacekeeping was subordinate to conquest, and the extensive colonial empires of the great powers in the 19th century were more intent on exploiting natural resources than on peacekeeping.

In one rare instance, France, inspired by a romantic age in Europe, sent "peacekeepers" to Greece during the Greek revolt against the Turks in 1831 and ended up in tenuous circumstances between two Greek factions competing to fill the power vacuum. [31]

Perhaps the first example of multinational action against a common threat was in 1900 during the Boxer Rebellion in China, when a 50,000-strong force from Japan, Russia, Britain, France, the United States, German, Italy and Austro-Hungary came to protect the international community in Beijing from the Boxer mobs. [32]

The 20th century, ruptured by two world wars, saw few attempts at peacemaking. In 1919, at the end of World War I — "the war to end all wars" — the international community established the League of Nations to maintain peace. But as World War II approached, the fledgling world body floundered, discredited by its failure to prevent Japanese expansion into China and by Italy's conquest of Ethiopia and Germany's annexation of Austria. [33]

The United Nations was born in 1945 from the rubble of World War II and the ultimate failure of the League of Nations. Britain's Urquhart notes that the U.N.'s most critical task was to prevent doomsday — war between the Soviet Union and the United States. "During the Cold War," he says, "the most important consideration . . . was to prevent regional conflict from triggering an East-West nuclear confrontation."

German Navy Captain Wolfgang Schuchardt joined his once-divided nation's military in the midst of the Cold War, in 1968. "We had a totally different situation then," he recalls. "We had [certain] positions and those were to be defended" against the Soviet Union. Now, priorities have changed and Schuchardt works on strategic planning for the U.N.'s peace-keeping operation in Lebanon, one of the Middle East's most volatile areas.

The United Nations established its first peace-keeping observer operation to monitor the truce that followed the first Arab-Israeli war in 1948. Based in Jerusalem, it proved ineffective in the long term, unable to prevent the next three major Arab-Israeli wars.

In 1949 the United Nations deployed a peace-keeping observer mission to a similarly tense India and Pakistan, then quarreling over a disputed area of Kashmir.

When communist North Korea invaded South Korea in 1950, the U.N.'s forceful response was unprecedented. The Korean War was actually fought under the U.N. flag, with troops from dozens of nations defending South Korea.

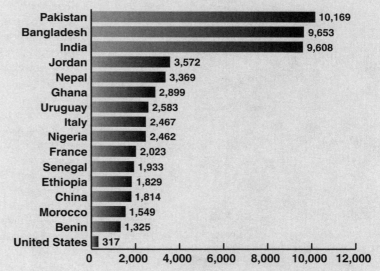

Developing Countries Provide Most Peacekeepers

Developing nations provide the most manpower to U.N. peacekeeping forces. Pakistan, Bangladesh and India were providing half of the U.N.'s nearly 58,000 personnel in early 2007.

U.N. Peacekeeping Forces by Country
(as of February 2007)

Country	Personnel
Pakistan	10,169
Bangladesh	9,653
India	9,608
Jordan	3,572
Nepal	3,369
Ghana	2,899
Uruguay	2,583
Italy	2,467
Nigeria	2,462
France	2,023
Senegal	1,933
Ethiopia	1,829
China	1,814
Morocco	1,549
Benin	1,325
United States	317

Source: "Ranking of Military and Police Contributions to UN Operations," Department of Peacekeeping Operations, United Nations, February 28, 2007

But the war was authorized through a diplomatic fluke. The Soviet Union, which would have vetoed the American-led invasion, was boycotting the Security Council when the vote to take U.N. action in Korea arose. [34]

As a child, Secretary-General Ban Ki-moon saw the U.N. in action. "As I was growing up in a war-torn and destitute Korea, the United Nations stood by my people in our darkest hour," he recalled. "For the Korean people of that era, the United Nations flag was a beacon of better days to come." [35]

During the Suez Crisis in 1956, the U.N. deployed forces to Egypt, where President Gamal Abdel Nassar had nationalized the Suez Canal, an international waterway that had long been linked to British and French interests. An Israeli invasion and a secretly planned joint French-British air action combined to confront Egypt,

U.N. Photo/Maher Attar

Sometimes they fight to keep the peace. In Marrakeh, Lebanon, a French soldier of the United Nations' peacekeeping contingent exchanges gunfire with insurgents of the Shiite militia movement, AMAL.

then a client state of the Soviet Union. The move brought East-West tensions to a boil.

To cool the situation, Canada's secretary of state for external affairs, Lester Pearson, suggested sending a U.N. Emergency Force to Egypt. The troops had to be rounded up in a week, but their distinctive light-blue berets had not arrived. So Urquhart had surplus army helmets spray-painted. U.N. peacekeepers henceforth would be recognized around the world as "the blue helmets." [36]

Eventually, pressure from the United States forced Britain, France and Israel to withdraw from the canal. Pearson won the Nobel Prize for his efforts.

Congo Quagmire

In the early 1960s U.N. peacekeepers became embroiled in chaos in the fractious, newly created nation of Congo. After gaining independence from Belgium, Congo erupted when strongman Joseph Mobuto seized power,

and Prime Minister Patrice Lumumba was assassinated. The struggle quickly turned into a proxy Cold War battle between the United States and the Soviet Union for influence in the region. [37]

Sweden's Dag Hammarskjold, then the U.N. secretary-general, saw in the Congo crisis "an opportunity for the United Nations to assert itself as the world authority in controlling and resolving major international conflicts," writes Poland's Andrzej Sitkowski. "It was his determination, personal commitment and effort which launched the clumsy ship of the organization full speed into the stormy and uncharted waters of Congo. He knew how to start the big gamble, but could not have known how and where it would end." [38]

While shuttling around Congo, a territory the size of Western Europe, Hammarskjold died in a plane crash that was "never sufficiently explained," Sitkowski continues. "It is a tragedy that his commitment and talents were applied, and, ultimately, laid waste in what he himself called a political bordello with a clutch of foreign madams."

The Congo mission cost the lives of 250 peacekeepers but yielded tepid results. Forty years later, U.N. peacekeepers would be back in the country, now known as the Democratic Republic of the Congo.

Other operations have successfully stabilized long-running disputes. In 1964 a U.N. force was deployed to stand between Greece and Turkey over a divided Cyprus. The operation began in 1964, but the island is still divided, and the U.N. force is still present. [39]

During the Cold War stalemate, U.N. peacekeeping had limited goals. As a result, however, it missed the opportunity (some would say moral duty) to stop Cambodian dictator Pol Pot's reign of genocidal terror against his own people. Well more than a million died in Cambodia's "killing fields," where piles of victims' skulls on display to visitors still mark that dark era. Yet the United Nations didn't enter Cambodia until years after the killing ended. [40]

During the 1980s, according to some observers, the United Nations was often stalemated while the Soviet Union and the United States fought over influence at the U.N., and peacekeeping's modest aims reflected the times. "I don't think it was ever designed for victory," Urquhart says. "The peacekeeping business was designed to freeze a potentially very dangerous situation until you got around to negotiating. It was quite successful in that."

Does the world community have a "responsibility to protect"?

YES

Gareth Evans
President, International Crisis Group
Former Co-Chair, International Commission
on Intervention and State Sovereignty

From a speech at Stanford University, Feb. 7, 2007

While the primary responsibility to protect its own people from genocide and other such man-made catastrophes is that of the state itself, when a state fails to meet that responsibility . . . then the responsibility to protect shifts to the international community. . . .

The concept of the "responsibility to protect" [was] formally and unanimously embraced by the whole international community at the U.N. 60th Anniversary World Summit in September 2005 . . . reaffirmed . . . by the Security Council in April 2006, and begun to be incorporated in country-specific resolutions, in particular on Darfur. . . .

But old habits of non-intervention died very hard. Even when situations cried out for some kind of response — and the international community did react through the U.N. — it was too often erratically, incompletely or counter-productively, as in Somalia in 1993, Rwanda in 1994 and Srebrenica in 1995. Then came Kosovo in 1999, when the international community did, in fact, intervene as it probably should have, but did so without the authority of the Security Council. . . .

It is one thing to develop a concept like the responsibility to protect, but quite another to get any policy maker to take any notice of it. . . . We simply cannot be at all confident that the world will respond quickly, effectively and appropriately to new human catastrophes as they arise, as the current case of Darfur is all too unhappily demonstrating. . . .

As always . . . the biggest and hardest piece of unfinished business [is] finding the necessary political will to do anything hard or expensive or politically sensitive or seen as not directly relevant to national interests. . . . We can . . . always justify [the] responsibility to protect . . . on hard-headed, practical, national-interest grounds: States that can't or won't stop internal atrocity crimes are the kind of rogue . . . or failed or failing states that can't or won't stop terrorism, weapons proliferation, drug and people trafficking, the spread of health pandemics and other global risks.

But at the end of the day, the case for responsibility to protect rests simply on our common humanity: the impossibility of ignoring the cries of pain and distress of our fellow human beings. . . . We should be united in our determination to not let that happen, and there is no greater or nobler cause on which any of us could be embarked.

NO

Ambassador Zhenmin Liu
Deputy Permanent Representative
Permanent Mission of the People's Republic of
China to the United Nations

From a statement before the U.N. Security Council, Dec. 4, 2006

The important Security Council Resolution 1674 . . . sets out comprehensive provisions pertaining to the protection of civilians in armed conflict. . . . What is needed now is effective implementation. . . .

First, in accordance with the Charter of the United Nations and international humanitarian law, the responsibility to protect civilians lies primarily with the Governments of the countries concerned. While the international community and other external parties can provide support and assistance . . . they should not infringe upon the sovereignty and territorial integrity of the countries concerned, nor should they enforce intervention by circumventing the governments of the countries concerned.

Second, it is imperative to make clear differentiation between protection of civilians and provision of humanitarian assistance. Efforts made by humanitarian agencies in the spirit of humanitarianism to provide assistance to the civilians affected by armed conflicts . . . should . . . at all times abide by the principles of impartiality, neutrality, objectivity and independence in order to . . . avoid getting involved in local political disputes or negatively affecting a peace process.

Third, to protect civilians, greater emphasis should be placed on prevention as well as addressing both symptoms and root causes of a conflict. Should the Security Council . . . manage to effectively prevent and resolve various conflicts, it would successfully provide the best protection to the civilians. . . . The best protection for civilians is to provide them with a safe and reliable living environment by actively exploring methods to prevent conflicts and effectively redressing the occurring conflicts.

While discussing the issue of protection of civilians in armed conflict, the concept of "responsibility to protect" should continue to be approached with caution by the Security Council. The World Summit Outcome last year gave an extensive and very cautious representation of "the responsibility to protect populations from genocide, war crimes, ethnic cleansing and crimes against humanity." . . . Since many member States have expressed their concern and misgivings in this regard, we believe, it is, therefore, not appropriate to expand, willfully interpret or even abuse this concept. . . .

Finally, we hope that . . . full consideration will be taken of the specific characteristics and circumstances of each conflict so as to adopt appropriate measures with a view to effectively achieving the objective of protecting civilians.

U.S., Japan Pay Most U.N. Peacekeeping Costs

The United States and Japan account for nearly two-thirds of the funds contributed by industrial nations to support the various peacekeeping missions at the United Nations. The U.S. share alone is about 38 percent of the total.

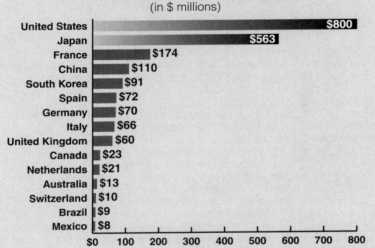

U.N. Peacekeeping Contributions in 2006
(in $ millions)

United States	$800
Japan	$563
France	$174
China	$110
South Korea	$91
Spain	$72
Germany	$70
Italy	$66
United Kingdom	$60
Canada	$23
Netherlands	$21
Australia	$13
Switzerland	$10
Brazil	$9
Mexico	$8

Source: "2006 Status of Contributions to the Regular Budget, International Tribunals, Peacekeeping Operations and Capital Master Plan," United Nations

Failed Missions

The fall of the Berlin Wall in 1989 heralded the end of the Cold War between the United States and the Soviet Union, as well as an extraordinarily promising start for U.N. action.

In 1991, the Security Council authorized the Persian Gulf War coalition that dislodged Iraqi troops from Kuwait. Though it wasn't fought under a U.N. flag, as in Korea, the first Gulf War demonstrated the U.N.'s clear exercise of military action over words.

Saddam Hussein's 1991 invasion of Kuwait was an unprovoked action by a sovereign nation against another, and clearly prohibited by the U.N. charter. "I always tell my students," notes international law Professor Smith, "that Saddam was the one guy on Earth dumb enough to do precisely the thing the United Nations was established to prevent."

Heady from that success, U.N. member states sought to transform the new post-Cold War cooperation into a dramatic expansion of United Nations peacekeeping. But its efforts were met by mixed results, and well-known bloody failures in the 1990s when it tried to intervene in critical situations in Africa and Bosnia.

In Somalia, on Africa's eastern horn, ultimately failed peacekeeping efforts led to the rise of warlord Mohamed Farah Aidid and the deaths of 18 U.S. soldiers in the infamous First Battle of Mogadishu. The book and film, "Black Hawk Down," told how a U.S. helicopter was shot down and the bodies of American soldiers were dragged through the streets. The battle left 700 Somalis dead along with a Malaysian and two Pakistanis. [41] Somalia would end up lapsing in lawlessness, and the psychological ramifications of the Somalia debacle still haunt the specter of tough peacekeeping operations. The 1994 Rwandan genocide occurred in central Africa, far from the power centers and concerns of Western aid agencies. The international community, the Clinton administration and the United Nations were all slow to respond, and ineffectual when they did. Canada led U.N. peacekeeping troops in Rwanda, but the reduced force was not authorized or likely able to intervene to prevent the killings.

Former Canadian General Romeo Dallaire, who headed U.N. peacekeeping forces during the Rwandan genocide in 1994, has written the best-selling *Shake Hands with the Devil* in which he criticizes the U.N.'s approach to the conflict. "I have been taking the position from the start that the United Nations is nothing but the front man in this failure," Dallaire states in a BBC interview. "The true culprits are the sovereign states that influence the Security Council, that influence other nations into participating or not." [42]

Bosnia was also a symbol of peacekeeping helplessness. U.N. peacekeepers carved out what they called "safe havens" to protect civilians against the euphemistically called practice of "ethnic cleansing." "Unfortunately, that only created an illusion of safety in an area where there wasn't safety at all," says former New Zealand Ambassador Keating. "That's because there wasn't sufficient personnel."

International expert Smith argues the U.N.'s Bosnia effort was doomed from the start. "They planned it as a humanitarian exercise," he says. "They planned not to use force. And they hamstrung themselves."

The most public example of the United Nations' inability to bring protection or peace, he notes, was when lightly armed Dutch peacekeeping troops were held hostage by Bosnian Serb forces in Srebrenica in July 1995, and turned over thousands of Bosnian Muslims in exchange for the release of 14 Dutch soldiers. The Serbs eventually massacred some 8,000 Bosnian Muslim men and boys in Srebrenica. Photographs of the hapless Dutch were flashed around the world as visible proof that U.N. peacekeepers lacked the ability to defend even themselves.

The Somali and Bosnian experiences were diplomatic, military and humanitarian disasters. "There was no clear operational doctrine for the kinds of things they were doing," says Keating, who served on the U.N. Security Council during that bleak period. "So they made it up as they went along."

Successful Missions

A U.N. mission that helped bring Namibia to independence in 1989 is often cited as a major peacekeeping success story. The U.N. negotiated a protocol allowing the peaceful withdrawal of Marxist rebels from the South-West African Peoples Organization (SWAPO) and Cuban and South African troops.

"Never before had the U.N. devised a peace and independence plan supported by such a web of political agreements, institutional arrangements and administrative buildup," writes Sitkowski, who served with the operation.

In Liberia, a watershed election in 2005 — monitored by the United Nations, the European Union and the Economic Community of West African States — appears to have ended decades of turmoil and violence and translated "security gains into meaningful, political and economic progress," according to the U.N.-supported *Annual Review of Global Peace Operations.*[43]

Liberia's newly elected president, Ellen Johnson-Sirleaf, has become increasingly visible on the world stage. An economist and former U.N. development offi-

The first all-female U.N. force, more than 100 policewomen from India, arrives at Liberia's Roberts International Airport in Monrovia on Jan. 30, 2007. The women will spend at least six months in Liberia, a nation emerging from years of brutal civil war.

AFP/Getty Images/Issouf Sanogo

cial with a Harvard master's degree, she has earned the nickname "Iron Lady" for her ability to do tough jobs normally undertaken by "strongmen" in Africa.[44]

"Our peace is so fragile," she said, "that we need a continuation of the U.N. peacekeeping force for at least three to four years, until our own security forces have been restructured and professionalized."[45]

Since 2005 the United Nations' first all-female peacekeeping unit, 103 women from India, has been stationed in Liberia. (*See sidebar, p. 82.*) "The women have quickly become part of Monrovia's urban landscape in their distinctive blue camouflage fatigues and flak jackets," said *The Christian Science Monitor.* "They guard the Ministry of Foreign Affairs, patrol the streets day and night, control crowds at rallies and soccer games and respond to calls for armed backup from the national police who, unlike the Indian unit, do not carry weapons."[46]

CURRENT SITUATION

Force Expansion

The Security Council voted on Jan. 11, 2007, to set up a modest political mission in Nepal to oversee a disarmament and cease-fire accord between the government and former Maoist rebels.[47]

AFP/Getty Images/Joe Klamar

Jasmina Zukic, a Muslim who lost 16 family members in the Balkans war, prays at the cemetery in Potocari, Bosnia, where she is waiting for the arrival and reburial of the remains of 610 Bosnian Muslim men, discovered in a mass grave on July 9, 2005. Local Serbs had killed more than 8,000 men and boys under the eyes of U.N. peacekeepers from The Netherlands.

The action came after a spate of significant growth for robust U.N. peacekeeping operations. During the last six months of 2006, the Security Council sent peacekeepers to maintain peace in southern Lebanon, prepare East Timor for reconciliation and stem the violence in Darfur. This built on rapid growth in the numbers and size of peace operations in recent years.

Secretary-General Ban wants to create a new office from the United Nations' 700-person peacekeeping department. It would focus entirely on supporting field operations and provide "a clear line of command, point of responsibility and accountability for field support," says U.N. spokeswoman Montas. That effort would bolster the R2P concept, she says, which is "to protect as rapidly as possible."

Montas points to the confusion and hesitation of the dark moments in the 1990s. "The U.N. had that painful experience of Rwanda and the former Yugoslavia," she says. "Things will have to be done better."

But Ban's peacekeeping reform efforts have been met with hesitation by the General Assembly, leading one European envoy to warn of "death by a thousand meetings." [48]

A major challenge looming for U.N. peacekeeping is the expansion of the force itself. With a potential 40 percent increase in the number of peacekeepers looming in 2007, the Security Council may have to cut short existing operations. That would be a mistake, says former

Ambassador Keating. "Leave too early," he says, "chances are you'll be back again in five years."

China and Sudan

In Sudan, mistrust has complicated efforts to get more peacekeeping troops to curb the horrors of Darfur. Sudan's regime, seen as both hostile and uncooperative by the West, is equally suspicious about U.N. involvement.

Sudan's U.N. Ambassador Abdalhaleem accuses Western nations of withholding support for the African Union in order to promote U.N. peacekeepers. "Their objective is to make it weak because their objective is to bring blue helmets in Darfur," he charges.

On Feb. 7, during the first visit ever by a Chinese leader to Sudan, President Hu Jintao asked Sudan's President Omar al-Bashir to give the United Nations a bigger role in trying to resolve the conflict in Darfur. Hu also said China wanted to do more business with its key African ally, according to Sudan state media reports.

Beijing has at least a two-fold strategy in courting Africa: political interest in influencing the 50-plus nations in Africa and a commercial interest in fueling its increasingly voracious economic engine with Sudanese oil and the continent's plentiful natural resources. [49]

Hu had been under Western pressure to do more to use his clout as Sudan's largest oil customer and international investor to push it to accept U.N. peacekeepers in Darfur.

A month later al-Bashir continued his defiance, telling an Arab League meeting in Riyadh, Saudi Arabia, that the proposed U.N.-AU force would be "a violation of Sudan's sovereignty and a submission by Sudan to outside custodianship." [50]

Arab leaders have been asked to step in to pressure Bashir. After a two-hour meeting with al-Bashir, Saudi Arabian King Abdullah and high-level Arab League and AU representatives, U.N. Secretary-General Ban told reporters, "I think we made progress where there had been an impasse. The king's intervention very much supported my position."

By April 4, as news broke that five AU peacekeepers had been killed in Darfur, Britain and the United States said they were drafting a U.N. resolution to impose financial sanctions and a possible "no-fly" zone over Darfur to punish Sudan's continued intransigence. Secretary-General Ban asked that a sanction vote be delayed to give him time for more negotiations planned in Africa and New York. [51]

On April 15, Saudi officials said Bashir told King Abdullah that an agreement had been reached for the hybrid AU-U.N. force. But given Bashir and Sudan's record of seeming to cooperate — and then pulling back after reports of agreement — the situation will be uncertain until more peacekeepers are actually in place in Darfur.

Meanwhile, China announced a new military cooperation deal with Sudan, a move one U.N. diplomat described as "pre-emptive." China appeared to be rushing to sign as many deals as possible with Sudan before economic and military sanctions are imposed on Khartoum, he said. [52]

Before Hu's February trip, Western observers, including Deller of the group Responsibility to Protect, had described China as "the great obstructer" in efforts to resolve the Darfur crisis.

Not surprisingly, Hen Wenping, director of African studies at the Chinese Academy of Sciences in Beijing, defended communist China's approach to Darfur: "China's strategy remains the same, and as always, it used quiet diplomacy to keep a constructive engagement, rather than waving a stick." [53]

Traditionally, none of the five permanent, veto-wielding members of the U.N. Security Council contributes many U.N. peacekeeping troops, since their influence in world affairs would compromise their neutrality. But China, one of the five, has emerged as a newly enthusiastic supporter of peacekeeping.

"China firmly supports and actively participates in U.N. peacekeeping operations," said Chinese Ambassador to the U.N. Zhang Yishan in late February. "Up till now, China's contribution in terms of personnel to 15 U.N. peacekeeping operations has reached the level of more than 5,000, and as we speak, there are about 1,000 Chinese peacekeepers serving in 13 mission areas." [54]

"China could flood the market of U.N. peacekeeping if they wanted to," French defense official Guicherd remarks. "Just like they are flooding other markets."

Afghanistan and Beyond

European nations responded tepidly last winter when the U.S.-led alliance in Afghanistan called for more NATO troops, frustrating the Bush administration and NATO officials. The alliance had sought more troops to combat an expected offensive by Taliban insurgents, and top officials warned of dire consequences if European nations didn't deliver. Frustrating NATO military efforts even more, Germany, France and Italy restricted the number of their troops taking part in the heavy fighting in southeastern Afghanistan, where the insurgency has shown its greatest strength. [55]

"I do not think it is right to talk about more and more military means," said German Defense Minster Franz Josef Jung. "When the Russians were in Afghanistan, they had 100,000 troops and didn't win."

Nonetheless, the German cabinet voted in February to send at least six Tornado jets to the front for surveillance operations against the Taliban. "Without security there is no reconstruction," said a chastened Jung, "and without reconstruction there's no security." [56]

The cost of continued combat duty in Afghanistan may influence the debate among NATO nations. Afghanistan has given the NATO organization "their very first taste of significant ground combat," says international law Professor Smith. "They're suffering casualties in ways they had not anticipated. NATO states are beginning to see people coming home in body bags and are wondering why they are involved at all."

Failure in Afghanistan could affect NATO's desire to project its military might in any new peacekeeping operations beyond Europe. "In the long run, there will be enough uncertainty in the world that members of NATO will understand that they must remain capable to some extent, but how far they are willing to stretch themselves will remain under consideration and debate," Smith adds.

Meanwhile, NATO intervention to serve as a buffer between Israel and the Palestinians remains a future possibility, but French defense official Guicherd says NATO is linked too closely with U.S. policy. Given the tension and the acute anti-Americanism in the region, she says, "it wouldn't be a very good idea for the time being." [57]

But NATO member Turkey could provide an entré into the Middle East, points out Smith. Turkey enjoys good relations with Israel and is a majority-Muslim country whose troops might be more acceptable to Arab populations. Smith calls it an "interesting idea. . . . Turkey has NATO [military] capabilities. They might actually play a meaningful role."

As *Turkish Daily News* columnist Hans De Wit put it, "The current situation in the Middle East is, in fact, a perfect chance for Turkey to show its negotiating skills, since its has good relations with all countries in this region.

"But somehow, its image as a former conqueror doesn't help. Turkey has done a terrible job in convincing the world that its intentions . . . are sincere; that it can bring mediation to the region and can be a stabilizer of importance." [58]

OUTLOOK

Is the World Ready?

As the still-uncertain response to Darfur indicates, countries around the world and at the United Nations are not rushing to every emergency call. "The international community has to prove that it is willing to step into difficult situations — and it may yet again," says former New Zealand Ambassador Keating. "But I wouldn't assume that it would every time."

The high ideals and bold aims articulated by the Responsibility to Protect doctrine may be tempered not only by whether the world has the will to send troops in to halt a massacre but also by whether there will be enough troops.

While it strives to play an increasing role around the world, NATO may be tied down at home. Kosovo is set to receive some form of U.N.-decreed independence from a reluctant Serbia, but the Balkans could again be rocked by the kind of bloody ethnic violence that marked the 1990s.

Such renewed ethnic hostility could challenge the NATO stabilization force, requiring the alliance to bolster its troop counts in Kosovo — and slow NATO efforts to export its peacekeeping influence elsewhere.

As the R2P concept takes root, however, pressure may increase for the kind of muscular intervention that only military forces like NATO troops can deliver.

"The right of an individual to live is a higher priority, at least in theory, than the right of states to do as they please," says former U.S. diplomat Feinstein. "Something important is happening in theory, and practice is lagging very far behind."

More than just words will be needed to make the Responsibility to Protect viable, says U.N. spokeswoman Montas. "The political will has to be there," she says, "and the political will has to come from the Security Council."

There is plenty of military might around the world to translate "theory into reality," according to former Australian foreign minister Evans. "The U.N. is feeling desperately overstretched . . . but with the world's armed services currently involving some 20 million men and women in uniform (with another 50 million reservists, and 11 million paramilitaries)," he observes, "it hardly seems beyond the wit of man to work out a way of making some of that capacity available . . . to prevent and react to man-made catastrophe." [59]

For many people, U.N. police official Lopes says, "We are the last port before Hell."

Having served on the Security Council during the Rwanda bloodbath, former Ambassador Keating knows all too well the limitations of U.N. action. Each case is weighed on "its own particular location in time as well as geography — and whether or not the resources are physically available to undertake the task that's envisaged," he says.

In Darfur, for example, there is the additional problem of mistakenly harming civilians, he says, so the council must weigh the "kind of scenario in which the bad guys and the good guys are almost stuck together." That's "one of the daunting things that's confronting any action with respect to Sudan — being "realistic" about the situation," he says.

"It's unforgivable, really, when you think about the 'Never Again' statements" made after the Holocaust, Keating says, "but the reality is at the moment there's no willingness to do it."

Peacekeeping expert Holt, at the Stimson Center, calls peacekeeping "an enduring tool," even though "it's always criticized for falling short of our hopes. But we keep turning back to it.

"A lot of these lessons are learnable and fixable," she adds. "Peacekeeping continues to evolve, it's a moving exercise," with very real global stakes. "Millions of people's lives remain in the balance if we don't get this right."

NOTES

1. Speech by Ban Ki-moon on Jan. 29, 2007, delivered as a video message.

2. Feinstein's comments on the civilian and military issues involved in the right to protect can be found at the Council on Foreign Relations Web site: www.cfr.org/publication/12458/priority_for_new_un_secretarygeneral.html?breadcrumb=%2Fpublication%2Fby_type%2Fnews_release%3Fid%3D328.

3. Quoted in Lee Michael Katz, "The Man Behind The Movie," *National Journal*, April 22, 2006.

4. From U.N. Secretary-General Ban Ki-moon's address to the Center for Strategic and International Studies in Washington, D.C., Jan. 16, 2007.

5. U.N. Department of Peacekeeping Operations, "Fact Sheet," May 2006.

6. "Peacekeeping and Related Stabilization Operations," CRS Report for Congress, Congressional Research Service, July 13, 2006.

7. U.N. Department of Peacekeeping Operations, *op. cit.*

8. Quoted in "From Cologne to Berlin and Beyond — Operations, Institutions and Capabilities," address to European Security and Defense Policy Conference, Jan. 29, 2007.

9. Organization for Security and Co-operation in Europe (OSCE); www.osce.org/activities.

10. "The Responsibility to Protect," Report of the International Commission on Intervention and State Sovereignty, December 2001, p. VII.

11. Gareth Evans, *The Responsibility to Protect: The New Global Moral Compact* (forthcoming, 2007).

12. "World Summit Outcome," U.N. General Assembly, 60th Session, Sept. 20, 2005, Item 39, p. 31.

13. Quoted in United Nations summary of Holocaust Commemoration speeches, Jan. 29, 2007.

14. Quoted in Luiza Ch. Savage, "Canada's 'Responsibility to Protect' Doctrine Gaining Ground at the UN, *Maclean's*, July 18, 2005.

15. "Chávez Criticizes U.N. Reform in Speech," The Associated Press, Sept. 17, 2005.

16. Luiza Ch. Savage, *op. cit.*; and Paul Reynolds, "Western Pressure Fails to Move Sudan," BBC Online, Oct. 23, 2006; http://news.bbc.co.uk/2/hi/africa/6076698.stm.

17. Quoted in "Gadhafi: U.N. Darfur Force is Ruse to Grab Sudan's Oil," Reuters, Nov. 20, 2006, Global Research online; www.globalresearch.ca/index.php?context=viewArticle&code=20061120&articleId=3934.

18. Chinua Akukwe, "Why the Darfur Tragedy Will Likely Occur Again," July 28, 2004, Worldpress.org; www.worldpress.org/Africa/1905.cfm.

19. William G. O'Neill, "The Responsibility to Protect," *The Christian Science Monitor*, Sept. 28, 2006; www.csmonitor.com/2006/0928/p0928/p09s01-coop.html. O'Neill is senior adviser to the Brookings Institution Project on Internal Displacement.

20. African Union, *Protocol Relating to the Establishment of the Peace and Security Council of the African Union* (Durban: African Union, July 2002).

21. David Newman and Joel Peters, "Kosovo as the West Bank, Macedonia as Israel," commentary, *Ha'aretz*, Oct. 30, 2002.

22. For an analysis of the problems and potential of an African peacekeeping force, see World Politics Watch; www.worldpoliticswatch.com/article.aspx?id=429.

23. "Aid Agencies Urge Donor Support for African Union Mission in Darfur," *Oxfam America* online, July 20, 2006; www.oxfamamerica.org/.

24. See United Nations Security Council Meeting on cooperation with regional organizations, Sept. 20, 2006, http://daccessdds.un.org/doc/UNDOC/PRO/N06/528/73/PDF/N065287.pdf?OpenElement.

25. Roland Paris, from *Review of International Studies*, British International Studies Association (2002), pp. 637-656.

26. Center for International Cooperation, *Annual Review of Global Peace Operations*, February 2006; www.cic.nyu.edu.

27. Alex Diceanu, "For Many Haitians, MINUSTAH Has Been Closer to a Foreign Occupation Force than a U.N. Peacekeeping Mission," *Peace Magazine*, April 2006; www.globalpolicy.org/security/issues/haiti/2006/04better.htm.

28. Marc Lacey, "U.N. Troops Fight Haiti Gangs One Battered Street at a Time," *New York Times*, Feb. 10 2007, p. A1.

29. See *World History*, McDougal Litell (2005).

30. *Encyclopedia Britannica* online; http://concise.britannica.com/ebc/article-9039167/Hanseatic-League.

31. David Brewer, *The Greek War of Independence: The Struggle for Freedom from Ottoman Oppression and the Birth of the Modern Greek Nation* (2001).

32. Naval Historical Center, "The Boxer Rebellion and the U.S. Navy, 1900-1901"; www.history.navy.mil/faqs/faq86-1.htm.

33. For background, see www.answers.com/topic/league-of-nations.

34. For background, see www.historylearningsite.co.uk/korea.htm.

35. Quoted in "Ban Ki-moon calls on new generation to take better care of Planet Earth than his own," U.N. News Centre, March 1, 2007; www.un.org/apps/news/story.asp?NewsID=21720&Cr=global&Cr1=warming.

36. James Traub, interviewed on "Fresh Air," National Public Radio, Oct. 31, 2006.

37. For a summary of the Congo's ongoing war, see Simon Robinson and Vivienne Walt, "The Deadliest War In The World," *Time*, May 28, 2006; www.time.com/time/magazine/article/0,9171,1198921-1,00.html.

38. Adrzej Sitkowski, *UN Peacekeeping Myth and Reality* (2006).

39. For background on the Congo crisis, see Justin Pearce, "DR Congo's Troubled History," BBC Online, Jan. 16, 2001; http://news.bbc.co.uk/1/hi/world/africa/1120825.stm.

40. The Cambodia Genocide Project at Yale University includes a definition of genocide as well as information on a Responsibility to Protect Initiative at Yale University Online; www.yale.edu/cgp/.

41. For a detailed account of the Somalia action, see Mark Bowden, "Black Hawk Down: An American War Story," *The Philadelphia Enquirer*, Nov. 16, 1997.

42. Interview with BBC, "Eyewitness: UN in Rwanda 1994," Sept. 6, 2000, news.bbc.co.uk.

43. *Annual Review of Global Peace Operations 2006, op. cit.*

44. For background, see http://africanhistory.about.com/od/liberia/p/Sirleaf.htm.

45. Quoted in "Liberia's New President," News Hour Online, March 23, 2006; www.pbs.org/newshour/bb/africa/jan-june06/liberia_3-23.html.

46. Tristan McConnell, "All female unit keeps peace in Liberia," *The Christian Science Monitor online*, March 21, 2005; http://news.yahoo.com/s/csm/20070321/ts_csm/ofemmeforce_1.

47. Warren Hoge, "World Briefing: Asia: Nepal: U.N. Creating New Political Mission," *The New York Times*, Jan. 24, 2007.

48. Evelyn Leopold, "U.N. Chief's Reform Plans May Be Stalled in Meetings," Reuters, Feb. 5, 2007.

49. Alfred de Montesquiou, "Chinese president tells Sudan counterpart he must do more for peace in Darfur," The Associated Press, Feb. 2, 2007.

50. Quoted in Warren Hoge, "Arabs and U.N. Chief Press Sudan's Leader to End Darfur Crisis," *The New York Times*, March 29, 2007, p. A5.

51. See Colum Lynch, "U.N. Chief Seeks to Delay Sanctions Against Sudan," *The Washington Post*, April 3, 2007, p. A15.

52. *Ibid.*

53. Howard W. French, with Fan Wexin, "Chinese Leader to Visit Sudan for Talks on Darfur Conflict," *The New York Times* online, Jan. 25, 2007.

54. Statement by Ambassador Zhang Yishan at the 2006 Session of the Special Committee on Peacekeeping Operations, United Nations, Feb. 27, 2006. Full statement available at www.fmprc.gov.cn/ce/ceun/eng/xw/t237291.htm.

55. Michael Abramowitz, "Afghanistan Called 'Key Priority' For NATO," *The Washington Post*, Nov. 30, 2006.

56. Kate Connolly, "Germany beefs up Afghan presence with six fighter jets," *The Guardian* online, Feb. 8, 2007; full story at www.guardian.co.uk/afghanistan/story/0,,2008088,00.html.

57. For background, see Samuel Loewenberg, "Anti-Americanism," *CQ Global Researcher*, March 2007, pp. 51-74.

58. Hans A. H.C. DeWit, "Turkey Needs Confidence, Not Fear," *Turkish Daily News* online, Feb. 16, 2007; www.turkishdailynews.com.tr/article.php?enewsid=66304.

59. Evans, *op. cit.*

BIBLIOGRAPHY

Books

Cassidy, Robert, *Peacekeeping In The Abyss: British and American Peacekeeping Doctrine and Practice after the Cold War,* **Praeger, 2004.**
A Special Forces officer and international relations scholar examines and compares U.S. military efforts in Somalia and British operations in Bosnia in an effort to understand which military cultural traits and force structures are more suitable and adaptable for peace operations and asymmetric conflicts.

Danieli, Yael, *Sharing The Front Line And The Back Hills: Peacekeepers Humanitarian Aid Workers And The Media In The Midst Of Crisis,* **Baywood, 2002.**
A clinical psychologist who is co-founder of the Group

Project for Holocaust Survivors and Their Children gives voice to the victims of traumatic hotspots such as Kosovo, Haiti and Burundi.

Franke, Volker, ed., *Terrorism and Peacekeeping, New Security Challenges,* **Praeger, 2005.**
An associate professor of international studies at McDaniel College presents numerous case studies in order to examine the challenges to national security policymakers posed by peacekeeping and terrorism.

Johnstone, Ian, ed., *Annual Review of Global Peace Operations 2006,* **Lynne Rienner Publishers, 2006.**
A senior U.N. official and former senior associate at the International Peace Academy examines U.N. missions around the world; includes numerous statistics and also frank observations on peacekeeping's failures and limitations.

Luck, Edward, *The U.N. Security Council: Practice and Promise,* **Routledge, 2006.**
A Columbia University professor and longtime U.N. watcher examines the Security Council's roller-coaster history of military enforcement and sees a "politically awkward division of labor" between major powers and developing countries.

Sitkowski, Adrzej, *U.N. Peacekeeping Myth and Reality,* **Praeger Security International, 2006.**
A veteran U.N. official reflects on peacekeeping operations with a very critical eye; includes an inside look at serving in Namibia, regarded as a model of U.N. success.

Smith, Michael G., with Moreen Dee, *Peacekeeping In East Timor: The Path To Independence,* **International Peace Academy Occasional Series, Lynne Rienner Publishers, 2003.**
"General Mike" Smith, who led the U.N. force in East Timor, concludes broadly there are no "templates" for peacekeeping and that lessons from previous missions were not fully learned.

Traub, James, *The Best Intentions: Kofi Annan and the UN in the Era of American World Power,* **Farrar, Straus and Giroux, 2006.**
A *New York Times* reporter critically portrays U.N. operations through the eyes and staff machinations of the recently departed secretary-general.

Articles

Dalder, Ivo, and James Goldgeiger, "Global NATO," *Foreign Affairs,* **September/October, 2006, p. A1.**
The authors argue that expanding NATO membership, even beyond Europe, can boost the security organization's new peacekeeping role.

Katz, Lee Michael, "The Man Behind The Movie," *National Journal,* **April 22, 2006.**
In an interview, Paul Rusesabagina, the real-life Hotel Rwanda manager, offers a witness to genocide's first-hand perspective, finding the U.N. "useless" in Rwanda.

Lacey, Marc, "U.N. Troops Fight Haiti Gangs One Battered Street at a Time," *The New York Times,* **Feb. 10 2007, p. A1.**
A look at "Evans," a gang leader who controls the slums and lives of 300,000 people in Haiti's Port-au-Prince — and U.N. peacekeeping troops' attempts to take him down.

Reports and Studies

"Darfur and Beyond: What Is Needed To Prevent Mass Casualties," Council on Foreign Relations, January 2007.
A carefully timed report suggests actions that should be taken by the new U.N. secretary-general, NATO, the European and African unions and the United States to prevent future genocides.

"The Responsibility To Protect," Report Of The International Commission On Intervention and State Sovereignty, December 2001.
Diplomats from Australia to Russia provide the intellectual underpinnings of The Responsibility to Protect in this landmark report. Because of the report's timing, it doesn't address the aftermath of the Sept. 11, 2001, attacks in depth.

"The Responsibility To Protect: The U.N. World Summit and the Question of Unilateralism," *The Yale Law Journal,* **March 2006.**
This cautious look at The Responsibility to Protect argues that it limits military action to narrow and extreme circumstances and can be used as a pretext to invade another nation.

For More Information

African Union, P.O. Box 3243, Addis Ababa, Ethiopia; (251)-11-551-77-00; www.africa-union.org. Promotes cooperation among the nations of Africa.

European Union Force, Rue de la Loi, 175 B-1048 Brussels, Belgium; (32-2)-281-61-11; www.consilium.europa.eu. Military detachments currently in Bosnia and Herzegovina and the Democratic Republic of the Congo.

International Commission on Intervention and State Sovereignty, 125 Sussex Dr., Ottawa, Ontario K1A 0G2; www.iciss.ca. Independent commission established by the Canadian government that promotes humanitarian intervention.

International Crisis Group, 149 Avenue Louise, Level 24, B-1050 Brussels, Belgium; +32-(0)-2-502-90-38; www.crisisgroup.org. Non-governmental organization using field-based analysis and high-level advocacy to prevent violent conflict worldwide.

Multinational Force and Observers, +39-06-57-11-94-44; www.mfo.org. International peacekeeping force on Sinai Peninsula monitoring military build-up of Egypt and Israel.

North Atlantic Treaty Organization, Blvd. Leopold III, 1110 Brussels, Belgium; +32-(0)-2-707-50-41; www.nato.int. Safeguards NATO member countries via military and political means.

Organization for Security and Co-operation in Europe, Kaerntner Ring 5-7, 1010 Vienna, Austria; +43-1-514-36-0; www.osce.org. World's largest regional security organization serves as a forum for political negotiations and decision-making in conflict prevention and crisis management.

Responsibility to Protect, 708 Third Ave., 24th Fl., New York, NY 10017; (212) 599-1320; www.responsibilityto-protect.org. Advocacy group working to protect vulnerable populations from war crimes and crimes against humanity.

United Nations Department of Peacekeeping Operations, 760 U.N. Plaza, New York, NY 10017; (202) 963-1234; www.un.org/Depts/dpko/dpko. Responsible for all U.N. peacekeeping missions mandated by the Security Council.

International Crisis Group

Brussels
Sept. 2006

Darfur simply does not matter
"The sad reality is that Darfur simply does not matter enough, and Sudan matters too much, for the international community to do more to stop the atrocities. Much as governments in Europe and the U.S. are disturbed by what is happening in Darfur — and they genuinely are — almost without exception they are not prepared to commit their troops on the ground in Sudan. . . . The issue is problematic for the U.S. because it has a close intelligence relationship with the Sudanese government in its war on terror."

Kofi Annan

Secretary-General, United Nations
March 2005

Policy of zero tolerance
"I am especially troubled by instances in which United Nations peacekeepers are alleged to have sexually exploited minors and other vulnerable people, and I have enacted a policy of 'zero tolerance' towards such offences that applies to all personnel engaged in United Nations operations. I strongly encourage Member States to do the same with respect to their national contingents."

Centre for Research on Globalization

Canada
May 2006

Third World intervention
"We in the West tend to believe that if a white developed country is sending troops to the Third World, it must be a good thing. But until we can envision a situation where Third World intervention against the U.S. or other great powers is realistic and possible, the 'Responsibility to Protect' exists simply as a tool for 'us' in the West to continue subjugating and running the affairs of other countries. Those who would have us intervene in Sudan on the basis of combating unrest under the 'Responsibility to Protect' would have us face the ridiculous situation, as in Kosovo, of 'needing' to violate a country's sovereignty as a result of the West having previously violated it."

Walden Bello

Executive Director, Focus on the Global South (Bangkok)
Jan. 2006

Dump humanitarian intervention
"We must forcefully delegitimize this dangerous doctrine of humanitarian intervention to prevent its being employed again in the future against candidates for great power intervention like Iran and Venezuela. Like its counterpart concept of 'liberal imperialism,' there is only one thing to do with the concept of humanitarian intervention: dump it."

Oxford Research Group

United Kingdom
April 2004

Intervention should be widened
"Can a universally acceptable humanitarian doctrine still be articulated and defended by the international community? We believe that for the sake of humanity, the answer has to be yes. But this will require civil society doing more to hold governments to account, and building transparency and trust into the processes that lead to a decision to go to war. It will require a return to and further development of the concepts of the ICISS report on 'The Responsibility to Protect.' . . . The understanding of 'intervention' should be widened to include methods of conflict prevention and resolution other than the use of military force."

Nozizwe Madlala-Routledge

Deputy Minister of Health, South Africa
July 2004

Current approach pays lip service
"The current U.N. approach entails merely disarming combatants and does not address the dismantling of war economies and effectively re-integrating ex-combatants into society, which is at the root of the problem. The approach pays lip service to gender equality by not taking cognisance of the specific needs of women ex-combatants or the violation of the rights of women by peacekeepers. . . . The delay between the start of peacekeeping operations and the start of peace-building and socio-economic development interventions reduces the ability to absorb combatants into the formal economy and to dismantle the war economy."

M.e. Cohen@HumorInk.com 07.29

M.E. Cohen

5

Radical Islam in Europe

Sarah Glazer

Pakistani Muslims burn the Danish flag in Karachi on Feb. 14, 2006, to protest Danish newspaper cartoons they said blasphemed the Prophet Mohammed. Worldwide protests sparked by the cartoons reflected many young Muslims' feeling that the Muslim world is under attack by the West.

AP Photo/Shakil Adil

From *CQ Researcher*,
November 1, 2007.

A recent spate of attempted terrorist plots by Muslims in Europe has revived questions about how much of the threat is homegrown — the outgrowth of disaffection among European Muslims — and how much is orchestrated abroad.

On Sept. 4 German authorities announced they had foiled a plan to blow up an American military base in Frankfurt. Their arrest of a member of Germany's large Turkish community — long considered one of Europe's most peaceful Muslim immigrant groups — along with two German-born converts to Islam raised new questions about Germany as a locus of radicalization and its success at integrating Muslim residents.

Police said the planned explosion could have been more deadly than the 2004 train bombings in Madrid, which killed 191 people, and the 2005 London transit attack that killed 52 commuters. [1]

On the same day as the announcement of the German arrests, Muslims in Copenhagen were charged with planning a bombing attack in Denmark, suggesting that domestic discontent in the country — where Muslim immigrants complain of job discrimination and a newspaper triggered worldwide protests among Muslims two years ago by publishing cartoons seen as ridiculing Mohammed — may have provided fertile ground for Islamic terrorism. [2]

This past summer, Britons were shocked to learn that Muslims suspected of trying to blow up the Glasgow, Scotland, airport on June 30 included middle-class Indian and Middle Eastern doctors working for the National Health Service — not alienated youths without jobs. The news came the day after the same suspects had allegedly tried to set off a car bomb outside a London nightclub and just before the anniversary of the July 7, 2005, London transit

More European Muslims Favor Suicide Bombings

Muslims in France, Spain and Great Britain are twice as likely as American Muslims to condone suicide bombings of civilians. About one in six Muslims in the three countries say bombing civilians to defend Islam is justifiable.

Can the suicide bombing of civilians to defend Islam be justified?

Muslims who said yes in . . .

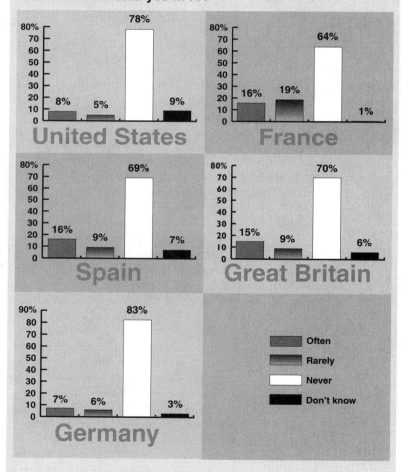

Often
Rarely
Never
Don't know

* Percentages may not total 100 due to rounding.

Source: "Muslim Americans: Middle Class and Mostly Mainstream," Pew Research Center, May 2007

bombings. One of the suicide bombers from that attack had left a video in a strong Yorkshire accent — a startling reminder that "a British lad" had been radicalized at home even if he also had links to militants abroad. [3]

All three events spurred soul-searching in Britain, Germany, Denmark, Scotland and elsewhere. Experts often blame Western foreign policies, including the war in Iraq, for the young Muslims' outrage and their feeling that the Muslim world is under attack by the West. But the long-held belief by some European leaders that opposing the Iraq War would immunize their countries from Muslim terrorist attacks appeared dashed by the plot in Germany, which opposed the war. Authorities said the bombing scheme was linked to Germany's military presence in Afghanistan. [4]

To what extent does the violence that Europe is experiencing reflect a failure to integrate immigrants and their children into Western society?

"There is a sense in our societies that the radicalism was not created by the United States [foreign policy] but caused by the lack of integration," Christoph Bertram, the former director of the Institute of Security Affairs in Berlin, told *The New York Times* the week after the German and Danish arrests. [5]

Reflecting that concern, British Prime Minister Gordon Brown in July announced that in addition to beefing up border police he was proposing a fourfold increase in "hearts and minds" programs like citizenship classes in Britain's 1,000 *madrasas* (Islamic religious schools, usually attached to a mosque), and

English-language training for imams.

"A tough security response is vital, but to be safe in the longer term we need to reach people before they are drawn into violent extremism," said Hazel Blears, Britain's Secretary of State for Communities and Local Government. [6]

Other analysts argue that radical fundamentalism originates from increasingly well-organized international networks seeking out and finding the few estranged individuals ready to commit violence. The German and Danish plotters were said to have received training and instructions in Pakistan. And in September, European authorities warned that a newly strengthened al Qaeda, operating from the lawless, tribal border region between Pakistan and Afghanistan, was stepping up plans to target Europe and the United States. [7]

Meanwhile, a recent New York City Police Department (NYPD) intelligence report concluded that the terrorists involved in the 2004 Madrid bombings, the London transit attack and the group in Hamburg, Germany, that planned the Sept. 11, 2001, terrorist attacks in the United States were "unremarkable" local residents, some with advanced degrees from European universities. Moreover, the report said, the process of radicalization seems to be accelerating, and terrorists are getting younger. "We now believe it is critical to identify the al Qaeda-inspired threat at the point where radicalization begins," the report said, a conclusion shared by a 2006 British intelligence report. [8]

Jytte Klausen, a professor of comparative politics at Brandeis University who has studied the profiles of 550 alleged terrorists arrested since the 9/11 attacks, disputes the idea that terrorism is primarily the fruit of "homegrown" radicals who have not been integrated into society. "This is not primarily about integration, though better integration might be preventative," she says. "It has a lot to do with transnational networks and ethnic origins: Political developments in Pakistan are getting filtered through Britain's back door; the radical groups piggyback on the migrant stream."

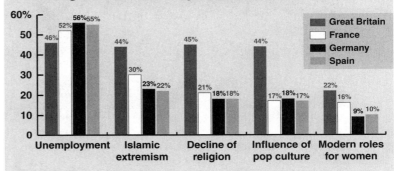

Jobs Are Top Muslim Concern

Most Muslims in Europe worry more about unemployment than about religious and cultural issues, such as the rise of extremism and the decline of religion. They are least concerned about the role of women in modern society.

Percentage of Muslims very worried about . . .

Legend: Great Britain, France, Germany, Spain

- Unemployment: 46%, 52%, 56%, 55%
- Islamic extremism: 44%, 30%, 23%, 22%
- Decline of religion: 45%, 21%, 18%, 18%
- Influence of pop culture: 44%, 17%, 18%, 17%
- Modern roles for women: 22%, 16%, 9%, 10%

Source: "Muslims in Europe: Economic Worries Top Concerns About Religious and Cultural Identity," Pew Global Attitudes Project, July 2006

British writer Ed Husain describes his recruitment in the 1990s in London by Islamists — Muslims who advocate an Islamic state, in some cases by violent means — in his 2007 memoir *The Islamist*. Husain argues that two factors prompt those drawn to political Islamic ideology to contemplate violence: the scorn heaped on non-Muslims by radical fundamentalists and the growing conviction that the world's Muslims need their own transnational state — or caliphate — governed by strict religious law, called sharia.

But others, like sociologist Tahir Abbas of England's University of Birmingham, say the notion of a Muslim caliphate is still an abstract one — an aspiration that isn't much different from European nations joining together in the European Union. And some of the London organizations where Husain says he was radicalized, such as Hizb ut-Tahrir and the controversial East London Mosque, claim they do not advocate violence to achieve the goal of a global Islamic state. Some groups say they only advocate the return of an Islamic state in Muslim countries. For example, Hizb ut-Tahrir says it works to bring "the Muslim world" under the caliphate but that in the West it does "not work to change the system of government." [9] (*See sidebar, p. 122.*)

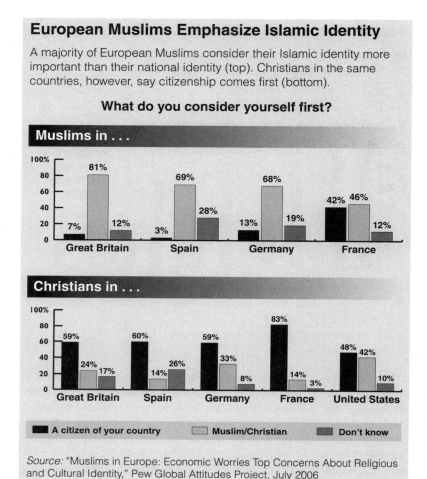

European Muslims Emphasize Islamic Identity

A majority of European Muslims consider their Islamic identity more important than their national identity (top). Christians in the same countries, however, say citizenship comes first (bottom).

What do you consider yourself first?

Muslims in . . .

Great Britain: 7%, 81%, 12%
Spain: 3%, 69%, 28%
Germany: 13%, 68%, 19%
France: 42%, 46%, 12%

Christians in . . .

Great Britain: 59%, 24%, 17%
Spain: 60%, 14%, 26%
Germany: 59%, 33%, 8%
France: 83%, 14%, 3%
United States: 48%, 42%, 10%

■ A citizen of your country   ▢ Muslim/Christian   ▣ Don't know

Source: "Muslims in Europe: Economic Worries Top Concerns About Religious and Cultural Identity," Pew Global Attitudes Project, July 2006

as they have in the United States, which might explain their openness to radical ideas. Polls show Muslims in France, Spain and Britain are twice as likely as U.S. Muslims to say suicide bombs can be justified. (*See graph, p. 106.*) Notably, support in Europe for suicide bombings is highest among Muslim adults under age 30 — supporters make up 35 percent of young Muslims in Great Britain and 42 percent in France. There were an estimated 15 million Muslims in the European Union in 2006, not counting the 70 million Muslims in Turkey. [12]

One measure of European Muslims' alienation from Western governments and news sources is the surprisingly large majorities who don't accept that recent terrorist acts were carried out by Muslims. An astonishing 56 percent of British Muslims don't believe Arabs carried out the 9/11 attacks, according to a poll by the Pew Research Center, a result commonly explained as acceptance of one of the conspiracy theories blaming Jews, Israel's secret police or the Bush administration. [13] But Abbas, who is Muslim himself, suggests another explanation for the widespread skepticism: Most Muslims are in denial because they are so shocked at the thought that fellow Muslims could carry out such a violent act.

Experts on Islam also hasten to point out that sympathizing with suicide bombers or sharing fundamentalist beliefs doesn't mean one will become a terrorist. Some of the fear about the call for an Islamic state by groups like Hizb ut-Tahrir — a group that calls for the end of Israel and which Britain has considered banning — is misplaced, Abbas believes. "People look at the surface, see dogma and . . . see it as a menacing threat. Yes, lots of people are hotheaded and mad, but they dip in and out of these organizations just as often as they're sprouting up. Young people need to find themselves, need to search for meaning to their lives," he says.

Some Muslim leaders in Britain, including Syed Aziz Pasha, secretary general of the Union of Muslim Organizations of the UK and Ireland, have pushed for sharia law in Britain — but only as it pertains to family matters like marriage, and only for Muslims. One poll shows about a third of British Muslims would rather live under sharia. [10]

Husain, a former member of Hizb ut-Tahrir, remains skeptical of the group's nonviolent stance: "The only difference between Islamists from Hizb ut-Tahrir and jihadists is that the former are waiting for their state and caliph before they commence jihad, while the latter believes the time for jihad is now." [11]

Meanwhile, most experts agree that Muslims in Europe have not been as easily incorporated into society

Yet, even if a group doesn't advocate terrorism to achieve an Islamic state, parties advocating Islamic rule through peaceful means should also be resisted because they aim to establish a "totalitarian" theocracy, argues Martin Bright, a journalist who has investigated radical links to Muslim groups in Britain. "We make a mistake if we think that just because people are engaged in the electoral process that's necessarily a good thing; Mussolini and Hitler were also engaged in the electoral process," says Bright, political editor at the *New Statesman*, a left-leaning political weekly published in London. Radical asylum seekers are often careful not to commit violence in Britain and other European countries that accept them for fear of deportation, he says, but still support jihad abroad.

When Muhammad Abdul Bari — secretary general of the British Muslim Council, an umbrella group representing Muslims — suggested last year that British non-Muslims adopt more Islamic ways, including arranged marriages, one critic interpreted it as a call for adopting sharia law. [14] A recent BBC documentary reported that sharia courts in Nigeria, operating strictly according to Koranic prescriptions, have ordered limbs amputated as a punishment for thievery, public flogging and stoning of women accused of adultery. [15] Critics like Bright say that given the potential for such brutal punishments, accompanying repressive attitudes towards women and frequently virulent anti-Semitism, the real struggle facing the West is about ideology, not terrorism.

The recent foiled bombing attempts have prompted calls in England and France to allow police to detain terrorist suspects for longer periods to give police more time to investigate. But groups like Human Rights Watch say Muslims are already bearing the brunt of law enforcement and immigration policies that violate their human rights. [16] In the long run, terrorist crackdowns can be counter-productive if they merely alienate mainstream Muslims, say civil liberties advocates.

By failing to heed moderate Muslims' warnings in the 1990s that clerics were preaching violence, law-enforcement services in Britain alienated the very communities they need to help them, says Hisham A. Hellyer, Senior Research Fellow at the University of Warwick and author of a forthcoming report from the Brookings Institution in Washington on counterterrorism lessons from Britain for the West. An important lesson for the West, he says, is to not cut off contact with

AP Photo/Peter MacDiarmid

A mangled bus is a grim reminder of the four rush-hour suicide bombings by Muslim terrorists that killed 52 London commuters and injured hundreds in July 2005. The attacks added to Europeans' concerns about how well they were integrating Muslim immigrants and their children.

Muslim groups who may be conservatively religious but not violent.

Some experts, including Director of National Intelligence Mike McConnell, fear the United States could be the next target of European terrorists. McConnell told the Senate Judiciary Committee in September that al Qaeda is recruiting Europeans for explosives training in Pakistan because they can more easily enter the United States without a visa. [17]

Peter Skerry, a professor of political science at Boston College who is writing a book about Muslims in America, says homegrown terrorists are less likely in the United States because there is more ethnic diversity among American Muslims, and they are more educated and wealthier than European Muslims. They are also less of a

Foreign Domination Sparked Radical Islamic Thought

Muslim writers protested British, U.S. interventions

The radicalization of Islam has historic roots reaching back to the 1930s, '40s and '50s, when Muslim writers were also protesting colonialism and what they saw as imperialistic British and U.S. interventions in the Middle East.

The Muslim Brotherhood, founded in Egypt in 1928, sought to couple resistance to foreign domination with establishment of an Islamic state run by sharia law, which imposes strict interpretations of the *Koran*. The Brotherhood at first worked closely with the secret Free Officers revolutionary movement led by Gamal Abdel Nasser and Anwar al-Sadat, which aimed at overthrowing the British regime and the Egyptian royal family.

But after the group's military coup toppled the Egyptian monarchy in 1952, Nasser's regime sorely disappointed the Brotherhood as insufficiently Islamic. A failed assassination attempt on Nasser by an embittered Brotherhood member in 1954 prompted the secular government to brutally suppress the movement and imprison its leaders.

One of those imprisoned leaders was Sayyid Qutb, known by his followers as "The Martyr," whose anti-Western writings would become extremely influential in the jihadist movement. In 1948, while on a study mission to the United States, he wrote with distaste of the sexual permissiveness and consumerism he saw, comparing the typical American to a primitive "caveman." [1] Alienated by America's hedonism, he argued the only way to protect the Islamic world from such influences would be to return to strict Islamic teachings.

Qutb spent most of the last decade of his life imprisoned in Egypt, where he was tortured. While in prison he wrote *Milestones*, his famous work espousing his vision of Islam as inseparable from the political state, and concluded the regime was a legitimate target of jihad. [2] He was convicted of sedition in 1966 and hanged.

The ideas of writers like Qutb have been adopted by radical Islamic groups (Islamists) today, generating concern in the West. An updated version of *Milestones*, published in Birmingham, England, in 2006 and prominently displayed at the bookstore next to the controversial East London Mosque contains a 1940s-era instruction manual by another member of the Muslim Brotherhood with chapter headings like "The Virtues of Killing a Non-Believer for the Sake of Allah" and "The Virtues of Martyrdom." [3]

The Muslim Brotherhood was "really the first organization to develop the idea that you could have an Islamic state within the modern world," according to *New Statesman* political editor Martin Bright. [4]

Although the Brotherhood is sometimes represented as moderate in comparison to jihadist groups like al Qaeda, Bright notes its motto remains to this day: "Allah is our objective. The Prophet is our Leader. The *Qu'uran* [*Koran*] is our constitution. Jihad is our way. Dying in the way of Allah is our highest hope." In 1981, Sadat, who had become Egypt's president, was assassinated by four members of a Brotherhood splinter group. [5]

Robert S. Leiken, director of the Immigration and National Security Program at the Nixon Center in Washington, D.C., recently interviewed leaders of the Brotherhood in Europe and the Middle East. He concluded the organization "depends on winning hearts through gradual and peaceful Islamization" and is committed to the electoral process. However, the group does authorize jihad in countries it considers occupied by a foreign power. [6]

For instance, Yusuf al-Qaradawi, the Brotherhood's spiritual leader, has supported suicide bombing in the Palestinian occupied territories and called it a duty of every Muslim to resist American and British forces in Iraq. [7]

Jamaat-e-Islami, the radical Asian offshoot of the Muslim Brotherhood, originated in British India first as a religious movement in 1941 and then as a political party committed to an Islamic state in 1947. It is the oldest religious party in Pakistan and also has wings in Bangladesh and Kashmir.

presence. Muslims constitute less than 1 percent of the U.S. population, compared to an estimated 8-9 percent in France, 5.6 percent in the Netherlands, 3.6 percent in Germany and 3 percent in Britain. [18]

But the European experience has American law enforcers casting a worried glance eastward, and some are redoubling efforts to forge links with American Muslims. [19] As they do, here are some of the debates taking place in academic, political and citizen arenas in Europe and the United States:

The party was founded by Abdul A'la Maududi, a Pakistani journalist who promoted a highly politicized, anti-Western brand of Islam. In his writings, Maududi asserts that Islamic democracy is the antithesis of secular Western democracy because the latter is based on the sovereignty of the people, rather than God.

Maududi was the first Muslim to reject Islam as a religion and re-brand it as an ideology — political Islam. His writing strongly influenced Qutb during his years in prison. British former radical Ed Husain writes that the organizations in London where he first heard Islam described as a political ideology in the 1990s — the Young Muslim Organization and the East London Mosque — both venerated Maududi. [8]

But while Maududi urged gradual change through a takeover of political institutions, Qutb argued for "religious war," seizing political authority "wherever an Islamic community exists," and jihad "to make this system of life dominant in the world." [9]

In support, Qutb cited the Prophet Mohammed's declaration of war on the infidels of Mecca. Qutb tarred all Christian, Jewish and Muslim societies of his time as *jahili* — disregarding divine precepts — because their leaders usurped Allah's legislative authority. "When I read *Milestones*, I felt growing animosity toward the *kuffar* (non-Muslims)," Husain writes. [10]

Husain would eventually move on to an even more radical group, Hizb ut-Tahrir (Party of Liberation), founded in Jerusalem in 1953 by Palestinian theologian and political activist Taqiuddin an-Nabhani. While Qutb and Maududi argued that Muslims had a religious duty to establish an Islamic state, Nabhani "provided the details of how to achieve it," writes Husain — through military coups or assassinations of political leaders. [11]

Today, Hizb ut-Tahrir says it seeks to establish a caliphate, or Islamic state governing all Muslims, through an "exclusively political" rather than violent method. [12] However, the group was recently denounced by a former senior member, Maajid Nawaz, who told the BBC that according to the group's own literature, the caliphate is "a state that they are prepared to kill millions of people to expand." [13]

Today, reverence for the writings of Qutb or Maududi should be a litmus test for any Islamist group's level of radicalism, according to Husain. But University of Birmingham sociologist Tahir Abbas cautions that Maududi's writing "is about trying to fight off the yoke of colonialism as much as developing a pan-Islamic identity. When it comes to Maududi, he's writing for his time — and people take it out of context."

Indeed, to the uninitiated, the writings of both Qutb and Maududi come across as rather dry, if fiercely loyal, interpretations of the *Koran* as the supreme word.

Still, Maududi's party, Jamaat-e-Islami, has spawned its share of leaders preaching violent hatred against the West. Hossain Sayeedi, a Jamaat-e-Islami member of the Bangladesh Parliament, has compared Hindus to excrement. In public rallies in Bangladesh, he has urged that unless they convert to Islam, "let all the American soldiers be buried in the soil of Iraq and let them never return to their homes." [14]

---

[1] Sayyid Qutb, *Milestones* (2006), p. 8.

[2] For background, see Peter Katel, "Global Jihad," *CQ Researcher*, Oct. 14, 2005, pp. 857-880.

[3] Qutb, *op. cit.*, p. 266.

[4] Martin Bright, "When Progressives Treat with Reactionaries: The British State's Flirtation with Radical Islamism," *Policy Exchange*, 2006, p. 21.

[5] *Ibid.*, p. 14.

[6] Robert S. Leiken and Steven Brooke, "The Moderate Muslim Brotherhood," *Foreign Affairs*, March/April 2007, pp. 107-119.

[7] Bright, *op. cit.*, p. 20.

[8] Ed Husain, *The Islamist* (2007), p. 24. In this book, Maududi is spelled Mawdudi.

[9] Qutb, *op. cit.*, p. 86.

[10] *Ibid.*

[11] *Ibid.*, pp. 91, 96.

[12] "Radicalisation, Extremism & 'Islamism,'" *Hizb ut-Tahrir Britain*, July 2007, www.hizb.org.uk/hizb/images/PDFs/htb_radicalisation_report.pdf.

[13] Richard Watson, "Why Newsnight's Interview with Former HT Member is Essential Viewing," BBC, Sept. 13, 2007, www.bbc.co.uk/blogs/newsnight/2007/09/why_newsnights_interview_with_former_ht_member_is.html.

[14] Quoted in Bright, *op. cit.*, p. 22.

Has Europe's terrorism been caused by a failure to integrate Muslims into society?

In the early 1990s, the isolation of the Bangladeshi neighborhood in East London where writer Husain grew up made it relatively easy for radical Islamist groups to recruit him to their vision of a transnational Islamic state, he writes in his memoir.

The lack of contact with mainstream British culture and society helps explain why many young Muslims insist that the recent attack on the Glasgow airport and

Europe Has Many Low-Income Muslims

Approximately one-fifth of Muslims in Europe are considered low-income, leading some terrorism experts to conclude that economic deprivation triggers extremism. In the United States, where there have been few terrorist attacks, only 2 percent of Muslims are considered low-income.

Percentage of Muslims Considered Low-income

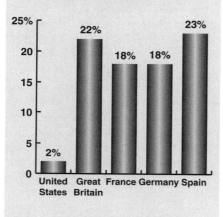

Source: "Muslim Americans: Middle Class and Mostly Mainstream," Pew Research Center, May 2007

major terrorist attack was likely in their country in the next 12 months, to consider Muslims a threat to national security and to believe Muslims had too much political power in their country. [20]

French immigration historian Patrick Weil, a senior research fellow at the University of Paris' National Center for Scientific Research, says France accepts Muslims as fellow citizens and friends more easily than the British.

"The English have fought [work and educational] discrimination among the elite, and they've been quite successful, but they've been bad at cultural integration," he says. In France, it's the opposite: "We're very bad at ending discrimination but much better at integration."

Among the Europeans polled, the French are the most likely to have Muslim friends, accept a son or daughter marrying a Muslim and think Muslims are unjustly the subject of prejudice. [21] In the same vein, more French Muslims think of themselves as French first and Muslim second than in the other three countries polled, according to a Pew survey. [22] (*See graph, p. 166.*)

That may help explain why France has been spared a major Muslim terrorist attack since the mid-1990s. The 2005 riots in Paris' poorer, heavily Muslim suburbs were protests against racial and economic discrimination driven by a desire to be part of France, rather than a separatist Muslim movement, Weil and other experts believe. Even when Muslims were protesting France's 2004 head-scarf ban in public schools, their chant was decidedly Francophile: "First, Second, Third Generation: We don't give a damn: Our home is Here!" [23]

Weil, a member of a commission appointed in 2003 by former French President Jacques Chirac that recommended banning "conspicuous religious symbols" in schools, claims the headscarf ban has helped to integrate Muslims into France's secular system and has given Muslim girls a better chance at educational equality. As evidence, he points out the ban was implemented without the need for police enforcement. The *Koran* became a bestseller during the head-scarf debate, a sign that non-Muslims wanted to learn more about Islam, he says. The head-scarf rule "includes you in the system" of basic French values, he says.

But John R. Bowen, an anthropologist at Washington University in St. Louis and author of *Why the French Don't Like Headscarves*, thinks the ban incurred resentment in the Muslim community. Nevertheless, he argues in a recent article, Muslims and non-Muslims in France

9/11 itself must be the creation of the government and the media, Husain believes. "When you're in that world, what others say [has] no meaning," he says. "You see them as non-believers headed for hell anyway."

But integration is a two-way street, and Husain says the traditional coldness of the English toward outsiders makes it difficult for anyone to easily enter their society.

Supporting that view is a *Financial Times* poll conducted last August that found Britons are more suspicious of Muslims than are other Europeans or Americans. Only 59 percent of Britons thought it possible to be both a Muslim and a citizen of their country, a smaller proportion than in France, Germany, Spain, Italy or the United States. British citizens also were the most likely to think a

"are far more willing to get on with the task of building a multireligious society than are the Dutch, British or Spanish — or even Americans." [24]

French Muslims, for instance, are not calling for sharia law, as do many British Muslims, he notes. Partly that's historical: Many North Africans arrive speaking fluent French and have a sense of affiliation to their former colonial power. Most French Muslims also tend to live in more ethnically mixed areas, while in England entire Bangladeshi villages seem to have been plopped down in single neighborhoods.

Most experts also give credit to the French police and domestic intelligence service. "The French really monitor their Muslims closely, so if someone is preaching a radical sermon they'll know right away and have much less compunction than the British to say, 'You can't do that,' or find a way to get rid of the guy" by deporting him, says Bowen.

Surprisingly, a French government adviser on religious affairs, Bernard Godard, who specialized in Muslim neighborhoods while serving with the French police and domestic intelligence service, ascribes France's lack of Muslim terrorism not to the country's policing efforts but to its policy of non-engagement in Iraq. "France is a little country that is not considered dangerous," he says. And it is harder to recruit North African Muslims for terrorism than Middle Easterners, he suggests. "They have no reason to do something against France."

The French also are much more inclusive toward newcomers than their neighbors. The French government gives newly arrived immigrants hundreds of hours of free French-language lessons to help qualify them for employment. In contrast, observes Bowen, the Netherlands recently required would-be immigrants — even the spouses of Dutch residents — to prove that they already speak good Dutch before they arrive, but provide no help in learning the language. "The Dutch are using language to exclude Muslims, the French to integrate them," he says. [25]

Similarly, Germany recently proposed requiring that immigrants show on their naturalization applications that they agree with German public opinion — a tactic some have called the policing of "un-German" thought. Turks and other Muslims see the plan as discriminatory, according to a study by the International Crisis Group (ICG). Nevertheless, the report concluded that Germany's approach to its mainly Turkish Muslim population was "paying off" — judging from the lack of ter-

rorist incidents or riots in Germany compared to the experiences of Britain and France. [26] (The ICG report was issued before the recent foiled German plot.)

But Boston College political scientist Jonathan Laurence, the author of the ICG report on Germany and a book published last year on integration in France, says the recent German plot involving a Turkish resident doesn't change his "cautious optimism." [27]

Since Germany has traditionally treated Turkish immigrants as "guestworkers" rather than citizens, most of today's Turkish population still holds only Turkish citizenship even though half were born in Germany. A 2000 law opened the door to citizenship but under very restrictive rules. Laurence says German Turks have less "political frustration" than Muslims in other European countries because they have lower expectations as a result of German citizenship laws. "They don't feel as entitled to success or mobility because they have not been included in the German dream," he says.

But he doubts that there are "any direct causal links" between a lack of integration and recent terrorist attempts in Europe. "There are too many other poorly integrated groups that don't turn to terror," he says.

If failure to integrate were the cause, "We'd have masses of people joining the jihad, which is not happening," says Jocelyne Cesari, director of Harvard University's Paris-based Islam in the West study group and author of the 2004 book *When Islam and Democracy Meet: Muslims in Europe and the United States.*

In fact, she continues, "All national ideologies in Europe are in crisis," as indicated by France's failure to ratify the EU constitution. [28] And for some young people, Islamic ideologies fill the vacuum left by national identity, she says.

That's what has happened in Britain, argues British *Daily Mail* journalist Melanie Phillips in her book *Londonistan.* England has become the epicenter of Islamic terrorism, she argues, in part because of shame about British national identity. "British society presented a moral and philosophical vacuum that was ripe for colonization by predatory Islamism," she writes. [29] "Driven by postcolonial guilt . . . Britain's elites have come to believe that the country's identity and values are by definition racist, nationalist and discriminatory." [30]

Ironically, points out Brandeis political scientist Klausen, England has the most terrorism in Europe even though it is one of Europe's most integrated countries by

Kafeel Ahmed died of severe burns a month after his attempted car bombing of Glasgow International Airport on June 30, 2007. Iraqi doctor Bilal Abdullah was also in the car and was charged with attempting a bombing. Ahmed, an engineer from India, was among eight Muslims — including three physicians working for Britain's National Health Service — charged in connection with attempted car bombings in Glasgow and London.

ing study of 550 people arrested for terrorism since 9/11, she was surprised to find a high degree of petty-criminal histories, suggesting these are not mainstream Muslims. And a highly traditional, religious background does not seem to be a predictor either. "The argument that democracy is illegitimate is what turns them on," she says.

Although unemployment is high among young Muslim men in Britain, it isn't among terrorists arrested there, according to Klausen, suggesting only a tenuous link between inequality or discrimination and political anger. [31]

So is terrorism the result of a lack of integration or the influence of external terrorist networks? "It's both," according to Robert S. Leiken, director of the Immigration and National Security Program at the Nixon Center, a think tank in Washington, D.C. Europe, he says, currently has two kinds of jihadists: "outsiders" — typically radical imams, asylum seekers or students fleeing from crackdowns against Islamist agitators in the Middle East — and "insiders" — second- or third-generation children of immigrants. [32]

"That's why Britain is the most dangerous country," according to Leiken. "It has the confluence of these two sources of jihad."

Has Britain's multiculturalism fostered social isolation and extremism?

Various books, columns and think-tank reports recently have blamed Britain's multicultural ethos for creating segregation along religious lines and, in some eyes, providing fertile ground for extremist Islamic ideas. Last year Prime Minister Tony Blair's Communities Secretary Ruth Kelly launched a study commission to examine whether multiculturalism * was causing greater ethnic-minority separateness. [33]

By the time the commission reported back in June, the term "multiculturalism" had disappeared from the report in favor of a new buzzword, "community cohesion," which some columnists took as a reflection of the government's growing anxiety about its earlier approach. [34]

Some critics say multiculturalism encourages Britons to elevate Islamic values over British values. Schools have ceased to transmit "either the values or the story of the nation" because in a multicultural classroom, the

measures like education. The young Islamist radicals described in Husain's memoir are all middle class and well integrated, she points out, including Husain, who worked in a bank. "We have a movement of radical groups recruiting among middle-class, upwardly mobile young Muslims," she says.

Klausen blames England's terrorism on international political networks and a generational counterculture that has found violence-prone individuals. In her study of four Danish-born Muslim teenagers convicted in connection with an October 2005 plot to blow up the U.S. embassy in Sarajevo, she found many similarities to the shooters at Colorado's Columbine High School in 1999. In her ongo-

---

* Multiculturalism is often described as the idea that all races, religions and ethnicities should be equally valued and respected.

"majoritarian culture is viewed as illegitimate and a source of shame," writes Phillips in *Londonistan*. [35]

In that vacuum, it's easy for Islamic radicalism to step in, some argue. For instance, in the state school Husain attended in Britain, Muslim children attended separate assemblies managed by a front organization for the revolutionary Islamic movement Jamaat-e-Islami. It then administered tests promoting Islam as an ideology that sought political power. [36]

The debate over British schools' abdication of responsibility for teaching about Islam is strikingly different from the debate in the United States, where the struggle has usually been over whether officially authorized textbooks or curricula should give more prominence to the nation's traditionally ignored ethnic groups. Compared to Canada, where multiculturalism is a curriculum taught from kindergarten, the term in Britain is "a bit murky," creating a "confused debate," says Canadian-born Abdul-Rehman Malik, a contributing editor at *Q-News*, an edgy magazine aimed at young British Muslim professionals.

To some critics, multiculturalism means the funding of local religious groups, which the critics blame for increasing tensions between Muslims and people of other faiths. A report issued this year by Policy Exchange, a conservative London think tank, concludes that the growth of radical Muslim politics has been "strongly nurtured by multicultural policies at the local and national level since the 1980s." [37]

Muslims' focus on religious identity and their sense that they are victims of discrimination "feeds into the broader narrative of victimhood that radical Islam in Britain is all about," says lead author Munira Mirza. "A lot of radical Islam in Britain is about saying, 'We Muslims are under attack; the West is against us.'"

Yet aside from legislation outlawing discrimination, which has been broadened to include religious discrimination, it's hard to point to any one government policy that's explicitly multicultural, says Sarah Spencer, associate director at the University of Oxford's Centre on Migration, Policy and Society and former deputy chairwoman of the government's Commission for Racial Equality.

Rather than multiculturalism causing the separation, "the factors that promote separation are socioeconomic ones," she maintains, such as housing clustered in poor neighborhoods.

Nevertheless, some critics argue that multiculturalism pervades both the public and private sectors in myriad ways, sometimes by just leaving Muslim communities alone.

The London-based Centre for Social Cohesion recently reported that the Islamic sections in public libraries in Tower Hamlets, London's most heavily Muslim borough, were dominated by fundamentalist literature — preaching terrorism and violence against women and non-Muslims. [38] This is a prime example of taxpayer-funded multicultural policy promoting radical Islam, according to center director Douglas Murray. A Muslim seeking to learn more about his faith from the library "couldn't help but be pushed toward the more extreme interpretation," he says.

The "most horrifying example" of let-them-alone multiculturalism, says Murray, is the estimated dozen Muslim women who are murdered in Britain each year in "honor killings" by fathers and brothers. An independent commission is investigating how police handled the case of a 20-year-old Kurdish woman killed by her father after she repeatedly sought help from authorities.

Police "may be worried that they will be seen as racist if they interfere in another culture," said Diana Sammi, director of the Iranian and Kurdish Women's Rights Organization. [39]

Women's advocates have sought legislation to protect women from forced marriages — already outlawed in Norway and Denmark — which they see as strongly linked to honor killings (*see p. 129*). But University of Chicago anthropologist Richard Schweder cautions it's not clear that honor killings in the Muslim community occur with more frequency than passion killings of adulterous partners by Western husbands. Other experts suggest that police may have failed to follow through on these cases for other reasons, perhaps having more to do with their own racism or their attitudes towards domestic violence.

Leiken of the Nixon Center says Britain's "separatist form of multiculturalism" offered radical Islamists from Algeria and other Muslim countries refuge and the opportunity to preach openly during the 1990s at a time when the French government was denying asylum to radical Muslims. [40] Britain's multicultural ideology "meant the legal system was lenient, and police often found themselves in a situation where they couldn't do anything" when moderate Muslims complained about radical clerics taking over their mosques, Leiken says.

CHRONOLOGY

19th Century *European nations colonize much of Muslim world. British colonization of India sparks mass Muslim immigration to Europe by end of century.*

1900-1960s *European rule in Islamic world ends. Muslims establish their own states. . . . Fundamentalist (Islamist) political groups emerge, some espousing a pan-Muslim caliphate. Muslim workers begin emigrating to Europe.*

1928 Radical Muslim Brotherhood is founded in Egypt.

1941 Islamist Jamaat-e-Islami party is founded in Pakistan.

1947-48 Pakistan becomes world's first avowedly Islamist state. . . . Israel is established, displacing Palestinians and creating lasting conflict with Arabs, Muslims.

1952 Col. Gamal Abdel Nasser topples Egyptian monarchy.

1953 Radical Islamic party Hizb ut-Tahrir is founded in Jerusalem.

1954 Brotherhood member tries to assassinate Nasser, who then imprisons leaders, including Sayyid Qutb. Qutb writes *Milestones* — manifesto of political Islam.

1964 *Milestones* is published.

1970s *Movement for Islamic state advances; Europe limits immigration to families, causing more Muslim emigration.*

1979 Iranian Revolution ousts U.S.-backed Reza Shah Pahlavi, brings Ayatollah Ruholla Khomeini to power.

1980s *Saudi Arabia, India, Pakistan and Iran seek to dominate Muslim world, send missionaries to Europe.*

1981 Scarman Report blames racial discrimination for South London Brixton riots, calls for multicultural approach toward Muslims.

1986 French pass strong terrorist-detention laws after spate of bombings.

1987 Saudi millionaire Osama bin Laden forms al Qaeda terrorist network.

1989 Iran's Khomeini calls for murder of Salmon Rushdie for his allegedly blasphemous depiction of Mohammed in *The Satanic Verses.*

1990s *Al Qaeda, other Islamist groups shift from national liberation to terrorism.*

1995 Algerian terrorists bomb Paris Metro.

1998 Al Qaeda calls on Muslims to kill Americans and their allies.

2000s *Islamist terrorists target Europe.*

Sept. 11, 2001 Terrorists attack World Trade Center and Pentagon.

December 2001 British Muslim Richard Reid tries to ignite "shoe bomb" aboard Paris-Miami flight.

2004 France bans Muslim head scarves in public schools. . . . Muslim terrorists kill 191 people in Madrid subway bombing. . . . Radical Islamist kills Dutch filmmaker Theo Van Gogh.

2005 London transit bombings kill 52. . . . Riots erupt in Muslim suburbs of Paris, other French cities.

2006 Danish cartoonist's depictions of Mohammed provoke protests worldwide. . . . Group of 23 mostly British Muslims are arrested on Aug. 10 on suspicion of planning to blow up transatlantic planes. . . . On Sept. 1 Muslims are arrested for running a terrorist camp in Sussex, Britain. . . . Britain expands detention powers against suspected terrorists.

2007 Europe and U.S. reported to be targets of revived al Qaeda. . . . Eight Muslims charged in failed car bombings in London, Glasgow; Bombing plots foiled in Germany, Denmark. British Prime Minister Gordon Brown proposes longer detention for terror suspects; British government encourages expansion of Muslim schools. . . . Spanish court convicts 21 in connection with 2004 Madrid train bombing; clears 3 alleged leaders.

Outspoken multiculturalism critic Kenan Malik, an Indian-born writer and lecturer living in London, complains government leaders were "subcontracting out" their relationship with Muslim citizens by dealing almost exclusively with clerics or official groups like the British Muslim Council, which has been accused of having radical links. And in a report published last year, journalist Bright criticized government officials for championing a group that promotes "a highly politicised version of Islam." [41]

"Why should British citizens who happen to be Muslim rely on clerics?" Malik asks. "It encourages Muslims to see themselves as semi-detached Britons."

Many French experts tend to agree the British laissez faire approach to multiculturalism failed because the government "created a higher identification with the [religious] group and left all authority with the religious leaders," in the words of Riva Kastoryano, a senior research fellow at the University of Paris' National Center for Scientific Research, who has written a book on multiculturalism in Europe.

Indeed, when it comes to local government funding, Malik said, "multiculturalism has helped to segregate communities far more effectively than racism." [42]

For example, during the 2005 Birmingham riots in Britain, blacks and Asians turned against one another. But 20 years earlier, black and Asian youths had joined together in riots there to protest police harassment and poverty. What changed, according to Malik, was the local government's "multicultural response" — setting up consultation groups and allocating funding along faith lines. "Different groups started fighting one another for funding, and the friction led to the riots between the two communities" in 2005, he says.

But the University of Birmingham's Abbas claims the 2005 riots were triggered by economic issues, ignited by a bogus radio story about a 14-year-old Caribbean girl who supposedly had been raped repeatedly by several Asian men. Abbas says that urban legend fed existing resentments over Asian takeovers of traditionally Caribbean businesses, like hair salons, in an area already suffering from declining jobs and ethnic rivalry over the drug market.

"It had nothing to do with multiculturalism," says Abbas.

Multiculturalism is more of an ideal about how to approach diversity and rid the country of its historic colonial baggage rather than a specific policy, in Abbas' view. To the extent it's been tried it varies greatly from one city to another, he stresses. "Multiculturalism hasn't been given its full testing period yet," he says. "We cannot easily say that because of multiculturalism we have the problems we have."

Would cracking down on terrorism violate civil liberties?

After the most recent foiled bombing plots in Britain, the Labor government proposed extending from 28 days to up to 56 days the period police can hold terrorist suspects without charge — a proposal opposed by both the Conservative and the Liberal Democratic parties.

The government says plots have become so complicated that police need more time to investigate. According to British police, big terrorism cases against one or two suspects can involve the investigation of 200 phones, 400 computers, 8,000 CDs, 6,000 gigabytes of data and 70 premises across three continents. [43]

In unveiling his anti-terror measures, Prime Minister Gordon Brown anticipated resistance from Parliament, which two years earlier had ratcheted down Blair's 90-day detention proposal to 28 days — a doubling of the then-14-day detention period.

"Liberty is the first and founding value of our country," Brown said. "Security is the first duty of our government." [44]

But Human Rights Watch says the extension would violate human rights law. The proposed 28 days is still more than twice as much as any other European country, and the government now releases more than half those accused in terrorism cases without charge, the group points out. [45]

Longer detentions would "clearly discriminate" against Muslim communities and be "counterproductive in making Muslims willing to cooperate with police" because they arouse such resentment, says Ben Ward, associate director for Europe and Central Asia at Human Rights Watch in London. Polls show that more than half of British Muslims already lack confidence in the police, he says. Muslim groups like the Muslim Council of Britain oppose the extension on similar grounds.

Allowing telephone wiretap evidence in court — another change being considered by the government — would be more effective in pursuing terrorist cases, says Ward. Britain is the only Western country that bans wiretap evidence in criminal prosecutions, he says, because its security services oppose revealing their methods.

What Makes a Person "British"?

Stereotypical views are challenged

At a North London pub, young professionals with pints in hand were engaged in a favorite national pastime — the Pub Quiz, a competition usually focused on trivia or sports.

But this quiz was different: It came from the test immigrants must take when applying for citizenship — popularly known as the "Britishness test." The 24-question exam was introduced in 2005 after former Home Secretary David Blunkett insisted that new immigrants should have a command of the English language and understand the nature of British life, customs and culture.

Not one of the 100 (mostly British) volunteers passed, an announcement greeted with applause, hilarity and shouts of "Deported!"

Teams with ad hoc names — like "As British as a pint of Guinness" — competed to answer such questions as, How many members are in Northern Ireland's Assembly? Who is the monarch not allowed to marry? and, curiously, What proportion of the United Kingdom population has used illegal drugs?

The highest score was 17, by Rohan Thanotheran, a Sri Lanka-born accountant who has lived in England since 1962. [1]

"Who would bother to learn those facts?" he asked later, suggesting the quiz was a desperate attempt by the government to reclaim nationalism at a time when symbols like the English flag are being hijacked by the far right.

Pub-goers are not the only British citizens who have failed. Member of Parliament Mike Gapes — who has supported the test, saying, "Nationalism is something that should be earned and not just given away" — flunked when 10 of the questions were posed to him during an interview. [2]

The test has been criticized for lengthening the application process and promoting a "siege mentality" among Britons towards foreigners. [3]

Many young people in the pub clearly found the questions comical, and several questioned the very idea of testing someone's "Britishness."

"The meaning of citizenship is not about knowing what percent of Christians in the U.K. are Catholics. Those are things most British citizens don't know. It doesn't make us any less British," said Munira Mirza, a writer, graduate student and founding member of The Manifesto Club, which organized the event to challenge stereotypical views of identity and Britishness.

A slim 29-year-old with shoulder-length black hair, Mirza was born in England of Pakistani Muslim parents. She describes herself as British-Asian but is quick to add that such ethnic and religious labels are "increasingly irrelevant to people, especially of my age, who grow up here and don't think of ourselves as ethnic categories." For example, she resists requests from TV producers to present the Muslim point of view. "You know what they're thinking: 'Only Muslims can connect with other Muslims.' It's quite a close-minded view," she says.

Two other quiz-takers from Muslim backgrounds in this distinctly secular crowd said they sometimes felt forced

Of all the counterterrorism measures being proposed in Europe, Human Rights Watch is "most concerned" about the United Kingdom, says Ward. But when it comes to existing practice, many experts consider France the most draconian.

From September 2001 to September 2006, France deported more than 70 people it considers "Islamic fundamentalists," including 15 Muslim imams, according to a recent Human Rights Watch report. [46]

The advocacy group argues that deportations require a much lower standard of evidence than judicial prosecutions and violate human rights because they often expose deportees to torture in their home countries. "Our point is not that all these guys are completely innocent, but even if someone is guilty of involvement in terrorism, France has a duty to make sure they're not sending them back to a place where they're facing threat of torture" — a serious risk even for an innocent person returned home once he's slapped with a terrorist label, says Judith Sunderland, author of the Human Rights Watch report on France's deportations.

"When we talk to people in Muslim communities, there's a lot of fear; they know they're being watched, and they're concerned about what they can say," says

to identify with their parents' foreign heritage because English peers persisted in seeing them as foreigners.

Lani Homeri, 26, a fashionably dressed law student with striking dark eyes and long raven hair, was born in Britain of Iraqi Kurdish parents who emigrated in the 1970s. She finds it odd how frequently she is asked whether she is Muslim, especially, she says, since she wears Western clothing and is "not a practicing Muslim."

A 28-year-old male pub-goer born in Sweden of Iranian parents who had fled the Islamic revolution said hostile questions about Islam from native-born Britons often made him defensive. "I'm agnostic, but when people attack Islam, I start defending it, even though it messed up my country," he said. "People like me, who want a secular government, start to protect their government because it's attacked on stupid grounds."

Misperceptions about Islam could help explain a recent poll conducted by Harris Interactive for the *Financial Times*, which found the British are more suspicious of Muslims than other Europeans or Americans. Only 59 per cent of Britons thought it possible to be both a Muslim and a citizen of their country, a smaller proportion than in France, Germany, Spain, Italy or the United States. [4]

Although the poll was taken before the foiled attacks in London and Glasgow in June, the memory of previous attacks, like the 7/7 transit bombings of July 7, 2005, may have hardened British attitudes. British citizens were also the most likely to predict a major terrorist attack in their country in the next 12 months, to consider Muslims a threat to national security and to believe Muslims had too much political power in their country. [5]

Mirza says those polls didn't reflect her own experience living in Britain. But she blames a "multicultural ethos" for forcing people to increasingly identify themselves with a particular ethnic or religious community, whether it is students taught to identify with people of their own race in history class or community leaders jockeying with ethnic groups for government funding.

A report Mirza coauthored for the London think tank Policy Exchange blames the methods Britain uses to encourage multiculturalism — such as providing local funding that can only be claimed by groups defined by ethnic or religious identity — for nurturing "a culture of victimhood" among Muslims, laying the groundwork for young people to turn to Muslim political groups. [6]

The rise of extremist groups is somewhat understandable "at a time when other political identities like 'left' and 'right' are not very appealing," Mirza observes, noting that young people are also gravitating to other forms of extremism, such as violence in the name of animal rights.

"We should be winning these young people over to other ideas," she says. "Unless you deal with that major problem, you will always find people will turn to something else that's offering a vision."

[1] Justin Gest, "How Many of 100 Britons Passed the Citizenship Exam? Not One," Sept. 29, 2007, *The Times* (London), www.timesonline.co.uk/tol/news/uk/article2554235.ece.

[2] Daniel Adam, "Redbridge Fails Britishness Test," *Rising East*, May 2006, www.uel.ac.uk/risingeast/archive04/journalism/adam.htm.

[3] *Ibid.*

[4] Daniel Dombey and Simon Kuper, "Britons 'More Suspicious' of Muslims," *Financial Times*, Aug. 19, 2007, www.FT.com.

[5] *Ibid.*

[6] Munira Mirza, *et al.*, "Living Apart Together: British Muslims and the Paradox of Multiculturalism," *Policy Exchange*, 2007, p. 18.

Sunderland. "We spoke to imams who said anytime they say anything in defense of someone accused of terrorism, they know they will be on someone's watch list." This fear erodes Muslims' trust in law enforcement and makes them less willing to cooperate in terrorism cases, she says.

But Godard, the adviser to the French Interior Ministry who has served as a specialist on Arab communities in both the national police and security services, dismisses her concerns. "Fifteen imams [removed] in 10 years — it's nothing," he says with a shrug.

Human Rights Watch is also concerned about France's use of its "criminal conspiracy" charge, which it says requires a low standard of evidence. "People are being detained for up to two years on very flimsy evidence," says Ward.

Godard shares this concern, complaining that the prosecutorial judges in France's special terrorism courts have "too much power" and that the source of evidence is not made public.

But many French citizens are happy with the system because they think it has kept them safe from terrorism, concedes Sunderland. France's surveillance system may curtail civil liberties, agrees Kastoryano, at the National Center for Scientific Research, but she adds, "This debate is in America, not here; no one here will talk about civil liberties."

As for the government's contention that its spying, secret files, deportations and special courts have been effective against terrorism, Sunderland says, "We don't have the information the French intelligence services have and have no way of verifying if they dismantled terrorist networks and prevented specific attacks, which is what the French government repeatedly claims."

When someone appeals a deportation in France, the only thing the government provides is an unsigned and undated "white paper" summarizing intelligence information, Sunderland says, "but not the sources or methodology, and the defendant can't go behind the information and figure out where it's coming from."

Proponents of expanded powers for the state argue that an exaggerated concern for human rights in England has inhibited authorities from pursuing terrorist suspects compared to France.

After France's experience with terrorists in the mid-1980s, new legislation extended the detention period for suspects. Using the 1986 law, the French "cleaned out outsiders, and the [radicals] went to Britain if they didn't go to jail," claims the Nixon Center's Leiken. By 1994, "that was a big problem in Britain."

By contrast, Britain's 30 years of experience with the Irish Republican Army (IRA) left British police unprepared for today's brand of Islamic terrorism, with no foreign-intelligence capacity and insufficient time to investigate the computer technology used by Islamic plotters, according to Peter Clarke, head of the Metropolitan Police Counter Terrorism Command. That inexperience was evident in the police shooting in the London underground of Brazilian electrician Jean Charles de Menezes on July 22, 2005, mistaken for one of the terrorists who had tried to detonate bombs on London's transit system the day before. The London Metropolitan police force was found guilty Nov. 1 of putting the public at risk during the bungled operation.

Unlike the IRA, Clarke says, today's terrorism threat is global, with players willing to die who are quickly replaced. Networks re-form quickly, no warnings are given and weaponry (like fertilizer bombs) is unconventional, he says. [47]

He cites the case of Dhiren Barot, an al Qaeda plotter who left plans on his laptop computer for killing thousands of people in Britain (and the United States) by detonating underground bombs.

After Barot's arrest in 2004, British police had to "race against time" to retrieve enough evidence from the seized computers and other equipment to justify charges at the end of the permitted period of detention. [48] After that experience, the Terrorism Act of 2006 criminalized "acts preparatory to terrorism," and police proposed extending the period terrorist suspects can be held without charge. [49]

In addition, since 2001 British anti-terror laws have given the government — with public support — more leeway to mine databases for information about individuals. "There was an assumption that if it was necessary to hand over our privacy to the state to provide protection, that it was a price worth paying," says Gareth Crossman, policy director at Liberty, a London-based civil liberties advocacy group. Now, the country has so many cameras trained on citizens "the government's privacy watchdog describes England as 'the surveillance society.'" [50]

A recent Liberty report warns privacy could be invaded in the future because of the government's ability to mine data and watch people on the street. Surveillance cameras, more prevalent in Britain than any other country, are credited with tracing autos involved in past terrorist attempts. But Liberty wants the government to regulate where they're placed and how they're operated (many are installed by private companies) to protect ordinary citizens' privacy. [51]

Legislation passed in Britain would authorize a national ID card, though it hasn't been implemented and may never be because of the cost. But Crossman warns the government could use it to trawl through databases for personal information by profiling "the sort of person that might be involved in terrorist activity — purely on the basis of demographic information. It's a real minefield. A young, Muslim male is basically where it will end up. That's hugely sensitive."

BACKGROUND

Muslim Migration

Modern Muslim immigration to Europe began in the late 19th century as a result of Europe's colonial and trading activity, which largely explains the different ethnic groups in each country and to some extent their degree of acceptance by those societies.

The French conquest of Algiers in 1830 eventually led to French control of Algeria, Morocco and Tunisia. Together, British colonization of India (which included modern-day Pakistan and Bangladesh) and Dutch domination of trade in Asia gave the three European countries control over most of the world's Muslims.

At the end of the 19th century, immigration began on a large scale, as France imported low-paid workers from Algeria and other African territories and other countries recruited workers from their colonies and territories.

Following World War II, countries like England sought workers, including many Muslims, to help with reconstruction. By the 1960s, entire Muslim families had begun to settle in Europe.

By 1974, however, a global economic recession had led many countries to limit migration, allowing entry only for family reunification or political asylum. Paradoxically, the policy led to further immigration by families, the only means of entry. The recession also increased Europeans' resentment of immigrants and their children, who were viewed as competing for jobs.

During the 1980s, Muslims' religious identity became more pronounced as young Muslims — frustrated by job discrimination — turned to their religion as a source of identity. Islamic political movements in Iran, North Africa and South Asia also influenced this trend.

The rise of political Islam encouraged Muslims in Europe to form associations based on religion, which heightened Europeans' fears of Islam as growing numbers of Muslim refugees were arriving from wars in Iran, Iraq, Lebanon, Palestine and Bosnia. At this time, as rivalry broke out between different groups in Saudi Arabia, India, Pakistan and Iran for domination of

More Muslims Identify With Moderates

More than half of the Muslims in France and Great Britain believe a struggle is going on in their countries between moderate and fundamentalist Islamic ideologies (top). Those who see such a struggle identify overwhelmingly with the moderates (bottom). Britain has the largest percentage of Muslims identifying with the fundamentalists.

Do you see a struggle in your country between moderate Muslims and fundamentalists?

Muslims answering "yes" in . . .

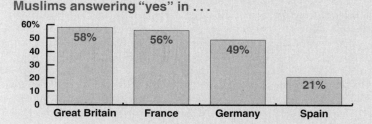

If so, do you identify more with moderates or fundamentalists?

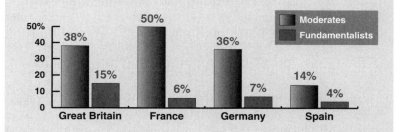

Source: "Muslims in Europe: Economic Worries Top Concerns About Religious and Cultural Identity," Pew Global Attitudes Project, July 2006

Muslim ideology, Europe became a target of missionary and proselytizing efforts, helped along by the distribution of petrodollars — mainly from Saudi Arabia — to create mosques, Islamic schools and even university chairs. [52]

Saudi money supported the spread and teaching of the Wahhabi strand of Islam, the official religion of Saudi Arabia and the guiding spiritual doctrine of al Qaeda. Wahhabism is a fundamentalist form of Islam that preaches strict adherence to Islam's injunctions, including abiding by sharia law.

Radical Mosque Says It Has Changed

But skeptics say its hard-core views are hidden

The atmosphere at the East London Mosque during a dinner held recently with non-Muslim neighbors could not have been more congenial or ecumenical. Ministers from a local interfaith group and executives in suits from a local hospital philanthropy joined bearded Muslims in skullcaps over plates of Indian food as they broke the Ramadan fast. They had just listened to a mosque lecturer declare, "We're all children of Adam" and "The meaning of Islam isn't terrorism, destruction or violence."

But these reassurances seem at odds with the reputation the mosque developed in the 1990s as a center for radical, young Muslims. And some observers of the London Muslim scene say that beneath its smooth public relations efforts the mosque remains a major center for radical Islam.

"The East London Mosque is at the center of a very sophisticated Jamaat-e-Islami network in Britain," says Martin Bright, political editor for the left-leaning *New Statesman* magazine, referring to the extremist Islamic political party based in Pakistan. "It is essentially the dominant force in the formation of Islamist ideology in Britain — and Europe." Jamaat-e-Islami and other Islamists espouse an Islamic state governed by sharia law.

But on two recent visits to the mosque, including the imam's weekly Friday sermon, talk of radicalism was absent. Instead the imam admonished the congregation for giving too little to charity. ("You give rice, but it's probably not even Basmati.")

Sumaia Begum, 19, a Londoner of Bangladeshi parentage dressed in black from head scarf to figure-concealing skirt, had just listened to the sermon in the secluded second-floor women's section, crowded with Bangladeshis and Somalis in somber black head-coverings. She seemed unaware of the mosque's reputation. "I'd love to live in an Islamic state, but bombing innocent people here — that's

not right," she said. "Bearing and raising children — for us, that is our jihad."

Critics of Islamist ideology say mosques like East London often have two faces — a moderate one for the public and a hard-core ideology they might only reveal at summer indoctrination camps for young people.

"At the Friday sermon, which is open to the public, they would not preach hatred," says Irfan Al Alawi, international director of the Center for Islamic Pluralism, a London think tank that promotes religious tolerance. "They would have before 7/7" (the July 7, 2005, London transit bombings). "But when it became obvious they were being investigated because of links with jihadists in Pakistan, they became somewhat cautious."

Throughout the late 1980s, the mosque, located at the heart of London's densest Bangladeshi neighborhood, was home to rival Jamaat-e-Islami factions in Britain, according to British author Ed Husain, a former radical who says he first encountered extremist rhetoric at the mosque in the 1990s, when most of its committee members were affiliated with the movement. [1]

Today, he writes, the Saudi-trained imam of the big mosque continues to lead a faction opposed to modernizing elements and prohibits gatherings of opponents of Islamism and of the strict Saudi version of Islam — Wahhabism. [2]

But Dilowar Khan, the director of the mosque and the gleaming London Muslim Center next door (built with government, private and Saudi funding), says he and his fellow Muslims at the mosque, like Husain, have moved away from the separatist views espoused in the 1990s, with their single-minded focus on replacing secular regimes in the Muslim world with religious states.

Back then, people were interested in Bangladeshi politics, in which Jamaat-e-Islami was very active, he explains.

As Harvard's Cesari explains, since Sept. 11 the apolitical nature of fundamentalist groups has been increasingly questioned as these groups have radicalized their rhetoric against non-Muslims and the West. These movements preach "a theology of intolerance" — referring to all non-Muslims as *kaffir* (or infidel) and aspects

of modern life as *haram* (forbidden) — "which can easily become . . . a theology of hate," she writes. Since the 1967 Israeli victory over the Arabs, a feeling of humiliation has combined with a warlike insistence on Islam's superiority over everything Western, democratic and secular. [53]

"Now we're more interested in how to improve our life and image here." For instance, he says, the mosque invites local political candidates as speakers and offers various services, ranging from job counseling to computer education.

While the mosque still may have members who are Wahhabis or followers of Jamaat, it does not define itself by any of those sects, according to Khan. He denies any "formal links" to those groups or to the Tablighi-Jamaat, a hard-line Islamic missionary movement that Al Alawi says has also captured much of the mosque's leadership.

As for Jamaat-e-Islami's central mission — to establish a Muslim state — Khan says, "We believe Islam is a complete code of life. . . . What's wrong with a Muslim country establishing an Islamic state by majority rule?"

What about the party's call for establishing sharia rule? "We're not interested in implementing sharia law in this country," he claims. "If the majority of people in Muslim countries want to implement certain laws in their own country, who am I to tell them, 'Don't do that'?" Later, he emphasized that sharia is the very essence of the religion, adding, "People who are against sharia law are enemies of Islam."

Does he advocate sharia courts like those in Nigeria, which order the amputation of limbs and stoning of women as punishments straight from the *Koran*? "That's only about 1 percent of sharia law," he says, which refers to the vast body of religious observance in Islam, including fasting at Ramadan.

Hisham A. Hellyer, an expert on counterterrorism at the University of Warwick and a former visiting fellow at the Washington-based Brookings Institution think tank, says that while Jamaat-e-Islami did have a presence in Britain's activist groups in the 1980s because of members' involvement in their home countries, "It's a bit of a stretch to say they were the direct wings of these organizations in the U.K." He points out, "It's not unusual for politicians in Britain to have been communists as students, but they mature and grow up. That's what happened to leaders in the Muslim community."

Muslim religious attire is common in the Bangladeshi East London neighborhood of Whitechapel, home to the East London Mosque, one of Britain's largest.

A recent TV documentary dramatized the perception that Muslim mosques are not always what they seem, reporting that Muslim clerics engaged in far more radical language — justifying terrorist bombings, for instance — in private meetings than in public sermons. Since the broadcast, however, some clerics have charged their words were taken out of context. The complaints are being investigated by Britain's broadcasting watchdog. [3]

Such charges and countercharges reflect a problem that Jason Burke, a veteran reporter on the Muslim world for the *British Observer* (of London), says "confronts me daily as a journalist working in the field. Who are our interlocutors? Whose voices best represent the complex, diverse and dynamic societies that are bundled together in that terrible generalization, the 'Muslim world'?" [4]

---

[1] Ed Husain, *The Islamist* (2007), p. 24.

[2] *Ibid.*, p. 280.

[3] BBC, "C4 Distorted Mosque Programme," Aug. 8, 2007, http://news.bbc.co.uk/1/hi/englan.

[4] Preface by Jason Burke in Martin Bright, "When Progressives Treat with Reactionaries," *Policy Exchange*, 2006, p. 7.

Individual acts of political terrorism in the 1990s and early 2000s fueled fears of radical Islam in Europe. Between 1995 and 1996, a radical Algerian group seeking an Islamic state in Algeria set off bombs on Paris subways and trains. And, prior to the 1998 World Cup soccer tournament in France, the French arrested 100 members of the group in a

preventive action. Radical preachers in Paris and London began to attract young Muslims from the poorer suburbs and cities. Some went to fight in Afghanistan or Iraq, while a few committed terrorist acts at home.

Increased immigration from Muslim countries and high birthrates combined to make Islam the fastest-

Railway workers and police in Madrid examine a train destroyed in a terrorist bombing in March 2004 that killed 191 and injured thousands. In late October, 21 of the 29 people charged were found guilty, including North African men from Algeria, Tunisia and Morocco.

growing religion on the continent, even as ethnic and religious tensions grew. In October 2005 riots erupted in the Muslim suburbs of Paris and other French cities, with the participants complaining of joblessness and discrimination. Muslims also demonstrated against the proposed ban on Muslim girls wearing head scarves at school, which took effect in 2004.

The Madrid train bombings, the 2004 assassination of Dutch filmmaker Theo Van Gogh by a Dutch-Moroccan and the 2005 London subway explosions — all committed by radical Muslims — led European countries to question how well they were integrating Muslim immigrants and their children.

Anthropologist Bowen attributes the differences in how Muslim communities have been absorbed and the types of politics they've adopted in various European countries to the different ways each country treated its colonies and immigrants from those colonies.

In France, Muslim immigrants are clustered in poor, outer suburbs that include a mix of North Africans — such as Algerians, Moroccans and Tunisians — all of whom speak French and grew up under French rule. North Africans often arrived feeling that they were quasi-French citizens, even if they were second-class citizens, says Bowen.

But in Britain many Muslims live in ethnic enclaves in Bangladeshi or Pakistani neighborhoods where Bengali is spoken in stores and banks, and parents of London-born children often speak no English. As

schools in these neighborhoods become 100 percent Asian, some educators are concerned the teaching of English as a first language is being thwarted. [54]

"The French [immigration] story goes back to the beginning of the 20th century," Bowen adds, "whereas in Britain the immigration is much more recent, and the communities are much more closed off."

In addition, he notes, "The French kids from North Africa are more tied into the Muslim Brotherhood, which says, 'Obey the laws of the country you're in, and try to create conditions to live as a Muslim.' There's none of this talk about creating a separate Islamic state that [the radical group] Hizb-ut-Tahrir runs on."

"Londonistan"

The shift to religiously oriented politics in Britain took place in the 1980s and '90s with the increasing embrace of identity politics and the arrival of Islamist political refugees.

After the 1981 rioting in the impoverished Brixton neighborhood of south London, the Scarman Report called for a multiracial, multicultural approach that would recognize the uniquely different needs of ethnic groups. National and local governments awarded funds to groups identifying themselves as ethnic or racial minorities, including ethnic housing associations, arts centers, radio channels and voluntary organizations. Local governments helped set up representative bodies to consult with Muslims over local issues. The funding of conservative religious organizations like the East London Mosque sometimes came at the expense of secular groups, say critics. [55]

The Rushdie affair led to a seminal moment in Muslim identity politics. In 1988 author Salman Rushdie's novel *The Satanic Verses* infuriated Muslims who felt it ridiculed the Prophet Mohammed. British Muslims formed the U.K. Action Committee on Islamic Affairs to protest the perceived blasphemy. Eventually Iran's supreme religious leader, the late Ayatollah Khomeini, issued a religious edict known as a *fatwa* condemning Rushdie to death. But the anti-Rushdie campaign was led primarily from Pakistan by disciples of the deceased Islamist ideologue Abul A'la Maududi, who founded the Jamaat-e-Islami party in India in 1941.

Book burnings in Bradford, England, widely covered by the media, also raised the profile of radical Islamism among young Muslims. The first Gulf War, the Palestinian intifadas of the late 1980s and early '90s and the slaughter of Muslims in Bosnia also discomfited Muslims about their loyalties.

Radical Islam in Britain has evolved under the influence of Islamist groups operating from Pakistan, Bangladesh and the Middle East. According to Policy Exchange, the conservative think tank in London, money poured in from Saudi Arabia and Pakistan for new religious, publishing and education facilities in Britain, shifting the balance "from more traditional and apolitical Muslim organisations toward more internationalist and politically radical groups," especially those leaning toward Wahhabism. [56]

Indeed, as France and other nations forced Islamists to leave in the 1990s, members of the French secret service dubbed the British capital "Londonistan" for its role as a refuge for Islamist groups. [57]

In the weeks following the attacks on the World Trade Center and the Pentagon, many mainstream British news organizations — including the *Guardian* — accepted that the attacks were a response to suffering in the Palestinian territories and to American support of Israel. In interviews, young British Muslims said 9/11 and later the London bombings of 2005 made them identify as Muslims more than they had before. After the Iraq War started in 2003, Islamists joined with left-wing groups and created the Respect Party on an anti-war platform. "Radical Islam's narrative of the victimised *ummah* [Muslim community] has drawn sustenance from broader public anger at U.S. and U.K. foreign policy," says Policy Exchange. [58]

Terrorist Attacks

The current wave of terrorism can be traced to Feb. 23, 1998, when al Qaeda issued a *fatwa* stating that all Muslims had a duty to kill Americans and their allies — civilian or military. Islamic liberation movements began to shift their emphasis to localized, violent jihad. [59]

The Sept. 11, 2001, attacks were directly tied to al Qaeda, as was the attempt three months later by British-born Muslim Richard Reid to blow up an American Airlines flight from Paris to Miami by lighting explosives in his shoes.

Twenty-nine Muslims living in Spain — including first-generation North Africans from Algeria, Tunisia and Morocco — were charged in connection with the March 2004 bombing of four Madrid trains at rush hour, which killed 191 people and injured more than 1,800. [60] The group included petty drug traffickers as well as university students. Jamal Ahmidan, the plot's Moroccan mastermind, was said to be happily integrated into Spanish society. In October, a Spanish court found 21 people guilty of involvement in the bombing, but three alleged leaders were cleared. [61]

That November, Dutch filmmaker Van Gogh, who had made a film critical of Islam's treatment of women, was stabbed to death on an Amsterdam street by Mohammed Bouyeri, 26, the Amsterdam-born son of Moroccans. Bouyeri, whose radicalism began during a seven-month period in prison, belonged to the Hofsted Group, which had considered bombing the Dutch parliament. [62]

Until the most recent plots, post-2001 terrorist attempts in Europe had been seen as independently planned, even if the organizers took their inspiration from al Qaeda. That appears to have been the case in the 2005 London bus and subway suicide-bomb attacks. The first attack, on July 7, involved four British Muslims — three Pakistanis from West Yorkshire and an Afro-Caribbean Muslim convert. All four had Westernized, unremarkable backgrounds, according to the NYPD. A second attack, intended for three underground trains and a bus on July 21, failed because the bombs did not detonate.

On Aug. 10, 2006, 23 individuals — most British citizens and nearly all Muslim — were arrested on suspicion of plotting to blow up transatlantic airliners using liquid explosives. Three weeks later a group of Muslims was arrested for running a terrorist training camp at a former convent school in Sussex. A total of 68 people were arrested, and al Qaeda is suspected of being centrally involved in the bomb plot. [63]

Several doctors in England were arrested in two incidents — trying to blow up cars near a London nightclub on June 29 and driving a burning jeep into the Glasgow airport the next day.

Although the Sept. 11, 2001, attacks were directed by al Qaeda, they were planned by a group of English-speaking Muslims at a mosque in Hamburg, where they had been radicalized.

"Without a group of radicalized jihadists who had been homegrown in the West to lead this plot, the chances of 9/11 being a success would have been reduced considerably," concluded the NYPD intelligence report. "The Hamburg group underwent a process of homegrown radicalization that matched almost exactly those of Madrid, London, Amsterdam."

British writer Ed Husain describes his recruitment in the 1990s in London by radical Islamists in his 2007 memoir. Today Husain, a former member of the group Hizb ut-Rahrir, remains skeptical of its nonviolent stance.

But unlike the 7/7 bombers who attacked London, the NYPD observes, when members of the Hamburg group went to Afghanistan to fight, they were re-directed to another target in the West, not to their place of residence. [64]

The North London Central Mosque, better known as the Finsbury Park Mosque, became infamous in the early 2000s for its support of radical Islam under the leadership of its fiery imam, Abu Hamza al-Masri. The mosque's attendees included shoe bomber Reid and 9/11 conspirator Zacarias Moussaoui. After British police raided the mosque on Jan. 20, 2003, it eventually was reclaimed by mainstream Muslims.

However, the London-based think tank Policy Exchange found extremist anti-Western, anti-Semitic literature at the mosque and claims a mosque trustee has said he is prepared to be a suicide bomber against Israel, according to a report released Oct. 30. [65]

Since the 2003 raid, law enforcement and security forces have tried to work with other mosque leaders to prevent the incitement to violence that emanated from Finsbury Park and other Salafi mosques in London in the 1990s. * Among the most notorious clerics were:

---

* Salafi is a term applied broadly to sects that adhere to a supposedly pure form of Islam that they believe was practiced by Islam's ancestors; it often refers to Wahhabis and sometimes to Deobandis, the Muslim Brotherhood and Jamaat-e-Islami.

- Al-Masri, who was sentenced to seven years for incitement to murder in February 2006;
- Abdullah el-Faisal, a Jamaican-born convert sentenced to nine years in 2003 for soliciting the murder of Jews, Americans and Hindus and inciting racial hatred. [66]
- Syrian-born self-styled cleric Omar Bakri Mohammed, who helped establish the radical group Al Muhajiroun and called the 9/11 hijackers the "Magnificent 19," has been banned from Britain and currently lives abroad. [67]

Action against radical clerics was authorized by amendments to Britain's Terrorism Act adopted in 2001, 2005 and 2006, which expanded the definition of terrorist offenses. The most recent changes criminalized "incitement to terrorism," providing assistance to terrorists and providing instruction in the use of firearms and explosives. The British government also has been given greater ability to ban political groups. Last year it considered banning both Hizb ut-Tahrir and Al Muhajiroun, which are both active on college campuses. [68]

CURRENT SITUATION

Worsening Threat

The recent string of disrupted plots in Europe signals a "continuing and worsening" radicalization within Europe's Islamic diaspora and a renewed leadership role for al Qaeda, according to a recent report from the International Institute for Strategic Studies (IISS), a leading security think tank in London. Al Qaeda has regrouped as an organization and now has the capacity to carry out another 9/11-magnitude attack, according to the IISS. [69]

Britain is considered the main target, with up to 30 terrorist plots discovered there — some that would have involved mass-casualty suicide attacks, said British intelligence officials last November. [70] Al Qaeda's Pakistan-based leadership was directing its British followers "on an extensive and growing scale," the officials said, and British authorities said they have their eye on 2,000 individuals involved in such plots. In fact, said Britain's domestic intelligence chief Jonathan Evans on Nov. 5, terrorist recruitment is accelerating so quickly that there could now be twice that many — up to 4,000 — potential terrorists living in Britain. Terrorists are grooming British youths as young as 15 to aid in terrorism and

Should the British government fund Muslim faith schools?

YES   Ibrahim Hewitt
Vice Chairman, Association of Muslim Schools, U.K.

Written for *CQ Researcher*, October 2007

The right of any group to establish a school and have it paid for by the state is enshrined in the 1944 Education Act. This is not limited to people of any particular religious or political background. Section 76 of the act goes on to say that "pupils are to be educated in accordance with the wishes of their parents." These provisions grew out of a compromise between church and state concerning the church-run schools then in operation. The state took over control of some of the schools while leaving others more or less in the control of the church. That is the context in which the state funding of Muslim schools exists.

Critics of faith schools — read "Muslim schools" — claim state funding is a historical anomaly that should be abolished. Proponents believe that parental choice has a firm basis in history, as made clear by Section 76. Choice has long been exercised by Anglican, Roman Catholic and Jewish parents, to little or no criticism. Now, many of the criticisms of faith schools are surfacing with the existence of Muslim schools, which were established by parents not unreasonably asking for the same choice in return for paying the same taxes toward education as everyone else.

Faith plays a hugely important part in the life of most Muslims — the notion of a "secular Muslim" is actually a contradiction in terms — and we are enjoined by the *Qu'ran* to "enter into Islam wholeheartedly" and not make any differentiation between religious and secular. It follows, therefore, that the education of our children should be within a framework that recognizes the existence and importance of their faith background.

As parents, we have a legal, moral and religious duty to raise and educate our children to become upright and honest citizens. The fact that the law of the land encourages the existence of faith schools as a core education provision in Britain means that parents from all faiths and none have a choice about their children's schools. Those who would have all schools as religion-free zones offer no such choice while overlooking conveniently that a secular approach is not a neutral approach; it is a conscious desire to remove religion from public life — hardly tolerant in a society where many faiths are represented across different communities.

Human-rights legislation makes clear that people should have freedom of religion; to insist on schools in which faith is the only forbidden f-word is both unreasonable and undemocratic. Muslims' taxes pay for schools of all faiths and none, so why shouldn't some of those taxes be used to fund Muslim schools as well?

NO   Terry Sanderson
President, National Secular Society

Written for *CQ Researcher*, October 2007

In a country increasingly divided by religion, the prospect of a hundred or more Muslim schools being brought into the state sector is truly terrifying. The British government, by some upside-down logic, has convinced itself that separating children in schools along religious lines will somehow help create "community cohesion."

The government clings to this opinion in the face of all the evidence. Its own advisers have said Muslim communities are "leading parallel lives," that we as a nation are "sleepwalking into segregation" and that segregated schools are a "ticking time bomb."

At present, there are seven Muslim schools paid for by the state. The rest are operating privately. There is little control over what goes on in the fee-paying schools, and the government argues that by bringing them under state control it would be easier to oversee them and ensure that they teach the national curriculum to an acceptable standard.

But the Muslim parents who took their children out of the state system in the first place did so because they felt that what the state offered was not what they wanted. If the state is not going to provide the strictly Islamic education they desire for their children, then they will simply opt out again and set up more private schools. The state will have to compromise if it wants these people on board.

So, rather than the national curriculum changing Muslim schools, it will be Muslim schools that force the national curriculum to change. Before long we will have schools where girls are forced to wear veils. (This has already been advocated by a leading Muslim educator, even for non-Muslim pupils who might seek a place in the school.) We will have state schools where swimming lessons are not permitted, where male teachers cannot teach girls, where there is no music, no representative art and no sporting activities for females unless they are "modestly dressed" in flowing garments.

Because the Church of England and the Catholic Church have traditionally operated about one-third of Britain's state school system, it is now difficult to argue that other religions should not be permitted to have their own "faith schools." But by permitting Islamic schools into the state system, the government is colluding in the very thing it insists it is against — the further separation of an already-isolated community.

The only way out of this unholy mess is to dismantle the whole system of state-operated religious schools and return them to community control.

have expanded their training bases beyond Pakistan, specifically to Somalia and other areas in East Africa. [71]

Meanwhile, U.S. officials fear Europe's terrorist problems could be exported to the United States because of the ease with which Europeans travel to America. "When you talk to intelligence officials, that's their nightmare," says the Nixon Center's Leiken.

Intelligence officials in Denmark and Washington said at least one suspect in the abortive Copenhagen bombing had direct ties to leading al Qaeda figures. Jakob Scharf, head of Danish intelligence, said Muslim extremists typically are young men, ages 16-25, courted by mentors who identify those predisposed toward a jihadi mindset, radicalize them and put them in touch with others who could help them plan violent action. Denmark became the target of terrorist groups after a conservative Danish newspaper published cartoons two years ago widely seen as mocking Islam. [72]

Fertile Ground

In the past two decades, Europe and the United States have become "crucial battlegrounds" in the rapidly intensifying competition between groups in Saudi Arabia, India, Pakistan and Iran for control of Muslim ideology, according to Harvard's Cesari. [73]

The Saudis spent an estimated $85 billion between 1975 and 2005 to spread fundamentalist Islam by distributing Wahhabi prayer books, dispatching missionaries and imams and building grand mosques in Madrid, Rome, Copenhagen and Great Britain. [74]

The report released last week by *Policy Exchange* found extremist literature — preaching stoning of adulterers, jihad and hatred for non-Muslims — at a quarter of 100 leading mosques and educational institutions visited in England, including the East London Mosque. (*See sidebar, p. 122.*) Much of the material was distributed by Saudi organizations, found in Saudi-funded institutions or written by members of the Wahhabi religious establishment, the report said.

Historically, there have been two paths to violent extremism, notes Brandeis University's Klausen. A political movement seeking Islamic sovereignty includes the Muslim Brotherhood, the Pakistani party Jamaat-e-Islami, Hizb ut-Tahrir, Hamas and Al Muhajiroun.

Competing with them are puritanical groups like the Deobandi sect and the ultra-conservative Tablighi-Jamaat movement, which consider "recent" innovations, such as

the mystically oriented practices of the Sufi Muslims and the worship of saints, as impermissible. Like the political groups, these groups glorify suicide but tend to stress theological and moral, rather than political, arguments.

Europe may have proven fertile ground for strict interpretations of Islam, according to Cesari, because some Muslims react to the bewildering range of moral choices in today's globalized Western society with a certain "rigidity of thought and total rejections of cultural pluralism." [75]

But the variety of those arrested for terrorism in recent years suggests there are many reasons young Muslims are drawn to radicalism. For example, about 9 percent are converts, who might have been drawn to other kinds of radical political groups in another era. [76]

For author Husain, one of the few ex-radicals to publicly describe his journey into that world, "it was the serious lack of a sense of belonging here in Britain. We're all left alone like atoms to do our own thing. There's no collective entity. In that vacuum, extremists point to other coherent forms of identity, which are very easy to sign up to."

Questioning Integration

As concern about radical extremism grows, some European governments are rethinking their approach to integrating Muslims and are demanding more from immigrants who want citizenship, including acceptance of their national values.

"It's clear the Dutch and British laissez faire models have outlived their usefulness," says Laurence of Boston College. "No longer will a blank check be given to religious communities to govern themselves. It led to isolation in which a certain extremism thrived."

In the Netherlands the 90-year-old policy of "pillarization," which permits each faith to set up its own faith schools and organizations, is falling out of favor among the Dutch as they see their own socially progressive mores conflicting with Muslim values.

Increasingly, politicians on both the left and right in the Netherlands are saying about Muslims: "We have to be intolerant of the intolerant," says Jan Duyvendak, a professor of sociology at the University of Amsterdam. Applicants for citizenship are shown a film of topless women and two men kissing. The message it's supposed to send: "If you want to come to the Netherlands, you should be tolerant of this," he says.

Scandinavian countries also feel that their culture and values, including gender equality, are increasingly threatened by Muslim communities that "we have quite failed to integrate," Unni Wikan, a professor of social anthropology at the University of Oslo, told a panel recently in London. [77]

Several Scandinavian governments, for example, have outlawed forced marriages of minors, often imported from a Muslim man's native village or clan. In Norway participation in a forced marriage brings up to 60 years in prison. Denmark requires that spouses brought into the country be at least 24 years old. Other European countries are considering similar laws, says Wikan, because "we're afraid we're leading toward a society that's breaking up into ethnic tribes."

Scandinavians and the Dutch also have become concerned about honor killings of young Muslim women thought to have dishonored the clan. "That kind of honor code sacrifices women on the altar of culture," Wikan said. "We don't want such values to become part of Europe."

In France, President Nicolas Sarkozy, who campaigned on a law-and-order immigration platform, proposed DNA testing of immigrants' children seeking to enter the country to prove they're relatives. He has vowed to expel 25,000 illegal immigrants a year. Sarkozy would also set quotas by geographic regions of the world, an approach immigration historian Weil calls "xenophobic" and which he suspects would be focused on disliked minorities. Sarkozy's proposed immigration package will produce a "backlash from Arabs and blacks," Weil warns.

A Belgian proposal to take a tougher stance on immigration, pushed by parties of the right but increasingly adopted by mainstream parties, has been widely interpreted as targeting Muslims. [78]

Changing Course

A British government report earlier this year moved away from the language of multiculturalism, saying friendships with people from other ethnic groups are the best way to prevent prejudice. Prime Minister Brown has also said a sense of Britishness should be the "glue" tying different ethnic groups together. But some teachers are uncomfortable with new requirements that schools teach patriotism, because they are unsure what it is. [79]

After the foiled June plots in Britain and Glasgow, Brown proposed a three-year, $114-million program to win the hearts and minds of Muslims by conducting citizenship classes in Britain's 1,000 *madrasas* and English-language training for imams.

But Faiz Siddiqui, convenor of the Muslim Action Committee representing more than 700 mosques and imams in Britain, pointed out that "excessive sums of money" — by one estimate $14 billion over the last 25 years — were already coming into the country from Saudi Arabia and other countries to support "radical ideology." He also noted that some imams accused of inciting people to murder, like Abu Hamza, already spoke English. [80]

In an investigative report published last year, the New Statesman's Bright found that the British government's main partner in the Muslim community — the Muslim Council of Britain — had links to the religious right both at home and abroad. Leaked memos revealed that the government's decision to make the group its main link to the Muslim community had been heavily influenced by the British Foreign Office, which wanted to maintain connections with opposition movements abroad. [81]

After the report was published, then-Communities Secretary Kelly focused on reaching out to other groups in the community and halted communication altogether with the council, says Bright. One reason for the switch, she said, was the council's boycott of Britain's Holocaust Memorial Day. How Brown will eventually re-connect with the nation's Muslim community remains uncertain.

However, in a speech delivered Oct. 31, Brown's Communities Secretary Blears said the current government "remains absolutely committed" to Blair's shift in priority away from reliance on a few national organizations and toward Muslim groups "actively working to tackle violent extremism." [82]

Muslim Schools

Britain's education department in September recommended that the more than 100 private Muslim schools enter the state-supported system and that faith schools generally should be expanded. The proposal received a deeply divided response. [83] (*See "At Issue," p. 127.*)

The nation's teachers' union expressed concern that the proposal could further divide children ethnically. Moreover, there's no requirement that Muslim schools cover other religions in depth, "which we consider appropriate," said Alison Ryan, policy adviser to the Association of Teachers and Lecturers.

Some moderate Muslims worry the faith schools could become breeding grounds for extremism. Earlier this year, the principal of King Fahd Academy in London confirmed its textbooks described Jews as "apes" and Christians as "pigs" and refused to withdraw them. [84]

Almost half of Britain's mosques are under the control of the conservative Deobandis, who gave rise to the Taliban in Afghanistan, according to a police report cited by the *London Times* in September. [85] And many of them run after-school *madrasas* that could be expanded into state-funded faith schools, some moderate Muslims fear.

But even groups concerned about ethnic separateness acknowledge that a country that supports nearly 7,000 faith schools — mostly Church of England and Catholic — cannot discriminate against Muslims, who currently have only seven state-supported schools. [86] And some hope that with greater government oversight of the curriculum, any tendency toward extremism would be limited.

OUTLOOK

Encouraging Moderation

Concerned that its terrorism problem is largely homegrown, the British government is now trying to curb radicalism. Among other things, the government is trying to encourage moderation by creating a program to educate imams in communicating with young people to reject extremist views and minimum standards for Muslim clerics in prisons and other public institutions to give them the skills to confront and isolate extremists. It is also supporting local governments that are developing their own accreditation programs for imams employed in their city to help them deliver sermons in English, reach out to young people and resist extremist ideology. All these steps are part of a $114 million program announced by Communities Secretary Blears Oct. 31 to build resilience to violent extremism, including citizenship classes in mosque schools. [87]

The government is also using community-policing techniques to get to know Muslims in the neighborhoods where they think terrorists may be living. Dutch, Spanish and Danish authorities are closely watching Britain's approach to see if it stems the tide of radical recruitment.

Next year, a year-old government-backed group aimed at encouraging moderation in mosques, the Mosques and Imams Advisory Board, plans to issue a code of standards to allow its member mosques and imams to be supervised and regulated. The draft code, the Observer reported, would require members to offer programs "that actively combat all forms of violent extremism." Imams would also be expected to make clear to their followers that forced marriages are completely "unIslamic" — as is violence in domestic disputes. [88]

As Oxford University Professor of European Studies Timothy Garton Ash recently observed: "So much now depends on whether the 10 percent" who sympathize with suicide bombers "veer toward the barbaric 1 percent" who thought the London subway bombers were justified or "rejoin the civilized majority." [89]

But Klausen of Brandeis University says that while Britain's new approach has succeeded in establishing links to Muslim leaders, so far it "has failed to build trust among the general Muslim public." [90]

British author Husain says government officials mistakenly think they can deal with radical Islamists' demands rationally. Secular Western leaders have trouble connecting with the annihilation of the West as a religious duty, he says, because they "don't do God."

"Which Islamist demand do you want to do business with?" he asks. "The destruction of Israel? The overthrow of secular government? The establishment of the caliphate? I don't see any of those being up for negotiation," Husain says.

At the same time, it's important not to confuse all conservative religious groups with those committed to terrorism, warns counterterrorism expert Hellyer.

"In a lot of public discourse we have accusations," he says, such as, "This Salafi mosque or this Salafi preacher is 100 percent guilty of all the radical ideologies in the U.K." In fact, he notes, most Salafi Muslims are zealously conservative but not necessarily violent. Those at the Brixton London mosque first attended by shoe bomber Reid tried to dissuade him from radical theologies that preached violence, and as he became increasingly radical he left the mosque. [91]

"I would hate for us to waste resources going after people we don't like rather than people who are a dangerous threat," Hellyer says.

Following the 2005 bombings, the British government launched an Islamic "Scholars' Roadshow" aimed at winning the minds of under-30 Muslims on issues like jihad and extremism. The Muslim magazine *Q-News*, which came out early against suicide bombing, helped organize the event because it agreed with the government that "there needs to be a theological response to violent Islam-inspired radicalism," says contributing editor Malik.

More than 30,000 young Muslims attended — a sign of success. "But we also fought a significant segment of the Muslim community who said: 'Are you promoting Blair's Islam?' " Malik adds.

The British government's tactic of using 'good' Islam to fight 'bad' Islam is likely to be of limited success because it assumes that religious interpretation — not politics — drives radical movements, Brandeis University's Klausen suggests. Terrorists today meet at jihadist video stores, at Internet cafes and in prison — not in mosques, she says. Communities Secretary Blears recently acknowledged this reality, saying the government's new program to counter violent extremism would reach out to young people on the Internet, in cafes, bookshops and gyms. Yet it's hard for outsiders to know which theology to back. The roadshow, for instance, aroused bitter criticism in the press for supporting conservative interpretations of Islam. [92]

The German government, by contrast, has resisted efforts to create a "tame" Islam, saying the state shouldn't influence the theological development of Islam. [93]

Yet the need for Islam-based opposition to extremism is why political moderates like Malik think it was significant when a former senior member of Hizb-ut Tahir recently denounced the radical group on the BBC. "Here's a guy who in very measured language is saying, 'I reject on theological and philosophical grounds the ideology of an Islamic state,' " while remaining a Muslim, says Malik. He's opening a debate that "needs to happen on Muslim terms."

Winning that debate will be the real challenge, says journalist Bright, and not just because the West is frightened of terrorism. "If people are prepared to blow up individual innocents in atrocities, then we all know what we think about that," he observes. "More difficult is what we do about separatist, totalitarian ideologies and their effects on our young people. That to me is a more serious problem, because far more people are susceptible to that than to becoming terrorists."

NOTES

1. Jane Perlez, "Seeking Terror's Causes, Europe Looks Within," *The New York Times*, Sept. 11, 2007.

2. Nicholas Kulish, "New terrorism case confirms that Denmark is a target," *International Herald Tribune*, Sept. 16, 2007, p. 3, www.iht.com/articles/2007/09/17/europe/17denmark.php.

3. Paul Reynolds, "Bomber Video 'Points to al-Quaeda,' " BBC, Sept. 2, 2005, http://news.bbc.co.uk/1/hi/uk/4208250.stm.

4. See Perlez, *op. cit.*, and Souad Mekhennet and Nicholas Kulish, "Terrorist mastermind, or victim of mistaken identity?" *International Herald Tribune*, Oct. 12, 2007, p. 3.

5. Perlez, *op. cit.*

6. Karen McVeigh, "70 million [pounds] Promised for Citizenship Lessons in Schools and English-speaking Imams," *The Guardian*, July 26, 2007, p. 5.

7. Declan Walsh, "Resurgent Al-Qaida Plotting Attacks on West from Tribal Sanctuary, Officials Fear," *The Guardian*, Sept. 27, 2007. Also see, Jason Burke, "Target Europe," *The Observer*, Sept. 9, 2007, www.guardianunlimited. For background, see Roland Flamini, "Afghanistan on the Brink," *CQ Global Researcher*, June 2007, www.cqpress.com.

8. "Radicalization in the West: The Homegrown Threat," NYPD Intelligence Division, 2007, p. 5. Preventing terrorism by tackling the radicalization of individuals is one part of British intelligence service's four-point strategy: Prevent, Pursue, Protect and Prepare. See also "Countering International Terrorism: The United Kingdom's Strategy," *HM Government*, July 2006, presented to Parliament by the prime minister and secretary of state for the Home Department, www.intelligence.gov.uk.

9. Hizb ut-Tahrir, "Radicalisation, Extremism & 'Islamism,' " July 2007, p. 3, www.hizb.org.uk/hizb/images/PDFs/htb_radicalisation_report.pdf.

10. James Chapman, "Muslims Call for Special Bank Holidays," *Daily Mail*, Aug. 15, 2006.

11. Jane Perlez, "London Gathering Defends Vision of Radical Islam," *The New York Times*, Aug. 7, 2007.

12. Pew Research Center, "Muslim Americans: Middle Class and Mostly Mainstream," May 22, 2007, www.pewresearch.org, pp. 53-54. "Special Report: Islam, America and Europe: Look out, Europe, They Say," *The Economist*, June 22, 2006.

13. *Ibid.*, p. 51. A survey conducted by British Channel 4 in the summer of 2006 found half of Muslims 18-24 believed that 9/11 was a conspiracy by America and

Israel. Cited in Munira Mirza, *et al.*, "Living Apart Together: British Muslims and the Paradox of Multiculturalism," *Policy Exchange*, 2007, p. 58.

14. Cited in Melanie Phillips, *Londonistan: How Britain is Creating a Terror State Within* (2007), p. 302. Also see, "British Should Try Arranged Marriages," *Daily Telegraph*, July 10, 2006, www.telegraph.co.uk/news/main.jhtml?xml=/news/2006/06/10/nterr110.xml.

15. "Inside a Sharia Court," "This World," BBC 2, Oct. 1, 2007, http://news.bbc.co.uk/1/hi/programmes/this_world/7021676.stm.

16. "UK: Extended Pre-charge Detention Violates Rights," Human Rights Watch press release, July 26, 2007, and "In the Name of Prevention: Insufficient Safeguards in National Security Removals," Human Rights Watch, June 2007, http://hrw.org/reports/2007/france0607/1.htm#_Toc167263185.

17. The Associated Press, "Quaeda Using Europeans to Hit U.S., Official Says," *International Herald Tribune*, Sept. 26, 2007, p. 8. McConnell's testimony is at www.dni.gov/testimonies/20070925_testimony.pdf.

18. Peter Skerry, "The Muslim Exception: Why Muslims in the U.S. Aren't as Attracted to Jihad as Those in Europe," *Time*, Aug. 21, 2006.

19. Neil MacFarquhar, "Abandon Stereotype, Muslims in America Say," *The New York Times*, Sept. 4, 2007, p. A12.

20. Daniel Dombey and Simon Kuper, "Britons 'More Suspicious' of Muslims," *Financial Times*, Aug. 19, 2007.

21. *Ibid.*

22. Pew Global Attitudes Project, "Muslims in Europe: Economic Worries Top Concerns about Religious and Cultural Identity," July 6, 2006, http://pewglobal.org/reports/display.php?ReportID=254.

23. Presentation by John R. Bowen, University of Chicago International Forum, London, Sept. 29, 2007, as part of "Engaging Cultural Differences in Western Europe" panel.

24. John R. Bowen, "On Building a Multireligious Society," *San Francisco Chronicle*, Feb. 5, 2007.

25. *Ibid.*

26. International Crisis Group, "Islam and Identity in Germany," March 14, 2007, p. 19.

27. Jonathan Laurence and Justin Vaisse, *Integrating Islam: Political and Religious Challenges in Contemporary France* (2006).

28. For background, see Kenneth Jost, "Future of the European Union," *CQ Researcher*, Oct. 28, 2005, pp. 909-932.

29. Phillips, *op. cit.*, p. 22.

30. *Ibid.*, p. 24.

31. Jytte Klausen, "British Counter-Terrorism After 7/7: Adapting Community Policing to the Fight against Domestic Terrorism," *Journal of Ethnic and Migration Studies*, forthcoming, pp. 17-18.

32. See Robert S. Leiken, "Europe's Angry Muslims," *Foreign Affairs*, July/August 2005.

33. Will Woodward, "Kelly vows that new debate on immigration will engage critically with multiculturalism," *The Guardian*, Aug. 25, 2006.

34. Madeleine Bunting, "United Stand," *The Guardian*, June 13, 2007.

35. Phillips, *op. cit.*, p. 25.

36. Ed Husain, *The Islamist* (2007), p. 22.

37. Mirza, *et al.*, *op. cit.*, pp. 6, 18.

38. James Brandon and Douglas Murray, "How British Libraries Encourage Islamic Extremism," Centre for Social Cohesion, August 2007, www.socialcohesion.co.uk/pdf/HateOnTheState.pdf.

39. Emine Saner, "Dishonorable Acts," *The Guardian*, June 13, 2007, p. 18.

40. Leiken, *op. cit.*

41. Martin Bright, "When Progressives Treat with Reactionaries: The British State's Flirtation with Radical Islamism," *Policy Exchange*, 2006, p. 12, www.policyexchange.org.uk/images/libimages/176.pdf.

42. From "Connections," winter 2001, quoted in Tariq Modood, *Multiculturalism: A Civic Idea* (2007), pp. 10-11.

43. Patrick Wintour and Alan Travis, "Brown Sets out Sweeping but Risky 'Terror and Security Reforms,' " *The Guardian*, July 26, 2007, p. 1.

44. *Ibid.*

45. Since 2001, government figures show more than half of those arrested under the 2000 Terrorism Act have been released without charge. Human Rights Watch press release, "UK: Extended Pre-charge Detention Violates Rights," July 26, 2007.

46. Human Rights Watch, "In the Name of Prevention: Insufficient Safeguards in National Security Removals," June 2007, http://hrw.org/reports/2007/france0607/1.htm#_Toc167263185.

47. Peter Clarke, "Learning from Experience: Counter-terrorism in the UK Since 9/11," *Policy Exchange*, 2007, www.policyexchange.org.uk/images/libimages/252.pdf, pp. 19-20.

48. *Ibid.*, p. 27.

49. *Ibid.*

50. See www.liberty-human-rights.org.uk/publications/3-articles-and-speeched/index.shtml.

51. Liberty, "Overlooked: Surveillance and Personal Privacy in Britain," September 2007, www.liberty-human-rights.org.uk.

52. Jocelyne Cesari, *When Islam and Democracy Meet* (2004), pp. 15-16.

53. *Ibid.*, pp. 99-100.

54. Mirza, *op. cit.*, p. 24.

55. *Ibid.*

56. *Ibid.*, pp. 27-28.

57. *Ibid.*

58. *Ibid.*, p. 29.

59. Klausen, *op. cit.*, pp. 14-15. For background, see Peter Katel, "Global Jihad," *CQ Researcher*, Oct. 14, 2005, pp. 857-880.

60. See "Timeline: Madrid investigation," BBC News, April 28, 2004, http://news.bbc.co.uk/2/hi/europe/3597885.stm.

61. NYPD Intelligence Division, *op. cit.*

62. *Ibid.*

63. *Ibid.*, p. 15.

64. *Ibid.*

65. Denis MacEoin, "The Hijacking of Islam: How Extremist Literature is Subverting Mosques in the United Kingdom," *Policy Exchange*, 2007, www.policyexchange.org.uk.

66. See "Hate preaching cleric jailed," BBC News, March 7, 2003, http://news.bbc.co.uk/2/hi/uk_news/england/2829059.stm.

67. See "Cleric Bakri barred from Britain," BBC News, Aug. 12, 2005, http://news.bbc.co.uk/2/hi/uk_news/4144792.stm.

68. Klausen, *op. cit.*

69. Richard Norton-Taylor, "Al-Quaida has Revived, Spread and is Capable of a Spectacular," *The Guardian*, Sept. 13, 2007, www.guardian.co.uk/alqaida/story/0,,2167923,00.html. Also see "Strategic Survey 2007," International Institute for Strategic Studies, www.iiss.org/publications/strategic-survey-2007.

70. Peter Bergen, "How Osama Bin Laden Beat George W. Bush," *New Republic*, Oct. 15, 2007.

71. Norton-Taylor, *op. cit.* Jonathan Evans, "Address to the Society of Editors," Nov. 5, 2007, www.mi5.gov.uk.

72. Kulish, Sept. 17, 2007, *op. cit.*

73. Cesari, *op. cit.*, p. 96.

74. Jonathan Laurence, "Managing Transnational Islam: Muslims and the State in Western Europe," March 11, 2006, www.johnathanlaurence.net.

75. *Ibid.*, p. 92.

76. Robert S. Leiken and Steven Brooke, "The Quantitative Analysis of Terrorism and Immigration," *Terrorism and Political Violence* (2006), pp. 503-521.

77. University of Chicago International Forum, London, Sept. 29, 2007.

78. Dan Bilefsky, "Belgians Agree on One Issue: Foreigners," *International Herald Tribune*, Oct. 10, 2007.

79. Jessica Shepherd, "What does Britain Expect?" *The Guardian*, July 17, 2007, p. E1.

80. McVeigh, *op. cit.*

81. Bright, *op. cit.*, p. 28.

82. Hazel Blears, "Preventing Extremism: Strengthening Communities," Oct. 31, 2007, www.communities.gov.uk.

83. "Faith in the System," Department of Children, Schools and Families, Sept. 10, 2007.

84. "We Do Use Books that Call Jews 'Apes' Admits Head of Islamic School," *Evening Standard*, Feb. 7, 2007.

85. Andrew Norfolk, "Hardline Takeover of British Mosques," *The Times* (London), Sept. 7, 2007, www.timesonline.co.uk/tol/comment/faith/article2402973.ece.

86. BBC, "Faith Schools Set for Expansion," Sept. 10, 2007, www.bbc.co.uk.

87. "Major Increase in Work to Tackle Violent Extremism," Department of Communities and Local Government, U.K., Oct. 31, 2007, www.communities.gov.uk/news/corporate/529021.

88. Jo Revill, "Mosques Told to Obey New Code of Conduct," *The Observer*, Nov. 4, 2007, p. 24.

89. Timothy Garton Ash, "Battleground Europe," *Los Angeles Times*, Sept. 13, 2007, www.latimes.com/news/opinion/la-oe-garton13sep13,0,979657.story. Also see Klausen, *op. cit.*: One percent of UK Muslims felt the July 2005 London transit bombers were "right," according to a 2006 poll. Ten percent of Germans sympathized with suicide bombers.

90. Klausen, *op. cit.*

91. See "Who is Richard Reid?" BBC, Dec. 24, 2001, www.bbc.co.uk.

92. Klausen, *op. cit.*

93. International Crisis Group, *op. cit.*, p. 31.

BIBLIOGRAPHY

Books

Bowen, John R., *Why the French Don't Like Headscarves: Islam, the State, and Public Space*, Princeton University Press, 2007.
A Washington University anthropologist looks at the furor that led to the 2004 ban on head scarves in French schools.

Cesari, Jocelyne, *When Islam and Democracy Meet: Muslims in Europe and in the United States*, Palgrave, 2004.
The director of Harvard University's Islam in the West program compares the experiences of European and U.S. Muslims.

Husain, Ed, *The Islamist*, Penguin Books, 2007.
A former Muslim radical in London describes his recruitment by extremist Islamist groups in the 1990s.

Modood, Tariq, *Multiculturalism: A Civic Idea*, Polity, 2007.
A University of Bristol sociologist advocates "multicultural citizenship" to integrate Muslims in Britain.

Phillips, Melanie, *Londonistan: How Britain Is Creating a Terror State Within*, Gibson Square, 2006.
A journalist blames the rise of Muslim radicalism in London on persistent denial by the British government and a craven form of multiculturalism among leftists.

Qutb, Sayyid, *Milestones*, Maktabah Booksellers and Publishers, 2006.
A leader of the Muslim Brotherhood wrote this inspirational text for radical Islamist groups while in an Egyptian prison.

Articles

Bowen, John R., "On Building a Multireligious Society," *San Francisco Chronicle*, Feb. 5, 2007.
France is doing a better job of absorbing Muslims than other European countries.

Leiken, Robert S., and Steven Brook, "The Moderate Muslim Brotherhood," *Foreign Affairs*, March/April 2007.
The Muslim Brotherhood has moved away from violence in favor of using the electoral process to obtain its goal of an Islamic state in Egypt, France, Jordan, Spain, Syria, Tunisia and the United Kingdom, say leaders.

Perlez, Jane, "From Finding Radical Islam to Losing an Ideology," Sept. 12, 2007, *The New York Times*, www.nytimes.com/2007/09/12/world/europe/12britain.html?_r=1&oref=slogin.
A former senior member of the radical group Hizb ut-Tahrir says he left the group because it preached violence.

Ruthven, Malise, "How to Understand Islam," *The New York Review of Books*, Nov. 8, 2007, pp. 62-66.
Influential jihadist thinkers Maududi and Qutb held more rigid views of sharia than many scholars.

Reports and Studies

"In the Name of Prevention: Insufficient Safeguards in National Security Removals," Human Rights Watch, June 6, 2007, http://hrw.org/reports/2007/france0607/.

The group argues that France's policy of deporting imams and others it considers Islamic fundamentalists violates human rights.

"Islam and Identity in Germany," International Crisis Group, March 14, 2007, www.crisisgroup.org.
Issued before the latest foiled plot in Germany, this report downplayed the threat of homegrown terrorism in Germany's Turkish community.

"Radicalisation, Extremism & 'Islamism': Realities and Myths in the 'War on Terror,' " Hizb ut-Tahrir Britain, July 2007, www.hizb.org.uk.
The separatist British group lays out its argument for a caliphate in the Muslim world and denies it espouses violence.

"Radicalization in the West: The Homegrown Threat," New York City Police Department Intelligence Division, 2007, http://sethgodin.typepad.com/seths_blog/files/NYPD_Report-radicalization_in_the_West .pdf.
Muslim terrorists in Europe were generally "well-integrated" into their home countries, according to this study.

Bright, Martin, "When Progressives Treat with Reactionaries: The British State's Flirtation with Radical Islamism," *Policy Exchange*, 2006, www.policyexchange.org.uk.
The *New Statesman's* political editor says the government was pressured to maintain a relationship with radical Muslim groups.

MacEoin, Denis, "The Hijacking of Islam: How Extremist Literature is Subverting Mosques in the United Kingdom," *Policy Exchange*, 2007, www.policyexchange.org.uk/Publications.aspx?id=430.
The group visited leading mosques and schools in Britain and found extremist literature preaching hatred against non-Muslims, anti-Semitism and stoning of adulterers.

Mirza, Munira, *et al.*, "Living Apart Together: British Muslims and the Paradox of Multiculturalism," *Policy Exchange*, 2007, www.policyexchange.org.uk.
A conservative think tank in London blames British multiculturalism policies for dividing people along ethnic lines.

For More Information

Association of Muslim Schools UK, P.O. Box 14109, Birmingham B6 9BN, United Kingdom; +44-844-482-0407; www.ams-uk.org. A Birmingham-based group that "supports and develops excellence in full-time Muslim schools" in the United Kingdom.

Center for Islamic Pluralism, (202) 232-1750; www.islamicpluralism.eu. A Washington-based think tank that is critical of radical Muslim groups.

Centre for Social Cohesion, 77 Great Peter St., Westminster, London SW1P 2EZ, United Kingdom; +44-20-7799-6677; www.socialcohesion.co.uk. A British group critical of Britain's multicultural policy.

Hizb ut-Tahrir, www.hizb.org.uk. Considered one of the more radical Islamic organizations in Britain.

Human Rights Watch, 350 Fifth Ave., 34th Floor, New York, NY 10118-3299; (212) 290-4700; www.hrw.org. An international human rights organization.

Islam in the West Program, Harvard University, 59-61, Rue Pouchet, F-75849 Paris Cedex 17, France; +33-1-40-25-11-22; www.euro-islam.info. A network of scholars who conduct comparative research on Muslims in Europe.

Liberty, 21 Tabard St., London SE1 4LA, United Kingdom; +20-7403-3888; www.liberty-human-rights.org.uk. London-based group, also known as the National Council for Civil Liberties, that advocates for civil liberties.

Muslim Council of Britain, P.O. Box 57330, London E1 2WJ, United Kingdom; +44-845-26-26-786; www.mcb.org.uk. Represents more than 500 Muslim groups, mosques and schools in Britain.

National Secular Society, 25 Red Lion Square, London WC1R 4RL, United Kingdom; +44-20-7404-3126; www.secularism.org.uk. A London-based group that opposes faith schools in Britain.

Policy Exchange, Clutha House, 10 Storey's Gate, London SW1P 3AY, United Kingdom; +20-7340-2650; www.policyexchange.org.uk. A London-based think tank that opposes the British government's multicultural policy and choice of Muslim groups to support.

Saban Center for Middle East Policy, Brookings Institution, 1775 Massachusetts Ave., N.W., Washington, DC 20036; (202) 797-6000; www.brookings.edu/saban.aspx. A Washington-based think tank that studies terrorism.

Stop Islamisation of Europe, +44-122-854-7317; sioe.wordpress.com. A Danish group that has been coordinating street protests in Europe against Islamist stances on issues like sharia.

Mohamed Abdul Bari
Chairman, East London Mosque

Freedom of speech has limits
"Muslims [must] express their feelings peacefully and will call upon the newspapers concerned to apologise for the enormous offence [Mohammed cartoon] and distress caused. The hallmark of any civilized society is not just that it allows freedom of speech, but that it accepts this freedom also has limits."

— The Independent *(England), February 2006*

Ali Selim
Secretary-General Irish Council of Imams

Perpetrators don't speak for all
"In some parts of the world acts of violence against innocent people have created an unhealthy atmosphere which allowed Islamophobia to flourish. To stigmatise every Muslim for a crime perpetrated by a Muslim is just like stigmatising every Christian for a crime perpetrated by a Christian. It is not fair and is absurd."

— The Irish Times, *April 2007*

Salma Yaqoob
Councillor; Sparkbrook, Birmingham, England

Citizenship classes are useless
"Muslims in this country are already British. If Muslims are singled out for citizenship classes, it will only alienate them and make them feel like they are not really British at all. The Muslim community has already condemned extremism. You can't stop extremism through citizenship classes alone."

— Birmingham Evening Mail *(England), May 2006*

Wolfgang Schaeuble
Interior Minister Germany

Our country, our values
"Islam is part of us now. That means Muslims must adapt and not just pay lip service to doing so. They must put up with cartoons, gender equality, possibly insulting criticism — all this is part of our open society."

— Conference on Islam, Berlin, September 2006

Al-Maktoum Institute for Arabic and Islamic Studies
Dundee, Scotland

Education promotes understanding
"There must be better education at university level on Islam and Muslims in today's world, which reflects the needs of our contemporary multicultural society. It is only through multicultural education that we can work to eliminate extremism and fundamentalism."

— Time For Change report, October 2006

Dalil Boubakeur
Chairman, French Council of the Muslim Faith

A religion of peace
"The Prophet founded not a terrorist religion, but on the contrary, a religion of peace. We attach enormous importance to this image and we will not allow it to be distorted. I myself oppose the extremist forms of Islam; we reject this parallel."

— Libération.fr *(France), February 2006*

Tony Blair
Then-Prime Minister United Kingdom

Attacking absurd ideas is crucial
"This terrorism will not be defeated until its ideas, the poison that warps the minds of its adherents, are confronted, head-on, in their essence, at their core. By this I don't mean telling them terrorism is wrong. I mean telling them their attitude to America is absurd; their concept of governance pre-feudal; their positions on women and other faiths, reactionary and regressive."

— Evening Standard *(England), March 2006*

Bassam Tibi
Professor of International Relations, University of Gottingen, Germany

Riots in France pose warning for Europe
"The explosions now are in France, but other countries are sitting on the same time bomb; it's a European time bomb. This is a warning for Europe from the 'no-future' Muslim kids whose lives are wasting all over the continent. Without change, the fighting will come to the streets of Berlin, Amsterdam wherever."

— Boston Globe, *November 2005*

Christo Komarnitski, Bulgaria

6

Torture Debate

Seth Stern

Nurses Valentina Siropoulu, left, and Valia Cherveniashlka are among six Bulgarian medical workers who were tortured while imprisoned for eight years in Libya on charges they infected hundreds of Libyan children with HIV-AIDS. They were released in August. About 160 countries torture prisoners, despite six international treaties banning the practice.

From *CQ Researcher,*
September 1, 2007.

I t is called, simply, waterboarding. A prisoner is strapped to a board with his feet above his head, his mouth and nose covered, usually with cloth or cellophane. Water is then poured over his face, inducing gagging and a terrifying sense of drowning.

The U.S. government — which has been accused of using waterboarding on detainees it suspects are terrorists — denies that it practices torture or cruel, inhuman or degrading treatment. The Central Intelligence Agency (CIA) says it must use what it calls "enhanced interrogation techniques" — to obtain critical information from "enemy combatants" in the war on terrorism. [1] But human rights advocates say waterboarding and other abusive interrogation tactics are prohibited by international law.

To be sure, the United States is far from the worst offender when it comes to mistreating prisoners. Even human rights advocates who complain the most bitterly about the tactics used in America's war on terror say they don't compare to those utilized by the world's worst human rights abusers.

"Nothing the administration has done can compare in its scale to what happens every day to victims of cruel dictatorships around the world," Tom Malinowski, Human Rights Watch's Washington advocacy director, told the U.S. Senate Foreign Relations Committee on July 26. "The United States is not Sudan or Cuba or North Korea." [2]

Indeed, about 160 countries practice torture today, according to human rights groups and the U.S. State Department. [3] In July, for example, six Bulgarian medical workers freed after eight years in a Libyan prison said they had been tortured. "We were treated like animals," said Ashraf al-Hazouz, one of the prisoners, who had been accused of deliberately infecting Libyan children with the HIV-

Torture Still in Use Throughout the World

Some 160 countries practice torture, according to a 2005 survey of incidents reported by the U.S. Department of State and Amnesty International. Besides using torture to solicit information, some countries use it to punish or intimidate dissidents, separatists, insurgents and religious minorities. The Council of Europe accuses the U.S. Central Intelligence Agency (CIA) of using its rendition program to send kidnapped terror suspects to be interrogated in 11 cities — all in countries that practice torture.

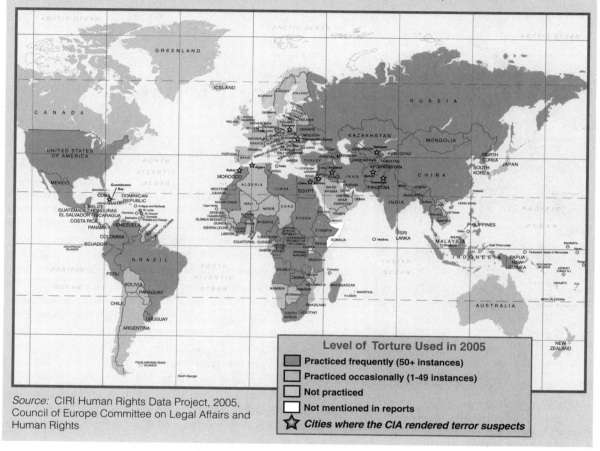

Source: CIRI Human Rights Data Project, 2005, Council of Europe Committee on Legal Affairs and Human Rights

Level of Torture Used in 2005
- Practiced frequently (50+ instances)
- Practiced occasionally (1-49 instances)
- Not practiced
- Not mentioned in reports
- ☆ Cities where the CIA rendered terror suspects

AIDS virus. Hazouz said the Libyans attached electrodes to his genitals and feet, unleashed attack dogs on him and tied his hands and legs to a metal bar, spinning him "like a chicken on a rotisserie." [4]

While other countries' abuse methods may seem more abhorrent, human rights advocates worldwide complain angrily that America's detention and interrogation practices in the post-9/11 war on terror have lowered the bar for torturers worldwide, giving habitual abusers a new justification for their behavior.

America's detention policies since Sept. 11, 2001, "are a gift to dictators everywhere" who "use America's poor example to shield themselves from international criticism and pressure," Malinowski said. Abusive governments now routinely "justify their own, longstanding practices of systematically violating basic human rights norms" by arguing that they — like the United States — must use torture to deal with the threat of international terrorism. [5]

U.S. counterterrorism policies that anger allies and human rights activists include the indefinite detentions

— without a guaranteed trial or right to counsel — of hundreds of alleged terrorists at Guantánamo Bay, Cuba, beginning shortly after 9/11. Then in April 2004 CBS' "60 Minutes II" televised explosive photographs that circulated around the world portraying harsh interrogation methods that reportedly had migrated from Guantánamo to the U.S.-run Abu Ghraib military prison near Baghdad. A year later *The Washington Post* revealed that the CIA was operating so-called "black sites" — secret prisons in Eastern Europe and Southeast Asia where detainees were subjected to extreme interrogation methods, allegedly including waterboarding. [6] Finally, news that the United States was kidnapping terror suspects from foreign locations and transporting them to interrogation sites in third countries with reputations for practicing torture — a tactic known as extraordinary rendition — triggered further global outrage. [7]

By adopting such measures, the United States has lost its moral authority to condemn torture and human rights abuses in other countries, say critics. "It's a very bad precedent for people to be able to say 'the U.S. — the biggest democracy promoter in the world — has to use it, why can't we?' " says physician Bhogendra Sharma, president of the Center for Victims of Torture in Nepal, which treats victims tortured by both the Nepalese government and Maoist guerrillas.

Few American ambassadors today "dare to protest another government's harsh interrogations, detentions without trial, or even 'disappearances,' knowing how easily an interlocutor could turn the

Severe Torture Still Used by Many Nations

According to the U.S. State Department and Human Rights Watch, the following nations are among those condoning widespread and particularly severe forms of torture:

 China: Prison guards are forbidden from using torture, but former detainees report the use of electric shock, beatings and shackles. Among those targeted for abuse are adherents of the outlawed Falun Gong spiritual movement, Tibetans and Muslim Uighur prisoners.

 Egypt: Government interrogators from the State Security Investigations arm of the Ministry of the Interior regularly torture suspected Islamic militants, including prisoners transferred to Egypt by the United States. Victims were kicked, burned with cigarettes, shackled, forcibly stripped, beaten with water hoses and dragged on the floor.

 Indonesia: Security officers in Aceh Province systematically torture suspected supporters of the armed Free Aceh movement, using beatings, cigarette burning and electric shock.

 Iran: Political prisoners are subjected to sensory deprivation known as "white torture" — they are held in all-white cells with no windows, with prison clothes and even meals all in white.

 Morocco: Terrorism suspects detained after a May 2003 attack in Casablanca were subjected to torture and mistreatment, including severe beatings.

 Nepal: Both government security personnel and Maoist rebels employ torture, including beating the soles of victims' feet, submersion in water and sexual humiliation.

 Nigeria: Armed robbery and murder suspects are subjected to beatings with batons, horse whips, iron bars and cables.

 North Korea: Captors routinely tortured and mistreated prisoners using electric shock, prolonged periods of exposure, humiliations such as public nakedness, being hung by the wrists and forcing mothers recently repatriated from China to watch the infanticide of their newborn infants.

 Russia: Russian security forces conducting so-called anti-terror operations in Chechnya mutilate victims and dump their bodies on the sides of roads.

 Uganda: Government security forces in unregistered detention facilities torture prisoners with caning and severe beatings and by inflicting pain to the genitals.

 Uzbekistan: Police, prison guards and members of the National Security Service routinely employ suffocation, electric shock, deprivation of food and water and sexual abuse. Prison regulations in 2005 permitted beatings under medical supervision.

Sources: "Human Rights Watch's 2007 World Report;" U.S. State Department "2006 Country Reports on Human Rights Practices"

Views Differ on U.S. Interrogation Tactics

A wide gulf exists between Americans' and Europeans' views of how the United States treats terrorism suspects. Americans are almost evenly split on whether the United States uses torture, but three-quarters of Germans and nearly two-thirds of Britons believe it does. And while just over half of Americans think U.S. detention policies are legal, 85 percent of Germans and 65 percent of Britons think they are illegal.

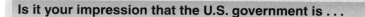

Is it your impression that the U.S. government is . . .

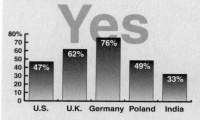

. . . currently allowing interrogators to use torture to get information from suspected terrorists?

Yes

U.S.	U.K.	Germany	Poland	India
47%	62%	76%	49%	33%

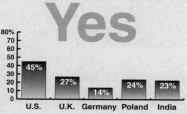

. . . making every effort to make sure that interrogators never use torture?

Yes

U.S.	U.K.	Germany	Poland	India
45%	27%	14%	24%	23%

Is it your impression that current U.S. policies for detaining people it has captured and is holding in Guantánamo Bay are or are not legal, according to international treaties on the treatment of detainees?

Are legal

U.S.	U.K.	Germany	Poland	India
52%	22%	8%	18%	28%

Are not legal

U.S.	U.K.	Germany	Poland	India
38%	65%	85%	50%	34%

Source: "American and International Opinion on the Rights of Terrorism Suspects, International Questionnaire," WorldPublicOpinion.org, June 2006

The worldwide anger triggered by America's post-9/11 detention and interrogation policies stems not only from the perception that notorious governments now feel free to continue torturing prisoners. It also stems from widespread perceptions that:

• The United States' overwhelming military and technological superiority have made it arrogant, immune from having to abide by international norms.

• America's pervasive cultural influence has, since 9/11, "normalized" torture by spreading the concept across the globe that torture works and can be legally or morally justified.

• The United States has squandered its historic position as the world's leader in the fight against human rights abuses, opening itself to charges of being a hypocrite.

When the U.S. State Department released its annual report on human rights violators in 2005, both China and Russia said the United States has its own abuses to explain. "Unfortunately, [the report] once again gives us reason to say that double standards are a characteristic of the American approach to such an important theme," said a statement issued by the Russian foreign ministry. "Characteristically off-screen is the ambiguous record of the United States itself." [9]

Disappointment over U.S. tactics has been widespread. *El Tiempo*, a leading newspaper in Bogotá, Colombia, editorialized in 2005: "It seems incredible that these kind of un-civilizing backward steps are coming from a country which declares itself a defender of Western values and which has been so on more than one occasion." [10]

A 2006 survey of 26,000 people in 25 countries found that 67 percent disapproved of U.S. treatment of detainees in Guantánamo and other prisons. Some of the

tables and cite U.S. misconduct as an excuse for his government's own abuses," said a 2007 Human Rights Watch (HRW) report. [8]

Sarah Leah Whitson, HRW's director for the Middle East and North Africa, says when she visits officials in those regions to discuss their use of torture, their first reply now is often, "What about the United States? Go talk to the U.S. government."

highest disapproval rates were among America's closest allies in Europe — which have suffered their own terrorist attacks since 9/11 — and Middle Eastern allies such as Lebanon and Egypt, who fear the growing influence of Islamic extremists. [11]

But the 9/11 attacks did more than raise the profile of the torture debate in the United States. An Australian law professor has become one of the world's most vocal advocates for "life-saving compassionate torture," which he says is justified if it elicits crucial information needed to prevent future terrorist attacks and save innocent lives. (*See "At Issue," p. 155.*)

But critics of that argument point out that torture is not only used to extract life-saving information from terrorists but also to punish political dissidents, suspected criminals — who sometimes are innocent — and religious minorities. China, for instance, tortures members of the Falun Gong spiritual movement, Tibetan dissidents and Muslims from the Uighur region, according to Human Rights Watch.

In Iraq — where former leader Saddam Hussein was notorious for torturing political enemies — the U.S. occupation has not curbed the prevalence of torture by government agents or insurgents. In fact, say human rights advocates, the level of torture perpetrated by the Shiite-dominated Iraqi government and affiliated militias reportedly has escalated as the country has descended into civil strife. (*See sidebar, p. 144.*)

Despite the damage done to America's reputation by its counterterrorism tactics, President Bush in July said he was authorizing the CIA to reopen its overseas black sites. Bush had announced last September that the use of secret prisons had been suspended and that the prisoners were being transferred to Guantánamo. That decision was prompted by the U.S. Supreme Court's ruling that all U.S. detainees, including those held by the CIA, were covered by the Geneva Conventions' guidelines for the treatment of wartime detainees.

The administration said in July 2007 the CIA would comply with the conventions in its treatment of prisoners at the sites. But Bush's new order did not ban waterboarding or any other controversial interrogation techniques and gave interrogators wide latitude if their purpose is to gather intelligence needed to prevent terrorist attacks. [12]

The Bush administration and its supporters argue the United States is operating within the confines of U.S.

AP Photo/Jerry Harmer

Vann Nath, one of only seven people to survive the Khmer Rouge's infamous Tuol Sleng prison, looks at a photo of Kaing Guek Eav, who ran the murderous regime's security service. Eav was recently found living in Cambodia as a born-again Christian. He was indicted by a U.N.-backed tribunal in July for his role in the torture and deaths of 14,000 men, women and children at the facility. His trial is expected to begin in 2008.

and international law and that aggressive interrogation methods are needed to protect against future terrorist attacks. "These are dangerous men with unparalleled knowledge about terrorist networks and their plans for new attacks," President Bush said in 2006. "The security of our nation and the lives of our citizens depend on our ability to learn what these terrorists know." [13]

With America seen as abandoning its role as the world's ethical standard-bearer, human rights groups complain that the European Union (EU) has not stepped up to fill the void. The EU has dragged its feet in questioning U.S. interrogation policies, say critics, and some EU countries have secretly allowed U.S. aircraft to use their airports for rendition flights. Some renditions involved innocent citizens who were tortured in countries long known to abuse prisoners, such as Egypt and

Torture Has Escalated in Iraq

Saddam's brutal legacy survives

The fall of Saddam Hussein and more than four years of U.S. occupation have done little to curb torture in Iraq. In fact, the level of torture perpetrated by government personnel and militias reportedly has escalated as the country has descended into what many consider a civil war.

The use of torture in Iraq is "totally out of hand," said Manfred Nowak, a U.N. official appointed to study torture around the world, and "many people say it is worse than it had been in the times of Saddam Hussein." [1]

Bodies brought to the Baghdad morgue often bear signs of acid-induced injuries, broken limbs and wounds caused by power drills and nails, said U.N. investigators. [2] The torture is mostly being perpetrated by the largely Shiite ministries of the Interior and Defense as well as by private Shiite militias, according to Sarah Leah Whitson, Human Rights Watch's program director for the Middle East and North Africa.

"The torture committed in the Ministry of Interior facilities we documented is certainly comparable to torture and abuse that's been recorded in the Baath prisons prior to the war," says Whitson.

In 2006 U.S. and Iraqi troops discovered a secret Baghdad prison run by the Interior Ministry, known as Site 4, where some of the more than 1,400 prisoners were found to have been subjected to systematic abuse.

Human rights advocates say the widespread use of torture is being fueled by the breakdown of law and order and the continued employment of officials who previously used torture during Saddam's regime. The weakened Iraqi central government has been unable to rein in the abuse of prisoners in these facilities, despite promises to do so. There has been less documented evidence of torture by Sunni insurgents, Whitson points out. Sunnis usually execute their victims, often by beheading.

A January 2005 report by Human Rights Watch found that police, jailers and intelligence agents — many of whom had similar jobs under Saddam — were "committing systematic torture and other abuses." Despite being "in the throes of a significant insurgency" in which thousands of police officers and civilians are being killed, the report said, "no government — not Saddam Hussein's, not the occupying powers and not

Syria. Besides generating outrage among close U.S. allies such as Canada, the incidents have led to prosecutions in Germany and Italy of Americans allegedly involved in the renditions.

As the Bush administration continues to defend itself against global criticism of its counterterrorism policies, these are some of the questions being asked:

Is torture effective?

Advocates and opponents of torture and other coercive techniques can look at the same evidence about their effectiveness and come to very different conclusions.

Take the case of Khalid Shaikh Mohammed, a senior al Qaeda operative and the alleged principal architect of the 9/11 attacks. He was captured in Pakistan in 2003 and interrogated by U.S. intelligence agents — reportedly using waterboarding — before being transferred to military custody at Guantánamo. [14] In a military hearing in March 2007 the Defense Department released a tran-

script of his confession in which he took credit for 31 different terrorist operations, including planning the 9/11 attacks in the United States and the beheading of *Wall Street Journal* reporter Daniel Pearl.

CIA Director Michael Hayden cited coercive interrogation techniques employed against detainees such as Mohammed (dubbed K.S.M. by intelligence agents) as an "irreplaceable" tool that helped yield information that has helped disrupt several terrorist plots since 9/11. "K.S.M. is the poster boy for using tough but legal tactics," said Michael Sheehan, a former State Department counterterrorism official. "He's the reason these techniques exist." [15]

But opponents of aggressive interrogation techniques, like Col. Dwight Sullivan, head defense lawyer at the Office of Military Commissions, cite Mohammed's serial confessions as "a textbook example of why we shouldn't allow coercive methods." [16]

Some intelligence experts doubt the veracity of portions of Mohammed's information. For one thing they

the Iraqi interim government — can justify ill-treatment of persons in custody in the name of security." [3]

The government of Iraqi Prime Minister Nuri Kamal al-Maliki has been slow to respond to reports of torture by governmental personnel, say human rights advocates. The Iraqi government "made all kinds of promises and commitments to investigate and review" allegations of torture in 2005, Whitson says, but since then the Interior Ministry "has only gone further outside control of the government," as war and sectarian violence have escalated. "There's not a commitment to making this issue a priority."

When British and Iraqi special forces raided the office of an Iraqi government intelligence agency in the southern city of Basra in March 2007, they found prisoners exhibiting signs of torture. Al-Maliki condemned the raid, but not the abuse it uncovered. [4]

Torture has continued since the start of the U.S. military occupation in Iraq. A 2004 report by the International Committee of the Red Cross found that after Saddam's fall Iraqi authorities beat detainees with cables, kicked them in the genitals and hung them by handcuffs from iron bars of cell windows for several hours at a time. [5]

Torture is also being employed in Kurdistan, a semi-autonomous region in northern Iraq that is the most stable part of the country. Human Rights Watch reported in July 2007 that detainees accused of anti-government activities were subjected to torture and other mistreatment. [6]

The torturers are security forces and personnel at detention facilities operated by the two major Kurdish political parties — the Kurdistan Democratic Party and the Patriotic Union of Kurdistan — which operate outside control of the region's government, the report said. Detainees have been beaten, put in stress positions and handcuffed for several days at a time.

Nonetheless, the abuses in Kurdistan do not equal those occurring elsewhere in Iraq. "Certainly the situation in mainland Iraq is much worse," says Whitson.

---

[1] BBC News, "Iraq Torture 'worse than Saddam,' " Sept. 21, 2006.

[2] *Ibid.*

[3] Doug Struck, "Torture in Iraq Still Routine, Report Says," *The Washington Post*, Jan. 25, 2005, p. A10.

[4] Kirk Semple, "Basra Raid Finds Dozens Detained by Iraqi Unit," *The New York Times*, March 5, 2007.

[5] "Report of the International Committee of the Red Cross on the Treatment by the Coalition Forces of Prisoners of War and Other Protected Persons by the Geneva Conventions in Iraq During Arrest, Internment and Interrogation," February 2004, www.globalsecurity.org/military/library/report/2004/icrc_report_iraq_feb2004.pdf.

[6] "Caught in the Whirlwind: Torture and Denial of Due Process by the Kurdistan Security Forces," Human Rights Watch, July 3, 2007, http://hrw.org/reports/2007/kurdistan0707/.

---

don't think a single operative — even one as high ranking as he — could have been involved in 31 separate terrorist plots. And those intimately associated with the Pearl case are highly skeptical that Mohammed himself murdered Pearl, as he claimed.

"My old colleagues say with 100-percent certainty that it was not K.S.M. who killed Pearl," former CIA officer Robert Baer told *New Yorker* writer Jane Mayer. And Special Agent Randall Bennett, who oversaw security at the U.S. consulate in Karachi when Pearl was killed, said "K.S.M.'s name never came up" during his interviews with those convicted in 2002 of the murder. [17]

Skeptics of torture's effectiveness say most people — to end their suffering — will provide false information. For instance, a torture victim deprived of his clothes will feel so "ashamed and humiliated and cold," said retired FBI counterterrorism agent Dan Coleman, "he'll tell you anything you want to hear to get his clothing back. There's no value in it." [18]

Others say torture doesn't work against zealots. "People who are committed to their ideology or religion . . . would rather die than speak up," says Sharma at the Center for Victims of Torture in Nepal.

Both opponents and supporters of coercive interrogation methods, however, agree torture is useful for other purposes. Many countries use torture to punish dissidents, separatists or guerrillas and to intimidate others from joining such groups. "The real purpose of torture is oppression of one or the other kind, to send a signal to anyone who is an opponent that there is a very, very grave risk," says Sune Segal, head of communications for the Copenhagen-based International Rehabilitation Council for Torture Victims, which collaborates with 131 treatment centers around the world. "It's not about soliciting information."

Underlying the debate is the fact that little scientific evidence exists about whether torture works. A recent Intelligence Science Board study concluded that "virtually none" of the limited number of techniques used by

U.S. personnel in recent decades "are based on scientific research or have even been subjected to scientific or systematic inquiry or evaluation." [19]

Darius Rejali, a political science professor at Reed College in Portland, Ore., says regimes that employ torture aren't likely to divulge their findings, and torturers themselves have very little incentive to boast about their work, which is punishable under international law. "Torture travels by back routes," Rejali says. "There's rarely training, so there is no particular mechanism for determining whether it works."

Experienced interrogators who have talked about their work say pain and coercion are often counterproductive. John Rothrock, who as a U.S. Air Force captain in Vietnam headed a combat interrogation team, said he didn't know "any professional intelligence officers of my generation who would think this is a good idea." [20]

Experts say the most effective interrogations require a trained interrogator. Coleman says he learned to build a rapport with even the worst suspects rather than trying to intimidate them. He would patiently work to build a relationship in which the target of his interrogation would begin to trust him and ultimately share information.

You try to "get them to the point, in the intelligence world, where they commit treason," he said. [21]

Is torture ever justified?

Australian law Professor Mirko Bagaric at Deakin University in Melbourne prompted a vigorous public debate in May 2005 when he suggested that torture is sometimes morally justified.

"Given the choice between inflicting a relatively small level of harm on a wrongdoer and saving an innocent person, it is verging on moral indecency to prefer the interests of the wrongdoer," Bagaric wrote in *The Age*, a leading daily paper in Melbourne. Such cases are analogous to a situation in which a wrongdoer threatens to kill a hostage unless his demands are met, he said. "In such a case, it is not only permissible but desirable for police to shoot (and kill) the wrongdoer if they get a 'clear shot.' " [22]

In the United States, Harvard Law Professor Alan Dershowitz has argued that the legal system should adjust to the reality that if it could prevent a catastrophic terrorist attack that could kill millions, interrogators will probably torture a suspect whether or not it's legal. In emergencies, he contends, courts should issue "torture warrants" to interrogators trying to prevent such attacks.

"A formal, visible, accountable and centralized system is somewhat easier to control than an ad hoc, off-the-books and under-the-radar-screen non-system," Dershowitz wrote. [23]

Those who justify torture in certain situations usually invoke a hypothetical "ticking time bomb" scenario in which interrogators torture a suspect to obtain information that can help prevent an imminent attack. Twenty-five years ago, long before the rise of Islamist terrorists, philosophy Professor Michael Levin of the City University of New York hypothesized a similar scenario in *Newsweek*.

"Suppose a terrorist has hidden a bomb on Manhattan Island, which will detonate at noon on 4 July. . . . Suppose, further, that he is caught at 10 a.m. that fateful day, but — preferring death to failure — won't disclose where the bomb is. . . . If the only way to save those lives is to subject the terrorist to the most excruciating possible pain, what grounds can there be for not doing so?" [24]

But opponents of torture say such perfect "ticking time bomb" scenarios occur in the movies, but rarely in real life. Interrogators usually aren't positive they have captured the one person with knowledge of a real plot. And even if they torture such a suspect, it usually won't prevent the attack because his accomplices will proceed without him, critics say.

"I was in the Army for 25 years, and I talked to lots of military people who had been in lots of wars. I talked to lots of people in law enforcement," says James Jay Carafano, a fellow at the conservative Heritage Foundation. "I've never yet ever found anyone that's ever confronted the ticking time bomb scenario. That's not the moral dilemma that people normally face." [25]

"The United States is a nation of laws," says Sen. Patrick J. Leahy, a Vermont Democrat who chairs the Senate Judiciary Committee, "and I categorically reject the view that torture, even in such compelling circumstances, can be justified." Even if harsh interrogation techniques do not rise to the level of torture, he said, they are probably illegal under international laws that prohibit cruel, inhumane or degrading treatment of prisoners.

Law professors and philosophers widely agree that torture is always immoral and should not be legalized. Once torture is allowed in extreme circumstances, they point out, it quickly spreads to less urgent situations. "It has a tendency to just proliferate," says Raimond Gaita, a professor of moral philosophy at King's College in London.

He cites the experience of Israel, which authorized coercive interrogation techniques in 1987 in limited circumstances. But interrogators in the field used more aggressive techniques with more suspects than intended.

Eitan Felner, former director of the Israeli Information Center for Human Rights in the Occupied Territories, writes the lesson of Israel's experience is "the fallacy of believing — as some influential American opinion-makers do today — that it is possible to legitimize the use of torture to thwart terrorist attacks and at the same time restrict its use to exceptional cases." [26]

Instead, torture should remain illegal and interrogators faced with the time-bomb scenario should be in the same legal position as someone who commits civil disobedience, say opponents. "Anyone who thinks an act of torture is justified should have . . . to convince a group of peers in a public trial that all necessary conditions for a morally permissible act were indeed satisfied," writes Henry Shue, a professor of politics and international relations at the University of Oxford. [27]

Human Rights advocates say that — while not explicitly endorsing torture — U.S. policies have changed the dialogue about torture around world. "It used to be these things were automatically bad," says Jumana Musa, advocacy director for Amnesty USA. "Now, there's a cost-benefit analysis and the notion that this isn't really that bad."

Have U.S. attitudes toward torture changed?

Some prominent American politicians and some soldiers, albeit anonymously, have recently endorsed torture as a way to prevent terrorist attacks or save lives.

At a May 2007 GOP presidential debate, Rudolph W. Giuliani, the mayor of New York during the Sept. 11 terror attacks, said if elected president he would advise interrogators "to use every method they could think of" to prevent an imminent catastrophic terror attack. Other candidates were even more explicit, embracing torture with an openness that would have been unheard of before 9/11. California Rep. Duncan Hunter said he would tell the Defense secretary: "Get the information," while Colorado Rep. Tom Tancredo endorsed waterboarding. [28]

Some U.S. military personnel who have served in Iraq express similar attitudes. More than a third of the 1,700 American soldiers and Marines who responded to a 2006 survey said torture would be acceptable if it helped save the life of a fellow soldier or helped get information, and

An American soldier threatens an Iraqi detainee with an attack dog in one of the graphic Abu Ghraib prison abuse photos that shocked the world in 2004. Human rights advocates worldwide say America's harsh post-9/11 detention and interrogation practices lowered the bar for torturers worldwide. Twelve low-level U.S. military personnel have since been convicted for their roles in the abuse, which an Army investigation described as "sadistic, blatant and wanton criminal" abuse.

Getty Images/The Washington Post

10 percent admitted to using force against Iraqi civilians or damaging their property when it wasn't necessary. [29]

But many top U.S. military leaders, interrogators and veterans denounce torture as ineffective and say it will only make it more likely that American captives will be tortured in the future. Sen. John McCain, R-Ariz., who was tortured while a prisoner of war in Vietnam, has spoken out forcefully against torture and led the 2005 effort in Congress to limit the kinds of interrogation methods U.S. military personnel can use.

"We've sent a message to the world that the United States is not like the terrorists. [W]e are a nation that upholds values and standards of behavior and treatment of all people, no matter how evil or bad they are," McCain said. Furthermore, he added, disavowing torture will "help us enormously in winning the war for the hearts and minds of people throughout the world in the war on terror." [30]

A 2006 public opinion survey by the University of Maryland's Program on International Policy Attitudes (PIPA) suggests that most Americans reject the use of torture. The PIPA poll found that 75 percent of Americans agreed that terror detainees had "the right not to be tortured." Fifty-seven percent said the United States should

CHRONOLOGY

1700s *Torture is banned in Europe.*

1754 Prussia becomes first European state to abolish torture; other European countries soon follow suit.

1900-1950 *Torture re-emerges, then is prohibited.*

1917 Russian Revolution gives birth to communism, which will foster totalitarian regimes that will torture perceived enemies of the state.

1933 Nazis take over Germany and soon begin torturing civilian prisoners.

1948 U.N. adopts Universal Declaration of Human Rights banning torture.

1949 Geneva Conventions ban all use of "mutilation, cruel treatment and torture" of prisoners of war.

1950s-1960s *Torture continues, despite international ban.*

1954 France tortures thousands of Algerians during Algeria's war for independence.

1961 Amnesty International is founded after two Portuguese students are jailed for seven years for toasting freedom.

1970s-1990s *Democracies — as well as authoritarian regimes — continue to torture.*

1971 British interrogators use the "five techniques" against Irish Republican Army suspects. European Court of Human Rights calls the methods illegal.

1975 Khmer Rouge takes over Cambodia and soon begins torturing and murdering thousands of detainees.

1978 Human Rights Watch is founded.

1987 Israel authorizes use of aggressive interrogation techniques during widespread Palestinian unrest.

1999 Israel's Supreme Court bans torture and abusive interrogation methods.

2000s-Present *Rise of Islamic terrorist attacks sparks increasing use of torture.*

2001 Muslim terrorists kill 3,000 in Sept. 11 attacks. . . . Hundreds of Muslims are detained in the United States and Afghanistan. . . . Fox Television's "24" begins showing U.S. agents using torture.

2002 First "enemy combatants" captured in Afghanistan arrive at Guantánamo naval base in Cuba. President Bush says they will be treated humanely, but that they are not protected by Geneva Conventions. . . . In September Syrian-born Canadian Maher Arar is detained during a stopover in New York and is sent to Syria for interrogation, where he is tortured.

March 30, 2004 U.S. Supreme Court rules Alien Tort Claims Act can be used to sue human rights abusers.

April 27, 2004 CBS News' "60 Minutes II" airs photographs of U.S. troops abusing prisoners at Abu Ghraib prison in Iraq.

November 2005 *Washington Post* reports the CIA detains terror suspects in secret prisons where detainees allegedly are subjected to coercive interrogation techniques. . . . U.S. government insists it does not torture. Congress passes Detainee Treatment Act, prohibiting torture and mistreatment of prisoners but limiting detainees' rights to challenge their detentions.

2006 On June 29, Supreme Court rules U.S. detainees are subject to the Geneva Conventions. . . . Military Commissions Act authorizes new courtroom procedures for enemy combatants but allows greater flexibility for CIA interrogations.

2007 A German court orders 13 U.S. intelligence agents arrested for their alleged role in rendering a German citizen to Afghanistan. . . . Canada apologizes to Arar for allowing him to be taken to Syria. . . . In July, President Bush authorizes the CIA to reopen secret overseas prisons. . . . International war crimes tribunal in Cambodia indicts former Khmer Rouge leader Kaing Geuk Eav for the torture and murder of thousands of prisoners. . . . Libya admits it tortured Bulgarian medical personnel imprisoned for eight years.

not be permitted to send terror suspects to countries known to torture, and 73 percent said government officials who engage in or order torture should be punished. Fifty-eight percent of Americans said torture was impermissible under any circumstances — about the same percentage as those in countries like Ukraine, Turkey and Kenya — but lower than the percentages in Australia, Canada and France. [31]

Some critics fear that since 9/11 U.S. television shows and movies have changed the way torture is portrayed, making torture more palatable to Americans and the rest of the world.

"It used to be the bad guys who used these techniques," says David Danzig of Human Rights First, a New York-based advocacy group that works to combat genocide, torture and human rights abuses. "You saw it infrequently — an average of four or five times a year — and when you did see it, it was space aliens or Nazis doing it, and it almost never worked. Now it's often the heroes who are using these techniques."

The number of instances of torture portrayed on television jumped from almost none in 1996 to 228 in 2003, according to the Parents Television Council. [32]

Fox Television's "24" has come to symbolize that almost tectonic shift in TV's treatment of torture. The hero of the show — which debuted two months after 9/11 — is Jack Bauer, a member of a unit charged with preventing catastrophic terrorist attacks, including nuclear and poison gas attacks on American cities such as Los Angeles. Bauer and his comrades have been shown using electrical wires, heart defibrillators, physical assaults and chemical injections to obtain information vital to preventing the attacks. [33]

The show's creator has insisted he is not trying to present a realistic — or glamorized — view of torture and that Bauer is portrayed as paying a high psychological price for using torture. [34]

But critics say the show — enormously popular in the United States and throughout the world — is changing how American citizens and soldiers view torture. "The biggest lie that has gained currency through television is that torture is an acceptable weapon for the 'good guys' to use if the stakes are high enough. . . . It is a lie," wrote John McCarthy, a journalist who was held hostage in Lebanon in the late 1980s. He accused the entertainment industry of "minimizing the true horrors of torture by failing to show the very profound impact it has on victims' lives." [35]

THE RACK.

Cuthbert Simpson, a Protestant martyr, suffers on the rack in the Tower of London in 1563. Torture has been used over the centuries to solicit information and to punish political and religious dissenters.

AFP/Getty Images/Hulton Archive

The show "leaves a message with junior soldiers that it's OK to cross the line in order to gather intelligence and save lives," said Danzig.

Senior American military officials were so worried about the show's impact that Brig. Gen. Patrick Finnegan, dean of the United States Military Academy, and top FBI and military interrogators visited the set in 2006. Finnegan told the show's creators it gives U.S. military personnel the wrong idea and has hurt America's image abroad by suggesting the United States condones torture. [36]

The show's impact on world opinion of Americans has been the subject of numerous debates — both in the United States and abroad — including a 2006 panel discussion at the Heritage Foundation. The show reinforces a world view of Americans as people who succeed by "breaking the law, by torturing people, by circumventing the chain of command," said David Heyman, director of Homeland Security at the nonpartisan Center for Strategic and International Studies, which focuses on security issues. [37]

Carafano, the Heritage fellow, said the program "just sort of confirms [the] prejudice" of those "who think ill of us" already. [38]

The show was also debated in June at a conference of North American and European judges in Ottawa, Canada. U.S. Supreme Court Justice Antonin Scalia argued that government agents should have more latitude

Careful Training Creates Soldiers Who Torture

Most defy sadistic stereotype

Torturers are made, not born. That was the finding of a Greek psychology professor who studied the military regime that came to power in Greece after a 1967 coup.

Until it fell in 1974, the dictatorship carefully trained soldiers to gather information and squelch dissent through torture. That's when Professor Mika Haritos-Fatouros tried to understand how the soldiers had been turned into torturers. In one of the most in-depth studies of torturers ever conducted, she interviewed 16 former soldiers and reviewed the testimony of 21 others and their victims. [1]

Many of her interviewees defy the stereotype of sadistic men who take pleasure in abuse. Haritos-Fatouros found that the torturers were simply plucked from the ranks of ordinary soldiers and trained. One, from a farm family, was a 33-year-old high school teacher married with two children by the time Haritos-Fatouros interviewed him. But for 18 months he had tortured prisoners and ordered others to do so.

The army sought young recruits from rural, conservative families who were physically healthy, of normal intelligence, conformist in nature and compliant. They underwent three months of intensive "training," during which they were broken down physically and mentally — a process that began almost before they arrived at the training facility. The abuse of the torturers-in-training intensified during the subsequent weeks as they were allowed little sleep and ordered to run or hop everywhere they went.

The aim "was to minimize all resistance by instilling in the cadets the habit of obeying without question an order without logic," Haritos-Fatouros wrote. [2] In short, they were programmed to blindly obey authority and dehumanize their victims.

Gradually, they were desensitized to torture. First, they participated in group beatings. One of the torturers said the first time he participated in a group beating he went to his cousin's house and cried. But it got easier each time, he said. Later, they ratcheted up to inflicting electric shocks and other serious abuse.

The underlying goal, Haritos-Fatouros concluded, was making the torturers believe they were "not, in fact, inflicting a savage and horrifying violation upon another human being."

"They brainwashed us," one torturer said. "It was only later we realized that what we did was inhuman. It was only after I finished my military service that it occurred to me that most of us beat up prisoners because we'd been beaten up ourselves." [3]

Another torturer told her, "When I tortured, basically, I felt it was my duty. A lot of the time I found myself repeating the phrases I'd heard in the lessons, like 'bloody communists' and so on. I think I became worse as time went on. I became more a part of the system. I believed in the whole system." [4]

Haritos-Fatouros' chilling conclusion: "We are all, under the right conditions, capable of becoming torturers." [5]

---

[1] Mika Haritos-Fatouros, *The Psychological Origins of Institutionalized Torture* (2003).

[2] *Ibid.*, p. 46.

[3] *Ibid.*, p. 95.

[4] *Ibid.*, p. 82.

[5] *Ibid.*, p. 229.

---

in times of crisis. "Jack Bauer saved Los Angeles," said Scalia. "He saved hundreds of thousands of lives." [39]

Scalia's comments sparked heated retorts from the other judges and a subsequent *Globe and Mail* editorial. "Jack Bauer is a creation of wishful thinking. . . . He personifies the wish to be free of moral and legal constraints. . . . That's why constitutions exist; it's so tempting when fighting perceived evil to call for Jack Bauer." But, left unchecked, the commentary concluded, "Jack Bauer will poison liberty's fount." [40]

The popular TV program, however, doesn't seem to have clouded the vision of a group of American high school students invited to the White House in June to receive the prestigious Presidential Scholar award. They handed President Bush a handwritten letter urging him to halt "violations of the human rights" of terror suspects. "We do not want America to represent torture," said the letter. [41]

BACKGROUND

Ancient Practice

Torture has been embraced by some of the world's most enlightened civilizations. Egyptian wall paintings and friezes depict scenes of horrific treatment of enemies. [42] In ancient Greece, slaves and foreigners could be tortured lawfully but free citizens could not. The same held true in ancient Rome, where free citizens could only be tortured in cases of treason. Slaves could be beaten, whipped, stretched on the rack or burned with hot irons — as long they were not permanently injured or killed. [43]

The use of torture in Europe expanded in the 13th century after Italian city-states began to require stricter proof of guilt in criminal trials. Before that, guilt or innocence was proven by combat or endurance trials in which God was expected to favor the innocent. [44] Under the reforms, defendants could only be found guilty if two witnesses testified against them or the accused confessed to the crime. When there were no witnesses, torture was used to produce confessions, a practice that would persist for the next 500 years in Europe.

Torture was also used to punish prisoners in public spectacles, often attended by cheering crowds. In the technique known as "pressing to plead" weights were piled on the prisoner's body, crushing him until he confessed — or died. Victims were also stretched on a device called the rack — sometimes until their bones were pulled out of their sockets. Britain's King Henry VIII used torture against those who challenged his position as head of the Church of England. Queen Elizabeth I employed torture against those suspected of treason.

Particularly brutal torture methods gained religious sanction during the inquisitions conducted by the Roman Catholic Church to stamp out heresy. In 1252, Pope Innocent IV formally authorized the use of torture against heretics. In Spain for instance, victims were bound to a turning wheel as various body parts — the soles of their feet or the eyes — were brought closer and closer to a fire. In Italy, victims were suspended by their arms — tied behind their backs — from a pulley attached to a beam. The "strappado," as it was called, was then repeatedly jerked to increase the pain. Weights sometimes were attached to the victim's feet to increase the agony, often fracturing bones and tearing limbs from the body. [45]

In the early 17th century, some Europeans tried to regulate torture. Dutch legal scholar Johannes Voet, for instance, argued that torture should only be used when there are "grave presumptions" against the accused. He also suggested that the youngest member of any group of defendants be tortured first, because the youngest was thought most likely to talk. [46]

In 1754 Prussia became the first modern European state to abolish torture. Ten years later, in his seminal book *On Crimes and Punishments*, Italian philosopher and penal reformer Cesare Beccaria denounced torture as "a sure route for the acquittal of robust ruffians and the conviction of weak innocents." The book reflected emerging Enlightenment-era ideals about individual rights and the proper limits on punishment. [47] Within a century, most of Europe had banned torture, in part because convictions without eyewitness testimony or confessions were increasingly allowed, reducing the need for torture. But torture continued to thrive in Africa, Asia and the Middle East. In 1852, for example, leaders of an outlawed religious group in Persia — modern-day Iran — were "made into candlesticks" — with holes dug into their flesh into which lighted candles were inserted. [48]

By 1874, French author Victor Hugo naively declared "torture has ceased to exist." But torture continued to be used against insurgents in Austria and Italy and against opponents of the Tsarist government in Russia.

Changing Norms

By the 20th century, social norms about punishment had changed; the upper classes no longer wanted to watch gruesome public spectacles. Torture sessions became secretive affairs, conducted in prison basements and detention centers. [49]

In the first half of the 20th century, torture was employed by totalitarian governments in countries such as Germany, Russia, Italy and Japan. [50] The Nazis tortured prisoners of war to get information and conducted horrific medical experiments on Jewish and Gypsy civilians in concentration camps. Japanese soldiers severely abused and tortured Allied prisoners.

After the horrors of World War II, torture and lesser forms of abuse known as cruel, inhumane and degrading treatment were outlawed by a series of treaties: the 1948 Universal Declaration of Human Rights, the Geneva Conventions of 1949 and the 1984 Convention Against Torture. (*See box, p. 152.*)

Five International Treaties Ban Torture

Torture has been banned by international treaties since 1948. Key provisions include:

Universal Declaration of Human Rights (1948)

No one shall be subjected to torture or to cruel, inhuman or degrading treatment or punishment.

Adopted by U.N. General Assembly on Dec. 10, 1948, www.un.org/Overview/rights.html.

Third Geneva Convention, Common Article 3 (1949)

Regarding the treatment of civilians and prisoners of war, "the following acts are and shall remain prohibited at any time:

    (a) violence to life and person, in particular murder of all kinds, mutilation, cruel treatment and torture;
    (b) taking of hostages;
    (c) outrages upon personal dignity, in particular humiliating and degrading treatment . . ."

Adopted on Aug. 12, 1949, by the Diplomatic Conference for the Establishment of International Conventions for the Protection of Victims of War, held in Geneva, Switzerland; effective Oct. 21, 1950, www.icrc.org/ihl.nsf/0/e160550475c4b133c12563cd0051aa66?OpenDocument.

International Covenant on Civil and Political Rights (1966)

Article 7
No one shall be subjected to torture or to cruel, inhuman or degrading treatment or punishment. In particular, no one shall be subjected without his free consent to medical or scientific experimentation.

Article 10
All persons deprived of their liberty shall be treated with humanity and with respect for the inherent dignity of the human person.

Adopted the U.N. General Assembly on Dec. 16, 1966, and opened for signature and ratification; became effective on March 23, 1976, www.unhchr.ch/html/menu3/b/a_ccpr.htm.

Torture persisted during the second half of the century, however, particularly in authoritarian countries. For instance, Soviet and Chinese communist regimes tortured political and religious dissidents. Cambodia's murderous Khmer Rouge military regime had a 42-page interrogation manual for use at its Tuol Sleng torture center during the 1970s.

Many repressive regimes were supported by the United States, which was fighting a proxy Cold War with the Soviet Union in developing countries like Vietnam, El Salvador and Guatemala. Because such governments were resisting socialist or communist insurgencies, the United States often provided them with guns, military aid and training, even though they were known to use torture.

In the 1970s, President Jimmy Carter broke with the past by announcing that the nation's foreign policy henceforth would be based on advancing human rights. Congress passed a law requiring the State Department to issue annual reports on the human rights records of any country that received U.S. economic or military aid. [51] Although the law remains on the books and the State Department continues to issue its annual human rights "country reports," the foreign policy focus on human rights faded under Carter's successor, Ronald Reagan, who placed fighting communism above protecting human rights.

Since the 1970s, however, greater scrutiny by Western governments, the U.N., the EU and human rights groups has prompted changes in how countries torture. Increasingly, methods were adopted that don't leave visible scars, such as beating the soles of feet, sleep deprivation, sexual humiliation and electric shock.

Democracies' Experience

It wasn't only communists and dictators who tortured captives after World War II. Democratic countries — including Great Britain, France and Israel — all used torture or other forms of abuse during the last half of the century, usually in response to what they viewed as imminent threats from religious or political dissidents.

But the democracies ended up alienating their own citizens as well as the occupied populations, according to

Protocol Additional to the Geneva Conventions of Aug. 12, 1949, relating to the Protection of Victims of International Armed Conflicts (1977)

Article 75: Fundamental guarantees

1. . . . persons who are in the power of a Party to the conflict . . . shall be treated humanely in all circumstances and shall enjoy, as a minimum, the protection provided by this Article without any adverse distinction based upon race, colour, sex, language, religion or belief, political or other opinion, national or social origin, wealth, birth or other status, or on any other similar criteria. Each Party shall respect the person, honour, convictions and religious practices of all such persons.

2. The following acts are and shall remain prohibited at any time and in any place whatsoever, whether committed by civilian or by military agents:

(a) Violence to the life, health, or physical or mental well-being of persons, in particular:
   (i) Murder;
   (ii) Torture of all kinds, whether physical or mental;
   (iii) Corporal punishment; and
   (iv) Mutilation;
(b) Outrages upon personal dignity, in particular humiliating and degrading treatment, enforced prostitution and any form of indecent assault;
(c) The taking of hostages;
(d) Collective punishments; and
(e) Threats to commit any of the foregoing acts.

Adopted by the Diplomatic Conference on the Reaffirmation and Development of International Humanitarian Law applicable in Armed Conflicts on June 8, 1977; became effective on Dec. 7, 1979, www.unhchr.ch/html/menu3/b/93.htm.

Convention Against Torture and Other Cruel, Inhuman or Degrading Treatment or Punishment (1984)

Article 1

. . . the term 'torture' means any act by which severe pain or suffering, whether physical or mental, is intentionally inflicted on a person for such purposes as obtaining from him or a third person information or a confession, punishing him for an act he or a third person has committed or is suspected of having committed, or intimidating or coercing him or a third person, or for any reason based on discrimination of any kind, . . .

Article 2

1. Each State Party shall take effective legislative, administrative, judicial or other measures to prevent acts of torture in any territory under its jurisdiction.
2. No exceptional circumstances whatsoever, whether a state of war or a threat of war, internal political instability or any other public emergency, may be invoked as a justification of torture.
3. An order from a superior officer or a public authority may not be invoked as a justification of torture.

Article 3

1. No State Party shall expel, return ("refouler") or extradite a person to another State where there are substantial grounds for believing that he would be in danger of being subjected to torture.
2. For the purpose of determining whether there are such grounds, the competent authorities shall take into account all relevant considerations including, where applicable, the existence in the State concerned of a consistent pattern of gross, flagrant or mass violations of human rights.

Adopted by the U.N. General Assembly on Dec. 10, 1984, and opened for signature and ratification; became effective on June 26, 1987, www.unhchr.ch/html/menu3/b/h_cat39.htm.

Christopher Einolf, a University of Richmond sociologist who has studied the history of torture. Torture also proved difficult to control once it was authorized.

For instance, France initiated an intensive counterinsurgency strategy — which included torture — in Algeria after the Algerian National Liberation Front began a terrorist bombing campaign in 1956 to force France to cede control of the colony. France's strategy sometimes is cited as evidence that torture works. [52]

But Rejali at Reed College says France succeeded in gathering information because informants voluntarily cooperated — not as a result of torture. And tortured suspects often gave their interrogators the names of rival insurgents, dead militants or old hiding places rather than good information, he says.

Lou DiMarco, a retired U.S. Army lieutenant colonel who teaches at the Command and General Staff College, Fort Leavenworth, Kan., contends the French experience

Syrian-born Canadian citizen Maher Arar was picked up by the CIA in 2002 at John F. Kennedy International Airport in New York and taken to Syria, where he was imprisoned for a year and tortured with electric cables. He was later cleared of any links to terrorism. Human rights advocates say the CIA's so-called extraordinary rendition program "outsources" torture to countries known to abuse prisoners. The U.S. Justice Department said Syria had assured the United States it would not torture Arar.

in Algeria also proves the difficulty of controlling torture. "In Algeria, officially condoned torture quickly escalated to prolonged abuse, which resulted in permanent physical and psychological damage as well as death," he wrote. [53]

Similarly, the British, facing a spike in Irish Republican Army (IRA) violence in Northern Ireland in 1971, turned to aggressive interrogation techniques, including the "five techniques" — a combination of hooding, noise bombardment, food and sleep deprivation and forced standing. Individually, any one of these techniques could be painful, but taken together, "they induced a state of psychosis, a temporary madness with long-lasting after-effects," wrote John Conroy in his book, *Unspeakable Acts, Ordinary People: The Dynamics of Torture.* [54]

Tom Parker, a former British counterterrorism agent, says extreme interrogation methods had "huge" adverse consequences for Britain: They alienated Ireland — not a natural ally of the IRA — and enabled Ireland to successfully challenge British interrogation methods in the European Court of Human Rights.

Israel approved similar methods in 1987 after its security services were found to be using illegal interrogation techniques on Palestinian detainees in the occupied territories. Officials felt it would be better to allow a few psychological methods and "moderate physical pressure." But coercive methods proved hard to regulate and keep under control. [55]

In 1999, Israel's Supreme Court outlawed such techniques as cruel and inhuman treatment.

Post-9/11 Crackdown

After the 9/11 attacks, aggressive interrogation of suspects became a key — and highly controversial — part of U.S. antiterrorism strategy. On Nov. 13, 2001, President Bush signed an executive order allowing the military to detain and try "enemy combatants" outside the United States.

Defense Secretary Donald H. Rumsfeld announced the next month that enemy combatants detained in Afghanistan would be transferred to Guantánamo. In February 2002 Bush said the United States would treat the detainees humanely but did not consider them legitimate prisoners of war protected by the Geneva Conventions, which ban torture and "cruel, inhuman and degrading treatment."

U.S. interrogators used the same harsh methods designed to train American personnel to resist torture if captured. The so-called "Survival, Evasion, Resistance and Escape" (SERE) techniques included physical and mental pressure ("stress and duress") and sleep deprivation.

Rumsfeld formally approved many of these techniques in December 2002, including prolonged standing, use of dogs and the removal of clothing; he later rescinded approval for some of the methods. [56] Mohammed al-Qhatani — the alleged 20th 9/11 hijacker who had been captured along the Pakistani-Afghan border — says he was interrogated for 20-hour stretches, forced to stand naked while being menaced by dogs and barred from praying during Ramadan unless he drank water, which Islam forbids during Ramadan's fasting periods. The Pentagon said such techniques were designed to "prevent future attacks on America." [57]

Is torture ever justified?

YES

Mirko Bagaric
Professor of Law, Deakin University Melbourne, Australia

Written for *CQ Researcher*, August 2007

Despite its pejorative overtone, we should never say never to torture. Torture is bad. Killing innocent people is worse. Some people are so depraved they combine these evils and torture innocent people to death. Khalid Shaikh Mohammed, who is still gloating about personally beheading American journalist Daniel Pearl with his "blessed right hand," is but just one exhibit.

Torture opponents must take responsibility for the murder of innocent people if they reject torture if it is the only way to save innocent lives. We are responsible not only for what we do but also for the things we can, but fail, to prevent.

Life-saving torture is not cruel. It is morally justifiable because the right to life of innocent people trumps the physical integrity of wrongdoers. Thus, torture has the same moral justification as other practices in which we sacrifice the interests of one person for the greater good. A close analogy is life-saving organ and tissue transplants. Kidney and bone marrow transplants inflict high levels of pain and discomfort on donors, but their pain is normally outweighed by the benefit to the recipient.

Such is the case with life-saving compassionate torture. The pain inflicted on the wrongdoer is manifestly outweighed by the benefit from the lives saved. The fact that wrongdoers don't consent to their mistreatment is irrelevant. Prisoners and enemy soldiers don't consent to being incarcerated or shot at, yet we're not about to empty our prisons or stop trying to kill enemy soldiers.

Most proponents of banning torture say it does not produce reliable information. Yet there are countless counter-examples. Israeli authorities claim to have foiled 90 terrorist attacks by using coercive interrogation. In more mundane situations, courts across the world routinely throw out confessions that are corroborated by objective evidence because they were only made because the criminals were beaten up.

It is also contended that life-saving torture will lead down the slippery slope of other cruel practices. This is an intellectually defeatist argument. It tries to move the debate from what is on the table (life-saving torture) to situations where torture is used for reasons of domination and punishment — which is never justifiable.

Fanatics who oppose torture in all cases are adopting their own form of extremism. It is well-intentioned, but extremism in all its manifestations can lead to catastrophic consequences. Cruelty that is motivated by misguided kindness hurts no less.

NO

Sune Segal
Head of Communications Unit International Rehabilitation Council for Torture Victims Copenhagen, Denmark

Written for *CQ Researcher*, August 2007

Taking a utilitarian "greater good" approach in the wake of 9/11/2001, some scholars argue that torture is justified if used to prevent large-scale terror attacks. That argument rests on several flawed assumptions.

The claim that torture — or what is now euphemistically referred to as "enhanced interrogation techniques" — extracts reliable information is unfounded. The 2006 *U.S. Army Field Manual* states that "the use of force . . . yields unreliable results [and] may damage subsequent collection efforts." As laid out in a recent *Vanity Fair* article, it was humane treatment — not torture — of a detainee that led to the arrest of alleged 9/11 mastermind Khalid Shaikh Mohammed. In the same article, a U.S. Air Force Reserve colonel and expert in human-intelligence operations, drives home the point: "When [CIA psychologists argue that coercive interrogation] can make people talk, I have one question: 'About what?' "

But even if torture did "work," is it justified when a suspect is in custody and presumed to possess information about an imminent attack likely to kill thousands of people?

No, for several reasons. First, the above scenario assumes the person in custody has the pertinent information — a presumption that is never foolproof. Thus, by allowing torture there would be cases in which innocent detainees would be at risk of prolonged torture because they would not possess the desired information.

Second, it might be argued that mere circumstantial evidence suggesting the detainee is the right suspect is enough to justify torture or that torturing a relative into revealing the suspect's whereabouts is acceptable.

Third, if one form of torture — such as "waterboarding" — is allowed to preserve the "greater good," where do we go if it doesn't work? To breaking bones? Ripping out nails? Torturing the suspect's 5-year-old daughter?

Fourth, torture is not a momentary infliction of pain. In most cases the victim — innocent or guilty — is marked for life, as is the torturer. As a former CIA officer and friend of one of Mohammed's interrogators told *The New Yorker* in an Aug. 13, 2007, article: "[My friend] has horrible nightmares. . . . When you cross over that line, it's hard to come back. You lose your soul."

That's why we refrain from torture: to keep our souls intact. Torture is the hallmark of history's most abhorrent regimes and a violation of civilized values. Taking the "greater good" approach to torture is intellectually and morally bankrupt.

But some within the administration disapproved. In July 2004 Alberto J. Mora, the Navy's general counsel, warned in a 22-page memo that circumventing the Geneva Conventions was an invitation for U.S. interrogators to abuse prisoners. [58]

His prediction was prescient. SERE techniques apparently migrated to U.S. facilities in Afghanistan and Iraq, where they were reportedly employed by inadequately trained and unsupervised personnel. What began as "a set of special treatments" had become routine, wrote Tony Lagouranis, a former Army interrogator in Iraq. [59]

In late 2003 American military personnel at Abu Ghraib prison committed the abuses that generated the most public outrage, thanks to graphic photographs taken by the soldiers involved that eventually were circulated by news media around the world. An Army investigation later detailed "sadistic, blatant and wanton criminal" abuse that included beating detainees with a broom handle, threatening male detainees with rape, sodomizing another with a chemical light stick and frightening them with dogs. [60] Twelve U.S. military personnel have since been convicted for their roles in the abuse.

Mistreatment of Iraqi detainees was not just limited to Abu Ghraib. A military jury convicted Chief Warrant Officer Lewis Welshofer of negligent homicide after an interrogation in a facility in western Iraq in which he put a sleeping bag over the head of Iraqi Gen. Abed Hamed Mowhoush, sat on his chest and covered the general's mouth while asking him questions. American civilian contractors working alongside CIA and military interrogators in Iraq have also been accused of mistreating detainees.

Ever since the 9/11 attacks, a furious legal debate, both inside and outside the Bush administration, has examined the kinds of coercive interrogation methods the military and CIA can employ and the extent to which the United States must abide by international law. In 2005 Congress sought to limit the use by U.S. personnel of cruel, inhumane and degrading treatment in the Detainee Treatment Act. [61]

Then in 2006 the Supreme Court ruled that all prisoners held by the United States — including those in CIA custody — were subject to Common Article 3 of the Geneva Conventions, which outlaws torture or cruel and inhuman treatment of wartime detainees. (See box, p. 152.) [62] Later that year Congress passed another bill, the Military Commissions Act, endorsed by the Bush administration. It limited military interrogators to techniques that would be detailed in an updated *Army Field Manual.* The law did not specify, however, which interrogation methods CIA personnel can use — an omission designed to provide flexibility for interrogators at secret CIA facilities where "high value" prisoners are interrogated.

When *The Washington Post* revealed in 2005 that the CIA was operating secret prisons in eight countries in Eastern Europe, Thailand and Afghanistan, the administration had at first refused to confirm the story. [63] In 2006 Bush finally acknowledged the facilities existed, pointing out that, "Questioning the detainees in this program has given us information that has saved innocent lives by helping us stop new attacks — here in the United States and across the world." [64]

In 2007, Human Rights Watch and *The Post* detailed the experience of one former CIA detainee — Marwan Jabour, a Palestinian accused of being an al-Qaeda paymaster — who spent two years in a CIA-operated prison.

Jabour says he was kept naked for the first three months of his detention in Afghanistan. The lights were kept on 24 hours a day, and when loud music wasn't blasted through speakers into his cell, white noise buzzed in the background. And while he was frequently threatened with physical abuse, he says he was never beaten during 45 interrogations. He was also deprived of sleep and left for hours in painful positions. He was ultimately transferred to Jordanian and then Israeli custody, where a judge ordered his release in September 2006. [65]

CIA detainees also reportedly have been subjected to waterboarding and had their food spiked with drugs to loosen their inhibitions about speaking. [66]

The United States did not allow the International Committee of the Red Cross (ICRC) to visit the CIA's detainees until 2006. A subsequent ICRC report based on interviews with 15 former CIA detainees concluded that the detention and interrogation methods used at the "black sites" were tantamount to torture, according to confidential sources quoted in *The New Yorker.* [67]

The United States has strongly denied the ICRC's conclusions and claims the program is closely monitored by agency lawyers. "The CIA's interrogations were nothing like Abu Ghraib or Guantánamo," said Robert Grenier, a former head of the CIA's Counterterrorism Center. "They were very, very regimented. Very meticulous." The program is "completely legal." [68]

Unlike the CIA's secret prisons, the agency's use of so-called "extraordinary renditions" predated the 9/11 attacks. The first terror suspects were rendered to Egypt in the mid-1990s. [69] But the practice expanded greatly after 9/11, with up to 150 people sent to countries such as Morocco, Syria and Egypt between 2001 and 2005. Many, like Abu Omar — an imam with alleged links to terrorist groups — were snatched off the street. Omar, an Egyptian refugee, was kidnapped from Milan in February 2003 and sent to Egypt where he says he was tortured for four years before being released in 2007. [70]

U.S. officials have repeatedly insisted the United States does not send detainees to countries where they believe or know they'll be tortured. [71] But such declarations ring hollow for human rights advocates like Malinowski. "The administration says that it does not render people to torture," he told the Senate Foreign Relations Committee. "But the only safeguard it appears to have obtained in these cases was a promise from the receiving state that it would not mistreat the rendered prisoners. Such promises, coming from countries like Egypt and Syria and Uzbekistan where torture is routine, are unverifiable and utterly untrustworthy. I seriously doubt that anyone in the administration actually believed them." [72]

Renditions usually require the complicity of the countries where the suspects are grabbed. A 2006 report by the Council of Europe's Parliamentary Assembly tried to identify all the member countries that have allowed rendition flights to cross their airspace or land at their airports. [73]

One was the Czech Republic, which reportedly allowed three different jets to land at Prague's Ruzyne Airport during at least 20 different rendition flights, triggering anger from some Czechs. "No 'law enforcement,' 'intelligence,' or 'security' argument in support of torture can ever be anything but inhumane," wrote Gwendolyn Albert, director of the Czech League of Human Rights, in 2006 in *The Prague Post*. [74]

Former CIA operative Melissa Boyle Mahle condemns torture but has defended renditions and the need for absolute secrecy. "Renditions should be conducted in the shadows for optimal impact and should not, I must add, leave elephant-sized footprints so as to not embarrass our allies in Europe," she wrote in a 2005 blog entry. "During my career at the CIA, I was involved in these types of operations and know firsthand that they can save American lives." [75]

CURRENT SITUATION

Rendition Fallout

Kidnapping and shipping off allies' citizens to be harshly interrogated in foreign countries has strained relations with America's friends. Prosecutors in Germany and Italy are attempting to prosecute U.S. personnel for their role in renditions, and the rendition of Canadian citizen Maher Arar to Syria has chilled relations between Canada and the United States.

In Italy, the former chief of Italy's intelligence service is on trial for Omar's 2003 abduction in a case that threatens to ensnare top officials of the current and past Italian governments. A U.S. Air Force colonel and 25 CIA operatives also were indicted but are being tried in absentia because the United States has blocked their extradition. [76]

Similarly, a court in Munich ordered the arrest of 13 American intelligence operatives in January 2007 for their role in the kidnapping of a German citizen interrogated for five months at a secret prison in Afghanistan. But Germany, unlike Italy, does not allow trials in absentia, so an actual trial is unlikely because the United States will not extradite the defendants. [77]

Other European governments may be called to task for their role in U.S. renditions. Investigations have been initiated by Spain, and the Most Rev. John Neill — archbishop of Dublin — said the Irish government compromised itself by allowing rendition flights to land at Shannon Airport.

Meanwhile, on this side of the Atlantic, Canadian-U.S. relations are strained by the case of Syrian-born Canadian citizen Maher Arar. The McGill University graduate was returning to Canada from Tunisia in September 2002 when he landed at John F. Kennedy International Airport in New York during a stopover. U.S. immigration authorities detained him after seeing his name on a terrorist "watch" list.

After two weeks of questioning, he was flown to Jordan and then driven to Syria. During a yearlong detention by Syrian military intelligence, Arar says he was beaten with two-inch-thick electric cables. "Not even animals could withstand it," he said later. [78]

He was released in October 2003. A Canadian inquiry cleared Arar of any links to terrorism and said the Royal Canadian Mounted Police had given U.S. authorities erroneous information about him. Canada's prime minister apologized to Arar in January 2007 and announced an $8.9 million compensation package. Canada has also demanded an apology from the U.S. government and asked that Arar's name be removed from terrorist watch lists. [79]

U.S. federal courts have dismissed a lawsuit by Arar, and Attorney General Alberto R. Gonzales said Syria had assured the United States it would not torture Arar before he was sent there.

But Paul Cavalluzzo, a Toronto lawyer who led the government investigation of Arar's case, calls Gonzales' claim "graphic hypocrisy," pointing out that the U.S. State Department's own Web site lists Syria as one of the "worst offenders of torture."

"At one time, the United States was a beacon for the protection of human rights, whether internationally or domestically. Certainly, the Arar case was one example that lessened [that] view [among] Canadians."

Suing Torturers

Criminal prosecutions and civil lawsuits are pending against alleged torturers in several courts around the world.

In the United States, Iraqis claiming they were mistreated by American military personnel and private contractors are seeking redress under a little-used 18th-century law. The Alien Tort Claims Act, which originally targeted piracy, allows federal courts to hear claims by foreigners injured "in violation of the law of nations or a treaty of the United States."

In May 2007, the American Civil Liberties Union used the law to sue Jeppesen Dataplan Inc., a subsidiary of the Boeing Co., on behalf of three plaintiffs subjected to renditions. The company is accused of providing rendition flight services to the CIA. Two additional plaintiffs joined the suit in August. [80]

The law also was used in a class-action suit against Titan Corp. and CACI International Inc., military contractors that provided translators and interrogation services at Abu Ghraib. The suit asserts the two companies participated in a "scheme to torture, rape and in some instances, summarily execute plaintiffs." CACI called it a "malicious recitation of false statements and intentional distortions." [81]

The law was rarely used until the late 1970s, when human rights groups began suing abusive foreign officials. Since then it has been used to sue a Paraguayan police chief living in Brooklyn accused of torturing and killing a young man in Paraguay, an Ethiopian official, a

Guatemalan defense minister and the self-proclaimed president of the Bosnian Serbs.

Advocates of such suits say they are important tools in holding abusers accountable. "It is truly a mechanism that provides for policing international human rights abuses where a criminal prosecution may not necessarily be feasible," says John M. Eubanks, a South Carolinas lawyer involved in a suit that relies on the statute. The home countries of human rights abusers often lack legal systems that enable perpetrators to be held accountable.

"America is the only venue where they're going to be able to get their case heard," says Rachel Chambers, a British lawyer who has studied the statute.

Although the U.S. Supreme Court affirmed the use of the statute in 2004, legal experts disagree about just how much leeway the court left for future plaintiffs. [82]

Moreover, the statute can't provide redress in lawsuits against the U.S. government for the mistreatment of prisoners. The United States has successfully challenged such lawsuits by claiming sovereign immunity, a doctrine that protects governments against suits. The same defense has protected individuals sued in their official government capacity, according to Beth Stephens, a professor at Rutgers School of Law, in Camden, N.J. It is unclear how much protection private contractors such as CACI can claim for providing support services for interrogations.

Meanwhile, in Cambodia a U.N.-backed tribunal in July accused former Khmer Rouge leader Kaing Guek Eav of crimes against humanity for his role in the torture and deaths of 14,000 prisoners at Tuol Sleng. Only seven people who entered the prison emerged alive. The trial is expected to begin in 2008. [83]

And in Sierra Leone former Liberian President Charles Taylor is facing a U.N.-backed war-crimes tribunal for his role in financing and encouraging atrocities — including torture — committed during the civil war in neighboring Sierra Leone. The trial has been delayed until January 2008. [84]

The "Black Sites"

In July, when President Bush authorized the CIA's secret prisons to be reopened, the executive order laid out the administration's position on how the "enhanced interrogation" program will fully comply "with the obligations of the United States under Common Article 3" of the Geneva Conventions, which bans "outrages upon personal dignity, in particular humiliating and degrading treatment."

The president's order said the United States would satisfy the conventions if the CIA's interrogation methods don't violate federal law or constitute "willful and outrageous acts of personal abuse done for the purpose of humiliating the individual in a manner so serious that any reasonable person, considering the circumstances would deem the acts to be beyond the bounds of human decency."

The language appears to allow abusive techniques if the purpose is to gather intelligence or prevent attacks, say critics. "The president has given the CIA carte blanche to engage in 'willful and outrageous acts of personal abuse,' " wrote former Marine Corps Commandant P. X. Kelley and Robert Turner, a former Reagan administration lawyer. [85]

Human rights advocates are troubled by the executive order's lack of an explicit ban on coercive interrogation techniques such as stress positions or extreme sleep deprivation, which military interrogators are explicitly barred from using in the latest *Army Field Manual*, issued in 2006.

Media reports suggested the Bush administration also has sought to maintain other methods, such as inducing hypothermia, forced standing and manipulating sound and light. [86]

"What we're left with is a history of these kinds of techniques having been authorized, no explicit prohibition and we don't know what the CIA is authorized to do," says Devon Chaffee, an attorney with Human Rights First. "This creates a real problematic precedent."

Human rights advocates worry that foreign governments may cite Bush's executive order to justify their own coercive interrogations. "What they did is lower the bar for anybody," says Musa, the advocacy director for Amnesty USA.

In August, the American Bar Association passed a resolution urging Congress to override the executive order. [87] Also that month, Democratic Sen. Ron Wyden of Oregon vowed to block President Bush's nominee to become the CIA's top lawyer. Wyden said he was concerned that the agency's senior deputy general counsel, John Rizzo, had not objected to a 2002 CIA memo authorizing interrogation techniques that stopped just short of inflicting enough pain to cause organ failure or death.

"I'm going to keep the hold [on Rizzo] until the detention and interrogation program is on firm footing, both in terms of effectiveness and legality," Wyden said. [88]

OUTLOOK

No Panaceas

Human rights advocates worry countries that have tortured in the past will feel more emboldened to do so in the future as a result of U.S. government policies.

"This is just empowering the dictators and torturing governments around the world," said Whitson of Human Rights Watch.

They also worry that China, a rising superpower, is an abuser itself and has proven willing to do business with countries with histories of abuse in Central Asia and Africa.

HRW Executive Director Kenneth Roth also complains that — as its membership swells and the difficulty of reaching consensus grows — the European Union appears unable or unwilling to act. "Its efforts to achieve consensus among its diverse membership have become so laborious that it yields a faint shadow of its potential," he says.

The future direction of U.S. interrogation policies could depend heavily on the outcome of the 2008 American presidential election, which will likely determine the fate of what has become the most important symbol of U.S. detention policies: the prison for enemy combatants at Guantánamo. All the Democratic presidential candidates say they would close the facility, according to a study of candidate positions by the Council on Foreign Relations. [89]

On the Republican side, only two candidates — Rep. Ron Paul, R-Texas, and Sen. McCain — have advocated shutting the facility, and neither has been among the leaders in the polls. Mitt Romney, the former Massachusetts governor who has been among the front-runners this summer, suggested doubling the size of Guantánamo if he became president.

But regardless of who wins the election, human rights advocates do not look to a new occupant of the White House as a panacea. Amnesty USA's Musa says new administrations are often skittish about radically changing course from predecessors' foreign policies.

"It's not the absolute cure for all ills," she says.

NOTES

1. See Jonathan S. Landay, "VP confirms use of waterboarding," *Chicago Tribune*, Oct. 27, 2006, p. C5; and "Interview of the Vice President by Scott

Hennen, WDAY at Radio Day at the White House," www.whitehouse.gov/news/releases/2006/10/20061024-7.html. Also see John Crewdson, "Spilling Al Qaeda's secrets; 'Waterboarding' used on 9/11 mastermind, who eventually talked," *Chicago Tribune*, Dec. 28, 2005, p. C15. Also see Brian Ross and Richard Esposito, "CIA's Harsh Interrogation Techniques Described," ABC News, Nov. 18, 2005, www.abcnews.com.

2. Testimony by Tom Malinowski before Senate Committee on Foreign Relations, July 26, 2007.

3. David Cingranelli and David L. Richards, CIRI Human Rights Data Project, 2005, http://ciri.binghamton.edu/about.asp.

4. Quoted in Molly Moore, "Gaddafi's Son: Bulgarians Were Tortured," *The Washington Post*, Aug. 10, 2007, p. A8.

5. "In the Name of Security: Counterterrorism and Human Rights Abuses Under Malaysia's Internal Security Act," Human Rights Watch, http://hrw.org/reports/2004/malaysia0504/.

6. Dana Priest, "CIA Holds Terror Suspects in Secret Prisons," *The Washington Post*, Nov. 2, 2005, p. A1; also see Rosa Brooks, "The GOP's Torture Enthusiasts," *Los Angeles Times*, May 18, 2007, www.latimes.com/news/opinion/commentary/la-oe-brooks18may18,0,732795.column?coll=la-news-comment-opinions.

7. For background see Peter Katel and Kenneth Jost, "Treatment of Detainees," *CQ Researcher*, Aug. 25, 2006, pp. 673-696.

8. Kenneth Roth, "Filling the Leadership Void: Where is the European Union?" *World Report 2007*, Human Rights Watch.

9. Edward Cody, "China, Others Criticize U.S. Report on Rights: Double Standard at State Department Alleged" *The Washington Post*, March 4, 2005, p A14.

10. Lisa Haugaard, "Tarnished Image: Latin America Perceives the United States," Latin American Working Group, March 2006.

11. "World View of U.S. Role Goes from Bad to Worse," Program on International Policy Attitudes, January 2007, www.worldpublicopinion.org/pipa/pdf/jan07/BBC_USRole_Jan07_quaire.pdf.

12. See Karen DeYoung, "Bush Approves New CIA Methods," *The Washington Post*, July 21, 2007, p. A1.

13. See "President Discusses Creation of Military Commissions to Try Suspected Terrorists," Sept. 6, 2006, www.whitehouse.gov/news/releases/2006/09/20060906-3.html.

14. Crewdson, *op. cit.*

15. Jane Mayer, "The Black Sites," *The New Yorker*, Aug. 13, 2007, pp. 46-57.

16. *Ibid.*

17. *Ibid.*

18. Jane Mayer, "Outsourcing Torture," *The New Yorker*, Feb. 14, 2005, p. 106.

19. Intelligence Science Board, "Educing Information, Interrogation: Science and Art," Center for Strategic Intelligence Research, National Defense Intelligence College, December 2006, www.fas.org/irp/dni/educing.pdf.

20. Anne Applebaum, "The Torture Myth," *The Washington Post*, Jan. 12, 2005, p. A21.

21. Henry Schuster, "The Al Qaeda Hunter," CNN, http://edition.cnn.com/2005/US/03/02/schuster.column/index.html.

22. Mirko Bagaric, "A Case for Torture," *The Age*, May 17, 2005, www.theage.com.au/news/Opinion/A-case-for-torture/2005/05/16/1116095904947.html.

23. Alan Dershowitz, *Why Terrorism Works: Understanding the Threat, Responding to the Challenge*, Yale University Press, 2003, pp. 158-159.

24. Michael Levin, "The Case for Torture," *Newsweek*, June 7, 1982.

25. " '24' and America's Image in Fighting Terrorism," Heritage Foundation Symposium, June 30, 2006.

26. Eitan Felner, "Torture and Terrorism: Painful Lessons from Israel," in Kenneth Roth, *et al.*, eds., *Torture: Does it Make Us Safer? Is It Ever OK? A Human Rights Perspective* (2005).

27. Henry Shue, "Torture," in Sanford Levinson, ed., *Torture: A Collection* (2006), p. 58.

28. See Brooks, *op. cit.*

29. Humphrey Hawksley, "US Iraq Troops 'condone torture,' " BBC News, May 4, 2007, http://news.bbc.co.uk/2/hi/middle_east/6627055.stm.

30. "Bush, McCain Agree on Torture Ban," CNN, Dec. 15, 2005, www.cnn.com/2005/POLITICS/12/15/torture.bill/index.html.

31. "American and International Opinion on the Rights of Terrorism Suspects," Program on International Policy Attitudes, July 17, 2006, www.worldpublicopinion.org/pipa/pdf/jul06/TerrSuspect_Jul06_rpt.pdf.

32. Allison Hanes, "Prime time torture: A U.S. Brigadier-General voices concern about the message the show '24' might be sending to the public and impressionable recruits," *National Post*, March 19, 2007.

33. Evan Thomas, " '24' Versus the Real World," *Newsweek Online*, Sept. 22, 2006, www.msnbc.msn.com/id/14924664/site/newsweek/.

34. Jane Mayer, "Whatever It Takes," *The New Yorker*, Feb. 19, 2007, www.newyorker.com/reporting/2007/02/19/070219fa-fact_mayer?printable=true.

35. John McCarthy, "Television is making torture acceptable," *The Independent*, May 24, 2007, http://comment.independent.co.uk/commentators/article2578453.ece.

36. Mayer, Feb. 19, 2007, *ibid.*

37. Heritage symposium, *op. cit.*

38. *Ibid.*

39. Colin Freeze, "What would Jack Bauer do?," *Globe and Mail*, June 16, 2007, www.theglobeandmail.com/servlet/story/LAC.20070616.BAUER16/TPStory/TPNational/Television/.

40. "Don't Go to Bat for Jack Bauer," *Globe and Mail*, July 9, 2007, www.theglobeandmail.com/servlet/story/RTGAM.20070709.wxetorture09/BNStory/specialComment/home.

41. The Associated Press, "Scholars Urge Bush to Ban Use of Torture," *The Washington Post*, June 25, 2007, www.washingtonpost.com/wp-dyn/content/article/2007/06/25/AR2007062501437.html.

42. See David Masci, "Torture," *CQ Researcher*, April 18, 2003, pp. 345-368.

43. James Ross, "A History of Torture," in Roth, *op. cit.*

44. John Langbein, "The Legal History of Torture," in Levinson, *op. cit.*

45. Brian Innes, *The History of Torture* (1998), pp. 13, 43.

46. Roth, p. 8.

47. Ross, p. 12.

48. Darius M. Rejali, *Torture & Modernity: Self, Society, and State in Modern Iran* (1994), p. 11.

49. *Ibid.*, p. 13.

50. Christopher J. Einolf, "The Fall and Rise of Torture: A Comparative and Historical Analysis," *Sociological Theory* 25:2, June 2007.

51. For background, see R. C. Schroeder, "Human Rights Policy," in *Editorial Research Reports 1979* (Vol. I), available in *CQ Researcher Plus Archive*, http://library.cqpress.com. Also see "Foreign Aid: Human Rights Compromise," in *CQ Almanac*, 1977.

52. Darius Rejali, "Does Torture Work?" *Salon*, June 21, 2004, http://archive.salon.com/opinion/feature/2004/06/21/torture_algiers/index_np.html.

53. Lou DiMarco, "Losing the Moral Compass: Torture & Guerre Revolutionnaire in the Algerian War," *Parameters*, Summer 2006.

54. John Conroy, *Unspeakable Acts, Ordinary People: The Dynamics of Torture* (2001).

55. Miriam Gur-Arye, "Can the War against Terror Justify the Use of Force in Interrogations? Reflections in Light of the Israeli Experience," in Levinson, *op. cit.*, p. 185.

56. Jess Bravin and Greg Jaffe, "Rumsfeld Approved Methods for Guantánamo Interrogation," *The Wall Street Journal*, June 10, 2004.

57. Department of Defense press release, June 12, 2005, www.defenselink.mil/Releases/Release.aspx?ReleaseID=8583.

58. Jane Mayer, "The Memo," *The New Yorker*, Feb. 27, 2006, pp. 32-41.

59. Tony Lagouranis, *Fear Up Harsh: An Army Interrogator's Dark Journey Through Iraq* (2007), p. 93.

60. A summary of the Taguba report can be found at www.fas.org/irp/agency/dod/taguba.pdf.

61. "Bush Signs Defense Authorization Measure With Detainee Provision," *CQ Almanac 2005 Online Edition*, available at http://library.cqpress.com.

62. The case is *Hamdan v. Rumsfeld*, 126 S. Ct. 2749 (2006).

63. Priest, *op. cit.*

64. "President Discusses Creation of Military Commissions to Try Suspected Terrorists," *op. cit.*

65. Dafna Linzer and Julie Tate, "New Light Shed on CIA's 'Black Site' Prisons," *The Washington Post*, Feb. 28, 2007, p. A1.

66. Mark Bowden, "The Dark Art of Interrogation," *The Atlantic*, October 2003.

67. Mayer, Aug. 13, 2007, *op. cit.*

68. *Ibid.*

69. Mayer, Feb. 14, 2005, *op. cit.*

70. Ian Fisher and Elisabetta Povoledo, "Italy Braces for Legal Fight Over Secret CIA Program," *The New York Times*, June 8, 2007.

71. Jeffrey R. Smith, "Gonzales Defends Transfer of Detainees," *The Washington Post*, March 8, 2005, p. A3.

72. Malinowski testimony, *op. cit.*

73. Council of Europe Parliamentary Assembly, "Alleged secret detentions in Council of Europe member states, 2006," http://assembly.coe.int/CommitteeDocs/2006/20060606_Ejdoc162006Part II-FINAL.pdf.

74. Gwendolyn Albert, "With Impunity," *Prague Post*, April 12, 2006, www.praguepost.com/articles/2006/04/12/with-impunity.php.

75. http://melissamahlecommentary.blogspot.com/2005/12/cia-and-torture.html.

76. Elisabetta Povoledo, "Trial of CIA Operatives is delayed in Italy," *The International Herald Tribune*, June 18, 2007.

77. Jeffrey Fleishman, "Germany Orders Arrest of 13 CIA Operatives in Kidnapping of Khaled el-Masri" *Los Angeles Times*, Jan. 31, 2007.

78. Mayer, Feb. 14, 2005, *op. cit.*

79. "Arar Case Timeline," Canadian Broadcasting Company, www.cbc.ca/news/background/arar.

80. Christine Kearney, "Iraqi, Yemeni men join lawsuit over CIA flights," Reuters, Aug. 1, 2007.

81. Marie Beaudette, "Standing at the Floodgates," *Legal Times*, June 28, 2004.

82. The case is *Sosa v. Alvarez-Machain*, 2004, 542 U.S. 692 (2004).

83. Ian MacKinnon, "War crimes panel charges Khmer Rouge chief," *The Guardian*, Aug. 1, 2007.

84. "Taylor Trial Delayed until 2008," BBC News, Aug. 20, 2007, http://news.bbc.co.uk/2/hi/africa/6954627.stm.

85. P. X. Kelley and Robert F. Turner, "War Crimes and the White House," *The Washington Post*, July 26, 2007.

86. Thomas, *op. cit.*

87. Henry Weinstein, "ABA targets CIA methods, secret law," *Los Angeles Times*, Aug. 14, 2007.

88. The Associated Press, "Dem blocking Bush pick for CIA lawyer," MSNBC, Aug. 16, 2007, www.msnbc.msn.com/id/20294826.

89. "The Candidates on Military Tribunals and Guantánamo Bay," Council on Foreign Relations, July 17, 2007, www.cfr.org/publication/13816/.

BIBLIOGRAPHY

Books

Bagaric, Mirko, and Julie Clarke, *Torture: When the Unthinkable Is Morally Permissible*, State University of New York Press, 2007.
Bagaric, an Australian law professor, argues torture is sometimes morally justified and should be legally excusable.

Conroy, John, *Unspeakable Acts, Ordinary People: The Dynamics of Torture*, Random House, 2000.
A reporter examines the history of torture.

Dershowitz, Alan M., *Why Torture Works: Understanding the Threat, Responding to the Challenge*, Yale University Press, 2003.
A Harvard law professor argues that torture will be employed by interrogators, so courts should issue "torture warrants" to bring some legal oversight to the process.

Haritos-Fatouros, Mika, *The Psychological Origins of Institutionalized Torture*, Routledge, 2003.
A sociologist explores the indoctrination of Greek torturers during military rule of the country during the 1970s.

Lagouranis, Tony, *Fear Up Harsh: An Army Interrogator's Dark Journey Through Iraq*, NAL Hardcover, 2007.
A former U.S. Army interrogator describes the use of coercive techniques by American soldiers.

Levinson, Sanford, ed., *Torture: A Collection*, **Oxford University Press, 2004.**
Essays by academics and human rights advocates examine the historical, moral and political implications of torture.

Rejali, Darius, *Torture and Democracy*, **Princeton University Press, 2007.**
A Reed College professor and expert on torture traces its history from the 19th century through the U.S. occupation of Iraq.

Articles

"Torture in the Name of Freedom," *Der Spiegel*, **Feb. 20, 2006, www.spiegel.de/international/spiegel/ 0,1518,401899,00.html.**
The German news magazine concludes the United States is ceding its moral authority on the issue of torture.

Bowden, Mark, "The Dark Art of Interrogation," *The Atlantic Monthly*, **October 2003, www.theatlantic .com/doc/200310/bowden.**
An American journalist examines interrogation methods employed by U.S. personnel since the 9/11 terrorist attacks.

Einolf, Christopher J., "The Fall and Rise of Torture: A Comparative and Historical Analysis," *Sociological Theory*, **June 2007, www.asanet.org/galleries/default-file/June07STFeature.pdf.**
A University of Richmond sociology professor explains the continued prevalence of torture during the 20th century.

Mayer, Jane, "Outsourcing Torture," *The New Yorker*, **Feb. 14, 2005, www.newyorker.com/archive/ 2005/02/14/050214fa_fact6.**
The reporter traces the history of the U.S.'s "extraordinary rendition" policy.

Mayer, Jane, "Whatever It Takes," *The New Yorker*, **Feb. 19, 2007, www.newyorker.com/reporting/2007/ 02/19/070219fa_fact_mayer.**
The article examines the popular television show "24" and its role in "normalizing" perceptions of torture.

Mayer, Jane, "The Black Sites," *The New Yorker*, **Aug. 13, 2007, p. 46, www.newyorker.com/reporting/ 2007/08/13/070813fa_fact_mayer.**
A journalist examines the history of the CIA's secret "black site" prisons for high-value terror suspects.

Ozdemir, Cem, "Beyond the Valley of the Wolves," *Der Spiegel*, **Feb. 22, 2006, www.spiegel.de/international/0,1518,401565,00.html.**
A Turkish member of parliament discusses a popular Turkish movie that depicts American soldiers mistreating Iraqi civilians.

Reports and Studies

"Alleged secret detentions and unlawful inter-state transfers involving Council of Europe member states," Committee on Legal Affairs and Human Rights Council of Europe Parliamentary Assembly, June 7, 2006, http://assembly.coe.int/CommitteeDocs/2006/2006060 6_Ejdoc162006PartII-FINAL.pdf.
An organization of European lawmakers examines the role of European governments in U.S. renditions.

"Educing Information, Interrogation: Science and Art," Foundations for the Future Phase 1 Report, Intelligence Science Board, December 2006, www.fas. org/irp/dni/educing.pdf.
Too little is known about which interrogation methods are effective.

"Tarnished Image: Latin America Perceives the United States," Latin American Working Group, www.lawg.org/docs/tarnishedimage.pdf.
A nonprofit group examines Latin American press coverage of U.S. policies, including its interrogation of detainees.

For More Information

Amnesty International USA, 5 Penn Plaza, New York, NY 10001; (212) 807-8400; www.amnestyusa.org. U.S.-affiliate of London-based international human rights organization.

Center for Victims of Torture, 717 East River Rd., Minneapolis, MN 55455; (612) 436-4800; www.cvt.org. Operates healing centers in Minneapolis-St. Paul and Liberia and Sierra Leone. Also trains religious leaders, teachers, caregivers and staff from other NGOs about the effects of torture and trauma.

Human Rights First, 333 Seventh Ave., 13th Floor, New York, NY 10001-5108; (212) 845-5200; www.humanrights-first.org. A New York-based advocacy group that combats genocide, torture and other human rights abuses; founded in 1978 as the Lawyers Committee for Human Rights.

Human Rights Watch, 350 Fifth Ave., 34th floor, New York, NY 10118-3299; (212) 290-4700; www.hrw.org. Advocates for human rights around the world.

International Rehabilitation Council for Torture Victims, Borgergade 13, P.O. Box 9049 DK-1022; Copenhagen K, Denmark; +45 33 76 06 00; www.irct.org. Umbrella organization for worldwide network of centers that treat torture victims.

Medical Foundation for the Care of Victims of Torture, 111 Isledon Rd., Islington, London N7 7JW; (020) 7697 7777; www.torturecare.org.uk. Trains and provides medical personnel to aid victims of torture.

Office of the High Commissioner for Human Rights, 8-14 Ave. de la Paix, 1211 Geneva 10, Switzerland; (41-22) 917-9000; www.unhchr.ch. United Nations agency that opposes human rights violations.

Tony Blair

Then-Prime Minister, United Kingdom

What's the actual threat?
"People devote the most extraordinary amount of time in trying to say that the Americans, on rendition, are basically deporting people . . . and people spend very little time in actually looking at what the threat is that we face and America faces, from terrorism and how we have to deal with it."

— The Independent *(United Kingdom), February 2006*

Michael Ignatieff

Member of Parliament, Canada

Taking the high ground
"The moral imperative, 'Do not torture, any time, anywhere, in any circumstances,' is mandated by the United Nations convention against torture and other cruel, inhuman or degrading treatment or punishment. The fact that terrorists torture does not change these imperatives. Compliance does not depend on reciprocity."

— Business Day *(South Africa), April 2006*

Basil Fernando

Executive Director, Asian Human Rights Council

A benefit to the elite
"There is still reluctance on the part of Thai elite to eliminate torture. . . . [Those in power fear] police will no longer be an instrument in their hand. They have to accept that police can investigate everyone and that the police will become a friend of the ordinary man."

— Bangkok Post, *July 2006*

Editorial

The Indian Express

We are all capable of torture
"Living in a country where torture has become banal, we know it is just as likely to emanate from disgruntled and disaffected fellow citizens as it is from the institutions mandated to protect us — the army, the police, the paramilitary. When authoritarianism and violence become common currency across classes . . . then nobody has qualms disrespecting the basic tenets of civilised political discourse, behaviour, and transaction."

— November 2005

Manfred Nowak

Anti-Torture Investigator, United Nations

Torturers should pay the costs
"Countries where torture is widespread or even systematic should be held accountable to pay. . . . If individual torturers would have to pay all the long-term rehabilitation costs, this would have a much stronger deterrent effect on torture than some kind of disciplinary or lenient criminal punishment."

— Address before U.N. Human Rights Council, Geneva, April 2007

Narmin Uthman

Minister of Human Rights, Iraq

No torture in Abu Ghraib
"Abu Ghraib prison is currently under the supervision of the Human Rights Ministry, and our [inspection] committees have not found evidence of any use of torture. . . . The change in the treatment of [prisoners by] the jail guards in Abu Ghraib prison has had a great impact on changing the Americans' policy towards Iraqi prisoners in general."

— Al-Arabiya TV *(Dubai), February 2006*

Larry Cox

Executive Director, Amnesty International

EU needs better policies
"By the EU adopting anemic rules for the commerce of torture instruments, it essentially allows the practice to continue, now with an official wink and nod. These directives fail to provide broad and tough policies to guarantee that businesses do not profit by the sale of these repulsive tools."

— U.S. Newswire, February 2007

Kofi Annan

Then-Secretary-General, United Nations

Torture is torture, by any name
"Fifty-seven years after the Universal Declaration of Human Rights prohibited all forms of torture and cruel, inhuman or degrading treatment or punishment, torture remains an unacceptable vice. . . . Nor is torture permissible when it is called something else. . . . Humanity faces grave challenges today. The threat of terror is real and immediate. Fear of terrorists can never justify adopting their methods."

— Speech during International Human Rights Day, December 2005

7

Ending Poverty in Africa

Peter Katel and Alan Greenblatt

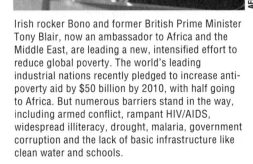

Irish rocker Bono and former British Prime Minister Tony Blair, now an ambassador to Africa and the Middle East, are leading a new, intensified effort to reduce global poverty. The world's leading industrial nations recently pledged to increase anti-poverty aid by $50 billion by 2010, with half going to Africa. But numerous barriers stand in the way, including armed conflict, rampant HIV/AIDS, widespread illiteracy, drought, malaria, government corruption and the lack of basic infrastructure like clean water and schools.

From *CQ Researcher,*
September 9, 2005 (updated October 2007).

During a June 2007 visit to Senegal, first lady Laura Bush sampled eggplant and beets — not as part of some fancy embassy dinner, but as pickings from a garden at a Dakar clinic for people with HIV or AIDS. The hospital keeps a vegetable garden that patients themselves tend as part of a treatment regimen that emphasizes the importance of nutrition. The facility has received nearly $600,000 in direct aid from the U.S. Agency for International Development (USAID) — a small part of the $15 billion the Bush administration has pledged toward the fight against AIDS, particularly in Africa. [1]

The garden is also emblematic of a larger effort to improve agriculture in sub-Saharan Africa. An effort spearheaded by USAID to improve the quality of Rwandan coffee, for example, has led 5,000 Starbucks outlets in the U.S. to sell the country's coffee; Green Mountain Coffee Roasters in 2007 called the country "the hottest emerging origin in specialty coffee." [2] Three months after Laura Bush's visit to Senegal, the Gates and Rockefeller foundations announced plans to spend $150 million over five years to boost agricultural productivity throughout Africa. More than 80 percent of the continent's soil is considered seriously degraded, with many areas "on the verge of permanent failure." [3]

Governments, charities and corporations have pledged tens of billions of dollars in the hope of wiping out massive killers such as AIDS and malaria while raising living standards and life expectancy for millions of Africans living in extreme poverty, defined as less than $1 a day.

Besides Africa, many other nations also are beset by extreme poverty, among them Haiti, Honduras and Cambodia. [4] But Africa is the only continent unlikely to meet any of the Millennium

U.S. Donates Low Percentage of National Income

The U.S. donates more money to poor countries — $19 billion in 2004 — than any other wealthy country (top graph) but ranks second to last when aid is calculated as a percentage of national wealth (bottom graph). The U.S. donates only 0.16 percent of its national income to poor countries, far less than the 0.7 percent goal set by the U.N. in 2000. Five countries, all from Northern Europe, already meet that goal.

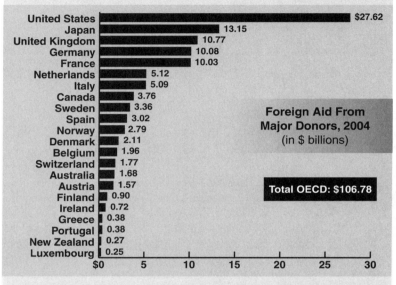

Foreign Aid From Major Donors, 2004 (in $ billions)

Country	$ billions
United States	$27.62
Japan	13.15
United Kingdom	10.77
Germany	10.08
France	10.03
Netherlands	5.12
Italy	5.09
Canada	3.76
Sweden	3.36
Spain	3.02
Norway	2.79
Denmark	2.11
Belgium	1.96
Switzerland	1.77
Australia	1.68
Austria	1.57
Finland	0.90
Ireland	0.72
Greece	0.38
Portugal	0.38
New Zealand	0.27
Luxembourg	0.25

Total OECD: $106.78

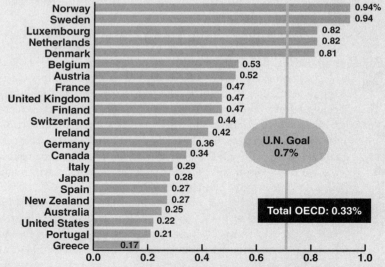

Foreign Aid as Percentage of Gross National Income, 2004

Country	%
Norway	0.94%
Sweden	0.94
Luxembourg	0.82
Netherlands	0.82
Denmark	0.81
Belgium	0.53
Austria	0.52
France	0.47
United Kingdom	0.47
Finland	0.47
Switzerland	0.44
Ireland	0.42
Germany	0.36
Canada	0.34
Italy	0.29
Japan	0.28
Spain	0.27
New Zealand	0.27
Australia	0.25
United States	0.22
Portugal	0.21
Greece	0.17

U.N. Goal 0.7%

Total OECD: 0.33%

Source: Organisation for Economic Development and Co-operation (OEDC), Development Co-operation Report 2006, Vol. 8, No. 1, 2007

Development Goals set by the U.N. in 2000 and 2001 as part of an effort to reduce extreme poverty worldwide by 50 percent by 2015. [5] Since 1990, life expectancy in Africa has fallen from 50 years to 46 years, and gross national income per capita has dropped from $550 to $490, according to the World Bank. [6]

The needs are clear, but the solutions remain evasive. Pilot programs show promise but are difficult to replicate on a massive scale. Even country-wide successes in reducing poverty have proved difficult to replicate in neighboring nations. The biggest pledges are not always fulfilled. Even when they are, the money can be slow in reaching intended recipients. One survey, for instance, found that less than 1 percent of the funds released by the Chad Ministry of Finance to help rural health clinics actually reached them. [7] Even after the World Bank insisted that Chad adopt anti-corruption laws and promise to spend most of its oil money on programs such as health care and rural development in order to receive loans, Idriss Deby, Chad's president, spent the first $4.5 million he received as a "signing bonus" from oil companies to buy weapons to use against rebels. [8]

Poverty keeps a tight grip on Africa despite billions of dollars in aid that have poured in since the continent's former European colonies gained independence in the 1960s. Drought, pestilence and armed conflict also are holding the continent back, as are corruption, traditional tribal culture and the lack of basic infrastructure like clean water, paved roads, schools and hospitals. All of this contributes to the severe malnutrition of more than 206 million people in sub-Saharan Africa, according to Action Against Hunger. [9]

In 2004, the entire combined gross domestic product for the 47 countries of sub-Saharan Africa was $385.6 billion — about that of the state of New Jersey. [10] Although the extreme poverty rate in Africa fell from 46 percent in 1999 to 41 percent in 2004, that is still a long way from meeting the United Nation's 2015 Millennium Development Goal of 22 percent. [11]

The Millennium Development Goals, announced in 2000, helped highlight the issue of global poverty, which has since become a central concern of world leaders. The world's leading industrialized nations in 2007 pledged a collective $60 billion — half from the U.S. — to fight AIDS, malaria and tuberculosis, mainly in Africa. They also agreed to provide $60 billion worth of debt relief and to work with 30 African countries to cut the number of deaths from malaria in half. [12] These commitments were the latest commitment in a series made by wealthy nations to fight poverty and disease on the African continent.

Much fanfare surrounded top leaders of the West's richest nations — known as the G-8 — when they met in Gleneagles, Scotland, in 2005 and vowed to double anti-poverty spending to $50 billion a year by 2010 — with half the new money going to Africa. The rest was earmarked for anti-poverty programs elsewhere in the world.

The G-8 meeting was held in the glow cast by rock star and anti-poverty crusader Bono and by "Live 8" pop concerts that year in London, Philadelphia and Johannesburg that sought to rally millions of young people to push their national leaders to finally end African poverty. That event helped renew Western attention to Africa, as did subsequent high-profile visits by celebrities

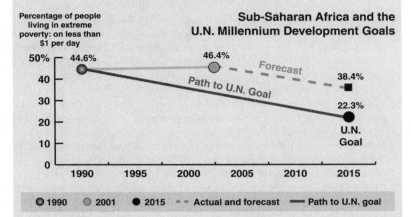

Africa Won't Meet U.N. Goals

Sub-Saharan Africa will be far from meeting the U.N.'s goal of reducing extreme poverty worldwide by 50 percent by 2015. Africa is the only continent not expected to meet the goals.

Percentage of people living in extreme poverty: on less than $1 per day

Sub-Saharan Africa and the U.N. Millennium Development Goals

44.6% — 46.4% — Forecast — 38.4%
Path to U.N. Goal — 22.3% — U.N. Goal

● 1990   ● 2001   ● 2015   - - Actual and forecast   — Path to U.N. goal

Number of People Living on Less Than $1 Per Day
(in millions)

	1990	2001	2015
East Asia and Pacific	472	271	19
China	375	212	16
Europe and Central Asia	2	17	2
Latin America and the Caribbean	49	50	43
Middle East and North Africa	6	7	4
South Asia	462	431	216
Sub-Saharan Africa	227	313	340
Average/Total	**1,219**	**1,089**	**622**

Source: World Bank, "Global Monitoring Report 2005"

such as Madonna, Angelina Jolie and Don Cheadle. Bill Clinton has made African health and anti-poverty efforts a priority of his post-presidential foundations, attracting major support from corporations and helping to cut the price of anti-retroviral drug prices for AIDS patients.

And the G-8 pledge represented a sea change in attitudes about dealing with extreme poverty. In earlier decades, rich countries and international aid organizations such as the World Bank operated under the theory that helping poor countries build up their agriculture and industry would enable them to eventually climb out

Can Jeffrey Sachs End Global Poverty?

There's Bono hobnobbing with President Bush at the White House, advising U.N. Secretary-General Kofi Annan and rocking at the Live 8 concert in London. The charismatic frontman for the Irish rock group U2 certainly seems to be at the epicenter of recent efforts to end African poverty. While Bono did help focus the world's attention on Africa's dire poverty, *the* big player in the fight against global poverty these days is superstar economist Jeffrey Sachs.

Indeed, Bono calls Sachs "my professor," adding, "In time, his autograph will be worth a lot more than mine." [1]

Operating from well within established institutions, first as director of Harvard University's Institute for International Development, then as director of the U.N. Millennium Project and now as director of Columbia's Earth Institute, Sachs, who was born in 1954, provides the intellectual backing for the key demand of activists worldwide: End poverty fast.

More precisely, Sachs has laid out a plan to end extreme poverty by 2025. His ideas spring from the central thesis that desperately poor countries — nearly all of sub-Saharan Africa — are beset by problematic geography (including a climate that's uniquely hospitable to drought and mosquitoes) and ugly colonial history. Moreover, because they weren't on the Cold War front lines during the 1980s and '90s, they didn't rate the big-time U.S. aid that helped lift South Korea and Taiwan into prosperity.

Only massive and well-targeted aid can break through Africa's "poverty trap," Sachs told *Mother Jones* magazine. "Once they're on the first rung of the ladder of development, they'll start climbing just like the rest of the world." [2]

By traditional global-development standards, which measured progress in tiny steps, Sachs' vision is breathtakingly ambitious. But, as he reminds doubters, ending slavery and then the Jim Crow system seemed like unattainable goals for America, as did throwing the colonial powers out of Africa and Asia. "They took decades to bring to fruition; perseverance was the key," he writes. "In the same way, the end of poverty will come quickly, marked by a rapid transition." [3]

Sachs knows about rapid transitions. As a young professor, he virtually stumbled into advising the Bolivian government in 1985, when it was fighting ruinous inflation. Sachs' plan worked, and he went on to advise the post-Soviet governments of Poland and Russia. Those assignments led him into the intensive, firsthand study of deep poverty.

Following the 9/11 terrorist attacks, Sachs, who was already working with U.N. agencies, offered to help Annan "lead the world in fulfillment of the hopes of the new millennium." Sachs got the assignment of figuring out how to see that the U.N.'s Millennium Development Goals — aimed at halving extreme poverty by 2015 — were met.

Not surprisingly for a professor who has cast himself as a key player on the world stage, Sachs has his critics. "There is, for one thing, the matter of Sachs' ego," wrote Daniel W. Drezner, a University of Chicago political scientist, in reviewing Sachs' widely praised new book, *The End of Poverty.* "Anyone who writes that 'as a young faculty member, I lectured widely to high acclaim, published broadly and was on a rapid academic climb to tenure, which I received in 1983, when I was 28,' clearly lacks the gift of understatement." [4]

Drezner and others also note that some of Sachs' ideas are really reheated policies from the early years of development economics. If ending poverty is, as Sachs argues, so

of deep poverty themselves. Now, some development experts argue that a massive aid effort mainly targeting the conditions of poverty themselves — such as lack of access to clean water — can improve poor peoples' lives in a shorter amount of time.

"I'm talking about a plan to help Africa feed itself, deliver basic infrastructure and get the major killer diseases under control over a 10-year period," said Jeffrey Sachs, the Columbia University economist who was a special adviser to the U.N. and the development of its Millennium Development Goals project, and the leading theoretician of the latest campaign against African poverty. [13]

Making that vision reality depends on spending the pledged money effectively. Expenditure details are works in progress, but the broad outlines are clear:

- Expand anti-HIV/AIDS prevention and treatment, including care of AIDS orphans;
- Expand family-planning services;
- Provide more access to clean water;
- Expand malaria-mitigation efforts, and;
- Begin training some of the 4 million new teachers Africa needs. [14]

easy, "Why haven't five decades of effort gotten the job done?" William Easterly, a former World Bank economist now at New York University, asked in another — and largely critical — review of Sachs' book. "Sachs should redirect some of his outrage at the question of why the previous $2.3 trillion didn't reach the poor so that the next $2.3 trillion does. In fact, ending poverty is not easy at all." [5]

Easterly's review sent Sachs, characteristically, into counter-attack mode. "Easterly's World Bank experience made him into a dystopian, seeing the worst in everything and expecting failure everywhere," he wrote. "I have had the good fortune to participate in successful efforts to stop hyperinflations, introduce new and stable national currencies, convert centrally planned economies to market economies and establish the Global Fund to Fight AIDS, TB and Malaria." [6]

Sachs has been an impressive fundraiser. But even he can't raise the hundreds of billions his vision would require to build the roads, farms, schools and hospitals Africa needs. Instead, he has picked poor rural villages — 79 so far — in countries with fairly stable governments and persuaded corporations, foundations and wealthy individuals to fund his programs there at a cost of $300,000 a year for five years. [7]

Economist Jeffrey Sachs says massive infusions of well-targeted aid can end extreme poverty.

In September 2006, Sachs persuaded George Soros, a financier well known for funding democracy campaigns and the campaigns of Democratic candidates, to donate $50 million to his project. [8]

Other anti-poverty veterans profess amusement at Sachs' lack of modesty but concede that his supreme self-confidence has helped focus attention and money on a region that needs plenty of both.

One Africa expert who has tangled with Sachs but respects him doesn't want to discuss him on the record. "I need to deal with him," the expert says. "He's The Man."

[1] Bono, "Foreward" in Jeffrey Sachs, *The End of Poverty* (2005), p. xv.

[2] Onnesha Roychoudhuri, "The End of Poverty: An Interview with Jeffrey Sachs," *MotherJones.com*, May 6, 2005, www.motherjones.com.

[3] Sachs, *op. cit.*, p. 364.

[4] Daniel Drezner, "Brother, Can You Spare $195 Billion?," *The New York Times Book Review*, April 24, 2005, p. 18.

[5] William Easterly, "A Modest Proposal," *The Washington Post Book World*, March 13, 2005, p. T3.

[6] Jeffrey Sachs, "Letters," *The Washington Post Book World*, March 27, 2005, p. T12.

[7] Joe Nocera, "Can a Vision Save All of Africa?" *The New York Times*, June 16, 2007, p. C1.

[8] Celia W. Dugger, "Philanthropist Gives $50 Million to Help Aid the Poor in Africa," *The New York Times*, Sept. 13, 2006, p. A18.

The G-8 also endorsed a major goal of anti-poverty activists — removing trade barriers to Africa's exports of cotton and other commodities set by affluent countries. Stepping up African exports by only 1 percent would generate $70 billion for the region per year, or more than all the aid money pledged by the G-8 over the next five years, according to Oxfam, a major British anti-poverty organization. [15]

But will reality match the ambitious plans? Skeptics point out that few of the leaders who made the pledges will still be in office in 2010, and that aid promised in the past has often failed to materialize. A 2007 study by Bono's advocacy group found that the G-8 nations had increased aid by less than half the amount needed to reach their goal of doubling aid by 2010. [16]

Congress took two years to pass legislation setting up Bush's program to meet the Millennium Challenge goals. The president set those goals — including sending $5 billion a year to poor countries by 2006 — in 2002, but his funding requests have never come near that total. And, of the total of $6 billion that had been appropriated by the middle of 2007, only about $71 million had actu-

New Foreign Aid Program Comes to Town

Accustomed to thinking of themselves as the world's most generous people, Americans tend to think their government's foreign-aid spending is high — too high.

In 2004, for instance, 64 percent of Americans responding to a Gallup Poll said the United States was spending "too much" on foreign aid. Most respondents to another survey guessed that the United States spent 15 percent of its budget on foreign aid. [1]

In fact, the United States spends 1 percent of its federal budget and slightly more than two-tenths of 1 percent — 0.22 percent — of its gross national income (GNI) on foreign aid, consistently ranking last in giving among wealthy nations. (*See graph, p. 168.*) Top contributors Norway and Sweden pony up 0.94 percent. Looked at another way, the United States contributed about $51 per citizen in fiscal 2003, whereas Norwegians gave $381 per person.

In 2002, President Bush proposed increasing the $11 billion the U.S. spends on foreign aid by $5 billion over three years. The new money was to be channeled through a new agency, the Millennium Challenge Corporation (MCC), which was designed to make economic-development grants to countries that embrace capitalism and meet U.S.-set standards for democratic governance.

Officially, the MCC has a radically different mission from the U.S. Agency for International Development (USAID), which for four decades has been the government's major anti-poverty funding arm.

The MCC focuses "less on the issue of poverty alleviation itself" than on "rewarding countries who are making the right policy choices" through grants that allow for faster economic growth than they would achieve via traditional development funding, says Jeffrey Grieco, the USAID deputy assistant administrator for public affairs. His own agency aims to "sustain growth over a long period of time while alleviating suffering from poverty."

"We work for prosperity and opportunity because they're right; it's the right thing to do," Bush said in proposing the MCC. "We also work for prosperity and opportunity because they help defeat terror."

The MCC was also designed to remedy what foreign-aid critics have long said is a tendency for development funds to end up fattening rulers' wallets or be channeled into useless projects. [2]

But critics of the Bush administration say the agency has been slow to gear up, with Congress providing fewer

dollars each year than the administration has requested. Program funding grew rapidly to $2 billion in fiscal 2007, but its budget looked likely to be slashed for 2008.' Of the total of $6 billion that had been appropriated by the middle of 2007, only about $71 million had actually been spent. [3]

In 2005, Rep. Jim Kolbe, R-Ariz., defended the agency, saying that complaining about the MCC's slowness to act was not fair. "A plane doesn't take off at 500 miles, and it doesn't take off at 30,000 feet," he said. "It takes off slower, and it climbs. And we do the same thing with programs, which is how you ramp them up." [4]

Fair or not, the agency's first administrator, Paul Applegarth, resigned under fire in June 2005. His departure was announced two days after five African leaders complained personally to Bush that the grant-making process was proceeding at a snail's pace. [5] John J. Danilovich, a former ambassador to Costa Rica and Brazil, was appointed CEO five months after Applegarth's departure.

The MCC's slow start has dampened earlier fears that it would supplant USAID. "This is a terrible blow to USAID — a vote of no confidence in how they are giving out aid," Lael Brainard, a Brookings Institution scholar, said when the MCC was created. [6] In fact, most foreign-aid spending still is being channeled through USAID.

"MCC is so new that it's hard to say it's in competition," says Mvemba Dizolele, a policy analyst at the Center for Global Development. However, he adds, it's possible that the MCC's mandate to finance programs proposed by the beneficiary countries may be superior to the traditional approach of paying for projects that Washington-based experts have deemed important.

[1] Gallup Poll, March 4, 2004, and Mary H. Cooper, "Reassessing Foreign Aid," *CQ Researcher*, Sept. 27, 1996, pp. 841-864.

[2] Paul Blustein, "Bush Seeks Foreign Aid Boost," *The Washington Post*, March 15, 2002, p. A1.

[3] "The Millennium Challenge," *The Washington Post*, July 16, 2007, p. A14.

[4] Quoted in Celia Dugger, "Bush Aid Initiative For Poor Nations Faces Sharp Budget Cuts and Criticism of Slow Pace," *The New York Times*, June 17, 2005, p. A12; Richard W. Stevenson, "Bush Promotes His Plans to Help Africa," *The New York Times*, July 11, 2003, p. A7.

[5] Dugger, *ibid.*

[6] Elizabeth Becker, "With Record Rise in Foreign Aid Comes Change in How It Is Measured," *The New York Times*, Dec. 7, 2003, p. A10.

ally been spent. [17] What's more, Bush's budget request for 2008 would have cut funding for USAID by nearly one-third, including a 9 percent cut to its child survival program and an 18 percent cut to its famine efforts. At the time he submitted his request, the agency had already lost 100 Foreign Service officers and 30 percent of the doctors in its Africa bureau. [18]

After Democrats took control of Congress in 2007, however, they adopted a budget that devoted $1 billion more for Africa than Bush requested, mostly to fight AIDS and malaria. "We're on a trajectory to exceed the target laid out by the president at Gleneagles," Bobby Pittman, senior director of African affairs at the National Security Council, told *The New York Times.* [19]

But even if the rich countries do fulfill their pledges — and if trade barriers for African products fall — experts say practical problems could pose obstacles. Africa's poorly developed ports and roads would be overwhelmed by a big increase in exports. In addition, the G-8 didn't make any firm commitments on trade. (As one of its final acts, the Republican-controlled Congress in December 2006 passed an extension of a trade law that gives special treatment to countries in Africa. [20])

As the Gleneagles summit was nearing an end, Thailand's Supachai Panitchipakdi, director-general of the World Trade Organization, said its rhetoric stood in contrast to a near-standstill on the present round of global trade negotiations. [21] Likewise, John Page, the World Bank's senior economist for Africa, says the "prevailing opinion" of trade-watchers is that rich countries will not lower their politically popular trade barriers.

However, many countries have used trade as a route out of poverty. In the 1960s, gross domestic product (GDP) per capita throughout Africa was about $2,000 a year, or roughly twice the rate in East Asia. Today, East Asia is one of the world's largest exporting regions, with a per capita GDP of $4,000. [22] By contrast, per capita GDP in Africa has dropped to $1,000.

Meanwhile, two of East Asia's "economic tigers" — South Korea and Taiwan — are also cited as proof that massive aid delivers results. The two countries — together with South Vietnam, which no longer exists as a separate country — received half of all U.S. bilateral aid * in the 1950s and '60s. [23] During the same period, Africa was receiving 1 to 5 percent of U.S. bilateral aid.

The massive aid strategy aimed at Africa is known as The Big Push. "The Big-Push approach is the only one that can address Africa's challenges with the urgency and effectiveness required," concluded a March 2005 report of the Commission for Africa, formed in 2004 by Tony Blair, then Britain's prime minister. [24]

But skeptics note that earlier waves of development aid for Africa, also accompanied by star-studded concern, had little long-term impact. Among the best-known were the July 13, 1985, "Live Aid" concerts to raise money for famine victims in Ethiopia and other African nations and the song and video "We Are the World," sung by dozens of American stars earlier that same year. Yet per capita income in Ethiopia has fallen from $110 to $90 in this decade, and 85 percent of the population still depends on farming in the drought-plagued country. [25]

And hunger stalks other African countries as well — most recently Niger and several West African nations. [26]

Skeptics, like George Ayittey, a Ghanaian-born economist at American University in Washington, D.C., insist the G-8's massive-aid strategy is "fundamentally flawed." He contends that corruption, which costs Africa $148 billion a year in lost funds, is the single, biggest obstacle to fighting poverty. [27]

"If these governments were to get serious and cut that in half, they will get more money than the $50 billion Tony Blair wants to raise for them," Ayittey says, noting that wealthy nations usually are more willing to send aid to honest governments. Paul Wolfowitz, who was forced out as president of the World Bank in 2007, had sought to make anti-corruption efforts a priority but was resisted by many staffers who worried that such efforts would penalize the poor twice by curtailing lending in their countries.

Mo Ibrahim, a billionaire Sudanese businessman, sought to make good government more personally rewarding for sub-Saharan leaders by giving out $5 million prizes to those with clean hands who left office voluntarily. Yet critics said that wouldn't be enough — that there was much more money to be looted from the treasuries of even tiny countries. "Those inclined towards repression and corruption aren't going to be dissuaded by this award," said Peter Lewis, director of the African Studies program at Johns Hopkins University. [28]

While critics like Ayittey say Africa suffers mainly because of bad governments, aid advocates like Sachs blame geography, history and the West's indifference to the con-

---

* Bilateral aid is foreign aid from one country to another.

tinent's plight. For instance, poverty and malaria, which kills more than a million Africans a year, reinforce one another. [29] In Nigeria alone, according to Nigeria's Society for Family Health, malaria causes more than $1 billion worth of job absenteeism annually, consumes 45 percent of health-care spending and kills thousands of children.

Two of the continent's other plagues, AIDS and armed conflict, are mutually reinforcing as well, largely because the disease helps swell the under-29 age group in hard-hit countries. "Several studies show that countries that had such radically large youth bulges in the period between 1990 and 2000 were three times more likely to suffer civil war, coups or armed insurrections," writes author Laurie Garrett, a leading scholar of global infections. Of the 37 countries experiencing the "bulge," nearly all are in Africa. And when the violence provokes mass rape, HIV spreads even more quickly, she points out. [30]

"You can't look at Africa without looking at conflict and HIV/AIDS," says Michael Wessells, a child-protection specialist with the Richmond, Va.-based Christian Children's Fund. "In West Africa right now, we're seeing the rise of a generation of mercenary soldiers. This means that cycles of violence that amplify poverty will continue until we get serious about protection."

The G-8 nations promised "extra resources" so that Africa's peacekeeping forces "can better deter, prevent and resolve conflicts." [31]

In the wake of all these issues, here are some of the questions about global poverty being debated:

Is massive aid the best strategy for saving Africa?

Eritrea is a secretive society that is turning inward. President Isaias Afwerki, who has led the nation since it won independence from Ethiopia in 2003, has cut his country off from foreign donors, turning down more than $200 million in aid in 2006-07 alone, including food from the U.N., development loans from the World Bank and grants from international charities seeking to cover road construction and health care. Billions of dollars in post-colonial aid have done little to lift Africa from chronic poverty, he told the *Los Angeles Times*.

Still, Afwerki's attitude represents an extreme version of what some critics of aid believe — that it does more to foster dependency than better economic health. "These are crippled societies," Afwerki said. "You can't keep these people living on handouts because that doesn't change their lives." [32]

Advocates of massive aid to Africa often cite the success of the Marshall Plan in rebuilding post-World War II Europe as a shining example of such a strategy. But critics doubt it can work in Africa, pointing out that Western Europe was already an industrial region with democratic traditions and a literate population.

"Africa, in contrast, is a continent of 10,000 peoples shoehorned into 40 countries by colonial powers who sought to divide and conquer," Scottish journalist Alison Rowat writes, summing up the debate. "Sub-Saharan Africa has desperately poor people, a tiny, self-serving elite, a largely agrarian economy and widespread illiteracy." [33]

However, proponents of massive-aid strategies say they have worked in countries — such as Taiwan and South Korea — where conditions were similar to those existing in Africa. "The Asian nations that Africa is being told to emulate may have pulled themselves up by their bootstraps, but at least they were provided with boots," economic-affairs writer James Surowiecki observed in *The New Yorker*. "Between 1946 and 1978, in fact, South Korea received nearly as much U.S. aid as the whole of Africa." [34] (During the Cold War, U.S. foreign aid was targeted at supporting anti-communist regimes. Allies, like South Korea and Taiwan, which neighbor communist countries, were some of the largest beneficiaries.)

Not everyone agrees that massive aid explains Asia's success. One of the toughest critics of the G-8 nations' Big Push strategy notes that economic data do not show a connection between aid and growth in Southeast Asia's "tiger" countries like Hong Kong and Singapore, nor between aid and the timing of South Korea's economic takeoff. [35]

"If there was any evidence that the Big Push worked, I would be all for it," says William Easterly, a former World Bank economist who now teaches at New York University. "I just don't think there is any evidence that it works. It's been tried over and over in Africa and elsewhere."

Some development experts who have worked in both Africa and Asia also say they've noticed dramatic differences in the political cultures of the two regions. Asian leaders, they say, usually adopt policies that enable private producers to be more competitive, while African politicians generally are preoccupied with maintaining power.

Big Push proponents acknowledge that while it may not be the right approach for all countries, some countries do need an anti-poverty offensive beyond funding individual development projects. Economist Stephen C. Smith of George Washington University points out, for instance, that a Big Push can solve the problem of unequal progress, which occurs when foreign investors won't invest in a country because it lacks skilled workers yet the workforce is too poor to afford training — and even if individuals could afford training there aren't any jobs.

"It's the chicken-and-egg problem," Smith says. "The Big Push is designed to deal with the chicken-and-egg problem."

But a Big Push should not try to overhaul an entire economy at once, Smith cautions. "You really need to think critically about sectors and which investments to make in those sectors. Successful cases of high growth have really been about stringing together bursts of growth. We may need to think of The Big Push as something occurring over time. I call it a Smart Push."

To that end, former President Bill Clinton has helped corporations and the wealthy target their investments in Africa. In 2006, Clinton launched a sustainable growth program with a $100 million grant from British billionaire Sir Tom Hunter. [36]

Others do not trust African governments to spend the aid on the right kinds of projects. "In the Blair Commission [for Africa] and the G-8 action plan you have a fairly strong statement about trusting countries," the World Bank's Page says, adding that the donors then recommend that the money be used for infrastructure, HIV/AIDS, education and malaria mitigation. "Aren't we saying that we trust countries, but they're not doing enough in these categories?"

Moreover, Page says, conditions in Africa vary greatly. Tanzania has its own anti-poverty programs and tells donors how aid will be spent. But in barely functioning governments like Sierra Leone and Liberia, "donors get together and say, 'This is what we're going to do,'" Page says. " 'We don't trust you to be representative of your constituency or a responsible implementing government.' "

Other Big Push critics worry about Africa becoming too dependent on foreign aid.

"For the last 40 years, Africa has been getting more, not less, aid — we've received more than $500 billion," says Andrew Mwenda, a journalist in Uganda who is now a research fellow at Stanford University. "But we are getting poorer, not richer. Uganda is considered one of Africa's economic success stories. Yet we rely on foreign aid for nearly half the country's budget. Parliament is so foreign-aid dependent that even the chairs and desks are funded by Denmark." [37]

A woman carries away grain supplied by a humanitarian organization in Dogo, Niger, where a severe food shortage threatens thousands with starvation. U.N. Secretary-General Kofi Annan has acknowledged the U.N. was slow in sending aid to Niger, where drought and a locust plague last year wiped out much of the harvest.

Giving massive amounts of aid to a government creates an incentive for capable people to line up and get money rather than work, says Yaw Nyarko, a Ghanaian-born economist who is vice provost for globalization and multicultural affairs at New York University (NYU). The same principle would apply in the United States, he says.

"You've got to get people to sit down and admit that transferring money for development is not easy — get people to try different things, evaluate those that work and those that don't, with no preconceived notions about giving [aid] to governments or NGOs [non-governmental organizations] or banks," he continues. Just handing out large amounts of aid to governments promotes corruption, he says. "The industrialized world has given lots of aid; we know for sure what will happen if you give it carte blanche to governments."

The more people know about Africa, the more likely they are to point out the practical complications of applying a massive aid program throughout the region. Some of these people see the Big Push as a statement of purpose rather than a roadmap.

"The best way to look at it is to see it as a vision, see it as a framework," says Sarah Newhall, president and CEO of Pact, a Washington-based aid contractor that specializes in training and management.

Foreign Aid Is Tiny Fraction of U.S. Spending

U.S. aid to other countries constituted 1 percent of overall U.S. government spending in fiscal 2005. Social Security and defense were the two biggest expense categories.

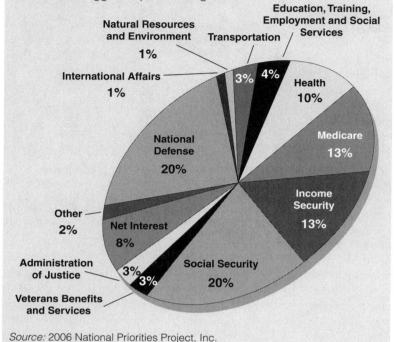

Natural Resources and Environment **1%**

International Affairs **1%**

Transportation

Education, Training, Employment and Social Services

3% **4%**

Health **10%**

National Defense **20%**

Medicare **13%**

Income Security **13%**

Other **2%**

Net Interest **8%**

Administration of Justice **3%**

Veterans Benefits and Services **3%**

Social Security **20%**

Source: 2006 National Priorities Project, Inc.

Will forgiving the debts of Africa's poorest countries help end poverty?

After years of campaigning by activists in both rich and poor countries, the G-8 — just before the Gleneagles meeting in 2005 — agreed to cancel the debts that some of the world's poorest countries owe to multilateral lenders such as the World Bank. In 2007, the G-8 agreed to forgive an additional $60 billion in debt.

Proponents argued that asking poor countries to keep up their debt payments as a condition for receiving more aid left them unable to provide basic survival needs. "A lot of the poorest countries are still [spending] more servicing old debts than on health care and education. That's unacceptable," Bono told CNN in 2002. [38]

"There is no question that the amount of debt exceeded domestic budgets of health and education," says GWU's Smith. "There is a tradeoff between debt and services."

But others claim the central premise of that argument — that impoverished countries must choose between making debt payments and providing services to the poor citizens — is faulty, because the countries whose debts were forgiven weren't repaying them in the first place. Thus, they say, the debt cancellation announced at Gleneagles did not produce any net income for African countries to spend on social programs.

"Does debt relief represent a net transfer of resources to poor countries?" asks NYU's Nyarko. "I doubt it. The whole thing is a sham. You get up and say you're going to forgive the debt that was not being paid and could not have been paid anyway. What are you getting besides a sound bite?"

"There is a lot of smoke and mirrors in the aid business," says the World Bank's Page, noting that a $6.7 billion debt-forgiveness action for Africa in 2003 by individual country donors was mostly "a book-keeping transaction."

The G-8 policy would cancel about $40 billion owed by 38 heavily indebted countries, on which they pay about $1.5 billion a year to the World Bank, the International Monetary Fund (IMF) and the African Development Fund. [39] The countries would be allowed to cancel that debt if they comply with World Bank-IMF economic-reform and poverty-reduction standards. So far, 14 sub-Saharan and four Latin American countries have met those standards and thus have already been forgiven about 90 percent of their bilateral debts (those owed to individual countries) and about half of the debt they owe to international financial institutions (multilateral debt). Some countries were still making payments on those debts but others were not.

In addition, points out Steven Radelet, a senior fellow with the Center on Global Development, the looming presence of debt "kept countries going back every year to borrow new money to pay old loans." Canceling the debt allows African countries to "get off the treadmill, restore credibility to the system and allow finance ministers to pay attention to important development issues."

But Page says that rather than moving a column of figures from the "payments owed" to the "write-off" column, officials should be discussing whether new aid money will flow into poor countries. To answer that question, he says, one must figure out how much aid goes to consultants, how much to crisis relief (as opposed to development) and how much to administrative costs. "That deserves a much more open discussion, but it has not caught the interest of the Bonos of the world," he says.

Other critics of debt-forgiveness complain that it effectively penalizes countries that owed money and managed to make their payments. "Those faithful in servicing their debt like Kenya are being ignored," said Kenyan Planning and National Development Minister Peter Anyang Nyongo after the G-8 decision. [40]

American University's Ayittey has another interpretation. He suggests that the G-8 applied political rather than humanitarian standards in deciding which countries get relief, similar to Cold War-era decisions that targeted aid to anti-communist regimes. "What are the criteria" being used today, he asks, if economically responsible countries like Malawi, Kenya and Botswana are not granted debt relief? Apparently, countries seen as allies in the war on terror, such as Ethiopia, are being favored, he says.

"The Cold War is gone," he says, "but we are going into Cold War-style considerations, where geopolitical factors are being taken into account."

Will corruption prevent development from taking place in Africa?

Debates about aid to Africa inevitably lead to a discussion of Africa's widespread government corruption, because most development money is channeled through governments. But the debates often begin with the question of whether corruption is more widespread in Africa than elsewhere.

According to Transparency International, which monitors government corruption around the world, "corruption in Africa is a major concern, more so than on any other continent."

The Berlin-based group agrees with the African Union's estimate that corruption in Africa ends up siphoning off $148 billion a year. The Commission for Africa puts it another way, estimating that corruption adds

USAID/Patricia Mantey (both)

Microfinancing at Work

Poor people around the world, mostly women, are using microfinancing loans to start businesses; borrowers include a chicken farmer in Kenya (top) and a woman applying for a loan in Senegal. Some 7,000 microfinance institutions are serving 13 million to 16 million poor people worldwide, including some 2.5 million in Africa.

at least 25 percent to the cost of government contracts, ultimately raising the cost of goods and services and thus taking even more money from the poor. In eastern and southern Africa alone, corruption cost up to $18 billion in 1999, according to Transparency International. [41]

"If only foreign aid could be shifted from lining corrupt politicians' and bureaucrats' pockets to developing private enterprise, then Africa would have hope," wrote Ugandan radio journalist Mwenda. [42]

CHRONOLOGY

1940s-1950s *Economists begin developing aid plans for war-ravaged and underdeveloped nations.*

1943 Polish-born British economist Paul Rosenstein-Rodan publishes his influential plan — dubbed "The Big Push" for reviving southern and Eastern Europe.

1944 World Bank is founded at a conference in Bretton Woods, N.H.

1945 U.N. is founded in San Francisco.

1948-1952 United States spends $13 billion under the Marshall Plan to revive war-torn Western Europe.

1956-1957 The first sub-Saharan nations to gain independence — Sudan from Egypt and Great Britain in 1956 and Ghana from Britain in 1957 — foreshadow the departure of all European colonial powers from Africa in the next decade.

1960s-1970s *Aiding "underdeveloped" countries becomes a major U.S. goal as it competes with the Soviet Union for global influence.*

1960 President John F. Kennedy pledges in his inaugural speech to aid people "in huts and villages," and goes on to create the U.S. Agency for International Development (USAID) and the Peace Corps.

1961 University of Chicago economist Theodore Schultz begins developing the thesis that "human capital" — investing in people — is as important as investment in factories and roads.

1973 World Bank President Robert S. McNamara declares the goal of ending poverty by the end of the century.

1973-1979 Skyrocketing oil prices hit poor countries hard, prompt McNamara to launch a policy of "structural adjustment," which effectively requires poor countries to cut back on services to qualify for loans.

1980s-1990s *Activists force aid agencies to shift from "structural adjustment" to lending policies aimed at fighting corruption and increasing accountability of governments to their poor citizens.*

1981 World Bank economists warn that many of the institution's loans are unpayable and should be cancelled.

July 13, 1985 "Live Aid" rock concerts in London, Philadelphia and Sydney focus worldwide attention on famine

in Ethiopia and the ravages of poverty throughout Africa.

1994 Activists disrupt the World Bank's annual meeting in Madrid, charging it promotes poverty, not development.

1996 U.S. investment banker James Wolfensohn becomes the World Bank's new president and denounces the "cancer of corruption" in developing countries.

2000s *World Bank and other development institutions vow to quickly wipe out the worst effects of poverty.*

2000 Secretary-General Kofi Annan announces the U.N.'s "Millennium Development Goals," including a 50 percent reduction by 2015 in the number of people living in poverty.

2002 *March 14:* President Bush proposes giving $5 billion to poor countries that take measures against corruption and adopt pro-market economic policies. *March 22:* Most U.N. nations sign the "Monterrey Consensus," which calls for rich nations to donate up to 0.7 percent of their gross national product to anti-poverty development.

Feb. 2004 British Prime Minister Tony Blair forms the 17-member Commission for Africa to help fight poverty.

2005 *July:* Leaders of the world's leading industrialized countries — the G-8 — pledge to step up development aid by $50 billion by 2010, with half of the increase going to Africa. *Sept.:* Former U.S. President Bill Clinton and British billionaire Sir Tom Hunter announce a $100 million initiative to foster sustainable growth in two African nations.

2006 *Sept.:* The Gates and Rockefeller foundations announce plans to spend $150 million over five years to promote agriculture in Africa. That same day, George Soros announces that he will contribute $50 million to support economist Jeffrey Sachs' efforts to help African villages escape poverty. *Oct.:* Muhammad Yunus and Grameen Bank of Bangladesh, which pioneered microcredit loans, are awarded the Nobel Peace Prize. *Dec.:* The White House hosts its first-ever summit on malaria

2007 *Jan.:* Oprah Winfrey opens a $40 million school for African girls outside of Johannesburg. *Feb.:* President Bush's proposed 2008 budget would cut funding for programs such as education, health care and child welfare in the USAID by 31 percent, while boosting support for economic programs through the State Department. *June:* The world's leading industrialized nations pledge $60 billion to fight AIDS, malaria and tuberculosis, primarily in Africa, while also granting $60 billion in debt relief.

"There are countries, such as South Africa and Botswana, whose perceived levels of corruption are comparable to developed countries such as Italy, Greece, Hungary and Taiwan," says Transparency International, "while others score much more poorly." Among the worst are Nigeria, Chad, the Democratic Republic of Congo, Angola and Cote d'Ivoire. [43]

Even in countries with severe corruption, like oil-rich Nigeria, the corruption is relative. Former Nigerian dictator Gen. Sani Abacha, for instance, reportedly headed a corruption network that stole billions of dollars in oil revenues in the 1990s. [44] But Uzo Gilpin, director of the Society for Family Health, a Nigeria-based health-care program, says she and her colleagues simply ignore the corrupt practices they constantly encounter. "No one is going to come up to me or to members of the society and demand a bribe," she says. But if her group were not known for its honesty, she concedes, it would have to pay local officials to work in their territories.

Transparency International says foreign companies that pay bribes to obtain market access have helped foster corruption in Africa. [45] Corporations claim that if they refuse to pay a bribe, corrupt governments merely award their contracts to companies that will.

To get around the corruption Catch-22, the G-8 leaders urged expansion of the Extractive Industries Transparency Initiative, unveiled by Blair in 2002 and advocated by anti-corruption activists for years. The new policy would require oil, gas and mining companies — lucrative sources of bribes to the government officials who award licenses and concessions — to publish all payments made to foreign governments. [46] That would remove the veil of secrecy that allows corruption to flourish.

Large-scale corruption is hardly limited to Africa. In 1996, the late Indonesian dictator Mohamed Suharto — whose regime was notorious for thievery on an epic scale — told World Bank President James Wolfensohn, "What you regard as corruption in your part of the world, we regard as family values." [47]

But corruption in Asia appears to have done less economic damage than corruption in Africa. NYU's Easterly compared, for example, corruption in Indonesia and in the Democratic Republic of Congo (the former Zaire), which was once ruled by one of Africa's most notorious kleptocrats, the late Mobutu Sese Seko. He is thought to have stolen up to $8 billion of his country's resources. [48]

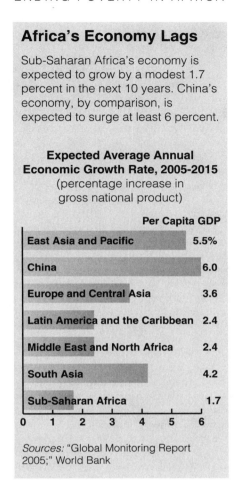

Africa's Economy Lags

Sub-Saharan Africa's economy is expected to grow by a modest 1.7 percent in the next 10 years. China's economy, by comparison, is expected to surge at least 6 percent.

Expected Average Annual Economic Growth Rate, 2005-2015
(percentage increase in gross national product)

	Per Capita GDP
East Asia and Pacific	5.5%
China	6.0
Europe and Central Asia	3.6
Latin America and the Caribbean	2.4
Middle East and North Africa	2.4
South Asia	4.2
Sub-Saharan Africa	1.7

Sources: "Global Monitoring Report 2005;" World Bank

"A strong dictator will choose a level of corruption that does not harm growth too badly, because he knows his rake-off depends on the size of the economy," Easterly writes, referring to Suharto. [49] Unlike Suharto, Mobutu did not promote the development of an economic infrastructure and left his country in a shambles.

But economist Sachs says the extent of corruption in Africa is hyped and then used by Western politicians as an excuse for stinginess. [50] "Our stereotypes about African corruption are a near-obsession on our part," he said. "They're not the reality." [51]

American University's Ayittey, however, says African corruption is so rampant that all aid should be channeled through NGOs rather than through governments. "For God's sake, learn from your own mistakes," he practi-

That Rare Species: The African Success Story

Amid the constant, dreary news about poverty, violence and disease in the 47 countries of sub-Saharan Africa, success stories are rare. But they do exist, often thanks to international aid. Yet even the region's success stories face unhappy new endings, as AIDS and violence threaten to undo their progress.

Topping most experts' success-story lists is tiny, diamond-producing Botswana. The landlocked former British colony, population 1.7 million, is considered the jewel of southern Africa, achieving an impressive 7 percent average annual economic growth rate over the past 20 years. That's in the same ballpark as flourishing Singapore, whose annual growth usually has ranged from 5 percent to 10 percent since 1994.

Botswana is among sub-Saharan Africa's few upper-middle-income nations. This World Bank classification is based on the country's gross national income per person of $3,530, or seven times the $506 average income in the rest of the region. [1] Democratically governed since gaining independence from Great Britain in 1966, Botswana at that time was among the world's poorest countries. [2] But Botswana prevented corruption from gaining a foothold, creating a favorable climate for business investment and ensuring that banks kept credit flowing to private business, building up a market-driven economy. Experts say these measures were more influential than revenue from Botswana's diamonds. Indeed, in most other countries, the Commission for Africa recently concluded, "Natural resources bring war. They enrich the elite but for most people they merely increase corruption, poverty, environmental degradation and political instability." [3]

Yet HIV/AIDS could be Botswana's undoing. An estimated 38 percent of the adult population is infected — bringing average life expectancy down to 38 years — below even the disastrous continental average of 45.8 years. Experts predict that by 2010 one in five Botswanean children will be orphaned by AIDS. [4] The U.N. Development Program says Botswana was late in initiating an anti-HIV/AIDS campaign and blames the government's "widespread denial, misinformation and generally limited understanding" of the problem. [5]

Mozambique, whose $210 per capita income in 2003 made it one of the world's poorest countries, nonetheless has steadily reduced the percentage of its citizens living in absolute poverty from 69 percent in 1996-97 to 54.5 percent in 2002. [6] The achievement is especially noteworthy because Mozambique is still recovering from 25 years of war. A struggle for independence from colonial master Portugal, which began in 1964, eventually evolved into a civil war with one side supported by apartheid-era South Africa. After a 1992 peace treaty, the country became a big aid recipient but kept its economy growing, even when assistance dropped. [7] Actions included such simple-sounding moves as clearing away red tape in the customs system — which allowed imports and exports to get to their destinations 40 times faster and increased customs revenue by 38 percent in two years. Perhaps just as important, Mozambique was able to maintain peace. [8]

Aid also was put to good use in Uganda, which cut its HIV-prevalence rate from 20 percent in 1991 to 6.5 percent in 2001 by launching an aggressive prevention campaign based on open discussions of HIV. Uganda also maintained economic growth by privatizing state-owned firms, encouraging foreign investment and channeling tax revenues and aid into health and education. "Public-sector spending on community services, which donor support made possible, explains a significant part of Uganda's high economic growth," Britain's Department for International Development concluded. [9] Although child mortality fell from 160 deaths per 1,000 children in 1990 to 141 in 2002, poverty indicators remain high. [10]

Uganda's success, however, is mostly limited to the South. The North is plagued by a 19-year-old insurrection led by the brutal Lord's Resistance Army (LRA), which has abducted some 30,000 children and forced them to terrorize the countryside by beating, maiming or killing civilians and kidnapping still more children. Human Rights Watch reports that some 40,000 Ugandan children nightly flee their homes in the unprotected countryside to sleep in churches, hospitals and bus stations to avoid capture by the

cally shouts. "We all know that government-to-government aid never worked."

If NGOs are to become substitute aid recipients for corrupt governments, George Washington University's Smith says the organizations will have to be trained to administer

larger programs than they are accustomed to handling. The solution is not to merely "throw money" at NGOs, he says.

Radelet, of the Center for Global Development, agrees that in countries with corrupt or dysfunctional governments — such as dictator-ruled Zimbabwe or

LRA. And some 1.3 million civilians live fulltime in refugee camps because of the LRA threat. [11]

In West Africa, Ghana has reduced the proportion of people living in poverty from 51.7 percent in 1991-92 to an estimated 28.6 percent in 2004. Most experts credit the authoritarian regime of President Jerry Rawlings for igniting the turnaround. Flight Lt. Rawlings seized power in a military coup in 1979 and was elected to office in 1992 and 1996. In the 1980s, Rawlings switched from Soviet-style economic management to the market-system approach that the World Bank and other international donors embrace. "Policy reforms implemented after 1983 served to enhance the effectiveness of aid and other public investments and helped to increase exports," the Commission for Africa concluded. Rawlings' rare willingness to leave power in 2000 when his two-term limit was up is also seen as having bolstered stability and investor confidence. [12]

Even Rwanda, which endured horrific genocidal slaughters in 1994, reduced the proportion of its poor from 72 percent in 1995 to 60 percent in 2001. Much of that progress reflected the torrent of aid that flowed following the slaughter of approximately 900,000 Tutsis by Hutus, the country's other main ethnic group. "Aid was effective not only for humanitarian purposes but also to stimulate economic growth and reduce poverty over an extended period," the Commission for Africa concluded. [13]

For development professionals, such success stories prove the value of major infusions of aid. "There are

Rita Lazaro, an entrepreneur in Mozambique, makes soy milk with a VitaGoat machine, which can turn out 30 liters an hour of the highly nutritious product. USAID partner Africare asked her to lead the pilot rural-enterprise project to teach other Mozambicans improved agriculture and nutrition practices.

USAID/Melissa Thompson

some countries where a rapid scale-up of aid makes lot of sense," says Steven Radelet, a senior fellow at the Center for Global Development in Washington. "In the popular debate, this distinction gets lost."

[1] World Bank, "African Development Indicators 2005"; http://worldbank.org.

[2] "Introduction, the UN in Botswana," www.unbotswana.org.bw.

[3] "Our Common Interest: Report of the Commission for Africa," pp. 43, 355-356; www.commissionforafrica.org/english/report/introduction.html.

[4] UNAIDS, "Statistics," Botswana; www.unbotswana.org.bw/unaids.html.

[5] "Moving Upstream and Engaging Governments in Strategic Policy Advocacy: The Case of UNDP Botswana's HIV & AIDS Programme," [undated], www.undp.org/hiv/botswana.pdf.

[6] World Bank, "Mozambique, Data and Statistics"; http://worldbank.org.

[7] "Chronology of War and Peace in Mozambique," *Conciliation Resources* (1997); www.c-r.org/accord/moz/accord3/chronol.shtml; and "Our Common Interest," *op. cit.*, p. 299.

[8] "Our Common Interest," *ibid.*, pp. 50, 165.

[9] John A. Okidi, "Operationalizing Pro-Poor Growth: A Country Case Study on Uganda," UK Department for International Development, pp. 15-18; www.dfid.gov.uk/casestudies/files/africa/uganda-growth.asp.

[10] World Bank, "Millennium Development Goals, Uganda"; http:worldbank.org., and "Our Common Interest," *op. cit.*, p. 299.

[11] Human Rights Watch, "New Photo, Video Essays Tell Story of Uganda's Child 'Night Commuters," Aug. 22, 2005; http://hrw.org/english/docs/2005/08/21/uganda11647.htm; " Uganda: Human Rights Overview," Human Rights Watch, World Report, 2005, http://hrw.org/english/docs/2005/01/13/uganda9862.htm.

[12] Ann M. Simmons, "Ghana Election Seen as Test; Marks End of an Era," *Los Angeles Times*, Dec. 8, 2000, p. A19.

[13] Ann Ansoms and Stefaan Marysse, "The Evolution and Characteristics of Poverty in Rwanda," United Nations, World Institute for Development, Economics Research, June 4, 2004, p. 3; www.wider.unu.edu/conference/conference-2004-1/conference%202004-1-papers/Ansoms-Marysse-1905.pdf.

war-torn Ivory Coast and Somalia — aid should be funneled through NGOs. "But you'd have a different approach in Ghana or Mozambique," he says, "where you've got pretty well-functioning governments and more of a thriving press."

Radelet points out that Western politicians sometimes appear hypocritical, condemning corruption in poor countries while tolerating it back home. "Yes, there's corruption [in Africa]," he says. "And if a scandal broke out in Mozambique, a bunch of congressmen

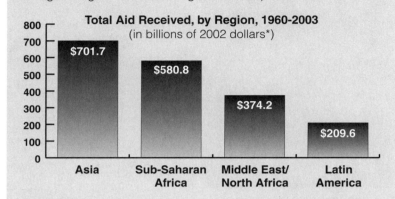

Africa Is Second-Highest Aid Recipient

Over the last four decades, the 47 countries in sub-Saharan Africa received $581 billion in foreign aid from the U.S. and other donors, making the region the second-highest aid recipient.

Total Aid Received, by Region, 1960-2003
(in billions of 2002 dollars*)

- Asia: $701.7
- Sub-Saharan Africa: $580.8
- Middle East/North Africa: $374.2
- Latin America: $209.6

* Adjusted for inflation, using 2002 as the base year. Includes aid from both individual nations (bilateral) and international organizations (multilateral). The figures from individual nations represent donations from members of the Organization for Economic Cooperation and Development and do not include aid that may have been donated by either the former Soviet Union or China.

Source: Organization for Economic Cooperation and Development

would stand up and say, 'Cut off aid to Mozambique.' But they'd never say, 'Cut off aid to New York state.' "

Poor countries that are trying to halt corruption lack police, courts and records-keeping systems that Americans take for granted, he points out. But countries with sincere anti-corruption policies deserve bigger aid investments, he maintains.

BACKGROUND

From the Ashes

A plan to revive Europe began taking shape even before World War II ended, when British economist Paul Rosenstein-Rodan in 1943 published a strategy — dubbed The Big Push — to spur recovery in Eastern and Southeastern Europe once the shooting stopped. [52]

Indeed, development economics first began by pushing for recovery rather than poverty alleviation, hence the formal name of the World Bank — International Bank for Reconstruction and Development — founded in 1944 at a conference in Bretton Woods, N.H. [53]

In keeping with its reconstruction mission, the bank made its first loans to war-weary France, Holland, Denmark and Luxembourg. But the bank's role in rebuilding Western Europe was soon overshadowed by the sweeping Marshall Plan, named after its creator, Secretary of State Gen. George C. Marshall. By 1953, the United States had spent $13 million on the phenomenally successful program. [54]

President Franklin D. Roosevelt, who had pushed to establish the World Bank and the IMF, had formulated ambitious anti-poverty goals even before the two institutions were created. In his 1941 State of the Union address — 11 months before the United States entered World War II — Roosevelt declared "freedom from want" as one of the "four essential human freedoms" that would emerge from the ashes of the worldwide conflict already under way.

After the war, the theme of fighting global poverty echoed through the newly formed United Nations. A 1948 General Assembly resolution called for "urgent consideration to the whole problem of the economic development of underdeveloped countries." The next year, a U.N. report said economic development "must not serve merely to augment the wealth and power of a small section of the population." [55]

In the 1950s, the de-colonization wave reached Africa, with the independence of Sudan in 1956 and of Ghana in 1957. In the 1960s, all of sub-Saharan Africa would gain independence.

In the World Bank's early days, dams, railroads and irrigation systems — the building blocks of industrial production — were seen as the magic bullets against poverty and also against the influence of the Soviet Union, the United States' Cold War enemy.

That viewpoint got a powerful boost in 1960 with the publication of economist W. W. Rostow's influential *The Stages of Economic Growth*, which argued that poor countries needed outside assistance in order to launch economic "take-offs."

"We must demonstrate that the underdeveloped nations — now the main focus of communist hopes — can move successfully . . . into a well established take-off within the orbit of the democratic world, resisting the blandishments and temptations of communism," Rostow wrote. "This is, I believe, the most important single item on the Western agenda." [56]

In his 1960 inaugural speech, President John F. Kennedy borrowed a page from Rostow's book when he declared: "To those peoples in the huts and villages of half the globe struggling to break the bonds of mass misery, we pledge our best efforts to help them help themselves."

Kennedy set up the first U.S. agency whose mission was to help poor countries: the U.S. Agency for International Development — then as now under the wing of the State Department. He also established the Peace Corps, which since 1961 has sent 187,000 volunteers to work in 139 developing countries.

But in the flurry of development-aid expansion, Africa's poor got relatively little attention. The Cold Warriors of the Kennedy and Lyndon B. Johnson administrations focused most development aid on Asia and Latin America. In Latin America, for instance, the Alliance for Progress, launched by Kennedy in 1961 in response to the Cuban revolution, was designed to send Latin America $10 billion in U.S. government aid and $300 million in private capital. [57]

The program largely failed after land reform — a key goal — proved illusory. Private investment declined, and the United States ended up supporting military dictatorships just because they were anti-communist. [58] All told, the United States spent $22 billion a year during the Cold War years, mostly divided between Latin America and Asia. That spending dropped to $16 billion after 1974, when the Vietnam War was almost over. [59]

During the same period, no Marshall Plan or Alliance for Progress was announced to kick-start African development. Instead, aid to Africa focused on building political alliances rather than on promoting reform, largely because African countries were not seen as sources of critical resources or as Cold War security threats.

"It is highly unlikely that most African countries will obtain external assistance or investment on anything approaching the scale required for sustained economic development," says a 1965 CIA assessment that Sachs cites

Hundreds of thousands of Kenyans young and old are living with the AIDS virus, including 200,000 infants and children, according to the World Bank. The AIDS epidemic has claimed 1.5 million Kenyans since 1984; Kenya has 1.8 million AIDS orphans.

World Bank

in his book, *The End of Poverty.* [60] "No African raw materials or other resources are essential to U.S. security." [61]

Instead, America's Cold War policy in Africa focused on buying the support of political allies in resisting Soviet designs on the continent. Among the beneficiaries of U.S. funds during the period were strongmen such as Mobutu, the late Jonas Savimbi of Angola and Hissene Habre of Chad — all notorious thieves and human-rights abusers. [62]

Big Loans, Big Debts

Despite the Cold War support of strongmen, the idea of helping the world's poor had embedded itself in Western foreign policy, even as some development theorists began arguing that building dams would not, by itself, do the job. Over the next 40 years the World Bank would promote aid strategies ranging from developing human capital to structural adjustment in the 1980s to today's emphasis on improving governance and producing measurable results.

In 1961, for instance, University of Chicago economist Theodore Schultz said investing in education was as critical as investing in machines and infrastructure. In 1968, newly appointed World Bank President Robert S. McNamara declared that relieving human suffering should be the main goal of anti-poverty agencies. Indeed, McNamara also declared that the goal of development should be "to eradicate poverty by the end of this cen-

Getty Images

Villagers in Obalanga, Uganda, prepare human remains for burial in June 2005, many of them child victims of the Lord's Resistance Army (LRA), which has terrorized northern Uganda for years.

tury." [63] Fresh from his disillusioning service as Defense secretary during the Vietnam War, McNamara doubled lending within five years. During his 13-year tenure, bank lending rose from $1 billion to $13 billion a year. [64]

In the 1970s, noting that after more than a quarter-century of aid most of the world's poor were still poor, McNamara called for "integrated rural development," focusing on agricultural and social projects that combined land reform, easier access to farm credits and the creation of organizations, to give the rural poor a political voice. [65]

But world events thwarted McNamara's ambitious plans. In 1973, Middle Eastern oil producers launched an oil embargo against the West in retaliation for U.S. support of Israel in the Yom Kippur War. As world energy prices skyrocketed, poor countries were able to absorb the shock only because McNamara convinced oil-producing countries to step up their contributions to the bank, allowing it to make more long-term, zero-interest loans to poor countries to help pay for higher energy costs.

In exchange, McNamara insisted that poor countries adopt "structural adjustment" policies — revamping their economies by lowering the value of their currencies to make their exports more attractive, shrinking their bloated bureaucracies and privatizing state-run enterprises. Although McNamara called it a temporary measure, adjustment hardened into full-fledged World Bank policy. A second, major oil-price shock in 1979 only strengthened the bank's demands for structural reforms. [66]

Whatever their merits, structural-adjustment policies cast the World Bank and IMF as "bad guys" for the next two decades, as politicians and activists around the globe charged their policies forced governments to service loans rather than their own people.

Activists soon began calling for debt cancellation, and eventually so did aid bureaucrats, stumped by how to make new loans to countries whose obligations on older loans were piling up. By 1981, World Bank economist Easterly writes, a bank report advised, "longer-term solutions for debt crises should be sought" for five African countries. Five years later, another report said many African countries needed "debt relief" — the preferred bureaucratic term. [67]

After oil prices skyrocketed following the two oil shocks of the 1970s, the commercial-banking industry was awash in petro-dollars deposited by Mideast oil exporters. Bankers roamed Asia and Latin America — and Africa to a lesser extent — throughout the 1970s lending money to Third World countries. But in 1982, when Mexico — one of the biggest borrowers — announced that it couldn't pay its foreign bank loans unless new loan money flowed in, private banks began fleeing much of the developing world.

The job of keeping those by-now heavily indebted countries financially afloat fell to the World Bank and IMF. Easterly argues that the results were "much lending, little adjustment and little growth." [68] And financial crises recurred — in 1994-95 in Mexico and in 1997-98 in East Asia.

Activists in both rich and poor countries began charging with increasing fury that the development institutions seemed either blind — or clueless — to the developing world's growing poverty, and they began filling the vacuum left by officialdom. [69]

On July 13, 1985, "Live Aid" concerts in London, Philadelphia and Sydney raised money for famine victims in Ethiopia and turned African poverty into a cause

Will the G-8 summit at Gleneagles ultimately help Africa?

YES

Stephen C. Smith
Professor of Economics and International Affairs, George Washington University

Written for *CQ Researcher*, August 2005

We have a moral obligation to help end extreme poverty. It is also in America's self-interest to help. Poverty sows seeds of international conflict, accelerates global environmental destruction as the desperate poor overuse natural resources and makes the world vulnerable to the spread of disease without regard to borders.

Stronger, less impoverished societies provide a bulwark against violent extremism. Poverty does not cause terrorism, but it increases susceptibility to terrorist activity.

Although improving government capacity and freeing market forces are both necessary, they are not sufficient. Locally, a smart push is often needed to free the poor from vicious cycles of poverty. Even in high-growth economies such as India's, substantial pockets of self-reinforcing poverty persist. If parents are too unskilled to support their family, the children have to work. But if children work, they can't get enough education to later avoid sending their own children to work.

If entrepreneurs have too small an inventory to make many sales, they gain too little profit to build a larger inventory. Similarly, if people are too undernourished or ill to work productively, their resulting wages will be too small to pay for sufficient food or medicine to make them more productive. Moreover, people desperate for food will overuse their land.

The push out of poverty traps doesn't have to be the purely statist enterprise that skeptics depict. Successful development and poverty reduction rest on a three-legged stool of government, business and citizen groups. In Africa, improvements in education, community capabilities and technology, such as the Internet and cell phones, are boosting the capacity of community and non-governmental organizations (NGOs).

Government is needed to provide the institutional framework and balance competing interests. But to reach the poor we must emphasize bottom-up market development and support indigenous community efforts. Foreign investment usually follows rather than initiates growth. Markets must have rich soil in which to grow, fertilized by a vibrant citizen sector — which can also demand government accountability.

NGOs help provide escape routes from poverty traps, utilizing comparative advantage in innovation, program flexibility, specialized knowledge, targeted public goods, common property management, trust and credibility and advocacy. We can increase grants to programs passing effectiveness criteria and supporting local citizen groups through training, capacity building and technical assistance. By helping build capacities of the African people, we can empower their own efforts to escape from poverty.

NO

George B. N. Ayittey
Distinguished Economist, American University; President, Free Africa Foundation

Written for *CQ Researcher*, August 2005

After their July summit in Scotland, the G-8 leaders provided debt relief and promised to increase aid to Africa by $50 billion annually. The only item of substance in the deal was the $40 billion debt relief granted to 18 of the poorest nations, of which 14 are African. Actually, the debt-cancellation agreement was reached before the summit.

Furthermore, the promised increase in aid won't materialize until 2010. By then, all the signatories would have left office! Even then, of the $50 billion promised, only $20 billion represents new money. The rest represents a reshuffling of existing aid commitments and the honoring of previous, unfulfilled pledges.

And there was no agreement on key trade issues, such as subsidies to Western farmers and trade barriers to Africans. The G-8 leaders agreed in principle to phase out subsidies for farm exports but set no deadlines.

Thus, the G-8 summit was a sham and won't make much difference on the ground in Africa.

Helping Africa is a noble cause, but the entire aid business has become a theater of the absurd with the blind leading the clueless. More than $400 billion in foreign aid — the equivalent of four Marshall Plans — has been pumped into Africa between 1960 and 1997, with negligible results. The fact of the matter is, Africa's begging bowl leaks horribly. In August 2004, an African Union report claimed that Africa loses an estimated $148 billion annually to corrupt practices, a figure that represents 25 percent of the continent's gross domestic product (GDP). Two years earlier, at an African civic groups meeting in Addis Ababa, Ethiopia, Nigerian President Olusegun Obasanjo claimed, "corrupt African leaders have stolen at least $140 billion (£95 billion) from their people in the decades since independence."

Civil wars continue to wreak devastation on African economies, costing at least $15 billion annually in lost output and destruction of infrastructure. The crisis in Zimbabwe, for example, has exacted an enormous toll on Africa. In 2001, *The* [London] *Observer* estimated that Zimbabwe's economic collapse had caused $37 billion worth of damage to South Africa and other neighboring countries.

And Africa can't feed itself. It spends nearly $19 billion on food imports, slightly more than the $18.6 billion in global aid it receives.

Clearly, Africa can find all the aid resources it needs in Africa itself — if only its leaders would put their houses in order.

for the world's youth. Irish rock singer Bob Geldof was the event's sparkplug, and it led him to become virtually a fulltime rock philanthropist/activist, and a role model for fellow Irish rocker Bono.

"Corruption Cancer"

But poor countries stayed poor, and activists around the world stoked resentment against the World Bank and other development agencies. Fury exploded at the bank's 1994 annual meeting in Madrid. Demonstrators got into the meeting hall and all but took over the event, accusing the bank of perpetuating poverty rather than fighting it.

The demonstrations had their effect. The bank's next president, James Wolfensohn, turned the institution into an ally of all but the most radical bank critics among the world's NGOs.

Wolfensohn also confronted another huge problem: the bank's working relationships with corrupt rulers who pocketed billions of dollars in aid funds. Instead of ignoring the problem, Wolfensohn in 1996 denounced what he called the "cancer of corruption" as one reason poor countries were not pulling themselves out of poverty. [70]

As if to illustrate his point, the notoriously corrupt Indonesian economy imploded the next year. Indonesia's banking system had been weakened by years of bad loans to bankers' cronies. And when the IMF tried to get failing banks closed, politically connected institutions were exempted.

Also during the mid-1990s, a development strategy that had been kicking around in Bangladesh since 1976 suddenly captured global attention. "Microfinancing" — making nominal loans largely to women to start small businesses — turned out to work remarkably well. Over the next few years, microfinancing was exported around the world, replacing the view of poor people as passive recipients of aid with a view of them — especially of poor women — as inventive, entrepreneurial and reliable and only needing a bit of a boost.

The concept received additional prominence in 2006, when pioneers Muhammad Yunus and the Grameen Bank of Bangladesh won the Nobel Peace Prize. Today, some 7,000 microfinance institutions are serving 13 million to 16 million poor people worldwide. The recipients owe a total of about $7 billion. [71] In Africa, some 2.5 million people are micro-borrowers.

Millennial Change

Another strategic shift has taken place at the United Nations, which has its own constellation of anti-poverty agencies. In 2000 and 2001, the U.N. announced an ambitious series of Millennium Development Goals (MDGs), aimed at achieving minimum standards of life — such as schooling and access to clean water — for the world's poorest people by 2015. Among the goals, perhaps the most ambitious is a plan to halve the number of people living in extreme poverty — defined as existing on less than $1 a day — by 2015. Other goals include achieving universal primary education and reducing by two-thirds the incidence of mortality in infants and children under age 5. [72]

The MDGs got little notice outside the global anti-poverty bureaucracy until a U.N.-sponsored meeting on development financing in Monterrey, Mexico, in March 2002. The leaders of 50 nations agreed that rich nations should step up aid and that poor countries should crack down on corruption and open their economies as conditions for getting help. The wealthy countries agreed to take "concrete steps" to spend at least 0.7 percent of their national GNPs on anti-poverty programs designed to meet the program's goals.

President Bush joined the anti-poverty chorus. He announced at Monterrey that the United States would increase its anti-poverty spending by $5 billion a year. Under a program called the Millennium Challenge Account, the money would go to countries that had honest, democratic governments and realistic plans for the money. [73] Bush's move surprised his critics, who had been preparing to denounce U.S. stinginess. [74]

Inevitably, as the big powers focused on global poverty, Africa came in for special attention. At a 2002 G-8 meeting in the Canadian Rockies, the leaders crafted an African Action Plan aimed at increasing rich-country aid to peacekeeping and essential health services while increasing aid to Africa by $6 billion a year. Oxfam, the aid organization, promptly called that sum "peanuts." [75]

By then the stage was already being set for the massive aid strategy approved in 2005. Two weeks after the Monterrey Consensus was signed, the U.N. Development Program appointed economist Sachs to study how to meet the MDGs. There is "not a place in the world," he said, that couldn't meet the MDGs, provided it got the right help. [76]

CURRENT SITUATION

Hunger in West Africa

As drought and a locust plague caused food shortages in West Africa in 2005, international relief agencies began pouring food aid into Niger. The U.N. alone hoped to help 2.5 million people. [77] Doctors Without Borders treated hundreds of malnutrition victims a day in the provincial city of Maradi.

However, anger at the U.N. for what some called a late response was strong enough that when Secretary-General Annan toured Niger, members of a crowd that greeted him in the town of Zinder erupted in cries of "hunger, hunger." [78]

Even before Annan's visit, private humanitarian agencies had been criticizing the U.N. "The international community should have responded three months ago," Mego Terzain, field emergency coordinator for Doctors Without Borders, said in late July 2005. [79]

Annan admitted as much in the *Financial Times* after returning from Niger. "All the relevant actors — governments in the region, donors, international financial institutions and aid groups — share responsibility for the crisis. Each of us, in our own way, was too slow to understand what was happening, get people in place and come up with the necessary resources," he wrote. [80]

Actually, officials in Niger and humanitarian agencies had warned for months that a crisis was brewing, but it wasn't until a British Broadcasting Corporation (BBC) television report aired images of children from Niger wasting from hunger that aid began flowing. [81]

Apart from the U.N. effort, the U.S. Agency for International Development sent 200 tons of food and $8.6 million in emergency funds. [82]

The food shortage was caused when much of the harvest was wiped out by drought and locusts during the 2004 harvest. This occurred just as the area was lifting price controls on farm products, so the growing shortage reportedly triggered a surge in food prices that led traders to hoard supplies in hope that prices would rise even more. [83]

The timing couldn't have been more ironic. Niger's food shortage was already killing children when the G-8 leaders were meeting in Scotland, and idealistic pop stars were holding concerts across the globe to drum up support for ending African poverty.

However, Niger wasn't the only country hit by the locusts. Nearby Mauritania, Mali and Burkina Faso lost all or most of their harvests as well. In fact, the U.N. Food and Agricultural Organization had paid for insecticide spraying to kill the locusts, but money ran out before all of the breeding grounds were reached. U.N.

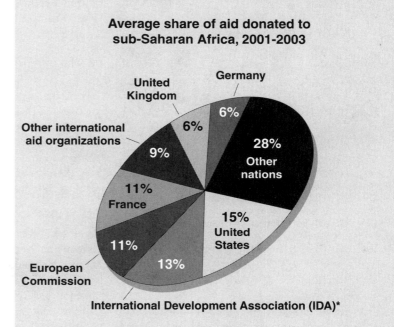

U.S. Gives Most to Sub-Saharan Africa

The United States was the largest individual donor to sub-Saharan Africa between 2001 and 2003, contributing 15 percent of the total aid.

Average share of aid donated to sub-Saharan Africa, 2001-2003

- Germany 6%
- Other nations 28%
- United States 15%
- International Development Association (IDA)* 13%
- European Commission 11%
- France 11%
- Other international aid organizations 9%
- United Kingdom 6%

Note: Percentages do not add to 100 due to rounding.

* A World Bank agency that funds economic-development programs in poor countries.

Source: Global Monitoring Report 2005

Shanghai's modern financial district reflects China's rapid leap from Third World country to economic powerhouse. Export-based policies helped China slash the number of people living in extreme poverty from 375 million in 1990 to 212 million in 2001 — a figure expected to drop to 16 million by 2015. To emulate China's growth, African countries want industrialized nations to lower their trade barriers to African agricultural exports, an unlikely prospect for now.

officials reported on the spraying shortfall and warned that the locusts would wreak havoc. [84]

The succession of warnings seemed to underscore one of the major reasons for the stepped-up aid to Africa: Money is often the only thing standing between life and death for hundreds of thousands of people. Indeed, in late August 2005, the U.N. World Food Program warned that more than 3 million people in drought-plagued Ethiopia face hunger that year unless the country received emergency food aid. [85]

War and Peace

Armed conflict is one of Africa's most deadly plagues. Warfare, usually between ethnic groups, claims lives by the thousands and makes anti-poverty work hard or impossible in strife-torn regions. In this context, the possible undoing of a long-sought peace deal in one of Africa's most violence-troubled countries is especially disheartening.

In July 2005 in Sudan, the two sides to one of Africa's longest-running civil wars signed a peace deal that elevated John Garang — leader of insurgent southern forces trying to secede from the north — to vice president. [86] At least 2 million people had been killed since the war began in 1983, a conflict unrelated to the ongoing mass killings in Sudan's western province of Darfur.

Massacres in Darfur began as retaliation for attacks on police and military posts by non-Muslim rebels opposed to the Islamic government. Militia known as "Janjaweed," widely reported to be organized and supported by the government, have killed as many as 400,000 and displaced thousands of others now living in refugee camps on the border. The Bush administration has defined the killings as genocide. [87]

The killings have remained a central concern in the West, with 18 states and numerous universities having divested their holdings in companies that arm or finance the Sudanese government. Attempts at altering events on the ground, however, have been largely unsuccessful. In September 2007, rebels destroyed an African Union compound, killing 10 peacekeepers and further complicating efforts to send U.N. troops there.

Action Plan

After the G-8 meeting, the World Bank was assigned to draw up an "action plan" for Africa that would outline measurable results that could be expected from the massive infusion of aid. The plan was expected to be ready in time for the U.N.'s Millennium Review Summit in New York in early September 2005.

Page, the bank's chief economist for Africa, vowed to produce a plan with a list of checkable goals. "We will be defining priorities, setting out instruments for data monitoring and evaluation," he said. "We feel a tremendous need to improve our ability to help countries do this." If all works well, Page continued, quantifiable results on such basic tasks as improving child mortality and eradicating malaria will be available.

Targets are being emphasized, said the Commission for Africa, because, "What is measured and monitored usually gets results." Past development efforts have not been distinguished by the availability of reliable data on achievements and failures. [88]

In fact, development veterans in general are obsessed by the need to show good outcomes on a continent that is short of them. "We have to think big, but we also have to pay very careful attention to quality and to making a difference at the local level," says Wessells of the Christian Children's Fund. "It's a big challenge and something that keeps me up at night."

Furthermore, he worries, "If we scale up too quickly, we'll exceed local capacities, raise expectations and create frustrations, and the quality won't be what is necessary to achieve results."

As noted earlier, the United States has been slow in making good on aid pledges made at Gleneagles and through other programs. However, aid has been growing and the U.S. pledged half of the $60 billion in new aid announced at the G-8 meeting in 2007.

Radelet, of the Center for Global Development, says that would "send a signal to other countries that look to the United States for leadership" on anti-poverty strategy and financing. "If the United States backs off, it's easier for other countries to do that as well."

Women Wanted

School enrollment and literacy are traditional standards by which poor countries' socioeconomic advancement or retreat is measured. But development experts today insist that educating girls — something considered frivolous in some Third World countries — is crucial.

Investing in educating girls "may well be the highest-return investment available in the developing world," said World Bank Chief Economist Lawrence H. Summers (later the U.S. Treasury secretary and president of Harvard) in 1992. [89]

Studies have long concluded that better-educated girls are statistically less vulnerable to HIV/AIDS and have healthier babies. [90] "The impacts of education on development . . . are stronger when girls are educated," the Commission for Africa reported. [91] Gender equality in schooling is one of the Millennium Development Goals, yet only 30 percent of African girls complete secondary school, where they can reap the greatest benefits. [92]

In fact, modern development strategies focus on elevating the role of women in general, because studies show it is a major key to progress. "We don't know quite why that is," says Pact's Newhall. One possible reason, she suggests: "If you are the one who did the birth work, you want a return on your investment, because that's hard work."

No overall statistics are available on how the gender-equality-in-education drive is faring. In countries that do publish statistics, results vary widely. In Chad, for every 10 boys in primary and secondary school, fewer than six girls are in class. But in Kenya, the result is only slightly below South Africa's perfect one-boy-to-one-girl ratio. [93]

Even in Kenya, however, getting girls into secondary school in some areas can require complicated negotia-

tions, as Margery Kabuya can testify. She is seeking permission from Masai tribal leaders to establish a girls' secondary school in Kenya's Rift Valley. In 2006, some 250 12-to-14-year-old girls — who are of marriage age by local standards — graduated from a primary boarding school Kabuya established in 1999. The girls will have to return to village life, probably to be married, unless an alternative exists.

Kabuya, who is East Africa representative of the Christian Children's Fund, told the community leaders that educated girls "will feed their children better, which means more children will survive," improving maternal mortality. And, in a country where members of the Kikuyu ethnic group are seen as go-getters, she added this surefire pitch: "They will be like Kikuyus. What got Kikuyus where they are is that they took girls to school."

Eventually, Kabuya was allowed to "book" the girls for school at infancy — a substitute for the custom of booking baby girls for marriage. So far, she has booked 840 girls. She also got promises that the girls would not be married off while they were in school.

Fragile Hope

The 2005 G-8 meeting opened a period of hope for Africa, but in many countries, that hope is fragile. "The way it is now in Africa cannot continue, because at the moment we are getting more new crises faster than we are solving old crises," Jan Egeland, the U.N. emergency relief coordinator, said in 2005. [94]

Apart from the famines and looming famines in the Sahel, violence continues in Darfur, food shortages in Zambia, Zimbabwe, Swaziland and Mozambique, Ethiopia and Eritrea, civil war in northern Uganda, and fighting in Togo and Chad. [95] Organized violence also plagues Burundi and Somalia, and a dictatorship that practices state terrorism is running Zimbabwe, says Wessells of Christian Children's Fund.

The scale of these tragedies and the level of human suffering they bring would be enough to cloud anyone's hopes. Nevertheless, Wessell and others say that well-designed grass-roots programs do work. He cites a project in Sierra Leone in which ex-soldiers on opposing sides worked together to build schools and clinics — which among other things ensured that former combatants wouldn't return to violence.

Economist Easterly sees another source of hope in African expatriate communities that send money and new ways of doing things back home. One example: Patrick Awuah, a Ghanaian who was an engineer and program manager for Microsoft during the 1990s, founded Ashesi University in Accra, Ghana's capital. The private university — whose U.S. advisers include Kofi Bonner, a former executive vice president of the Cleveland Browns working on development projects in San Francisco, and Henry Louis Gates Jr., director of Harvard University's W.E.B. DuBois Center for Afro-American Research — aims at nothing less than training "a new generation of ethical and entrepreneurial leaders in Africa." [96]

Expatriates make their decisions to return, or to work from abroad, independently of what the G-8, the World Bank and the U.N. decide. "This is a decision I took about my life," says Gilpin, who returned to her home country of Nigeria to fight malaria, HIV/AIDS and other health dangers. As a physician's daughter, she says, "In our family we've always felt that if you are so privileged that you studied abroad and have skills, you need to put them into practice where it counts."

But she is realistic about the limitations of development work. "For every successful intervention, there are hundreds of people you didn't reach," she says. "You become aware of how complex the problem is."

Complexities or no, Africa boasts more than a few development workers at the local level, where their work is keeping people alive, getting them healthier and educating kids. But the rich countries and multilateral lenders are promising more than local victories. They are promising to make huge, continent-wide advances against the ravages of poverty.

For now, though, expectations run higher for the smaller-scale projects than for the mega-programs aimed at pushing entire countries along the road to prosperity. Experience may not have brought most Africans to despair, but it has not led them to expect much from promises alone.

"Nigerians have seen this kind of thing before," says Gilpin of the Society for Family Health. But that hard-eyed realism shouldn't be mistaken for despair, she adds. "No matter how bad things get, people get up in the morning and go, go, go. Civil society is growing, there is much more awareness of democracy, of the rights of the individual, the rights of the child, of the cycle of poverty. Things are looking up, not down."

OUTLOOK

Poverty in Africa has been a hot topic in the West in recent years, receiving stepped-up aid from rich nations, including the United States — as well as attention from celebrities, corporations and the media. High-profile magazine packages and benefit concerts — including an "American Idol" telethon — have helped keep pressure on politicians to make good on their recent aid package promises.

The case can be made that Africa is being helped more, however, by its growing economy. Its growth has hovered at around 5 or 6 percent in recent years — or about double the rate of growth in the U.S. economy. Growth of average living standards from 2001 to 2006 was the highest in Africa's history. Foreign private capital into Africa reached $38 billion in 2006 — more than foreign aid. [97]

Congress renewed special trade breaks for sub-Saharan countries in 2006. In recent years, China has emerged as an important trading partner for Africa. Like the United States, China is concerned with maintaining access to oil and other natural resources in Africa. Africa's level of trade with China grew from $10.6 billion in 2000 to almost $40 billion in 2005 and is expected to reach $100 billion by 2010. [98]

Poverty rates have been falling rapidly in emerging economies such as China and India but remain stubbornly high in most African countries. Despite recent gains, Africa will not meet the U.N.'s goals for universal school enrollment or improved nutrition. The proportion of children under five who are underweight has declined only slightly, from 33 percent in 1990 to 29 percent in 2005. [99] Africa has easily the highest proportion of working children in the world. About one in four children under 14 works, about the same percentage as was true worldwide back in 1960. [100]

However, a poll conducted in 2007 by *The New York Times* and the Pew Global Attitudes Project found residents of 10 sub-Saharan countries guardedly optimistic. A majority of respondents in seven of the countries said that their economies were at least somewhat good. But disease, corruption and the lack of basics such as clean water and adequate schools remain essential concerns. [101]

Although its overall economy is growing and some countries, such as Rwanda, have vastly improved cell-phone coverage, Africa is not fully integrated into the global economy. Less than 4 percent of Africa's population is connected to the Web, with the bulk of those with Internet connections located in South Africa or northern Africa countries such as Egypt. "Unless you can offer Internet access that is the same as the rest of the world, Africa can't be part of the global economy or academic environment," said Lawrence H. Landweber, a retired University of Wisconsin computer scientist. "The benefits of the Internet age will bypass the continent." [102]

Philanthropy remains a key concern for Western nations, celebrities and corporations. Many of the new donors, including Bush's Millennium Challenge Corporation and the Gates Foundation, have standards of accountability and transparency that are more familiar to the business realm than to charitable giving. This approach has been widely influential, however. "There's been a paradigm shift in how people view the potential contribution of the private sector," says Nick Hellman, who has inspected African drug disbursal programs for the Gates Foundation. [103]

But some worry about what will happen when corporations move on and new executives find charitable concerns other than fighting malaria. The Bush administration, for all its high-profile humanitarian efforts, has decided to cut back on funding for areas such as health care, education and child welfare and concentrate more on development efforts. Its 2008 budget would cut USAID funding by 31 percent while boosting funding for the State Department's economic support fund by 27 percent. [104]

Still, even critics of aid concede that, although an imperfect mechanism, it can certainly be helpful to poor countries. In his book *The Bottom Billion*, economist Paul Collier notes that Nigeria has "depressingly little to show" for the $280 billion in aid it has received over the past 30 years, yet estimates that aid has added a percentage point to economic growth among the poor.

"Aid has been a holding operation preventing things from falling apart," he writes. [105]

NOTES

1. Mark Silva, "A Garden of Possibility," *Chicago Tribune*, June 27, 2007, p. 13.

2. Alex Perry, "Seeds of Change," *Time International*, Oct. 8, 2007, p. 32.

3. Christine Gorman, "Seeds of Hope," *Time*, Sept. 25, 2006, p. 59.

4. See individual country statistics at http://worldbank.org. For background see Peter Katel, "Haiti's Dilemma," *CQ Researcher*, Feb. 18, 2005, pp. 149-172.

5. "The Gleneagles Communiqué," G-8, July 8, 2005, p. 11, www.g8.gov.uk. For background see David Masci, "Aiding Africa," *CQ Researcher*, Aug. 29, 2003, pp. 697-720.

6. Statistics available at http://worldbank.org.

7. Niall Ferguson, "The Least Among Us," *The New York Times*, July 1, 2007, p. 7:10.

8. Daphne Eviatar, "Striking It Poor: Oil as a Curse," *The New York Times*, June 7, 2003, p. B9.

9. Nan Dale and David Blanc, "Sub-Saharan Africa: A Less Encouraging View," *The New York Times*, Aug. 2, 2007, p. A16.

10. Stephen Kotkin, "In Africa, One Step Forward and Two Back," *The New York Times*, July 8, 2007, p. B5.

11. "The Eight Commandments — Millennium Development Goals," *The Economist*, July 7, 2007.

12. Christian Retzlaff and Jeffrey Fleishman, "G-8's Pledge to Africa Criticized," *Los Angeles Times*, June 9, 2007, p. A9.

13. Council on Foreign Relations, "Can We End Global Poverty," June 14, 2005.

14. "G-8 Fact sheet: Investing in Africa's People (AIDS, Health, Education, Water)," undated, www.g8.gov.uk.

15. "Rigged Rules and Double Standards," Oxfam, 2002, p. 10.

16. Celia W. Dugger, "Rock Star Still Hasn't Found the African Aid He's Looking For," *The New York Times*, May 15, 2007, p. A6.

17. "The Millennium Challenge," *The Washington Post*, July 16, 2007, p. A14.

18. Roya Wolverson, *et al.*, "Influence the New Bush Politics of Aid," *Newsweek International*, Sept. 17, 2007.

19. Dugger, *op. cit.*

20. "Congress Wraps Up With a Barrage of Bills," *Los Angeles Times*, Dec. 10, 2006, p. A27.

21. Alan Beattie, "G8 mood and Doha talks 'show disconnect,'" *Financial Times* (London), July 9, 2005,

p. 8; Commission for Africa, "Our Common Interest," March 11, 2005, p. 252, www.commission-forafrica.org/english/report/introduction.html.

22. Commission for Africa, *ibid.*, pp. 96-97.

23. "The Role of Foreign Aid in Development," Congressional Budget Office, May 1997, p. xii. For background see Mary H. Cooper, "Foreign Aid After Sept. 11," *CQ Researcher*, April 26, 2002, pp. 361-392.

24. Commission for Africa, *op. cit.*, p. 81.

25. *Ibid.*, pp. 333-335; "Ethiopia Country Data Profile," http://worldbank.org.

26. For background, see David Masci, "Famine in Africa," *CQ Researcher*, Nov. 8, 2002, pp. 921-944.

27. "What Does Corruption Cost Africa?" Transparency International, http://transparency.org/in_focus_archive/g8/faqs.html#cost.

28. Emily Flynn Vincent, "A Reward for Good Behavior," *Newsweek*, Oct. 1, 2007, p. 74.

29. "UK Takes the Lead in Preventing Malaria Deaths," Department for International Development [UK], Jan. 27, 2005.

30. Laurie Garrett, "The Lessons of HIV/AIDS," *Foreign Affairs*, July-August 2005, p. 51.

31. "Chair's Summary," www.g8.gov.uk.

32. Edmund Sanders, "Struggling Eritrea Puts Self-Reliance Before Aid," *Los Angeles Times*, Oct. 2, 2007, p. A1.

33. Alison Rowat, "Without Sorting Out How Africa is Run, Nothing is Going to Work," *The Herald* [Glasgow], June 6, 2005, p. 6.

34. James Surowiecki, "A Farewell to Alms," *The New Yorker*, July 25, 2005, p. 40.

35. William Easterly, "Reliving the 50s: the Big Push, Poverty Traps, and takeoffs in Economic Development," New York University, June 2005.

36. "The Brand of Clinton," *The Economist*, Sept. 22, 2007.

37. Andrew Mwenda, in "Africans on Africa: Debt," BBC News, July 7, 2005.

38. "U2 star Bono: 'Drop the Debt,' " Jan. 2, 2002, CNN.com.

39. Paul Bluestein, "Debt Cut is Set for Poorest Nations," *The Washington Post*, June 12, 2005, p. A1.

40. *Ibid.*

41. Commission for Africa, *op. cit.*, pp. 33, 145.

42. Mwenda, *op. cit.*

43. "Frequently Asked Questions About Corruption and Africa," *Transparency International*, July 7, 2005.

44. James Rupert, "Corruption Flourished in Abacha's Regime," *The Washington Post*, June 9, 1998, p. A1.

45. *Ibid.*

46. "The Extractive Industries Transparency Initiative," undated gateway page by Department for International Development (UK), www2.dfid.gov.uk/news/files/extractiveindustries.asp.

47. Sebastian Mallaby, *The World's Banker: A Story of Failed States, Financial Crises, and the Wealth and Poverty of Nations* (2004), p. 179.

48. Howard W. French, "In Africa, There's More Than One Great Dictator," *The New York Times*, Oct. 5, 1997, Sec. 4, p. 16.

49. William Easterly, *The Elusive Quest for Growth* (2002), pp. 247-248.

50. Jeffrey Sachs, *The End of Poverty: Economic Possibilities For Our Time* (2005), pp. 311-315.

51. Council on Foreign Relations, *op. cit.*

52. Easterly, *op. cit.*, June 2005.

53. Unless otherwise indicated, the sources for this section are Mallaby, *op. cit.*, and Richard N. Cooper, A Half-Century of Development (2005).

54. "The Marshall Plan," U.S. Department of State.

55. Louis Emmerij, *et al.*, "UN Contributions to Development Thinking and Practice," conference paper, Jan. 24, 2005, pp. 1-4.

56. W. W. Rostow, *The Stages of Economic Growth: A Non-Communist Manifesto* (1960), p. 134.

57. Glenn P. Hasted, *American Foreign Policy: Past, Present, Future* (2003), pp. 275-278.

58. *Ibid.*

59. Hoyt Gimlin, "Foreign Aid: A Declining Commitment," *Editorial Research Reports*, Sept. 23, 1988, p. 470.

60. Sachs, *op. cit.*, p. 190.

61. Department of State, *Foreign Relations of the United States, 1964-1968*, Vol. XXIV (Africa).

62. Howard W. French, "Exit Savimbi, and the Cold War in Africa," *The New York Times*, March 3, 2002, Sec. 4, p. 5, and "An Anatomy of Autocracy: Mobutu's Era," *The New York Times*, May 17, 1997, p. A1; Norimitsi Onishu, "An African Dictator Faces Trial in His Place of Refuge," *The New York Times*, March 1, 2000, p. A3.

63. Mallaby, *op. cit.*, p. 35.

64. World Bank, "Robert Strange McNamara, 5th President of the world Bank Group, 1968-1981."

65. Kenneth Ruddle and Dennis A. Rondinelli, *Transforming Natural Resources for Human Development: A Resource Systems Framework for Development Policy* (1983), Chap. 2, Sect. 3.

66. For background, see Kathy Koch, "Africa: Strategies for Economic Turnabout," *Editorial Research Reports*, Nov. 7, 1986, pp. 815-832.

67. Easterly, *op. cit.*, p. 125.

68. *Ibid.*, p. 102.

69. For background, see Brian Hansen, "Globalization Backlash," *CQ Researcher*, Sept. 28, 2001, pp. 761-784.

70. Mallaby, *op. cit.*, p. 176.

71. "Microfacts: Data Snapshots on Microfinance," Global Development Research Center, site updated Aug. 3, 2005, www.gdrc.org/icm.

72. United Nations Development Programme, "Millennium Development Goals."

73. Barely any money was spent in the program's first three years, leading to the director's replacement.

74. John Authers and Alan Beattie, "US wakes from 20-year slumber in development field," *Financial Times* (London), March 25, 2002, p. 12.

75. Rupert Cornwell, "Western Powers Pledge 4bn for Africa," *The Independent* (London), June 28, 2002, p. 14.

76. Alan Beattie, "Aid boost allows greater UN goals," *Financial Times* (London), March 21, 2002, p. 12.

77. Marie-Louise Gumuchian, "UN Condemned Over Niger Famine as Annan Visits Worst-Hit Area," *The Independent* (London), Aug. 24, 2005, p. 23.

78. *Ibid.*

79. Christian Allen Purefoy, "400,000 children risk starvation in Niger," *The Guardian* (London), July 25, 2005, p. 12.

80. Kofi Annan, "Africa cannot grow or be free on an empty stomach," *Financial Times* (London), Aug. 29, 2005, p. 13.

81. Craig Timberg, "Global Aid System Stalled As Niger's Crisis Deepened," *The Washington Post*, Aug. 17, 2005, p. A8.

82. "U.S. Sending Emergency Food Aid to Niger," The Associated Press, Aug. 5, 2005.

83. Craig Timberg, "The Rise of a Market Mentality Means Many Go Hungry in Niger," *The Washington Post*, Aug. 11, 2005, p. A17.

84. *Ibid.*

85. "Three Million Ethiopians Face Famine — UN," UN Integrated Regional Information Network, Aug. 25, 2005.

86. Marc Lacey, "New No. 2 in Sudan, an ex-Rebel Leader, Dies in Copter Crash," *The New York Times*, Aug. 1, 2005, p. A5.

87. Joel Brinkley, "Sudan Still Paying Militias Harassing Darfur, U.S. Says," *The New York Times*, July 20, 2005, p. A3.

88. Commission on Africa, *op. cit.*

89. "Chair's Summary," *Evian*, June 3, 2003.

90. "Confronting the challenges of financing for development: a global response," March 21-22, 2002.

91. "Educating Girls: Changing Lives for Generations," in *The State of the World's Children 1999*, UNICEF.

92. "Education, Frequently Asked Questions," *World Bank*, undated.

93. Commission for Africa, *op. cit.*, p. 177.

94. "Regional Fact Sheet," *World Development Indicators 2005*, World Bank.

95. For background see Mary H. Cooper, "Women and Human Rights," *CQ Researcher*, April 30, 1999, pp. 353-376.

96. Warren Hoge, "U.N. Relief Director Appeals for Help in Crises Throughout Africa," *The New York Times*, May 10, 2005, p. A8.

97. William Easterly, "What Bono Doesn't Say About Africa," *Los Angeles Times*, July 6, 2007, p. A23.

98. Craig Timberg, "From Competitors to Trading Partners," *The Washington Post*, Dec. 2006, p. A23.

99. "The Eight Commandments," *The Economist*, July 7, 2007.

100. Michael Wines, "Africa Adds to Miserable Ranks of Child Workers," *The New York Times*, Aug. 24, 2006, p. A1.

101. Lydia Polgreen and Marjorie Connelly, "Poll Shows Africans Wary, But Hopeful About Future," *The New York Times*, July 25, 2007, p. A6.

102. Ron Nixon, "Africa, Offline: Waiting for the Web," *The New York Times*, July 22, 2007, p. B1.

103. "The Halo Effect," *Time International*, Oct. 1, 2007.

104. Wolverson, *op. cit.*

105. "Springing the Traps," *The Economist*, Aug. 4, 2007.

BIBLIOGRAPHY

Books

Ayittey, George, *Africa Unchained: The Blueprint for Africa's Future*, Palgrave Macmillan, 2005.
A Ghanain-born economist at American University argues that rich nations' development plans for Africa will do more harm than good until African nations themselves build genuinely representative governments.

Collier, Paul, *The Bottom Billion*, Oxford University Press, 2007.
The economics professor says that four conditions keep people in extreme poverty: natural resources that promote corruption rather than wealth creation, lack of geographic access to markets, unchecked violence (including civil wars) and weak governments and institutions.

Easterly, William, *The White Man's Burden*, Penguin Press, 2006.
The economist argues that Western foreign aid programs have been ineffective and created perverse incentives. Rather than grand visions of eliminating poverty, he recommends piecemeal solutions for small, soluble problems.

Mallaby, Sebastian, *The World's Banker: A Story of Failed States, Financial Crises, and the Wealth and Poverty of Nations*, Council on Foreign Relations Press, 2004.
A *Washington Post* columnist chronicles the career of former World Bank President James Wolfensohn (1995-2005) and describes the evolution of global anti-poverty strategy.

Rostow, W. W., *The Stages of Economic Growth: A Non-Communist Manifesto*, Cambridge University Press, 1960.
An economist who became a top adviser to Presidents John F. Kennedy and Lyndon B. Johnson helped launch U.S. anti-poverty aid to poor countries with this influential book.

Sachs, Jeffrey, *The End of Poverty: Economic Possibilities for Our Time*, Penguin Press, 2005.
The Columbia University theorist and gadfly behind the wave of attention to the world's poorest people combines a memoir of his anti-poverty fieldwork with a plan to end extreme poverty by 2025.

Smith, Stephen C., *Ending Global Poverty: A Guide to What Works*, Palgrave Macmillan, 2005.
A George Washington University economist examines grass-roots strategies that have produced results in poor communities around the world.

Articles

"The Brand of Clinton," *The Economist*, Sept. 22, 2007.
How the former president has found partners to drive down the price of drugs in Africa while building up multiple economic development initiatives.

"The Eight Commandments — Millennium Development Goals," *The Economist*, July 7, 2007.
The British magazine measure progress toward the U.N.'s anti-poverty goals and finds signs of progress but no hope of meeting the most ambitious goals for Africa.

"Ranking the Rich," *Foreign Policy*, May-June 2004; www.foreignpolicy.com.
Together with the Center for Global Development, a Washington think tank, the magazine charts the foreign-aid performance of 21 rich nations using a variety of measures.

"The $25 Billion Question," *The Economist,* July 2-8, 2005, p. 24.

The G-8 leaders should keep in mind the failures of past development strategies in Africa, a leading newsmagazine concludes.

Blustein, Paul, "After G-8 Aid Pledges, Doubts on 'Doing It,' " *The Washington Post,* July 10, 2005, p. A14.

A reporter who covered the Gleneagles summit analyzes the possibility that the global promise of aid could produce little but — in the words of one activist — a "compliance deficit."

Fletcher, Michael A., "Bush Has Quietly Tripled Aid to Africa," *The Washington Post,* Dec. 31, 2006, p. A4.

The president has tripled humanitarian aid to the world's poorest continent and promises to double the amount of help again by 2010.

Garrett, Laurie, "The Lessons of HIV/AIDS," *Foreign Affairs,* July-August 2005, p. 51.

A journalist who has become a leading scholar of global plagues examines the likely near-term future of the world's worst epidemic, with special attention to Africa.

Nixon, Ron, "Africa, Offline: Waiting for the Web," *The New York Times,* July 22, 2007, p. B1.

Very little of sub-Saharan Africa is connected to the Internet.

Peel, Michael, "The Resource Curse," *Financial Times Weekend Magazine,* March 26, 2005, p. 16.

In Nigeria, Africa's most populous country, widespread poverty coexists with vast oil wealth.

Sanders, Edmund, "Struggling Eritrea Puts Self-Reliance Before Aid," *Los Angeles Times,* Oct. 2, 2007, p. A1.

Eritrea's president refuses help from outside donors, arguing that charity has kept his neighbors poor.

Weisberg, Jacob, "The War on African Poverty: Tony Blair's LBJ Problem," *Slate,* June 28, 2005; http://slate.com.

In a skeptical take on anti-poverty strategies, the editor of the popular online magazine faults both the Bush administration for an underperforming plan to help well-governed poor countries, and Tony Blair for a centralist, statist vision of development.

Reports

Commission for Africa, "Our Common Interest," March 11, 2005; www.commissionforafrica.org.

A 453-page report by a commission formed by British Prime Minister Tony Blair examines the extent, reasons for and possible solutions to Africa's deepening poverty.

Rajan, Raghuram G., and Arvind Subramanian, "Aid and Growth: What Does the Cross-Country Evidence Really Show?" International Monetary Fund Working Paper, June 2005.

Two IMF economists conclude that evidence is lacking concerning the effectiveness of aid programs in stimulating economic growth in poor countries.

U.N. Millennium Project, "Investing in Development: A Practical Plan to Achieve the Millennium Development Goals," 2005; www.unmillenniumproject.org/reports.

The team formed by U.N. Secretary-General Kofi Annan lays out a strategy for halving the number of people in extreme poverty by 2015.

For More Information

African Union, P.O. Box 3243, Addis Ababa, Ethiopia; (251) 11 551 77 00; www.africa-union.org. A diplomatic organization that fosters economic and social cooperation among the continent's countries.

Center for Global Development, 1776 Massachusetts Ave., N.W., Suite 301, Washington DC 20036; (202) 416-0700; www.cgdev.org. A think tank that studies ways to reduce poverty.

Christian Children's Fund, 2821 Emerywood Parkway, Richmond, VA 23294; (800) 776-6767; www.christian-childrensfund.org. A 67-year-old, nonsectarian organization that arranges sponsorships for children in poor countries and also sponsors programs and research in education, health and sanitation.

Earth Institute at Columbia University, 405 Low Library, MC 4335, 535 West 116th St., New York, NY 10027; (845) 365-8565; www.earthinstitute.columbia.edu. Headed by economist Jeffrey Sachs, the institute studies the relationship between anti-poverty projects, environmental protection, health and technology.

ONE, The Campaign to Make Poverty History, 1400 Eye St., N.W., Suite 601, Washington, DC 20005; (202) 552-4990; www.one.org. The U.S. arm of the Web-based global coalition of anti-poverty activists has partners such as CARE USA, the U.N. Foundation and several church-based, anti-poverty organizations.

Overseas Development Institute, 111 Westminster Bridge Road, London SE1 7JD, UK, +44 (0) 20 7922-0300; www.odi.org.uk. The leading British think tank on development and emergency relief policy and strategy.

Oxfam America, 226 Causeway St., Boston, MA 02114; (800) 776-9326; oxfamamerica.org. The U.S. arm of a famed British organization supports a wide range of projects in 26 countries to build peace, security and equality for women.

Pact, 1200 18th St., N.W., Suite 350, Washington, DC 20036; (202) 466-5666; www.pactworld.org. A nonprofit specializing in training community leaders in poor countries to work on a variety of democracy-building programs.

Population Services International, 1120 19th St., N.W., Suite 600, Washington, DC 20036; (202) 785-0072; www.psi.org. A nonprofit that distributes health products for HIV/AIDS and other health issues in 70 poor countries.

Transparency International, Alt Moabit 96, 10559 Berlin, Germany; (011-49-30) 343 8200; www.transparency.org. An 11-year-old organization dedicated to fighting global corruption; publishes index of corruption levels perceived in each country.

U.N. Millennium Project, 1 United Nations Plaza, 21st Floor, Rm. 2160, New York, NY 10017; (212) 906 5735; www.unmillenniumproject.org. An advisory group, directed by Jeffrey Sachs, dedicated to finding and publicizing ways to meet the Millennium Development Goals.

World Bank, 1818 H St., N.W., Washington, DC 20433; (202) 473-1000; www.worldbank.org. The world's major anti-poverty lender.

8

Energy Nationalism

Peter Behr

The Caspian Sea oil town of Neft Dashlari ("Oil Rocks") produces more than half of Azerbaijan's crude oil. Built in 1947 on a chain of artificial islands, the facility contains 124 miles of streets, schools, libraries and eight-story apartments housing some 5,000 oil workers. Energy companies are targeting the Caspian Sea and other areas in the search for non-Persian Gulf oil sources.

From *CQ Researcher*, July 1, 2007.

Westerners saw the Soviet Union's 1991 collapse as a defining triumph of democracy, but Russian President Vladimir Putin has called it "the greatest geopolitical catastrophe of the century." [1] Today, to the growing unease of leaders in Washington and Europe, Putin is bent on erasing the wounds of what some Russian leaders call the "16 lost years" since the break-up and reclaiming Russia's position as a superpower. His weapon: the country's considerable energy resources.

With $500 million pouring into its coffers daily from oil and gas exports, Moscow is raising its voice — and using its elbows — in international business negotiations. During the winter of 2005-06, Russia temporarily cut off natural gas deliveries to Ukraine and Western Europe over a pricing dispute. [2] Putin also jailed Russian oil tycoon Mikhail Khodorkovsky after he challenged government energy plans and political control. And to the dismay of Washington, Moscow is considering energy investments in increasingly bellicose Iran and enticing former Soviet states Turkmenistan and Kazakhstan to channel new Caspian Sea natural gas production through Russia's existing and planned pipelines — supplies that will be vital to Europe.

"The truth is that Russia, having first scared its neighbors into [joining] NATO by its bullying behavior, is currently outmaneuvering a divided and indecisive West on almost every front, and especially on energy," said *The Economist*, the respected British newsweekly. [3]

Oil and politics have always made a volatile blend — particularly in the Middle East. But Russia's recent in-your-face actions represent a new strain of energy nationalism being practiced by Russia and a handful of emerging petrostates in Africa, Central Asia and Latin America that are nationalizing or taking greater control over

"Hot Spots" to Supply Most of World's Energy

To reduce dependence on the unstable Persian Gulf, an oil-hungry world is turning to sources in Central Asia, Africa and Russia. But most of these "emerging" producers have either nationalized their oil industries or are considered vulnerable to terrorists or dissidents. By 2010, according to the U.S. Energy Information Agency, 58 percent of global daily oil production will be at risk because it originates or passes through one of the world's oil "hot spots," including Saudi Arabia, Russia, Iraq, Nigeria, the Caspian region, Venezuela and the straits of Hormuz and Malacca.

Source: U.S. Department of Energy

their oil resources. Moreover, the leaders of some petrostates are imposing new political agendas on their oil sectors, notably Putin and Venezuela's combative socialist president Hugo Chávez.

"Everywhere there is a return to oil nationalism," says Jean-Marie Chevalier, director of the energy geopolitics center at Paris-Dauphine University. [4]

In the three decades since the world's first great oil shock in 1973, oil prices have periodically climbed and crashed as shortages were followed by surpluses. But this time around, the high prices are likely to stay high, many experts warn. To be sure, the war in Iraq and a looming confrontation over Iran's nuclear program are feeding the high prices. And escalating global markets, led by booming China and India, also intensify demand.

But rising energy nationalism is also triggering anxiety in global oil markets. A dramatic shift has occurred in world oil supplies since 30 years ago, when roughly three-quarters of the world's oil production was managed by private multinational oil companies — the so-called Seven Sisters — and the rest belonged to a handful of state-owned oil companies. "Today, that is about reversed," Former CIA Director John M. Deutch succinctly told the House Foreign Affairs Committee. [5]

As of 2005, 12 of the world's top 20 petroleum companies were state-owned or state-controlled, according to *Petroleum Intelligence Weekly* (PIW). [6] (*See chart, p. 210.*) "There has been a very significant change in the balance of power between international oil companies, and it's clear today that it is the national companies that have the upper hand," said Olivier Appert, president of the French Oil Institute. [7]

"One of the favorites of headline writers is 'Big Oil,'" says Daniel Yergin, author of *The Prize: The Epic Quest for Oil, Money & Power.* "But it's the wrong Big Oil. 'Big Oil' today means the national oil companies."

The nationalization of foreign oil company interests in Venezuela and Bolivia in the past two years is the hard edge of this new chapter in oil politics, echoing the same raging denunciations of Western governments and oil companies that accompanied Iran and Libya's nationalizations of foreign oil interests in the 1950s and '60s. [8] "The nationalization of Venezuela's oil is now for real," said Chávez at a ceremony in May marking the takeover of the country's last foreign-run oil fields. "Down with the U.S. empire!" he shouted as newly purchased Russian jet fighters roared overhead. [9]

Oil-production arrangements vary widely among the dozen leading national oil companies. In Nigeria and Brazil,

Pipeline Politics Play Pivotal Role

New and proposed oil and gas pipelines from fields in Russia, the Caspian region and Africa will likely play crucial roles in meeting the world's future energy needs. But global politics will influence when, where and whether the pipelines will be built. For instance, China covets oil and gas from eastern Siberia, but Russia's leaders have delayed building a proposed pipeline into Daqing, China. They want the pipeline to go to Russia's Pacific coast, to serve competing customers in Asia and the United States.

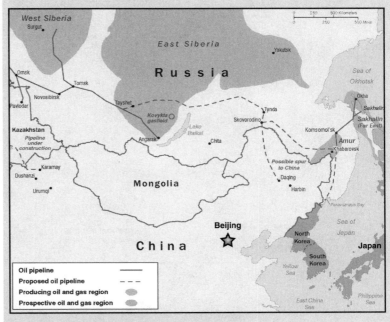

Source: U.S. Department of Energy

the government invites foreign companies to develop their oil regions, while Kuwait keeps them out. Ecuadorian President Rafael Correa, a Chávez ally who took office in January, has demanded a higher share of revenues from foreign oil companies but needs outside help to expand refining facilities. [10] Russia is forcing Shell and BP to give up majority positions in oil and gas joint ventures but hasn't thrown them out. And neither have Chávez and Correa.

Kazakhstan, after becoming independent in 1991, combined existing state firms into KazMunaiGaz — a new company that it intends to take public — while maintaining government influence through a parent company. The China National Offshore Oil Corp. is publicly traded but state-controlled.

World Oil Prices Respond to Events

Oil prices reached an all-time high of $78* a barrel in 1981, two years after the U.S.-Iran hostage crisis began. Prices dropped for the next 17 years as new non-OPEC (Organization of Petroleum Exporting Countries) supplies came online and demand declined. After bottoming out at $15.50 a barrel in 1998, prices have risen, largely due to increased demand from India and China, Middle East conflicts and the growing state control of oil operations around the world.

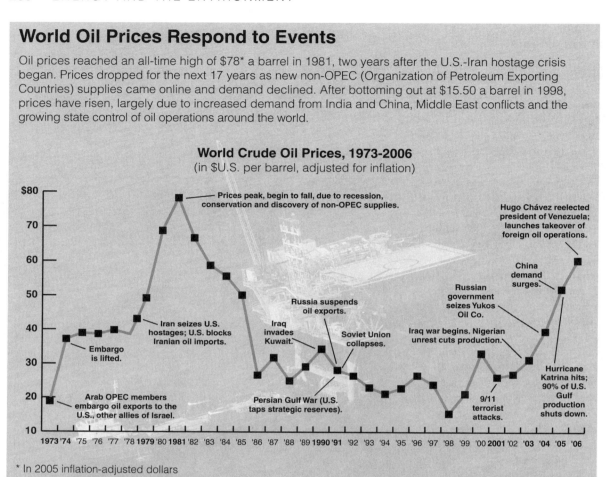

World Crude Oil Prices, 1973-2006
(in $U.S. per barrel, adjusted for inflation)

Prices peak, begin to fall, due to recession, conservation and discovery of non-OPEC supplies.

Hugo Chávez reelected president of Venezuela; launches takeover of foreign oil operations.

China demand surges.

Russian government seizes Yukos Oil Co.

Iraq war begins. Nigerian unrest cuts production.

Russia suspends oil exports.

Iran seizes U.S. hostages; U.S. blocks Iranian oil imports.

Iraq invades Kuwait.

Soviet Union collapses.

Embargo is lifted.

Hurricane Katrina hits; 90% of U.S. Gulf production shuts down.

Arab OPEC members embargo oil exports to the U.S., other allies of Israel.

Persian Gulf War (U.S. taps strategic reserves).

9/11 terrorist attacks.

* In 2005 inflation-adjusted dollars

Source: Energy Information Administration

But whatever model a petrostate adopts, *PIW* says the trend is largely the same: Major oil companies are finding their interests "increasingly subordinated to the nationalistic political agendas of key reserve-holding host countries." [11]

The new oil nationalism has been fed by energy prices at or near peak levels — when adjusted for inflation — reached after the 1970s oil shocks. (*See "Background," p. 211, and chart above.*) [12]

Rising energy prices also have produced a vast shift in wealth — over $970 billion in 2006 — from consuming nations to producing countries, a $670 billion jump in four years, and most has gone to a handful of countries, according to the Federal Reserve Bank of New York. [13]

Some industry experts say new sources of oil coming online — often from politically unstable hot spots in Africa and Central Asia — could mean lower consumer prices if Russia and the Central Asian petrostates remain independent of the Organization of Petroleum Exporting Countries (OPEC), which seeks to set international oil prices. On the other hand, the dramatic changes occurring in the industry could boost prices and — eventually — lead to declining supplies if state-run companies reduce exploration investments or botch operations, as some have done.

The International Energy Agency estimates that at least $2.2 trillion will need to be invested in the global oil sector over the next 30 years to meet rising demand for oil, but oil nationalism "is slowing or even discouraging this needed investment," according to the James A. Baker III Institute for Public Policy at Rice University. [14]

Consolidation of the world's oil supplies into government hands also raises questions about whether the new oil producers will break the historic "curse of oil" pattern, in which petrostate leaders used oil profits to line their pockets and buy arms rather than lift indigent populations out of poverty. Still others worry that intensified competition for energy between nations will sow new conflicts around the globe.

In addition to oil shortages and high prices, the International Energy Agency says Earth is facing "twin energy-related threats" — inadequate and insecure supplies of affordable oil and, paradoxically, environmental harm caused by excessive oil consumption. [15]

High prices and dangerous climate-changing energy emissions are fostering conservation-oriented responses similar to those prompted by skyrocketing oil prices in the 1970s, including the use of smaller cars and investments in energy-efficient manufacturing, construction and appliances. [16]

But short supplies also can trigger intense competition between consuming nations, and experts are closely watching the political fallout as major powers vie for control over oil and gas resources. The construction of new pipelines to carry oil and gas from Central Asia to Asia and Europe has already sparked disputes among Russia, China and the United States, and more could follow. [17]

China's worldwide search for oil is causing particular concern because its aggressive attempts to secure important new reserves in countries such as Sudan and Myanmar (formerly Burma) have ignored human rights abuses in those countries that the international community is trying to halt, critics say. [18]

Trends in oil discoveries and price moves have long defied accurate forecasting. An escalation of Persian Gulf conflicts, a terrorist attack on Saudi Arabian oil facilities or congested sea channels could shoot oil prices past $100 a barrel. [19]

For the moment, the world is consuming oil faster than it is finding new supplies, and the historic trend of gradual increases in the world's hydrocarbon reserves has shifted to one of "stagnation and modest decline." Global oil reserves were down by nearly 1 percent in 2006, according to the *PIW's* latest reserves survey. [20]

A banner at a natural gas plant in Tarija, Bolivia, proclaims: "Nationalized: Property of the Bolivians," after President Evo Morales nationalized foreign oil and gas operations in May 2006. "The looting by the foreign companies has ended," he declared.

As increased oil nationalism and global conditions trigger tight supplies, high prices, nervous markets and potential conflict, here are some questions being asked by the oil industry, its investors and critics:

Will emerging petrostates undermine OPEC's control over oil prices, benefiting consumers?

The first Arab oil embargo, in 1973, established oil as a pivotal political and economic lever. Since then, the OPEC cartel has sought to keep world oil prices high enough to maximize producers' returns without tipping global economies into recession.

It is widely assumed that OPEC's continued control over prices depends on whether emerging African, Caspian and Latin American producers reject OPEC membership and create excess global supply.

Of course, a widespread economic recession or financial crisis could slash oil demand, generating a surplus and a collapse in oil prices. In the past, OPEC has responded by cutting production to shore up prices, with mixed results.

So far, Russia has rejected OPEC requests to limit production. Neither Russia nor its Caspian neighbors are strong candidates to join OPEC, says Robert E. Ebel, senior adviser at the Center for Strategic and International Studies (CSIS). "Why would they want to join? Why

Have the World's Oil Supplies Peaked?

After 50 years, the debate continues

It's called the "peak oil" theory, and ever since American geologist M. King Hubbert developed it in 1956, oil experts have been divided into two camps — those who believe Earth's oil supplies have peaked, and those who don't.

If proponents of the theory are correct — that the world has used up half of the planet's oil stocks and the remaining supplies will face rapid depletion — the future promises even higher prices and more energy shocks. But critics of the theory say the high point in oil production is still 20 or 30 years away, that oil production is not likely to decline precipitously thereafter and that political events and energy prices — not hydrocarbon shortages — will dictate the industry's course until near the mid-century mark.

According to industry estimates, world oil reserves increased by 24 billion barrels during 2006 to 1.3 trillion barrels — a gain of about 2 percent over 2005. [1] Reserve estimates are periodically recalculated based on new geological and engineering data and new discoveries. But the 2006 increase cannot be documented because two of the countries reporting the greatest increases were Iran and Saudi Arabia, and their governments don't let outsiders check their figures.

"No one knows the amount of oil really contained in reservoirs," says Leonardo Maugeri, an economist and oil industry analyst with the Italian oil and gas company ENI. Such knowledge evolves over time after new wells are drilled and more sophisticated technology is developed.

"In fact," he adds, "countries such as Saudi Arabia or Iraq (which together hold about 35 percent of the world's proven reserves of oil) produce petroleum only from a few old fields, although they have discovered, but not developed, more than 50 new fields each." [2]

The peak oil argument begins with the controversial 1956 prediction by Hubbert that oil production from the lower U.S. 48 states would top out in 1968. The actual peak occurred two to four years later, depending on which measure of oil production is used. As a result of Hubbert's controversial prediction, "He found himself being harassed and vilified," says one of Hubbert's champions, Chris Skrebowski, editor of the monthly magazine *Petroleum Review*, published by the Energy Institute in London. [3]

But Peter M. Jackson, a director of the international research firm Cambridge Energy Research Associates (CERA), argues Hubbert erred in not considering how new drilling technologies could increase output from older fields or how energy prices affect exploration and production. [4]

He is even more critical of Hubbert's present-day disciples who say an oil field peaks when half of its available oil has been extracted. Their model is illustrated with a simple, smoothly rising and falling bell-shape curve.

Jackson says Hubbert's curve ignores the typical expansion of oil field dimensions as more exploration and development occurs. Oil production from the lower 48 states since 1970 has been 66 percent higher and 15 billion barrels greater that Hubbert predicted, Jackson writes, citing U.S. Geological Survey findings and his company's oil field analysis.

When admittedly high-priced, "unconventional" sources such as shale and tar sands or Arctic fields are counted, the world's total supply of oil is 4.8 trillion barrels,

---

would they want other people telling them what they can produce and export? They can derive all the benefits [of OPEC's pricing strategies] without being a member."

But experts disagree over whether Russia might support creation of an OPEC-style cartel for natural gas — of which it has the world's largest supply. In November 2006, a confidential NATO economic study warned Russia may be seeking to assemble a gas cartel with Algeria, Qatar, Libya, the countries of Central Asia and perhaps Iran. [21]

But Dmitry Peskov, deputy Kremlin spokesman, has denied the suggestion. "Our main thesis is interdependence of producers and consumers. Only a madman could think that Russia would start to blackmail Europe using gas, because we depend to the same extent on European customers." [22]

Whatever Russia does, the supply-demand balance is running tight for oil and gas, even with new petrostate supplies coming online, and new conflicts in oil-rich "hot spots" would only worsen conditions. "Many of the world's major oil-producing regions are also locations of geopolitical tension," said Daniel S. Sullivan, assistant secretary of State for economic, energy and business affairs. "Instability

Jackson stated. That is enough, at current growth rates, to delay a peak until 2030 or later, and even then, the peak will not be followed by a sharp decline, he said.

BP chief economist Peter Davies complains that Hubbert's theory also ignores the impact of increased conservation and the switching to alterative fuels that occurs as oil prices rise, which tend to extend oil supplies. Since 1980, for instance, the world's economic output has doubled while oil consumption has only increased by a third, he noted in a June 14, 2006, speech in London. "Year by year, a combination of exploration, investment and the application of technology is ensuring that every unit of oil and gas that is produced is replaced by new proved reserves," he said. [5]

Jackson likened peak oil advocates to sidewalk doomsayers who predict the end of the world. "Peakists continue to criticize those who disagree, but their projections of the date of the peak continue to come and go," he said in his CERA report. "One of the most recent peak oil dates was supposed to have occurred just after the U.S. Thanksgiving Day 2005, and we still wait for the evidence."

Skrebowski replied furiously that Jackson and the anti-peak oil crowd were either Polyannas or paid shills for an oil industry that must persuade investors that untapped oil abounds. [6]

But, when one gets beyond the name calling, the two sides appear less far apart. Skrebowski says Jackson's 4.8 trillion barrels may be technically available "but is only of interest if it can be discovered, mobilised and marketed within a reasonable time period. "This," he says, "is the entire debate: Can all the unfound and unproven resources be exploited quickly enough to more than offset the peaking and decline of the known and proven reserves?"

A leading peak oil advocate, Dallas energy financier Matthew R. Simmons, argues that Saudi Arabia's reserves are being greatly overestimated. [7] But he also says more than half the world's conventional oil and a larger share of its unconventional oil remain to be extracted. "What the world is running out of is cheap oil — the $20 oil we built our civilization around," he writes. [8]

That sounds close to the views of CERA chairman Daniel Yergin. However, he asks, will economics and government decisions in a politicized oil world permit enough new exploration and production to keep pipelines full?

Although energy companies will be prospecting in more difficult environments, he says, "the major obstacle to the development of new supplies is not geology but what happens above ground: namely, international affairs, politics, decision-making by governments and energy investment and new technological development." [9]

[1] "World Proved Reserves of Oil and Natural Gas," Energy Information Administration, Jan. 9, 2007; www.eia.doe.gov/emeu/international/reserves.html.

[2] "The Cheap Oil Era is Far from Over," *Alexander's Oil and Gas Connections*, June 2, 2004; www.gasandoil.com/goc/features/fex 42299.htm.

[3] Chris Skrebowski, "Open letter to Peter Jackson of CERA," *Energy Bulletin*, Dec. 21, 2006; www.energybulletin.net/23977.html.

[4] Peter M. Jackson, "Why the 'Peak Oil' Theory Falls Down," Cambridge Energy Research Associates, Inc., Nov. 10, 2006; http://cera.ecnext.com/ coms2/summary_0236-821_ITM.

[5] Peter Davies, "BP Statistical Review of World Energy 2005," presentation, London, June 14, 2006, p. 9.

[6] Skrebowski, *op. cit.*

[7] "Twilight in the Desert," *The Oil Drum*, June 13, 2005; www.theoildrum.com/classic/2005/06/twilight-in-desert.html.

[8] Randy Udall and Matthew R. Simmons, "CERA's Rosy Oil Forecast — Pabulum to the People," *ASPO-USA's Peak Oil Review/Energy Bulletin*, Aug. 21, 2006.

[9] Daniel Yergin, "Ensuring Energy Security," *Foreign Affairs*, March/April 2006, p. 75; www.foreignaffairs.org/20060301faessay85206/daniel-yergin/ ensuring-energy-security.html.

in producing countries is the biggest challenge we face, and it adds a significant premium to world oil prices." [23]

When supplies are tight, consumers lose. And tight supplies could persist since government-controlled energy operations may not develop new reserves or build pipelines as aggressively as the international oil companies. Instead, national oil companies tend to use more of their profits to fund social improvements and provide cheap, subsidized energy for citizens. [24]

To make matters worse, demand for more energy — led by booming China and India — is accelerating. Assuming their growth bubbles don't burst, experts predict China's energy use would have to grow by 150 percent by 2020 and India's to double to maintain current economic expansion. [25]

However, China's continued growth is not a certainty, according to a study from the Stanley Foundation, in Muscatine, Iowa. [26] "China faces immense problems, including pollution, disease, poverty, inequality, corruption, abuses of power, an aging population and a shrinking labor force," contend authors Michael Schiffer, a foundation program officer,

Saudi Arabia and Russia Have Biggest Reserves

Saudi Arabia and Canada lead the world in oil reserves, with nearly 450 billion barrels — more than half as much as the next 10 nations combined. Russia has the most natural gas reserves, with 1.68 quadrillion cubic feet — almost three-quarters more than Iran.

Oil Reserves*			Natural Gas Reserves*		
Rank	Country	Barrels (in billions)	Rank	Country	Cubic ft. (in trillions)
1.	Saudi Arabia	262.3	1.	Russia	1,680.0
2.	Canada	179.2	2.	Iran	974.0
3.	Iran	136.3	3.	Qatar	910.5
4.	Iraq	115.0	4.	Saudi Arabia	240.0
5.	Kuwait	101.5	5.	United Arab Emirates	214.4
6.	United Arab Emirates	97.8	6.	United States	204.4
7.	Venezuela	80.0	7.	Nigeria	181.9
8.	Russia	60.0	8.	Algeria	161.7
9.	Libya	41.5	9.	Venezuela	152.4
10.	Nigeria	36.2	10.	Iraq	112.0
11.	Kazakhstan	30.0	11.	Kazakhstan (tie)	100.0
12.	United States	21.8	11.	Turkmenistan (tie)	100.0

* As of Jan. 1, 2007

Source: "World Proved Reserves of Oil and Natural Gas, Most Recent Estimates," Energy Information Administration, Jan. 9, 2007

and Gary Schmitt, director of the American Enterprise Institute's advanced-strategic studies program. "China's leaders today are, thus, holding a tiger by the tail. They have built the legitimacy of their continued rule largely on meeting the rising expectations of a billion-plus people, but to meet those expectations they eventually have to release the reins of economic and political power they are clutching so tightly." [27]

Some experts hope China and India — which are eyeing Persian Gulf oil — could eventually add their considerable consumer weight to efforts by others to restrain OPEC's pricing strategies. "Much of the recent discussion in Washington about the growing oil demand of China — and to a lesser extent India — has focused on the threats posed to the U.S. economy and foreign policy, but that often obscures the fact that the oil interests of China, India and the United States are also broadly aligned," writes Xuecheng Liu, a senior fellow at China's Institute of International Studies. [28]

Will nationalizing oil wealth help the poor?

In May 2006, newly elected President Evo Morales ordered troops to occupy Bolivia's oil and gas fields and gave foreign companies 180 days to renegotiate their energy leases or leave the country. "The looting by the foreign companies has ended," he declared. [29]

Morales was elected partly on a populist platform to take over energy resources in Bolivia, which has Latin America's second-largest gas reserves after Venezuela. "We are the owners of this noble land," he said during the campaign, "and it is not possible that [natural resources] be in the hands of the transnationals." [30]

Echoing former Mexican President Lazaro Cardenas, who nationalized 17 foreign oil companies in 1938, leaders of Bolivia, Ecuador and Venezuela have called their energy reserves a critical tool for helping poor, indigenous populations.

Since the oil age began more than a century ago, governments in the developing world — on both the right and left — have promised their people a fair share of the wealth created by geological forces. But few leaders have followed through. Instead, "black gold" has spawned corruption, economic hardship, vast class differences and civil war.

"Look what oil is doing to us, to the oil-exporting countries," said OPEC founder Juan Pablo Pérez Alfonzo, a Venezuelan, nearly 30 years ago. [31] "It is the excrement of the devil."

Oil bonanzas often leave developing economies worse off — a phenomenon economists call the "resource curse." [32] PEMEX, Mexico's state-run oil company, pays an estimated 60 percent of oil earnings to fund government programs. But Mexico has overborrowed to keep production going and has more than $30 billion in pension liabilities, leaving it with a huge longstanding debt and too little money for maintaining old oil fields or finding new ones. [33] And Mexico's biggest field is in decline, raising fears that a chronic slippage in oil revenues could trigger a budget disaster. [34]

Similarly, OPEC members had an average gain of 1.3 percent in per capita gross domestic product (GDP) between 1965 and 1980, while the rest of the world saw GDP grow 2.2 percent annually. [35]

Sudden oil windfalls have also triggered what economists call the "Dutch disease" — skyrocketing currency values that depress local manufacturers' exports and trigger huge jumps in imports. The economic paradox got its nickname from a drastic decline in economic growth in the Netherlands after natural gas was discovered there in the 1960s. [36]

Oil's easy money also often ends up filling government officials' Swiss bank accounts rather than benefiting public health or education. Some of the most egregious excesses are in Africa. Since oil was discovered in Nigeria's Niger Delta in 1956, for example, the country's infamous kleptocracy has used oil billions to enrich elites, leaving delta residents trapped in pollution and poverty. "Everything looked possible — but everything went wrong," *National Geographic*'s Tom O'Neill reports. [37]

Now the situation "has gone from bad to worse to disastrous," said Senan Murray of BBC News. [38] The Movement for the Emancipation of the Niger Delta (MEND) has stepped up attacks on foreign oil facilities and the police who protect them, including an oil rig 40 miles offshore. In May, six Chevron employees were kidnapped and released after a month, but other kidnappings followed. [39] The oil companies — in conjunction with the Nigerian government — have pledged to support rural education, environmental cleanup and other social programs, but armed rebels in the delta say improvements aren't being implemented fast enough. [40]

In Venezuela, Chávez has kept his promises to channel petrodollars to health care, roads and housing. The percentage of Venezuelans living in poverty has shrunk from 42.8 percent to 30.4 percent under Chávez, according to government statistics. Researchers at Catholic University, near Caracas, estimate that about 45 percent of the population lives in poverty, less than in 1999. [41]

Chávez also uses oil money to promote his anti-capitalism ideology by investing in social programs in other Latin American countries. But he hasn't made a dent in Venezuela's chronic corruption, according to Transparency International. The Berlin-based nonprofit puts Venezuela in the bottom quarter of its 2002 and 2006 rankings. [42]

A forest of oil derricks lines the Caspian shore just outside of Azerbaijan's capital Baku. The oil-rich Caucasus republic is expected to be a significant source of the world's oil in the future, some of it delivered via new pipelines.

At the same time, the Washington-based advocacy group Freedom House says Chávez has presided over the "deterioration of the country's democratic institutions," replacing the Supreme Court, filling civilian government posts with military personnel, blacklisting political opponents from government positions and shutting down a leading opposition television station. [43]

Russia, China, Mexico and Iran also provide cheap, subsidized energy to their populations, in a tradeoff that carries a stiff economic price. The policy has backfired in Iran, where the government imposed gasoline rationing in June 2007, triggering violent protests that led to more than a dozen gas stations being set on fire. [44] Iran's subsidized gasoline prices are among the lowest in the world, so Iranian motor fuel consumption has been climbing fast. But the government was forced to ration gasoline because it has not used its oil profits to build enough refinery capacity, and gasoline imports have not kept up with demand.

Oil wealth has generated violence and even civil war in many developing countries. For instance, factions from northern and southern Sudan, where oil was discovered in 1978, fought a civil war in the 1980s over the nation's oil revenue. Although a peace accord was signed in 2005, the largely Arab and Islamist ruling party in the north has dragged its feet on sharing the oil wealth with the largely black, Christian southerners.

Meanwhile, some analysts say oil has played a key role in the international community's failure to stop the rape,

CHRONOLOGY

1951-1979 *Oil surpluses keep crude prices low; U.S. restricts oil production to maintain prices.*

1951 Soviet Union builds first deep-sea oil platform.

1956 Geologist M. King Hubbert's "peak oil" theory contends half of U.S. oil stocks would be depleted by the 1960s, and the remaining supplies face rapid depletion.

1960 Iran, Iraq, Kuwait, Saudi Arabia and Venezuela form the Organization of Petroleum Exporting Countries (OPEC) to stabilize world oil prices.

1970s OPEC gains control of global oil pricing; Arab countries begin using oil as a political weapon.

1972 Oil production from Lower 48 states peaks; limits on U.S. production are lifted.

1973 Major Arab oil producers impose embargo on oil exports to United States and several allies in retaliation for their support of Israel in Yon Kippur War; oil prices quadruple.

1979 Shah flees Iran; Iranian students seize hostages at U.S. Embassy, triggering more price shocks.

1980s *Oil from non-OPEC sources breaks the cartel's market hold, helping to create an oil glut.*

1980 Iraq attacks Iran, triggering an eight-year war.

1981 Global oil prices drop after a severe recession.

1983 Production from the North Sea and Alaska's North Slope swells global oil supply.

1985 Saudis boost output; prices plummet.

1988 Iran-Iraq War ends.

1990s *Breakup of Soviet Union raises hope for development of Caspian Sea oil and gas; oil production increases in Africa; global warming emerges as environmental issue.*

1990 Iraq invades Kuwait.

1991 U.S.-led coalition drives Iraq from Kuwait; Soviet Union collapses.

1993 Crude prices drop to $15 a barrel.

1996 Giant Sakhalin oil project announced in Russian Far East.

1997 Violence, protests disrupt Nigerian and Colombian production; Caspian pipeline consortium formed to deliver Caspian Sea oil to Black Sea ports; Kyoto global warming protocol drafted.

1999 Oil production flattens; prices rise.

2000s *Terrorist attacks in U.S. lead to new Iraq war; China becomes fastest-growing oil importer; oil prices climb.*

Sept. 11, 2001 Arab terrorists attack World Trade Center, Pentagon; oil prices surge.

2002 Oil workers strike in Venezuela.

2003 Iraq War begins; attacks close some oil platforms in Nigeria. . . . Major Iraq pipeline is sabotaged; violence escalates.

2004 Oil production in Russia, former Soviet states continues to recover, surpassing 1991 Soviet Union totals.

2005 China's oil demand soars. . . . Hurricane Katrina strikes the U.S. Gulf Coast, shutting down nearly 90 percent of oil and gas production in federal waters.

2006 Venezuelan President Hugo Chávez reelected, launches takeover of foreign-run oil operations. . . . Bolivian President Evo Morales announces the nationalization of all remaining natural gas reserves in the country. . . . Baku-Tblisi-Ceyhan pipeline opens, bypassing the Bosporus Strait.

2007 In a tariff dispute with Belarus, Russia's state-owned Transneft oil company shuts down a pipeline supplying oil to several European countries. . . . Dissidents attack three major pipelines in Nigeria's Niger Delta. . . . On May 1, Chávez takes control of the last remaining privately run oil operations in Venezuela.

murder and wholesale destruction of villages in western Sudan's Darfur region, where the Coalition for Darfur says as of 2005 Sudanese militia reportedly had killed 140,000 villagers, 250,000 have perished from disease, famine or exposure and 2 million more are homeless. The Sudanese government disputes the figures. [45]

Until recently, U.N. Security Council efforts to sanction Sudan have been hampered by China, which buys two-thirds of Sudan's oil and has invested more than $8 billion in its oil sector. [46] "Business is business," said Deputy Foreign Minister Zhou Wenzhong in 2004. "We try to separate politics from business." [47]

But this year, after critics threatened to make Darfur an issue during China's preparations to host the 2008 Summer Olympic Games, China shifted course. It now supports a combined U.N.-African Union peacekeeping force in Sudan, which Sudan agreed to accept in June. However, skeptics doubt the agreement will be fully carried out. [48]

In an effort to buffer the negative impact of oil wealth on developing countries, industrialized nations have launched the Extractive Industries Transparency Initiative, announced by then British Prime Minister Tony Blair in October 2002. By requiring oil, gas and other "extractive" companies to report what they pay foreign governments for their natural resources, the initiative aims to expose corruption and foster accurate reporting of oil revenues and spending.

"Knowing what companies pay and what governments receive is a critical first step" to creating accountability in the handling of oil wealth, says the initiative's statement of purpose. [49] Members include industrialized countries as well as the World Bank, major oil companies and about 20 oil-producing developing nations.

However, transparency efforts are still hampered by national oil companies that keep their energy books closed and ignore international accountability guidelines. Nevertheless, BP chief economist Peter Davies is optimistic about the initiative. "There is still a broad tendency toward transparency," he says. "There are forces that counteract this from time to time, [but] the forces for progress are there."

Will the growing competition for energy trigger new international conflicts?

The Cold War that dominated the last half of the 20th century was about ideology. As a new century begins, a widely shared concern is that energy will become a new arena for superpower or regional confrontations.

Conflicts over oil historically have centered in the Middle East. Now, because of the new petrostates, other hot spots claim attention in Central Asia, Africa and Latin America. The risks are magnified by the recent escalation of energy prices, which have made oil and natural gas resources an even bigger prize for rulers seeking to take or keep power.

New York Times columnist Thomas L. Friedman recently described a perverse relationship between oil prices and democracy: The higher oil prices go, the more democracy suffers and authoritarianism grows in the countries with oil. "Not only will some of the worst regimes in the world have extra cash for longer than ever to do the worst things," Friedman wrote, "but decent, democratic countries — India and Japan, for instance — will be forced to kowtow or turn a blind eye to the behavior of petro-authoritarians, such as Iran or Sudan, because of their heavy dependence on them for oil. That cannot be good for global stability." [50]

Japan and China see themselves competing for access to natural gas reserves in eastern Russia. Poland fears that Russia's construction of a new "North Stream" natural gas pipeline to Germany, now under way, will enable Russia to cut gas deliveries to Poland if tensions between those two countries erupt. [51] (A large portion of Russia's lucrative gas sales to Germany now transit through Poland, but that route could be bypassed by the North Stream project, Polish leaders fear.)

In Latin America, Bolivia's seizure of majority control over its natural gas industry in 2006 was a direct challenge to Brazil, which needs Bolivia's gas and whose state energy company Petrobras is a major gas producer in Bolivia. [52]

Some experts especially worry about the possibility of conflicts over energy between the United States and China, which is on a path to challenge U.S. economic and military leadership within two decades unless its hyper-growth spins out of control. Maureen S. Crandall, a professor of economics at the Industrial College of the Armed Forces, says that while China badly wants to import oil and natural gas from eastern Russia, it is not clear that pipelines will be built to deliver those resources. So China is looking hard at Caspian gas production and at the prospects for a pipeline through Iran to bring gas to seaports for export in liquefied form aboard tankers. [53]

World Crude Supplies Remain Vulnerable

Oil "hot spots" are most at risk

On Feb. 24, 2006, a small band of al Qaeda gunmen attacked Saudi Arabia's giant oil processing facility at Abqaiq — the first such attack since terrorist leader Osama bin Laden publicly targeted Saudi oil installations in a 2004 audio message.

Although the Saudis repulsed the assault, the incident was a wake-up call as to what terrorists' intentions were concerning oil supplies, warned Simon Henderson, director of the Gulf and Energy Policy Program at the Washington Institute for Near East Policy. "Saudi oil production remains extremely vulnerable to sabotage," he wrote shortly after the attack, and the kingdom's estimated 12,000 miles of pipelines are also "at particular risk." A Saudi police raid on a terrorist hideout the previous year had reportedly uncovered copies of maps and plans of the new Shaybah oil field, he pointed out. [1]

Had the terrorists succeeded in destroying the sulfur-clearing towers at Abqaiq — through which about two-thirds of Saudi crude passes — it would have driven the price of crude to more than $100 a barrel for months, perhaps even up to bin Laden's goal of $200 a barrel, according to R. James Woolsey, a former CIA director. [2]

World leaders have been warning since the onset of the Industrial Age that the key to energy security lies in diversification of supplies. When Winston Churchill — then the First Lord of the Admiralty — shifted the Royal Navy from coal to oil on the eve of the First World War, he presciently warned, "Safety and certainty in oil lie in variety and variety alone." [3]

The conflicts and crises that have periodically disrupted Middle East oil supplies — from the oil shocks of the 1970s to Saddam Hussein's invasion of Kuwait in 1990 — have repeatedly reinforced the wisdom of Churchill's advice: find more sources of oil outside the Persian Gulf.

Today, the world is once again seeking to diversify its energy supplies, turning to sources in Central Asia, Africa and Russia. But while the emergence of these rising petrostates has increased the diversity of energy supplies, it has not increased energy security. Many of those new producers appear along with Saudi Arabia on the U.S. Energy Information Administration (EIA) list of various "hot spots" in world oil markets.

Saudi Arabia tops the list, but it is followed by other "emerging" oil producing states: Russia, Iran, Iraq, Nigeria, the Caspian region, Sudan, Venezuela and seven other countries where energy facilities are considered at risk from saboteurs or unstable domestic policies. [4] The EIA projects that by 2010 at least 50 million barrels of oil per day — 58 percent of worldwide daily production — will be in jeopardy because it originates or passes through oil hot spots.

"The security of the energy infrastructure is becoming progressively in doubt," says Massachusetts Institute of Technology Professor John Deutch, also a former CIA director. "Oil facilities, pipelines [and] control systems for the energy distribution systems are all very much more vulnerable to terrorist attack and national disaster." [5]

The choke points for seaborne oil — and, increasingly, natural gas — create some of the worst risks. According to Daniel Yergin, author of *The Prize: The Epic Quest for Oil, Money & Power*, those ocean chokepoints include the:

- Strait of Hormuz, at the entrance to the Persian Gulf;
- Suez Canal, which connects the Red Sea and the Mediterranean;
- Bab el Mandeb Strait at the Red Sea's entrance;
- Bosporus Strait, a major transit channel for Russian and Caspian oil; and
- Strait of Malacca between Malaysia and Indonesia, a conduit for 80 percent of the oil used by Japan and South Korea and about half of China's oil. [6]

That puts China in opposition to the Bush administration's top-priority campaign to isolate Iran to prevent it from developing nuclear weapons — a goal Iran denies it is seeking. The Iran issue headed America's agenda for the U.S.-China Senior Dialogue between top diplomats from both nations in June 2007, while China pushed for assurances the United States was not boosting its support for China's rival, Taiwan. [54]

The two nations are not consciously pointed toward conflict, says the National Intelligence Council's 2020

The Malacca strait is only 1.5 miles wide at its narrowest point, and if terrorists or pirates scuttled a ship at that choke point it could disrupt supplies for a long time, Yergin warns.

"It may take only one asymmetric or conventional attack on a Ghawar [Saudi oil field] or tankers in the Strait of Hormuz to throw the market into a spiral, warns Anthony H. Cordesman, a scholar at the Center for Strategic and International Studies in Washington. [7]

"Assuring the security of global energy markets will require coordination on both an international and a national basis among companies and governments, including energy, environmental, military, law enforcement and intelligence agencies," Yergin writes. "But in the United States, as in other countries, the lines of responsibility — and the sources of funding — for protecting critical infrastructures, such as energy, are far from clear."

Countries are trying a wide range of policies and practices to increase security of energy production and delivery, experts say. Colombia has military units — trained and partly supplied by the United States — tasked with combating rebel attacks on oil pipelines. The natural gas networks of Qatar and the United Arab Emirates are being connected to shipping terminals in Oman that lie outside the vulnerable Strait of Hormuz. [8] China is expanding its naval forces in order to protect oil shipments through Asian sea lanes where piracy is a threat.

But Gal Luft, executive director of the Institute for the Analysis of Global Security in Washington, says security efforts have been hampered by uncertainty over whether private companies or governments should pay for the additional security.

"NATO is looking into defining the roles of industry and government," Luft says. "Each wants the other to do more. In places where you can introduce technology or more manpower economically, you do it. But on the ground not a lot is happening."

Building in redundancy and the availability of alternative sources are also popular strategies for assuring energy deliveries, says Mariano Gurfinkel, associate head of the Center for Energy Economics at the University of Texas.

Separatist rebels show their firepower in Nigeria's oil-rich Niger Delta in February 2006. Insurgents have kidnapped foreign oil workers and sabotaged oil facilities to protest the slow pace of economic development in the delta.

AFP Photo/Dave Clark

"Since it is very hard to avoid all incidents on all elements of the energy infrastructure, efforts are made to minimize the consequences."

[1] Simon Henderson, "Al-Qaeda Attack on Abqaiq: The Vulnerability of Saudi Oil," Washington Institute for Near East Policy, www.washingtoninstitute. org/templateC05.php?CID=2446.

[2] R. James Woolsey, "Global implications of Rising Oil Dependence and Global Warming," testimony before the House Select Committee on Energy Independence and Global Warming, April 18, 2007, p. 2.

[3] Daniel Yergin, "Ensuring Energy Security," *Foreign Affairs*, March/April 2006, p. 69.

[4] "World Energy Hotspots," Energy Information Administration, Sept. 2005, www.eia.doe.gov/emeu/cabs/World_Energy_Hotspots/Full.html.

[5] John M. Deutch, testimony before the House Foreign Affairs Committee, March 22, 2007.

[6] Yergin, *op. cit.*, p. 79.

[7] Anthony H. Cordesman, "Global Oil Security," Center for Strategic and International Studies, Nov. 13, 2006, p. 14.

[8] Energy Information Administration, "Oman" country analysis, April 2007, www.eia.doe.gov/emeu/cabs/Oman/NaturalGas.html.

Project report — the most recent public forecast by the CIA's research arm. "[T]he growing dependence on global financial and trade networks increasingly will act as a deterrent to conflict among the great powers — the U.S., Europe, China, India, Japan and Russia," says the report. [55]

But, the report adds, inadvertent conflicts could erupt as a result of growing oil nationalism, the lack of effective international conflict-resolution processes or raw emotions exploding over key issues. For instance, a naval arms race could develop between China, intent on pro-

Majority of Oil Companies Are State-Owned

Thirteen of the world's 25-largest oil companies are entirely owned or controlled by national governments, including all the companies in the Middle East; three other oil firms are partially state-owned. In 1973, by comparison, roughly three-quarters of the world's oil production was managed by the privately owned "Seven Sisters" — the seven major Western oil companies.*

World's Largest Oil Companies

Rank (2005)	Company	Country of origin	Percentage of firm owned by state
1	Saudi Aramco	Saudi Arabia	100
2	Exxon Mobil	United States	0
3	NIOC	Iran	100
4	PDVSA	Venezuela	100
5	BP	United Kingdom	0
6	Royal Dutch Shell	United Kingdom/Netherlands	0
7	PetroChina	China	90
8	Chevron	United States	0
8	Total	France	0
10	Pemex	Mexico	100
11	ConocoPhillips	United States	0
12	Sonatrach	Algeria	100
13	KPC	Kuwait	100
14	Petrobras	Brazil	32
15	Gazprom	Russia	50.002
16	Lukoil	Russia	0
17	Adnoc	United Arab Emirates	100
18	Eni	Italy	0
19	Petronas	Malaysia	100
20	NNPC	Nigeria	100
21	Repsol YPF	Spain	0
22	Libya NOC	Libya	100
23	INOC	Iraq	100
24	EGPC	Egypt	100
24	QP	Qatar	100

* The Seven Sisters were: Exxon, Mobil, Chevron, Texaco, Gulf, Shell, British Petroleum

Source: *Petroleum Intelligence Weekly*

favors maintaining a credible U.S. military posture in Asia, they argue, but if U.S. actions are seen as a bid for supremacy or a check on China's rightful regional role, "it might fuel further resentments and incite precisely the reaction we don't seek, a redoubling of counter-vailing military, economic and diplomatic strategies."

"The United States and China are not seeking to make war on one another," agrees Michael Klare, a political science professor at Hampshire College. "But they are inadvertently contributing to the risk of conflict in Africa and Central Asia by using arms transfers as an instrument of influence."

China, for instance, has sent troops to Sudan to protect its energy investment there, he points out, and the U.S. military maintains a presence in Central Asia. In the same vein, former Chinese deputy chief of staff Gen. Xiong Guangkai told an international conference on energy security last December that "the strategic race for the world's energy may result in regional tension and even trigger a military clash." [57]

The recent deterioration of U.S.-Russian relations is a case study of what should not be allowed to happen between the United States and China, say some experts. The dialogue has grown raw, escalated by Russia's sharp swing toward an aggressive nationalism. But the division also has been fostered by arrogant and short-sighted U.S. moves over the past 15 years that treated Russia as a defeated world power and dictated terms to them instead of seeking a working relationship, says Blair Ruble, director of the Kennan Institute in Washington.

"It has been a bipartisan failure," adds Ruble's colleague, program associate F. Joseph Dresen. After the

tecting vital seaborne oil shipments, and the United States, determined to maintain strategic leverage in Asian waters. While China's interest "lies with a peaceful and stable regional and international order," write Schiffer and Schmitt, China's ambitions or internal political conflicts could take it in a different direction. [56] Prudence

Soviet Union's collapse, the United States "had tons of leverage" but "we needed more influence. It starts with diplomacy."

A win-win relationship with China that minimizes potential for conflict "will take far more sophistication than U.S. policymakers from either political party have previously shown," Schiffer and Schmitt conclude. [58]

BACKGROUND

OPEC Is Born

In 1960, representatives of Iran, Iraq, Kuwait, Saudi Arabia and Venezuela met in Baghdad to form a cartel designed to stabilize world oil markets. Today the 12-member Organization of Petroleum Exporting Countries — now based in Vienna, Austria — also includes Qatar, Indonesia, Libya, the United Arab Emirates, Algeria, Nigeria and Angola. Ecuador and Gabon joined in the '70s but dropped out in the '90s. [59]

Despite the cartel's promise of stability, oil markets have been chaotic since the 1970s, characterized by four distinct periods.

Two oil shocks hit world energy markets in the 1970s. Resentful of U.S. efforts to suppress oil prices and angered by U.S. support for Israel in the 1973 Yom Kippur War, several Arab OPEC members on Oct. 17, 1973, imposed an oil embargo on the United States and other countries aiding Israel, followed by a production cut. [60] The world suddenly faced a crude-oil shortage of 4 million barrels a day, 7 percent below demand. Prices shot up from $3 a barrel to $12. [61] Long lines formed at gasoline pumps in the United States and some European countries.

To limit the impact on American consumers, President Richard M. Nixon imposed price controls on the U.S. economy, and President Gerald Ford created the U.S. Strategic Petroleum Reserve, which today holds more than 688 million barrels of crude oil in underground caverns. [62]

The embargo ended five months later — in March 1974 — after Arab-Israeli tensions eased. Egyptian President Anwar el-Sadat, intent on moving toward a peace agreement, argued successfully that the "oil weapon had served its purpose." [63]

But memories of the embargo continued to drive a search for new energy policies. On April 18, 1977, shortly

Motorists in London queue up for petrol in 1973. The world's first oil shock was caused by an Arab oil embargo, which established oil as a pivotal political and economic lever.

Keystone/Hulton Archive/Getty Images

after being inaugurated, President Jimmy Carter warned about America's overdependence on foreign oil supplies, calling the energy crisis "the moral equivalent of war." With the exception of preventing war, Carter said, "this is the greatest challenge our country will face during our lifetimes." [64]

Then in early 1979, after a year of paralyzing strikes and demonstrations by supporters of militant Iranian Shia Muslim cleric Ayatollah Ruhollah Khomeini, Iran's Shah Mohammad Reza Pahlavi fled Tehran, opening the door to the founding of an Islamic republic.

As the impact of the Iranian Revolution on world oil prices began to be felt, Carter in July 1979 unveiled a comprehensive energy plan to help America combat its overdependence on unstable Middle Eastern oil, promoting conservation, alternative fuels and higher taxes on gasoline and gas-guzzling cars. [65]

Four months later, on Nov. 4, Islamist zealots and students took over the U.S. Embassy in Tehran, holding 52 hostages for 444 days — until Ronald Reagan replaced Carter. [66] During the crisis, oil prices nearly doubled. [67] World oil markets got even tighter in 1980, when Iran's oil production nearly dried up after Iraq invaded — beginning an eight-year-long conflict. Panic

Pollution and poverty abound in the swampy Niger Delta region of Nigeria, where international oil companies are drilling for the country's rich oil resources. Shanties reflect the slow rate of development, which has sparked violent protests in recent years.

drilling crews, path-breaking technology and platforms able to withstand crushing waves and 130-mile-per-hour winds. [69] By the early 1980s, daily North Sea production had reached 3.5 million barrels — more than Kuwait and Libya combined — and a new 800-mile pipeline to the port of Valdez from Alaska's landlocked North Slope was supplying up to 2 million barrels of oil a day to the Lower 48 states — a quarter of U.S. production. [70] In 1985, non-OPEC production had increased by 10 million barrels a day over 1974 levels, more than double the cartel's daily output. [71]

Moreover, by 1983 energy conservation was working. Americans were consuming less gasoline than in 1973, even with more cars on the road, and the U.S. economy had become 25 percent more energy efficient. Conservation efforts in Europe and Japan also were cutting consumption. [72] The two trends sent energy prices into a nosedive. By 1985 crude was below $10 a barrel ($20 in inflation-adjusted, 2006 prices), prompting Saudi Arabia to abandon efforts to control cartel production and boost its own output. Analysts have since interpreted the Saudis' decision as a strategic move to hamper the ability of Iran and Iraq to continue their war, raging just across the Saudi border. Others say the move hastened the demise of communism — by draining the Soviet Union's treasury at a time when it was facing rising internal pressures and fighting a war in Afghanistan.

But the lower oil prices also knocked the wind out of the conservation movement. The push to continue raising vehicle performance stalled in Congress, and gas-slurping minivans and SUVs became wildly popular. [73]

New Petrostates

Oil prices spiked briefly in 1991 after Saddam Hussein invaded Kuwait, and the U.S.-led coalition counterattacked, knocking out 3 percent of world oil output. After Iraq's defeat, the oil industry focused on the rising petrostates in Africa and Central Asia and on the collapse — and stunning recovery — of Russia's oil production. [74]

The Caspian Sea — about the size of California — holds one of the world's oldest-known concentrations of petroleum. The Caspian has long triggered fears that its oil, known since Alexander the Great's day, would become a conflict flashpoint. "It will be sad to see how the magnet of oil draws great armies to the Caucasus," wrote journalist Louis Fischer in 1926. [75]

purchases by governments, companies and consumers made the shortage worse, and, once again, motorists in industrialized countries queued up at gas stations.

The 1970s price shocks triggered a determined campaign to reduce energy dependence. Congress in 1975 directed U.S. auto manufacturers to double the efficiency of their cars within a decade, and businesses made serious efforts to shrink energy use. [68]

But the pendulum would soon be reversed. A sharp recession stunted energy demand, the search for oil outside the Persian Gulf intensified and the balance between supply and demand was set to shift again.

Oil Glut

Discoveries and exploitation of vast oil and gas reserves in the North Sea, Mexico and Alaska's North Slope in the early 1980s led to a tide of new production, tipping events in consumers' favor.

North Sea development, called "one of the greatest investment projects in the world," required intrepid

The Caspian is bordered by Russia on the northwest, Kazakhstan on the north and east, Turkmenistan to the east, Iran to the south and Azerbaijan in the west. (*See map, p. 199.*) The rise of the independent former Soviet satellites triggered extravagant hopes that the Caspian could become "the Middle East of the next millennium." The State Department fanned the hyperbole, estimating Caspian oil reserves at 200 billion barrels, or 10 percent of the world's total potential reserves. [76]

Then developers began hitting dry holes, and war and separatist violence spread through the region. Caspian countries disagreed over how to divide the Caspian's energy reserves and whether the Caspian is, in fact, a "sea" or a "lake" — a definition that could affect the ultimate distribution. "The dreams have faded as the hard realities of energy development and politics have set in," says economist Crandall at the Industrial College of the Armed Forces, who predicts Caspian reserves will top out at 33-48 billion barrels, or 3 percent of the world's total. [77]

But even with the lower estimates, the Caspian reserves still are larger than Alaska's North Slope, big enough to attract not only Russia and Iran but also Europe and China. By 2010, the Energy Information Agency projects the Caspian region will be producing 2.9-3.8 million barrels a day — more than Venezuela. [78]

Dreams for a birth of democracy in the region also have faded. Most of the region's governments have become more authoritarian and corrupt since the demise of the Soviet Union, says Martha Brill Olcott, a senior associate at the Carnegie Endowment for International Peace. [79] Indeed, says Crandall, most Central Asian states are "one-bullet regimes" that would fall into chaos if current leaders were deposed. [80]

In Africa, the discovery of oil in Algeria in 1955 — and later in the Niger Delta and Libya — seemed like gifts from the gods for the planet's poorest continent. The riches lured flocks of petroleum companies.

As exploration expanded, Africa's proven reserves more than doubled from 1980 to 2005, to 114.3 billion barrels, far ahead of overall reserve gains worldwide. In 2004, Nigeria ranked eighth among the world's biggest oil exporters, followed by No. 10 Algeria and 12th-place Libya. [81] Angola soon joined Africa's oil club: In the past 10 years, Angola's estimated oil reserves have nearly tripled and its crude oil production doubled. [82]

Oil also was found in Sudan, where production has been climbing since completion in 1999 of an oil

In the shadow of Istanbul's historic Blue Mosque (left), the Hagia Sophia Museum (center) and Topkapi Palace (right), an oil tanker enters the Bosporus Strait. The 21-mile-long waterway is the sole route for Caspian oil shipped through pipelines to the Black Sea, where it is then loaded onto tankers for the trip through the strait to the Mediterranean. Turkey fears increased tanker traffic could bring an environmental catastrophe to the already busy Bosporus, so it has encouraged development of an overland pipeline that would bypass the strait.

pipeline for exports, despite years of civil war. In 2006, estimates of proven reserves topped 5 billion barrels, a 10-fold increase over the year before. [83]

Africa also has abundant natural gas. Nigeria has the continent's largest reserves and the world's seventh-biggest, while Algeria's reserves rank eighth. [84] Both are on a par with Saudi Arabia and the United States. Algeria in 1964 became the first nation to ship liquified natural gas (LNG) aboard tankers. But Nigeria, convulsed by tribal wars and coups, has been unable to capitalize on its gas deposits until recently. It still "flares," or burns away, 40 percent of the natural gas produced with its oil, although Nigeria is beginning to expand LNG production. [85]

The New Nationalism

China's staggering expansion and modernization have overtaken its energy resources. Twenty years ago, China was the largest oil exporter in East Asia. Now it is the world's second-largest oil purchaser, accounting for nearly one-third of the global increase in oil demand, note David Zweig and Bi Jianhai of the Hong Kong University of Science. [86] Similarly, India's oil consumption doubled

President Vladimir Putin addresses executives of Russia's Rosneft oil company in September 2005 after visiting the Tuapse oil terminal, pictured behind him. Putin is attempting to reclaim Russia's position as a superpower by harnessing its considerable energy resources.

between 1990 and 2004, and other industrializing Asian nations nearly matched that pace. [87]

Fortunately for the world's consumers, the explosive growth of China's oil demand was matched by a remarkable recovery in Russia's oil output. The fall of the Soviet Union and a financial credit crisis had devastated Russia's oil industry. Starved for capital and leadership, it was producing only 6 million barrels a day in 1995. But oil output had rebounded to average 9.4 million barrels a day this year, making Russia currently the world's largest oil producer, ahead of Saudi Arabia, which has trimmed its output. With the world's largest production and reserves of natural gas, it is poised to be Europe's prime supplier while developing its immense Far East gas reserves for eventual use by China, the rest of Asia and North America.

Russia's energy wealth also has transformed its self-image and ambitions, as it pulls away from the West. "In the late 19th century, Russia's success was said to rest on its army and its navy; today, its success rests on its oil and gas," writes Dmitri Trenin, deputy director of the Carnegie Moscow Center. [88]

Today, says Leonid Grigoriev, president of the Institute for Energy and Finance in Moscow, "We see ourselves as a great power." [89]

That power has frightened Russia's neighbors, especially after the Putin government took control of major petroleum reserves and energy pipelines, forcing Western energy companies to surrender equity positions in the country's largest new gas fields. Putin "has a very traditional Soviet view of the nature of power," says the Kennan Institute's Ruble. "He views oil and gas as strategic playing cards to reassert Russia in the world scene."

Now Europe anxiously faces growing dependence on Russia for its energy. "Russia is a natural, reliable and stable supplier" for Europe, insists Grigoriev.

"They see things strictly through the eyes of Russia: What is in their national interest?" responds CSIS's Ebel.

"The issue of security of supply is critical for European consumers," says BP economist Davies. "That debate is continuing."

Like Putin, Venezuela's Chávez is an architect of oil's rising nationalism. Following in the footsteps of Argentinean strongman Juan Perón and Cuba's Fidel Castro, Chávez is using Venezuela's oil and gas reserves — the Western Hemisphere's largest — to promote his socialist "Bolivarian Revolution." [90] While Chávez delights in confronting U.S. policy goals in Latin America, he also finds willing listeners in the Middle East and Asia. Having survived a coup attempt and an oil-workers' strike that stunted output in the winter of 2002-03, the former rebel paratrooper is firmly in control.

At home, Chávez has steered energy export earnings toward the three-quarters of the population that comprise Venezuela's poor. Their plight worsened in the 1980s and '90s despite market reforms recommended by globalization advocates at the International Monetary Fund (IMF) and World Bank. Chávez rejects free-market, capitalist economic approaches and vows to establish a socialist, classless society. [91] Social spending by Petróleos de Venezuela S.A. (PDVSA), the state-run oil and natural gas company, has increased 10-fold since 1997.

Abroad, Chávez seeks a coalition of allies who will help him parry opposition from the United States and pursue his agenda. He has offered low-priced oil to Latin America. (He also has donated heating oil to the poor in the United States.) PDVSA has forced major oil companies to give up majority holdings in Venezuela's oil fields and has signed oil deals with China, Iran, Vietnam, Brazil and Belarus. [92]

Has a new Cold War begun over oil that could lead to conflict?

YES Michael T. Klare
Five College Professor of Peace and World Security Studies (Amherst, Hampshire, Mount Holyoke and Smith colleges and the University of Massachusetts, Amherst)

Written for *CQ Researcher*, June 2007

Two simultaneous developments are likely to intensify future conflicts over oil. On one hand, increasing competition for a finite resource will become more intense in the years ahead. With China and India leading the growth in demand, competition is going to soar, and supply isn't likely to expand nearly as fast as demand. In addition, oil supplies increasingly will be located in areas of tension and inherent friction — the Middle East, Africa, Central Asia and other unstable places.

During the Cold War, the superpowers competed for influence by providing arms for various proxies in Africa, the Middle East and Asia. We are seeing the same thing happening in the oil cold war.

The United States, Russia and China, in their pursuit of oil allies, are again providing arms to proxies and suppliers, which is intensifying the risk of internal conflicts. It is an exceedingly dangerous development. The United States and China are not seeking to make war on one another. But they are inadvertently contributing to the risk of conflict in Africa and Central Asia by using arms transfers as an instrument of influence.

Ultimately, the only solution will be to reduce our craving for imported oil. That is easier said than done. It is a craving, and cravings lead to irrational behavior. For China, its close embrace of the Sudanese government — including supplying arms — is bringing the Chinese terrible criticism. The United States, for its part, engages in equally irrational behavior in creating close ties with — for example — the leaders of Kazakhstan and Azerbaijan — alienating the pro-democracy movements in those countries.

Ultimately, the most dangerous piece in all of this is the U.S.-China competition for energy. We have a cold war today, but it could become a hot war, although not through a deliberate act over oil. But we are engaged in competitive arms competition in Africa and Asia, and this could lead to inadvertent local conflicts and an accidental clash between the United States and China, much the way World War I began.

Neither side would choose such a conflict, but it would arise from a clash of proxies, eventually involving U.S. and Chinese advisers and troops.

Such an outcome may not be highly probable, but it is an exceedingly dangerous possibility.

NO Amy Myers Jaffe
Wallace S. Wilson Fellow in Energy Studies, James A. Baker III Institute for Public Policy; Associate Director, Rice University Energy Program

Written for *CQ Researcher*, June 2007

Competition over energy may contribute to fundamental global conflicts, but the conflicts would have happened with or without the energy situation. North Korea is not an oil issue. Kosovo was not about oil. The Iran confrontation is not an oil issue.

The Persian Gulf remains a special case. Saudi Arabia controls most of the world's excess oil production. In the case of the Iraq War in 1991 — which followed Iraq's invasion of oil-rich Kuwait — the United States was not going to let Saddam Hussein control 40-50 percent of the world's oil reserves. Saudi oil facilities have been targeted by terrorists, and Iran has threatened in the past to use military force to interfere with oil shipments through the Strait of Hormuz.

A future confrontation with Iran would greatly increase the risk to essential oil exports through the Persian Gulf. On the other hand, Iran is critically dependent upon revenues from its own oil sales and must import gasoline from foreign refiners to meet its population's requirements.

The overriding concern, however, is that the sudden loss of the Saudi oil network would paralyze the global economy. The United States — and the rest of the world — has a concrete interest in preventing that. But most conflicts facing the United States today, like North Korea or Afghanistan, are not going to change whether the price of oil is $50 a barrel or $70 a barrel.

Nor is Central Asia likely to become a flash point. We have been watching a revival of the so-called Great Game competition over Caspian oil for a decade. Why? Because the leaders in those countries have chosen to delay, trying to get the best economic and geopolitical deals they can. The Russians play the Japanese off the Chinese. The Chinese are trying to take care of their needs. Their motivations vary from country to country, but it is a dynamic that is very unlikely to lead to conflict. We are not likely to go to war with Russia over a pipeline in Kazakhstan.

The United States and China, as the world's largest oil importers, are economic partners by virtue of their trade and, consequently, potential political rivals. But both share a common interest in reasonable oil prices.

If the United States and China ever go to war over Taiwan, oil will not be the trigger.

Nigerians work on a French gas-drilling installation in Nigeria's Niger Delta, aided by Chinese contractors. The Chinese are competing with other international oil companies for the delta's rich oil reserves.

But Venezuela now spends more on social programs than on maintaining and expanding its oil production capacity, according to the Baker Institute. The current production rate of 2.4 million barrels a day is down from 3.1 million barrels when Chávez took office in 1999. [93]

"He is good at giving oil away, but he's not good at producing oil," says Chávez opponent Luis Giusti, who headed PDVSA in the 1990s.

While Chávez is a thorn in the side to the U.S. government and international oil companies, his overtures to China and Iran and his willingness to slow future development in favor of higher returns today represent a new reality in the world's energy story. [94]

CURRENT SITUATION

Majors Shut Out

Government-owned or controlled petroleum companies today control a majority of the world's hydrocarbon reserves and production. By 2005, nationalized oil companies had taken over 77 percent of the world's 1.1 trillion barrels of oil reserves. And, while Western oil companies have absorbed their share of the short-term windfall created by recent higher prices, their long-term future does not look particularly rosy. Major oil firms now control only 10 percent of global petroleum reserves. [95]

"International majors have been relegated to second-tier status," concluded the Baker Institute. In the 1970s and '80s, Western companies were invited to explore the new fields in the North Sea, Alaska and the Gulf of Mexico, but today key future resources in Russia and Central Asia are government-controlled.

"The bulk of the resources remain in a number of key countries, which are dominated by states, and we have to be dependent on governments and state companies to deliver the capacity," says BP's Davies.

"Access really is a consideration," adds Cambridge Energy Research Associates chairman Yergin. "Where can you go to invest money, apply technology and develop resources and bring them to market? Terms get very tough. The decision-making slows down, if you can get there at all."

China's strategy for feeding its oil appetite is a major source of concern, says former CIA Director Deutch. Its oil companies scour the world seeking access to oil and gas resources, effectively reducing supplies on the world market.

"China — and now India — are making extensive efforts in Africa and elsewhere in the world to lock up oil supplies," says Deutch. These state-to-state deals typically are not based solely on market terms but include sweeteners such as political incentives, military assistance, economic aid or trade concessions, he explains.

International oil companies, while banking record profits, are facing higher taxes or demands to surrender parts of their stakes in projects. For instance, say Western analysts, Putin's government has shown its knuckles to Royal Dutch Shell and Exxon Mobil in disputes over control of two huge projects on Sakhalin Island, off Russia's Pacific coast. Shell had to give up controlling interest in the Sakhalin-2 pipeline project to Russia's natural gas monopoly Gazprom after suffering cost overruns. Russia wants to determine where the gas goes, says its oil minister. [96]

Emboldened by rising oil prices, Russia and nations in South America and West Africa that once relied on Western oil companies are now "increasingly calling the shots," said *The Wall Street Journal*. [97]

Producer Windfalls

Oil prices have more than tripled since 2002, sparking an unprecedented transfer of wealth from consuming to producing nations. The amount energy-importing nations must spend for oil has leaped from $300 billion in 2002 to nearly $1 trillion in 2006 (roughly the gross domestic product of Spain or South Korea). [98] The higher prices, of course, affect not only oil production but also the current value of oil in the ground. The IMF reports the value of energy exporters' oil reserves increased by more than $40 trillion between 1999 and 2005. Thus if prices stay at current levels, it would translate into an enormous increase in future wealth for the exporting nations, concentrated in the Middle East, Russia, Central Asia and Africa. [99]

Higher oil prices leave all consumers with less to spend and save, but the impact is harshest in poor countries with no oil. Without oil or other high-value exports to offset increased energy costs, poor countries go deeper in debt.

"Debt is the central inhibitor of economic development," says former CIA Director R. James Woolsey Jr. "Importing expensive oil is helping bind hundreds of millions of the world's poor more firmly into poverty." [100]

The flow of petrodollars also is profoundly affecting the United States — the world's richest nation but also its largest oil consumer. When the U.S. buys oil from abroad, dollars pile up in the exporting nations' coffers. The oil-dollar outflow has added enormously to the U.S. "current account" deficit, or the dollar difference between U.S. imports and exports and international financial transactions. The United States is the only major nation that pays for its oil imports by borrowing heavily from the rest of the world. [101]

"The U.S. now borrows from its creditors — such as China and Saudi Arabia — over $300 billion per year, approaching a billion dollars a day of national IOU-writing, to import oil," according to Woolsey. [102]

A consequence of the increasing role of national oil companies is that most U.S. dollars paid for oil go into accounts controlled by foreign governments, according to the Federal Reserve Bank of New York. A crucial question is what those governments will do with their petrodollars, bank experts said. [103]

The outward tide of U.S. petrodollars has been matched by purchases of U.S. securities and properties by exporting countries, providing crucial support for U.S. stock and bond markets, the Federal Reserve report notes. In a dramatic example, China recently purchased $3 billion in stock of the Blackstone Group, a prominent U.S. equity firm that buys and turns around distressed companies.

Uncertainty over the construction of new oil and gas pipelines is heightening political tensions among the central players in the global competition for energy. New pipelines will be increasingly vital in moving energy resources from new fields in Russia, Central Asia and Africa.

"Officials in Beijing have $1.2 trillion of reserves they want to invest more profitably than in U.S. Treasuries. They lack the expertise to do it themselves and don't want to pay money managers millions in fees," said financial columnist William Pesek. [104]

For its part, Blackstone will get the increased access to China's surging economy that it covets. [105]

But such purchases are full of complexities, the Federal Reserve report notes. The Blackstone stock purchase was made by China's new state-owned investment fund, and other oil exporters have set up similar "sovereign wealth funds" to make direct investments in the United States and other oil-buying countries, writes

Gas stations in Tehran were torched and looted on June 26, 2007, after the Iranian government announced plans to begin fuel rationing. The state-controlled National Iranian Oil Co. has subsidized consumer fuel prices, sparking increased demand for oil.

columnist Sebastian Mallaby. "Chunks of corporate America could be bought by Beijing's government — or, for that matter, by the Kremlin." The economic and political fallout could be seismic, he adds. [106]

If events make oil exporters less willing to put dollars back into the United States, U.S. interest rates could increase to keep the foreign investment coming. Otherwise, U.S. consumers would have to cut their spending to reduce the outflow of dollars. A big shift of petrodollars away from the United States would pull a vital prop out from under stock markets. [107]

The flow of untraceable petrodollars also affects world security. Because so much oil revenue goes into the Middle East and from there into untraceable channels, some of it is being used to finance terrorist organizations opposed to the United States. "Thus . . . when we pay for Middle Eastern oil today, this long war in which we are engaged becomes the only war the U.S. has ever fought in which we pay for both sides," Woolsey says. [108]

Pipeline Politics

Over the next quarter-century, the world will rely on new oil and gas fields in Russia, Central Asia and Africa for a critical part of its energy needs. But uncertainty over when, where and if new pipelines will be built to access those new fields is heightening political tensions among the central players in the global competition for energy.

China covets oil and gas from eastern Siberia, but Russia's leaders have delayed building a pipeline into China, unwilling to hinge such a costly project on a single customer. Instead, Russia wants to channel those resources to its Pacific coast, where they can be shipped to competing customers not only in China but also in Japan, the rest of Asia and the United States.

Europe depends on Russian natural gas delivered over a Soviet-era pipeline network, which must be expanded to handle future growth. But Russia itself needs more gas and thus wants to build new pipelines into Central Asia to transport gas from Caspian fields — at market prices — to Europe.

Many Russian pipelines carrying Caspian oil terminate at the Black Sea. But Turkey opposes plans to expand that route because it fears a catastrophic oil spill from tanker traffic through the Bosporus Strait.

The most direct export route for Caspian oil is southward, by pipeline through Iran — a project China would welcome. But the United States opposes the route because it seeks to block Tehran's suspected nuclear-weapons development. [109]

Pipeline infighting is further reflected in BP's controversial $4 billion, 1,100-mile BTC pipeline from Baku, Azerbaijan, past Tbilisi, Georgia, and on to the Mediterranean port of Ceyhan, Turkey. The world's second-longest pipeline threads through mountains and volcanic regions and had to withstand unrest in Georgia, environmental opposition and sabotage threats. Its completion in 2005 fulfilled a hardball strategy by the United States to keep the pipeline out of Russian territory and block a shorter, cheaper route through Iran. [110] Leaders in Moscow and Tehran were infuriated.

"We really put all our cards on the table on that one," said Ebel, of CSIS.

But Russia has high cards to play, too, in the current pipeline tug-of-war over the undeveloped natural gas riches on the Caspian's eastern coast. The only gas pipeline through this region now leads north from Turkmenistan, through Kazakhstan into Russia, and Moscow controls it. [111]

The United States is pushing for a new pipeline across the Caspian seabed to carry Turkmenistan's gas westward to Baku.

From there it could travel into Turkey and connect with a new pipeline that the European Union wants to see built into Austria, (the "Nabucco" project), thus completing a pathway for Caspian gas to Europe without setting foot on Russian soil.

"We would love to see the Trans-Caspian Gas Pipeline put in place," Deputy Assistant Secretary of State for European and Eurasian Affairs Matthew Bryza said in January. [112]

Putin has other ideas. He is pressing Turkmenistan and Kazakhstan to support a Russian-built pipeline around the north end of the Caspian into Russia to move the gas into Europe over old and new Russian lines. Russia insists that no pipeline may cross the Caspian Sea unless all five adjoining nations agree — and Moscow is ready with its veto.

Speaking in Turkey recently, Bryza took a shot at Gazprom's natural gas pipeline monopoly, saying Russia uses its pipelines to intimidate governments in Europe that depend on them. "Europeans are finally waking up to the reality, I'm sorry to say, that Gazprom isn't always the most reliable partner for them. The more gas that moves from Central Asia and Azerbaijan to Europe via Turkey, the better." [113]

Russian officials contend the United States is still trying to throw its weight around, telling Moscow what to do.

In May, Moscow claimed the advantage after Putin and President Gurbanguly Berdymukhammedov of Turkmenistan agreed to the Russian plan for moving Caspian gas, but the United States says the door is still open for its favored route. [114] "These two pipelines are different," Bryza said in June, speaking of the Russian plan and trans-Caspian pipeline.

Meanwhile, Turkmenistan continues to talk with China about an eastward pipeline connection for its gas.

Currently, however, most of the pipeline-route disputes remain on paper. Soaring steel prices continue to inflate the costs of the billion-dollar pipeline networks. "The watchword today is delay," says Yergin of Cambridge Energy Research Associates, "not only because of political issues, but also because construction costs are going through the roof."

OUTLOOK

Curbing Demand

The race for Earth's remaining energy resources increasingly is splitting the world into two camps: countries that sell oil and natural gas and those that buy them.

The buyers — led by the United States, Europe, China and India and Japan — have a clear imperative, according to the International Energy Agency (IEA) and other energy experts: Start curbing demand. [115]

Energy security is the primary reason. Two-thirds of the growth in oil supplies over the next quarter-century will likely come from the Middle East, Russia, the Caspian region, Africa and Venezuela — areas beset by conflict or political instability. [116]

Climate change is also driving the need to curb demand. Total world economic output is projected to more than double by 2030, accelerating the discharge of greenhouse gases into the atmosphere. Eighty percent of the growth will come from China, India, Brazil and other developing countries. [117]

To avert potentially catastrophic climate disasters before the end of this century, both industrial and developing countries must agree on strategies for conserving energy and reducing greenhouse gases without halting economic growth, says the Intergovernmental Panel on Climate Change. [118]

Both energy insecurity and climate threats demand greater international cooperation than in the past decade, experts say. The United States has, until now, mainly sought to deal with its energy challenges by producing more oil and gas outside its borders, said a 2004 report for the Baker Institute for Public Policy.

After the Sept. 11, 2001, terrorist attacks, influential members of the Bush administration saw regime change in Iraq as a way to shake OPEC's hold on oil production, the Baker Institute authors wrote. Instead of taking responsibility for reducing energy consumption, however, the U.S. addressed the challenge "by attempting to control the Middle East." [119] But the strategy "has fallen flat on its face," the authors have asserted.

No matter how the Iraq War ends, the authors continue, the United States must move more decisively to reduce its energy demands if it wants credibility in seeking cooperation from China. China is quickly catching up to the United States in energy production and greenhouse-gas emissions, according to a recent report by U.S. climate experts Jeffrey Logan, Joanna Lewis and Michael B. Cummings. [120]

China has been building on average one new electric power plant a week for the past few years, and its automobile sales are booming (though they're small by U.S. standards). [121] But by the end of the decade, China will have 90 times more motor vehicles than it had in 1990, and by 2030 — or sooner — there may be more cars in China than in the United States. [122]

This year China announced new climate goals, including a 10 percent reduction in carbon-dioxide emissions over five years. "[W]e have to take responsibility for lowering greenhouse emissions," said Zhang Zhang Guobao, vice chairman of the energy-policy-setting National Development and Reform Commission. [123]

But China has adopted a "wait-and-see" attitude toward international climate-change agreements, unwilling to make binding commitments until it is clear what the United States and the developed world will do, according to Logan, Lewis and Cummings. The United States must lead by example, they said.

"Thinking about how to alter our energy-consumption patterns to bring down the price of oil is no longer simply a hobby for high-minded environmentalists or some personal virtue," says *Times* columnist Friedman. "It is a national-security imperative." [124]

"It must be recognized," says Yergin of Cambridge Energy Research Associates, "that energy security does not stand by itself but is lodged in the larger relations among nations and how they interact with one another." [125]

NOTES

1. The Associated Press, "Putin: Soviet Collapse a 'Genuine Tragedy,' " MSNBC, April 25, 2005, www.msnbc.msn.com/id/7632057.

2. "Russia Cuts Ukraine Gas Supplies," BBC News, Jan. 1, 2006; http://news.bbc.co.uk/1/hi/world/europe/4572712.stm.

3. "Russia and the West; No Divide, No Rule," *The Economist*, May 17, 2007, p. 12.

4. "Oil Nationalism Troubling Multinationals," *Iran Daily*, Oct. 23, 2006, p. 11, http://irandaily.ir/1385/2691/pdf/i11.pdf.

5. John M. Deutch, testimony before the House Foreign Affairs Committee, March 22, 2007.

6. "PIW Ranks the World's Top Oil Companies," *Energy Intelligence*, www.energyintel.com/DocumentDetail.asp?document_id=137158.

7. *Iran Daily, op. cit.*

8. Peter Katel, "Change in Latin America," *CQ Researcher*, July 21, 2006, pp. 601-624.

9. Natalie Obiko Pearson, "Chávez takes over Venezuela's last private oil fields," The Associated Press Worldstream, May 2, 2007.

10. Alexandra Valencia, "Ecuador says started review of oil contracts," Reuters, June 6, 2007; www.reuters.com/article/companyNewsAndPR/idUSN0645081020070607.

11. *Energy Intelligence, op. cit.*

12. U.S. motorists were paying over $1.42 a gallon for regular gasoline in March 1981. Adjusted at 2006 price levels to account for inflation, that cost would be $3.22 a gallon; www.eia.doe.gov/emeu/steo/pub/fsheets/petroleumprices.xls.

13. Matthew Higgins, Thomas Klitgaard and Robert Lerman, "Recycling Petrodollars: Current Issues in Economics and Finance," Federal Reserve Bank of New York, December 2006, p. 1; www.newyork-fed.org/research/current_issues/ci12-9.pdf.

14. "The Changing Role of National Oil Companies in International Energy Markets," James A. Baker III Institute for Public Policy, April 2007; http://bakerinstitute.org/Pubs/BI_ Pol%20Rep_35.pdf, page 2; see all reports www.rice.edu/energy/publications/nocs.html.

15. "World Energy Outlook 2006," International Energy Agency, p. 1; www.worldenergyoutlook.org/summaries2006/English.pdf.

16. For background, see Colin Woodard, "Curbing Climate Change," *CQ Global Researcher*, February 2007, pp. 27-50; and the following *CQ Researchers*: Barbara Mantel, "Energy Efficiency," May 19, 2006, pp. 433-456; Marcia Clemmitt, "Climate Change," Jan. 27, 2006, pp. 73-96; Mary H. Cooper, "Energy Policy," May 25, 2001, pp. 441-464; Mary H. Cooper, "Global Warming Treaty," Jan. 26, 2001, pp. 41-64; Mary H. Cooper, "Global Warming Update," Nov. 1, 1996, pp. 961-984.

17. Maureen S. Crandall, *Energy, Economics and Politics in the Caspian Region: Dreams and Realities* (2006), pp. 23, 46.

18. Amy Myers Jaffe and Matthew E. Chen, James A. Baker III Institute for Public Policy, testimony before the U.S.-China Economic and Security

Review Commission, hearing on China's Role in the World, Aug. 4, 2006; www.uscc.gov/hearings/2006hearings/written_testimonies/06_08_3_4wrts/06_08_3_4_jaffe_amy_statement.php.

19. R. James Woolsey, "Global Implications of Rising Oil Dependence and Global Warming," testimony before the House Select Committee on Energy Independence and Global Warming, April 18, 2007, p. 2.

20. "PIW Survey: Oil Reserves Are Not Rising," *Petroleum Intelligence Weekly*, April 16, 2007; www.energyintel.com/DocumentDetail.asp?document_id=199949. See also "Performance Profiles of Major Energy Producers 2005," Energy Information Agency, pp. 20-21; www.eia.doe.gov/emeu/perfpro/020605.pdf.

21. Michael Connolly, "Fragmented Market Would Hamper Russian-Iranian 'Gas OPEC,' " *Wall Street Journal* online, Feb. 2, 2007.

22. Daniel Dombey, Neil Buckley, Carola Hoyos, "NATO fears Russian plans for 'gas OPEC,' " *Financial Times*, Nov. 13, 2006.

23. Daniel S. Sullivan addressed the Energy Council's Federal Energy & Environmental Matters Conference, March 9, 2007.

24. James A. Baker III Institute for Public Policy Report, *op. cit.*; also Baker Institute Report, "Introductions and Summary Conclusions," pp. 7-19; www.rice.edu/energy/publications/docs/NOCs/Presentations/Hou-Jaffe-KeyFindings.pdf.

25. "Mapping the Global Future: Report of the National Intelligence Council's 2020 Project," National Intelligence Council, December 2004; www.dni.gov/nic/NIC_globaltrend2020.html.

26. Michael Schiffer and Gary Schmitt, "Keeping Tabs on China's Rise," The Stanley Foundation, May 2007, p. 1; www.stanleyfoundation.org/publications/other/SchifferSchimitt07.pdf.

27. *Ibid.*, p. 9.

28. Xuecheng Liu, "China's Energy Security and Its Grand Strategy," The Stanley Foundation, September 2006, p. 13; www.stanleyfoundation.org/publications/pab/pab06chinasenergy.pdf.

29. Quoted in Paulo Prada, "Bolivian Nationalizes the Oil and Gas Sector," *The New York Times*, May 2, 2006, p. A9.

30. Quoted in Juan Forero, "Presidential Vote Could Alter Bolivia, and Strain Ties With U.S.," *The New York Times*, Dec. 18, 2005, p. A13.

31. Alfonzo quoted by Stanford University's Terry Lynn Karl, Senior Fellow at the Institute for International Studies, Stanford University, in "The Oil Trap," Transparency International, September 2003; ww1.transparency.org/newsletters/2003.3/tiq-Sept 2003.pdf.

32. Richard M. Auty, *Sustaining Development in Mineral Economies: The Resource Curse Thesis* (Routledge), 1993. Summarized in Richard M. Auty, "The 'Resource Curse' in Developing Countries Can Be Avoided," United Nations University, Helsinki; www.wider.unu.edu/research/pr9899d2/pr9899d2s.htm.

33. "Country Analysis Briefs: Mexico," Energy Information Administration, January 2007; www.eia.doe.gov/emeu/cabs/Mexico/Oil.html; and "Major Non-OPEC Countries' Oil Revenues," www.eia.doe.gov/cabs/opecnon.html.

34. Robert Collier, "Mexico's Oil Bonanza Starts to Dry Up," *San Francisco Chronicle*; www.sfgate.com/cgi-bin/article.cgi?file=/c/a/2006/06/30/MNGAAJN 9JG1.DTL.

35. Karl, Transparency International, *op. cit.*, p. 1.

36. See "The 'Dutch Disease': Theory and Evidence," *Poverty and Growth Blog*, The World Bank, http://pgpblog.worldbank.org/the_dutch_disease_theory_and_evidence.

37. Tom O'Neill, "Hope and Betrayal in the Niger Delta," *National Geographic*, February 2007, p. 97.

38. Senan Murray, "Tackling Nigeria's Violent Oil Swamps," BBC News, May 30, 2007; http://news.bbc.co.uk/2/hi/africa/6698433.stm.

39. Karl Maier, "Nigeria Militants Release Six Chevron Oil Workers," Bloomberg, June 2, 2007; www.bloomberg.com/apps/news?pid=20601087&sid=aXT6yOlwMVGY&refer=home.

40. Daniel Balint Kurti, "New Militia is a Potent Force," *The Christian Science Monitor*, March 7, 2007; www.csmonitor.com/2006/0307/p04s01-woaf.html.

41. Bernd Debusmann, "In Venezuela, obstacles to 21st Century socialism," Reuters, June 20, 2007.

42. Transparency International, Corruption Perceptions Index, 2006; www.transparency.org/policy_research/surveys_indices/cpi/2006.

43. Freedom House, "Countries at the Crossroads 2006; Country Report: Venezuela," www.freedomhouse.org/template.cfm?page=140&edition=7&ccrpage=31&ccrcountry=141.

44. "Iran fuel rations spark anger, pump stations burn," Reuters, June 27, 2007, www.reuters.com/article/worldNews/idUSDAH72595420070627.

45. "New Analysis Claims Darfur Deaths Near 400,000," Coalition for Darfur, April 25, 2005, http://coalitionfordarfur.blogspot.com/2005/04/new-analysis-claims-darfur-deaths-near.html.

46. Jaffe, *op. cit.*

47. David Zweig and Bi Jianhai, "China's Global Hunt for Energy," *Foreign Affairs*, Sept./Oct. 2005, p. 32.

48. Scott McDonald, "China Welcomes Darfur Agreement," The Associated Press, June 14, 2007; www.boston.com/news/world/asia/articles/2007/06/14/china_welcomes_darfur_agreement/.

49. "Fact Sheet," Extractive Industries Transparency Initiative, 2007; www.eitransparency.org/section/abouteiti.

50. Thomas L. Friedman, "The First Law of Petropolitics," *Foreign Policy*, May/June 2006, p. 4; www.foreignpolicy.com/story/cms.php?story_id=3426.

51. Ariel Cohen, the Heritage Foundation, "The North Eureopean Gas Pipeline Threatens Europe's Energy Security," Oct. 26, 2006; www.heritage.org/Research/Europe/bg1980.cfm.

52. Alexandre Rocha, "Burned by Bolivia, Brazil Goes to Africa and Middle East Looking for Gas," *Brazzil Magazine* (online), June 20, 2007; www.brazzilmag.com/content/view/8368/1/.

53. Crandall, *op. cit.*, p. 143.

54. Foster Klug, "U.S. Presses China on Iran in Latest Talks," The Associated Press, June 20, 2007.

55. "Mapping the Global Future," *op. cit.*

56. Schiffer and Schmitt, *op. cit.*, p 14.

57. Evan Osnos, "U.S., China vie for oil, allies on new Silk Road," *Chicago Tribune*, Dec. 19, 2006, p. 4.

58. Schiffer and Schmitt, *op. cit.*, p. 15.

59. "About Us," Organization of Petroleum Exporting Countries, www.opec.org/aboutus/history/history.htm.

60. Until 1972 production limits set by the Texas Railroad Commission effectively set a ceiling on oil prices in the United States and the rest of the world. But U.S. output peaked then, opening the way for OPEC's moves to control oil markets; http://tonto.eia.doe.gov/dnav/pet/hist/mcrfpus1m.htm.

61. For background, see Mary H. Cooper, "OPEC: Ten Years After the Arab Oil Boycott," *Editorial Research Reports*, Sept. 23, 1983; available in *CQ Researcher Plus Archive*, www.cqpress.com.

62. "U.S. Strategic Petroleum Reserve," Fact Sheet, U.S. Department of Energy, May 30, 2007; www.fossil.energy.gov/programs/reserves.

63. Daniel Yergin, *The Prize: The Epic Quest for Oil, Money & Power* (1991), p. 631.

64. "Carter Energy Program," *CQ Historic Documents Series Online Edition.* Originally published in *Historic Documents of 1977*, CQ Press (1978), CQ Electronic Library; http://library.cqpress.com/historicdocuments/hsdc77-0000106610.

65. *Ibid.*

66. "Iranian Hostage Crisis, 1980 Special Report," *Congress and the Nation, 1977-1980* (Vol. 5); CQ Press; available at CQ Congress Collection, CQ Electronic Library, http://library.cqpress.com/congress/catn77-0010173673.

67. "Real Gasoline Prices," Energy Information Administration; www.eia.doe.gov/emeu/steo/pub/fsheets/real_prices.html.

68. For background, see R. Thompson, "Quest for Energy Independence," *Editorial Research Reports*, Dec. 23, 1983, available in *CQ Researcher Plus Archive*, CQ Electronic Library, http://library.cqpress.com.

69. Yergin, *op. cit.*, p. 669.

70. *Ibid.*, p. 666.

71. "Annual Energy Review 2005, World Crude Oil Production, 1960-2005," Energy Information Administration; www.eia.doe.gov/emeu/aer/pdf/pages/sec11_11.pdf.

72. Yergin, *op. cit.*, p. 718.

73. Mary H. Cooper, "SUV Debate," *CQ Researcher*, May 16, 2003, pp. 449-472.

74. For background, see Kenneth Jost, "Russia and the Former Soviet Republics," *CQ Researcher*, June 17, 2005; pp. 541-564.

75. Louis Fischer, *Oil Imperialism* (1926), cited by Robert E. Ebel, Center for Strategic and International Studies, July 25, 2006.

76. Bruce W. Nelan, "The Rush for Caspian Oil," *Time*, May 4, 1998, p. 40.

77. Crandall, *op. cit.*, p. 1.

78. "Caspian Sea," Energy Information Administration, 2007; www.eia.doe.gov/emeu/cabs/Caspian/Full.html.

79. Martha Brill Olcott, "Will Central Asia Have Another 'Second Chance'?" speech, Carnegie Endowment for International Peace, Sept. 15, 2005.

80. Crandall, *op. cit.*, p. 3.

81. "Top World Oil Producers, Exporters, Consumers, and Importers 2004," Information Please Database, 2007; www.infoplease.com/ipa/A0922041.html.

82. "BP Statistical Review 2006," *British Petroleum*, p. 8; www.bp.com/sectiongenericarticle.do?categoryId=9017903&contentId=7033469.

83. "Sudan," Energy Information Administration, April 2007; www.eia.doe.gov/emeu/cabs/Sudan/Background.html.

84. "Libya — Natural Gas," Energy Information Administration, March 2006; www.eia.doe.gov/emeu/cabs/Libya/NaturalGas.html.

85. "Nigeria/Natural Gas," Energy Information Administration, April 2007, www.eia.doe.gov/emeu/cabs/Nigeria/NaturalGas.html.

86. Zweig and Jianhai, *op. cit.*, p. 25.

87. "International Energy Outlook, 2007," Energy Information Administration, p. 83; www.eia.doe.gov/oiaf/ieo/pdf/ieorefcase.pdf.

88. Dmitri Trenin, Deputy Director, Carnegie Moscow Center, "Russia Leaves the West," *Foreign Affairs*, July/August 2006.

89. Leonid Grigoriev, speaking at the Kennan Institute, Feb. 5, 2007; www.wilsoncenter.org/index.cfm?topic_id=1424&fuseaction=topics.event_summary&event_id=215229.

90. *Oil and Gas Journal*, quoted in www.eia.doe.gov/emeu/cabs/Venezuela/Oil.html. Conventional reserves do not include the extensive Canadian tar sands or Venezuela's extra-heavy oil and bitumen deposits.

91. Michael Shifter, "In search of Hugo Chávez," *Foreign Affairs*, May/June 2006, p. 47. For background, see Peter Katel, "Change in Latin America," *CQ Researcher*, July 21, 2006, pp. 601-624.

92. Baker Institute for Public Policy, *op. cit.*, p. 6.

93. "Venezuela," Energy Information Administration, September 2006; www.eia.doe.gov/emeu/cabs/Venezuela/Oil.html.

94. Baker Institute, *op. cit.*, p. 5.

95. *Ibid.*, p. 1.

96. Gregory L. White and Jeffrey Ball, "Huge Sakhalin Project Is Mostly on Track, As Shell Feels Pinch," *The Wall Street Journal*, May 7, 2007, p. 1.

97. *Ibid.*, p. 1. Also see Amy Myers Jaffe, James A. Baker III Institute for Public Policy, "Russia: Back to the Future?" testimony before the Senate Committee on Foreign Relations, June 29, 2006, p. 1.

98. Higgins, Klitgaard and Lerman, *op. cit.*, p. 1.

99. "World Economic Outlook, April 2006," Chapter 2, p. 24, International Monetary Fund; www.imf.org/external/pubs/ft/weo/2006/01/pdf/c2.pdf.

100. Woolsey, *op. cit.*, p. 3.

101. Higgins, Klitgaard and Lerman, *op. cit.*, p. 6.

102. Woolsey, *op. cit.*, p. 3.

103. Higgins, Klitgaard and Lerman, *op. cit.*, pp. 3-4.

104. William Pesek, "Blackstone + China = Bubble," Bloomberg, May 23, 2007; www.bloomberg.com/apps/news?pid=20601039&sid=aU7bs9CJazGI&refer=columnist_pesek.

105. Ransdell Pierson and Tamora Vidaillet, "China flexes FX muscle with $3 bln Blackstone deal," Reuters, May 21, 2007.

106. Sebastian Mallaby, "The Next Globalization Backlash," *The Washington Post*, June 25, 2007, p. A19.

107. Higgins, Klitgaard and Lerman, *op. cit.*, p. 6.

108. Woolsey, *op. cit.*, p. 4.

109. The United States has its own huge pipeline project on the table, a plan to transport natural gas from Alaska's North Slope into the U.S. Midwest, which would reduce some of the future need for natural gas imports by LNG tankers from Russia and the Middle East.

110. Robert E. Ebel, "Russian Energy Policy," Center for Strategic and International Studies, testimony before the U.S. Senate Committee on Foreign Relations, June 21, 2005; Crandall, *op. cit.*, p. 23.

111. "Central Asia," Energy Information Administration, September 2005; www.eia.doe.gov/emeu/cabs/Centasia/NaturalGas.html.

112. "Washington Pushes for Trans-Caspian Pipeline," *New Europe*, Jan. 15, 2007; www.neurope.eu/view_news.php?id=69019.

113. Press statement, State Department, Consulate General-Istanbul, Remarks by Matthew Bryza, deputy assistant secretary of State for European and Eurasian affairs, May 11, 2007; http://istanbul.usconsulate.gov/bryza_speech_051107.html.

114. "Turkmenistan open oil, gas to Russia," UPI, June 13, 2007.

115. "World Energy Outlook 2006," International Energy Agency, p. 3; www.worldenergyoutlook.org/summaries2006/English.pdf.

116. "International Energy Outlook 2007," Energy Information Administration, p. 187; www.eia.doe.gov/oiaf/ieo/pdf/ieopol.pdf.

117. "Fighting Climate Change Through Energy Efficiency," United Nations Environment Program, May 30, 2006; www.unep.org/Documents.Multilingual/Default.asp?DocumentID=477&ArticleID=5276&l=en.

118. "Working Group III Report," Intergovernmental Panel on Climate Change, May 2007; www.mnp.nl/ipcc/pages_media/AR4-chapters.html.

119. Joe Barnes, Amy Myers Jaffe, Edward L. Morse, "The Energy Dimension in Russian Global Strategy," James A. Baker III Institute for Public Policy," 2004, p. 5; www.rice.edu/energy/publications/docs/PEC_BarnesJaffeMorse_10_2004.pdf.

120. Jeffrey Logan, Joanna Lewis and Michael B. Cummings, "For China, the Shift to Climate-Friendly Energy Depends on International Collaboration," *Boston Review*, January/February 2007; www.pewclimate.org/press_room/discussions/jlbostonreview.cfm.

121. Logan, Lewis and Cummings, *op. cit.*

122. Global Insight Forecast, "Outlook Still Buoyant for Chinese Auto Market," March 2007; www.globalinsight.com/SDA/SDADetail9307.htm.

123. Catherine Brahic, "China to promise cuts in greenhouse gases," NewScientist.com news services, Feb. 14, 2007, http://environment.newscientist.com/article/dn11184.

124. Friedman, *op. cit.*, p. 10.

125. Yergin, "Ensuring Energy Security," *op. cit.*, p. 69.

BIBLIOGRAPHY

Books

Crandall, Maureen S., *Energy, Economics, and Politics in the Caspian Region: Dreams and Realities*, Praeger Security International, 2006.
An economics professor at the National Defense University argues that the Caspian region's oil development will accelerate global and regional military, ethnic and religious conflict.

Klare, Michael, *Resource Wars: The New Landscape of Global Conflict*, Henry Holt, 2001.
A political science professor describes how the demand for scarce resources among growing populations has led to wars over the past century.

Yergin, Daniel, *The Prize: The Epic Quest for Oil, Money & Power*, Simon & Schuster, 1991.
In a Pulitzer Prize-winning work, the chairman of Cambridge Energy Research Associates chronicles the political and economic history of the oil industry.

Articles

"PIW Ranks the World's Top Oil Companies," *Energy Intelligence*, www.energyintel.com.
Petroleum Intelligence Weekly, a leading industry publication, ranks Saudi Aramco of Saudi Arabia and Exxon Mobil of the United States as the world's top two oil companies.

O'Neill, Tom, "Curse of the Black Gold," *National Geographic*, February 2007, p. 88.
The writer examines the politics and corruption of multinational petroleum companies that critics claim have created poverty and violence in the wake of Nigeria's oil boom.

Schiffer, Michael and Gary Schmitt, "Keeping Tabs on China's Rise," The Stanley Foundation, May 2007, www.stanleyfoundation.org.
Two foreign policy experts encourage the West to continue diplomatic relations with the Beijing government amid China's rise as a global superpower.

Shifter, Michael, "In Search of Hugo Chávez," *Foreign Affairs*, May-June 2006, p. 45.
According to a vice president of the Inter-American Dialogue, the profits from nationalization of Venezuela's oil have yielded only modest gains for the country's poor.

Trenin, Dmitri, "Russia Leaves the West," *Foreign Affairs*, July-Aug. 2006, p. 87.
Russia's vast energy resources make it a potential threat to the United States and other Western nations, according to the deputy director of the Carnegie Moscow Center.

Udall, Randy, and Matthew R. Simmons, "CERA's Rosy Oil Forecast — Pabulum to the People," *ASPO-USA's Peak Oil Review/Energy Bulletin*, Aug. 21, 2006, www.energy bulletin.net.
Two energy experts refute a recent optimistic oil study by Cambridge Energy Research Associates, contending that in actuality oil will be in shorter supply and more expensive by 2015.

Yergin, Daniel, "Ensuring Energy Security," *Foreign Affairs*, March-April 2006, p. 69.
The chairman of Cambridge Energy Research Associates explores new tactics for safeguarding the world's energy supplies and alleviating energy-related conflicts.

Zweig, David, and Bi Jianhai, "China's Global Hunt for Energy," *Foreign Affairs*, Sept.-Oct. 2005, p. 25.
Two foreign policy professors at Hong Kong University argue that China must find new energy sources if it wants to maintain rapid economic growth.

Reports

"Challenge and Opportunity, Charting a New Energy Future," Energy Future Coalition, 2002, www.energyfuturecoalition.org.
A bipartisan energy research group advocates alternative energy strategies to reduce dependence on foreign oil.

"The Changing Role of National Oil Companies in International Markets," James A. Baker III Institute for Public Policy, Rice University, May 1, 2007, www.rice.edu.
Energy researchers provide case studies analyzing the problems of private petroleum companies amid the rise of oil nationalism.

Ebel, Robert E., "Russian Energy Policy," testimony before Senate Foreign Relations Committee, June 21, 2005.
A senior energy adviser at the Center for Strategic and International Studies stresses the United States' need for a diplomatic energy-policy dialogue with Russia.

Jaffe, Amy Myers, "Russia: Back to the Future?" testimony before Senate Foreign Relations Committee, June 29, 2006.
A noted energy analyst reviews Russia's increasingly nationalistic energy policies.

Woolsey, R. James, "Geopolitical Implications of Rising Oil Dependence and Global Warming," testimony before Select Committee on Energy Independence and Global Warming, April 18, 2007.
A former CIA director offers solutions for curbing the United States' dependence on oil and natural gas.

For More Information

American Enterprise Institute, 1150 17th St., N.W., Washington, DC 20036; (202) 862-5800; www.aei.org. Public-policy research group studying economic and social issues.

American Petroleum Institute, 1220 L St., N.W., Washington, DC 20005-4070; (202) 682-8000; www.api.org. Industry group representing oil and gas producers.

Cambridge Energy Research Associates, 55 Cambridge Parkway, Cambridge, MA 02142; (617) 866-5000; www.cera.com. Renowned energy consultancy to international energy firms, financial institutions, foreign governments and technology providers.

Center for Strategic and International Studies, 800 K St., N.W., Washington, DC 20006; (202) 887-0200; www.csis.org. Public-policy research group specializing in defense, security and energy issues.

Council on Foreign Relations, 1779 Massachusetts Ave., N.W., Washington, DC 20036; (202) 518-3400; www.cfr.org. Think tank focusing on international issues; publishes Foreign Affairs.

Energy Future Coalition, 1800 Massachusetts Ave., N.W., Washington, DC 20036; (202) 463-1947; www.energyfuturecoalition.org. A bipartisan advocacy group for energy conservation and alternative fuels.

Energy Information Administration, 1000 Independence Ave., S.W., Washington, DC 20585; (202) 586-8800; www.eia.doe.gov. The primary source of federal data and analysis on energy.

Extractive Industries Transparency Initiative, Ruseløkkveien 26, 0251 Oslo, Norway; +47 2224 2110; www.eitransparency.org. Advocates responsible energy use and public disclosure of energy-based revenues and expenditures on behalf of more than 20 nations.

Human Rights Watch, 350 Fifth Ave., 34th floor, New York, NY 10118-3299; (212) 290-4700; www.hrw.org. Advocates for human rights.

International Energy Agency, 9 rue de la Fédération, 75739 Paris Cedex 15, France; 33 1 40 57 65 00/01; www.iea.org. The principal international forum for global energy data and analysis.

James A. Baker III Institute, 6100 Main St., Rice University, Baker Hall, Suite 120, Houston, TX 77005; (713) 348-4683; http://bakerinstitute.org. Academic research group specializing in energy.

Kennan Institute, Woodrow Wilson International Center for Scholars, Ronald Reagan Building and International Trade Center, One Woodrow Wilson Plaza, 1300 Pennsylvania Ave., N.W., Washington, DC 20004-3027; (202) 691-4000; www.wilsoncenter.org. Think tank specializing in social, political and economic developments in Russia and the former Soviet states.

Organization of the Petroleum Exporting Countries, Obere Donaustrasse 93, A-1020 Vienna, Austria; +43-1-21112-279; www.opec.org. Coordinates and unifies petroleum policies among its 12 oil-exporting member nations.

Transparency International, Alt-Moabit 96, 10559 Berlin, Germany; 49-30-3438 20-0; www.transparency.org. Advocacy group that campaigns against corruption worldwide.

World Bank, 1818 H St., N.W., Washington, DC 20433; (202) 473-1000; www.worldbank.org. Provides financial and technical assistance to developing countries.

VOICES FROM ABROAD

Abdalla Salem El-Badri

Secretary General, OPEC

Oil is important to all

"Any talk of energy security must take into account both supply and demand perspectives. The role of oil is equally important to the economic growth and prosperity of consuming-importing countries, as well as to the development and social progress of producing-exporting countries."

— *Speech, Second Asian Ministerial Energy Roundtable, May 2007*

Ngozi Okonjo-Iweala

Minister of Finance, Nigeria

Niger Delta problems present an opportunity

"The government is determined to address the genuine problems of the Niger Delta people but will not allow gangsterism to prevail. . . . There will be no going back on the present reforms no matter what political configuration is in place, because Nigeria can not afford to miss this opportunity."

— This Day *(Nigeria), April 2006*

Editorial

Gazeta *(Russia)*

Russia: 'Oil is its everything'

"In 2009 oil prices will fall. [Putin] understands perfectly well that it is the falling of oil prices and not at all the elections that could return the demand for liberal reforms. This is the kind of country Russia is — oil is its everything."

— *February 2006*

Rafael Ramírez

Minister of Energy and Petroleum, Venezuela

Oil stability requires social stability

"There cannot be stability in the international oil market if there is no stability within the oil producing countries, which in turn presupposes political and social stability, justice and a truly national and fair distribution of the oil rent."

— *Speech during Third OPEC International Seminar, September 2006*

Xu Weizhong

African Studies Director
China Institute of Contemporary International Relations

It's not just about oil

"[Western media] believed that China became interested in Africa only because of oil. But . . . Africa has always been a focus of China's foreign policy over the past half-century. . . . China has broad cooperation with African countries, including both energy-rich countries and resource-lacking ones. Western media's accusation against China [regarding Darfur] was not objective."

— *Xinhua news agency (China), October 2006*

Luiz Inacio Lula da Silva

President, Brazil

Brazil has rights too

"Bolivia's nationalization of its gas reserves was a necessary adjustment for a suffering people seeking a greater measure of control over their own resources. However, the fact that Bolivia has rights does not deny the fact that Brazil has rights in the matter as well."

— *AP Worldstream, May 2006*

Dmitry Peskov

Deputy Presidential Spokesman, Russia

Russia depends on Europe, too

"I think the authors of such an idea [gas OPEC] simply fail to understand our thesis about energy security. Our main thesis is interdependence of producers and consumers. Only a madman could think that Russia would start to blackmail Europe using gas, because we depend to the same extent on European customers."

—Financial Times, *November 2006*

Carlos Lopes

Political Analyst, Brazil

Lula is weak

"Presidential meetings don't resolve technical questions. They're symbolic, and the symbolism was bad from Brazil's viewpoint. Bolivia's sovereignty defends Bolivia, not Brazil. Brazil's role is to defend its interests. . . . Its attitude was very weak, but that's Lula."

— *AP Worldstream, May 2006*

Uzeir Jafarov

Military Expert, Azerbaijan

Iran threatens U.S. oil interests

"Even if Azerbaijan gives no consent to using its territory by U.S. troops, it should be not ruled out that Tehran, being in a desperate situation, would strike objects of U.S. economic interests in Azerbaijan: works in the Caspian Sea, the Baku-Tbilisi-Ceyhan pipeline."

— *United Press International, April 2006*

VENE-ZUELA

Arcadio Esquivel/La Prensa, Panama

9

Curbing Climate Change

Colin Woodard

In front of the U.S. Embassy in London, the "Statue of Taking Liberties" holds the torch of protest against the U.S. withdrawal from the Kyoto Protocol, which places limits on greenhouse gases created by burning fossil fuels.

From *CQ Researcher,*
February 1, 2007.

From the shores of Jokulsarlon Lagoon, the view of Iceland's ice cap is breathtaking: A vast dome of snow and ice, 3,000 feet tall, smothers the jagged mountains; a glacier spills the 12 miles down to the water's edge.

More stunning is how fast it's all vanishing.

A century ago there was no lagoon, and this spot was under 100 feet of glacial ice. The glacier, the Breidamerkurjokull, extended to within 250 yards of the ocean. Now the Atlantic is more than two miles away from the glacier's massive, miles-wide snout, which stands in an expanding lake of its own melt water. Jokulsarlon — "glacier lake" in Icelandic — is now more than 350 feet deep and has more than doubled its size in the past 15 years, threatening to wash out Iceland's principal highway.

In the 250 miles between the lake and Reykjavik, Iceland's capital, the highway passes by another dozen glaciers, all of them steadily retreating back up the valleys they once filled. Stand on their snouts and you hear cracking, moans and the gurgle of the many streams of water pouring from their insides, feeding unruly brown rivers that rush toward the sea. As they retreat, a new landscape scrolls out from underneath, places that haven't seen the light of day since medieval times.

Iceland is losing its ice, and it's not alone. Greenland's 10,000-year-old ice sheet is retreating at a rate that has astonished scientists who study it. Arctic Ocean sea ice has shrunk by 6 percent since 1978, while the average thickness has declined by 40 percent in recent decades, threatening polar bears, seals and the Inuit people who hunt them. (*See sidebar, p. 239.*)

In Antarctica enormous floating ice shelves have disintegrated, and many of the glaciers that empty the West Antarctic ice sheet

Japanese activists and advocates for now-endangered polar bears cheer the signing of the Kyoto Protocol in 2005, requiring cuts in carbon emissions. The treaty has the support of 169 nations; among industrialized nations, only Australia and the United States, refused to join.

have picked up speed, raising the possibility that a large portion of the southern ice cap may break up, which would quickly raise world sea levels by 20 feet.

Mid-latitude glaciers are vanishing as well. All appear to be the result of significant increases in average temperatures: 0.6 degrees Celsius (1.1 degrees Fahrenheit) globally and 1.6 degrees Celsius in the Arctic during the 20th century. [1]

Iceland's president, Olafur Ragnar Grimsson, has invited fellow world leaders to come to Iceland and bear witness. "Nowhere in the world can you see traces of climate change as clearly as in the North," he said. "It's an important mission." [2]

The vast majority of the world's scientists are now convinced that the warming of the past 50 years has largely come from greenhouse gas emissions, mostly created by the burning of fossil fuels. The "greenhouse effect" is how the Earth retains much of its warmth from the sun, as certain gases in the atmosphere trap some of the radiation reflected off the planet's surface and warm the planet.

Greenhouse gases (GHG) occur naturally in the atmosphere and include water vapor, carbon dioxide, methane, nitrous oxide and ozone. But human activity has been boosting the concentrations of some of them, most notoriously the carbon dioxide (CO_2), which is released by burning fossil fuels. The overproduction of man-made gases has been blamed for much of the excess retention of heat in the atmosphere that has contributed to global warming.

"Everything we're seeing in the Arctic is 100 percent consistent with that," says Robert Corell, a senior fellow at the American Meteorological Society in Washington, D.C., who oversaw the Arctic Climate Impact Assessment, a four-year study involving 300 scientists from around the world.

A climate study conducted by the U.N. Intergovernmental Panel on Climate Change (IPCC), released on Feb. 2, 2007, flatly states that the climate-change debate is over. [3] "Feb. 2 will be remembered as the date when uncertainty was removed as to whether humans had anything to do with climate change on this planet," said IPCC Executive Director Achim Steiner. "The evidence is on the table."

Made up of more than 1,000 scientists from 113 countries, the IPCC said new research over the last six years shows with 90 percent certainty that human-generated greenhouse gases have caused most of the rise in global temperatures over the past half-century. "Warming of the climate system is unequivocal," said the IPCC's "Summary for Policymakers" — one of four reports scheduled for release this year. [4] The IPCC generally is considered a cautious body because all participating governments must sign off on its conclusions.

"We know the climate is changing and that we have a 10- or 20-year window to address it," says Hermann Ott, a climate expert at Germany's Wuppertal Institute. "It's very urgent that we act at both the national and international level pretty soon."

The industrial powers, which produce most of the world's pollutants, are in the best position to act. And it has been the 27 nations of the European Union (EU) that have spearheaded efforts to reduce greenhouse gas emissions. They have acted in large part because of widespread public concern — sparked by recent climactic extremes witnessed in their home countries.

Europe was hit with a devastating summer heat wave in 2003 that killed 25,000 people; roads buckled in Germany and water levels on the Danube plunged to record lows, forcing a suspension of the Budapest-Vienna hovercraft service and allowing illegal migrants to wade between Romania and Bulgaria. The year before, torrential rains triggered devastating floods across Central Europe, causing $15 billion in damages. Last winter many Austrian ski resorts were unable to open in December because it was not cold enough to make snow. [5]

European leaders are so convinced of the seriousness of global warming that — in a dramatic announcement on March 9 — they unilaterally committed themselves to more than double the amount of greenhouse gases they had promised earlier to scour from their emissions. [6]

Yet skeptics remain, even in Europe. Henrik Svensmark, a weather scientist at the Danish National Space Center, for instance, believes that changes in the sun's magnetic field — and the corresponding impact on cosmic rays — not greenhouse gas emissions, may be the key to global warming. [7]

Habibullo Abdussamatov, head of the research laboratory at Pulkovo Astronomical Observatory in St. Petersburg, Russia, takes a similar non-mainstream position. [8]

That global warming exists is not new to the Inuit. The Inuit Circumpolar Conference, which represents 150,000 people living in the High Arctic, recently filed a protest with the Inter-American Commission on Human Rights, charging that U.S. greenhouse gases are destroying their homes and livelihoods. (*See sidebar, p. 239.*)

And residents of low-lying Pacific island nations fear their entire countries may be eliminated as melting ice causes oceans to rise. [9] (*See sidebar, p. 234.*)

"We are frightened and worried. And we cannot think of another Tuvalu to move to . . . if nothing is done urgently and we are forced out of our islands," Tuvalu Ambassador Enele Sosene Sopoaga told the U.N. General Assembly last fall. [10]

Climate experts in the United States and abroad say they expect the United States to become more aggressive about climate change after the 2008 presidential election, regardless of which party wins. They cite many factors, including the Republican defeats in the 2006 midterm elections, muscular action by state and city governments to reduce emissions and increasing pressure for substantive action from corporate and religious leaders such as Boeing, General Electric, BP, the U.S. Conference of Catholic Bishops and the Baptist General Convention of Texas. [11]

"The rest of us are waiting to see when and how the U.S. will re-engage in climate issues, says Harald

Global Carbon Dioxide Emissions: 1850-2030

For most of human history, carbon-dioxide emissions were irrelevant to climate. But only decades after the dawn of the Industrial Age, the accumulation of carbon dioxide generated by the burning of fossil fuels began to noticeably change the lower atmosphere. Now carbon emissions threaten to spiral past our ability to control their effects on global warming.

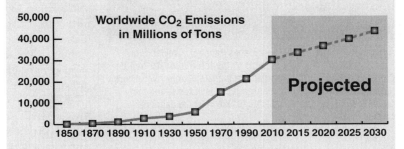

Source: "Climate Change 101: International Action," Pew Center on Global Climate Change

Winkler, principal scientific officer at the University of Cape Town Energy Research Center in South Africa. "The large, carbon-emitting developing countries aren't going to make a move until the U.S. federal government moves."

Uncertainty over U.S. action has complicated international efforts to develop a successor to the Kyoto Protocol, the international agreement that expires in 2012, under which 41 of the world's industrialized countries — but not the United States — agreed to reduce their greenhouse gas emissions. Experts say that significantly reducing global GHG emissions hinges not only on U.S. participation but also participation by large developing countries like China, India and Brazil. [12] China, where the economy has been growing at more than 9 percent a year for more than two decades, is expected to surpass the United States as the world's largest carbon emitter in 2009. [13]

Critics of Kyoto — led by the United States — say the protocol has little hope of significantly reducing emissions as long as China and India are exempt. But these countries say they are lifting tens of millions out of poverty and that they should not be penalized for pursuing the same heavily polluting development path the rich industrial nations followed.

A rush-hour cloud of pollution drapes Bangkok, Thailand, on Feb. 2, 2007, the day that a report by the International Panel on Climate Change (IPCC) asserted that climate changes very likely have been caused by human burning of fossil fuels, and that global temperatures are expected to rise by three degrees Celsius by 2100.

To address the challenge of global warming, many argue, the international community must find a mechanism by which rich nations help poorer ones adopt clean energy and transportation technologies and adapt to the effects of a changing climate.

As the world's leaders grapple with climate change, here are some of the questions being debated:

Are all countries doing their part to control global warming?

The short answer is no, although most are doing far more than the United States.

To date, 169 countries have signed the Kyoto Protocol, including every industrial nation except Australia and the United States. Kyoto, which went into effect in 2005, has been a polarizing agreement. Its supporters call it only a baby step toward confronting climate change; its detractors — most of whom now agree that global warming is real — say it already has slowed economic growth without making a meaningful reduction in greenhouse gas emissions.

Under the agreement, the 41 wealthy countries agreed to collectively reduce their emissions 5.2 percent below 1990 levels by 2012. The EU committed to an overall 8 percent reduction, Japan and Canada to 6 percent. But few countries appear on target to meet their commitments. As of 2004, Canada's emissions had increased 26.6 percent over 1990 levels, and Japan's by 6.5 percent; European Union (EU) emissions had decreased by just 0.6 percent.

Within the EU, Great Britain reduced its emissions by 14.3 percent and Germany by 17.3 percent, but those gains were offset by substantial increases in Greece (26.6 percent), Portugal (41 percent) and Spain (49 percent). [14]

In their March 9 announcement of new emission-reduction goals, however, EU leaders agreed to unilaterally reduce their overall emissions to 20 percent of 1990 levels within 13 years and use renewable sources for one-fifth of their electric power. They also vowed to use bio-fuels in 10 percent of road vehicles by 2020. [15]

French President Jacques Chirac called the decision to make unilateral reductions one of the "great moments in European history." And in a clear challenge to the United States, China and India, German Chancellor Angela Merkel said the EU's 27 members would commit to a 30 percent reduction if other countries followed suit. The plan will be presented to President Bush and other world leaders in June. [16]

Why has the United States been so cool to Kyoto? Some American critics see the treaty as a misguided piece of "one-worldism" that will wreck the U.S. economy. Others argue that it doesn't really matter, that following Kyoto guidelines is unlikely to have a significant effect on global warming, primarily because new mega-economies such as China, India and Brazil have not signed on to control their emissions.

Thomas H. Wigley, a senior scientist at the National Center for Atmospheric Research in Boulder, Colo., estimated that even if the United States had joined Kyoto and all countries met and stuck to their targets, warming in 2100 would be reduced by a mere 8 percent. Wigley is against Kyoto, but only because he advocates a far stronger commitment to reducing gases.

Many around the world saw the hesitation of the United States as self-serving. "Of course, the consensus is that the president is paying his dues to Big Oil and Big Metal for supporting his election," wrote Scottish columnist Charles Fletcher, "and of course that is, to us, outrageous. But money is unsentimental. The fight against global warming and pollution should be equally clear-eyed in its assessment of what just happened."

In Fletcher's eyes, "What happened was that the American president was honest and spoke plainly, and we should start dealing with it. He said: 'I will not accept anything that will harm our economy and hurt our American workers.'" [17]

Kyoto's proponents argue that it has been an essential first step and has yielded benefits simply by focusing attention on the need to reduce emissions. "It is only the first battle in the war against climate change," says Tony Juniper, vice chair of the Amsterdam-based Friends of the Earth International, since "the commitments made by governments under Kyoto do not go anywhere near far enough." [18]

Unfortunately, nobody knows exactly what "far enough" is. Scientists do know that since the Industrial Revolution, greenhouse gas concentrations in Earth's atmosphere have increased from 280 parts per million (ppm) of carbon dioxide to 379 in 2005, while the world has warmed by more than 0.6 degrees Celsius. A British government study suggests that if current emissions trends hold, the concentration will reach 550 ppm by 2035 and likely increase average temperatures by another 2 degrees C. While 2 degrees may not sound like much, average temperatures during the last Ice Age were only 5 degrees Celsius lower than they are today. [19]

"At Kyoto, the countries of the world sat down and talked about what reductions they could manage," says Alex Evans, a senior policy associate at the Center on International Cooperation (CIC) at New York University. "Now we need to ask ourselves what level of risk we are actually prepared to tolerate."

One of the most important accomplishments of the European Union is the creation of the Emission Trading Scheme (ETS), which is based on the premise that the free market is the most cost-effective way to reduce carbon emis-

Bangladesh Faces Catastrophic Flooding

Thirty million residents of Bangladesh would lose their homes if the sea level rises three feet at the end of the century, which some experts predict (red line on map). Pedicabs slosh through flooded streets in Dhaka. The low-lying, densely populated region of the Indian subcontinent lies mostly in the Ganges River delta and is vulnerable to sea-level rises that may be caused by melting polar glaciers.

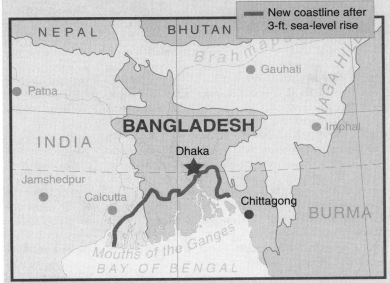

Sources: ESRI and UNEP

AFP/Getty Images/Farjana K. Godhuly

Pacific Islanders' Sinking Feeling

Tiny nations face inundation

People in the Republic of the Marshall Islands have a lot to lose if global warming causes the seas to rise as much as scientists think they could. Their entire nation would cease to exist.

The Marshallese live on 1,100 islands spread across three-quarters of a million square miles of the central Pacific Ocean. Most of the islands are small, so small that if you added them all together, you would have a parcel of land no bigger than the District of Columbia.

A few are no more than a couple hundred yards wide, and their average elevation is just seven feet above sea level. They're arranged in 29 sandy, ring-shaped chains called atolls. Stand most anywhere on Majuro Atoll, the capital and home to one-third of the country's 58,000 people, and you can hear the surf crashing on either side of you. [1]

Small island states are among the most vulnerable to climate change. Many of them will not be able to adapt by retreating from the coastal zone. There isn't anywhere else to go. The International Panel on Climate Change (IPCC) notes that land lost to sea-level rise and associated effects "is likely to be of a magnitude that would disrupt virtually all economic and social sectors in these countries." [2]

Understandably, the governments of places like the Bahamas, Fiji and the Federated States of Micronesia have been among the most vocal critics of the U.S. and other governments that have opposed aggressive action on climate change.

Atoll nations like Kiribati, the Maldives, Tuvalu and the Marshall Islands are doubly vulnerable because they are literally built on the backs of reef-building corals that formed the islands and today protect them from storms. According to a study by the Tyndall Centre for Climate Change Research in the United Kingdom, the predicted increase in sea-surface temperatures can be expected to damage and kill the relevant corals through bleaching, preventing them from keeping pace with rising seas. [3]

Signs of erosion are everywhere on Majuro. Beaches have vanished, seawalls have been battered down and chunks of the main road have been swept away by the sea. At a cemetery in the middle of town, islanders have to keep reburying their relatives because the sea keeps uncovering their coffins during storms. There are no rivers in the Marshall Islands; people rely on a thin "lens" of fresh groundwater for drinking and irrigation, but more and more of those lenses are becoming contaminated with brine.

On Majuro, some of those changes may be the result of poorly conceived developments and the mining of lagoon sand for use in construction, acknowledges Holly Barker, a senior adviser to the Marshallese ambassador to the United States "It's true that on Majuro there are some human impacts, but we see exactly the same effects on the outer islands, where people are still living sustainably off the land and there is no industry whatsoever," says Barker, who previously lived on remote Mille Atoll as a Peace Corps volunteer. "On Mille there are these huge gun turrets that the Japanese built 100 yards inshore during World War II so that U.S. vessels coming in wouldn't see them. Now they're standing out in the water."

sions. First, member governments assigned binding carbon-emission quotas to large polluters, effectively creating an artificial "shortage" in polluting rights. Then an emissions commodity market was set up. Companies needing to emit more carbon dioxide could buy credits from those producing less, or from developing nations, who could use the money on U.N.-certified projects that cut or absorb emissions.

The system has its downsides, such as sharp increases in electricity prices as utilities pass the cost of buying credits on to consumers. In Germany, for instance, off-peak prices for electricity doubled in just two years, largely because much of the power there comes from burning coal, which produces more greenhouse gases than other fossil fuels.

"ETS has had its share of problems, but it has been a really very valuable learning experience," says Eileen Claussen, president of the Pew Center on Global Climate Change. "They've figured out how to make it work well and have gotten a lot of private-sector players invested in the new carbon-trading market. It's definitely part of the way forward for the rest of us." [20]

A 1992 study of Majuro Atoll by the National Oceanic and Atmospheric Administration (NOAA) determined that if sea levels rise by three feet, the atoll will cease to exist. Defending the atoll from a 50-year storm event would be impossible in such a case, and NOAA has issued a sober policy recommendation: "Full retreat of the entire population of Majuro Atoll and the Marshall Islands must be considered in planning for worst-case [sea-rise] and climate-change scenarios." [4]

"For the Marshall Islands, climate change is an issue of sovereignty," Barker says. "The Marshallese have extremely low carbon emissions. Other countries' lifestyle habits don't give them the right to take away a nation. Where will the Marshallese go? Will they still have a voice at the United Nations? Will they cease to be a nation?"

In 2001, Tuvalu, another Pacific atoll nation, convinced New Zealand to take an annual quota of refugees, so as to allow an orderly evacuation of the nation. "While New Zealand responded positively in the true Pacific way of helping one's neighbors, Australia on the other hand has slammed the door in our face," Paani Laupepa of the Tuvalu Ministry of Natural Resources, said at the time.

He also had sharp words for the United States, saying that its refusal to ratify the Kyoto Protocol had "effectively denied future generations of Tuvaluan their fundamental freedom to live where our ancestors have lived for thousands of years." [5]

Should it come to that, the most likely refuge for the Marshallese would be the United States, which governed the islands for more than 40 years after World War II under a mandate from the United Nations. The U.S. Postal Service still delivers the mail within the country, and Marshallese serve in the U.S. military in relatively large numbers.

Children of the Marshall Islands in the South Pacific may lose their world if the oceans rise even a few feet. The islands are spread across low-lying atolls. Refugees from the Marshalls are already immigrating to New Zealand as the global temperature rises.

Mieco Beach Yacht Club

---

[1] The author has reported on climate change from the Marshall Islands in both 1997 and 1999. For a full report see Colin Woodard, *Ocean's End* (2000), pp. 163-189.

[2] International Panel on Climate Change, "Climate Change 2001," Section 17.2.2.1.

[3] Jon Barnett and Neil Adger, *Climate Dangers and Atoll Countries*, Tyndall Centre, October 2001, p. 4.

[4] P. Holthus, *et al.*, "Vulnerability Assessment of Accelerated Sea-level Rise, Case Study: Majuro Atoll, Marshall Islands, Apia, Western Samoa," South Pacific Regional Environment Program, 1992.

[5] "Pacific islanders flee rising seas," BBC, Oct. 9, 2001, 20:29 GMT.

Denmark has become a global leader in developing technologies and policies to reduce greenhouse gas emissions. Its government supports the wind-energy industry, which now provides a quarter of Denmark's electricity and supplies the majority of wind turbines in use elsewhere in the world. Wind turbines dot the countryside like giant pinwheels, while huge offshore wind farms capture the stiff winds in the Baltic and North seas.

Authorities in the Danish capital, Copenhagen, have deployed 2,000 bicycles in public locations around the city, which can be borrowed for free; a heavy sales tax on automobiles discourages their purchase. The country is home to the world's largest solar-powered district heating station — a 12-megawatt facility on the island of Aero — and hundreds of special plants that process kitchen and farm wastes into fertilizers and clean-burning methane fuels.

"Planning for the environment has always been popular in Denmark," explains Christian Matthiessen, a geographer at the University of Copenhagen. "We're an agricultural nation where nobody lives more than 30 miles from the sea. The environment has always played a role for everybody." [21]

Wind turbines harness the stiff winds on the Baltic Sea, in the channel between Denmark and Sweden. More than 20 percent of Denmark's electricity is generated by wind, an alternative to the burning of fossil fuels, blamed for global warming.

Tiny Iceland, population 280,000, intends to go even further by withdrawing from the carbon economy altogether. In 1998 the government committed itself to using the island's enormous geothermal resources to charge hydrogen fuel cells, whose only waste product is water vapor. Cells would then be used to power cars, boats and other energy needs that can't be directly met by geothermal and hydro resources.

"Our vision is that when we have transformed Iceland into a hydrogen economy, then we are completely independent of imported fossil fuel," says the father of the plan, Bragi Arnason of the University of Reykjavik. "There will be no greenhouse gas emissions from our fuel." [22]

But Iceland and Denmark are tiny nations, and it is clear that meaningful reductions of global emissions would have to include not only the United States but also China, India and other rapidly industrializing nations.

Between 1990 and 2004, U.S. annual greenhouse gas emissions increased by 16 percent, the equivalent of the total combined annual emissions of Great Britain, the Netherlands and Finland. India's emissions increased by about 60 percent and China's by roughly 70 percent. [23]

"China's environmental issues are no longer just China's issues," says Jianguo Liu, who holds the Rachel Carson Chair in Sustainability at Michigan State University and is a guest professor of the Chinese Academy of Sciences. "They've become global issues.

Should rich nations assist poor ones in fighting global warming?

As the world decides what to do after Kyoto expires, perhaps the paramount question has become how to fairly and effectively engage the developing world. Most critical will be working out a compromise under which rich countries agree to help poor ones reduce their emissions and adapt to the disasters and dislocations expected to follow the ongoing change in climate.

Rich countries are likely to help poorer ones with emissions reductions because it is in their own interest to do so, at least with regard to the largest polluters. "Basically there is no way that we can force China and India to contribute to mitigating climate change," says Ott of the Wuppertal Institute. "They're saying, 'we are developing the way we learned it from you, and when we reach your level of wealth, we'll start caring about the climate, just as you did.'" For this reason, many experts say rich countries will need to help developing ones help themselves.

Various developing countries require different sets of expectations, argues Ott, who convened a series of meetings with experts from developing countries to try to find equitable solutions. In short, he says, newly industrialized countries, such as South Korea and Taiwan, should be reducing emissions without outside support, while rich countries should help rapidly industrializing nations such as China, India and Brazil with investments that will put them on a cleaner path. Other nations with little culpability for the problem and even fewer resources to confront it, such as Liberia and Bangladesh, shouldn't be expected to do much on their own.

"Most of the additional greenhouse gases in the atmosphere today are due to the past industrialization of the developed countries, so they must take the lead in combating climate change," says Winkler of the University of Cape Town. "We all need to be doing something, but each of us will be doing different things based on what we are responsible for and what we are capable of, given our situation."

Assistance could yield considerable benefits. China

alone expects to build more than 500 new power plants in the next five years. Left to its own devices, China would build conventional plants that would be used for decades. If the outside world were to help transfer the latest pollution-control technology, the growth in China's emissions would be considerably slower.

"Give them a chance to develop, but by leapfrogging over that phase with bad windows, bad air conditioners, dirty coal plants and the internal combustion engine," says Stephen Schneider, co-director of Stanford University's Center for Environmental Science and Policy. Such technology transfers would also provide a cost-effective means for Western companies to earn credits under an ETS.

Building a high-tech, low-emissions plant in India, for example, where labor and material costs are low, would be far cheaper than replacing an existing high-emissions plant in, say, Indiana. "For the planet, a ton of carbon in Beijing is the same as a ton of carbon in Boston or Brussels," Schneider notes. "So everyone wins."

Western companies are reluctant to deploy new technologies to many developing countries, largely because of the poor state of intellectual-property protection in the Third World. "You don't want to give up a more efficient technology if it is just going to be copied, because then, what do you have left?" says C. S. Kiang, dean of the College of Environmental Sciences at Peking University in Beijing. Part of the solution, he says, would be to give recipient countries ownership of some subset of the deployed technology. "China's never had intellectual property of its own before, but once they own some they will respect it," he says, creating a "win-win situation" for both parties and the environment.

While the ETS gives Western countries incentives to help rapidly developing parts of the world, they have fewer incentives to help poor countries adapt. Building Dutch-style defenses to protect densely populated, low-lying areas of Bangladesh from rising seas and stronger storms, for example, would cost billions of dollars, with little or no financial return for rich countries. The argument, therefore, is a moral one.

The expected impacts of global warming — more frequent and severe floods, droughts, heat waves and storms — are expected to fall most heavily on poor nations. An estimated 97 percent of deaths related to natural disasters occur in developing countries, which generally have poorer sanitation, flood control and health-care infrastructure. [24]

Even when Hurricane Katrina hit New Orleans, the poor suffered the most. "People with resources can move and rebuild and start new lives in the event of hurricanes or other disasters," says the Pew Center's Claussen. "But poor people often have nowhere else to go, nowhere else to turn, no resources to make the changes in their lives that will protect them from this global problem." In this respect, she suggests, the world is like New Orleans writ large. [25]

A draft IPCC report offers stark predictions — based on new research — on the coming effects of global warming, especially on poor people. Leaked to The Associated Press in March, the report — the second of four IPCC studies being issued this year — predicts that hundreds of millions of Africans and tens of millions of Latin Americans could face water shortages within 20 years, and more than 1 billion people in Asia could face water shortages by 2050.

While some regions may produce more food thanks to a longer growing season, that will be only temporary, the report said. By 2080, between 200 million and 600 million people could face starvation, water shortages could threaten 1.1 to 3.2 billion people and about 100 million people could be flooded each year, according to the report. [26]

Will reducing greenhouse gases harm the global economy?

Despite some bravado, virtually everyone agrees that a lot of money will have to be spent if the world is to see a substantial reduction in greenhouse gas emissions. The biggest disagreements lie in whether the cost of mitigating climate change is greater or lower than the cost of the damages expected to be wrought by global warming.

Myron Ebell, director of global warming policy at the Competitive Enterprise Institute, a Washington think tank that received funding from Exxon Mobil, says global warming is too expensive to be worth addressing. Until recently, Ebell maintained global warming wasn't taking place. [27] Now he concedes it's real but that achieving meaningful emissions reductions will cost hundreds of trillions of dollars. That's far more than even rich countries can afford, he says, and, in any case, considerably less than the cost of simply adapting to the new situation.

"By far the best strategy at present is to build resiliencies in societies so they are better able to handle environmental challenges," Ebell argues. "Rather than promoting

CHRONOLOGY

1800s–1920s *Scientists sound early warnings about climate change.*

1886 Swedish chemist Svante Arrhenius theorizes that carbon dioxide (CO_2) buildup caused by industrialization will warm the atmosphere.

1924 American physicist Alfred Lotka predicts that humans will double atmospheric CO_2 in 500 years.

1950s *Concern about greenhouse gases (GHG) grows.*

1954 Embryo ecologist G. Evelyn Hutchinson of Yale University predicts deforestation will increase CO_2 levels.

1957 Climate-science pioneer David Keeling of the Scripps Institution begins monitoring CO_2 levels and finds them rising yearly.

1970s–1980s *Scientists predict sharp rises in temperatures and sea levels.*

1979 First World Climate Conference in Geneva, Switzerland, calls on governments to prevent human-caused climate changes. . . . National Academy of Sciences warns a "wait and see" attitude may mean "waiting until it is too late."

1985 Scientific conference in Villach, Austria, predicts sharp rise in global temperatures and sea levels and calls for treaty to limit CO_2.

1988 U.N. establishes Intergovernmental Panel on Climate Change (IPCC).

1990s *Kyoto Protocol sets global goals for reducing use of fossil fuels.*

1990 Pope John Paul II declares the greenhouse effect has reached "crisis proportions."

1992 At summit in Rio de Janeiro 154 nations sign U.N. Framework Convention on Climate Change pledging to reduce GHG emissions to 1990 levels by 2000.

1994 Fearing catastrophic flooding, the Alliance of Small Islands States asks for a 20 percent cut in global GHG emissions by 2005. . . . Climate-change convention becomes effective, with 184 signatories.

1997 Climate convention signatories meet in Kyoto, Japan; adopt legally binding goals to cut greenhouse emissions to 5.2 percent below 1990 levels by 2012. . . . GOP-controlled U.S. Senate vows not to ratify resulting Kyoto Protocol.

1998 Despite the Senate action, Clinton administration signs treaty on Nov. 12.

2000s–Present *U.S. backs away from Kyoto treaty. Antarctic glaciers begin to crumble; heat wave hits Europe.*

2001 President George W. Bush repudiates Kyoto Protocol, reneging on campaign pledges. . . . National Academy of Sciences and 18 foreign counterparts say it's "evident" human activities contribute to climate change.

2002 Antarctica's gigantic Larsen-B ice shelf disintegrates. . . . Bush recommends tax incentives for companies to voluntarily reduce GHG emissions.

2003 Heat wave kills thousands in Europe.

2004 Swiss reinsurance company says global warming could cause $150 billion in yearly damages. . . . Scientists report unexpectedly rapid warming of the Arctic region and predict half of its sea ice will disappear by 2010.

2005 Kyoto Protocol takes effect on Feb. 16 after ratification by Russia; U.S. and Australia are only industrialized non-participants.

2007 On Feb. 2 the IPCC declares with 90 percent certainty that human activity causes global warming. On March 9 European leaders agree unilaterally to cut overall greenhouse emissions to 20 percent below 1990 levels by 2020. Leaked IPCC draft says water shortages will affect hundreds of millions of Africans and tens of millions of Latin Americans within 20 years and more than 1 billion Asians by 2050. By 2080, millions more could face starvation, and up to 3 billion could face water shortages.

Inuit Confront Hard Reality

Melting Arctic ice is changing ancient ways

Like the residents of tropical Pacific atolls, the Inuit people of the High Arctic have a lot to lose from climate change. For them, however, profoundly disruptive changes are already underway.

Some parts of the Arctic — in Alaska, Western Canada and Eastern Russia — have warmed by 4 to 7 degrees Fahrenheit in the past 50 years, a single lifetime — causing the destruction of Inuit villages along with the sea ice that once protected them from winter storms. Ice and permafrost are no longer reliable, causing hunting deaths and damage to roads, infrastructure and forests. [1]

"Climate change isn't some abstract discussion or theory for us, it's a harsh and stark reality we live with every day," says Patricia Cochran, the Anchorage-based chair of the Inuit Circumpolar Conference (ICC), which represents 150,000 Inuit living in Greenland, Canada, Russia and Alaska. "Members of our community are dying because of extreme changes in sea and river ice conditions that are making it difficult for our people to hunt, trap, fish and snowmobile, which are critical activities for us."

Inuit elders report that weather, and the location and characteristics of plant and animal species, are becoming increasingly unpredictable. Seals and other important game species that forage near the sea ice edge are in trouble, with serious economic consequences for Inuit hunting communities.

The village of Shishmaref, Alaska, was forced to move off an island because of erosion caused by powerful winter storms. Many others are not able to store meat the traditional way — burying it in the permafrost — because the Earth is no longer reliably cold enough. [2]

Inuit leaders spent years trying to get developed countries to act to curb their emissions, but their efforts in climate change summits were complicated by the fact that they, unlike small island states, do not have a nation-state and, therefore, no seat at the table. Shelia Watt-Cloutier of Iqaluit, Canada, attended the 2003 climate change summit in Milan but couldn't get anyone to pay attention.

"I couldn't even get our Canadian negotiators to express our views on the plenary floor," recalls Cloutier, the past chair of the ICC. "We ended up asking Samoa" — a small island state — "to say something about the Arctic and, thankfully, they did."

The Inuits' relationship with both Canada and small island states has since developed, but Inuit leaders have been discouraged by the world's failure to act forcefully to reduce greenhouse gas emissions. In December 2005 they took a radical step, filing an official legal petition with the Inter-American Commission on Human Rights (IACHR), charging the United States with violating their human rights by not cutting emissions.

An Inuit woman from Igloolik hunts for seal in the melting ice of the Foxe Basin, near Canada's Baffin Island.

"This was not an act of aggression or anger, it was a gift of generosity from our hunters who see what is happening," Cloutier says. "It's meant to educate and inform and, yes, add pressure to the United States and other countries around the world to do the right thing."

In November 2006, the Washington-based IACHR responded to the 163-page petition with a short letter saying "it will not be possible to process your petition at present." The petition did not provide sufficient evidence to allow proper evaluation.

"I was shocked," Cloutier says. "It wasn't a ruling, it was sort of an ambiguous response." The Inuit plan to continue to draw attention to the situation in the Arctic, at the IACHR and elsewhere, for as long as it takes.

---

[1] Petition to the Inter-American Commission on Human Rights: Violations resulting from global warming caused by the United States, Dec. 7, 2005, pp. 33-37.

[2] *Ibid.*

Arctic Ice Is Shrinking

The ice cap that usually covers the seas surrounding the North Pole is quickly receding, at the rate of 9 percent each decade. Since 1979, when ice filled out the area inside the red outline, it has withdrawn from the north shore of Alaska and the coastline of Siberia.

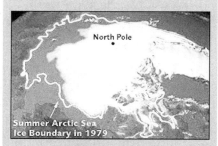

North Pole

Summer Arctic Sea
Ice Boundary in 1979

Sources: NASA and Natural Resources Defense Council

policies that would impoverish the world by putting it on an energy-starvation diet, [one] should be advocating policies that lead to wealthier and more creative societies . . . free markets, private property and the rule of law." [28]

Sir Nicolas Stern, former chief economist of the World Bank and head of Britain's Government Economic Service, dismisses the concern about cost. Stern directed a 700-page study on climate change for the British government that was released in October 2006. It concluded that failure to act could wind up costing the world as much as 20 percent of its annual income — $7 trillion — while greenhouse gas emissions could be brought under meaningful control for an annual cost of just 1 percent of global gross domestic product, or about $350 billion.

"Costs of mitigation," the Stern Review reads, "are small relative to the costs and risks of the climate change that will be avoided." [29]

Left to business as usual, the study says, greenhouse gas concentrations in the atmosphere could reach more than triple their pre-industrial level by century's end, potentially causing "a radical change in the physical geography of the world," including sudden shifts in the pattern of monsoon rains in Asia, drying out of the Amazon rain forest and the destruction of ice caps with

an attendant rise in sea levels that would threaten the homes of 1 in 20 humans.

Far-northern nations such as Sweden, Russia and Canada will see net economic benefits through higher crop yields and lowered heating requirements. [30]

Benefits will include, among other things, "new Arctic shipping routes, a boom in trade with Russia, corn instead of wheat on the Prairies, golf instead of skiing in Ontario, Chardonnay instead of ice wine in Niagara, lower heating bills and fewer deaths due to pneumonia," writes Jacqueline Thorp in Toronto's *Financial Post.* [31]

But much of the rest of the world will see net losses from floods, extreme weather events and changes in environmental conditions. Even for Canada, there could be a grim tradeoff: Rising waters will inundate low-lying farmland in Canada's Maritime Provinces as well as in the Fraser River delta on the west coast, displacing millions of acres and hundreds of communities. Warmer temperatures will force farmers to plant new kinds of crops and allow the in-migration of warm-weather diseases such as Hantavirus, West Nile virus, chytrid fungus, dengue fever and Lyme disease. [32]

The Stern Review suggests governments should enact measures that:

- Set up and expand ETS schemes that, in effect, put a price on greenhouse gas emissions;
- Encourage the development and adoption of renewable-energy technologies, and
- Establish energy-efficiency standards for buildings and appliances.

The report cautions that funds will still have to be spent to adapt to the changing climate — an estimated $15 billion to $50 billion a year among the 24 relatively wealthy nations that comprise the Organization for Economic Cooperation and Development (OECD) alone — but many of these investments represent infrastructure that will provide tangible benefits unrelated to climate change. [33]

If the world does decide to take substantive action, is there money to be made from the technological revolution that would follow? "In general, it's hard to see an economic upside to responding to global warming," says Raymond J. Kopp, a senior fellow at Resources for the Future in Washington. "But some companies will definitely be able to take advantage of this. It all depends on how you are positioned." Companies committed to the status quo, he notes, stand to lose ground to competitors that have a head start in adapting to a carbon-constrained world.

For example, Toyota has jumped to the head of the pack in developing low-emission cars. Its Prius, a gas-electric hybrid, is the market leader. In the United States, the dominant automobile market in the world, Toyota has had difficulty keeping up with demand for the mid-size Prius, which gets 45-50 miles to the gallon with substantially less emission than comparable conventional vehicles. Ironically, Toyota developed the Prius in an effort to catch up to General Motors (GM), which had invested billions in low-emission vehicles. But GM soon turned to large sport utility vehicles instead and is now losing sales to Toyota's more fuel-efficient cars.

In 2004, Toyota had a sales goal of 28,000 cars in the United States; instead it has sold at a rate of 110,000 annually, and the company expects to sell nearly 300,000 this year, once a new North American assembly line allows dealers to keep them in stock. It also sells well in Europe and Japan. "Many thought the Prius would get things started and fade away," says Toyota spokesman John Hanson. "Instead it has become an icon for what a hybrid is, and demand continues to increase."

Similarly, British energy giant BP, which supports efforts to curtail greenhouse gas emissions, is better positioned for a low-carbon future than Exxon Mobil, which opposes such action. BP is investing $8 billion over the next decade in solar, combined-cycle gas turbines, hydrogen and wind technologies.

"We think the political commitment to renewables around the world will grow, and we'll have more of the answers than our competitors will," Chris Mottershead, BP's adviser on energy and the environment, told *The Economist.* "We're happier with our position than we were three years ago, because the world seems more inclined to change." [34]

Billionaire CNN founder Ted Turner is also bearish on the economic opportunities offered by global warming. "The greatest fortunes in the history of the world will be made in this new energy business," Turner told the World Affairs Council in February in Houston, center of the U.S. oil business.

BACKGROUND

Complex Problem

Earth's climate has alternated between hot and cold, glacial and inter-glacial, for millions of years, a fact that

Environmental activists stack sandbags for a symbolic dike in The Hague, Netherlands, one of the lowest countries in the world. Knowing their vulnerability, the Dutch plan to spend as much as $25 billion to upgrade their dike system in preparation for possible rises in sea-level elevations.

gives comfort to those who downplay the dramatic warming of the last few decades. They note that climate is affected by numerous factors, including latitude, elevation and proximity to the ocean, and is periodically disrupted by such anomalies as El Niño, the periodic rise in sea temperatures in the eastern Pacific.

As early as the 1890s, however, scientists speculated that the build-up of carbon dioxide in the atmosphere might be another cause of climate change. The process has been called the "greenhouse effect" although garden greenhouses work on different principles. The greenhouse effect is an increase in the temperature of the planet as radiant energy from sunlight is trapped in the atmosphere by carbon dioxide and other gases, collectively called "greenhouse gases." This dynamic keeps the surface of the planet warm, even when turned toward the cold void of space.

A global-warming problem exists because humans have been increasing the natural level of CO_2 by burning fossil fuels for power, heat and transportation and have added other greenhouse gases such as methane (from refineries and animal feedlots) and chlorofluorocarbons (from refrigeration and air conditioners). There is now the equivalent of 60 percent more CO_2 in the atmosphere than before the Industrial Revolution. [35]

Top 25 Greenhouse-Gas Emitters

Australia emits 6.8 tons of carbon per year for every member of its 20 million population — the world's highest per-capita emissions rate. The United States is a close second, at 6.6 tons of carbon per capita — or about 1.9 billion tons. China, India and other rapidly developing nations have far lower emissions rates.

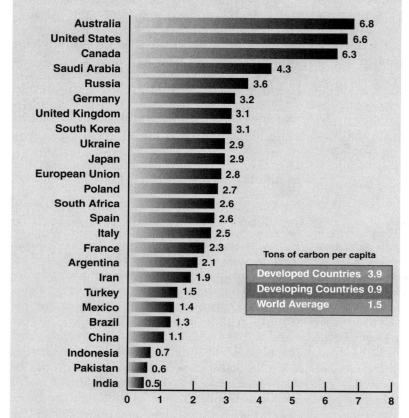

	Tons of carbon per capita
Australia	6.8
United States	6.6
Canada	6.3
Saudi Arabia	4.3
Russia	3.6
Germany	3.2
United Kingdom	3.1
South Korea	3.1
Ukraine	2.9
Japan	2.9
European Union	2.8
Poland	2.7
South Africa	2.6
Spain	2.6
Italy	2.5
France	2.3
Argentina	2.1
Iran	1.9
Turkey	1.5
Mexico	1.4
Brazil	1.3
China	1.1
Indonesia	0.7
Pakistan	0.6
India	0.5

Developed Countries	3.9
Developing Countries	0.9
World Average	1.5

Source: Kevin Baumert, *et al.*, "Climate Data: Insights and Observations," Pew Center on Global Climate Change, November 2004

Climate Change has updated its predictions on the causes and consequences of climate change in 1995, 2000 and in February 2007. The latest update predicts that greenhouse gas emissions will cause the Earth to warm by 2 to 4.5 degrees Celsius by the end of the century, causing further reduction of winter snowfall and polar sea ice, stronger hurricanes and typhoons and an increase in the frequency of heat waves and other extreme weather events. Sea levels could rise by one to two feet.

Bitter Debate

Countries have reacted in very different ways to such predictions. Europeans, by and large, have taken the threat seriously and invested accordingly. The United States has generally taken a wait-and-see approach, fearful of slowing economic growth. The current Republican administration, in particular, has been reluctant to take action until science can report with certainty that climate change is an imminent danger. Yet scientists warn that it is nearly impossible to provide certainty before it's too late for governments to take meaningful action. President George W. Bush also strongly believes that new technologies will solve the problem if the free market is allowed to respond on its own.

Unfortunately, nobody knows exactly how the world's climate will behave as greenhouse gases increase. Although scientists feel confident of the general trend — more severe weather events, melting polar ice and changing sea levels and currents — knowing exactly how, when and where the changes will occur remains a matter of educated guesswork.

Meanwhile, scientists continue to study the problem. The United Nations Intergovernmental Panel on

But political and scientific pressures convinced the president to address the issue in his State of the Union message in January 2007. Bush said that new energy technology would "help us to confront the serious challenge of global climate change." That was enough to encourage a raft of optimism from industries ready to ramp up alternative-energy projects. And the White House itself claimed that the president's new technology proposals will stop the projected growth in carbon-dioxide emissions from cars, light trucks and SUVs within 10 years. [36]

The first international attempt to regulate greenhouse gases — the 1992 U.N. Framework Convention on Climate Change — sought to stabilize emissions at 1990 levels through voluntary measures. The United States ratified the agreement, and ultimately 189 nations signed on to it. Unfortunately, it became clear within a few years that voluntary pledges were not going to work. This led to the 1997 Kyoto Protocol, which featured legally binding cuts in emissions.

While the United States was deeply involved in creating the treaty — and signed it during the Clinton administration — the Republican-controlled Congress did not ratify it, in large part because it did not require emissions cuts from China and India. In March 2001, shortly after his inauguration, Bush repudiated the protocol on the grounds that it would hurt the U.S. economy, reneging on campaign pledges to require cuts in greenhouse gas emissions if elected.

Instead, he came out a year later with a plan offering tax incentives to get companies to voluntarily cut their emissions by 18 percent over 10 years. The scheme backfired; emissions increased steeply, discrediting the notion that voluntary targets could address the problem. [37]

Other countries, notably the Netherlands, began preparing for the effects of climate change. With a quarter of its territory below sea level and much of the rest vulnerable to flooding, the country had little choice. The Dutch plan to spend an extra $10 billion to $25 billion to upgrade their vast network of dikes, pumping stations and sea defenses.

"It's better to be safe than sorry when you live below sea level," notes Peter C.G. Glas, director of inland water systems at Delft Hydraulics, which designed and built much of the dike infrastructure. [38]

While the U.S. government dithered over improving the flood defenses of New Orleans, which is also largely below sea level, the Dutch were busy strengthening sea walls and modifying a large dam at the mouth of the Zuider Sea against a future sea-level rise.

The real threat to the Netherlands from global warming, however, isn't rising seas but surging rivers, Dutch experts say, because the country straddles the flood-prone Rhine River delta. Climate models suggest that rainfall in northern Europe could increase by 5 to 10 percent, while melting Alpine glaciers could increase the flow of rivers.

The famed snows of Kilimanjaro are nearly gone. Global warming is blamed for the meltdown on Africa's highest peak, which lies near the Equator in Kenya.

Over the centuries, ever-higher dikes have been constructed to keep the river contained, but they've been proving less and less adequate with time. In 1995 the Rhine nearly breached the defenses, and with some dikes 20 feet high, failure would have caused catastrophic flooding.

The prospect of worsening floods has prompted the Dutch to change tactics. Instead of building higher levees, the government plans to allow the rivers to flood certain areas when necessary. Some 220,000 acres of land will be surrendered to the rivers by 2050, creating a natural flood zone of marshlands and forest. An additional 62,000 acres will be made into pastures, from which livestock will be evacuated during floods.

Because the Netherlands is so densely populated, sacrificing all that land won't be easy, and engineers are trying to minimize the dislocations. Dura Vermeer, a Dutch construction company, has designed giant floating greenhouses, commercial buildings and even towns that can be deployed in the new sacrifice zones. Such planning is expected to be a growth industry.

"This could be the future for many countries," says Jeroen van der Sommen of the Delft-based Netherlands Water Partnership, which promotes the country's water know-how abroad.

Rapid Meltdown

Recent events — notably thawing in both polar regions — leads many scientists to fear far greater climate disruptions than even the IPCC has predicted.

One of the most dramatic events was the 2002 collapse of Antarctica's Larsen-B ice shelf, a 10,000-year-old, 650-foot-thick expanse of floating ice the size of Rhode Island. Pedro Skvarca, a glaciologist with the Argentine Antarctic Institute, flew over the shelf's seaward edge as it decomposed.

"The surface of the ice shelf was almost totally covered by melt ponds and lakes, and waterfalls were spilling over the top," he recalls. Bits and pieces of the shelf had broken off, filling the Weddell Sea with bergs and slush. Two weeks later almost the entire shelf was gone. "It was unbelievable to see how fast it had broken up," Skvarca says. "The coastline hadn't changed for more than 9,000 years and then it changed completely in just a few weeks."

Scientists say the collapse will likely have worldwide effects. The collapse of Larsen-B as well as the smaller Larsen-A and Wordie ice shelves was caused by a steep increase in summertime temperatures in the Antarctic Peninsula region. With the ice shelves gone, the far larger glaciers and ice sheets behind them have begun sliding into the sea between two and six times faster than before.

"The glaciers took off like race horses after the ice shelves were removed," says Ted Scambos, lead scientist at the National Snow and Ice Data Center in Boulder, Colo. "We're seeing things that we didn't think glaciers could do in terms of the speed of their response." Similar changes have been recorded in the Amundsen Sea in West Antarctica, where glaciers drain the West Antarctic Ice Sheet, a precariously balanced portion of the southern ice cap containing enough ice to raise world sea levels by 20 feet. [39]

In the Arctic, warmer winter temperatures have caused the rapid thinning of the Greenland Ice Sheet, a reduction of Arctic Sea ice and the thawing of permafrost. The thawing has damaged roads, buildings, pipelines and airports in Russia and shrunk the Alaskan ice-road season to 100 days a year, down from 300 just 30 years ago. In addition, melting permafrost releases carbon dioxide trapped underneath, adding to atmospheric CO_2 levels and speeding up global warming even faster than expected.

The loss of sea ice is leaving polar bears with fewer places to hunt, and in late 2006 the Bush administration placed them on the endangered species list. [40]

CURRENT SITUATION

Frustration in Europe

In Europe there is increasing impatience with the United States, not only because Washington has failed to regulate greenhouse gas emissions but also because that failure has put European industry at a competitive disadvantage. "Right now, the EU is on its way, but the U.S. and the rest of the world are still in the station," says Kopp of Resources for the Future. "At the end of the day, EU nations are in a global economy, so they can't run too far ahead of the U.S. or they will disadvantage their economy too much and run into political problems. They need U.S. involvement."

Some European countries are tired of waiting. In November 2006 the EU's high-level group on competitiveness, energy and the environment proposed introducing a "border" tax on products imported from countries that have not signed the Kyoto Protocol. The measure, which has the backing of French Prime Minister Dominique de Villepin and EU Vice President for Enterprise and Industry Gunter Verheugen, of Germany, aims to even the playing field for European industries, which have incurred the costs of participating in the European emissions trading scheme. [41]

"It's an idea that's gaining momentum, but it's also very controversial," says John Hontelez, secretary-general of the European Environmental Bureau in Brussels. "If you are serious about Europe taking the lead and fulfilling its Kyoto obligations, a border-tax adjustment is one of the few easy ways to ensure you do not simply become a hostage of those countries that don't see that fighting climate change is necessary."

Hontelez, who heads a federation of more than 140 European environmental organizations, favors enacting a tax against the United States and Australia, the only other industrial nation to reject the Kyoto Protocol, but not against developing countries like China. "The U.S. and Australia are really acting irresponsibly toward the global population," he says.

But EU Trade Commissioner Peter Mandelson, of Great Britain, opposes the proposal. "Not participating in the Kyoto process is not illegal," he said in a December 2006 speech. "Collective responsibility will only be fostered by policies of dialogue, incentive and cooperation" rather than "coercive measures."

AT ISSUE

Should a trade tax be imposed on the U.S. and other countries that don't sign the Kyoto Protocol?

YES
John Hontelez
Secretary-General, European Environmental Bureau, Brussels, Belgium

Written for *CQ Researcher*, January 2007

If we are serious about Europe taking the lead and fulfilling its Kyoto obligations, border tax adjustments based on carbon emissions are one of the few easy ways to ensure we do not simply become a hostage of those countries that don't see that fighting climate change is necessary.

I am very much in favor of taking measures with the United States and Australia, two countries that should have accepted Kyoto and are really acting irresponsibly toward the global population.

But you can't use this tax in the same way for products from China and India and so on because these countries haven't made or violated Kyoto Protocol commitments, and in 1997 it was quite right not to require them to make the same commitments as developed nations.

The tax would increase the possibilities for the European Union (EU) to achieve greater greenhouse gas reductions without damaging important parts of our industry. It would also show the outside world that the EU is very serious about climate policies, even understanding that it is very difficult, in practice, to measure the CO_2 inputs of the products that are being considered.

For example, if you use aluminum for cans or pipes that are produced in Europe, the cost includes the CO_2 emissions right that this company has had to buy. So the price includes their payment down on the mechanisms to reduce CO_2 emissions, while the products outside the EU aren't including that cost. A border tax adjustment would prevent that. You ensure that all the EU aluminum products are not wiped out simply for the reason that other countries are not reducing CO_2.

The money generated from this tax would probably go to a kind of export support for products that are leaving the EU. It's not what I would like to have happen, but for the sake of compromise, I suppose the money has to go both ways.

The refusal of the U.S. administration to implement Kyoto has a devastating effect because now we see what the fast-developing countries like China, India and Brazil are doing, and of course we should not put the same restrictions on them. Nevertheless, it is an issue, of course.

But as long as the U.S. is not joining in the effort, these countries will have all the reasons in the world to say: Why should we limit our economic development and start controlling emissions when the world is refusing to take part? That's the message the U.S. sends to the rest of the world.

NO
Peter Mendelson
Trade Commissioner, European Union

From Speech to EU, Brussels, Dec. 18, 2006

We in the developed world are responsible for 80 percent of historical carbon emissions. We have an historical environmental debt, as well as a self-interest in our own survival, which both mean we must lead in finding solutions.

Our leadership is necessary. But it is not enough. China will become the biggest emitter of CO_2 in or around 2010. A billion Indians will not be far behind. And assuming that countries like China, India and Brazil continue to move towards Western levels of economic growth, we are confronted with the urgent challenge of greening that growth.

I see three essential parts to the political challenge we face. The first is public education to build a constituency for difficult change and break current patterns of behavior. The second challenge is greater efficiency in the way we use energy. We also need to help China, India and others dramatically to improve their energy efficiency. The third outstanding challenge is to lower greenhouse gas emissions.

But it is also essential to establish that economic growth — and the trade that drives it — are not inherently at odds with sustainable climate policy. Economic growth is what gives us the resources to manage the human impact on the environment at the local level. But growth's impact on the environment will have to change. Efficiency gains can help. But we have to do more than stabilize our impact — we need to reverse it. We will not achieve this without a global shift to renewable-energy sources and green technologies. And here trade policy has an important role.

There is one trade-policy response to climate change about which I have serious doubts. That is the idea of a specific "climate" tariff [or "border" tax] on countries that have not ratified the Kyoto Protocol. This would be highly problematic under current WTO [World Trade Organization] rules. I also suspect it would not be good politics.

Not participating in the Kyoto process is not illegal. Nor is it a subsidy under WTO rules.

How would we choose what goods to target? China has ratified Kyoto but has no Kyoto targets because of its developing-country status. The U.S. has not ratified, but states like California have ambitious climate-change policies.

Above all, dealing with climate change is an international challenge. It requires international cooperation. Coercive policies will harm this. Collective responsibility will only be fostered by policies of dialogue, incentive and cooperation.

Carbon Dioxide Emissions of Major Economies

Despite Kyoto Treaty carbon-reduction goals established by 169 nations in 2005, major economic powers have largely failed to reduce carbon emissions. The United States, not a signatory to the treaty, shows a steady rise, while EU and Japanese emissions have flattened out. Emerging giant China presents the most precipitous climb in emissions as it industrializes.

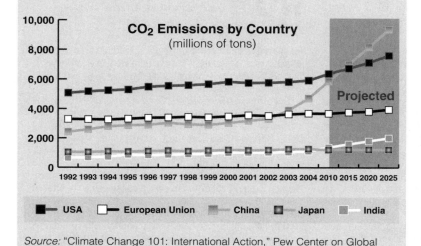

CO₂ Emissions by Country
(millions of tons)

Projected

■ USA   □ European Union   ▨ China   ▨ Japan   ■ India

Source: "Climate Change 101: International Action," Pew Center on Global Climate Change

It is also unclear if the measure would be allowed under World Trade Organization (WTO) rules, which prevent foreign products from being treated differently than domestic ones. [42]

But Hontelez says the EU should consider the measure regardless of what the WTO allows. "I don't think trade has a higher moral standing than fighting for sustainable development and against climate change," he explains. "It's irresponsible not to act because we have some trade rules."

China's Efficiency Drive

While China's government has resisted mandatory CO_2 reductions, it is extremely concerned about reducing pollution and increasing energy efficiency. The primary motivation is economic: If current trends continue, the combined costs of acid rain, dirty air and rampant energy consumption could slow the country's phenomenal growth.

To meet energy demands, China builds a new power plant every week, on average. That's enough additional capacity every year to power a country the size of England. Since 70 percent of China's electricity comes from burning coal, the effect on the environment is baleful. Sulfur-dioxide pollution — another by-product of burning coal — contributes to 400,000 premature deaths a year and produces the acid rain that now falls on a third of China, damaging lakes, forests and crops. If coal-consumption trends continue, officials worry pollution effects will become untenable. [43]

"If China wants to continue to grow, they need more energy, and one way to deal with that is with greater energy efficiency," says Kiang of Peking University, noting that the country uses energy only a tenth as efficiently as Japan. "China wants to do something to improve its energy efficiency, and in the end that will improve the climate-change situation even though it was not the original target."

Under its 11th five-year plan, issued in 2006, the Chinese government has set some of the world's most aggressive efficiency targets, including a 20 percent cut in energy use per unit of gross domestic product (GDP) by 2010. New regulations include automobile fuel-efficiency standards that are higher than those in the United States and construction codes that encourage the use of insulated windows and efficient lighting.

In addition, China intends to generate 16 percent of its energy from renewable sources by 2020. State-owned utilities are building wind farms. In Dunhuang, the construction of a 100-megawatt solar-generating plant — one of the world's largest — should prevent 400,000 tons of greenhouse gas emissions each year. [44]

"The government pays more attention to climate change now because it is expected to have a huge impact on water resources," says Liu of Michigan State and the Chinese Academy of Sciences. "Water shortages are already a serious problem in northern China, while southern China is afflicted by flooding. In the long term, the government will be very interested and willing to reduce emissions of greenhouse gases."

"The government is fully aware of the possible impacts of climate change on China," says Kiang. "But the climate-change issue hasn't reached the general public" in large part because of the small number of non-governmental organizations, the sector that focused attention on the issue in the West.

For now, at least, the government rejects international calls for mandatory greenhouse gas cuts, citing fairness. "You cannot tell people who are struggling to earn enough to eat that they need to reduce their emissions," said Lu Xuedu, deputy director general of China's Office of Global Environmental Affairs, in October 2006. [45]

Son of Kyoto

Delegates to a climate change summit in Nairobi, Kenya, in 2006 sought to construct a successor agreement to the Kyoto Protocol but were handicapped by the non-participation of the United States, the world's largest emitter of man-made greenhouse gases.

"We're living in this two-track world at the moment," says Winkler of the University of Cape Town. "We're expected to build on the architecture of the Kyoto Protocol, but without U.S. participation, we can't expect any engagement from the big developing countries."

Delegates were unable to reach agreement on a timetable for future emission cuts or other key elements, and many expressed frustration with the U.S. policy articulated by Undersecretary of State Paula J. Dobriansky, who maintained that the best way to address climate change was through voluntary international partnerships "that are integrated with economic growth." [46]

China indicated it was not ready to adopt mandatory cuts, while India's environment minister said it was "surreal" to expect his country to slash emissions when its per capita emissions are so much lower than those of the developed world and so many of its people live in poverty.

The Bush administration's newest climate policy is centered not on the Kyoto process but on the new Asia-Pacific Partnership on Clean Development, which promotes the development of clean-energy technologies by the private sector. Created in July 2006, the initiative involves the United States, Australia, China, India, South Korea and Japan and features no mandatory emissions limits. Administration officials say it is a "growth-oriented strategy" that "enables investment in the technologies and practices we need to address these important issues." [47]

"The fairness and effectiveness of this proposal will be superior to the Kyoto Protocol," said Australian Prime Minister John Howard. "It demonstrates the very strong commitment of Australia to reducing greenhouse gas emissions, according to an understanding that it's fair in Australia and not something that will destroy Australian jobs and unfairly penalize Australian industries." [48]

For Schneider of Stanford's Center for Environmental Science and Policy, the most revealing element of the Bush administration plan was the amount it pledged to invest in the project: $50 million — less than the cost of a single clean-energy power plant. "That number is off by a factor of a hundred," he says. "They put up nothing. This is purely cover. If they truly have a climate policy they had better make some real investments, many billions a year."

OUTLOOK

Will the U.S. Act?

The future direction of international climate policy clearly is tied to domestic U.S. politics. Advocates for robust action say meaningful progress can only occur if and when the United States engages with the issue. They are encouraged, however, by growing signs that opinion in Washington is shifting toward action.

Former Vice President Al Gore's Academy Award-winning documentary on global warming, "An Inconvenient Truth," has focused public opinion on the issue, and the takeover of Congress by the Democrats increases prospects for congressional action on climate change. New House Speaker Nancy Pelosi appointed a Select Committee on Energy Independence and Global Warming to recommend legislation.

"[House] debate on global warming has been stifled for 12 years," said Pelosi, a California Democrat. "We can't wait any longer." [49]

In the Senate, global-warming naysayer James M. Inhofe, R-Okla., was replaced as chairman of the Senate Environment and Public Works Committee by Barbara Boxer, another California Democrat and a strong advocate of climate action. At least four climate-change measures have been introduced in the Senate so far in 2007, mostly to establish a carbon-emission trading system.

"Things are moving right now at an incredibly quick pace," said Antonia Herzog, a scientist with the Natural Resources Defense Council. But even if both chambers were to pass legislation this year, it is unclear whether Bush would sign such a measure. [50]

Pushing for action in Congress is an unlikely alliance of environmentalists, evangelical Christians and large companies seeking to burnish their good-citizen images and get a consistent national policy to replace the growing patchwork of state carbon-emission limits. In January the United States Climate Action Partnership (USCAP) — a coalition of nearly a dozen energy companies and environmental activists — called for action to "slow, stop and reverse the growth of greenhouse gas emissions over the shortest period of time reasonably achievable." [51]

A wide range of religious leaders — from the Ecumenical Patriarch of the Christian Orthodox churches, Bartholomew I, to the more than 60 Jewish, Catholic, evangelical and mainstream protestant organizations in the National Religious Partnership for the Environment — are also pushing for action on global warming.

"Climate change was seen early on as the preeminent environmental challenge for people of faith," explains partnership Executive Director Paul Gorman. "It's deep religious insight and conviction that's moved this thing along." [52]

Meanwhile, many states have taken the issue into their own hands, creating regional emissions-trading schemes for power plants in the Northeast and in West Coast states.

Five Western governors announced on Feb. 26 that they would set limits on their emissions. Even in conservative Texas, the previously anti-global-warming power company TXU has agreed to be sold to a private investor group that plans to halt the building of coal-fired power plants and adopt green strategies.

Arnold Schwarzenegger, the Republican governor of California, said in June 2006 that the global-warming debate is over. "We know the science, we see the threat, and the time for action is now," he said, adding that his state would be "the leader in the fight against global warming." [53]

International observers hope that there will be major progress at the federal level in the United States after the 2008 presidential elections. "I see the U.S. leading in not very long," says Ott at the Wuppertal Institute in Germany. "The EU is very timid and cautious as an actor on the world stage. The U.S. often takes a long time to act, but when it does, it does it in full-scale. That gung-ho, 'we can do it' mentality would be helpful."

NOTES

1. Intergovernmental Panel on Climate Change, "Climate Change 2007: The Physical Science Basis — Summary for Policy Makers," Feb. 2, 2007; www.ipcc-wg2.org (global temperature increases); Arctic Climate Impact Assessment, "Impacts of a Warming Arctic," 2004, p. 23 (Arctic temperature increases).

2. "Iceland's president says the world should look to icebound North for global change help," The Associated Press, Sept. 20, 2006.

3. Elisabeth Rosenthal and Andrew C. Revkin, "Science Panel Calls Global Warming 'Unequivocal,' " *The New York Times* online, Feb. 3, 2007; www.nytimes.com.

4. Juliet Eilperin, "Humans Faulted For Global Warming; International Panel Of Climate Scientists Sounds Dire Alarm," *The Washington Post*, Feb. 3, 2007, p. A1; also see IPCC, "Climate Change 2007," *op. cit.*

5. See Colin Woodard, "Europe's scorching summer," *E Magazine*, Jan. 1, 2004; Dean Calbreath, "Changes in climate pose greatest challenge for insurers, say experts from around world," *San Diego Union-Tribune*, April 23, 2004, and "Lack of snow in Europe has skiers down," Reuters, Dec. 12, 2006.

6. Dan Bilefsky, "Europe Sets Ambitious Limits on Greenhouse Gases, and Challenges Others to Match It," *The New York Times*, March 10, 2007, p. A5.

7. Quoted by Lawrence Soloman, "The Deniers — Part VI," *National Post* online, Canada, Feb. 2, 2007.

8. *Ibid.*

9. Interview, John Hontelez, January 2007; Interview, Shelia Watt-Cloutier, December 2006; Colin Woodard, *Ocean's End: Travels through Endangered Seas* (2000), pp. 163-189.

10. Quoted in States News Service, Sept. 27, 2006.

11. Interviews with Philip Gorman, August 2005; Eileen Claussen, August 2005. For background see Tom Price, "The New Environmentalism," *CQ Researcher*, Dec. 1, 2006, pp. 985-1008.

12. For background see Marcia Clemmitt, "Climate Change," *CQ Researcher*, Jan. 27 2006, pp. 73-96.

13. *The Economist Pocket World in Figures* (2007), pp. 32-33; Keith Bradsher, "China to pass U.S. in 2009 in Emissions," *The New York Times*, Nov. 7, 2006, p. C1.

14. U.N. Framework Convention on Climate Change, "Report on the Implementation on its 25th Session," 2006, p. 12.

15. Bilefsky, *op. cit.*

16. *Ibid.*

17. Charlie Fletcher, *Scotland on Sunday*, Edinburgh, April 1, 2001.

18. Quoted in Tony Juniper, "A crucial first step," *The Guardian Unlimited*, Feb. 16, 2005.

19. "Stern Review on the Economics of Climate Change," HM Treasury, Oct. 30, 2006, pp. iii-iv; www.hm-treasury.gov.uk/about/about_index.cfm.

20. "Selling Hot Air," *The Economist*, Sept. 9, 2006, Survey on Climate Change, pp. 17-19.

21. Colin Woodard, "Europe: Planning Ahead," in *Feeling the Heat: Dispatches from the Frontlines of Climate Change* (2004), pp. 31-32; www.awea.org/faq/wwt_potential.

22. Quoted in "Hydrogen Economy," BBC Newsnight, Aug. 21, 2002; Asgeir Sigfusson, "Iceland: Pioneering the Hydrogen Economy," *Foreign Service Journal*, December 2003, pp. 62-65.

23. U.N. Framework, *op. cit.*, p. 12; Subodh Sharma, *et al.*, "Greenhouse Gas Emissions from India: A Perspective," *Current Science*, Vol. 90, No. 3, February 2006, p. 328.

24. *Ibid.*

25. Eileen Claussen, "Climate change: the state of the question and the search for the answer," speech given at St. Johns University, Oct. 5, 2006.

26. Seth Borenstein, "Draft of new international climate report warns of droughts, starvation, disease," The Associated Press, March 10, 2007.

27. Marlo Lewis, "The Snowe-Rockefeller Road to Kyoto," *American Spectator*, Nov. 3, 2006; Clemmitt, *op. cit.*, p. 80.

28. Myron Ebell, Letter to the Editor, *The Financial Times*, Sept. 28, 2005, p. 14.

29. Stern Review, *op. cit.*, pp. viii-x; Gaby Hinsliff, "The price of failing to act on climate change," *The Observer* (London), Oct. 29, 2006, p. 1.

30. Stern Review, *op. cit.*, pp. iv-x.

31. Jacqueline Thorpe, *Financial Post*; Canada.com, Jan. 27, 2007.

32. Canadian Institute for Climate Studies, Canada Impact, "Implications for Canada of recent IPCC Assessment Reports," prepared by the Canadian Climate Program Board and Canadian Global Change Program Board, Aug. 28, 1998.

33. *Ibid.*, pp. xviii-xi.

34. "A Coat of Green," *The Economist*, Survey on Climate Change, *op. cit.*, p. 20.

35. Stern Review, *op. cit.*, p. iii.

36. Alhouse, Peter, "Bush's address tackles energy and climate, Jan. 24, 2007, NewScientist.com news service, at http://environment.newscientist.com/channel/earth/dn11020-bushs-address-tackles-energy-and-climate.html.

37. Eric Pianin, "Bush Unveils Global Warming Plan; President's Approach Focuses on New Technology, Incentives for Industry," *The Washington Post*, Feb. 15, 2002, p. A9.

38. The author reported this section during a 2001 assignment in the Netherlands, published in Woodard (2004), *op. cit.*, pp. 25-30.

39. Stefan Lovegren, "Warming to Cause Catastrophic Rise in Sea Level?" *National Geographic News*, April 26, 2004.

40. Juliet Eilperin, "US Wants Polar Bears Listed as Threatened," *The Washington Post*, Dec. 27, 2006, p. A1.

41. Andrew Bounds, "EU Trade Chief to Reject 'Green' Tax Plan," *The Financial Times*, Dec. 17, 2006.

42. For a discussion, see Bill Curry, "French PM Wants to Hit Canada with Carbon Tax," *Globe & Mail* (Toronto), Nov. 15, 2006, p. A1.

43. Keith Bradsher and David Barboza, "The Cost of Coal," *The New York Times*, June 11, 2006, p. 1; "Anti-hero," *The Economist*, Survey of Climate Change, *op. cit.*, pp. 18-19.

44. "China to build one of the world's biggest solar power stations," Agence France-Presse, Nov. 21, 2006.

45. Quoted in Bradsher, *op. cit.*

46. Jeffrey Gettleman and Andrew C. Revkin, "Big Conference on Warming Ends, Achieving Modest Results," *The New York Times*, Nov. 17, 2006.

47. "US defends climate change policy ahead of Sydney conference," US Fed News, Jan. 7, 2006; testimony by James L Connaughton, Chairman, White House Council on Environmental Quality, CQ Congressional Testimony, Sept. 20, 2006.

48. "U.S. agrees to climate deal with Asia," BBC News Online, July 28, 2005.

49. Quoted in Manu Raju, "House Creates Global Warming Panel, Despite Skepticism in Both Parties," *CQ Today*, March 8, 2007.

50. Quoted in Karoun Demirjian, "Taking climate legislation to the Hill; 4 major bills battle for Congress' support," *Chicago Tribune*, March 8, 2007, p. C4.

51. Marie Horrigan, "Prioritizing Global Warming," CQPolitics.com, Feb. 23, 2007.

52. For background, see Colin Woodard, "Changes in the Air," *Trust*, spring 2006, pp. 18-25.

53. Quoted in Miguel Bustillo, "Gov. Vows Attack on Global Warming," *Los Angeles Times*, June 2, 2005, p. B1.

BIBLIOGRAPHY

Books

Flannery, Tim, *The Weather Makers: How Man Is Changing the Climate and What it Means for Life on Earth*, **Atlantic Monthly Press, 2006.**
An Australian scientist describes the evidence for climate change, the disturbances it is causing to coral reefs, polar bears and other creatures, and the efforts some coal and oil companies have made to delay or prevent political action on the issue.

Kolbert, Elizabeth, *Field Notes from a Catastrophe: Man, Nature, and Climate Change*, **Bloomsbury, 2006.**
A reporter for the *New Yorker* provides a readable account of how climate change is affecting the planet, with firsthand accounts from Iceland, Alaska and Greenland.

Michaels, Patrick J., *Meltdown: The Predictable Distortion of Global Warming by Scientists, Politicians, and the Media*, **Cato Institute, 2004.**
A prominent climate-change skeptic from the University of Virginia argues that global warming has been hyped by scientists, activists and the media.

Motovalli, Jim, ed., *Feeling the Heat: Dispatches from the Frontlines of Climate Change*, **Routledge, 2004.**
The editor of *E: The Environmental Magazine* dispatched a group of reporters to report on the effects of climate change worldwide.

Woodard, Colin, *Ocean's End: Travels Through Endangered Seas*, **Basic Books, 2000.**
Author Woodard describes the collapse of marine ecosystems and the potential link to climate change, including accounts of his travels to the Antarctic Peninsula — where glaciers and ice sheets are collapsing — to the Marshall Islands — whose people fear they will lose their country to rising seas — and to flood-ravaged New Orleans.

Articles

Calvin, William H., "The Great Climate Flip-flop," *Atlantic Monthly*, **January 1998.**
A professor of evolutionary biology at the University of Washington examines concerns that global warming could slow or stop the Gulf Stream and other ocean currents, possibly triggering the sudden onset of an Ice Age.

Easterbrook, Gregg, "Case Closed: The Debate about Global Warming is Over," *Issues in Governance Studies*, **June 2006.**
A Brookings Institution scholar summarizes scientific thinking on climate change and argues that reducing emissions will be easier and more affordable than commonly thought.

Oreskes, Naomi, "The Scientific Consensus on Climate Change," *Science*, **Dec. 3, 2004, p. 1686.**
A professor of history and science studies at the University of California, San Diego, refutes the popular notion that scientists disagree on whether or not global warming is happening.

Sharma, Subdoh, *et al.*, **"Greenhouse gas emissions from India: A perspective,"** *Current Science*, **Feb. 10, 2006, p. 326.**
A professor of optics at the S.N. Bose Centre for Basic Sciences in Calcutta discusses current and projected trends in India's greenhouse-gas emissions described by three Indian scientists.

Reports and Studies

"Climate Change 2007," International Panel on Climate Change, IPCC, Feb. 2, 2007, available online.
The U.N. panel provides the latest official scientific assessment of the causes and likely effects of climate change; additional reports will follow throughout the year, including region-by-region impact assessments.

Barnett, Jon, and Neal Adger, "Climate Dangers and Atoll Countries," Tyndall Centre Working Paper No. 9, October 2001, available online.
A British think tank summarizes the risks facing low-lying atoll nations from rising sea levels and extreme weather events associated with climate change.

"Impacts of a Warming Arctic," Arctic Climate Impact Assessment, Nov. 24, 2004, available online.
A 140-page report synthesizes the findings of an international team of scientists charged with studying global warming in the Arctic. It predicts dire consequences for the entire region, including the disappearance of Arctic sea ice and the continued decay of the Greenland ice sheet.

"South-north dialogue on equity in the greenhouse: a proposal for an adequate and equitable global climate agreement," Deutsche Gessellschaft fur Technische Zusammenarbeit (GTZ), May 2004, available online.
Leading climate-policy experts from both developed and developing countries discuss creating an equitable framework for future climate-change negotiations. In German.

Stern, Nicolas, *et al.*, **"Stern review on the Economics of Climate Change," H.M. Treasury Office, updated January 2007, available online.**
An independent review commissioned by the British government argues that addressing climate change would be far less costly than the economic damages expected from allowing greenhouse-gas emissions to continue unabated.

For More Information

American Meteorological Society, 45 Beacon St., Boston, MA 02108; (617) 227-2425; www.ametsoc.org. Promotes the development and dissemination of information on atmospheric and related sciences.

Arctic Climate Impact Assessment, University of Alaska — Fairbanks, P.O. Box 747740, Fairbanks, AK 99775; www.acia.uaf.edu. International project of the Arctic Council and International Arctic Science Committee for evaluating knowledge on climate variability, climate change and increased ultraviolet radiation.

Intergovernmental Panel on Climate Change, 7bis Avenue de la Paix, C.P. 2300, CH-1211 Geneva 2, Switzerland; (+41)-22-730-8208; www.ipcc.ch. U.N.-sponsored organization of scientists who assess findings on global warming.

Inuit Circumpolar Conference, 170 Laurier Ave. W., Suite 504, Ottawa, Ontario, Canada K1P 5V5; (613) 563-2642; inuitcircumpolar.com. International non-governmental organization representing 150,000 Inuit of Alaska, Canada, Greenland and Russia.

Pew Center on Global Climate Change, 2101 Wilson Blvd., Suite 550, Arlington, VA 22201; (703) 516-4146; www.pewclimate.org. Nonprofit organization that issues information and promotes policy discussion of global warming.

Resources for the Future, 1616 P St., N.W., Washington, DC 20036; (202) 328-5000; www.rff.org. Non-partisan think tank conducting independent research on environmental, energy and natural resource issues.

U.N. Environment Programme, United Nations Ave., Gigiri, P.O. Box 30552, 00100, Nairobi, Kenya; (254-20) 7621234; www.unep.org. Voice for the environment in the U.N. system.

Wuppertal Institute for Climate, Environment and Energy, Döppersberg 19, 42103 Wuppertal, Germany; +49 (0)202/2492-0; www.wupperinst.org. German research organization working towards sustainable development.

VOICES FROM ABROAD

Ian Campbell
Environmental Minister, Australia
July 2006

Don't lecture Australia on Kyoto.
"We do get lectured from time to time here in Queensland, in Australia, by Europeans and others that we should've signed Kyoto as some sort of magic silver bullet. . . . Unfortunately Kyoto ignored almost totally around 70 percent of the world's emissions."

Mikhail Gorbachev
former president, Soviet Union
Oct. 2006

We have very little time to act.
"When we speak of the environment, we say that the situation is five minutes to midnight. We are already in a global environmental crisis. The atmosphere has been polluted and it has had an impact on the global climate. We see the shrinking of arable land, deforestation . . . the pollution of the ocean.

Worldpress.org
Jón Knútur Ásmundsson, Iceland
Feb. 15, 2002

Iceland the Kuwait of the North?
"By the year 2040, scientists and politicians envision Iceland as the first country that will be almost entirely free from fossil fuel. It is a heady dream, but . . . [it is] the hope that the country will one day be known as the "Kuwait of the North.""

James Lovelock
The Independent, Great Britain
Feb. 2006

China builds too fast.
"It is most unlikely that anything we do as individuals or even as a nation will significantly reduce climate change. The United Kingdom produces only 2 per cent of global emissions. You have to ask, will any gesture we make stop the Chinese, for example, building a giant coal-burning power station every five days?"

Dr. Louis Verchot
World Agroforestry Center, Kenya
Feb. 2007

Devastating for agriculture.
"The impacts on agriculture in developing countries, and particularly on countries that depend on rain-fed agriculture, are likely to be devastating."

Sydney Morning Herald
Reuters
Jan. 2007

Pitting people against each other?
"Global warming could exacerbate the world's rich-poor divide and help to radicalise populations and fan terrorism in the countries worst affected. . . ."

Stavros Dimas
EU Environmental Commissioner, Berliner Zeitung
March 2007

Turn off the TV.
"Every individual contributes to greenhouse gas emissions. If we use energy-saving light bulbs or turn off the stand-by mode for televisions, then we will not only lower emissions, but also save money."

Jiang Yu
Foreign Ministry of China, Reuters
Feb. 2007

Don't blame us.
"Climate change has been caused by . . . developed countries and their high per-capita emissions. Developed countries bear an unshirkable responsibility."

House of Lords Select Committee on Economic Affairs
United Kingdom
July 2005

Doubts on IPCC approach.
"We have some concerns about the objectivity of the [International Panel on Climate Change] process, with some of its emissions scenarios and summary documentation apparently influenced by political considerations. There are significant doubts about some aspects of the IPCC's emissions scenario exercise. The government should press the IPCC to change their approach. There are some positive aspects to global warming and these appear to have been played down in the IPCC reports."

Yukiyashi, Japan

10

Ecotourism

Rachel S. Cox

Marine iguanas show little fear of visitors to the Galapagos Islands, where the Ecuadorian government tightly controls tourism. Ecotourism supporters say such "sustainable" travel brings environmental and economic benefits to isolated communities, but critics warn that even well-managed ecotourism can destroy the very attractions it promotes.

From *CQ Researcher,*
October 20, 2006.

A week-long cruise to the fabled Galapagos Islands last summer took members of the Sturc family of Washington, D.C., back into history. As they clambered out of their rubber landing raft, boobies and penguins, iguanas and sea lions greeted them as nonchalantly as their forebears had greeted British naturalist Charles Darwin when he arrived in 1835 to collect evidence that led to his theory of natural selection.

"It was beautiful in a very stark way," Susan Sturc recalls. "We were impressed at how clean everything was. There was no trash anywhere." But, she adds, the islands 600 miles off the coast of Ecuador were "not as untouched as I had thought they would be. I was surprised at how much development there was. I thought it would be pristine."

The Sturcs' experience typifies the paradox of ecotourism, a relatively new and increasingly popular form of tourism that The International Ecotourism Society defines as "responsible travel to natural areas that conserves the environment and improves the well-being of local people."

To its supporters, ecotourism offers a model with the potential to remake the travel industry, bringing environmental and economic benefits to destination communities while providing tourists with more meaningful experiences than conventional tourism offers. But critics warn that the environmental and social changes that accompany even well-managed ecotourism threaten to destroy the very attractions it promotes.

Over the last 25 years, travelers have enjoyed expanding opportunities to visit locations once considered impossibly remote. Even Antarctica is now visited by more than 10,000 travelers per year.

Hotels Going "Green" Around the World

Many tourism companies are trying to reduce their impact on the environment — and save money — by cutting consumption of water, energy and other resources and improving the disposal of waste.

Hotel "Greening" Success Stories

Hilton International

The chain saved 60 percent on gas costs and 30 percent on both electricity and water in recent years, cutting waste by 25 percent. Vienna Hilton and Vienna Plaza reduced laundry loads by 164,000 kilograms per year, minimizing water and chemical use.

Singapore Marriott and Tang Plaza Scandic

Efforts to save some 40,000 cubic meters of water per year have reduced water use by 20 percent per guest. The chain pioneered a 97 percent "recyclable" hotel room and is building or retrofitting 1,500 rooms annually.

Sheraton Rittenhouse Square, Philadelphia

Boasts a 93 percent recycled granite floor, organic cotton bedding, night tables made from discarded wooden shipping pallets, naturally dyed recycled carpeting and nontoxic wallpaper, carpeting, drapes and cleaning products. The extra 2 percent 'green' investment was recouped in the first six months.

Inter-Continental Hotels and Resorts

Each facility must implement a checklist of 134 environmental actions and meet specific energy, waste and water-management targets. Between 1988 and 1995, the chain reduced overall energy costs by 27 percent. In 1995, it saved $3.7 million, reducing sulfur dioxide emissions by 10,670 kilograms, and saved 610,866 cubic meters of water — an average water reduction of nearly 7 percent per hotel, despite higher occupancies.

Forte Brighouse, West Yorkshire, United Kingdom

Energy-efficient lamps reduced energy use by 45 percent, cut maintenance by 85 percent and lowered carbon emissions by 135 tons. The move paid for itself in less than a year.

Hyatt International

Energy-efficiency measures in the United States cut energy use by 15 percent and now save the chain an estimated $15 million annually.

Holiday Inn Crowne Plaza, Schiphol Airport, Netherlands

By offering guests the option of not changing their linens and towels each day, the hotel reduced laundry volume, water and detergent — as well as costs — by 20 percent.

Source: Lisa Mastny, "Traveling Light, New Paths for International Tourism"

than the tourism industry as a whole, according to the World Tourism Organization. [1]

Tourism activist Deborah McLaren, the founder of Indigenous Rights International, says many tourists are no longer interested in the fantasy tourism culture of "sand, sun, sea and sex" offered by packaged tours to beach resorts and cruise ships. [2] Many travelers now prefer what the industry calls "experiential" tourism — encounters with nature, heritage and culture. Many also want a sense of adventure and discovery or philanthropic activities, such as restoring historic buildings or teaching. [3]

While ecotourism has brought new income to isolated parts of the world, it has come at a price, critics say. When archeologist Richard Leventhal, director of the Museum of Archaeology and Anthropology at the University of Pennsylvania, began his field work in 1972 in Cancun, Mexico, grass huts bordered the island's white-sand beaches. Today, Cancun's 20,000 hotel rooms attract more than 2.6 million visitors a year, and a sprawling shanty town houses the 300,000 workers drawn to the new industry. [4]

"Ecotourism has brought a lot of attention to a lot of places that wouldn't have gotten it otherwise," Leventhal observes. "That's generally good, because the economies are so fragile." But "tourism is one of the most fickle stimuli that exist. A hurricane comes, and the tourists are gone."

"Ecotourism is not the cost-free business option that its supporters suggest," argues Rosaleen Duffy, a senior lecturer at the Centre for International Politics at Manchester University in England. "Because ecotourism often takes

Tourism in general is considered by many to be the world's largest industry, and one of the fastest growing. Indeed, eco/nature tourism is growing three times faster

place in relatively remote areas and small communities, the effects of establishing a small-scale hotel or food outlet can have the same impact as building a Hilton in a large town or city." [5]

As a Maya scholar, Leventhal has worked closely with communities throughout Central America, especially in Belize — considered a leading ecotourism success story similar to nearby Costa Rica. "What I always ask," he says, "is, 'Does it really benefit local people?'"

Development economists call the problem "leakage." Studies have shown that up to half of the tourism revenue entering the developing world reverts to the developed world in profits earned by foreign-owned businesses, promotional spending abroad or payments for imported labor and goods. [6]

And, as "ecotourism" has become a popular gimmick in travel marketing, another sort of leakage has emerged. "Ten years ago, I could tell you what ecotourism was," Leventhal says. "Today, everyone's trying to claim it, because it's a hook people really like."

Ron Mader, a Mexico-based travel writer and founder of the ecotourism Web site Planeta.com, agrees. "Look at national travel Web sites," he says. "Even Cancun has a page on ecotourism," with a picture of a contented drinker lounging at a pool bar, suggesting that just getting a sunburn is "practicing ecotourism."

Partly to clarify such public misperceptions, some ecotourism advocates support creation of a certification system reflecting a destination's environmental and cultural sensitivity. Conservation groups like the Rainforest Alliance and Conservation International see the plan as a way to encourage responsible ecotourism and sound environmental practices.

" 'Eco-travel' can come in many shades of green," senior editor Rene Ebersole writes in *Audubon* magazine. "Without a global certification label — something as recognizable as, say, the [U.S. Department of Agriculture] 'Organic' sticker on produce — it's hard to be sure" which trips qualify as genuine ecotourism. [7]

Critics contend, however, that ecotourism certification will further diminish the involvement of indigenous people and exacerbate many of the problems ecotourism already creates for its communities. "It really pits people against each other," says McLaren.

Conservation International and other major non-governmental conservation organizations (NGOs) say ecotourism can give indigenous people a stake in protecting

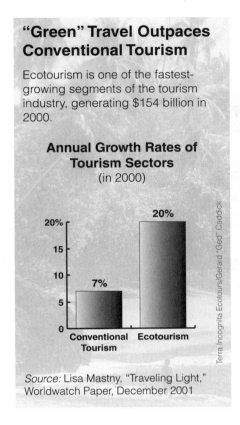

"Green" Travel Outpaces Conventional Tourism

Ecotourism is one of the fastest-growing segments of the tourism industry, generating $154 billion in 2000.

Annual Growth Rates of Tourism Sectors
(in 2000)

Conventional Tourism: 7%
Ecotourism: 20%

Source: Lisa Mastny, "Traveling Light," Worldwatch Paper, December 2001

Tierra Incognita Ecotours/Gerard "Ged" Caddick

their environment, with income from tourism compensating for the loss of traditional lifeways, such as hunting and slash-and-burn agriculture.

"Carefully planned and implemented tourism can . . . offer a powerful incentive to conserve and protect biodiversity," says Conservation International. "People who earn their living from ecotourism are more likely to protect their natural resources and support conservation efforts." [8]

But Luis Vivanco, an anthropology professor at the University of Vermont who has studied the effects of ecotourism in Costa Rica, is skeptical. "For elites and people with the ability to make money, it's a great opportunity," he says. But in real life, "ecotourism is redefining people's lives and landscapes. It's impossible not to wonder if they could be destroying what they love."

As conservationists, tourism operators, development banks and anthropologists evaluate ecotourism, here are some of the key questions in the debate:

Declining survival rates of African cheetahs have been linked to heavy tourism in game preserves. According to Conservation International, clamoring tourists frighten adult cheetahs and their young away from their kills, allowing hyenas to scavenge the food and forcing cubs to go hungry.

Does ecotourism threaten fragile ecosystems?

Traveling in Nepal in the early 1980s, Steve Powers, a tour operator in Long Beach, N.Y., witnessed the effects of uncontrolled tourism. "Nepal was a prime example of how not to do tourism in the Third World," he says. "The government policy was to let everybody in with no controls. Tourists just trashed the trekking sites, and backpackers living on $2 a day really weren't benefiting the community."

Even the native porters contributed to the problem. He remembers seeing them conscientiously collect all the trash at a campsite, then dump it in a river.

By 2003, more than 25,000 trekkers were visiting the Khumbu Valley near Mt. Everest. Much of the area that Sir Edmund Hillary described as being superbly forested in 1951 had become "an eroding desert." [9]

The main culprit in the area's massive deforestation was the tourists, and the demand they created not only for fuel to warm themselves and their porters but also to build the "teahouses" where they stayed.

"Do tourists who come here consider what their need for hot water costs in terms of wood?" asked Gian Pietro Verza, field manager at an Italian environmental research station near a Sherpa village. "One trekker can consume an average of five times more wood per day than an entire Sherpa family uses — and the porters and guides they bring with them need firewood, too." [10]

Other ecotourism skeptics tell the story of Brazil's first "eco-resort," Praia do Forte, a 247-room hotel whose developer bought thousands of acres of rain forest on a spectacular beach, then leveled much of the forest to build his hotel. [11]

In Africa, uncontrolled "nature" tourism has been linked to a decline in cheetah survival rates. As tourists clamor to watch the cats up close, according to Costas Christ, Sr., director of ecotourism at Conservation International, they frighten the cheetahs and their young away from hard-won kills, the food is scavenged by hyenas and the cubs go hungry. [12]

The Third World Network, a Malaysia-based coalition that supports development in developing countries, recently reported that tourism was destroying the "World's Eighth Wonder" — the Banaue rice terraces, a UNESCO World Heritage site in the northern Philippines. The group said timber cutting in the Banaue watershed to provide wood for handicrafts for tourists was reducing water flow to the terraces and encouraging giant earthworms to bore deeper into their banks.

In addition, a recent study by the Tebtebba Foundation, a Philippines-based indigenous peoples' advocacy and research center, found the terraces also were being damaged by the water demands of hotels, lodges and restaurants, as well as the conversion of rice paddies into lots for lodges and shops. At the same time, the study said, rice farmers are giving up their traditional livelihoods to take jobs in tourism. [13]

Similarly, the development in the Galapagos Islands that surprised ecotourist Susan Sturc reflected social changes brought about by increased tourism. The Ecuadorian government tightly controls Galapagos tourism, limiting the number of cruise ships, requiring visitors' groups to be accompanied by guides and prohibiting the carrying of food onto the islands. [14]

Nonetheless, the influx of tourists has attracted many Ecuadorians from the mainland who seek better economic opportunities. Between 1974 and 1997 the population of the Galapagos grew by almost 150 percent, and today there are about 27,000 year-round residents. In 2004, a study about the future of the Galapagos warned "tourism is the main economic driver, yet the migration it induces threatens the future of tourism." [15]

These and many other environmental impacts are being addressed by governments and NGOs. Tour operator Powers helped to establish Nepal's Kathmandu Environmental Education Project, now being run by Nepalis. It educates both tourists and locals by conducting eco-trekking workshops, encouraging trekking companies to be environmentally responsible and even paying porters for the trash they bring home. "It's better now," he says, but finding funds for such educational efforts is a perennial problem.

Powers believes organizations like the American Society of Travel Agents (ASTA) can help educate businesses, especially since its code of conduct includes respecting destination cultures and environments. But in-country operators — the local hotels and guides with whom travel agents arrange tours — also should be held accountable, he says.

But defining and measuring practices that promote environmental sustainability is a very new field, says David Weaver, a professor of tourism management and an ecotourism expert at the University of South Carolina in Columbia. "We're working to pin down the variables and criteria you would need to measure to determine whether an operation is sustainable," he says, but "we still have a long way to go. There aren't a lot of mature programs, and a lot of it is learn as you go."

For instance, a recent study of Magellanic penguins nesting at Punta Tombo, in Argentina, found that the birds adjusted relatively quickly to tourists. To study stress in the birds, researchers measured their number of head turns when humans approached and the level of stress-related hormones they secreted.

Greg Wetstone, U.S. director for the International Fund for Animal Welfare, calls the findings encouraging. "We still have a lot to learn, but this study reinforces the sense that responsible ecotourism can be a low-impact way to create economic pressure for protecting threatened wildlife." The study's authors cautioned, however, that "long-term consequences are much harder to document, especially in long-lived animals." [16]

Ecotourism consultant Megan Epler Wood, the first executive director of the Ecotourism Society (now The International Ecotourism Society), sees the problem of managing environmental effects more in terms of money than methodology. "With the participation of large conservation agencies, it has been shown that as long as an ecotourism project is appropriately planned, zoning the infrastructure well away from protected areas, people can visit without harming," she says.

But even in the United States, Epler Wood notes, the National Park Service has trouble implementing new methodologies because of funding gaps, a situation that is even more dire in developing countries. [17] "You may have one or two staff overseeing hundreds or thousands of acres," she says. "The idea of them controlling and managing so much requires a budgetary level that many can't approach."

Even the best-managed ecotourism facility can pave the way for less-benevolent permanent development, say other observers. In the remote Canadian province of Newfoundland, for instance, the tourism infrastructure gradually improved as the fishing industry gave out. "There has always been the hook and bullet crowd," says Larry Morris, president of the Quebec-Labrador Foundation/Atlantic Center for the Environment. "Now it's 'non-consumptive use.' "

The sophistication of the outfitters has increased dramatically, Morris notes, and the province is capitalizing on concerns about global warming by promoting itself as a reliable destination for snow lovers. Now some of the visitors are purchasing permanent homes — a trend the industry labels "amenity migration." The province just got its first gated community, in Deer Lake, and its "wilderness cottages" — next to a new golf course — are attracting buyers from the United Kingdom.

The University of South Carolina's Weaver suggests that environmental damage caused by ecotourism can be diminished if it is practiced in areas that are already heavily altered. In downtown Austin, Texas, for instance, crowds gather every night at the Congress Street Bridge between March and November to watch up to 1.5 million Mexican free-tailed bats — North America's largest urban bat colony — emerge from their nests in deep crevices.

"You can have very high-quality ecotourism in highly disturbed areas," he says. "People go to see whooping cranes in the stubble of farmers' fields in Saskatchewan."

"Green" Certification on the Rise

Tourism companies increasingly are participating in voluntary certification programs that provide a seal of approval to businesses that demonstrate environmentally or socially sound practices.

Selected Tourism-Certification Efforts Worldwide

Green Globe 21 — Has awarded logos to some 500 companies and destinations in more than 100 countries. Rewards efforts to incorporate social responsibility and sustainable resource management into business programs. But may confuse tourists by rewarding not only businesses that have achieved certification but also those that have simply committed to undertake the process.

ECOTEL® — Has certified 23 hotels in Latin America, seven in the United States and Mexico, five in Japan and one in India. Assigns hotels zero to five globes based on environmental commitment, waste management, energy efficiency, water conservation, environmental education and community involvement. Hotels must be reinspected every two years, and unannounced inspections can occur at any time. A project of the industry consulting group HVS International.

European Blue Flag Campaign — Includes more than 2,750 sites in 21 European countries; being adopted in South Africa and the Caribbean. Awards a yearly ecolabel to beaches and marinas for their high environmental standards and sanitary and safe facilities. Credited with improving the quality and desirability of European coastal sites. Run by the international nonprofit Foundation for Environmental Education.

Certification for Sustainable Tourism, Costa Rica — Has certified some 54 hotels since 1997. Gives hotels a ranking of one to five based on environmental and social criteria. Credited with raising environmental awareness among tourism businesses and tourists. But the rating is skewed toward large hotels that may be too big to really be sustainable.

SmartVoyager, Galapagos, Ecuador — Since 1999, has certified five of more than 80 ships that operate in the area. Gives a special seal to tour operators and boats that voluntarily comply with specified benchmarks for boat and dinghy maintenance and operation, dock operations and management of wastewater and fuels. A joint project of the Rainforest Alliance and a local conservation group.

Green Leaf, Thailand — Had certified 59 hotels as of October 2000. Awards hotels between one and five "green leaves" based on audits of their environmental policies and other measures. Aims to improve efficiency and raise awareness within the domestic hotel industry.

Source: Lisa Mastny, "Traveling Light, New Paths for International Tourism"

Others view peregrine falcons roosting in Pittsburgh skyscrapers, and even in the much-maligned New Jersey Meadowlands — just five miles from Manhattan — a bird-watching and fishing guidebook now promotes ecotourism. [18]

"The perception that [ecotourism] is a threat comes mostly from indigenous groups," says anthropologist Vivanco. "When you don't have control over tourism in your community, things leave." About five years ago, he points out, "bioprospecting" — in which pharmaceutical companies send people into the rain forest to see if they can find useful plants — became identified as ecotourism.

"Indigenous groups felt that things were being taken from them," he says, and it made them "very politicized," even though the evidence of biological theft was mostly anecdotal. "There is the notion that this is yet another effort to bring us into the modern world, to get control of our land — the latest version of the white man telling us what we should do with our land."

Some indigenous peoples involved with ecotourism projects are simply calling it quits. In Santa Maria, Costa Rica, where for several years Vivanco took his students on field trips, the community-based tourism project that sent paying guests to stay in local homes began to arouse resentment because not all families got guests. Recently, the villagers decided to end the program. "People are saying, 'We've had enough. It's causing division in the community,' " Vivanco says. "Their own conflicts play out in tourism."

Does ecotourism offer a realistic alternative to more traditional commercial development?

In the early 1990s, archeologist Leventhal worked with a group of Mayan Indians studying the future of their communities in southern Belize. At the time Belize — following Costa Rica's lead — was in the process of transforming itself into a major ecotourism destination. The group went on a tour of Mexico's popular Yucatan Peninsula.

"They were fascinated by being waited on by other Maya," Leventhal recalls. But not all the encounters were positive. When they'd walk into the big hotels, the Mayan security guards would immediately stop them.

"They really understood the impact of tourism," Leventhal says. "Yes, it brought money in, but they got very worried about certain aspects of it. They got involved with the idea that these were their cousins. Living in a subsistence economy in their own villages, they basically controlled the show. They didn't need to borrow money. When you borrow money, you have to pay it back." In the end they rejected ecotourism.

A 1999 study commissioned by the environmental group Greenpeace and conducted by American resource economist Christopher LaFranchi, however, suggests that while ecotourism may not be perfect, it is far more advantageous for indigenous peoples than "industrial" options such as logging and plantation-style agriculture. The study compared such traditional development tactics with small-scale development options, including ecotourism in the forest lands of the Marovo lagoon area in the Solomon Islands. It found negative long-term repercussions despite "rapid and considerable cash returns available from abruptly selling the forest for logging" and potential governmental revenues derived from taxing the timber industry.

"The rapid exploitation of tropical forests, although very profitable for international timber companies, has produced only limited long-term economic gain for the nations of the Pacific, and at great environmental and social cost," the study said. [19]

In comparing the costs and benefits of exploiting the reef and forest resources of the area, the study found that "the economic benefits of the small-scale options considerably exceed those of the industrial options. Moreover, they leave landowners in more direct control of their resources, distribute benefits more equitably and do not expose them to the high risks of fluctuations in international commodity markets." [20]

The present value of industrial options — mainly logging and palm oil — to landowners was estimated at $8.2 million, while small-scale options were valued at $29 million.

Tourism Professor Weaver calls this advantage the "one shot" angle. With traditional development, he says, "You get a lot of money in a limited time, but then it's done. With ecotourism, it's never exhausted."

Terra Incognita Ecotours/Gerard "Ged" Caddick

The Karawari Lodge in Papua New Guinea's East Sepik Province sits on the edge of a lowland rain forest in one of the country's most remote regions. Visitors can explore the area's varied flora and fauna and visit villages on the Karawari River.

Within the world of international aid agencies and development banks, says ecotourism consultant Epler Wood, ecotourism is "increasingly gaining credibility as a development tool because of its clear economic statistics and because there aren't that many other tools." Proposed development projects must now be sustainable, she says. "The economic growth potential is on a par with textiles. The reception is growing, and all the statistics have been clearly presented."

Often, she points out, the poorest countries stand to gain the most from ecotourism. Many studies show that traditional development strategies "have created a gap between rich and poor and between urban and rural," she explains. "Rural people have been left out of grand development schemes. But as long as they are an ecotourism attraction, rural people can get a nice growth trend."

Ecotourism has other advantages over traditional development schemes, she adds. Start-up takes a much lower investment and, thanks to the Internet, projects can be marketed directly to consumers, allowing the benefits to be delivered directly to the producer.

"It's very viable," says Benjamin Powell, a managing partner of Agora Partnerships, an American NGO that promotes Nicaraguan entrepreneurship. "Certain countries have completely branded themselves as ecotourism destinations to great effect. If it is done right, people are often willing to pay, and it often does trickle down to the locals."

Traditionally, institutional and cultural barriers have prevented native people from owning local businesses. Besides lacking a cultural tradition of entrepreneurship, Powell explains, "Most aspiring entrepreneurs in poor countries are caught in a development blind spot: They're too big for microfinance, yet too small for traditional lending."

Powell promotes the advantages to small investors of small investments in local businesses. "From an investment perspective, you have more leverage if you invest in a local operation because you can put some corporate-responsibility standards in place," he says. "There's no correlation with the stock market at all. It's a very specific market, very local. It's not affected by anything macro. But still, it is very risky."

Should ecotourism businesses and programs be certified?

As ecotourism has become highly marketable, numerous schemes have sprung up that offer a "green" imprimatur for businesses. Some certification proposals require high standards while others set the bar lower; some are operated for profit, others are run by nonprofit organizations; some can be purchased, others are awarded.

"We're seeing nearly 100 different programs," says Katie Maschman, a spokeswoman for The International Ecotourism Society. Some programs are worldwide, national or regional in scope and others relate to specific resources, such as Blue Flag certification for healthy beaches. Other examples include the worldwide program Green Globe 21 and the World Wildlife Fund's PAN Parks network in Europe. The American Hotel & Lodging Association lets its most energy-efficient members display a Good Earthkeeping logo. The association estimates 43 million domestic travelers each year are "environmentally minded."

In recent years, the Rainforest Alliance and the ecotourism society have spearheaded an effort to regularize certification, supported by the Inter-American Development Bank, foundations and other development groups. Now they are studying how to develop and judge standards and certify eco-ventures that practice sustainable tourism, inspired by successful certification programs in other industries — such as the Forest Stewardship Council's approval of sustainably harvested lumber and the fair trade movement's certification of "green" coffee beans and bananas.

Advocates argue that a more coherent certification system is the only way to protect the market advantages of genuine ecotourism and encourage development of sustainable practices in the broader marketplace.

But critics say certification programs now being discussed raise more questions than they answer. For one thing, deciding who qualifies is not a simple matter. At an ecolodge in Australia, for example, visitors can buy packets of seeds to feed the colorful, parrot-like lorikeets, which will then flock around and alight on tourists' arms and heads.

"It's a paradox that this park lodge has advanced accreditation," says tourism professor Weaver. "They do a lot of fantastic things," but the bird feeding is a "demonstrable ecological problem." It keeps a lot of weak birds alive, which spreads diseases, he explains, and when the birds, gorged on seeds, return to the wild and defecate, weeds and other invasive species are introduced.

Nonetheless, a good ecolabel or certification "would give the public some confidence in what they're buying," Weaver says.

The difficulties lie in deciding how such a system would be monitored, he says, and what penalties should be levied for violations. To Planeta.com founder Mader, certification based on sustainability does not address questions many travelers are concerned about. "Most of the travelers I talk to would love certification if it would tell them where there's a clean bathroom," he says. Mader sees a far greater need for certification in safety- and service-related areas such as scuba diving, rock climbing or massage therapy.

Certification efforts so far have been "prioritized far too ahead of the curve, before we have reliable information, let alone communication," Mader argues. "In countries that are developing rural travel, there are usually six to 12 state or federal entities involved — none of whom ever want to talk to one another. The tourism section and the environmental, labor, agriculture and forestry sections each want to protect its place in the pipeline. Communication that could improve the marketability of the ecotourism product is all too rare. They're not sharing information, and none is very transparent or public."

McLaren, of Indigenous Rights International, questions the parallel being drawn between products like lumber and ecotourism. "It's really hard, because tourism is a service instead of a product. You can follow the trail from farm to market with a potato, but it's much more difficult to certify all these different parts" of tourism.

McLaren says the certification process so far looks to some observers like "another grab at money and control" that has left the local communities out of the process.

"We need to talk to the businesses," says Mader, echoing her concern. "There's a lot of discussion at the consultancy level, but at the operator level we're just not speaking their language."

Martha Honey, executive director of The International Ecotourism Society and a leader of the certification effort, says that while many certification programs came into being without consultation with indigenous people, those involved in current efforts are "extremely concerned about and sensitive to" the issue. Last September, she notes, the first meeting in an effort to bring indigenous peoples to the table was held in Quito, Ecuador, and future meetings are scheduled in Fiji and Norway. She cites as a possible model the Respecting Our Culture program in Australia, run by indigenous peoples through a program called Aboriginal Tourism Australia.

Critics of certification also worry that it will be too costly. "The field is not ready for certification," says Epler Wood. "There's no identifiable market for it, and without a market driver you get a lot of investment in systems that are not selling with the public."

"Ecotourism is a small, micro-business phenomenon," she continues. "The profit margins barely justify staying in business." While certification could have a viable role in developing a bigger market, she says, until

the companies are more stable and profitable, they cannot afford it.

Honey agrees that cost is an issue. "Certification cannot be so expensive that it sets the bar too high for small-scale operators," she says, but she feels the problem is surmountable. One solution would be scaled fees, with larger operators paying more. Another might be government subsidies drawn from revenues such as airport taxes or "negative taxes" on less eco-friendly businesses, such as the cruise industry.

Honey explains that existing certification programs failed to develop a large market because most of them had virtually no marketing budget. And, she says, what marketing they did was misdirected. The key to greater success, she believes, is to market the label not to travelers — the ultimate consumers — but to the tourist industry's equivalent of dealers or middle men — tour operators who stand to save money by not having to investigate individual accommodations and attractions for themselves.

Honey also argues that a reliable certification program also would be extremely useful to guidebook publishers, national parks — which must evaluate the reliability of concessionaires — and development agencies like the U.N. Development Programme, the U.S. Agency for International Development and the World Bank.

But Xavier Font, a lecturer in tourism management at Leeds Metropolitan University in England, says "certification is most suited to those countries with well-established infrastructures and the finances to support industry to reduce its negative impacts. It is not the best tool for livelihood-based economies or sectors, be it tourism, forestry, agriculture or any other at the center of attention of certification today." [21]

Brian Mullis, president of Sustainable Travel International, a nonprofit organization that is developing the first certification program in North America, disagrees. "Having spent a good part of the last four years looking at the problem," Mullis says, "I don't think it is premature. At the end of the day, the only way sustainable travel can really be defined is to have verification that companies are doing what they say they're doing.

"More and more consumers are supporting businesses that define themselves as green," he continues. "But if they're not doing what they say they're doing, it doesn't really matter what they say."

CHRONOLOGY

1860s-1960s *Interest in nature travel grows after first being limited largely to the wealthy.*

1916 U.S. National Park Service is founded.

1920s "Bush walker" movement in Australia increases the popularity of wilderness excursions.

1953 Sir Edmund Hillary and Tenzing Norgay are the first to climb Mount Everest.

1970s *Tourism spreads into remote and fragile regions after wide-bodied jets make travel cheaper.*

1970 First cruise ship visits Antarctica. . . . First Earth Day on April 22 signals birth of environmental movement.

1980s *Environmental and cultural impact of tourism sparks concern.*

1980 Manila Declaration on World Tourism declares that "tourism does more harm than good" to people and societies in the Third World. . . . Ecumenical Coalition on Third World Tourism takes shape to fight such negative impacts as poverty, pollution and prostitution.

1989 Hague Declaration on Tourism calls on states "to strike a harmonious balance between economic and ecological considerations."

1990s *Ecotourism is promoted as a "win-win" for economic development and the environment. Tourism increases 66 percent in 10 years on the Galapagos Islands.*

1990 The Ecotourism Society (later renamed The International Ecotourism Society) is founded.

1992 First World Congress on Tourism and the Environment is held in Belize.

1995 *Conde Nast Traveler* magazine publishes its first annual "Green List" of top ecotourism destinations.

1996 World Tourism Organization, World Travel & Tourism Council and Earth Council draft Agenda 21 for the travel and tourism industry, outlining key steps governments and industry need to take for sustainability.

1997 Governments and private groups from 77 countries and territories pledge in the Manila Declaration on the Social Impact of Tourism to better involve local communities in tourism planning and to address social abuses.

1999 World Bank and World Tourism Organization agree to cooperate in encouraging sustainable tourism development.

2000s *"Sustainable travel" is embraced by governments and the travel industry. The number of tourists visiting Antarctica tops 10,000 a year.*

2000 Mohonk Agreement sets out terms for international ecotourism certification. . . . One-in-five international tourists travels from an industrial country to a developing one, compared to one-in-13 in the mid-1970s.

2002 U.N. celebrates International Year of Ecotourism; more than 1,000 participants at World Ecotourism Summit approve Quebec Declaration on Ecotourism — stressing the need to address tourism's economic, social and environmental impacts.

2003 The once heavily forested base of Mt. Everest has become an "eroding desert" due to 10,000 trekkers a year burning trees for fuel.

2004 A study about the Galapagos Islands warns that tourism-induced human migration "threatens the future of tourism."

2005 Between 1950 and 2004, the number of tourist arrivals worldwide grows by more than 3,000 percent — from 25 million arrivals to some 760 million in 2004.

2006 International tourist travel jumps 4.5 percent worldwide in the first three months. The fastest-growing destinations are Africa and the Middle East, each rising about 11 percent.

BACKGROUND

Tourism Is Born

Travel for pleasure came on the world scene with the emergence of wealth and leisure. Affluent Greeks and Romans vacationed at thermal baths and visited exotic locales around Europe and the Mediterranean. The first guidebook for travelers is credited to the French monk Aimeri de Picaud, who in 1130 wrote a tour guide for pilgrims traveling to Spain. In the 18th and 19th centuries, European and British aristocrats as well as wealthy Americans took the "grand tour" of continental Europe's natural and cultural attractions, including the Swiss Alps, and health spas became popular destinations. [22]

Until the Industrial Revolution, travel had more to do with its etymological root — the French word for "work," travailler — than with pleasure. The development of railroads, steamships and, later, the automobile and airplane, made travel easier and faster. The Englishman Thomas Cook set up a travel agency in 1841 and organized tourist excursions by train to temperance rallies in the English Midlands. By the mid-1850s he was offering railway tours of the Continent.

In the United States, the American Express Co. introduced Travelers Cheques and money orders, further easing the logistics of tourism. By the end of the 19th century, the tourism industry had fully emerged, complete with guidebooks, packaged tours, booking agents, hotels and railways with organized timetables. [23]

Earlier, the dawning of the Romantic era in around 1800 had fired a new passion for the exotic among Europeans and an upwelling of scientific curiosity that fueled journeys of exploration and discovery. Beginning in 1799, Alexander von Humboldt, a wealthy German, spent five years exploring in the uncharted reaches of Central and South America, gathering data and specimens. Three decades later, a young British aristocrat keen on biology, Charles Darwin, sailed to the Galapagos Islands and developed the foundations of his revolutionary theory of evolution. [24]

Armchair adventurers avidly sought reports of explorers supported by the British Royal Geographic Society, founded in 1830. Among them were the legendary missionary/explorer David Livingstone in Africa and the man who went to find him, journalist Henry Stanley, in the mid-19th century; Antarctic explorers Robert Scott, the British naval officer who perished on his journey to the South Pole, and Ernest Shackleton in the early 20th century; and Sir Edmund Hillary, the New Zealander who in 1953, with his Nepalese guide Tensing Norgay, first climbed Mt. Everest.

By the late 19th century, the beauty of unspoiled nature was attracting more and more ordinary visitors. In the United States, Congress set aside more than 2 million acres in 1872 to create Yellowstone National Park, the world's first national park. Reserving public lands for "public use, resort and recreation," became a guiding principle of the National Park Service, established in 1916.

Private tourism promoters also played a large role in the creation and expansion of the National Park System, with the Northern Pacific Railroad urging the creation of Yellowstone as a draw for its passengers. The railroads later played similar roles in promoting the creation of Sequoia and Yosemite (1890), Mount Rainier (1899) and Glacier (1910) national parks. [25]

Beginning in Australia in 1879, other countries also set aside protected areas for parks, including Mexico (1898), Argentina (1903) and Sweden (1909). The Sierra Club began its Outings program in 1901 with an expedition for 100 hikers, accompanied by Chinese chefs, pack mules and wagons, to the backcountry wilderness of the Sierra Nevada Mountains. The trips not only provided healthful diversion for the members but also encouraged them to "become active workers for the preservation of the forests and other natural features" of the area.

The political implications behind the early trips would continue to motivate nonprofit organizations to sponsor travel outings in the years ahead.

In the 1950s, big-game hunters began flocking to luxury safari lodges in Kenya, South Africa and, later, Tanzania. The creation of national parks and wildlife sanctuaries by Kenya's British colonial government, however, forced the nomadic Maasai people from their ancestral lands. The resulting resentments led to poaching and vandalism, problems that to this day complicate conservation efforts.

Rise of Ecotourism

The powerful combination of the labor movement and 20th-century industrialization brought tourism within reach of a vast, new universe — the burgeoning population of middle-class wage earners seeking diversion for their annual vacations.

Taking the Guilt Out of Ecotravel

Travel — even by the most dedicated ecotourists — invariably takes a toll on the environment. But now environmentally sensitive travelers are finding ways to compensate.

When the World Economic Forum sponsored a meeting of its Young Global Leaders Summit this year in Vancouver, British Columbia, the forum offered attendees the opportunity to "offset" the negative environmental effect of the emissions generated by their plane flights by contributing to the rehabilitation of a small hydropower plant in Indonesia.

Concerns about the negative impact of their own airplane emissions also prompted conservationists and community-development activists who gathered in Hungary in April 2006, to offset their emissions by planting trees on a Hungarian hillside.

Airplanes contribute 3 to 5 percent of global carbon dioxide emissions — 230 million tons in the United States alone in 2003 — and air transport is one of the world's fastest-growing sources of emissions of carbon dioxide and other so-called greenhouse gases, according to the Worldwatch Institute. [1]

The only sure-fire way to eliminate negative environmental impacts is to stay home — an option some travel writers actually are promoting. [2] But short of that, say those promoting ecotourism, travelers can "give back" to Mother Nature by donating "carbon offsets."

At the Web site for ClimateCare.org, a British organization started in 1998, travelers can learn how many tons of carbon dioxide their trip will produce and donate money to underwrite renewable-energy projects, energy-efficiency improvements and reforestation efforts in developing countries to produce a comparable reduction in carbon emissions. A round trip between New York and Chicago, for example, produces the equivalent of 0.27 tons of CO_2, which the organization translates into a $3 donation per traveler to renewable-energy projects.

A 2004 German program, atmosfair (www.atmosfair.de/index.php?id=08L=3) converts carbon emissions into euros, then contributes donated sums to climate-protection projects in India and Brazil. Its installation of solar power instead of diesel- and wood-fired equipment in 10 industrial kitchens in India, for example, will save roughly 570 tons of CO_2 — the equivalent of 2,000 round-trip flights between New York and Chicago.

The Portland, Ore.-based Better World Club claims it's "the first travel company in the world to offer a carbon-offset program." Its TravelCool! Program offers offsets in $11 increments, which it equates to roughly one ton of CO_2, or a tenth of the emissions produced annually by the typical automobile. The funds collected have helped replace old oil-burning boilers in Portland public schools.

The Web site nativeenergy.com, based in Charlotte, Vt., will calculate all the carbon dioxide emissions from an entire vacation, including hotel stays. The Native American group supports American Indian and farmer-owned wind, solar and methane projects. Contributions to offset automobile and other travel emissions can be made in the form of regular monthly contributions.

---

[1] Lisa Mastny, "Traveling Light: New Paths for International Tourism," Worldwatch Paper 159, December 2001, p. 29; and Esther Addley, "Boom in green holidays as ethical travel takes off, *The Guardian*, July 17, 2006; and P. W. McRandle, "Low-impact vacations (Green Guidance)," World Watch, July-August 2006.

[2] See Ian Jack and James Hamilton-Paterson, "Where Travel Writing Went Next," *Granta*, Summer 2006.

In 1936, the International Labor Organization called for a week's paid vacation every year. A 1970 ILO convention expanded the standard to three weeks with pay.

But it was the rise of the aviation industry after World War II that sparked mass, intercontinental tourism. In 1948 Pan American World Airways introduced tourist class, and the world suddenly grew smaller. In 1957 jet engines made commercial travel faster still.

The introduction of wide-bodied jets in the 1970s made international travel between developed and developing nations practical for holiday travelers. By 1975, international tourist arrivals had surpassed 200 million annually — and double that number by 1990. [26]

In the mid-1970s, 8 percent of all tourists were from developed countries traveling on holidays to developing countries. By the mid-1980s the number had jumped to 17 percent.

Developing countries and international aid institutions initially welcomed the burgeoning source of foreign exchange sparked by the spurt in tourism. The World Bank's first tourism-related loan was made in

1967 for a hotel in Kenya that was partly owned by a subsidiary of Pan American Airways. In the 1970s the bank loaned about $450 million directly to governments for 24 tourism projects in 18 developing countries, and other international aid and lending institutions followed suit.

But the bank's support of conventional tourism and large hotel projects provoked criticism that it encouraged indebtedness while failing to address the problems of poverty in Third World countries. Concern about the environmental effects of resort development, along with a string of financial failures, caused the bank to close down its Tourism Projects Department in 1979.

As the emergence of the environmental movement in the 1960s and '70s pushed international aid agencies to re-examine their commitments, other forces were also pushing the development of a less intrusive, more eco-friendly form of travel.

Despite setbacks among local operators and growing discontent among indigenous peoples, by the turn of the millennium the notion that tourism could be both more lucrative and less resource-intensive than heavy industry or plantation-style monoculture was gaining currency in the international community. In 1998 it was reported to be the only economic sector in which developing countries consistently ran a trade surplus. It represented roughly 10 percent of developing-world exports and accounted for more than 40 percent of the gross domestic product in some countries. [27]

In 2002, more than 1,000 participants from 132 countries gathered in Quebec, Canada, to attend the World Ecotourism Summit, organized by the U.N. Environment Programme and the World Tourism Organization. In adopting the Quebec Declaration on Ecotourism, they embraced "the principles of sustainable tourism, concerning the economic, social and environmental impacts of tourism" — which would come to be seen as the "triple bottom line" in development circles.

The declaration also pointed out that ecotourism differed from the broader concept of "sustainable tourism" by four key characteristics:
- contribution to the conservation of natural and cultural heritage;
- inclusion of local and indigenous communities;
- interpretation of natural and cultural heritage; and
- affinity for independent and small-group travelers. [28]

The summit also boosted ecotourism certification

Watched by local experts, an ecotourist gives a blowgun a try in Peru's Amazon rain forest. Tour groups now flock to the Amazon for trips up the river and forays into the forest in search of the region's animals and colorful birds.

efforts by endorsing "the use of certification as a tool for measuring sound ecotourism and sustainable tourism" while also stressing that certification systems "should reflect regional and local criteria." [29]

Giving native peoples a stake in conservation outcomes was a prime force behind the development of ecotourism, says Harold Goodwin, director of the International Centre for Responsible Tourism at the University of Greenwich in England. To win the support of indigenous peoples, international conservation organizations began creating environmentally responsible tourist accommodations near private conservation areas that would provide some income to native peoples. Foundations were established to return earnings to the community in the form of water projects and other physical improvements, educational opportunities, even clinics and health services. Besides being altruistic, the program had practical outcomes as well.

"You have to give the local community economic benefits so they don't poach," Goodwin says.

Ecotourism also opened up new marketing possibilities, Goodwin says. Costa Rica, for example, unable to compete in the world tourism market on the quality of its beaches, began promoting its rich, unspoiled biodiversity as an attraction — with great success. Belize followed suit.

Mixing People and Nature

Penguins in Antarctica show no fear of humans (top); tourists in Baja, Calif., watch a blue whale (middle); and a visitor gets acquainted with giant turtles in the Galapagos Islands (bottom).

Ecotourism also introduced a new type of competition, he says, because "there are only so many places to go and things to do," and only so much elasticity in pricing. Introducing the values of environmentalism, conservation and education, he says, "avoids competing on price. You can compete on interpretation."

But many of the first small, local ecotourism endeavors that sprang up in the 1990s failed because there was a disconnect between the international market and the local entrepreneurs, Goodwin says. Those that succeeded, however, transformed their surroundings.

"In the early 1990s, everybody was talking about ecotourism," says anthropologist Vivanco, who did his field research at that time near the private Monte Verde Cloud Forest Preserve, considered the jewel in the crown of Costa Rica's extensive park system. "Over 10 years ago, there were about 45,000 to 50,000 tourists a year in an area of about 3,500 to 4,000 inhabitants," he says. But as the number of visitors increased and new facilities went up, hundreds of Costa Rican workers moved to the area, creating a negative environmental impact on the fringe of the preserve — a problem that has afflicted ecotourism sites as remote as the Galapagos Islands.

"Nowadays, there are at least 140,000, and as many as 200,000 visitors, and it's grown up in a completely unmanaged way at the edge of the park," he says.

"The population explosion has an impact on their whole way of life," Vivanco continues. "Class differences emerged that didn't exist before. Locally, many people were saying, 'It's a bit out of hand, we need to get greater control.'"

Making Sure Your Travel Is Really "Green"

The term ecotourism is used so loosely by marketers these days that tourists may be getting "ecotourism lite," not a truly "green" experience, says Katie Maschman, a spokeswoman for The International Ecotourism Society.

"It's great to see ecotourism principles incorporated from a mass-tourism perspective," Maschman says, "but there is a lot of green-washing going on. A hotel simply advertising that they only change the sheets every three days does not, by any means, suggest they've given it real attention."

Research is vital to planning a trip that minimizes negative environmental and cultural impacts, experts say. And while a variety of Web sites and guidebooks focus on "green" travel, nothing substitutes for direct questioning of tour and facility operators and of other travelers. [1]

"The best thing to do is to ask to speak to former clients," says Steve Powers, of Hidden Treasure Tours, in Long Beach, N.Y. Like many other tour packagers, Powers tries to support small, grassroots programs. But it can be difficult to determine whether operators at a far-off destination are actually doing what they say.

A tourist also can ask travel companies for their policies, which may already be codified and thus easily communicated. "If you want to book a tour," says Ron Mader, founder of the ecotourism Web site planeta.com, "ask [tour operators] if they support conservation or local development projects. Many agencies and operators are very proud of their environmental conservation and community-development work." [2]

Helpful Web sites featuring ecotourism destinations are operated by nonprofit organizations, travel marketers and for-profit online travel clubs and information exchanges, including www.sustainabletravelinternational.org, eco-club.com, responsibletravel.com, eco-indextourism.org, ecotourism.org, ecotour.org, tourismconcern.org, traveler-sconservationtrust.org, and visit21.net.

Travel-award programs are another good source of ideas, such as the Tourism for Tomorrow awards of the World Travel & Tourism Council at www.tourismfortomorrow.com; the annual ecolodge award of the International Ecotourism Club, available at ecoclub.com; and the First Choice Responsible Tourism Awards from responsibletravel.com.

In addition to consulting those and similar sites, adding terms such as "green travel" or "ecotourism" to a country- or destination-based Internet search can bring results.

Here are the questions experts say travelers should ask their tour firm or the operator of the destination:

- Do you have an ethical ecotourism policy?
- What steps have you taken to reduce waste and water use?
- Do you practice recycling?
- How do you minimize damage to wildlife and marine environments?
- What community members do you employ and do they have opportunities for advancement? What local products do you purchase, and do you use local produce whenever possible? What community projects are you involved in?
- Do you donate to community organizations and/or conservation programs?
- What energy-saving activities do you practice?
- Are your buildings built with locally available materials?
- Do you use environmentally friendly products?

---

[1] P. W. McRandle, "Low-impact Vacations (Green Guidance)," World Watch, July-August 2006; and Esther Addley, "Boom in Green Holidays as Ethical Travel Takes Off," *The Guardian*, July 17, 2006.

[2] Quoted in Clay Hubbs, "Responsible Travel and Ecotourism," *Transitions Abroad*, May/June 2001, www.transitionsabroad.com/publications/magazine.

CURRENT SITUATION

Global Presence

Growing awareness of the environmental costs of travel, such as its contribution to global warming, increasingly affects travel decisions. More than three-quarters of U.S. travelers "feel it is important their visits not damage the environment," according to a study by the Travel Industry Association of America and *National Geographic Traveler* magazine. The study estimated that 17 million U.S. travelers consider environmental factors when deciding which travel companies to patronize. [30]

A survey by the International Hotels Environmental Initiative found that more than two-thirds of U.S. and Australian travelers and 90 percent of British tourists consider active protection of the environment — including support of local communities — to be part of a

Tourism is threatening the Philippines' ancient Banaue rice terraces, created 2,000 years ago by Ifugao tribesmen. The naturally irrigated paddies are endangered by deforestation to supply wood for tourist handicrafts and by the water demands of hotels and restaurants.

hotel's responsibility. [31] Another industry study found that 70 percent of U.S., British and Australian travelers would pay up to $150 more for a two-week stay in a hotel with a "responsible environmental attitude." [32]

Overall, the travel industry employs 200 million people, generates $3.6 trillion in economic activity and accounts for one in every 12 jobs worldwide. [33] Between 1950 and 2004, the number of tourist arrivals worldwide grew by more than 3,000 percent — from 25 million arrivals in 1950 to some 760 million in 2004. [34]

Moreover, travelers' destinations have shifted, with visits to the developing world increasing dramatically while travel to Europe and the Americas has dropped. By 2000, one-in-five international tourists from industrial countries traveled to a developing nation, compared to one-in-13 in the mid-1970s. [35] The fastest-growing areas for international travel in the first quarter of 2006 were Africa and the Middle East, with estimated increases of 11 percent each. [36]

For example, Wildland Adventures conducts tours to Central America, the Andes, Africa, Turkey, Egypt, Australia, New Zealand and Alaska. The Seattle-based tour operator created the nonprofit Traveler's Conservation Trust, which contributes a portion of the firm's earnings to community-improvement projects and conservation organizations in the countries they visit.

In the Ecuadorian Amazon rain forest, Yachana, an eco-lodge constructed in 1995 by the Foundation for Integrated Education and Development, attracts nearly 2,000 visitors a year — but limits the number to 40 at a time — who reach the lodge by canoe. Visitors spend time with indigenous families, participate in traditional rituals and visit the foundation's model farm and tree nursery. The lodge has generated more than $3.5 million for the foundation's programs in conservation, poverty reduction, health care and community development.

International Development

Nearly every country with national parks and protected areas is marketing some type of ecotourism," according to the Center on Ecotourism and Sustainable Development. "Lending and aid agencies are funneling hundreds of millions of dollars into projects that include ecotourism; major environmental organizations are sponsoring ecotourism projects and departments; and millions of travelers are going on ecotours."

"It's absolutely excellent," says ecotourism consultant Epler Wood. "I used to tell people I was a consultant on ecotourism, and they'd give me a blank stare. Now they are, like, 'Wow, you are so lucky.' It's been one of our greatest goals to make it an accepted, mainstream profession."

Moreover, many of the basic tenets of ecotourism are being embraced by the international development world as goals for economic development generally. In choosing which development projects to fund, the new "triple bottom line" adds environmental and social/cultural effects to the longstanding criterion of profitability — at least on paper.

At a tourism policy forum at George Washington University in October 2004 — the first of its kind — Inter-American Development Bank (IDB) President Enrique Iglesias and World Bank Vice President James Adams joined delegates from donor agencies, developing countries and academia in endorsing tourism's potential as a sustainable-development strategy. They also agreed, however, that the complex nature of the industry presents special challenges.

The IDB, after being involved with tourism projects for 30 years, has changed its focus from big infrastructure projects to more community-based projects, Iglesias said. Adams reported the World Bank had undertaken approximately 100 projects, including tourism in 56 countries — 3 percent of the bank's total investment. [37]

Will improved certification make ecotourism more marketable?

YES
Martha Honey
Executive Director, The International Ecotourism Society

Written for *CQ Researcher*, October 2006

Reputable "green" certification programs that measure environmental and social impacts will promote ecotourism — but it will take time to educate consumers. It took some 30 years to build the U.S. market for certified organic foods, and now consumer demand for organics is booming. In tourism, AAA and 5 Star quality-certification programs for hotels and restaurants have been around for nearly a century and are part of the "fabric" of the tourism industry.

U.S. consumers want to travel responsibly. But they are not yet actively asking for "green" certification, in part because there is no national program.

Around the world, my colleague Amos Bién notes there are some 60 to 80 "green" tourism-certification programs, but most are less than 10 years old. Costa Rica's Certification for Sustainable Tourism (CST) program, launched in 1998, awards one to five green leaves to hotels and tour operators. Lapa Rios Eco-lodge is one of only two hotels there to have earned five leaves. Owner Karen Lewis sees a link between certification, improved sustainability and increased marketability. "Certification is the best internal audit out there, for any owner and/or management team," she says.

Adriane Janer, of EcoBrazil, who has been involved in creating Brazil's new Sustainable Tourism Program, says "certification has been very successful in improving quality and reliability of products and services." In Guatemala, the Green Deal program principally certifies small businesses at a minimal cost of $300. In Costa Rica, certification is free, and the CST cannot keep up with all the hotels wanting to be audited.

In tourism, as in retailing, we're beginning to see the successful use of "retailers" — tour operators — who are choosing to use certified hotels and other "green" supplies. The Dutch tour operators association, which represents over 850 travel companies, requires all members to use hotels and other businesses that have a credible sustainability policy. In Costa Rica, seven leading tour operators are giving preference to CST-certified hotels, and at least two are hoping within three years to be using only certified hotels.

Indeed, without certification, the danger of 'greenwashing' — businesses that use "eco" language in their marketing but don't fit any of the criteria of ecotourism — greatly increases. Certification provides a necessary tool to separate the wheat from the chafe, the genuine ecotourism businesses from the scams and the shams.

As Glenn Jampol, owner of the Finca Rosa Blanca Inn, the other Costa Rican hotel to have earned five green leaves, puts it, "I envision a day when guests will routinely check for Rosa Blanca's green leaf rating as well as our star rating."

NO
Ron Mader
Founder, Planeta.com

Written for *CQ Researcher*, October 2006

Indigenous peoples, tour operators and others claim that many certification programs for ecotourism and sustainable travel do not deserve support. I agree.

Certification has a number of serious problems, starting with the lack of consumer demand. Moreover, most stakeholders have been left out of the process, including indigenous people, community representatives and owners of travel businesses. When invited to participate, many of these leaders opt out, reminding organizers they have other priorities.

Stakeholders around the world confided during the International Year of Ecotourism that certification does not enhance business. In fact, some leading tour operators believe certification and accreditation schemes are a scam that creates a cottage industry for consultants.

In short, ecotourism certification is not a "market-driven" option.

Said one tour operator during the Ethical Marketing of Ecotourism Conference: "First, get consumers to care, then worry about rating and certification. Doing it any other way is not only putting the cart before the horse, it is putting the wheel before the cart, the spoke before the wheels."

Much more effective are industry awards. They are conducted in the public eye and cost a fraction of formal certification programs. Likewise, an investment in Google ads pays better dividends than certification.

In 2006 Planeta.com invited tourism professionals — particularly those at the forefront of ecotourism — to participate in a candid review of tourism promotion. Respondents gave government marketing campaigns around the world a low mark. Comments indicate that in-country and outbound travel operators do not know the PR agencies that represent the country.

These are alarming results for those interested in ecotourism and responsible travel as they indicate that rather than promoting what's available, the promotion departments are seen as an obstacle, particularly for small- and medium-sized in-country businesses.

If our collective goal is to improve the marketing of ecotourism, the solution is simply to improve the dialogue among operators and national tourism campaigns. The reality is that by far the most "eco" and "community-focused" services are the ones that receive the least promotion.

While little or no consumer demand may exist for certified "eco" vacations, we should not accept the status quo. The emphasis needs to be placed on evaluating the industry and offering training and promotion for local providers who strive toward sustainability and ecotourism.

USAID Administrator Andrew Natsios similarly stressed the need for community involvement to ensure tourism is sustainable. "Properly planned tourism requires good natural-resource management and good local governance to protect and enhance the resources on which it depends," he said. [38]

Until recently, says Epler Wood, ecotourism funds typically were funneled through conservation-oriented NGOs, which often lacked the business experience needed to make new enterprises succeed. Another handicap was the paucity of small-scale loans. In 1995, she recalls, the International Finance Corp., profit-making arm of the World Bank, was investing no less than $500 million per project. Now, she says, they're down to about $1 million — still high for community-based ecotourism undertakings. And they're looking for partners with expertise in business development, not conservation.

"We're at the very beginning phase in a new era of enterprise development," Epler Wood says. "It's still a new paradigm. Economic growth still gets the big players and the big money, while the environmental and humanitarian development goals tend to be evaluative afterthoughts, instead of being integral to the projects."

But, she says, the big players are taking an interest. "The donor architecture is still not quite built to accommodate the potential of ecotourism as a sustainable-development tool. It's a very big, slow-moving world, but you do see change happening within it."

Variations on a Theme

As ecotourism joins the tourism mainstream, it is spinning off numerous new tourism genres. In Europe, especially, so-called pro-poor tourism, responsible tourism and ethical tourism aim to extend the benefits of tourism to developing countries while improving its effects on destination communities and the environment.

Evidence is mounting that travelers are embracing the concept's values. In England this past summer, ethical holidays reportedly were the fastest-growing travel sector. According to a recent survey, by 2010 the number of British visitors going on "ethical" holidays outside England will have grown to 2.5 million trips a year, or 5 percent of the market. The Web site ResponsibleTravel.com has seen bookings double in the last year. [39]

Other variations of ecotourism are viewed less favorably by ecotourism advocates. Adventure travel to exotic and often physically challenging destinations — "eco-tourism with a kick," ecotourism society executive director Honey calls it — has been a particularly fast-growing style of nature tourism.

Adventure travel proponents argue that adventurers, like ecotravelers, have an interest in protecting the resources they enjoy, but critics blame them for a wide range of damaging intrusions — helicopter trips causing noise and air pollution while taking skiers to pristine mountain tops; growing numbers of tourists struggling to ascend Mt. Everest (and risking their lives and the lives of others in the process); polar bear watchers who ride bus-like vehicles on monster-truck tires along the south shore of Hudson Bay in Manitoba in the fall, dangerously stressing the bears when they should be building up fat reserves for the long winter season. [40]

"Whereas nature, wildlife and adventure tourism are defined solely by the recreational activities of the tourist," Honey explains, "ecotourism is defined as well by its benefits to both conservation and people in the host country."

"Green" Chic

An essay in *The New York Times* fall travel magazine, "Easy Being Green," portrays ecotourism as the latest fashion trend. "In luxury resorts, eco is the flavor du jour," proclaims author Heidi S. Mitchell. [41]

"There has been a real movement toward high-end ecotourism," Honey said. A 2004 survey found that 38 percent would be willing to pay a premium to patronize travel companies that use sustainable environmental practices. [42]

But as green travel goes upscale, environmentalists worry that the original goals of environmental conservation paired with community betterment will be lost under a misleading "greenwash."

"Ecotourism has been watered down from the beginning," says Planeta.com founder Mader. "The NGOs have watered it down. They're even participating in Antarctic travel."

But others, like Honey, see the upscale trend as a sign that environmental sustainability — a key aspect of ecotourism — is having a real effect on the travel industry as a whole. In a less glamorous example, the Rainforest Alliance, with support from the Inter-American Development Bank, is working with small- and medium-sized travel businesses in Latin America to improve sustainable practices, whether or not the businesses meet all the requirements of classic ecotourism.

In Costa Rica, Guatemala, Belize and Ecuador, more than 200 tourism operations in or near sensitive or protected areas are receiving training in the "best practices" of sustainable tourism, including waste management and water and electricity conservation, as well as such social factors as paying adequate salaries and including local and indigenous people in decision-making.

Businesses that adopt best practices become eligible for certification by existing national programs and gain access to marketing networks and trade-show appearances organized by the Rainforest Alliance. The program has had two benefits, says Alliance marketing specialist Christina Suhr: "It has let people know what we do, and they have gained confidence in us."

OUTLOOK

Setting Limits

The latest worry for travelers who care about the Earth's environment is global warming, especially since air transport is one of the world's fastest-growing sources of emissions of carbon dioxide and other greenhouse gases. If global warming continues unabated, many of the attractions most favored by eco-travelers will be among the most vulnerable. A report for the United Kingdom's World Wide Fund for Nature warned of soaring temperatures, forest fires and other consequences that could drive wildlife from safari parks in Africa, damage Brazil's rain forest ecosystems and flood beaches and coastal destinations worldwide. [43]

Some observers say the costs of global travel in environmental damage, cultural homogenization and economic displacement are so serious that would-be travelers should just stay home.

"The more we flock to view the disappearing glaciers, the faster they will vanish," mused novelist James Hamilton-Paterson. [44]

Similarly, travel writer Anneli Rufus observes ruefully, "Colonialism isn't dead. Colonialism is alive and well every time you travel from the First World to the Third and come home bearing photographs of sharks and storms and slums . . . and then you tell your friends and co-workers, 'Oh man, it was so great, you gotta go.' "

But the quandary Rufus faces as she considers ending her travel writing is common to affluent travelers visiting poor countries: "Am I saving some tribe from extinction

Visitors can come within a few yards of wild mountain gorillas in Volcanoes National Park, on the Rwanda side of the Virunga Volcanoes. "I just about burst open with happiness every time I get within one or two feet of them," said naturalist Dian Fossey, who studied the gorillas for years.

Terra Incognita Ecotours/Gerard "Ged" Caddick

by not looking for it, much less telling you about it? Or am I starving some shopkeeper by not buying his sandals? Both. Neither. I am out of that [travel writing] game now." [45]

But indigenous-rights activist McLaren feels that the interpersonal connections and first-person impressions derived from independent travel are more important than ever. "In an age where the media dominates and shapes our views of the world," she writes, "it is imperative to utilize tourism as a means to effectively communicate with one another. In fact, there is no better way to understand the global crisis that we face together than through people-to-people communication." [46]

McLaren finds hope in the growing number of successful projects that blend tourism, environmentalism and sustainability, like Elephant Valley eco-resort in India.

"There are lots of good examples, though not everybody calls them ecotourism," McLaren says. "A lot of workable projects tend to be more regional, more of public-private partnerships." Elephant Valley, she says, is "a beautiful, low-impact place. Money is really being used to conserve the area, employ local people, produce food, teach about sustainability and work with schools in the region."

In Tasmania, ecotourism has been proposed as an alternative to logging in Australia's largest temperate rain forest, the Tarkine. [47]

In the Patagonia region of southern Chile, environmentalists are seeking to block plans to build a series of hydro-electric dams that would flood thousands of acres of rugged, pristine lands that, they say, could better serve as ecotourism attractions and ranchland. [48]

And in Puerto Rico, environmentalists and other groups are fighting the proposed development of resorts and residential complexes in one of the territory's "last remaining pristine coastal areas," seeking to preserve it "for wildlife, the citizens of Puerto Rico and ecotourism." According to the Waterkeeper Alliance, an organization leading the fight, the developments threaten local water supplies and also mean that "tourists who flock to Puerto Rico to enjoy its cultural and natural resources . . . will have one less reason to visit the island." [49]

NOTES

1. The International Ecotourism Society, Fact Sheet, June 2004, p. 2.

2. Deborah McLaren, "Rethinking Tourism," Planeta Forum, updated June 16, 2006, www.planeta.com/planeta/97/1197rtpro.html; Martha Honey, *Ecotourism and Sustainable Development: Who Owns Paradise?* (1999), p. 9.

3. A 2003 study by the Travel Industry Association of America and *National Geographic Traveler* found that 55.1 million U.S. travelers could be classified as "geo-tourists" interested in nature, culture and heritage tourism; see "The International Ecotourism Society, *op. cit.*

4. Jacob Park, "The Paradox of Paradise," *Environment*, October 1999. For a detailed discussion of the environmental costs of resort development, see Polly Pattullo, *Last Resorts: the Cost of Tourism in the Caribbean* (1996).

5. Rosaleen Duffy, *A Trip Too Far: Ecotourism, Politics & Exploitation* (2002), pp. x-xii.

6. Lisa Mastny, "Traveling Light," *Worldwatch Paper 159*, Worldwatch Institute, 2001, p. 10.

7. Rene Ebersole, "Take the High Road," *Audubon Travel Issue*, July-August 2006, p. 39.

8. Conservation International Web site; www.conservation.org/xp/CIWEB/programs/ecotourism/.

9. Finn-Olaf Jones, "Tourism Stripping Everest's Forests Bare," *National Geographic Traveler*, Aug. 29, 2003.

10. *Ibid.*

11. Simon Davis, "So Can Tourism Ever Really Be Ethical?" *The* [London] *Evening Standard*, July 19, 2006, p. 51.

12. Costas Christ Sr., "A Road Less Traveled," Conservation International Web site; www.conservation.org/xp/frontlines/partners/focus32-1.xml.

13. Maurice Malanes, "Tourism Killing World's Eighth Wonder," Third World Network, www.twnside.org.sg/title/mm-cn.htm.

14. An exception to the low-impact policy was recently permitted, allowing small kayaking groups to camp in preapproved sites on some islands.

15. Juliet Eilperin, "Despite Efforts, Some Tours Do Leave Footprints," *The Washington Post*, April 2, 2006, p. A1.

16. Juliet Eilperin, "Science Notebook," *The Washington Post*, Jan. 30, 2006, p. A5.

17. For background, see Thomas Arrandale, "National Parks Under Pressure," *CQ Researcher*, Oct. 6, 2006, pp. 817-840.

18. Janet Frankston, "State to push unlikely site for ecotourists: the Meadowlands," The Associated Press, Aug. 8, 2006.

19. Christopher LaFranchi and Greenpeace Pacific, "Islands Adrift: Comparing Industrial and Small-Scale Economic Options for Marovo Lagoon Region of the Solomon Islands," Greenpeace, 1999, p. 4; www.greenpeace.org/international.

20. *Ibid.*

21. Xavier Font, "Critical Review of Certification and Accreditation in Sustainable Tourism Governance," www.Planeta.com.

22. Unless otherwise noted, background drawn from Honey, *op. cit.*, pp. 7-8.

23. Mastny, *op. cit.*, p. 10.

24. For background, see Marcia Clemmitt, "Intelligent Design," *CQ Researcher*, July 29, 2005, pp. 637-660.

25. Rachel S. Cox, "Protecting the National Parks," *CQ Researcher*, June 16, 2000, pp. 521-544.

26. Mastny, *op. cit.*, p. 13.

27. *Ibid.*

28. See "Ecotourism: a UN Declaration," *The Irish Times*, Aug. 5, 2006.

29. Martha Honey, "Protecting Eden: Setting Green Standards for the Tourism Industry," *Environment*, July-August, 2003.

30. *Ibid.* For background, see Marcia Clemmitt, "Climate Change," *CQ Researcher*, Jan. 27, 2006, pp. 73-96.

31. Zoe Chafe, "Consumer Demand and Operator Support for Socially and Environmentally Responsible Tourism," CESD/TIES Working Paper No. 104, Center on Ecotourism and Sustainable Development and The International Ecotourism Society, revised April 2005, p. 4.

32. *Ibid.*, p. 6.

33. Mintel report cited in The International Ecotourism Society, Ecotourism Fact Sheet, "Eco and Ethical Tourism-UK," October 2003.

34. Mastny, *op. cit.*, and "Ecotourism Fact Sheet," The International Ecotourism Society and World Tourism Organization, *World Tourism Barometer*, January 2005, p. 2.

35. Martha Honey, *Ecotourism and Sustainable Development: Who Owns Paradise?* (1999), p. 8.

36. World Tourism Organization, news release, *op. cit.*

37. Cited in www.dantei.org/wto.forum/background-papers.html.

38. Theodoro Koumelis, "WTO Policy Forum: Tourism is top priority in fight against poverty," Oct. 22, 2004, TravelDailyNews.com.

39. Simon Davis, "So Can Tourism Ever Really Be Ethical?" *The* [London] *Evening Standard*, July 19, 2006, p. A51.

40. Mark Clayton, "When Ecotourism Kills," *The Christian Science Monitor*, Nov. 4, 2004, p. 13.

41. Heidi S. Mitchell, "Easy Being Green," *The New York Times Style Magazine*, fall travel 2006, Sept. 24, 2006, p. 14.

42. Christopher Solomon, "Where the High Life Comes Naturally," *The New York Times*, May 1, 2005, Sect. 5, Travel, p. 3.

43. Mastny, *op. cit.*, p. 29. The report is by David Viner and Maureen Agnew, "Climate Change and Its Impact on Tourism," 1999.

44. James Hamilton-Paterson, "The End of Travel," *Granta*, summer 2006, pp. 221-234.

45. Anneli Rufus, "There's No Such Thing as Eco-Tourism," AlterNet; posted Aug. 14, 2006; www.alternet.org/story/40174/.

46. McLaren, *op. cit.*

47. Leisa Tyler, "Next Time You're In . . . Tasmania," *Time International*, Dec. 27, 2004, p. 120.

48. Larry Rohter, "For Power or Beauty? Debating the Course of Chile's Rivers," *The New York Times*, Aug. 6, 2006, p. 3.

49. Waterkeeper Alliance Web site, "Marriott and Four Seasons: Do Not Disturb PR"; www.waterkeeper.org/mainarticledetails.aspx?articleid=262.)

BIBLIOGRAPHY

Books

Buckley, Ralf, ed., *Environmental Impacts of Ecotourism*, CABI Publishing, 2004.
This collection of articles analyzes the cost of various types of ecotourism and what is being done to mitigate negative impacts of the industry.

Duffy, Rosaleen, *A Trip Too Far: Ecotourism, Politics and Exploitation*, Earthscan, 2002.
Based on her field work in Belize, a senior lecturer at the Centre for International Politics at the University of Manchester in England critiques positive assumptions about ecotourism by examining its place in the complex web of "green capitalism."

Honey, Martha, *Ecotourism and Sustainable Development: Who Owns Paradise?* Island Press, 1999.
Using a clear, engaging writing style, Honey outlines the history and development of ecotourism, including a country-by-country study of the industry.

Weaver, David B., ed., *The Encyclopedia of Ecotourism*, CABI Publishing, 2001.
Papers by leading experts cover a range of ecotourism issues — from defining the term and its impact on host destinations to the practicalities of business planning and management.

Articles

Boynton, Graham, "The Search for Authenticity," *The Nation*, Oct. 6, 1997.
Paradoxes and compromises emerge when tourists search for "the real thing" in the developing world.

Duffy, Rosaleen, ed., "The Politics of Ecotourism and the Developing World," *Journal of Ecotourism*, Vol. 5, Nos. 1 and 2, September 2006.
An ecotourism scholar explores the range of issues raised by the politics of ecotourism in the developing world — from abstract theories to specific cases.

Ebersole, Rene, "Take the High Road," *Audubon Travel Issue*, July-August 2006, p. 39.
Without a globally recognizable certification label, travelers cannot be sure which trips and hotels qualify as genuinely ecologically friendly.

Honey, Martha, "Protecting Eden: Setting Green Standards for the Tourism Industry," *Environment*, July-August, 2003.
The writer provides an excellent overview of the background and rationale for creating a regularized certification program for ecotourism.

Jones, Finn-Olaf, "Tourism Stripping Everest's Forests Bare," *National Geographic Traveler*, Aug. 29, 2003.
As of 2003, more than 25,000 trekkers were visiting the Khumbu Valley near Mt. Everest, turning into "an eroding desert" much of the area described by Sir Edmund Hillary in 1951 as being superbly forested.

Nicholson-Lord, David, "The Politics of Travel: Is Tourism Just Colonialism in Another Guise?" *The Nation*, Oct. 6, 1997.
The writer offers a negative take on the cultural, political and economic conundrums posed by ecotourism.

Vivanco, Luis A., "The Prospects and Dilemmas of Indigenous Tourism Standards and Certification," in R. Black and A. Crabtree, eds., *Quality Control and Ecotourism Certification*, CAB International, in press.
An anthropologist examines ecotourism certification from the point of view of native peoples.

Reports and Studies

Chafe, Zoe, "Consumer Demand and Operator Support for Socially and Environmentally Responsible Tourism," *CESD/TIES Working Paper No. 104*, Center on Ecotourism and Sustainable Development/The International Ecotourism Society, revised April 2005.
Statistics and trends are presented from a range of studies focusing on the U.S., Europe, Costa Rica and Australia.

Christ, Costas, Oliver Hillel, Seleni Matus and Jamie Sweeting, "Tourism and Biodiversity: Mapping Tourism's Global Footprint," Conservation International, 2003, p. 7.
The authors document the overlap between biodiversity "hotspots" and tourist destinations, making a case for carefully managed, sustainable tourism.

LaFranchi, Christopher, and Greenpeace Pacific, "Islands Adrift? Comparing Industrial and Small-scale Economic Options for Marovo Lagoon Region of the Solomon Islands," Greenpeace, March 1999; www.greenpeace.org/international/press/reports/islands -adrift-comparing-indu.
An analysis of the subsistence-based economy of a small but biologically rich region illuminates the complex issues that arise when ecotourism is chosen over more conventional, extractive development routes.

Mastny, Lisa, "Traveling Light: New Paths for International Tourism," *Worldwatch Paper 159*, Worldwatch Institute 2001.
A well-documented study examines the environmental implications of global travel in light of the massive economic forces it entails and considers the challenges and opportunities of achieving sustainable travel.

For More Information

Center on Ecotourism and Sustainable Development, 1333 H St., N.W., Suite 300, East Tower, Washington, DC 20005; (202) 347-9203; www.ecotourismcesd.org. Designs, monitors, evaluates and seeks to improve ecotourism practices and principles.

Conservation International, 2011 Crystal Drive, Suite 500, Arlington, VA 22202; (703) 341-2400; www.conservation.org. Seeks to protect endangered plants and animals around the world.

EplerWood International, www.eplerwood.com. Consultancy that offers insights into the challenges and opportunities of ecotourism from specific projects to broader economic and organizational issues.

The International Ecotourism Society, 1333 H St., N.W., Suite 300, East Tower, Washington, DC 20005; (202) 347-9203; www.ecotourism.org. Works to foster responsible travel to natural areas that conserves the environment and improves the well-being of local people.

Planeta.com, www.planeta.com. An ecotourism Web site featuring news, blog articles and links to other relevant Internet sites.

Transitions Abroad, P.O. Box 745, Bennington, VT 05201; (802) 442-4827; www.transitionsabroad.com. Web site offering information on working, studying, traveling and living abroad.

World Tourism Organization, Calle Capitán Haya, 42, 28020 Madrid, Spain; +34 91 567 81 00; www.unwto.org. United Nations agency that promotes economic development through responsible, sustainable tourism.

11

Cuba's Future

Peter Katel

Since the Cuban revolution's first days, anti-Castro Cubans have been fleeing to the United States, such as these "boat people" in a raft off the Cuban coast in 1994. Some policy makers worry that Fidel Castro's departure from the political scene may lead to changes in Cuba that will spark another migration crisis.

From *CQ Researcher*, July 20, 2007.

The graybeard's voice is cracking. And, like many old men, he drifts easily into the past, reminiscing about a visit to Vietnam during the war. [1]

"Many years have passed since then," Fidel Castro, now 80, remarked during a 50-minute Cuban TV interview in June. [2]

Castro looked healthier than he has in recent brief TV clips, but gone is the dynamic revolutionary leader who would harangue Cuban crowds for hours — and who played a part in bringing the world to the brink of nuclear war. He even has traded his trademark green military fatigues for a red-and-white track suit — complete with an Adidas logo. [3]

The June 6 interview marked an official visit to Cuba by Nong Duc Manh, general secretary of Vietnam's Communist Party. But the real news was Castro's reappearance after a long illness, although he made no mention of returning to power.

In July 2006, while recuperating from intestinal surgery, he had transferred "provisional" authority to his brother, Raúl, Cuba's defense minister. [4]

Although the low-key Raúl remains officially in charge, many Cuba-watchers argue the real post-Castro era won't start until Fidel dies or becomes incapacitated. Still, the new era lies in sight, and the United States is starting to plan for it.

"One day, the good Lord will take Fidel Castro away," President George W. Bush said during a speech at the Naval War College, on June 29, 2007. After applause that seemed to embarrass the president, he said he was trying to focus attention on Cuba's future, not Castro's mortality. [5]

For a Caribbean island of only 11 million people, Cuba has

So Near and Yet So Far

Cuba is just 90 miles from Florida, but it might as well be a million miles away because of its tense relations with the United States. In recent years, the United States has been exporting medical supplies along with food and agricultural products. When Fidel Castro, now 80, leaves the scene, however, relations may improve.

Area: 42,800 square miles, slightly smaller than Pennsylvania

Population: 11.4 million (July 2007 est.)

Population growth: 0.3 percent per year (2007 est.)

Infant mortality: 6 deaths per 1,000 (2007 est.)

Labor force: 4.8 million, with 78 percent in the state sector and 22 percent in the non-state sector (2006 est.)

Unemployment rate: 1.9 percent (2006 est.)

Gross domestic product: $45.5 billion (2006)

Religion: nominally 85 percent Roman Catholic prior to Fidel Castro assuming power; Protestants, Jehovah's Witnesses, Jews and Santería are also represented.

Government: Communist state with Fidel Castro as president since December 1976. He served as prime minister from 1959 until he acquired the title of president. A Council of Ministers is proposed by the president and appointed by the National Assembly. Due to ongoing health problems, Castro provisionally transferred power to his brother Gen. Raúl Castro, minister of defense, on July 31, 2006, in accordance with the constitution. Fidel Castro has yet to reclaim control of the government.

Economy: The government continues to balance the need for more economic freedom against a desire for complete political control. It has rolled back limited economic reforms undertaken in the 1990s to increase efficiency and alleviate shortages of food, goods and services. Since 2000, Venezuela has been providing oil on preferential terms, with Cuba paying for the oil, in part, with the services of Cuban personnel, including around 20,000 medical professionals.

Source: The World Factbook 2007, Central Intelligence Agency, 2007

played an outsized role in U.S. political culture since Castro toppled dictator Fulgencio Batista in 1959.

In 1962, when Soviet nuclear missiles were discovered in Cuba, the United States and the Soviet Union came close to atomic war. The year before, Cuba had vanquished a force of invading Cuban exiles, trained and equipped by the United States. The "Bay of Pigs" defeat has gone down in history as a humiliating blow to the new John F. Kennedy administration and the Central Intelligence Agency.

In the 1980s and '90s, Castro allowed two mass refugee outflows that landed more than 125,000 Cubans in Florida and 25,000 in a detention camp at the U.S. Navy base at Guantánamo, an American outpost on Cuban soil. Then, in 1996, Cuban MiG fighters shot down two small American private airplanes, killing all four men on board. Cuba said the planes, sent by a group that had dropped anti-Castro leaflets in Havana, had violated Cuban airspace, a charge the United States called false.

The four were from the 750,000-strong, vociferously anti-Castro Cuban-American community in Miami, which has played a major role in keeping Cuba on presidential agendas. In Florida, Cuban-Americans formed a voting bloc that was crucial to the presidential victories of Bill Clinton in 1996 and Bush in both 2000 and 2004. [6]

Such events, coupled with the canny activism of Miami Cubans, help explain Cuba's hold on the American political imagination. There's also the irony that one of the world's last survivors of the era of communism lies only 90 miles from Florida. Indeed, with its history of defying the United States, Cuba is serving as inspiration to a new crop of nationalist Latin American politicians, especially Venezuelan President Hugo Chávez, who views Castro as a mentor.

"As Latin America moves away from the United States, there are increasing bonds between other Latin American states and Cuba," says Wayne S. Smith, once the top U.S. diplomat in Havana and now a critic of U.S. anti-Castro policy. He adds that other countries are likely not interested in adopting the Cuban model, with its state control of media, a near-absence of privately owned business, prohibition of travel without government authorization and other limitations on personal and political freedom.

Some experts, in fact, question the extent of Castro's regional influence. "He became more [of] an iconic figure, a figure mostly of Latin American nationalism and anti-Americanism," especially among youths, Jorge G. Castañeda, a former Mexican foreign minister, told National Public Radio. "I think that's what the kids like. . . . They know the Cuban experience is a failure, they know that they would never accept the kind of regime that exists in Havana. But they still say, 'Well, yes, but he stands up to the Americans.' " [7]

For the Bush administration, Castro's semi-retirement presents a new opportunity to encourage Cubans to democratize their repressive, Soviet-style system. "Something changed last July," says Caleb McCarry, the State Department's transition coordinator for Cuba. "For the first time in decades the future of Cuba is not certain for Cubans. What that reflects is the possibility for change."

To give change a nudge, the administration is asking Congress for $45.7 million to aid so-called civil society groups such as "Damas de Blanco" (Ladies in White), made up of the wives, mothers and sisters of some of the 75 anti-Castro activists arrested in a 2003 crackdown. That spending is part of a proposed $80 million package that would also fund U.S.-based efforts to deliver news

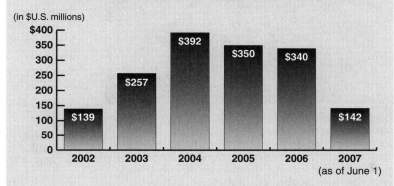

Trade Law Boosts U.S. Exports to Cuba

The United States exported $340 million in food and agricultural products to Cuba last year — more than double the exports in 2002. That was the first full year the Trade Sanctions Reform and Export Enhancement Act went into effect, permitting such trade.

Value of U.S. Food and Agricultural Exports to Cuba

(in $U.S. millions)

2002	$139
2003	$257
2004	$392
2005	$350
2006	$340
2007 (as of June 1)	$142

Source: John S. Kavulich II, "Economic Eye on Cuba: Monthly Report, U.S. Export Statistics for Cuba," U.S.-Cuba Trade and Economic Council, July 2007

to the island, where information about the world — and Cuba itself — is limited. "The civic movement needs additional support to present to their fellow Cubans a viable alternative to the failed policies of the Castro regime," the State Department's Commission for Assistance to a Free Cuba said in a July 2006 report. "It is critical that independent, Cuban civil society groups continue to gain greater access to basic modern equipment to help expand distribution of independent information and facilitate pro-democracy activities." [8]

A long-held fear, however, is that change could spark a breakdown in law and order that would spur thousands of Cubans to flee the island. "Massive, uncontrolled migration to Florida will be [among] the biggest challenges we will face from Cuba since Jan. 1, 1959," said a study published by the Army War College. [9] The specter of Cuban "boat people" haunts policy makers, says conservative Cuba-watcher Philip Peters, vice president of the Lexington Institute, a military-affairs think tank, and former State Department Cuba policy official. "Deep down in their hearts, when they really think about policy objectives, [American officials] don't want to have a migration crisis."

Provisional Cuban President Raúl Castro, right, meets in Havana with visiting Venezuelan President Hugo Chávez on June 13, 2007. Chávez spent several hours with Fidel Castro, whom he considers his mentor. While Cuba is serving as inspiration to a new crop of nationalist Latin American politicians like Chávez, some experts question how deep that influence runs.

Cuba's main newspaper, the Communist Party daily *Granma*, called the transition commission report a blueprint for "terror and annexation," also noting the report had criticized Cuba's much-vaunted health-care system. [10]

Cuba's free medical system has long been touted as outpacing the rest of the developing world — and the United States — in providing health care to all citizens. But some say Cuba's health system is in serious decline (*see p. 294*).

Within the United States, debate over Cuba often comes down to those who believe change is imminent and those who foresee a slower transformation.

"Clearly, there will not be a rapid transition to democracy in Cuba," said Rep. William Delahunt, D-Mass., who is sponsoring a bill to relax travel restrictions against Cuban-Americans. Family visits, which the Bush administration cut in 2004 from once a year to once every three years, foster the process of change, Delahunt argues. [11]

Others say the present system will disappear when Castro goes. "It's his army and his regime," says Havana-born Rep. Lincoln Diaz-Balart, R-Fla., a pillar of the Miami-Cuban establishment. Without Castro, he says, "That regime will dissolve like a sugar cube in a glass of water." Indeed, when Castro relinquished power last year he was, among other things, first secretary of the central

committee of the Communist Party of Cuba; commander-in-chief of the Revolutionary Armed Forces and president of the Council of State. [12]

As for the society Castro created, says dissident Laura Pollán of the Damas de Blanco, it remains full of fear and struggle. But when Castro is gone, she says from Havana, "There is no one else in the high spheres of power who has that charisma. Things won't be the same." [13]

Meanwhile, documents released on June 26 by the CIA were a somber reminder that Castro has outlived U.S. assassination attempts — including the recruiting of a Mafia boss to kill the Cuban leader in the 1960s. [14]

The latest disclosures showed again the U.S. government's obsession with *el comandante's* mortality — and gave him yet another chance to jab at his favorite adversary. "Now I understand why I survived Bush's plans and those of presidents who ordered my assassination," Castro said in a written statement poking fun at Bush's oft-displayed piety. "The good Lord protected me." [15]

As Cuba-watchers monitor developments on the island, these are some of the top issues being debated:

Is Cuba on the verge of change?

Although speculation about Cuba's future intensified after Fidel Castro's recent illness, questions were raised after the 1991 collapse of the Soviet Union and picked up steam in the new century.

Even before the State Department's Cuba transition coordinator was appointed two years ago, the U.S. Agency for International Development was financing a "Cuba Transition Project" at the University of Miami. Since 2002, it has produced more than two-dozen studies and seminars on Cuba, on topics such as maintaining a social "safety net," reforming the security services and the lessons of post-communist transformations in former Soviet satellites in central and Eastern Europe. [16]

In a 2003 study, Damian J. Fernandez, a Florida International University professor of international relations, detailed a grim view of "civic values" in Cuba. "The economy offers few rewards for those who follow the law, so lawlessness is rampant," he wrote. "Stealing from the state is not perceived as stealing, and as a consequence, corruption, both petty and official, is on the rise. Cubans seem to want to be free from politics rather than agents of it, while holding at the same time high expectations of what the state should deliver." [17]

Cubans will be no more receptive to indoctrination in U.S. political values than Eastern Europeans have been, Fernandez argued. [18]

A possibly complicating factor in any Cuba transition is the country's strong link with Castro's personality. From the moment Castro delivered his first speech, on Jan. 1, 1959, as leader of a victorious army, "He saw himself and the revolution as synonymous," wrote Brian Latell, the CIA's national intelligence officer for Latin America in 1990-94 and a veteran Cuba analyst. [19]

If Latell is correct about Castro's vision of his central place in Cuban life, the Cuban leader's bitterest enemies couldn't agree with him more. That explains the obsessive Castro health-watch that many Cuban-Americans have maintained for decades.

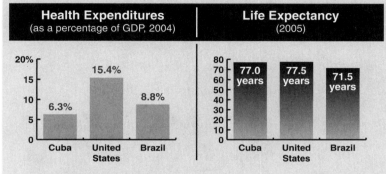

Low Health Spending But High Life Expectancy

Cuba spends only 6.3 percent of its gross domestic product (GDP) on free health care for all citizens; U.S. spending is more than twice that much. Life expectancies in Cuba and the United States are some five years longer than in Brazil, Latin America's largest country.

Health Expenditures (as a percentage of GDP, 2004)		
Cuba	United States	Brazil
6.3%	15.4%	8.8%

Life Expectancy (2005)		
Cuba	United States	Brazil
77.0 years	77.5 years	71.5 years

Source: World Health Organization, www.who.int

"At least 90 percent of the source of power of that regime is the life of Fidel Castro," says Diaz-Balart. "I never bought that bill of goods of Raúl as a power. That's a joke. Raúl Castro has been an administrator of the decisions of his brother in regard to the armed forces."

Diaz-Balart argues that Cuba can transform itself as Spain did after the 1975 death of longtime dictator Francisco Franco. Cuba, in fact, holds an advantage over Spain: It didn't suffer a civil war that reflected centuries-old class and ideological divisions. "The Cuban people ideologically are very united," Diaz-Balart says. "Nobody believes that communism baloney." The congressman is a member of a South Florida political dynasty rooted in Cuba; Fidel Castro joined it by marriage in 1948 when he wed Mirta Diaz-Balart, the congressman's aunt, in 1948; they were divorced in 1954. [20]

Raúl Castro's lifelong subordination to his brother lends strength to Diaz-Balart's prediction of collapse following Castro's permanent departure. But the Cuban system has shown greater resilience than its enemies are willing to acknowledge. Diaz-Balart concedes that he believed the Castro government was doomed by the collapse of the Soviet Union. But he adds that the American decision to grant 20,000 visas a year to Cubans — following a mass outflow of refugees in 1994 — breathed new life into a government that seemed to be on its last legs. The visas serve as a "safety valve," he argues, by refocusing the minds of discontented Cubans onto the possibility of leaving the island. Crackdowns such as the 2003 roundup of 75 dissidents that led to the creation of the Ladies in White protest group demonstrate, to critics of the government, that Castro hasn't relied exclusively on migration to maintain stability. Veteran dissident Vladimiro Roca says, "There are two actions that would indicate the beginning of a transition: economic reforms and the freeing of all political prisoners. Until then we can't speak of transition."

Others argue that Cuba's support from Venezuela and China — successors to the Soviet Union in helping keep Cuba afloat — makes the system less fragile than many claim.

With that economic support in place, and with the power shift from brother to brother having taken place in an unrushed fashion, "The transition is over," says John S. Kavulich II, a senior policy adviser at the U.S-Cuba Trade & Economic Council. "For the Cubans [in power], the manner by which Fidel Castro's illness has transitioned authority to Raúl Castro has been everything that they could have possibly dreamed for. When Fidel Castro does draw his last breath, it will be anti-climactic. There will no shock in the Cuban system."

Cuba's Booming Trade With China, Venezuela

Cuba's bilateral trade with China has more than tripled since 2004, reaching $1.8 billion in 2006. Its $2.6 billion 2006 trade with Venezuela was nearly double the 2004 amount. Reflecting the mounting competition to trade with Cuba, China promptly offered Cuba more financial credit after Cuba agreed with Venezuela in 2004 to barter and sell services — mainly medical — for oil. In return for telecommunications products and durable goods such as buses and refrigerators, Cuba has given China nickel and oil rights.

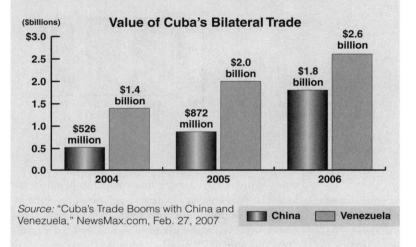

Value of Cuba's Bilateral Trade

($billions)

Source: "Cuba's Trade Booms with China and Venezuela," NewsMax.com, Feb. 27, 2007

Kavulich acknowledges Raúl may also leave the scene relatively soon — but the leadership group that is seen as ready to take charge at that point could prove as intractable as Fidel Castro, he argues. "These are people born under the revolution, raised under the revolution; they have the courage of their ignorance. They believe the economic data, the health-care statistics."

That group would include Foreign Minister Felipe Pérez Roque. Kavulich adds that another group of top officials, Economy and Planning Minister José Luís Rodriguez among them, tends to be more realistic in its views but may not have much influence unless reduced support from Venezuela and China creates a demand for its skills.

Even so, some who monitor Cuba closely say, living conditions are already so dire that even Castro's heirs can't kid themselves. "I don't think the current situation is sustainable," says Carlos Saladrigas of Miami, co-chair of the Cuba Study Group, a think tank that promotes peaceful change in Cuba. "Even the major accomplishments of the revolution that are such an important political force in the

country — the health-care and educational systems — are suffering for lack of resources."

Unlike Diaz-Balart and other leaders of the traditional Cuban-American political establishment in Miami, Saladrigas doesn't expect a sudden and overwhelming change to take place. "The Big Bang is not going to happen," he says. The Cuban elite are clearly going to start the ball rolling by making economic reforms. Reforms open spaces for people to get empowered independently of the state, spaces that civil society will fill and which add pressure for more reforms, and the cycle continues."

Yet the possibility of change moving at a measured pace depends on the government maintaining social and political stability. And, once Fidel Castro is out of the picture, stability depends on the government maintaining a level of repression that marked his time at the helm, some Cuba-watchers say.

"The Cuban government will not remain in control the day that the Cuban government is no longer willing to imprison and to kill people," says Frank Calzón, executive director of the Center for a Free Cuba. "I'm sure the government has some support, but what it cannot give up is the repression. If you know you're not going to be imprisoned — or killed — you're going to be out on the street."

Should the United States lift restrictions on travel to Cuba?

The Supreme Court has upheld the federal government's right to limit travel to Cuba. The court ruled 5-4 in 1984 that the executive branch could restrict Americans' movement abroad on national-security grounds. [21]

The restrictions aren't absolute. Working American journalists can visit — if Cuba gives them visas. And some access is allowed for academics and other professionals. But Congress explicitly prohibited tourist travel under the Trade Sanctions Reform and Export Enhancement Act of 2000. [22]

Executive branch travel limits date to 1962 and '63, when the Kennedy administration prohibited most transactions with Cuba. Over the next several decades, the travel ban was alternately toughened and softened. [23]

From 1977-1982, however, President Jimmy Carter lifted the ban entirely. His thanks, Cuban-Americans wryly note, was the Mariel refugee crisis of 1980. President Ronald Reagan reimposed restrictions in 1982 in retaliation for Cuba's support of left-wing guerrillas in El Salvador and the left-wing government of Nicaragua. However, Reagan kept in place previous exemptions for journalists and other professionals. [24]

President Clinton relaxed the rules again, but President Bush began tightening them in 2001 in response to demands by Cuban-Americans. Before the 2004 presidential election, Bush also imposed new limits on academic visits. [25]

Travel advocates argue that loosening the rules would force the Cuban government to relax control over its citizens. "Open travel would create a 'free flow of ideas' that 'would promote democratization,' as dissident Oscar Espinosa Chepe wrote shortly after his release from [a Cuban] prison in 2004," Reps. Jeff Flake, R-Ariz., and Charles Rangel, D-N.Y., wrote in April. [26] They are sponsoring one of two bills that would end travel restrictions entirely.

Supporters of restrictions say they deprive the Cuban government of hard currency — the main declared aim of travel restrictions. And they ask why Cuba's tougher restrictions on its own citizens' travel go virtually unmentioned in the United States. "For example, I cannot go to Cuba," says Calzón, who never gave up his Cuban citizenship, "not because the U.S. doesn't let me go, but because the Cuban government won't let me." Cubans who want to travel abroad also need permission.

Calzón also criticizes travel advocates who don't consider their role in what many Cubans call the "apartheid" system, which bars ordinary Cubans from facilities for tourists. [27]

"Americans talk about Martin Luther King, and how black Americans couldn't stay in a hotel or motel," Calzón says. "And those same people go to Cuba and stay in a hotel where Cubans are not allowed — and they say nothing."

But keeping Cuba isolated won't do anything to eliminate apartheid, travel advocates argue. "What doesn't hold together is that the people in the United States who are most strongly calling for change don't want to have any contact with Cuba," says Peters of the Lexington Institute. "They don't want diplomats to talk, they don't

Havana's skyline and nearby Varadero boast new luxury hotels built with European companies as partners. To help the economy, Cuba now encourages a new relationship with the thousands of exiles in the United States, whose aid to relatives has become essential to the economy.

want professors and students to go there. But if you care about post-Castro Cuba, the people who are post-Castro Cuba are there now. It just doesn't make any damn sense."

Separate rules govern Cuban-Americans' visits to see relatives — and generate a debate all their own. Family visits began when the travel ban was abolished in 1977-82, but in 2004 the Bush administration cut the visits from once a year to once every three years, limited to close relatives. [28]

Cuban-American leaders from their community's "historic" wing — those who arrived in the early '60s or '70s — had pushed for the tighter rules, arguing that they would further isolate and weaken the Castro government. "The only way to get rid of Fidel is to get tight on him," said Mario Guzman, 75. "The main reason why he's still in power is because the very Cubans he forced out are bringing him dollars back." [29]

Yet Cubans on the island who oppose Castro from less comfortable circumstances tend to oppose travel limits. "We're against all measures that restrict freedom of movement," says Vladimiro Roca, a longtime human-rights activist, speaking by phone from Havana. "The Cuban government, which limits the freedom of movement of Cubans, provides an example which shouldn't be imitated." Roca, a former Cuban Air Force fighter pilot and son of a legendary Cuban communist leader, was released from prison in 2002 after serving most of a five-year sentence for publishing a document attacking the one-party system. [30]

Does Cuba threaten the U.S.?

The Soviet Union's demise in 1991 not only ended the Cold War but also Cuba's alliance with a nuclear-armed adversary of the United States.

Today, nonetheless, Cuba is still viewed as a threat. It has earned a place on the U.S. government's "state sponsors of terrorism" list, in part because of its "close relationships" with Iran and North Korea. Last year, the State Department reported, "The Cuba-Iran Joint Commission met in Havana in January." Also, it noted, "Cuba and North Korea held military talks at the general staff level in May in Pyongyang. The North Korean trade minister visited Havana in November and signed a protocol for cooperation in the areas of science and trade." And, the report said, "Iran offered Cuba a 20-million Euro line of credit, ostensibly for investment in biotechnology." [31]

The reported line of credit echoed a much-disputed 2002 claim by a high Bush administration official that Cuban transfers of biomedical research and technology to other countries could be aimed at helping terrorist states develop germ-warfare capabilities.

"The United States believes that Cuba has at least a limited offensive biological warfare (BW) research and development effort," said John Bolton, then undersecretary of State for arms control and international security. "Cuba has provided dual-use biotechnology to other rogue states. We are concerned that such technology could support BW programs in those states." [32]

Fidel Castro immediately denounced Bolton's speech as a lie. Later, other American government experts charged that Bolton distorted intelligence to buttress his political claims. The Cuba bioweapons speech was "pure surmise, as far as I know," said Greg Thielmann, the recently retired head of the State Department's Strategic, Proliferation and Military Affairs Office. [33]

Bolton responded, "Thielmann knows nothing." [34]

In any event, U.S. officials no longer repeat Bolton's accusations. Asked if Cuba constitutes a threat, McCarry, the State Department's Cuba transition coordinator, says: "Cuba is a designated state sponsor of terrorism." He adds, "It's important to understand that an undemocratic Cuba is a destabilizing influence, and ultimately it is the Cuban people who suffer the consequences of a dictatorship whose purpose is to perpetuate itself in power."

Decoded, the administration position amounts to an admission that Cuba doesn't pose a threat, conservative Cuba-watcher Peters argues. The Bush administration, he says, "would have screamed to high heaven if there was some revival of Cuba's military capability or some actual activity that supports terrorism, or any effort to develop weapons of mass destruction." In fact, he says, "They haven't."

Peters acknowledges that Fidel Castro's mentorship of Venezuela's Chávez has energized Cuba's political proselytizing in the region, aided by the dispatch of Cuban doctors to various countries. "But that's normal political competition," Peters says. "It doesn't add up to a security threat."

Those who view Cuba as a danger cite U.S. military intelligence — but in a singular way. "At present, Cuba does not pose a significant military threat to the U.S. or to other countries in the region," the Defense Intelligence Agency (DIA) reported in 1998. "Cuba has little motivation to engage in military activity beyond defense of its territory and political system." [35]

But that conclusion was written by a Cuban spy. Ana Belen Montes, then the senior DIA analyst on Cuban affairs, was unmasked in 2001. She pleaded guilty the following year and is serving a 25-year sentence. Former CIA officer Latell, who knew Montes, wrote that he and his colleagues concluded after her arrest that all of their analyses had been transmitted to Cuba's spy agency. [36]

Rep. Diaz-Balart noted that other cases of Cuban espionage have surfaced in recent years. Among them: an infiltrator of the Brothers to the Rescue organization who returned to Havana before the shootdown of the two planes in 1996; 10 men and women arrested in 1998 in Florida and charged with spying (five pleaded guilty, and five were convicted at trial and are appealing); and an associate professor at Florida International University in Miami who is serving five years in prison after pleading guilty in February to filing reports to Cuban intelligence on the Cuban-American community. [37]

But while conceding that Cuba could hardly mount an invasion, Diaz-Balart cites the State Department's annual report on state sponsors of terrorism. "Combine that with the fact that the Cuban regime has killed American citizens in international waters. It has infiltrated the American government. The Cuban regime is certainly an asymmetric threat, mostly because of its deepening alliance with other state sponsors of terrorism." [38]

Notwithstanding the terrorism list, says Daniel Erikson, director of Carribean programs at Inter-American Dialogue, a centrist think tank, nothing indicates that the U.S. government treats Cuba as a high-priority danger. "It's talked about more in terms of promoting democracy," he says. "Allegations of bioweapons programs don't strike me as something that's keeping policy-makers up at night."

BACKGROUND

The Revolution

For two years, Fidel Castro led a rural guerrilla war against dictator Batista, while students and middle-class insurgents fought in the cities. Batista's forces finally collapsed in late 1958. On Jan. 8, 1959, after leading a column of his army across Cuba, Castro marched into Havana. Days earlier, Batista had fled.

Castro made extravagant promises. "If we do not give liberty to all parties to organize themselves, we will not be a democratic people," he told CBS television on Jan. 11. [39]

Later that month, he denied explicitly on two occasions that he was a communist. Historians have long debated whether Castro was flirting with Marxism-Leninism or already had committed to that doctrine.

In any event, Castro soon declared himself a communist; began purging "counterrevolutionaries," of whom an estimated 5,000 were executed; asked the Soviet Union to install nuclear missiles in Cuba; nationalized all business and industry and established a one-party state with no independent institutions of any kind, the Catholic Church excepted. [40]

From the revolution's first days, anti-Castro Cubans fled the island. By the end of the 1970s, nearly 500,000 had gone to the United States, most to South Florida. [41]

The first arrivals tended to be affluent businesspeople, followed by professionals and members of the middle class. By the late 1960s, small-scale merchants and workers predominated. [42]

In 1966, Congress enacted the Cuban Adjustment Act, which guaranteed lawful permanent residence (a "green card") to most Cubans, saving them the need to prove persecution.

Castro put the law to a severe test in 1980, when fleeing Cubans crashed a bus onto the diplomatically protected grounds of the Peruvian Embassy. In apparent retaliation for welcoming the gate-crashers, Cuba withdrew its embassy guards — and thousands more Cubans sought refuge.

Two weeks later, on April 15, 1980, Castro announced that foreigners could sail to Cuba to pick up departees. Thousands of Cuban-Americans set off in vessels of all kinds. Cuba established a debarkation point at the port of Mariel. By the time the "Mariel boatlift" ended on Oct. 31, about 125,000 Cubans had landed in Florida.

The exodus strained U.S. resources. In fact, the newcomers included hardened criminals whom Castro had ordered released from prison, an act viewed as a gesture of contempt for efforts by the Ford and Carter administrations to forge friendlier relations. [43]

Why did Castro reject the overtures? Possibly because he had learned about the perils of closer ties to the United States. In 1979, Castro had allowed exiles to visit family on the island, and about 100,000 arrived, many bearing consumer electronics and other products Cubans barely knew existed. The resulting discontent was among the factors that sparked the subsequent rush to the exits, including the embassy gate-crashing. [44]

Global Presence

Castro had declared the Cuban revolution a spark that would set the Americas ablaze. In his first few years in power, he aided insurgents in the Dominican Republic, Colombia, Venezuela and Argentina. In 1967, Castro's dashing Argentine comrade, Ernesto "Che" Guevara, was killed trying to launch a continent-wide uprising from Bolivia. In death, Guevara became a revolutionary icon — venerated to this day. [45]

Castro himself made a month-long trip to Chile in 1971 to build support for the newly elected socialist president, Salvador Allende. But the visit further inflamed military and upper-class fears of a communist takeover. These, along with covert U.S. aid to anti-Allende forces, helped set the stage for a 1973 coup. [46]

Shortly thereafter, Castro stepped onto a new stage — Africa — where Guevara had pioneered Cuban involvement. He fought in the Congo, during conflicts between African forces acting as proxies for the West and the Soviets.

In the 1970s and '80s, Castro sent thousands of Cuban troops to Angola to repel a 1975 South African invasion of the former Portuguese colony. According to documents made public in 2002, the United States was cooperating with South Africa, then ruled by a white-minority government. [47]

In 1977, Cuba sent 12,000 troops to help Ethiopian dictator Haile Mengistu repel an invasion by Somalia and

CHRONOLOGY

1959-1960 *Fidel Castro wins a guerrilla war against dictator Fulgencio Batista, then builds a Soviet-style communist state; U.S.-supported efforts fail to topple Castro.*

January 1959 Castro promises free elections.

April 17, 1961 Castro's forces rout U.S.-trained Cuban exiles who land at the Bay of Pigs in an effort to unseat Castro. . . . On Dec. 2, Castro announces he had been a communist for years.

September 1962 Soviet ships begin unloading nuclear missiles in Cuba, precipitating a major U.S.-Soviet crisis. President John F. Kennedy confronts Soviet leader Nikita Khrushchev, who agrees to remove the missiles.

1966 President Lyndon B. Johnson signs the Cuban Adjustment Act, which guarantees legal residence to Cubans who reach the United States.

Oct. 9, 1967 Ernesto "Che" Guevara, a dashing comrade of Castro's, is executed during his failed attempt to launch a South American revolution.

1970s-1980s *Cuba supports revolutionary efforts in Africa and Latin America, but discontent appears on the island.*

1971 Castro visits Chile for a month to build support for newly elected socialist President Salvador Allende, who is assassinated in 1973.

1975 Cuba sends military advisers to one of the guerrilla armies fighting for control of Angola.

Oct. 6, 1976 A bomb planted on a Cuban airliner by anti-Castro terrorists explodes in midair, killing 73.

1977 President Jimmy Carter lifts all restrictions on travel to Cuba.

1979 With Cuban support, Nicaragua's Sandinista guerrilla army topples onetime U.S.-backed strongman Anastasio Somoza.

April 15, 1980 Responding to domestic pressure, Castro permits the "Mariel boatlift," which brings 125,000 fleeing Cubans to Florida.

1982 President Ronald Reagan reimposes travel restrictions, partly in retaliation for Cuban support of Nicaragua.

1984 Academy Award-winning cinematographer Nestor Almendros releases a pioneering documentary on official Cuban persecution of homosexuals.

July 1989 Gen. Arnaldo Ochoa and three colleagues are sentenced to death for alleged drug trafficking and corruption.

1990s *Fall of Soviet Union leaves Cuba seemingly friendless and economically bereft, but predictions of imminent collapse prove inaccurate.*

1994 As Cubans continue to flee, Castro lifts restrictions on departures, leading to a U.S.-Cuba deal on migration.

Feb. 24, 1996 Cuban MiG shoots down two unarmed civilian American airplanes piloted by anti-Castro exiles. . . . President Bill Clinton signs law toughening economic sanctions against Cuba.

January 1998 Pope John Paul II makes the first papal visit to Cuba, denouncing prostitution linked to the new tourism industry.

2000s *Growing economic ties with Venezuela boost Cuba, but Castro's medical crisis reopens questions about a future without the charismatic comandante.*

Oct. 30, 2000 Venezuela agrees to supply oil to Cuba at rock-bottom prices.

2004 Bush administration tightens sanctions on Cuba, including restrictions on family visits by Cuban-Americans.

July 10, 2006 Bush administration's Cuba transition commission releases recommendations aimed at furthering the end of the communist system. . . . On July 31, 2006, an ailing Castro transfers top power to his brother, Raúl, Cuba's defense minister.

June 29, 2007 After President Bush refers to Castro's eventual death, Castro jokingly says God has been protecting him, tweaking Bush for his ostentatious piety.

a secessionist rebellion by guerrillas from the Eritrea region. Cuban troops helped Mozambique's newly formed government fight South African-backed guerrillas. [48]

Cuba's African adventures ended in the 1980s. Meanwhile, Castro refocused on his own neighborhood. Cuban advisers were active in the insurgency that toppled Nicaraguan dictator Anastasio Somoza in 1979 and in the new Sandinista government. And Cuba supported guerrillas fighting the U.S.-backed government in El Salvador. [49]

Frayed Safety Net

In 1989, Cuba shocked citizens and foreign observers alike when it tried a group of military and security officials for alleged drug trafficking and related crimes. After a televised trial, Gen. Arnaldo Ochoa — one of Cuba's most distinguished military men — and Antonio de la Guardia, a legendary Cuban secret agent, were sentenced to death. Both were executed by firing squad along with two associates. Ten others were sent to prison. [50]

All had confessed, but many Cuba-watchers thought they had been prosecuted for turning against the government, not because they had trafficked in drugs. Moreover, as potential rivals, they were seen as all the more threatening to Castro because the Soviet bloc, a major bulwark of the Cuban government, had begun to fall apart. [51]

The early 1990s saw Cubans go hungry. With the dissolution of the Soviet bloc, cheap food and fuel were no longer available. In response, Castro began rebuilding the tourist industry — formerly considered an unsavory relic of the Batista era, when the Mafia operated casinos in Havana. During the same period, scarcity created such high demand for legally unavailable goods of all kinds — from food to televisions — that a vast black market sprang up which proved far more efficient than creaky state enterprises. [52]

With European companies as partners, the government built luxury hotels in Havana and in nearby Varadero Beach. Cuba also encouraged a new relationship with the tens of thousands of Cuban exiles — traditionally insulted as "gusanos" (worms) — whose millions of dollars in aid to relatives had become essential to the economy. [53]

As Cuba's social safety net frayed, and well-to-do tourists arrived, prostitution, thought to have vanished with the Batista regime, reappeared. By the late 1990s, Cuba had become such a sex-tourism hotspot that Pope John Paul II raised the subject during a visit in 1998, condemning "prostitution hidden under different guises." [54]

"Boat People"

Many Cubans responded to the hardships by trying to flee. The early 1990s saw a boom in the number of Cubans heading for U.S. shores on virtually anything that floated, including rafts and windsurfers. [55]

In 1994, the exodus expanded. On July 13, a group of Cubans hijacked a tugboat, but a pursuit vessel sank the tug, killing 31 people. In the weeks that followed, two ferryboats were hijacked in Havana harbor and sailed into international waters, where the U.S. Coast Guard picked up the passengers, some of whom opted to go to the United States. [56]

Then, on Aug. 8, hijackers killed a Cuban Navy officer while seizing a vessel; they reached the United States and were admitted. Afterward, Castro announced Cuban forces would no longer intervene. "If the United States fails to adopt immediate and efficient measures to stop the encouragement of illegal departures from the country," he said, "we will instruct our coast guards not to intercept any boat leaving Cuba. I am not including hijacked boats." [57]

That month alone, the U.S. Coast Guard picked up more than 3,500 fleeing Cubans. Another 7,000 had crossed on their own. Faced with a growing problem, Clinton on Aug. 19 ordered all fleeing Cubans detained at the U.S. Navy base at Guantánamo. [58]

Over the next few weeks, the base took in more than 25,000 Cubans, while the United States and Cuba opened talks to settle the crisis. On Sept. 9, Cuba agreed to resume preventing unauthorized departures; for its part, the United States would stop admitting every intercepted Cuban. Instead, up to 20,000 visas a year to enter the United States would be granted to Cubans. U.S. officials soon chose to distribute some of these by lottery — a system still in place. [59]

The Clinton administration added a wrinkle to the new immigration system, quickly dubbed the "wet foot/dry foot" policy. Fleeing Cubans who managed to step onto U.S. shores were allowed to stay; those who reached within yards of land were sent back. [60]

U.S.-Cuba relations remained stormy through the 1990s despite the cooperation on fleeing Cubans. In 1996, a Cuban jet downed two small planes piloted by Miami Cuban-Americans flying in international airspace as part of a refugee-spotting organization, Brothers to the Rescue.

Led by a veteran of early CIA operations against Cuba, "Brothers" had begun expanding its operations in 1995 by dropping anti-Castro leaflets in Havana. Cuba

Miami Cubans Still Strong, But Divided

Powerful voting bloc sways policy

In 1999-2000, the drama over a Cuban youngster named Elián Gonzalez seemed to confirm the stereotype of Miami's Cuban-American community: a group so rabidly anti-Castro that it was willing to put politics ahead of reuniting a little boy with his father (*see p. 292*).

But seven years after Elián was sent home, Cuban-Americans attitudes are not so monolithic. The standard Cuban-American position toward Cuba used to be rigidly simple: Maintain the economic and travel embargoes until the death of Fidel Castro makes a non-communist government on the island a possibility.

"I don't feel like a minority at all," says Carlos Saladrigas, a Miami Cuban-American businessman who helps lead the Cuba Study Group, which fosters a gradual transition from the Soviet-style Cuban system. "I'm in a significant and growing majority. Miami is changing. Some people are changing out of frustration, some out of a deeper analysis of the facts."

Saladrigas cites a recent survey in which 65 percent of Cuban-Americans favor a dialogue with the Cuban government — an increase from about 40 percent in 1991 and 55.6 percent in 2004. And 55 percent of respondents favored unrestricted travel to Cuba. [1]

But Rep. Lincoln Diaz-Balart, R-Fla., a leading Cuban-American lawmaker, scoffs, "Anybody can do a poll. Remember, it's all in [how you ask] the question."

The bottom line, Diaz-Balart says, is whom Cuban-Americans elect. "The Cuban-American community has elected six members of Congress, four Republican and two Democrats, and there's no daylight between any of the six" on policy toward Cuba, he says. "That should say something."

Traditionally, Florida's Cuban-Americans have been solidly Republican (the two Democrats, Sen. Robert Menendez and Rep. Albio Sires, are from New Jersey). But, as Diaz-Balart notes, Cuban-American voters of both parties tend to agree on Cuba policy. From the left-liberal side, sociologist Max J. Castro argued recently that U.S. policy has been bent to the wishes of the "rich, entrenched, recalcitrant and demographically dwindling minority of that [Cuban-American] community." [2]

Among non-lawmakers, Cuban-American political views may always have been more diverse, especially in Spanish-language media, than most outsiders realized. The Elián saga served as a catalyst for making those differences even more public. "There has been a rethinking, and it began because of Elián, which was such a public relations disaster for the exiles," said Dario Moreno, a Florida International University (FIU) political science professor. [3]

During the Elián controversy, major exile organizations had been at odds over planned demonstrations timed for the Latin Grammy awards ceremony in Miami. The protests — sparked by the fact that some of the scheduled performers were Cubans still living on the island — led to the show being moved to Los Angeles. (Its date, Sept. 11, 2001 — the day terrorists attacked the U.S. — led to cancellation). [4]

---

then warned that it was entitled to take military action to safeguard its sovereignty. [61]

On Feb. 24, 1996, a Cuban MiG-29 shot down two "Brothers" planes (a third plane escaped). The United States said the planes had been in international territory; Cuba said otherwise. [62]

In response, President Clinton dropped his opposition to legislation by Sen. Jesse Helms, R-N.C., and Rep. Dan Burton, R-Ind., to step up the economic embargo against Cuba. The resulting Helms-Burton Act permitted the United States to prohibit entry by anyone with ties to a company doing business in Cuba or "trafficking" in property expropriated by its government. [63]

A Boy Named Elián

On Nov. 25, 1999, an American fishing boat rescued three Cubans floating on inner tubes off the Florida coast. The boat they'd been escaping on had sunk. One of the three was 5-year-old Elián González; his mother had drowned. [64]

Within days, the boy's father — along with the Cuban government — demanded his return. Cuban officials said Elián's mother, who was divorced from his father, had taken him without authorization. [65]

But Elián was taken in by relatives of his father — who said they'd never let him be sent back to Cuba. They were supported by the influential Cuban-American National Foundation. [66]

In any event, the initial selection of Miami was mind-boggling to many. Jorge Mas Santos, chairman of the Cuban-American National Foundation (CANF), was among those promoting the city as the site. Partly as a result, at least 22 board members of what had been considered the bulwark of the exile community resigned. [5]

Some said that Mas Santos had devalued the legacy of his late father, Jorge Mas Canosa, who made CANF a powerful political force. [6]

Arguments within the Cuban-American community remain as fiery as ever. That much was clear from a May 22, 2007, debate between two of its prominent members, Frank Calzón, executive director of the Committee for a Free Cuba, and Joe Garcia, a CANF board member. The debate was taped for a Miami Spanish-language station, Mega TV, but never aired; it is accessible on the Web. [7]

Garcia and Calzón argued so fiercely that Calzón finally stormed off the set. As he left, he let loose a final blast that goes to the heart of a divide among exiles — those who would talk to the Castro government and those who call that a betrayal.

"Go talk to Carlos Lage," Calzón sputtered, referring to the vice president of Cuba's Council of State. "I don't want to talk with you or with Mr. Lage." [8]

Residents of Miami's Little Havana neighborhood celebrate on July 31, 2006, after Fidel Castro transferred power to his younger brother Raúl.

Getty Images/Richard Patterson

Indeed, in 2003, then-CANF Chairman Jorge Mas Santos invited Lage and two other senior officials — not Fidel or Raúl Castro — to talk about the future. "In a change toward a democratic and free Cuba, they also have a place," he said. The offer produced no results. [9]

[1] See "2007 FIU Cuba Poll," Institute for Public Opinion Research, Cuban Research Institute, Florida International University, April 2, 2007; www.fiu.edu/%7Eipor/cuba8/.

[2] See Max J. Castro, "Miami Vise," *The Nation*, May 14, 2007; www.thenation.com/doc/20070514/castro.

[3] Quoted in Andres Viglucci, "Grammy Flap Exposes Split Among Exiles," *The Miami Herald*, Sept. 2, 2001, p. B1.

[4] See *ibid.* Also see Jacqueline Trescott and Sarah Kaufman, "Cultural Activities Pause After Tragedy," *The Washington Post*, Sept. 12, 2001, p. C1.

[5] See Luisa Yanez and Nancy San Martin, "20 CANF Board Members Resign," *The Miami Herald*, Aug. 8, 2001, p. A1; Elaine de Valle and Carol Rosenberg, "Radio Host Latest to Quit Cuban Foundation," *The Miami Herald*, July 20, 2001, p. A1.

[6] *Ibid.*

[7] See Glenn Garvin, "Changing Channels," blog, June 3, 2007; http://miamiherald.typepad.com/changing_channels/2007/06/the_lost_episod.html.

[8] See "Joe Garcia versus Frank Calzon," *Polos Opuestos*, May 22, 2007; www.youtube.com/watch?v=NJB50RAUSlY&mode=related&search=.

[9] Quoted in Andrea Elliott and Elaine de Valle, "Mas Santos Makes Offer to Talk with Cuba Leaders," *The Miami Herald*, Jan. 31, 2003, p. B1.

For six media-intensive months a battle raged, accompanied by frequent rallies outside the home in Miami's Little Havana where Elián was staying. Then on April 22, 2000, heavily armed immigration agents drove up to the home and seized Elián to take him to Washington, where his father had come to press his case in the federal courts. On July 28, 2000, the U.S. Supreme Court refused to consider a final attempt by the Miami family to keep the boy, now 6, and he flew home to Cuba with his father. [67]

Another legal battle ended better for a longtime hero of Miami's ultra-anti-Castro exiles — though it did little for their image. Luís Posada Carriles, a veteran of anti-Castro paramilitary and terrorist operations since the early 1960s, saw his last remaining indictment — for immigration fraud — dismissed by a federal judge in El Paso on May 9. [68]

Posada, who had worked closely with the CIA in the 1960s and '70s, is widely believed to have organized the 1976 bombing of a Cuban airliner by a bomb, killing all 73 people aboard. The most recent evidence came to light in 2005: a report by a Miami police detective of an informant's claim that Posada helped plan the bombing. The now-dead informant on another occasion denied Posada was involved; Posada denies involvement. [69]

Cuban officials have lost no opportunity to condemn the U.S. government's failure to charge Posada in the

Dissidents Face Harassment, Prison

Ladies in White won't back down

Cuba's tiny dissident movement has no illusions about toppling the government. But the government isn't taking any chances. Cubans who oppose the political system face harassment, arrest on charges including "social dangerousness" and prison. [1]

Even those who avoid prison court "acts of repudiation" in which government supporters (possibly including security agents) shout insults, pelt dissidents' homes and sometimes beat up their targets. A flurry of repudiations — first employed against those leaving Cuba in the 1980 Mariel boatlift — was reported last year. [2]

In one case, a member of Ladies in White, a group of about 30 wives, mothers, sisters and friends of imprisoned dissidents, was effectively put under house arrest by members of a "repudiation" squad so that she couldn't join the group's weekly demonstrations. "We didn't hurt her. We didn't strike her. But she couldn't leave her apartment," Isabel Prieto, one of the repudiators, told the *Chicago Tribune*. "As long as she doesn't threaten our rights, she can do what she wants." [3]

Another Ladies in White activist calls the tactic useless. "It doesn't matter to us," says Laura Pollán. "Our love for our dear ones is much greater."

Her husband, journalist Héctor Maseda, was one of 75 dissidents arrested in 2003 and sentenced to prison terms ranging from 12 to 25 years. Fourteen of those arrested were released the following year for ill health, possibly to avoid the embarrassment of a death behind bars. [4]

Imprisoning people practicing journalism outside the state-monopoly media or otherwise flouting the system's rules can be seen as authorized by the country's penal code, says a leading U.S.-based rights organization.

"Laws criminalizing enemy propaganda, the spreading of 'unauthorized news' and insults to patriotic symbols are used to restrict free speech under the guise of protecting state security," Human Rights Watch said in its 2006 annual report.

Vladimiro Roca, a former military pilot and son of famed communist leader Blas Roca, says he and his fellow oppositionists face a constant threat of imprisonment. "From one moment to the next, we could be sent to prison," he says. "We are at the mercy of the Cuban government." Still and all, he says, the dissident movement includes several thousand members.

Oswaldo Payá, the main organizer of the Varela Project, a 2002 call for a referendum on opening the political system to free elections, free speech and other civil liberties, said he and his colleagues were able to collect 11,000 signatures for their unprecedented public petition. [5]

Cuban officials insist the term "dissident" is a deliberately misleading label for what are really U.S.-sponsored enemies of the Cuban system. "There is no punishment in this country for expressing ideas that are different from than those of the government," said Roberto de Armas, a senior Cuban official, in 2004. "What's not tolerated is collaborating with a foreign government to overthrow the Cuban government." [6]

In 2003, Cuban officials released evidence of what they called a U.S. campaign to nurture political opposition and defamatory propaganda. Cuban intelligence agents who infiltrated dissident groups said they received American government money to subsidize their political activities. "It was

airliner bombing and others at Havana tourist spots in 1997. After Posada's latest legal victory, Cuba's top diplomat in Washington said the Bush administration had "done all it can to protect the bin Laden of this hemisphere." [70]

CURRENT SITUATION

Proposed Legislation

Several pending bills call for altering or scrapping major elements of U.S. policy toward Cuba, including the U.S. trade embargo and travel restrictions. Bills by Rep. Charles Rangel, D-N.Y., and Sens. Byron Dorgan, D-N.D., and Michael Enzi, R-Wyo., would remove all travel limits.

Rep. Delahunt, the Massachusetts Democrat, proposes just removing Bush administration restrictions on family visits to Cuba. Miami Democratic Chairman Joe Garcia supports the Delahunt bill, arguing it stands a better chance of passing than abolition of all restrictions. "Politics is the art of the possible," he says.

Supporters of the Delahunt proposal also argue that if the travel ban were lifted for all Americans, Cuban

a game," said Pedro Luis Veliz, recounting how he spun a tale of leading a 800-member dissident group, receiving financing in return from private U.S. organizations. Some of these organizations operated at least partly on funds from the U.S. Agency for International Development (AID). [7]

U.S. officials denied paying Cuban dissidents. "Since 1996, U.S. AID grantees sent over 1 million books, newsletters, videos and other informational materials to independent, non-governmental organizations and individuals in Cuba," said Adolfo Franco, then AID's assistant administrator for Latin America and the Caribbean. "No U.S. AID grantee is authorized to use grant funds to provide cash assistance to any individual or group in Cuba."

Since then, the Bush administration has recommended funding an "independent civil society" in Cuba, a designation that includes the Ladies in White.

Some critics of U.S. policy argue that building ties with dissident groups ends up hurting them. "All this prodding and provoking — the only thing it accomplishes is to get the kind of crackdowns that we've seen," said Wayne S. Smith, a former chief U.S. diplomat in Havana, now director of the Cuba program at the Center for International Policy. [8]

But Pollán has no objection to accepting help from wherever it's offered, noting that Cubans fighting for independence from Spain in the 19th century received aid from

The Ladies in White demonstrate in Havana on March 27, 2005, demanding the release of loved ones being held by the government.

AFP Photo/Adalberto Roque

Latin America, Europe and even the United States. "If Venezuela wants to help us economically, we'll accept," she adds, in an ironic reference to the close economic ties between that country and the Cuban government. "How wonderful if all countries helped us."

Meanwhile, the Ladies in White plan to keep up their weekly marches. "When we take to the street, more people tell us to keep going, and tell us that they feel solidarity with our cause. Their consciences are awakening."

[1] See "Cuba Frees Dissident Journalist, Reports Say," *Chicago Tribune*, Jan. 20, 2001, p. A4.

[2] See Frances Robles, "Mob attacks on Castro's critics are increasing," *The Miami Herald*, Jan. 22, 2006, p. A1.

[3] Quoted in Gary Marx, "Despite Fear, Some Step Forth," *Chicago Tribune*, May 1, 2006, p. A10.

[4] See "Cuba Releases Writer Imprisoned in 2003 Crackdown," (The Associated Press) *The New York Times*, Dec. 1, 2004, p. A5. See also, "Cuba: Heavy Sentences Are 'Totally Unjustified,' " Human Rights Watch, press release, April 7, 2003, http://hrw.org/english/docs/2003/04/07/cuba5520_txt.htm.

[5] See Christian Liberation Movement, "A Peaceful Path to Liberating Cuba," *The Miami Herald*, May 19, 2007, p. A20; Gary Marx, "Castro Foes Hold Meeting in Havana," *Chicago Tribune*, May 21, 2005, p. A3.

[6] Quoted in Tracey Eaton, "In Cuba, Castro Foes Wage Lonely Fight," *Dallas Morning News*, Dec. 19, 2004, p. A33.

[7] Quoted in Tracey Eaton, "Cuba Spies Say They Used Pro-Democracy Funds," *Dallas Morning News*, May 18, 2003, p. A24.

[8] *Ibid.*

authorities would feel free to block access by Cuban-Americans, who are seen, understandably, as carriers of the democracy virus. "My biggest worry is that they might have enough tourist dollars from all Americans that they might block Cuban-Americans from entering," says Saladrigas of the Cuba Study Group.

But those who support lifting the ban entirely argue that Delahunt's limited ban amounts to thinking small. "I'm worried about incrementalism — not because I don't think Cuban-Americans should be able to travel to Cuba; I think they should," said Julia Sweig, Latin America Studies director at the Council on Foreign Relations. "We need a broader policy that reflects our national interest, and right now we don't have one. . . . The better approach to take, in my view, is to say: Let a thousand flowers bloom legislatively, in terms of travel, in terms of getting rid of the embargo." [71]

Nevertheless, the incremental approach has cropped up elsewhere. A provision inserted in spending legislation would eliminate restrictions on agricultural sales to Cuba. Bush threatened to veto the bill if it reaches his desk. "Lifting the sanctions now . . . would provide assistance to a repressive regime at the expense of the Cuban people," Bush said. [72]

But the sales restrictions have long been unpopular in farm states. Rep. Jerry Moran, R-Kan., who authored the provision, noted that the United States trades freely with other repressive countries, including China. "Why the double standard?" he asked. [73]

The embargo argument has been under way for years. Rep. Diaz-Balart, a staunch sanctions supporter, expects no immediate major changes in Cuba policy. One indication, he says, was his success in getting the House to restore the administration's full request to a bill that would channel $45.7 million to Cuban pro-democracy organizations. He says an "overwhelming consensus" supports maintaining sanctions against Cuba until it meets democratic standards, including the release of political prisoners.

Good Health?

The summertime release of Michael Moore's latest movie, "Sicko," is turning up the volume on a long-running debate about Cuba's health system. In Moore's polemic, Cuba's free, universal health care easily bests the U.S. system, which leaves 45 million Americans without health insurance.

"There's a reason the World Health Organization [WHO] ranks [Cuba's] health-care system [among] the best in the Third World and that people from Latin America come there for their health care," Moore told *Time.* [74]

According to WHO, Cubans have virtually the same life expectancy as Americans and a better infant-mortality rate: six deaths per 1,000 live births vs. seven in the United States. In Brazil, Latin America's most populous country and not its poorest, the infant-mortality rate is 28 per 1,000 live births. [75]

Another new American film, "¡SALUD!" ("Health!") also portrays Cuba's universal-access medical system as a model. In an interview in the film, former President Jimmy Carter says, "Of all the so-called developing nations, Cuba has by far the best health system. And their outreach program to other countries is unequaled anywhere." [76]

The film's Web site does note that Cuba's health resources are being stretched, in large part because the country sends thousands of doctors abroad — mainly to Africa and Latin America. Some 20,000 Cuban physicians are in Venezuela alone. [77]

"It's true that Cuba until a few years ago enjoyed a public health system that compared favorably to those of other countries in the Caribbean and in Africa," Pollán of Ladies in White says from Havana. "But the Cuban people presently lack doctors and medicine. It's noticeable. In clinics where there had been five or six family-medicine doctors, there may be two. Where there were two, perhaps none. Doctors are going abroad; they're paid, and the money goes to the government. They're not serving the people."

Leonel Cordova, a Cuba-trained doctor in Miami who defected while working in Zimbabwe, said Moore and other visitors see only the tier of the health system reserved for party officials and foreigners. "It is as good as this one here [in Miami], with all the resources, the best doctors, the best medicines, and nobody pays a cent." [78]

But ordinary Cubans "have to bring their own food, soap, sheets — they have to bring everything," Cordova said. [79]

Bella Thomas, a British journalist who lived in Cuba in the 1990s, returned this year and found the health system "ragged." Cubans often have to pay bribes to get treatment, she wrote. At a hospital for ordinary Cubans, "I was appalled by the hygiene and amazed at the antiquity of the building and some of the equipment," she noted. [80]

Still, Cuba's ability to send so many doctors abroad testifies to the extent of its medical-education program. Other health advantages may come, paradoxically, from hardship. Cuba's strained transportation system means that people do plenty of walking, according to Richard N. Butler, an expert on aging and admirer of the Cuban medical system. Nor is obesity a problem. Cuba, he notes, does not enjoy a "surfeit of food." [81]

Raúl Who?

Outside Cuba, Fidel Castro's diminutive younger (by five years) brother would pass unrecognized, certainly in the United States (outside Miami).

Raúl may suffer from an image as his brother's puppet, but even a Cuba-watcher who has documented Raúl's subordinate status warns against underestimating the only defense minister Cuba has had since 1959. "Unlike his brother, he has never been motivated by an ego-charged quest for fame and glory or internationalist gratification," former CIA officer Latell writes. "He worries more about the economic hardships the Cuban people endure and has been the most influential advocate in the regime for liberalizing economic reforms." [82]

AT ISSUE

Is the Cuban government a threat to the United States?

YES
Frank Calzón
Executive Director, Center for a Free Cuba

Written for *CQ Researcher*, July 2007

The Department of State lists the Castro dynasty as a "state sponsor of terror." Castro provides safe haven for U.S. fugitives, including killers of American police officers. The Castros' 50-year effort to harm Americans did not start when Fidel urged Moscow to drop an atomic bomb on the United States in 1962 and did not end with the collapse of the Soviet Union. Today he nurtures like-minded regimes in Latin American nations, such as Venezuela and Bolivia, that share his hostility to American democracy.

Castro has always denied involvement in drug trafficking, but in July 1989 he brought Gen. Arnaldo Ochoa before a kangaroo court, charged him with narco-trafficking and promptly executed him. Ochoa, an unlikely suspect, had just returned from years in Africa leading Cuban armies. Cuba remains a transshipment point for drugs, and the U.S. Coast Guard — which has Castro's permission to return Cuban refugees captured on the high seas back to the island — is not allowed to enter Cuban waters when in hot pursuit of drug smugglers.

Castro's communist regime is a threat because it is just 90 miles from the U.S. coast, and whatever happens on the island is likely to spill over into the Southeast. Despite Castro's gloating about his health-care system, Cuba has suffered through several dengue fever epidemics; the AIDS crisis is partly due to the increase in prostitution and to Castro's refusal to reallocate resources he uses for propaganda and his penchant for inviting thousands to visit him with all expenses paid.

Those who minimize Castro's threat refuse to mention Ana Belen Montes, a high-ranking U.S. defense-intelligence analyst who pleaded guilty in March 2002 of spying for Havana. In her work for the Pentagon assessing the level of Castro's threat, she had access not only to intelligence about Cuba but also to American military secrets about hostile regimes. Havana shared the information she provided with America's enemies. She is now serving a 25-year sentence. Unfortunately, Montes' many years of telling American generals that Castro was not a threat continues to be accepted at face value by some who should know better.

If Washington were to forgive and forget, others thinking about doing harm to America will conclude that no matter how despicable their behavior — like the shooting down of American unarmed civilian aircraft in international airspace in the Florida Straits in 1996 — after a certain interval the U.S. would no longer hold them accountable for their crimes.

NO
Wayne S. Smith
Director, Cuba Program, Center for International Policy

Written for *CQ Researcher*, July 2007

The Cold War is long over. There are no longer Soviet troops in Cuba. Cuba has scaled back its own armed forces, and even without that would present no threat whatever to the United States. Some of its aircraft could reach Florida — but only if they could penetrate U.S. air defenses, which seems unlikely. But even if some got through, however, they have no weapons of mass destruction to deliver.

Back in March 2004, then-Undersecretary of State John Bolton charged that Cuba was "developing a limited biological weapons (BW) effort" and remained "a terrorist BW threat to the U.S."

But Bolton presented not a shred of evidence to back up his allegations, and, interestingly, in subsequent reports the State Department has not repeated his charge. Further, the Center for Defense Information and the Center for International Policy sent several delegations to investigate and found no evidence at all that Cuba was in any way involved in biological weapons. As retired Marine Gen. Charles Wilhelm put it after a visit: "While Cuba has the capability to develop and produce chemical and biological weapons, nothing that we saw or heard led us to the conclusion that they are proceeding on this path."

The State Department claims Cuba endorses terrorism as a policy and thus represents a threat. But, in fact, Cuba has condemned terrorism in all its manifestations, has signed all 12 U.N. anti-terrorist resolutions and offered to sign bilateral agreements with the United States to cooperate in efforts against terrorism. The Bush administration has consistently ignored the offer.

The United States has no evidence at all that Cuba is involved in terrorist activities. Not surprisingly, then, the annual State Department report on Cuba as a terrorist state puts forward what can only be described as misleading evidence. For example, it complains that "Cuba did not attempt to track, block or seize terrorist assets, although the authority to do so is contained in Cuba's Law 93 Against Acts of Terrorism."

But the obvious response to that is, "What assets?" There is no evidence that al Qaeda or any other foreign, terrorist organization has assets in Cuba. And so, there is nothing to seize. The statement does make clear, however, that Cuba has laws on the books against acts of terrorism.

As though grasping for something — anything — the report complains that Cuba "maintains friendly ties with Iran and North Korea." True, but unless there is some evidence that those ties extend to cooperation in terrorist activities or planning — and no such evidence is presented — they are not pertinent to the question of whether Cuba is or is not a "terrorist state."

To date, however, the U.S. has presented no evidence whatever that Cuba is a terrorist state.

But no one, Latell included, mistakes Raúl for a softy. Following the revolutionary army's victory, Raúl conducted the mass execution of 70 enemy prisoners, who were machine-gunned as they stood in front of a newly dug trench. [83]

Cuban artists and intellectuals have never forgotten Raúl's role in purges of the 1960s, in which longhairs and those identified as homosexuals were sent to labor camps run by the military. In a 1984 documentary on persecution of gays in the early revolutionary period, Heberto Padilla — a poet who left the country after falling out of favor with the government — traced the camps' origin to a trip by Raúl to then-communist Bulgaria. Officials there told him that they had found a way to deal with "antisocial" behavior. "'We have a special camp for antisocial elements, especially the homosexuals you're so concerned about,' " Padilla recounts. [84]

The Cuban government has repented its early views on homosexuals. In fact, one of Raúl's daughters, a psychologist, directs the National Center for Sexual Education and crusades for the rights of gays and transsexuals. Of her father's views, she told *The New York Times,* "He has told me he supports me, that he supports the personal rights of homosexuals." [85]

But Raúl's less benign side was on display long after the revolution. Appearing at the military tribunal in 1989 for his own long-time comrade-in-arms, Gen. Ochoa, and other high-ranking officials, Castro delivered an impassioned denunciation of Ochoa that was taken as a demand for the death sentence. Ochoa's crimes, he said, had been "'a stab in the back and a slap in the face of the fatherland." [86]

Yet, at Raúl Castro's first major public appearance following his brother's semiretirement, the heir apparent seemed to validate hopes that he's open to even more than economic change. "Let me take this opportunity to express our willingness to settle the long U.S.-Cuba disagreement at the negotiating table," Raúl said at a military parade in Havana on Dec. 2, 2006. "After almost half a century, we are prepared to wait patiently for the moment when common sense takes root in the halls of power in Washington." [87]

Some U.S.-based supporters of democratic change urged the Bush administration to accept the apparent invitation. "What Raúl was saying in his message to Washington was that a Cuba without [Fidel] Castro is a blank slate for everyone, and that it would be better if the two countries were to normalize relations," said Marifeli Pérez-Stable, vice president for democratic governance at Inter-American Dialogue. [88]

The Bush administration rejected the feeler. "I don't see how that really furthers the cause of democracy in that country, where you have dialogue with a dictator-in-waiting who wants to continue the form of governance that has really kept down the Cuban people for all these decades," State Department spokesman Sean McCormack said. [89]

Weeks later, when a congressional delegation visited Havana, it was not granted an audience with Raúl. [90]

The episode reinforced the atmosphere of mystery that surrounds Cuba's designated leader. "The most honest answer with Raúl is, 'Who the hell knows?' " says Erikson of Inter-American Dialogue. "You could argue he's going to collapse the day after [assuming full power]. You could argue he's going to manage things swimmingly."

OUTLOOK

"Economic Jewel"?

"What we would like to see is a transition along the lines of what we have seen in the Czech Republic, in Poland or in Spain," says Calzón of the Committee for a Free Cuba. That is political shorthand for the generally peaceful end to a dictatorship and the rapid building of a democracy.

The Cuban government rejects that vision and for years has called "transition," the term used by American officials, a euphemism for the overthrow of the Cuban government.

"We have the right to think the worst," said Ricardo Alarcón, a veteran Cuban diplomat who now presides over the country's congress, after the Bush administration unveiled its most recent transition plan last year. "We have the right to think about an attempt to assassinate Fidel, or a war."

War or assassination aside, whether Cuba in 10 years will bear any resemblance to, say, Poland 10 years after the Soviet collapse depends to a great extent on events that occur sooner than that.

If the Castro brothers die in relatively quick succession, says Kavulich of the U.S.-Cuba Trade & Economic Council, "At that point you've got a collective leadership that is heavy on military." Unlike their predecessors, the new leaders might have to figure out how to keep Cuba living within its means.

If Venezuela's Chávez remains in power, Cuba likely would still be able to count on him, Kavulich says. China is less of a sure bet.

A lessening of foreign subsidies would bring Cuba face-to-face with the need to carve out a new relationship with the United States — and for U.S. policy itself to change. But, says Peters of the Lexington Institute, "As Cuba changes, that will drive change here. After Fidel goes, I don't think the successor government is going to abandon socialism or rush to change the political system, but I do think they will open up the economy. And if there's any positive dynamic going on in Cuba, that will make people here pay closer attention."

Peters and others also foresee political changes in the Cuban-American community that will make more Cuban-Americans willing to deal with successors to Fidel Castro who haven't completely broken with the Marxist-Leninist model.

Regardless of how accurate that assessment of Cuban-Americans proves to be, one point on which politically opposite Cuban-Americans see eye-to-eye is Cuba's future.

"When Cubans can work hard for their families and retain the fruits of their labor, they will soon reconstruct Cuba," says Rep. Diaz-Balart, who argues that Cuban-Americans' views on Cuba remain largely unchanged. "Cuba is going to be an economic jewel within 10 years of the transition" from Fidel's rule.

Saladrigas, the Miami businessman who favors a more open attitude to Cuba's newest group of leaders, paints the future in similar colors. "Cuba's population is incredibly well-educated in relation to the rest of Latin America," he says. "And people forget that black markets are quintessentially free markets, so they have free market experience. And the Cuban-American community has a lot of knowledge, resources and goodwill to contribute."

But that community — whose first members, in the early 1960s, thought they'd be returning to Cuba in a matter of months — has lived with disappointment for decades. Hence, even some optimists temper their hopes. Democratic activist Garcia of Miami agrees with Saladrigas on Cuba's strengths among its own population and those of Miami Cubans. "If you can create call centers in Pakistan, I can only imagine what could happen 90 miles from the United States," he says.

But Cuban-Americans have seen their hopes dashed before. "I've sat at the dinner table of my home for the past 42 years and heard, 'Next year in Havana,' " says Garcia, who was born in the United States of Cuban refugee parents. "I know from my Jewish friends that it took them a few thousand years to reach Jerusalem. There is no question that Cuba will be a different nation, but how different depends on what the Cuban leadership decides to do and what the United States decides to do. Maybe it's in the interest of both to keep the status quo."

NOTES

1. For Spanish-speakers, the untranslated video can be seen at www.cubainformacion.tv/index.php?option= com_content&task=view&id=767&Itemid=86. For an English-language transcript see "Cuba's Fidel Castro gives TV interview," BBC Monitoring Latin America — Political, June 6, 2007. Castro visited Vietnam on Sept. 12-17, 1973. See "Castro Speech Database," Latin American Network Information Center, University of Texas, http://lanic.utexas.edu/ project/castro/1973/.

2. See "Cuba's Fidel Castro," *ibid*. On Castro's speech-making history, see Tad Szulc, *Fidel: A Critical Portrait* (2000), pp. 22-23.

3. See Will Weissert, "Healthier looking Castro gives long TV interview," The Associated Press, June 6, 2007.

4. See Manuel Roig-Franzia, "Ailing Castro Transfers Powers," *The Washington Post*, Aug. 1, 2006, p. A14.

5. Quoted in Jim Rutenberg, "Bush Touches on Cuba After Castro," *The New York Times*, June 29, 2007, p. A12.

6. See Lesley Clark and Beth Reinhard, "Cuba without Castro holds risks for GOP," *The Miami Herald*, Aug. 6, 2006, p. 21; Lesley Clark, "Kerry made inroads into Hispanic vote," *The Miami Herald*, Nov. 10, 2004, p. B6.

7. See Tom Gjelten, "Cuba's Castro an Inspiration, Not a Role Model," National Public Radio, Sept. 15, 2006.

8. See "Report to the President," Commission for Assistance to a Free Cuba, July, 2006, p. 19; www.cafc.gov/rpt/.

9. See Francisco Wong-Diaz, "Castro's Cuba: Quo Vadis?," U.S. Army War College, December 2006, p. 32; www.strategicstudiesinstitute.army.mil/pdf-files/PUB744.pdf.

10. Quoted in Frances Robles, "Cuban government blasts U.S. funding of anti-Castro activities," *The Miami Herald*, July 12, 2006.

11. See "After Fidel: A New Day for America's Relations with Cuba and Latin America?" NDN, Feb. 7, 2007 (video); www.ndn.org/media/afterfidelforumvideo.html; and "U.S.-Cuba Policy: Reflection on Failure," New America Foundation, April 18, 2007; http://newamerica.net/events/2007/us_cuba_policy_reflections_on_failure.

12. See "Proclama del Comandante en Jefe Fidel Castro al pueblo de Cuba," July 31, 2006; www.cadenagramonte.cu/noticias/agosto_06/010806_03.asp.

13. See Anita Snow, "Cuba Mourns Revolution's 'First Lady,'" The Associated Press, June 22, 2007.

14. The memo is accessible at www.gwu.edu/~nsarchiv/NSAEBB/NSAEBB222/family_jewels_pt1_ocr.pdf. Details concerning the CIA papers are accessible at the National Security Archive; www.gwu.edu/~nsarchiv/NSAEBB/NSAEBB222/index.htm.

15. Quoted in Will Weissert, "Cuba: 1960 plot to kill Castro reflects current U.S. policy," The Associated Press, June 30, 2007.

16. See "Cuba Transition Project," Institute for Cuban and Cuban-American Studies, University of Miami; http://ctp.iccas.miami.edu/main.htm.

17. See Damian J. Fernandez, "The Greatest Challenge: Civic Values in Post-Transition Cuba," Cuba Transition Project, University of Miami, 2003, p. ii; http://ctp.iccas.miami.edu/Research_Studies/DJFernandez.pdf.

18. *Ibid.*, p. 16.

19. See Brian Latell, *After Fidel: The Inside Story of Castro's Regime and Cuba's Next Leader* (2005), pp. 145-146.

20. See Hugh Thomas, *Cuba: The Pursuit of Freedom* (1971), pp. 817, 857-860.

21. See Mark P. Sullivan, "Cuba: U.S. Restrictions on Travel and Remittances," Congressional Research Service, updated May 3, 2007, pp. 3-4; www.fas.org/sgp/crs/row/RL31139.pdf. The case is *Regan v. Wald*, 468 U.S. 222 (1984).

22. *Ibid.*, p. 4.

23. See Sullivan, *op. cit.*, pp. 2-6.

24. See Barbara Crossette, "U.S., Linking Cuba to 'Violence,' Blocks Tourist and Business Trips," *The New York Times*, April 20, 1982, p. A1.

25. Sullivan, *op. cit.*, p. 5.

26. See Charles B. Rangel and Jeff Flake, "Time for America to be Relevant in Cuba," *The Washington Post* [op-ed], April 14, 2007, p. A19.

27. For reports of discrimination against Cubans, see Matthew Campbell, "Cuba's dissident democrats stir as the Castros lie low," *Sunday Times* (London), Aug. 13, 2006, p. A24; Clarence Page, "Cuba's Double Vision: Dollarized Socialism," *Chicago Tribune*, May 26, 2004, p. C9; Thomas Ginsberg, "Repression still the rule for Cubans," *Philadelphia Inquirer*, March 19, 2002, p. A1.

28. See Sullivan, *op. cit.*, p. 5.

29. Quoted in Abby Goodnough and Terry Aguayo, "Limits on Trips to Cuba Cause Split in Florida," *The New York Times*, June 24, 2004, p. A1.

30. For Roca's sentence and background see Juan O. Tamayo, "Four Cuban Dissidents Convicted," *The Miami Herald*, March 16, 1999, p. A1. For release, see "Former President Jimmy Carter Holds Press Conference in Havana, Cuba," CNN transcript, April 17, 2002; http://transcripts.cnn.com/TRANSCRIPTS/0205/17/se.02.html.

31. "State Sponsors of Terror Overview," U.S. State Department, April 28, 2006; www.state.gov/s/ct/rls/crt/2005/64337.htm.

32. See John R. Bolton, "Beyond the Axis of Evil: Additional Threats From Weapons of Mass Destruction," [speech transcript], May 6, 2002; www.state.gov/t/us/rm/9962.htm.

33. Quoted in Sonni Efron, "Threats Overstated by Bush Official, Critics Contend," *Los Angeles Times*, Nov. 3, 2003, p. A1.

34. *Ibid.*

35. See "The Cuban Threat to U.S. National Security," Defense Intelligence Agency, undated; www.fas.org/irp/dia/product/980507-dia-cubarpt.htm, and Department of Defense, press release, May 6, 1998; www.fas.org/irp/news/1998/05/b05061998_bt213-98.html.

36. See Latell, *op. cit.*, p. 227. See also Tim Golden, "Ex-U.S. Aide Sentenced to 25 Years for Spying for Cuba," *The New York Times*, Oct. 17, 2002, p. A14.

37. See in *The Miami Herald*, Jay Weaver, "FIU Couple Heading to Jail," Feb. 28, 2006, p. B1; "The Cuban Five Spy Case," Aug. 11, 2006 (chronology), p. B6; "Spy Case Reaches Crucial Point," Feb. 13, 2006, p. B1; Lydia Martin, "Spy Culture Takes Toll on Exiles' Psyche," Feb. 8, 2006, p. A1.

38. See Steven Metz and Douglas V. Johnson II, "Asymmetry and U.S. Military Strategy: Definition, Background and Strategic Concepts," Strategic Studies Institute, U.S. Army War College, January 2001.

39. Quoted in Hugh Thomas, *Cuba: The Pursuit of Freedom* (1971), pp. 1083-1084, 1460.

40. See Thomas, *ibid.*, pp. 1049-1064; Latell, *op. cit.*, pp. 124-129.

41. See Silvia Pedraza, "Cuba's Refugees: Manifold Migrations," paper presented at Fifth Annual Meeting of the Association for the Study of the Cuban Economy (ASCE), Aug. 10-12, 1995, p. 315; http://lanic.utexas.edu/la/cb/cuba/asce/cuba5/FILE2 6.PDF.

42. *Ibid.*, pp. 315-316.

43. See Latell, *op. cit.*, p. 152.

44. See Thomas H. Skidmore and Peter H. Smith, *Modern Latin America* (1989), p. 274.

45. See Jon Lee Anderson, *Che Guevara: A Revolutionary Life* (1997).

46. See Skidmore and Smith, *op. cit.*, pp. 130-137.

47. See "Conflicting Missions: Secret Cuban Documents on History of Africa Involvement," National Security Archive, April 1, 2002; www.gwu.edu/~nsarchiv/ NSAEBB/NSAEBB67.

48. See Pamela S. Falk, "Cuba in Africa," *Foreign Affairs*, summer 1987, p. 1077.

49. See Clifford Krauss, "U.S. and Soviets Jointly Urge Settlement in Salvador," *The New York Times*, Oct. 19, 1990, p. A3; James LeMoyne, "The Guerrilla Network," *The New York Times Magazine*, April 6, 1986, p. 16; Charles A. Krause, "Top Nicaraguan Minister on Undisclosed Mission to Cuba," *The Washington Post*, Aug. 16, 1979, p. A16.

50. Excerpts of the trial, which was filmed for Cuban television, are accessible at www. youtube.com/ watch?v=RrXX06kyI8c&mode=related&search=. See also Julia Preston, "Cuba Sentences Officers to Death for Corruption," *The Washington Post*, July 8, 1989, p. A1.

51. For a detailed account of the case, and the theories surrounding it, see Andrés Oppenheimer, *Castro's Final Hour* (1993).

52. Marjorie Miller, "Creeping Capitalist Tide Washes Up on Cuba Shores," *Los Angeles Times*, March 15, 1993, p. A4. Also, see Larry Rohter, "Cuba, Eager for Tourist Dollars, Dusts Off Its Vacancy Sign," *The New York Times*, Oct. 19, 1995, p. A14; Tim Golden, "Cuba's Economy, Cast Adrift, Grasps at Capitalist Solutions," *The New York Times*, July 12, 1993, p. A1; Howard W. French, "Cuba's New Hotels Dream of Dollars," *The New York Times*, March 31, 1991, Sect. 5 (Travel), p. 8.

53. See Peter Katel and Carroll Bogert, "The 'Worms' Become Butterflies," *Newsweek*, April 25, 1994, p. 38.

54. See Paul Knox, "Resist siren call of vice, Pope warns followers," *The Globe and Mail* (Toronto), Jan. 24, 1998, p. A14. Also, Linda Diebel, "Battle fatigue: A gaunt Castro and his weary (and wary) nation send a sad farewell to the Pope," *The Toronto Star*, Feb. 1, 1998, p. D4.

55. See "Teen flees Cuba on wind surfer," The Associated Press, March 4, 1990; "3 Cubans Windsurf to Freedom," *Chicago Tribune* (Knight Ridder-Tribune), May 1, 1994, p. A22; Phil Gunson, "Doctor's Epic Windsurf to Freedom of a Sort," *The Guardian* (London), Aug. 31, 1994, p. A7.

56. See Patrick J. Sloyan, "Refugee Flood; U.S. weighs plans to divert Cubans," *Newsday*, Aug. 19, 1994, p. A3.

57. See "Castro says Cuba will allow people to leave if USA fails to guard its coast," BBC Summary of World Broadcasts, Aug. 8, 1994. See also Sloyan, *ibid.*

58. See John M. Broder, "Clinton Halts Special Treatment for Cubans," *Los Angeles Times*, Aug. 20, p. A1.

59. See "Visa Lottery for Cubans," The Associated Press, Oct. 12, 1994.

60. See Yves Colon, "Touching Land Defines Who Stays, Goes," *The Miami Herald*, June 30, 1999, p. A15.

61. See Gail Epstein Nieves, "Basulto Warned Before First Trip," *The Miami Herald*, March 8, 2001, p. B1.

62. See Ann Devroy, "Clinton to Tighten Sanctions on Cuba," *The Washington Post*, Feb. 27, 1996, p. A1.

63. See Caroline Brothers, "Britain may retaliate for Helms-Burton Act," *Reuters*, May 3, 1996.

64. See "3 Who Survived Sinking Won't Be Deported," *The New York Times*, Nov. 27, 1999, p. A11.

65. See David Gonzalez, "Cuban Government Enters Fight for Boy," *The New York Times*, Nov. 30, 1999, p. A16.

66. See Mike Clary, "Two Nations Tug at 5-Year-Old Survivor," *Los Angeles Times*, Nov. 30, 1999, p. A1.

67. See Deborah Sharp, "Repatriation of 'miracle child' devastates exiles," *USA Today*, June 29, 2000, p. A3.

68. See Abby Goodnough and Marc Lacey, "Legal Victory by Militant Cuban Exile Brings Both Glee and Rage," *The New York Times*, May 10, 2007, p. A20.

69. See Oscar Corral, "Papers Connect Exile to Bomb Plot," *The Miami Herald*, May 10, 2005, p. A1. For a series of declassified government documents on Posada see "Luis Posada Carriles: The Declassified Record," National Security Archive, May 10, 2005; www.gwu.edu/~nsarchiv/NSAEBB/NSAEBB153/index.htm.

70. Quoted in Goodnough and Lacey, *op. cit.*

71. Latell, *op. cit.*

72. Quoted in Michael R. Crittenden, "House Keeps Trade Language in Spending Bill Despite Veto Threat," *CQ Today*, June 28, 2007.

73. *Ibid.*

74. Quoted in Jeffrey Kluger, "Moore in the E.R.," *Time*, May 28, 2007, p. 48.

75. See "Core Health Indicators," World Health Organization, regularly updated; www.who.int/whosis/database/core/core_select_process.cfm.

76. Quoted in "Is Michael Moore Right About Cuba?" PRNewswire, June 28, 2007; www.prnewswire.com/cgi-bin/stories.pl?ACCT=104&STORY=/www/story/06-28-2007/0004617479&EDATE=.

77. See "Cuba and Global Health" and "Cuba's Health System," in "¡SALUD!," 2006; www.saludthefilm.net/ns/main.html. See also, "Venezuela medics march over jobs," BBC, July 15, 2005; http://news.bbc.co.uk/1/hi/world/americas/4688117.stm.

78. Quoted in Anthony DePalma, " 'Sicko,' Cuba and the '120 Years Club,' " *The New York Times*, May 27, 2007, Sect. 4, p. 3.

79. *Ibid.*

80. See Bella Thomas, "A Cuban Death Rehearsal," *Prospect Magazine* (U.K.), June 2007; www.prospectmagazine.co.uk/article_details.php?id=9636.

81. Quoted in DePalma, *op. cit.*

82. See Latell, *op. cit.*, p. 246.

83. See Anderson, *op. cit.*, p. 388.

84. Quoted in Larry Kart, "Almendros — the Anti-Castro Director Who Put the Leftists on Guard," *Chicago Tribune*, Feb. 3, 1985, Arts Section, p. 28.

85. Quoted in Marc Lacey, "A Castro Strives to Open Cuban Society's Opinions on Sex," *The New York Times*, June 9, 2007, p. A4.

86. Quoted in Julia Preston, "Cuban General Said to Admit Crimes," *The Washington Post*, June 27, 1989, p. A10.

87. Quoted in Michael Langan, "Raúl Castro seeks negotiations with US," Agence France-Presse, Dec. 3, 2006.

88. *Ibid.*

89. *Ibid.*

90. See Julia Preston, "Castro to Recover but Not Return, Cubans Say," *The New York Times*, Dec. 18, 2006, p. A6.

BIBLIOGRAPHY

Books

Anderson, Jon Lee, *Che: A Revolutionary Life*, **Grove Press, 1997.**
An American journalist combed a wide range of sources to write a dispassionate, comprehensive account of the life of one of the most fascinating figures in Cuban revolutionary history.

Bardach, Ann Louise, *Cuba Confidential: Love and Vengeance in Havana and Miami*, **Vintage, 2003.**
An American journalist reports on the tangled family and political connections between Cuba and Miami, with a hard look at the Elián Gonzalez drama and exile politics in Florida.

Castro, Fidel, *War, Racism and Economic Injustice: The Global Ravages of Capitalism*, **Ocean Press, 2001.**
Castro expounds on numerous economic and political topics, including the "war on terror," in this collection of his speeches in several countries, including the United States.

Chomsky, Aviva, and Pamela Maria Smorkaloff, eds., *The Cuba Reader: History, Culture, Politics*, **Duke University Press, 2003.**
Selections from works by historians, poets, novelists and political figures provide an accessible introduction to Cuba.

Corbett, Ben, *This is Cuba: An Outlaw Culture Survives*, **Westview, 2002.**
An American freelance journalist digs into the gritty realities of day-to-day life in Cuba, including the black market, official corruption and prostitution.

Latell, Brian, *After Fidel: The Inside Story of Castro's Regime and Cuba's Next Leader*, **Palgrave, 2005.**
After a career monitoring Cuba for the CIA, Latell sketches the complicated relationship between the Castro brothers and its implications for the country's future.

Thomas, Hugh, *Cuba: The Pursuit of Freedom*, **Harper & Row, 1971.**
This 1,696-page work by a leading British historian of Spain and the Americas remains the basic reference on Cuba.

Articles

"Communist Party strengthened but may not take control — Cuban speaker," *Pagina/12* **(Buenos Aires), via BBC Monitoring Latin America — Political, Aug. 15, 2006.**
Ricardo Alarcón, speaker of Cuba's National Assembly and a veteran diplomat, offers a detailed, official explanation of the power shift from Fidel to Raúl Castro.

Adams, David, "Raúl, He's the Pragmatic Castro," *St. Petersburg Times*, **Aug. 13, 2006.**
A veteran Latin America correspondent reports on hopes that Raúl Castro will undertake economic reform.

Pérez-Stable, Marifeli, "Chinese-Style Reforms Would be an Improvement," *The Miami Herald*, **(op-ed), July 5, 2007.**
China's economically free if politically limited system offers more to its citizens than Cuba does to Cubans, writes a Cuban-American political scientist.

Thomas, Bella, "A Cuban Death Rehearsal," *Prospect* **(U.K.), June 2007.**
A British journalist and former Havana resident returns to the island to find a grim, pessimistic atmosphere.

Williams, Carol J., "Pressure Grows to Prosecute Cuban Exile," *Los Angeles Times*, **May 10, 2007, p. A3.**
The release of a Cuban exile suspected of involvement in blowing up a Cuban airliner arouses widespread indignation in Miami.

Reports and Studies

"Report on the Cuba Transition Conference," The Brookings Institution, April 2, 2007.
This is the centrist think tank's account of a meeting held by experts on Cuba and the Cuban-American community, including a former U.S. diplomat in Cuba, to examine the difficulty of helping Cubans change Cuba from within.

"Report to the President," Commission for Assistance to a Free Cuba, State Department, July 2006.
Released weeks before Fidel Castro announced he was temporarily relinquishing power, the report outlines an ambitious program of support for dissidents and aid to a post-Castro government if it asks for assistance from the United States.

Mesa-Lago, Carmelo, "Growing Economic and Social Disparities in Cuba: Impact and Recommendations for Change," Cuba Transition Project, Institute for Cuban and Cuban-American Studies, University of Miami, 2002.
An expert on the Cuban economy examines the deterioration of Cuba's social-services safety net and possible remedies, including more foreign aid.

Sullivan, Mark P., "Cuba: Issues for the 110th Congress," Congressional Research Service, updated May 8, 2007.
A foreign policy specialist lays out a clear summary of Cuba-related matters pending before lawmakers.

For More Information

Asociación Encuentro de la Cultura Cubana, Infanta Mercedes 43, 1º A, 28020 Madrid, España; (011-34-91) 425 04 04; www.cubaencuentro.com. (Spanish only). Web site of an intellectual and political journal published by Spain-based exiles that includes work by contributors from Cuba.

Center for a Free Cuba, 1320 19th St., N.W., Suite 600, Washington, DC 20036; (202) 463-8430; www.cubacenter.org. Promotes human rights and transition to democracy.

Cuba Study Group, 611 Pennsylvania Ave., S.E., Suite 208, Washington, DC; (202) 544-5088; www.cubastudygroup.org. Fosters transition to a democratic, capitalist society in Cuba.

Cuba Transition Project, Institute for Cuban and Cuban-American Studies, University of Miami, P.O. Box 248174, Coral Gables, FL 33124; (305) 284-2822; http://ctp.iccas.miami.edu/main.htm. Publishes research and holds conferences and seminars concerning directions that change might take.

Cuban American National Foundation, 1312 S.W. 27th Ave., Miami, FL 33145; (305) 592-7768; www.canf.org. Cuban exile organization influential in advocating economic and political isolation of the present Cuban government.

The Cuban Triangle (blog), http://cubantriangle.blogspot.com. A compendium of events and observations by Washington-based Cuba-watcher Philip Peters of the Lexington Institute.

Emergency Network of Cuban-American Scholars and Artists, http://encasa-us-cuba.org. Advocates abolishing travel restrictions and other elements of what it calls failed U.S. policy toward Cuba.

Granma, Havana, Cuba, www.granma.cu/ingles/index.html. English-language Web site of Cuba's leading newspaper, published by the Cuban Communist Party; includes links to other official Cuban sites.

12

Afghanistan on the Brink

Roland Flamini

A Pakistani army helicopter patrols the troubled tribal area of North Waziristan, along the Pakistan-Afghanistan border in February 2007. The region has been a refuge for Taliban and al Qaeda militants since a U.S.-led alliance toppled the fundamentalist Taliban regime in Afghanistan in 2001. Some experts question whether the U.S-NATO alliance is swimming against the historical tide in trying to reshape the destiny of Afghans, often called unconquerable and ungovernable.

From *CQ Researcher*,
June 1, 2007.

The fabled Khyber Pass — linking Pakistan and Afghanistan — has long been synonymous with warfare in Central Asia. Since before Alexander the Great, invaders have used the rugged route through the Kush Mountains as the gateway to the Indian subcontinent. The British marched through it as well, coming from India, in three unsuccessful attempts to conquer Afghanistan.

Today, the Khyber is a paved road jammed with trucks, cars and brightly colored "jingle buses," and thousands of Taliban fighters and al Qaeda terrorists freely use it to cross from safe havens in Pakistan to try to take back Afghanistan from its fragile, new government.

It's been five years since a U.S.-led alliance toppled the fundamentalist Taliban regime after it refused to give up al Qaeda leader Osama bin Laden following the Sept. 11, 2001, terrorist attacks in the United States. The defiance cost the Taliban dearly. Its ranks decimated, it fled with its al Qaeda allies into the mountainous border areas between Afghanistan and Pakistan. But bin Laden is still at large and the regime is attempting a comeback, leaving Afghanistan's future far from certain.

The West has been only partially successful in establishing secular statehood and political and economic stability. President Hamid Karzai maintains a tenuous hold on just part of the country. But the Taliban — flush with money from a revived and booming opium trade — has garnered new recruits and weapons and is pushing to restore its draconian version of Islamic law in Kabul, the capital. As summer approaches and melting mountain snows clear the routes into Afghanistan, the Taliban has vowed to renew its efforts.

Afghans Live in a Dangerous Neighborhood

As the gateway to Central Asia, Afghanistan serves as a link between China, the Middle East and the Indian subcontinent. But it's a dangerous neighborhood. To the east is nuclear-armed Pakistan, where the Taliban and al Qaeda find refuge in lawless tribal areas along the border. (*See map, p. 305.*) India and China — two other nuclear powers — are also in the neighborhood, which includes Iran, Tajikistan, Uzbekistan and Turkmenistan.

Afghanistan at a Glance

Area: 647,500 sq. km.

Population: 31.9 million; growing at 2.63%/year (July 2007 est.)

Infant mortality: 157 deaths per 1,000 (2007 est.)

Labor force: 15 million (2004)

Unemployment rate: 40% (2005)

Religion: Sunni Muslim, 80%; Shiite Muslim, 19%; other, 1%

Languages: Dari (Afghan Persian) and Pashtu spoken by 50% and 35% of the population, respectively. Turkic languages — primarily Turkmen and Uzbek — are spoken by 11%. Balochi and Pashai are among Afghanistan's 30 minor languages.

Government: The president and two vice presidents are elected by direct vote for five-year terms. A president can be elected for two terms. The bicameral National Assembly consists of the Wolesi Jirga (House of People), which is allotted no more than 249 seats via direct election, and the Meshrano Jirga (House of Elders), which has 102 seats.

Economy: Recovering from decades of conflict, the economy has improved significantly since the fall of the Taliban in 2001, largely due to an infusion of international aid, recovery of the agricultural sector and growth of the service sector. The gross domestic product was $8.8 billion in 2006, and the per-capita GDP was around $275. In 2003, 53% of the population was living below the poverty line.

Communications hardware: 280,000 telephones, 1.4 million mobile phones and 22 Internet hosts serving around 30,000 users (2005).

Source: The World Factbook 2007, Central Intelligence Agency, 2007

Meanwhile, the Afghanistan conflict has put NATO's credibility and role in the post-Cold War era at stake. The venerable alliance has 36,750 troops serving in Afghanistan — the first time its forces have been deployed outside Europe. Also on the line is the Bush post-9/11 doctrine to bring democracy to Islamist regimes that could breed global jihadists.

Some question whether the NATO alliance is swimming against the historical tide in trying to reshape the destiny of Afghans, often called unconquerable and ungovernable. Others say America's quick-fix mentality is the wrong approach. The international community "needs to operate on a 10-to-20-year horizon," says Ashraf Ghani, former Afghan minister of finance and now chancellor of Kabul University.

To improve strained relations between Kabul and Pakistan, considered crucial for Afghanistan's recovery, a telephone hotline was installed early this year linking Karzai's office and that of his Pakistani counterpart, Gen. Pervez Musharraf. But since neither leader wants to talk to the other, it remains silent.

Karzai complains Musharraf is not doing enough to halt attacks in Afghanistan by the Pakistan-based Taliban. [1] Musharraf, who faces growing political unrest at home, counters that Karzai merely wants a scapegoat for his own inability to provide security. Their open hostility blocks Afghanistan's recovery and undermines the bilateral relationship between the two countries, felt most strongly along their 1,400-mile border of rugged, mountain terrain. [2]

Taliban militants, who controlled most of Afghanistan from 1996 until 2001, openly cross the porous border

Tribal Areas Harbor Guns, Drugs and Terrorists

Pakistan's Federally Administered Tribal Areas, stretching along the Pakistan-Afghanistan border, consist of seven Pashtun-dominated "agencies": Khyber, Kurram, Orakzai, Mohmand, Bajaur, North Waziristan and South Waziristan. The British created the enclave to give maximum autonomy to the fiercely independent Pashtuns and to serve as a buffer between then-undivided India and Afghanistan. Smuggling, drug trafficking and gun-running flourish in the region, often described as "lawless." During the 1980s, the tribal areas served as a base for the mujaheddin fighting the Soviet occupiers in Afghanistan. Today they are a safe haven for Taliban and al Qaeda insurgents.

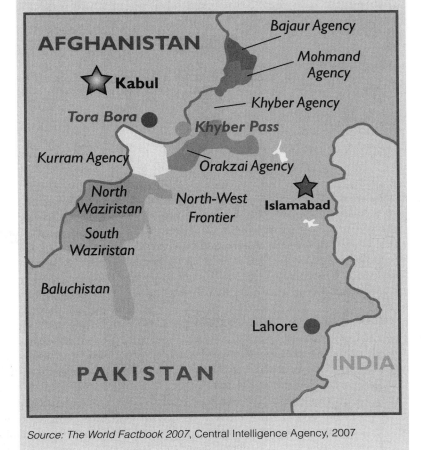

Source: The World Factbook 2007, Central Intelligence Agency, 2007

into Afghanistan and attack Afghan and Western troops or anyone thought to be cooperating with them. They then return to safety in Pakistan's North-West Frontier Province, Baluchistan and the lawless Federally

Foreign Troop Level Hits 50,000

Of the nearly 50,000 allied troops in Afghanistan, 27,000 are Americans: 12,000 serving in the U.S.-led coalition and 15,000 with NATO. The coalition has increased troop levels participating in Operation Enduring Freedom by only 2,800 since invading Afghanistan in 2001. NATO has more than quadrupled its troop levels since first deploying to Afghanistan in 2003.

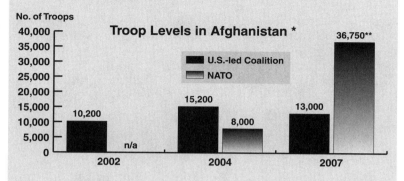

Troop Levels in Afghanistan *

No. of Troops

- U.S.-led Coalition
- NATO

2002: 10,200 (U.S.-led Coalition), n/a (NATO)
2004: 15,200 (U.S.-led Coalition), 8,000 (NATO)
2007: 13,000 (U.S.-led Coalition), 36,750** (NATO)

* U.S.-led coalition figures do not include U.S. troops serving under NATO.

** As of April 20, 2007

Sources: NATO, U.S. Department of Defense

Administered Tribal Areas (FATA) — all said to be sympathetic to or actually controlled by the Taliban.

"Waziristan [in the Federally Administered Tribal Areas] is virtually a criminal state, and Baluchistan is equally lawless," says Italian parliamentarian and foreign-policy specialist Margherita Boniver. "One has to wonder how much control Musharraf actually has over this situation."

Without question, his continued lack of determination in suppressing or denying refuge to the Taliban has been indispensable to its rapid recovery and resurgence. "Long-term prospects for eliminating the Taliban threat appear dim, so long as sanctuary remains in Pakistan," U.S. National Intelligence Director John Michael McConnell recently told the Senate Armed Services Committee. "And there are no encouraging signs that Pakistan is eliminating it." [3]

The cross-border antipathy doesn't help, and Karzai shares the blame for that. "Unless Afghanistan is good neighbors with Pakistan, it cannot survive," says Ishak Shahryar, Afghanistan's first ambassador to the United States after the defeat of the Taliban. "It doesn't make sense to antagonize Musharraf. For one thing, 90 percent

of Afghanistan's imports come through Pakistan."

But Pakistan is a tricky country with which to share a border, even without the Taliban threat. "We live in a very dangerous neighborhood," says former Afghan Foreign Minister Abdullah Abdullah. Indeed. Besides Pakistan, which has nuclear weapons, Afghanistan also shares the neighborhood with two other nuclear powers — India and China — plus Iran, Tajikistan, Uzbekistan and Turkmenistan.

The Taliban's re-emergence from its Pakistan sanctuary hampers the international community's efforts to establish a democracy in Afghanistan, as does Karzai's inability to control corruption or extend his authority over the entire country. With much of the country a patchwork of warlord-controlled fiefdoms, and the Taliban edging its way back into the south, critics derisively call Karzai "the mayor of Kabul."

There has been "an irrefutable loss of legitimacy [by] the government of Afghanistan among its people," said American Lt. Gen. Karl Eikenberry, deputy chairman of NATO's military committee. "People are asking, what is the government delivering? They have moved from a phase of pride in achieving democracy to disappointment in the government's delivery of services." [4]

In a 2002 speech to the Virginia Military Institute (VMI), President George W. Bush proclaimed his goal was "a stable government" in Afghanistan and launched a recovery plan he said would rival Gen. George C. Marshall's post-World War II reconstruction of Europe.

But has the international community lived up to its early promises to help? Close to $25 billion has been pledged in economic aid for reconstruction, but it's anyone's guess how much actually has been delivered or how it has been spent. Afghanistan became something of a black hole for foreign aid, analysts say, due to a dizzying combination of factors — security problems, questionable contracting practices, corruption, inefficiency, an initial preference for foreign contractors over cheaper

Afghan contractors, haste to show results at the expense of quality control and poor bookkeeping.

"Beltway bandits" — Washington-based contractors — saw to it that 80 cents of every U.S. aid dollar "went back to the United States," Ghani alleges.

So far, only about $13 billion of that $25 billion has been committed by the United States and Europe since 2001 — $10 billion of it from the United States — but those who keep track of the donations are unsure how much Japan and the Gulf States have contributed. [5] But even at $25 billion, the international community's pledge was less than the $30 billion over five years — plus another $15 billion in private investment — that Ghani and others have estimated would be needed to rebuild the war-torn country.

In February — five years after his VMI speech — Bush was less upbeat about progress in Afghanistan. The strengthened Taliban, operating out of "remote regions of Pakistan," was a renewed threat, he told the American Enterprise Institute (AEI), a conservative think tank in Washington. "We face a thinking [and] a tough enemy. They watch our actions. They adjust their tactics." [6]

With its military strength stretched due to the war in Iraq, the United States has turned to the North Atlantic military alliance for help, and Taliban fighters have been feeling the effect of battling modern, well-trained allied forces. The NATO deployment consists of troops from most of its 26 member countries, including 15,000 U.S. troops. Another 13,000 coalition forces (including 12,000 Americans) are still engaged in Operation Enduring Freedom, whose main task includes the continuing search for bin Laden.

Dutch Maj. Gen. Ton van Loon, until recently the NATO commander in Afghanistan's volatile south, told *The Washington Post* that insurgents have been pushed out of the southern regions where they had sought to gain a foothold, including Kandahar city and parts of Helmand province. The Taliban "will still be a force, but they don't have the initiative we have," van Loon said, and the anticipated major spring offensive had failed to materialize. [7] Military officials say they could hit the Taliban even harder if they were not barred from pursuing the enemy into their Pakistani hideouts.

But minor, daily clashes across the country are causing collateral damage among civilians — at least 380 deaths in the first four months of this year — and an angry, war-weary Afghan public is blaming U.S. and NATO firepower — especially airstrikes. [8]

Italian NATO soldiers guard a helicopter during a February 2007 operation in Herat province, where alliance forces are fighting Taliban insurgents. With most of its military resources tied up in Iraq, the Bush administration persuaded NATO to help fill the gap in Afghanistan. NATO now has nearly 38,000 troops in Afghanistan — 15,000 of them Americans.

AP Photo/Xinhua, Yu Zhixiao

A concerned President Bush dispatched Vice President Dick Cheney to the region in March to warn Musharraf that a new Democrat-dominated Congress intended to link further U.S. aid to Pakistan to greater efforts to restrain al Qaeda and the Taliban. On the same trip, Cheney also urged Karzai to beef up security and suppress Afghanistan's newly burgeoning $3 billion narcotics trade — a principal income source for Islamic militants and a major embarrassment to the Bush administration. (*See sidebar, p. 314.*) [9]

"Drug traffickers have a symbiotic relationship with insurgent and terrorist groups," wrote Antonio Maria Costa, executive director of the U.N. Office on Drugs and Crime. "Opium buys protection and pays for weapons and foot soldiers." [10] U.S. military forces in

Casting Off the Burqa: Still a Dream for Many

Taliban has executed those who teach, advocate for women

Television broadcasts of Afghan parliamentary sessions routinely show male and female members sitting side by side, and even show women rising to debate with their male colleagues. To the Afghan public — and to Afghan women in particular — such scenes are surreal.

In the real world, proximity between men and women is generally forbidden, and a woman who has the temerity to argue with a male, especially in public, could be putting herself in harm's way.

This disconnect captures the schizophrenic state in which Afghan women find themselves. The new constitution mandates that women, who make up 50 percent of the population, hold 27 percent of the parliamentary seats (68 out of 249 members) — a higher share than in the U.S. Congress. But in almost every other respect, the promise of a bright future for women in the "new" Afghanistan has faded.

In the "old" Afghanistan ruled by the repressive Taliban regime from 1996 to 2001, girls were barred from going to school, and women were forced to cover their bodies and faces in public. Even when they were encased in the famous, blue, face-hiding burqas, however, women could not leave their homes — to work or even to shop for food — unless accompanied by a male relative. Those who violated these or other rigid rules of behavior were subject to public punishment — and even execution. Thousands of women widowed by Afghanistan's decades of war — or who had no other male relative to accompany them — became prisoners in their own homes with no way of supporting their families — vividly portrayed in the critically acclaimed 2003 movie "Osama."

While the Taliban is no longer in charge and burqas are optional today, new laws passed to protect women are not being enforced. With the Taliban resurgent in some areas, Afghan women still live in fear. The burqa has returned to the streets, even in Kabul, and the continued savagery of a deep-rooted male-dominated culture coupled with disastrous economic conditions have combined to stifle hope and break the spirit.

Small wonder that 65 percent of Kabul's 50,000 widows, each responsible for an average of six dependents and left with no means of support, have told pollsters that they feel suicide is their only way out, reflecting their sense of helplessness even in today's society. [1] And it's not just the widows.

Despite new laws banning forced or child marriages or the exchange of girls to settle a debt or tribal score, up to 80 percent of Afghan women face forced marriages, and 57 percent of girls are married before the legal age of 16, according to the U.N. Development Fund for Women (UNIFEM). "Men in my country think that women are not . . . completely human," Afghan women's rights advocate Homa Sultani recently told CNN. [2] Some who see no escape from chronic abuse commit suicide by setting themselves on fire: 106 cases of self-immolation by women were reported in 2006, according to UNIFEM. [3]

"Young girls are killing themselves from frustration and because they feel there is no way out for them," Medica Mondiale spokeswoman Ancil Adrian-Paul told the BBC. [4] Why do they choose self-immolation? Kerosene and matches are easy to come by.

Small wonder, too, that the life expectancy of Afghan women is around 44 — some 20 years less than in Europe. [5] Afghanistan ranks second worldwide in deaths at childbirth, according to Hangama Anwari, commissioner of the Afghanistan Independent Human Rights Commission, who called the human rights situation of Afghan women "disastrous."

Speaking at a conference in Rome on Afghan womens'

Afghanistan originally resisted calls to help eradicate the country's poppy opium trade, arguing that it was not part of their assignment. But eventually the military agreed to provide logistical support once it became clear the illicit drug income was being used to arm the Taliban.

As the war in Afghanistan enters its sixth year, here are some of the questions being asked:

Did the United States desert Afghanistan for Iraq?

In February 2003, when the United States was mobilizing to invade Iraq, President Karzai flew to Washington to plead

rights in the post-Taliban era, she said, "Women do not have a place in the justice system and they are not guaranteed de facto equality of rights. The laws of divorce and the family need to be reviewed. Discrimination and abuse form part of a firmly rooted mentality, and rates of domestic violence and suicide are still high." [6]

President Karzai recently rebutted criticism of the lack of progress on women's rights by observing that women participate in government. But he has only one female cabinet minister, and she is responsible for women's affairs. Karzai also pointed out that 35 percent of Afghanistan's 6 million schoolchildren are girls — a major improvement from the days of the Taliban. [7]

But scholastic attendance has been dropping because the Taliban has been burning schools — 198 in 2006 — and murdering teachers, especially women who teach girls. [8] As of December, Taliban insurgents reportedly had killed at least 20 educators for teaching girls — dragging one male teacher from his school and beheading him. [9] According to a July 2006 Human Rights Watch report, most of the destroyed schools are in the southern provinces, where the Taliban has been most active. [10]

Karzai — who has told Western reporters that it will take a long time for attitudes about women to change in Afghanistan — shrugs off the burnings. "Schools get burned, but not every day," he told the Council on Foreign Relations in September 2006.

Last September the country was shocked when Taliban gunmen assassinated Safia Ama Jan, the local women's affairs director in the southern city of Kandahar and a well known, longtime champion of women's education. She was killed in broad daylight as she left for work.

So as they wait for long-held misogynist attitudes to change, many Afghan women are choosing to don the shapeless head-to-toe burqa again — just to be on the safe side in a land of hidden dangers.

AFP/Getty Images/Shah Marai

The face-hiding burqa is now optional in Afghanistan, but with the Taliban resurgent in some areas, many Afghan women, fearing violence, have donned them again.

[1] "Afghanistan: Democracy and Development: The Future Belongs to the Women," U.N. Development Fund for Women (UNIFEM), conference in Rome, Feb 15, 2007; and "Fact Sheet 2007," UNIFEM, May 2007.

[2] Anderson Cooper, Peter Bergen and Nic Robertson, "Afghanistan: The Unfinished War," transcript of "Anderson Cooper, 360 Degrees," CNN, May 10, 2007.

[3] UNIFEM, "Fact Sheet," *op. cit.*

[4] "Afghan women seek death by fire," BBC World News, Nov. 15, 2006.

[5] UNIFEM, "Fact Sheet," *op. cit.*

[6] Agenzia Italia, Feb. 16, 2007.

[7] "Afghanistan Five Years On," Council on Foreign Relations backgrounder, Oct. 5, 2006.

[8] Ann Jones, "Not the Same as Being Equal: Women in Afghanistan," www.truthout.org/docs_2006/020507H.shtml, Feb. 5, 2007.

[9] "Taliban Kills 2 Sisters for Crime of Teaching," The Associated Press, *The New York Times*, Dec. 10, 2006.

[10] See "Lessons in Terror Attacks on Education in Afghanistan," Human Rights Watch, July 2006; www.hrw.org/reports/2006/afghanistan0706/.

with the Bush administration not to abandon Afghanistan's recovery. [11] At the same time, seeing troops being rerouted from Afghanistan to Iraq, Foreign Minister Abdullah, complained, "The United States is leaving us in the lurch."

No reinforcements were arriving, Abdullah said, just when extra effort was needed to consolidate his country's recovery and finish mopping up remnants of the Taliban and al Qaeda. "Afghanistan is the real front line against terrorism, and yet the Bush administration is giving up," he said.

Two years later, Abdullah was more diplomatic, but the message was the same. He conceded, however, that

Getty Images/Paula Bronstein

Afghan officials count ballots after the Oct. 9, 2004, election in which Hamid Karzai was elected president. Karzai maintains a tenuous hold on only part of the country while the Taliban — flush with money from a revived and booming opium trade — has garnered new recruits and weapons.

after the fall of the Taliban the Afghans, in some cases, had unrealistic expectations.

Abdullah warned there was no quick fix for Afghanistan. "A country which was destroyed for 25 years couldn't be rebuilt in three-and-a-half years," he said, especially one that must rely on foreign support for its security and stability while it rebuilds. [12]

The U.S. Senate Foreign Relations Committee also cautioned the Bush administration not to detour from its efforts to rebuild Afghanistan and establish a secure democracy. "Our commitment to Afghanistan is also a demonstration of how we will approach post-conflict Iraq," said Chairman Richard G. Lugar, a Republican from Indiana. "Our credibility is on the line in these situations, and we must understand that failure to follow through could have extremely negative consequences." [13]

The belief that Afghanistan's recovery suffered when it slipped a few notches on the Bush administration's priorities list is widespread in the United States, Europe and Central Asia. Pakistani commentator Karamatullah Ghori calls it a blunder of "Himalayan" proportions. Neo-conservatives who were "calling the shots" misled Bush, Ghori continues, making him believe "Iraq would be a cakewalk."

Michael Scheuer, a former Central Intelligence Agency (CIA) officer in Afghanistan, agreed. "With the finite number of people who have any kind of pertinent experience," he said, "there was unquestionably a sucking away of resources from Afghanistan and al Qaeda to Iraq, just because it was a much bigger effort." [14]

Not surprisingly, conservative analysts reject this claim. "That's political posturing," snaps Danielle Pletka, vice president for foreign and defense policy at AEI. "We can certainly manage Afghanistan and Iraq. To suggest that the United States is only capable of handling one situation at a time is ridiculous. We certainly made some mistakes in Afghanistan, but we didn't neglect it." In fact, she contends, the United States was more effective at correcting mistakes in Afghanistan than in Iraq. "We woke up and smelled the coffee."

Defense specialist John Pike, who runs the globalsecurity.org Web site, says, "To say [Afghanistan] turned into a mess because of U.S. neglect, because Washington was too focused on Iraq, that's just a talking point. [It doesn't] explain what the U.S. mistakes are." [15]

Talking point or not, critics cite a variety of American mistakes in Afghanistan. At one period in 2004-2005, U.S. forces in Afghanistan had dropped to less than 10,000 personnel, compared to 130,000 in Iraq, and NATO was persuaded to step in to fill the gap. This was done by beefing up the International Security and Assistance Force (ISAF) originally established through U.N. mandate in 2002 to provide security and to train the Afghan army and police forces.

"The administration has picked the wrong fights at the wrong time, failing to finish the job in Afghanistan, which the world agreed was the central front in the war on radical fundamentalism, and instead rushing to war in Iraq," declared Sen. Joseph R. Biden, Jr., D-Del., now chairman of the Senate Foreign Relations Committee and an aspiring Democratic presidential candidate. [16]

Even former Republican House Speaker Newt Gingrich of Georgia is critical. "We are neither where we wanted to be, nor where we need to be: We have not defeated the Taliban in its sanctuaries in northwest Pakistan, and neither Afghanistan nor Pakistan is stable and secure," he told the AEI in 2006. [17]

U.S. economic-development aid also has been cut, even as reconstruction projects began to show signs of hasty and inferior workmanship. The aid budget request for Afghanistan fell from $2.2 billion in 2004 to $1.2 billion in 2005. In 2003 Congress earmarked $11 billion for Iraq and Afghan military operations, but less than $1 billion for reconstruction in Afghanistan. [18]

The United States wasn't the only country cutting back on aid. "The European Union . . . has not put into Afghanistan a tenth of the aid it has put into Iraq," despite the convening of four meetings of international donors, says Italian foreign policy specialist Boniver.

The Bush administration is defensive about charges of neglecting Afghanistan. "It was not possible to 'finish the job' in Afghanistan," Secretary of State Condoleezza Rice told Fox News last September. Bringing stability to Afghanistan "is going to be a long process." Nevertheless, she continued, "We have made enormous progress over the last four years. You actually have a national government that's elected. You now have for the people in Afghanistan the possibility of a better life." [19]

Still, the Taliban had returned "somewhat more organized and somewhat more capable than people would have expected," Rice admitted. But they were being beaten, she added. NATO "was destroying them in large numbers." [20]

Can Pakistan do more to clamp down on the Taliban?

In March 2007, Pakistani authorities arrested Mullah Obaidullah Akhund, a top Taliban strategist and the regime's former defense minister. Captured while visiting family in Quetta, the Baluchistan capital, Akhund is the most senior Taliban figure arrested in Pakistan since the U.S.-led Afghan offensive began in 2001. [21]

The timing of the arrest was seen as significant: Vice President Cheney was in Islamabad at the time, urging President Musharraf to do more to shut down the Taliban inside his country. "Akhund was arrested solely to keep Western governments at bay," former Pakistani Prime Minister Benazir Bhutto wrote a week later in *The Washington Post.* [22]

Since the 9/11 attacks the United States has paid Islamabad roughly $1 billion to apprehend terrorists. But according to *The New York Times*, Pakistan's patrols have diminished in the past eight months, in part because Musharraf signed a controversial agreement with border villages in September 2006 allowing local militias to secure the frontier. Musharraf agreed that tribal leaders in dangerous Waziristan province — an area bristling with AK-47s and rocket-propelled grenades — would prevent any Islamic militants from crossing into Afghanistan. In exchange, the Pakistani army would pull out of the region.

But Western military officials and diplomats say there is little sign the deal has lessened the flow of jihadists. Time

and again, NATO forces in Afghanistan have pursued fighters to the border, where the ban on hot pursuit into the latter's safe havens forces them to halt. But when NATO forces try to alert Pakistani authorities by radio of the location of the fighters, they get mixed results at best. [23]

"Calls to apprehend or detain or restrict these ongoing movements, as agreed, were sometimes not answered," said former NATO supreme commander from 2003 to 2006, Gen. James L. Jones. The Pakistani ambassador in Washington, however, denied any slackening of Pakistani border vigilance. [24]

Equally troubling are the insurgents' reported links with Pakistan's all-powerful Inter-Services Intelligence (ISI) agency. Its ties to the Taliban go back a long way. In 1992, it supported the Taliban's emerging drive to seize control in Afghanistan in hopes of establishing stability in a neighboring country that had been engulfed in violent unrest since the Soviet withdrawal in 1989.

U.S. journalist Arnaud de Borchgrave, a specialist on Pakistani affairs, says the ISI had 1,500 officers and operatives in Taliban-ruled Afghanistan in the late 1990s. "The country represented Pakistan's defense indepth in the event of an Indian invasion," de Borchgrave wrote, referring to Pakistan's neighboring nuclear arch rival. "Many of the ISI agents were veterans of the anti-Soviet guerrilla campaign that was fought by the mujaheddin under ISI direction, with funding and weapons from Saudi Arabia and the United States." [25]

Others question how much control Musharraf has over the lawless Pashtun area in the Federally Administered Tribal Areas. The Pakistani government has always conceded that its laws exist there only on the paved roads and cease where the pavement ends. The area is considered so perilous an outsider who enters a village without welcome is asking for death.

Musharraf frequently argues that hot pursuit by NATO forces inside Pakistan would make his government appear weak and undermine his position, potentially destabilizing Pakistan and opening the way for Islamic fundamentalists to take over Pakistan and its nuclear arsenal.

But his theory is disputed as self-serving. "The notion of Musharraf's regime as the only non-Islamist option is disingenuous and the worst type of fear mongering," writes former Prime Minister Bhutto. [26]

Islamic parties have never gained a majority in any free parliamentary elections in Pakistan, according to

1900s-1930s *Afghanistan becomes independent; tribal chiefs oppose reforms. Moscow's influence grows.*

1919 Afghanistan gains independence from Britain.

1926 Amanullah Khan begins push for a reformist monarchy.

1929 Nadir Shah becomes king.

1933 Shah is assassinated; his teenage son, Zahir Shah, succeeds him.

1940s-1960s *Afghanistan remains neutral in World War II. U.S. competes with Moscow for influence.*

1953 Gen. Madmoud Daoud, the king's cousin, becomes prime minister and begins to modernize, underwritten by the Soviets.

1964 Daoud resigns under pressure from U.S. . . . Zahir Shah establishes a constitutional monarchy, with free elections and female suffrage, triggering resistance.

1965 Women vote for the first time.

1970s *Monarchist Afghanistan is declared a republic. Power struggle leads to Soviet invasion.*

1973 King Shah is deposed; Afghanistan becomes republic under Daoud.

1978 Daoud is killed in leftist coup.

1979 Leftist Hafizullah Amin becomes president. Conservative Islamic and ethnic leaders revolt. . . . Moscow invades in December. Amin is executed.

1980s *Soviets occupy Afghanistan; U.S. backs anti-Soviet jihadists.*

1980 Soviet-backed Babrak Karmal becomes president.

1985 Islamic fighters resist Soviets.

1989 Last Soviet troops leave.

1990s *Taliban regime takes control of Afghanistan.*

1992 Mohammad Najibullah is overthrown as anti-Soviet resistance morphs into a civil war.

1996 Taliban seizes control in Kabul, hangs Najibullah, introduces hard-line Islamic policies.

1999 U.N. imposes air embargo and financial sanctions on Afghanistan, seeking handover of Osama bin Laden for the 1998 bombings of U.S. embassies in Africa.

2000-Present *U.S.-led coalition overthrows Taliban regime, but bin Laden escapes. Taliban makes a comeback, financed by opium trade.*

2001 Weeks after Sept. 11 terrorist attacks, Operation Enduring Freedom begins. Kabul falls; Taliban retreats. . . . Hamid Karzai is appointed to head interim government.

2002 International Security and Assistance Force is deployed in Kabul; international donors pledge $4.5 billion for Afghanistan's reconstruction.

2003 Special tribal council (*Loya Jirga*) drafts new Afghan constitution.

2004 Draft constitution is approved. . . . Karzai is elected president on Oct. 9 for five years.

2005 Voters elect lower house of parliament and provincial councils. Upper house is later appointed.

2006 NATO takes over security. . . . International donors pledge another $10.5 billion.

2007 Pakistan President Gen. Pervez Musharraf and Karzai agree to coordinate efforts to combat Taliban, al Qaeda. Allied troops kill top Taliban leader, Mullah Dadullah. Opium trade reaps $3 billion. . . . Taliban's threatened spring initiative fails to materialize. . . . U.S. Defense Secretary Robert M. Gates expresses guarded optimism that the military campaign against the resurgent Taliban is succeeding.

Bhutto. In Pakistan's last election, in 2002, religious political parties received only 11 percent of the vote, while Bhutto's secular party gained more than 28 percent. [27]

Besides, the military has been Pakistan's most dominant institution for decades. "I am not particularly worried about an extremist government coming to power and getting hold of nuclear weapons," said Robert Richer, who was associate director of operations in 2004 and 2005 for the Central Intelligence Agency. "If something happened to Musharraf tomorrow, another general would step in." [28]

Still, the Taliban has never been very concerned with votes and elections. If its growing strength is bottled up in Pakistani border areas with the Afghan escape valve shut off, Musharraf fears it could become his problem instead of Karzai's.

Is a Western-style democracy the best solution for Afghanistan?

At the 2001 U.N.-sponsored conference in Bonn, Germany, to determine Afghanistan's future, it was assumed the country would become a Western-style parliamentary democracy. Six months later, an interim administration in Kabul appointed by the tribal council, or *loya jirga*, representing all the main ethnic groups set out to draft a constitution and prepare for unfettered nationwide elections.

But work on the new constitution was immediately stalled by a debate among the drafters, clerics and jurists over the role of sharia, or Islamic law. The finished document was a compromise that allows individual judges wide latitude to give an Islamic interpretation to the country's new laws.

In retrospect, some critics contend that if Afghanistan is going to have a Western-style democratic parliamentary system, the first step should have been to form political parties. Because this was not done, says Italian parliamentarian Boniver, the elected parliament "includes warlords, drug lords and criminals of various kinds who got themselves elected and who have everything on their minds except democracy."

Shahir Zahine, a former mujaheddin fighter who now runs an Afghan non-governmental organization and publishes two newspapers, agrees. "The imposition on our society of a system called Western democracy has produced a mask of democracy, but not democracy

itself," he complained. Afghanistan needs to forget about further elections and create political parties effective enough to eliminate the warlords from the system, he insisted. [29]

A recent report by the Brussels-based International Crisis Group, a respected independent organization working to study and resolve crisis situations, agrees the lack of formalized political blocs "has seen powerbrokers of past eras try to dominate proceedings." To fix the problem, "New moderate forces need to move quickly now to establish formal [political] groups within the [parliamentary] houses to ensure their voices are heard." [30]

Another major problem is leadership — or the lack thereof — says former Ambassador Shahryar. "Karzai is very busy keeping everybody satisfied and forgets to be a leader," he says. And his lack of experience "comes out as indecisiveness." Once, when Karzai needed to appoint a new minister of industry, Shahryar recalls, the president offered the job to seven people and each time withdrew the offer before they could respond. Because of Karzai's unpopularity, Shahryar contends, many talented Afghans in the worldwide Afghan diaspora have not been interested in returning to their homeland to help with its recovery.

The nation's recovery has been hampered by poor security, corruption and lack of funds, and that too is blocking development of democracy, according to Shahryar. "After 9/11 we had the greatest opportunity to develop because the whole world was behind us," he declares. "We could have been a model for the Islamic world," he says. Instead, continued poverty and lack of reconstruction progress have created fertile ground for the return of the Taliban, he contends.

Afghanistan is "still lagging behind in . . . constructing an effective state," Afghanistan expert Barnett R. Rubin of New York University told the Carnegie Council, a New York think tank, in March 2006. "Basically, that territory does not produce enough wealth to pay for the costs of governing it." In fact, Afghanistan "is so poor we can't even tell how poor it is." In other words, Afghanistan doesn't produce enough reliable data to be included in international reports. [31]

Still, former Afghan finance minister Ghani believes, "There is actually more international attention focused on Afghanistan than in 2002." But that has not led to an increase in either aid or investment because of uncertainty over security and over the effectiveness of the cur-

Fighting Afghanistan's Narco Trade

Taliban uses drug profits to finance insurgency

When the fundamentalist Taliban regime ruled Afghanistan, it used a simple tactic to eradicate the country's opium poppy crop, according to New York University's Afghanistan expert Barnett R. Rubin. "Don't grow poppy," they would warn villagers. "We're going to come back in two months. If we see it, we'll hang you." [1]

Not surprisingly, the amount of opium poppy cultivated across Afghanistan plummeted. Between 1999 and 2001, the amount of land dedicated to growing poppies dropped from a high of 90,583 hectares to 7,606. (*See graph, p. 319.*) By 2005, four years after a U.S.-backed coalition ousted the Taliban, Afghanistan's poppy crop had reached record levels — 104,000 hectares, or about 257,000 acres — and is expected to hit a record high in 2007 for the third year in a row. Taliban insurgents — no longer opposed to poppy production — will reap about a third of the proceeds to buy recruits, weapons and bombs, according to the United Nations Office on Drugs and Crime. [2]

Afghanistan today is a virtual narco state, producing more than 90 percent of the world's opium, which is turned into heroin. Last year's harvest of 6,100 tons poured more than $2.8 billion in illicit revenue — 36 percent of the country's gross domestic product — into the pockets of warlords, traffickers and some government officials. [3]

"Drug-related crime and corruption are rife and permeate all levels of society," according to a recent British government memorandum to the House of Commons. The opium trade represents "one of the gravest threats to the long-term security, development and effective governance of Afghanistan," posing as much of a threat to the country's reconstruction as the resurgent Taliban, the report continued. [4]

Yet in Afghanistan's depressed economy, a hectare of poppies produces 27 times more income than a hectare of wheat, according to a 2005 Asian Development Bank report, so the poppy crop has become the primary source of income for millions of rural Afghans. [5] Thus, if the Afghan government wants to achieve its stated goal of reducing poppy cultivation by 70 percent by 2011 and altogether by 2016, it must provide alternative livelihoods for farmers.

That could prove a major challenge, given the slow progress of economic development and reconstruction.

Another complication: The Taliban now has "extensive financial and logistical links" to drug traffickers at all levels, according to the British memorandum. [6] Poppy farmers and drug traffickers in Taliban-controlled areas pay a "tax" to the insurgents for protection, who then hire "day fighters" from among the ranks of Afghanistan's unemployed. And smugglers who sneak the drugs out of Afghanistan return with weapons and bombs for the Taliban, say officials. [7]

Until recently, the U.S. military in Afghanistan refused to get involved in poppy eradication, despite signs the Taliban was using drug profits to finance its insurgency. The U.S. Army insisted that fighting the traffickers was the work of drug enforcement officers, in collaboration with the Afghan police. This brought complaints that the military was ignoring evidence that warlords and politicians friendly to the United States were involved in the illicit trade. The strategy was "the Afghan equivalent of failing to deal with looting in Baghdad," Andre D. Hollis, a former deputy assistant secretary of Defense for counternarcotics, told *The New York Times*. "If you are not dealing with those who are threatened by security and who undermine security, namely drug traffickers, all your other grandiose plans will come to naught." [8]

But after Donald H. Rumsfeld stepped down as secretary of Defense that policy changed. "Now people recognize that it's all related," said Thomas Schweich, the State Department's coordinator for counternarcotics in Afghanistan. "It's no longer just a drug problem. It is an economic problem, a political problem and a security problem." The U.S. military now provides logistical support for drug eradication — but still does not carry out operations. [9]

NATO officials also argue that expanding the alliance's mission to include drug eradication would alienate Afghans instead of winning their cooperation in fighting the Taliban. But under U.S. and U.N. pressure the multinational force is also cooperating — up to a point. The British memorandum specifies that NATO forces "can provide support to counternarcotics operations, such as training of

rent Afghan government, he says. Corruption and bureaucratic ineptitude are seen as barriers to the country's ability to handle aid.

Emma Bonino, Italy's minister of international trade and former head of humanitarian affairs at the European Union, says while problems remain, "Afghanistan has

Afghan counternarcotics forces and *in extremis* support (e.g. medical) to their operations within means and capabilities. . . . But they do not play a direct role on counternarcotics or take part in eradication." [10]

NATO's role is "to establish security throughout the country . . . not to dilute its focus in eradication and interdiction missions," writes Vanda Felbab-Brown, a research fellow at the Brookings Institution in Washington. Getting involved in the drug war, she adds, could jeopardize reconstruction efforts and weaken efforts at long-term development, potentially losing "the hearts and minds of the population." [11]

So what is the solution? Some commentators have suggested that if Western governments were to buy up the entire poppy crop, it would employ Afghan farmers while keeping the drugs off the world market. But that answer risks the international community being held for ransom by farmers threatening to sell to higher-paying drug traffickers, says Neil McKeganey, professor of drug misuse research at the University of Glasgow, Scotland. [12]

The Senlis Council, an international security and development policy group, advocates legalizing the poppy crop and using it to produce medicines like morphine. By locating the entire production process — from seed to tablet — in rural areas, Afghan villagers would have jobs and "an economic opportunity they would want to protect — particularly against drug traffickers," the group says. [13]

However, it will take at least 20 years to clean up the drug trade in Afghanistan, according to a U.N. report issued last November. And cutting demand in Iran, Pakistan, the United Kingdom, Italy, Spain and Germany — where the major consumers of Afghanistan's opium live — is a good way to start. But the current international approach to stemming the drug trade is wrong, according to Rubin.

"It should focus its efforts to removing big drug money from the political process," Rubin said. "But instead what we have done is put big drug traffickers in positions of power, failed to take or support strong actions against them while we attack the livelihoods of small farmers and laborers through eradication, and they then turn to the Taliban or warlords for protection." [14]

AP Photo/Rafiq Maqbool

Afghan police destroy opium poppies in Tarin Kowt in April. For the third year in a row, a record poppy crop is expected, despite eradication operations by Afghan and Western drug enforcement teams. In a policy reversal, the Taliban now uses profits from the illicit drug trade to buy arms and recruits.

Also see Anderson Cooper, Peter Bergen and Nic Robertson, "CNN's Anderson Cooper 360 Degrees," transcript of "Afghanistan: The Unfinished War," May 10, 2007.

[3] Grant Curtis, "Afghanistan's Opium Economy," *ADB Review*, Asian Development Bank, December 2005, p. 8. Also see James Risen, "Poppy Fields Are Now a Front Line in Afghanistan War," *The New York Times*, May 16, 2007, p. A1.

[4] "Afghanistan Counter Narcotics Strategy," Memorandum from the Afghan Drugs Inter-Departmental Unit (ADIDU), May 2, 2007; www.publications.parliament.uk/pa/cm200607/cmselect/cmdfence/memo/408/ucm11.htm.

[5] Grant Curtis, *op. cit.*

[6] "Afghanistan Counter Narcotics Strategy," *op. cit.*

[7] Risen, *op. cit.*

[8] Quoted in *ibid.*

[9] *Ibid.*

[10] *Ibid.*

[11] Vanda Felbab-Brown, Brookings Research Fellow, "Afghanistan's Opium Wars," *The Wall Street Journal*, Feb. 20, 2007, p. 12.

[12] Tanya Thompson, "Call to declare war on Afghan poppy fields," *The Scotsman*, May 22, 2007, p. 1.

[13] *Ibid.*

[14] Quoted in Jason Straziuso, "Afghan police aiding drug traffickers, fight will take 20 years to win, U.N. report says," The Associated Press, Nov. 28, 2006.

[1] Barnett Rubin, "The Forgotten War: Afghanistan," transcript of lecture at the Carnegie Council, New York, March 14, 2006.

[2] "World Drug Report 2006," U.N. Office on Drugs and Crime, 2006.

embarked on the road but it still needs to reach its destination." It was unrealistic, she says, to expect Afghanistan "to transform itself into a model of democracy in the past couple of years. Some say it has all gone bad and will get worse. I think the Afghans have reached the half-way mark, and to abandon them now would be irresponsible."

Donations Fall Short of Pledges So Far

Since the fall of the Taliban, the international community has pledged $25 billion to rebuild Afghanistan during donor conferences in Tokyo, Dubai, Berlin and London. However, only about half of that amount has actually been delivered so far.

International Aid to Afghan Reconstruction
(in $ billion U.S., as of May 2007)

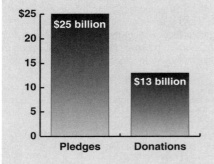

Source: U.N. Office for the Coordination of Humanitarian Affairs

BACKGROUND

Prey to Invaders

Afghanistan has been perpetually beset by foreign invaders due to its geographic position as the Gateway to Central Asia — the link between China, the Middle East and the Indian subcontinent. The list of invaders goes back to before Alexander the Great conquered Afghanistan in 328 B.C. White Huns, Kushans, Persians and Arabs came and went, and Ghenghis Khan's hordes swept over it in 1219 A.D. [32]

Resistance against foreign domination became a way of life for Afghans, and internal turmoil was almost continuous. Throughout most of the 17th century the Safavids of Persia were in control. But in 1747 Persian strongman Nadir Shah was assassinated, and the Afghans seized the ensuing uncertainty over succession to stage a

revolt and gain their independence. The uprising was led by Ahmad Shah Abdali, a member of the Pashtun ethnic group, which ruled the emergent Afghanistan nation in one form or another for the next 200 years. [33]

But Pashtun rule did not necessarily bring peace. The country was involved in at least 18 civil wars, foreign invasions or coups between 1816 and the U.S.-led invasion in 2001, including three wars with Persia and three with Britain.

While Pashtuns make up 42 percent of the population, the innumerable invasions and migrations have produced a demographically rich 31-million-plus Afghan population. Today, Afghanistan has at least a dozen other major ethnic groups, including Tajiks — the second-largest minority with 27 percent — Turkmen, Hazara, Uzbek, Nuristani, Arabs, Kirghiz and Persians. The Hazara and Uzbek are both at 9 percent, and the rest have much smaller percentages. [34]

The "Great Game"

In the 19th century, Britain and tsarist Russia competed for control of Central Asia in a rivalry dubbed by historians as the "Great Game." The main "battleground" was Afghanistan, where the two powers waged a long and secret war of espionage, diplomacy and exploration.

Britain moved preemptively and invaded Afghanistan for the first time in 1839. The British later went to war with Afghanistan in 1878, and again in 1919. The first occupation ended in disaster when an uprising by Muslim Afghan tribesmen forced the British to withdraw, and every member of the retreating force and their families were either massacred or died — except for one doctor. More than three decades later, a second British occupation force also withdrew, but not before London retained the right to control Kabul's foreign policy.

Afghanistan remained a British protectorate until 1919, when Afghan Emir Amanullah — backed by Moscow's new Bolshevik government — declared his country independent. With its hands full elsewhere in World War I, Britain conceded Afghanistan's independence after a brief war, started by Amanullah in May, 1919. [35]

An Afghan monarchy was reestablished in the same year when Amanullah Khan changed his title from emir to padshah (king). In the ensuing period of political turmoil, warlords wrestled one another for power until a new king emerged, Muhammad Nadir Shah. He was assassinated by a student dissident in 1931 and was succeeded by his 19-year-old son, Muhammad Zahir Shah — the last king of Afghanistan — who would rule for the next 40 years.

Until the 1960s the real power was vested in the king's uncles and other relatives, but in 1964 the king fired his prime minister and cousin, Mahmoud Daoud, and established a constitutional monarchy with a two-chamber parliament and free elections and gave women the right to vote.

In 1973, Zahir Shah went to London for an eye operation. While he was convalescing in Italy, Daoud seized control in a bloodless coup, establishing a republic with himself as its president. Zahir Shah remained in exile in Rome until summer 2001.

The Russians finally made it to Kabul after a pro-Moscow coup in April 1978 by the People's Democratic Party of Afghanistan. Daoud was killed and a pro-Moscow government formed with Nur Mohammad Taraki as president and prime minister. In September 1979 Taraki was assassinated, and Deputy Prime Minister Hafizullah Amin seized control. But on Dec. 25 and 26, 1979, the Soviet Union stunned the world by invading Afghanistan, airlifting some 4,000-5,000 troops into Kabul. Amin was, in turn, killed on Dec. 27 and replaced by Babrak Karmal. By 1982, Karmal's regime would be supported by a build-up of more than 100,000 Soviet troops, and by 1986 Moscow would replace Karmal with President Mohammad Najibullah. [36]

In the meantime, on Jan. 4, 1980, American President Jimmy Carter condemned the invasion, saying it "threatened both Iran and Pakistan and is a stepping-stone to possible control over much of the world's oil supplies." [37] In protest, no U.S. athletes competed in the Summer Olympics in Moscow that year. A more purposeful action was the CIA's support for Afghan resistance — the so-called mujaheddin — to the communist regime. According to *The New York Times*, the CIA shipped about $3 billion worth of weapons to Afghan commanders fighting the Soviets in the 1980s — in "a struggle that left perhaps 1 million Afghans dead and up to 3 million in exile in Pakistan." [38]

The Russians called it quits in 1988 after nearly a decade of severe losses (up to 15,000 soldiers) in nearly continuous fighting against the U.S.- and Pakistan-supported mujaheddin. The last Soviet forces withdrew in February 1989. After that, a chaotic sequence of warlords — many of them corrupt and brutally oppressive — seized power until challenged and overthrown by the next one.

President Bush meets last September with Afghan President Hamid Karzai, right, and Pakistani President Gen. Pervez Musharraf to urge more cooperation between the two countries. Karzai and Bush want Musharraf to do more to rein in Taliban and al Qaeda insurgents using Pakistan's border tribal areas as a refuge. A telephone hotline was installed early this year linking the two leaders, but so far neither wants to talk to the other.

Taliban Emerges

If the Taliban movement was not actually created by the Pakistani intelligence services concerned about the instability of its neighbor, as some suggest, the ISI was certainly present at its birth, and the link has never been broken.

The Taliban's first recruits came from Pakistani madrassas, or Muslim religious schools. A few dozen of the more conservative institutions served as de facto training grounds for the jihadists fighting the Soviet occupation of Afghanistan, according to British Foreign Office official Alexander Evans.

"Many of these jihadists went on to become foot soldiers in later campaigns," Evans writes. "They also helped form the Taliban and gave succor and support to Osama bin Laden." [39]

The Taliban began seizing power in Afghanistan in 1994. By 1996 the fundamentalists had expelled the government from Kabul and established a repressive Islamic theocracy. Among other restrictive measures, television

An Afghan Army soldier packs rocket-propelled grenades into Helmand province, where Afghans are fighting alongside 5,500 British forces trying to clear out Taliban insurgents. NATO forces hope to restore peace in Helmand so they can help upgrade a hydroelectric dam that powers much of Afghanistan.

and music were outlawed. Men had to wear beards and women had to be fully veiled and could no longer work or go out alone. Those who infringed on these rules were publicly punished and even executed. An armed Northern Alliance resistance movement made up of Uzbeks, Tajiks and other ethnic Afghan minorities — aided by Iran, India and Russia — held out in the north.

The Taliban welcomed bin Laden and his al Qaeda followers when they were asked to leave Sudan. Bin Laden had already been a conduit of Saudi Arabian contributions during the struggle against the Soviet occupation and had been active in the resistance. The Taliban not only allowed al Qaeda to set up training camps but also gave them legitimacy of a kind by making the terror organization a part of the ministry of defense.

The Taliban might still have Afghanistan in its fanatical grip were it not for the terrorist attacks on New York and the Pentagon. Once 9/11 was attributed to al Qaeda, the wrath of a vengeful United States came down on its protectors' heads. When Taliban leaders refused U.S. demands to surrender bin Laden, the United States began bombing Afghanistan on Oct. 7, 2001, and providing air cover for a Northern Alliance offensive. By early December the offensive had cleared the Taliban out of the main cities, with the remnants fleeing to Pakistan along with bin Laden and his followers. [40]

Unlike Iraq, the war in Afghanistan had bipartisan support in Washington and broad support among America's European allies. It was also welcomed in Afghanistan itself. "An overwhelming number of Afghanis recognized the need for international help," points out Marvin G. Weinbaum, a scholar in residence at the Middle East Institute, and the Afghans never viewed the coalition's presence as an "occupation." [41]

New Government

The United Nations convened an international conference in Bonn on Nov. 27, 2001, to lay out a road map for Afghanistan's route towards democracy.

But while the Northern Alliance may have helped win the war, it lost the fight for political dominance. With Washington's support, the majority Pashtun emerged as the dominant force in the new Afghan political structure, with a Pashtun — Karzai — leading the interim government, and the exiled king, also a Pashtun, returning as the "father of the nation."

By December 2003, a new Afghan constitution had been drafted establishing the Islamic Republic of Afghanistan with a strong presidency and a national assembly. Islam was to be the country's religion, but freedom of worship was guaranteed. The constitution also gave — at least on paper — equal rights to men and women. [42] Ten months later, the presidential election of Oct. 9, 2004, confirmed Karzai for five years. Due to security fears, national assembly elections were postponed until 2005, when they were held under U.N. supervision with a large voter turnout.

As the Bonn conference was getting underway, 1,000 U.S. Marines were landing in Afghanistan and taking over the Kandahar airport — establishing the first U.S. beachhead in the country. The primary aims of the U.S. military were to find bin Laden and provide security while the Afghan army and police were formed and trained to take over.

The closest the United States came to capturing the terrorist leader was in December 2001, when a large number of retreating Taliban were surrounded at Tora Bora near the Pakistan border. Bin Laden was widely believed to have been present at the four-day battle, but the Americans let anti-Taliban militia take the lead in the fighting, and bin Laden was among those who slipped through the cordon. It's widely believed that some of the attacking militia looked the other way while he made his escape. U.S. troops did not intervene directly until the last day of the battle, and by then there was no bin Laden. Today the bin Laden trail has reportedly gone ice cold.

Its hands full with Iraq, Washington has increasingly called upon the North Atlantic alliance to help ensure security in Afghanistan to enable democracy to establish roots. Initially, NATO's ISAF forces were to be centered in Kabul. By late 2005, however, NATO had agreed to take over security throughout all of Afghanistan and battle the re-emerging Taliban — the alliance's first deployment outside Europe.

CURRENT SITUATION

Resurgent Taliban

Five years after its Islamic emirate in Afghanistan was defeated, the Taliban remains "a formidable enemy," writes Francoise Chipaux, an Afghanistan specialist and correspondent for the French newspaper *Le Monde.* "Despite its superior strength and weaponry, NATO has not been able to guarantee the peace and security that the Afghan population has been hoping for since 2001." [43] She blamed what she called the "carelessness" of the Afghan government, mistakes made by the international community and the support given the Taliban by Pakistan and al Qaeda.

However, Dutch Maj. Gen. van Loon, lately commander of NATO's forces in Afghanistan's volatile south, was optimistic, telling *The Washington Post* that Taliban fighters had been driven out of the regions they had gained in 2006, when North Atlantic alliance forces were thinner on the ground. Van Loon said the Taliban "no longer had the initiative," and there was no longer any basis for thinking that the country was slipping back under its control. [44]

Military sources are encouraged by the fact that the Taliban's threatened major spring offensive failed to materialize and by the news that allied forces in May had killed Mullah Dadullah, the Taliban's foremost opera-

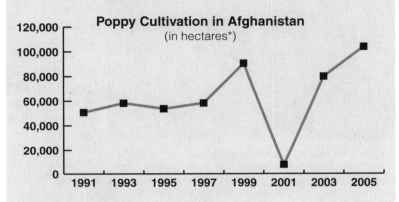

Opium Cultivation Increases Dramatically

Afghanistan's opium poppy crop has burgeoned to record levels since 2001, when the Taliban regime — which officially forbade poppy cultivation — was ousted. The booming drug trade now helps finance the growing Taliban insurgency.

Poppy Cultivation in Afghanistan
(in hectares*)

* 100 hectares = 247 acres

Source: "World Drug Report 2006," U.N. Office on Drugs and Crime, 2006

tional commander. [45] The Taliban, it seems, has learned from its defeat in open combat in September 2006 in southern Afghanistan against Canadian and British forces. [46] At the time, then-British commander Brig. Ed Butler said the insurgents had been "tactically defeated" for the time being. [47]

Even before the winter, the Taliban had switched from military-style coordinated attacks to guerrilla tactics, based on the "Iraq model." Small, highly mobile groups harass NATO forces, roadside bombs have become a standard hazard and suicide bomb attacks are on the increase. [48] But suicide bombs so far in 2007 are not up significantly over last year, even though they jumped fivefold between 2005 and 2006. [49]

The Pashtun Taliban has reportedly concentrated its efforts on southern Helmand province — which is also predominantly Pashtun — viewing it as a key area to test its ability to take and hold Afghan territory from NATO and Afghan troops. [50] But the Taliban also is following the money: Helmand produces 42 percent of Afghanistan's opium, a key source of the insurgents' income.

In April, Karzai and Musharraf, both under strong pressure from Washington to cooperate with one another, agreed to step up their efforts to halt terrorism

Afghans shout anti-American slogans during a March 6, 2007, protest in Nangarhar province after U.S. Marines reportedly fired on civilian cars and pedestrians following a suicide bombing. NATO and U.S. military officials fear a spike in civilian casualties could spark anti-Western sentiment among war-weary Afghans. At least 380 civilians were killed in the first four months of 2007.

and drug smuggling. Meeting in Ankara, Turkey, they vowed "to deny sanctuary, training and financing to terrorists and to elements involving subversive and anti-state activities in each other's countries." [51]

Many observers wonder how much Musharraf can deliver on his commitment to police the tribal areas where the Taliban receive shelter, even if he wants to. In May 2007, Musharraf's position at home appeared weakened following violent public protests over the president's suspension of Pakistan's chief justice, who had accused government officials of corruption. But the Bush administration is keenly aware that it cannot allow the three-sided U.S.-Pakistan-Afghanistan partnership to break up, or the key issue of stabilizing the border to slip from view.

Visiting Rawalpindi, Pakistan, in February, U.S. Defense Secretary Robert M. Gates said after meeting Musharraf, "If we weren't concerned about what was happening along the border, I wouldn't be here."

Hearts and Minds

An insurgency cannot succeed without the support of the population, but neither can a counterinsurgency. Thus, winning the hearts and minds of the Afghan population is NATO's biggest challenge, concedes Gen. Eikenberry. [52]

To further that goal, NATO has established provincial reconstruction teams (PRTs), which combine reconstruction and security efforts into one group.

Last July, for example, the British launched a $55 million economic program in Helmand designed to bring employment and other benefits to 600,000 people. The Helmand PRTs, which typically consist of both British combat troops and soldiers from the Royal Engineers, will spearhead reconstruction of roads and public buildings.

One of the goals of the PRTs is to maintain a cooperative relationship with the local population, a task made more difficult by NATO's increased reliance on the heavy airstrikes that have been a part of its offensive against Taliban strongholds. The civilian death tolls, such as the loss of 57 villagers — nearly half of them women and children — in a Herat village during U.S. airstrikes on April 27 and 29 — are turning Afghans against the NATO forces and undermining an Afghan government that is already considered shaky. In a similar incident on May 9 in Helmand, 21 civilians were killed by gunfire from planes supporting a ground operation. [53]

President Karzai has condemned the rise in peripheral casualties, including those shot at roadblocks and caught in crossfire during clashes. According to press reports, the most serious episodes of civilian deaths have involved U.S. counterterrorism and Special Operations forces, which has created tension inside the alliance and focused a lot of the protest against the U.S. military presence. [54]

Still, NATO officials point out there are often no clear battle lines between civilians and Taliban insurgents. Taliban fighters often endanger — and implicate — villagers by firing on NATO troops from their homes. NATO officials say the alliance has done a poor job of reminding the public — both inside and outside Afghanistan — that it is the Taliban that endangers civilians by hiding among the local population.

In another more sinister twist, alliance forces are sometimes deliberately given erroneous information about the whereabouts of the Taliban in order to incite attacks against a rival village. In at least one incident that resulted in civilian deaths, NATO troops were misled into thinking Taliban fighters were hiding in a nearby village and mounted an attack based on what turned out to be false information.

Commanders point out, however, that airstrikes are needed to make up for a shortage of ground forces. "Without air, we'd need hundreds of thousands of

Has U.S. policy in Afghanistan succeeded?

YES — James Phillips
Research Fellow, Allison Center for Foreign Policy Studies, The Heritage Foundation

Written for *CQ Researcher*, June 2007

The United States scored a major military victory in Afghanistan but has not yet been able to transform this military success into a stable peace. Less than three months after the Sept. 11, 2001, terrorist attacks, the United States overthrew the radical Taliban regime and uprooted the al Qaeda infrastructure in one of the most remote and inhospitable regions on Earth. Although Osama bin Laden escaped, he was forced to go to ground in the tribal badlands along the Afghanistan-Pakistan border, where he could not operate with impunity, as before. While Afghanistan remains a violent place, Taliban militants no longer have a free hand to massacre their opponents, violently repress freedom or provide secure bases for al Qaeda and other allies to export terrorism and Islamic radicalism.

The United States has made substantial progress in helping to create a democratic government, resettle over 3 million refugees, repair Afghanistan's war-torn infrastructure and build schools, hospitals and health clinics to raise living standards. Afghans enjoy much greater political, religious and social freedoms. Sunni zealots no longer systematically massacre Afghan Shiites. In contrast to life under the Taliban, women are free to attend school and work outside the home. There is a free press and lively political debate in the parliament.

Afghanistan still confronts major challenges. The Taliban movement has made a violent resurgence, in part because it enjoys sanctuary and support from Pushtun tribes inside Pakistan. The booming opium trade, which finances the Taliban and corrupts government officials, remains a long-term threat to stability. Warlords continue to thrive in the absence of law and order. But it is unrealistic to expect rapid change overnight. It will take at least a generation to consolidate a stable democracy in Afghanistan.

High-level U.S. attention is needed on a sustained basis to address Afghanistan's daunting problems. But all in all, most Afghans are far better off today than they were under the Taliban's harsh rule. Afghans have voted with their feet to return home from refugee camps in neighboring countries and from jobs farther away. Most important, Afghanistan is an ally, not an adversary, in the struggle against radical Islamic terrorism.

Washington must lead a coordinated international effort to bolster Afghanistan's embryonic democratic government and boost its capacity to provide services, security and higher living standards for its own people. In the long run, only Afghans — not Americans — can consolidate success in Afghanistan.

NO — Barnett R. Rubin
Director of Studies, Center on International Cooperation, New York University; Author, The Fragmentation of Afghanistan

Written for *CQ Researcher*, June 2007

U.S. policy has not achieved its principal objectives in Afghanistan but, in contrast to Iraq, it still could.

From the beginning the Bush administration defined Afghanistan primarily as a counterterrorism mission. In President Bush's words, we were to show that those who harbored terrorists would "share in their fate." In Secretary of Defense Donald H. Rumsfeld's words, the mission was to "kill and capture terrorists faster than the madrassas are turning them out."

According to President Bush, the United States has failed in that mission. Last February, Bush told the American Enterprise Institute, the principal neoconservative think tank:

"Across Afghanistan last year, the number of roadside bomb attacks almost doubled, direct fire attacks on international forces almost tripled and suicide bombings grew nearly five-fold. These escalating attacks were part of a Taliban offensive that made 2006 the most violent year in Afghanistan since the liberation of the country."

Afghanistan's production of opiates has reached a record high, accounting for more than 90 percent of the world's heroin supply. Money from this illicit trade funds insurgents who fight us and corrupts the Afghan government we are trying to support.

Blinded by its opposition to nation building, the Bush administration actively opposed the measures Afghanistan most needed after the initial victory. It opposed expansion of the International Security Assistance Force to the provinces. It refused to authorize the U.S. military to help demobilize and disarm militias. It allied with any anti-Taliban leader, turning a blind eye to both human rights violations and drug trafficking. It refused to lead the reconstruction effort. It treated Pakistan as its major ally in the war on terror, ignoring the conflict between Islamabad and Kabul and ignoring the establishment of Taliban bases there. Most of all, the United States diverted resources from Afghanistan to a disastrous war in Iraq.

In Afghanistan, however, unlike in Iraq, most of the people and most of the international community want the effort to succeed. Both military and financial aid have increased. The United States cooperates with the U.N., NATO and all major aid donors. Despite civilian casualties, Afghans have not yet decided they want us to leave. The internationally approved Afghanistan Compact and the Afghan government's National Development Strategy provide solid bases for success. If the United States disengages from Iraq, it can devote to Afghanistan the resources needed to succeed.

Plight of the Children

Decades of warfare have left poverty deeply entrenched in Afghanistan, especially among Kabul's 50,000 street children. Many are war orphans who help support themselves or their families by polishing shoes or collecting scraps from war-torn ruins and garbage dumps to recycle or use as fuel (top). Non-governmental organizations like Aschiana ("the nest") help provide education, vocational training and outreach services to street children and their families (bottom).

troops," a senior NATO official said. [55]

The deaths are occurring even as many Afghans are questioning the price of liberation from the Taliban. "There is no confidence in any justice system, security is still a huge problem and corruption is the biggest failing of all," said BBC correspondent Alistair Leithead, reporting from Helmand province. "People don't trust the police or the government departments, and that makes persuading them that all is well so much more difficult." [56]

In the south, the Taliban is considered less corrupt and more efficient than government bureaucrats appointed since the 2004 elections. [57] A disaffected generation of unemployed young Afghans — the result of setbacks in the economic recovery — has turned to crime or joined the Taliban, often more out of anger than religious fervor.

"Sixty-five percent of the population is under 20 years of age, and that's the source of new Taliban recruits," says Kabul University Chancellor Ghani. "I know of men who for $20 will put bombs under bridges. The number of people who will commit violence for pay is very high."

Some join the jihadists to avenge family members killed in the fighting. Taking blood for blood is a strong cultural belief among the Pashtun. "Today, it's not just the Taliban who are willing to blow themselves up," said Mullah Naceem-ur-Rahman Hashimi, who reportedly has been responsible for training suicide bombers. "Ordinary people do it because they have a father or brothers in prison, or because they themselves were released but their lives are finished, their dignity gone, and they know that if they die in a suicide operation, they'll go to heaven." [58]

The lack of security has seriously hindered the work of the 1,200 non-governmental organizations (NGOs) — 383 of them from overseas — operating in Afghanistan. To avoid kidnapping, many NGO workers now travel in old, unmarked cars, maintain secret addresses and work in offices with no identifying signs. In the villages, "getting around is very dangerous, and we always try to take along members of the local choura (council)," says Esmatullah Haidary, director of the Afghan Development Association, a leading local NGO.

"Members of smaller NGOs are sincere, but often naive," says Anja De Beer, coordinator of the Agency Coordinating Body for Afghan Relief. "They believe that because they are doing good work for people they will protect them, but that idea is no longer true." [59]

U.S. officials say the slow progress of reconstruction that had been a major disappointment to Afghans initially has been corrected. By 2004, the U.S. Agency for International Development (USAID) had spent $73 million and completed only 100 of 1,000 promised projects, according to *The Washington Post*. [60] But by 2005, the reconstruction pace had improved, said USAID's mission director in Kabul, Alonzo Fulgham, and the United States had built or refurbished 312 schools and 338 clinics, laid 500 miles of new asphalt roads and resurfaced another 500 miles. [61]

Quality of Life

Although the new Afghan constitution guarantees religious freedom, that freedom "remains restricted," according to a Council on Foreign Relations (CFR) backgrounder. In addition, the new constitution guarantees women's participation in the Afghan parliament, but the bright promise of women's rights of three years ago has somewhat dimmed. (*See sidebar, p. 308.*)

"Domestic abuse is rampant," according to the CFR report, noting an alarming jump in suicides — often by self-immolation — among young girls. New laws to raise the marriageable age and outlaw forced marriages are often ignored, especially in the villages. [62]

On the positive side, eight or nine private banks have opened in Afghanistan. Foreign companies have invested $800 million in the telecommunications sector; more than 1.5 million Afghans now have their own mostly mobile phones — a figure Ghani says is expected to double in three

Al Qaeda leader Osama bin Laden is thought to be hiding in Taliban-infested tribal areas on the border between Afghanistan and Pakistan, but his trail has grown cold.

years. And bids worth more than $60 million are coming in from U.S. firms to develop copper mining, he adds.

But progress has been uneven between the various regions, and the widespread mood among Afghans is one of increasing anger and frustration at what they perceive as unfulfilled promises and expectations.

Zarguna Saleh, an Afghan living in Virginia who used part of a family inheritance to build and start a vocational school for orphans in Jalalabad, says many Afghans believe the United States is pushing the wrong priorities. "They're thinking too much in American terms," says Saleh whose family moved to America after the Russian invasion but who now visits her homeland regularly.

"People are angry," she says. "There's no work, no infrastructure and all they hear about is women's rights. Right now, what Afghanistan needs is a strong government; the situation for women will take time to change."

On the other hand, there's no shortage of mass media, Saleh says. The people may "have nothing," she says, but "they have 300 newspapers." And while there are a dozen television channels, "they have no electricity" with which to watch them.

OUTLOOK

Political Solution

NATO's provincial reconstruction teams slowly are coming into their own — albeit modestly — after a shaky start. In April 2007, British troops wrested control of the strategic town of Sangin, a center of poppy cultivation and drug smuggling in Helmand province, that had been in Taliban hands for months. The town lies on the road to the Kajaki dam — the main source of power in southern Afghanistan — earmarked for a $10 million renovation by the U.S. government. But work had been delayed for more than a year because of the Taliban presence. [63]

"Afghanistan has emerged from hell to purgatory but is still a long way from heaven," says Italian parliamentarian Boniver, expressing a view widely held in the international community. "And the danger is that it could slide back into hell once more."

To prevent that slide back, NATO urgently needs to improve the security situation. "The mission hangs in the balance," says Lt. Gen. Eikenberry succinctly. [64] Certainly, routing the Taliban in the field without inadvertently triggering a backlash among villagers would significantly boost morale. But the Afghan problem is as much a weak government as it is a strong enemy. The government must reform its judiciary and clean up its corruption if it hopes to survive.

"Where we are losing in Afghanistan is in the battle to create a fair legal and judicial system; overcome rampant corruption; build a police force; control the drug-proliferation epidemic and bring job opportunities to the Afghan people," wrote Gen. Jones, the retired NATO supreme commander. [65]

Karzai will bear the brunt of the country's failures and might not survive the year as president, say knowledgeable Afghan expatriates. But if early elections are held, many well-qualified Afghans are ready to step into Karzai's shoes, they add.

Many Afghans also doubt America's long-term intentions, and that makes them hold back in their commitment to the international presence in Afghanistan. Most, however, generally agree their country cannot yet go it alone.

Political fragmentation, security problems and failure to meet public expectations after the defeat of the Taliban threaten the region's stability and offer opportunities for those same insurgents. Most Afghans and international observers agree the solution in Afghanistan is a political one, not a military one.

"To prevail in Afghanistan, more than military force is needed," wrote Jones. "Until Washington, Brussels and Kabul address that concept . . . the outcome will be too close to call." [66]

In the long run, says Pakistani analyst Ahmed Rashid, a coalition government — made up of the Taliban and the present Afghan administration, presumably without al Qaeda — might bring peace and stability to Afghanistan. [67]

Karzai himself revealed for the first time in April that he had held "reconciliation talks" with Taliban members, but most observers think he would be excluded from such an alliance. [68]

President Musharraf's own destiny is also linked to Afghanistan. Karzai's growing closeness to India, with workers from the subcontinent arriving in Kabul by the planeload, is a cause of rising concern in Islamabad. His other worry must surely be that the U.S. Congress might begin to ask why the administration has so far stopped short of declaring the Taliban a terrorist organization. Presumably, Washington has avoided that step because countries that harbor terrorists are declared state sponsors of terrorism.

The one certainty is that Afghanistan's recovery will be a long haul. "Many pieces seem to be going well, some are going badly, some change as you watch them," says Ronald E. Neumann, who until recently was U.S. ambassador to Kabul. "It's true that NATO is doing well. But you need a political process."

But can Afghanistan recover? "My sense is that it can be done," he says. "But it can't be done quickly."

NOTES

1. Roland Flamini, "Corridors of Power," www.world-politicswatch.com, March 3, 2007.

2. David Sanger, "Danger Signal in a Bombing," *The New York Times*, Feb. 28, 2007, p. A1.

3. Transcript of testimony by John Michael McConnell before the Senate Armed Services Committee, March 3, 2007.

4. Eikenberry was addressing the Brookings Institution on the situation in Afghanistan, April 30, 2007.

5. U.N. Office for the Coordination of Humanitarian Affairs.

6. Quoted from Bush speech to AEI on Feb. 12, 2007, White House text.

7. Jason Ukman, "NATO General Tells of Taliban Setbacks," *The Washington Post*, May 30, 2007, p. A10.

8. *Ibid.*

9. Afghan drug production statistics from www.unodc.org/pdf/afghanistan_2005/annex_opium-afghanistan-2005-09-09.pdf.

10. Antonio Maria Costa, "An Open Market Mystery," *The Washington Post*, April 25, 2007, p. A16.

11. "Karzai's Challenge: Remain a Priority; Afghanistan implores: 'Do more for us,' " *The Washington Post*, Feb. 28, 2003, p. A6.

12. "A Conversation with H. E. Abdullah Abdullah on U.S.-Afghanistan Relations," Council on Foreign Relations transcript, May 25, 2005.

13. Text of Lugar statement before Senate Committee on Foreign Relations, Feb. 12, 2003.

14. James Fallows, "Bush's Lost Year," *Atlantic Monthly*, October 2004, p. 18. Scheuer headed the special CIA unit formed to hunt for Osama bin Laden.

15. Quoted by Tim Harper, "Afghanistan: U.S. 'Handed off a Mess' to NATO Forces," *Toronto Star*, Sept. 16, 2006; www.commondreams.org/headlines06/0916-02.htm.

16. *Ibid.*

17. "Where Do We Go from Here? Lessons from the First Five Years of the War," American Enterprise Institute, transcript, Sept. 11, 2006.

18. U.S. Budget, fiscal 2004 and 2005.

19. Fox News, "Sunday with Chris Wallace," transcript, Sept. 10, 2006.

20. *Ibid.*

21. "Report: Pakistan arrests one of Taliban's top three," Reuters; March 2, 2007; www.intelligence-summit.blogspot.com/2007/03/report-pakistan-arrests-one-of-talibans.html.

22. Benazir Bhutto, "A False Choice for Pakistan," *The Washington Post*, March 12, 2007.

23. David E. Sanger and David Rohde, "U.S. Pays Pakistan to Fight Terror, but Patrols Ebb," *The New York Times*, May 20, 2007, p. A1.

24. *Ibid.*

25. Arnaud de Borchgrave, "Commentary: Shock and Awe About-face," *The Washington Times*, Dec. 12, 2006, p. A16.

26. Bhutto, *op. cit.*

27. Mark Mazzetti, "One Bullet Away from What?" *The New York Times*, March 11, 2007, Sec. 4, p. 1.

28. Quoted in *ibid.*

29. "Afghanistan: Una Strada Senza Uscita," Interpress Service News Agency, Italy, July 28, 2006.

30. "Afghanistan's New Legislature: Making Democracy Work," International Crisis Group, Asia Report No. 116, May 15, 2006.

31. Barnett R. Rubin, "Afghanistan: The Forgotten War," lecture at the Carnegie Council, March 10, 2006.

32. See "Chronological History of Afghanistan"; www.afghan-web.com/history/chron/index2.html.

33. *Ibid.*, and Adam Ritscher, "Brief History of Afghanistan," on the Afghanistan government's Web site, www.AfghanGovernment.com.

34. CIA *World Fact Book*, https://www.cia.gov/library/publications/the-world-factbook/index.html.

35. See "Chronological History of Afghanistan," *op. cit.*; also Ronan Thomas, "Once More Up the Khyber," *Asia Times*, www.atimes.com/atimes/South_Asia/HF20Df02.html.

36. For background, see *Political Handbook of the World*, CQ Press, http://library.cqpress.com.

37. See The American Presidency Project; www.presidency.ucsb.edu/ws/index.php?pid=32911.

38. Tim Weiner, "At Large in a Rugged Land," *Week in Review, The New York Times,* March 11, 2007, pp. 4, 14.

39. Alexander Evans, "Understanding Madrasahs: How Threatening Are They?" *Foreign Affairs,* January/February 2006, pp. 9-16.

40. For background, see Kenneth Jost, "Rebuilding Afghanistan," *CQ Researcher,* Dec. 21, 200l, pp. 1041-1064.

41. *Ibid.*

42. "Karzai signs Afghan constitution," BBC, Jan. 26, 2004; http://news.bbc.co.uk/2/hi/south_asia/3428935.stm. For English text of Afghan constitution, go to www.servat.unibe.ch/law/icl/af00000_.html.

43. Francoise Chipaux, "Afghanistan: Le Taliban sont de retour," *Le Monde,* April 29, 2007, p. 1.

44. Ukman, *op. cit.*

45. *Ibid.*

46. "Plus de 200 taliban tues dans le sud de l'Afghanistan," *L'Express,* quoted in www.casafree.com/modules/news/article.php?storyid=7187.

47. "British armed forces in Afghanistan," p. 3; Answers.com; www.answers.com/topic/operation-herrick.

48. Chipaux, *op. cit.*

49. See Jason Straziuso, "New U.S. commander in Afghanistan expects rise in suicide attacks in 2007," The Associated Press, Jan. 30, 2007.

50. http://news.bbc.co.uk/2/hi/south_asia/5189316.stm.

51. "Musharraf, Karzai meet in Turkey," United Press International, April 30, 2007.

52. Eikenberry, *op. cit.*

53. "Afghanistan: 21 civili uccisi in raid Nato," *Il Sole 24 Ore,* May 9, 2007, p. 2.

54. Gall and Sanger, *op. cit.*

55. *Ibid.*

56. http://news.bbc.co.uk/1/hi/world/south_asia/6607211.stm.

57. Chipaux, *op. cit.*

58. Francoise Chipaux, "Dans le provinces afghans, des conditions de travail difficiles pour les ONG," *Le Monde,* May 2, 2007, p. 1.

59. *Ibid.*

60. Joe Stephens and David B. Ottaway, "A Rebuilding Plan Full of Cracks," *The Washington Post,* Nov. 20, 2005, p. A1.

61. Carlotta Gall and David Rohde, "Problems with U.S. Aid Alienate Afghans," *International Herald Tribune,* Nov. 7, 2005; http://iht.com/articles/2005/11/07/news/rebuild.php/php.

62. *Ibid.*

63. *Ibid.*

64. Eikenberry, *op. cit.*

65. "What Is at Stake in Afghanistan," letter to the editor, *The Washington Post,* April 10, 2007, p. A16. The letter was also signed by Harlan Ullman, Gen. Jones' former senior adviser and now a senior associate at the Center for Strategic and International Studies in Washington.

66. *Ibid.*

67. Giandomenico Picco, "Afghanistan il prezzo della pace," *La Stampa,* Jan. 22, 2007.

68. Carlotta Gall, "Karzai Says He Has Met With Some Taliban Members in an Effort at Reconciliation," *The New York Times,* April 7, 2007, p. A1.

BIBLIOGRAPHY

Books

Bergen, Peter, *The Osama bin Laden I Know: An Oral History of Al-Qaida's Leader,* **Free Press, 2006.** A journalist and terrorism analyst chronicles bin Laden's life, based largely on the author's 1997 interview with the al Qaeda leader.

Coll, Steve, *Ghost Wars: The Secret History of the CIA, Afghanistan, and bin Laden, from the Soviet Invasion to September 10, 2001,* **Penguin, 2007.** A staff writer for *The New Yorker* — who covered Afghanistan from 1989 to 1992 for *The Washington Post* — recounts the CIA's involvement with the Taliban and al Qaeda in the years leading up to the Sept. 11, 2001, terrorist attacks.

De Long, Michael, Noah Lukeman and Anthony Zinni, *A General Speaks Out: The Truth about the Wars in Afghanistan and Iraq,* **Zenith Press, 2007.**

This critique of the U.S. war in Afghanistan is written by a retired Marine lieutenant general who was deputy to Gen. Tommy Franks, commander-in-chief at U.S. Central Command, (De Long); the former commander of Central Command (Zinni) and writer Lukeman.

Dupree, Louis, *Afghanistan*, Princeton University Press, 1980.

While dated, this book by a former senior research associate for Duke University's Program in Islamic and Arabian Development Studies and a founder of the Afghan Relief Committee is still widely regarded as the definitive work on Afghanistan.

Jones, Ann, *Kabul in Winter: Life Without Peace in Afghanistan*, Metropolitan, 2006.

A New York-based authority on women and violence, who worked in Kabul for a non-governmental organization that helped Afghan war widows, assesses women's conditions in Afghanistan.

Rashid, Ahmed, *Taliban, Islam, Oil, and the New Great Game in Central Asia*, IB Taurus, 2006.

A Pakistani journalist based in Lahore who has covered Central Asia for 25 years examines in meticulous detail the reasons why the Taliban came to power, and the circumstances of its alliance with Osama bin Laden.

Rodriguez, Deborah, and Kristin Ohlson, *Kabul Beauty School: An American Woman Goes Behind the Veil*, Random House, 2007.

Michigan-born Rodriguez originally volunteered to go to Afghanistan as a nurse's aide as the Taliban regime was ending. She stayed on first as a women's hairdresser and eventually opened a hairdressing school. The book has rare insights into current conditions among Afghan women in the post-Taliban era. Ohlson is a freelance writer.

Articles

Baker, Aryn, "The Truth About Talibanistan," *Time*, March 22, 2007.

Pakistan's tribal region has become a sanctuary for the Taliban and other extremists.

Moreau, Ron, *et al.*, "The Rise of Jihadistan," *Newsweek*, Oct. 2, 2006, pp. 24-28.

Five years after the U.S.-led invasion of Afghanistan, the Taliban is fighting back hard.

Rubin, Elizabeth, "In the Land of the Taliban," *The New York Times Sunday Magazine*, Oct. 22, 2006, pp. 86-97, 172-175.

Pakistan's mountainous border with Afghanistan has become "a Taliban spa for rehabilitation and inspiration," says a contributing editor of the magazine, with Quetta as an assembly point for Taliban incursions into Afghan territory.

Reports and Studies

Patel, Seema, and Steven Ross, "Breaking Point: Measuring Progress in Afghanistan," Washington Center for Strategic and International Studies, March 2007.

Two members of the Post Conflict Reconstruction Project say Afghans are losing trust in their government because of an escalation of violence, and conditions in the country have deteriorated in all key areas except the economy and women's rights.

Rubin, Barnett, "Afghanistan's Uncertain Transition from Turmoil to Normalcy," Council on Foreign Relations, 2006.

One of the world's foremost experts on Afghanistan and a former U.N. adviser on Afghanistan assesses the situation in Afghanistan.

Summers, Christina Hoff, "The Subjection of Islamic Women," American Enterprise Institute, 2007.

A resident AEI scholar researches culture, adolescents and morality in Afghan society.

United Nations Office on Drugs and Crime, "UNODC Afghanistan Opium Winter Rapid Assessment Survey," February 2007.

Opium production in Afghanistan continues to increase at a record rate. For an assessment of the previous year's crop see, "UNODC Afghanistan Opium Survey," October 2006.

For More Information

Afghanistan Research and Evaluation Unit, Flower St./Street No. 2, Shahr-i-Naw, Kabul, Afghanistan; +93-(0)-799-608-548; www.areu.org.af. Promotes a culture of research and learning in Afghanistan by strengthening analytical capacity and facilitating debate.

Carnegie Council, 170 E. 64th St., New York, NY 10065; (212) 838-4120; www.cceia.org. Think tank advocating ethical decision-making in international policy.

Council on Foreign Relations, 58 E. 68th St., New York, NY 10065; (212) 434-9400; www.cfr.org. Promotes a better understanding of the foreign-policy choices facing the United States and other governments.

International Crisis Group, 149 Avenue Louise, Level 24, B-1050 Brussels, Belgium; +32-(0)-2-502-90-38; www.crisisgroup.org. Nongovernmental organization using field-based analysis and high-level advocacy to prevent violent conflict worldwide.

International Institute for Strategic Studies, 13-15 Arundel St., Temple Place, London WC2R 3DX, United Kingdom; +44-(0)-20-7379-7676; www.iiss.org. Think tank focusing on international security with emphasis on political-military conflict.

Islamabad Policy Research Institute, House No. 2, Street No. 15, Margella Rd., Sector F-7/2, Islamabad, Pakistan; +92-51-921-3680-2; www.ipripak.org. Evaluates national and international political-strategic issues and developments affecting Pakistan and surrounding countries.

Middle East Institute, 1761 N St., N.W., Washington, DC 20036; (202) 785-1141; www.mideasti.org. Seeks better relations between Middle East nations and American policymakers.

North Atlantic Treaty Organisation, Boulevard Leopold III, 1110 Brussels, Belgium; +32-(0)-2-707-50-41; www.nato.int. Oversees International Security Assistance Force in Afghanistan, a U.N.-mandated mission established in 2001.

United Nations Development Fund for Women, 304 E. 45th St., 15th Floor, New York, NY 10017; (212) 906-6400; www.unifem.org. Promotes women's empowerment and gender equality.

United Nations Office on Drugs and Crime, Wagramer Strasse 5, A-1400 Vienna, Austria; +43-1-26060-0; www.unodc.org. Monitors the global trade in illicit drugs.

United States Agency for International Development, 1300 Pennsylvania Ave., N.W., Washington, DC 20523; (202) 712-0000; www.usaid.gov. Principal U.S. agency dispensing foreign aid.

VOICES FROM ABROAD

Pervez Musharraf
President, Pakistan

Repatriation requires cooperation

"Problems along the bordering regions of Pakistan and Afghanistan are compounded by the continuing presence of over 3 million Afghan refugees, some of them sympathetic to the Taliban. The incentives offered to the refugees for their voluntary return by the international community are minimal. A serious international commitment is required to facilitate their repatriation."

— *Statement before U.N. General Assembly, September 2006*

Mohammad Nader Nadery
Commissioner, Afghan Independent Human Rights Commission

Afghanistan is a narco state

"If the governors in many parts of the country are involved in the drug trade, if a minister is directly or indirectly getting benefits from drug trade, and if a chief of police gets money from drug traffickers, then how else do you define a narco-state?"

— *The Christian Science Monitor, May 2005*

Hamid Karzai
President, Afghanistan

The world was warned

"I did expect a rise in militant activity. And for two years I have systematically, consistently and on a daily basis warned the international community of what was developing in Afghanistan and of the need for a change of approach in this regard. . . . The international community [must] reassess the manner in which this war against terror is conducted."

— *BBC News, June 2006*

Des Browne
Defence Secretary Great Britain

Taliban stronger than expected

"We do have to accept that it's been even harder than we expected. The Taliban's tenacity in the face of massive losses has been a surprise, absorbing more of our effort than we predicted it would, and consequently slowing progress on reconstruction."

— *The Guardian (United Kingdom), September 2006*

Shukria Barakzai
Editor, Aina-E-Zan (Afghanistan)

A long way to go for women

"But we cannot allow 10 years of demagogy and oppression to be the sole scale by which we judge progress or the character of Afghan women today. . . . It is also illogical to say that every problem has been solved and that Afghan women are relieved from all the miseries they have suffered. There remains a long and difficult path of showing each Afghan how to recognize and protect the values of the liberty he or she possesses."

— *Worldpress.org, March 2005*

Jaap de Hoop Scheffer
Secretary General, NATO

Afghanistan is everybody's problem

"If we don't go to Afghanistan and if we are not here, Afghanistan will come to us. . . . Consequences will be felt not only in Afghanistan but in other nations as well . . . we will not give the terrorists an opportunity to win."

— *BBC Monitoring Europe, September 2006*

Karim Rahimi
Presidential Spokesman Afghanistan

Taliban help not welcome

"It is true that we still have some problems . . . but these problems do not mean that the people will give their support to the Taliban. The people of Afghanistan have proved in the past years that they have strongly rejected those who impose terrorism, oppression, war, manslaughter, cruelty and killing of innocents, and will never go to them."

— *Sapa — Agence France-Presse, October 2006*

Hamidullah
Farmer, Musa Qala Helmand Province

Our poppy is safe

"No [one] has destroyed my poppy and no one will be able to destroy it. We are not paying the Taliban, but they tell us, 'As long as we are here, no one can destroy your poppy.' This year we have grown more than ever."

— *Institute for War & Peace Reporting, March 2007*

Editorial
Anis (Afghanistan)

Stop Pakistan's support of the Taliban

"If NATO wants to bring permanent peace and stability to Afghanistan, prevent casualties among its forces and avoid facing huge economic burdens as well as avoiding pressure from the public in their own countries, they should try 100 per cent to ensure that Pakistan renounces its support for the Taliban and shuts down religious, terrorist training centres and the channels that breed fanaticism and suicide attacks."

— *September 2006*

Patrick Chappatte, Le Temps, Switzerland

13

The New Europe

Brian Beary

Poland's rising fortunes are on display at Warsaw's bustling Golden Terraces shopping mall on opening day Feb. 7, 2007. Poland and the nine other former communist countries that have joined the European Union since 2004 are enjoying economic growth that is the envy of their older EU counterparts.

From *CQ Researcher,*
August 1, 2007.

I t's difficult to imagine, but only 17 years ago the now vibrant 1,000-year-old capital of the Czech Republic was once part of the repressive Soviet bloc.

Today Prague has enthusiastically embraced Western ways. The old Russian-Czech "friendship" building, a potent symbol of Soviet domination, is now a bank. A renowned communist-style 1970s shopping mall has been bought by Britain's Tesco retail chain. Car manufacturer Skoda — once ridiculed for its dated image — is selling so many cars it cannot find enough engineers.

The latest technology is part of Prague's rebirth. Taxis arrive within minutes of being called because dispatchers use GPS technology to detect the closest car. At DVD stores, consumers use computers to check their rental history and get suggested movies to suit their tastes.

If there were ever any doubts the Czech Republic and nine other ex-communist nations — the so-called New Europe — could fit into the powerful European Union (EU), the concerns have long since faded. Three years ago eight of the 10 — Latvia, Lithuania, Estonia, Poland, Hungary, Slovakia, Slovenia and the Czech Republic — joined the EU, followed in January 2007 by Romania and Bulgaria. (*See map, p. 332.*) Today, the new kids on the block are growing faster than their older EU colleagues, with a gross domestic product (GDP) that has been rising on average 3.7 percent a year since 1997, compared to 2.5 percent in the 15 old member states — known as the EU-15.

But New Europe still has much catching up to do. Those living in the EU-15, known as Old Europe, enjoyed an average per capita GDP of $39,700 in 2006, compared to a New Europe range of

Former Communist Countries Are Now Part of Europe

The 15-member European Union (EU) was expanded in 2004 to include eight former communist countries — Estonia, Latvia, Lithuania, Poland, the Czech Republic, Slovakia, Hungary and Slovenia — along with Malta and Cyprus. Romania and Bulgaria joined in 2007, bringing EU membership to 27. Other countries being considered for membership include Croatia, Bosnia-Herzegovina, Serbia, Montenegro, Macedonia, Albania and Turkey.

EU Membership:
- EU-15 (Old Europe)
- As of May 1, 2004
- As of Jan. 1, 2007
- Candidates and/or potential candidates

Source: *The World Factbook 2007*, Central Intelligence Agency, 2007

from $4,900 in Bulgaria to $20,300 in Slovenia. Likewise, Old Europe — with four times as many people — has a $15.5 trillion GDP, which dwarfs New Europe's $1.1 trillion output. [1]

To catch up, the new members have adopted capitalism enthusiastically. "There is an irrational love of privatization — of utilities, gas, telecommunications," says Hana Rihovsky, a Czech-German who worked for sev-

A Region in Transition

The 10 former communist countries that joined the European Union (EU) since 2004 boast a combined population of 103 million — about a quarter of Old Europe's population — in an area covering about 416,000 square miles, roughly the size of France and Spain. Poland is the largest — both in size and population — followed by Romania. Before coming under Soviet influence after World War II, most of New Europe was ruled by either the Ottoman or Austro-Hungarian empires. Many of the countries — which are predominantly Roman Catholic or Orthodox — have weathered economic upheaval in transitioning from centrally controlled to free-market economies.

Country	President/ Prime Minister	Population*	Area (square miles)	Major religions	GDP per capita	Major exports
Bulgaria	Georgi Parvanov/ Sergei Stanishev	7.3 million	42,823, slightly larger than Tennessee	Bulgarian Orthodox 82.6 %, Muslim 12.2%	$4,932	Clothing, machinery and equipment, fuel.

Strategically located near the Turkish Straits and with a long Black Sea shore; controls key routes from Europe to Asia and the Middle East. Ruled by monarchies in the Middle Ages and the Ottoman Turks for 500 years until 1908. Rejected monarchy in 1946; dominated by Soviets until 1990. Initially elected socialists post-independence. Suffered severe economic difficulty during war in neighboring Kosovo, which cut main European trade routes. Has averaged 5.1 percent growth since 2000 due to low inflation, progress on structural reforms and new foreign investment.

Country	President/ Prime Minister	Population*	Area (square miles)	Major religions	GDP per capita	Major exports
Czech Republic	Vaclav Klaus/ Mirek Topolanek	10.2 million	30,450, slightly smaller than South Carolina	Roman Catholic 26.8%, Protestant 2.1%, unaffiliated 59%	$16,303	Machinery and transport equipment, raw materials, fuel.

Formerly part of Austro-Hungarian Empire; formed by Czechs and Slovaks after World War I. Liberalization efforts in spring 1968 quashed by Soviets. Declared independence after peaceful "Velvet Revolution" in 1989; followed by "Velvet Divorce" on Jan. 1, 1993, when split into Czech Republic and Slovakia. Among most stable and prosperous of the EU-10.

Country	President/ Prime Minister	Population*	Area (square miles)	Major religions	GDP per capita	Major exports
Estonia	Toomas Hendrik Ilves/Andrus Ansip	1.3 million	17,462, slightly smaller than New Hampshire and Vermont	Evangelical Lutheran 13.6%, Orthodox 12.8%, unaffiliated 35%, other and unspecified 32%, none 6.1%	$13,289	Machinery and equipment, wood, paper, textiles.

Northernmost of three former Soviet Baltic republics; borders Gulf of Finland and Baltic Sea. Became independent in 1918 after centuries of Danish, Swedish, German and Russian rule. Economic recovery after independence in 1991 aided by free-market reforms and return of "Baltic gold" held by Western banks since 1940. Strong electronics and telecommunications sectors. Balanced state budget, low public debt.

Country	President/ Prime Minister	Population*	Area (square miles)	Major religions	GDP per capita	Major exports
Hungary	Laszlo Solyom/ Ferenc Gyurcsany	10 million	35,919, slightly smaller than Indiana	Roman Catholic 51.9%, Calvinist 15.9%, Lutheran 3%, other Christian 3.6%, unspecified 11.1%, unaffiliated 14.5%	$12,194	Machinery and equipment.

Occupies fertile Middle Danube Plain. Former Kingdom of Hungary; once ruled by the Austro-Hungarian Empire; fell under communist rule in 1919, followed by 25 years of right-wing dictatorship. Joined Axis in World War II; occupied by Soviets in 1944. Historic 1956 revolt quelled by Moscow. Undertook economic liberalization ("Goulash Communism") in 1968. Initiated free-market economy after independence in 1989. Enjoys strong economic growth; per capita income nearly two-thirds EU average. Biggest challenge: low labor force participation (57 percent) is among lowest in industrialized world.

Country	President/ Prime Minister	Population*	Area (square miles)	Major religions	GDP per capita	Major exports
Latvia	Valdis Zatlers/ Aigars Kalvitis	2.2 million	24,938, slightly larger than West Virginia	Lutheran, Catholic, Orthodox (evenly divided)	$9,728	Wood/wood products, machinery and equipment, metals.

Second-largest of the Baltic States; ruled by Teutonic Knights, Poland, Sweden and then Russia. Independent between two world wars; annexed by U.S.S.R. in 1940. Had difficult transition to free-market policies: industrial, agricultural output plummeted; food, energy were scarce; GDP contracted 50 percent. Privatized most companies, banks, real estate since then. Enjoyed real GDP growth of 10.2% in 2006.

Country	President/Prime Minister	Population*	Area (square miles)	Major religions	GDP per capita	Major exports
Lithuania	Valdas Adamkus/ Gediminas Kirkilas	3.5 million	25,174, slightly larger than West Virginia	Roman Catholic 79%, Russian Orthodox 4.1%	$9,591	Minerals, textiles, clothing, machinery and equipment.

Largest of former Soviet Baltic republics; became industrialized after World War II. First of Baltics to declare independence in March 1990. Restructured economy for integration into EU after last Russian troops withdrew in 1993. Has rebounded since 1998 Russian financial crisis: Unemployment fell to 5.2% in 2007; wages grew 17.6%. Trades increasingly with the West rather than Russia. Has privatized most large, state-owned utilities.

Country	President/Prime Minister	Population*	Area (square miles)	Major religions	GDP per capita	Major exports
Poland	Lech Kaczynski/ Jaroslaw Kaczynski (twin brothers)	38.5 million	120,728, slightly smaller than New Mexico	Roman Catholic 89.8%, Eastern Orthodox 1.3%, unspecified 8.3%	$9,728	Machinery and transport equipment, manufactured goods.

Coveted by expansionist neighbors since its creation in mid-10th century; experienced a golden age in the 16th century. Was partitioned by Austria, Prussia and Russia in early 1790s. Re-emerged as independent state after World War I; overrun by Germany and the Soviets in World War II. Was comparatively tolerant and progressive Soviet satellite. Spawned independent trade union Solidarity in 1980. Economy transformed in the 1990s by "shock therapy" program; now one of most robust EU-10 economies. Still plagued by high unemployment, underdeveloped and dilapidated infrastructure and poor rural underclass.

Country	President/Prime Minister	Population*	Area (square miles)	Major religions	GDP per capita	Major exports
Romania	Traian Basescu/ Calin Popescu-Tariceanu	22.3 million	91,699, slightly smaller than Oregon	Eastern Orthodox 86.8%, Protestant 7.5%, Roman Catholic 4.7%	$6,166	Textiles, metals/metal products, machinery and equipment.

Freed from Ottomans in 1856, created by merger of Wallachia and Moldavia in 1859. As Axis partner in World War II participated in the 1941 German invasion of U.S.S.R.; overrun by Soviets three years later. Ruled for four decades by increasingly oppressive Nicolae Ceausescu, who enforced onerous fertility-boosting policies that resulted in overflowing orphanages and high numbers of "street children." Ceausescu and wife overthrown and executed in 1989. Elected former communists until 1996. Began instituting economic reforms, spurring creation of a middle class but hampered by corruption, red tape. Grew at 6.4% in 2006, strongest in a decade.

Country	President/Prime Minister	Population*	Area (square miles)	Major religions	GDP per capita	Major exports
Slovakia	Ivan Gasparovic/ Robert Fico	5.4 million	18,859, about twice the size of New Hampshire	Roman Catholic 68.9%, Protestant 10.8%, Greek Catholic 4.1%	$11,234	Vehicles, machinery and electrical equipment, base metals.

Consists of 40 percent of former Czechoslovakia; created when Slovaks and Czechs separated peacefully in 1989. Initially performed poorly due to authoritarian policies of post-separation governments. Increased privatization under center-right administration installed in 1998. Exceeded economic-growth expectations in 2001-06. Saw dramatic drop in joblessness — from 18% in 2003-04 to 10.2% in 2006 — but it remains economy's Achilles' heel.

Country	President/Prime Minister	Population*	Area (square miles)	Major religions	GDP per capita	Major exports
Slovenia	Janez Drnovsek/ Janez Jansa	2 million	7,827, slightly smaller than New Jersey	Catholic 57.8%, Muslim 2.4%, Orthodox 2.3%, other, unspecified or none 36.6%	$20,278	Iron, steel, automotive products, cement and sulfuric acid.

Ruled by Austro-Hungarian Empire until end of World War I; became part of the Kingdom of Serbs, Croats and Slovenes in 1918, which was renamed Yugoslavia in 1929. Went communist after World War II. Was most industrialized and economically advanced of former Yugoslav republics; per capita GDP was double Yugoslavia's. Enjoyed strong economy and stable democracy after independence in 1991. Has per capita GDP substantially higher than other EU-10 economies, thanks to excellent infrastructure, well-educated workforce and central location. Considered most successful former communist country.

* July 2007 estimate

Sources: *The World Factbook 2007*, Central Intelligence Agency, 2007; *Political Handbook of the World 2007*, CQ Press; and Eurostat, EU Statistics Agency

eral years in Prague for the Community of European Railways (CER), the European rail industry lobby. "Even the transport sector, although it is not fully privatized, is being opened up for competition."

Workers in New Europe — also known as the EU-10 — also put in longer days than their Western counterparts, clocking an average 2,000 hours a year compared to 1,400 hours for the average German. [2] The new members have emerged as pioneers of innovative fiscal policies — among them the controversial flat tax favored by conservative economists, in which all income levels are taxed at the same rate.

In a remarkable turnaround, New Europe is even inspiring economic reform among its Western neighbors. According to the Center for European Policy and Analysis (CEPA), "the extent to which the EU is able to reverse its downward economic spiral may depend on the effort that Western European countries make to imitate the pro-business, pro-growth economic policies of Central Europe." [3] Corporate tax rates already are falling across Western Europe, notably in Austria and Germany, as countries compete with one another to attract investment. [4]

In Poland "young people are amazingly motivated and active," observes Fearghas O'Beara, a European Parliament official. They are optimistic the country "has turned the economic corner" and "every dream seems possible," reminding him of the United States' can-do mood in the 1950s.

But despite the generally upbeat outlook, economic liberalization also has had its downside. For example, as communist-era price controls on housing are stripped away, lower-income households are feeling the pinch. "The average Czech salary is about $1,000 a month, yet it costs about the same for a newly rented two-bedroom apartment in Prague," notes Rihovsky. The situation is better in the countryside, she says, where people tend to own their homes. "Rural life is in some ways complete bliss. You see 30-year-old Skodas driving around, but the lifestyle is easygoing and the people more content."

In addition, as public-sector salaries fail to keep up with rising costs, a subculture of petty bribery — known as "gift-giving" — has emerged. Rihovsky recalls negotiating a reduction in a parking fine — from about $39 to $24 — by paying the Czech police officer directly instead of taking a parking ticket. People give doctors little gifts to get appointments, she adds, but "the situation is not as bad as it is in Bulgaria or Romania, where salaries are lower still." [5]

New Europe's free-market zeal — especially with regard to the free movement of labor across borders — has ruffled some feathers in higher-wage Old Europe, which fears an influx of EU-10 labor. A factory worker in Germany, for instance, earns on average $18.80 per hour compared with $1.96 in Hungary. [6]

A Bulgarian woman picks strawberries in southern Spain in 2006. Some 30,000 Eastern European women were recruited for the fruit harvest. Many workers from EU-10 countries have emigrated to Western Europe in search of better-paying jobs, often causing consternation among indigenous workers fearful that the influx of the lower-paid workers will cause wages to drop.

Not surprisingly, New Europe's workers are heading west in droves in search of better-paying jobs. Between May 2004 and April 2007, 630,000 residents of new member states registered to work in the United Kingdom (U.K.). Most were from Poland, Lithuania and Slovakia and primarily worked in factories and warehouses or as kitchen and catering staff, cleaners and farmhands. [7]

The British government insists the new workers contribute "to the success of the U.K. economy while making few demands on our welfare system." [8] But Britons aren't so sure. "Immigrants are now arriving at nearly one a minute and will require 200 new homes every day for the next 20 years," complains the advocacy group Migration Watch UK. [9] Some old member states — such as Austria, Germany and France — have temporarily denied EU-10 workers access to their job markets, but those restrictions will disappear by 2014.

And when the European Commission — the EU's executive arm — in 2004 proposed opening the borders to EU-10 workers offering skilled services, Old Europe's citizens balked, especially in the more socialist-oriented countries like France. Claiming such an influx would lower the quality of services, opponents conjured up the specter of France being inundated with thousands of Polish plumbers undercutting their French counterparts.

Ethnicity Still Matters in EU-10

Some minorities want greater autonomy

Despite the new unity between governments in Old and New Europe, ethnic minorities largely remain outsiders, clashing with authorities over language, education and political representation.

Since casting off the Soviet communist yoke, nationalist feelings are on the rise in New Europe, as countries bask in their new-found independence. At the same time, many have also become increasingly fearful of — and even hostile to — demands for greater autonomy from ethnic communities inside their boundaries.

For instance, most of Europe's 8 million Roma — commonly known as gypsies — live in Central and Eastern Europe. Thought to have migrated from India a thousand years ago, they speak their own language and usually live in Roma enclaves. Their darkest hour came during the Holocaust — called the "porrajmos" ("the devouring") by the Roma — when the Nazis and their allies murdered between 500,000 and 1 million gypsies. [1] More recently, it has emerged that up to 2,000 Roma women in the Czech Republic were sterilized without their consent during childbirth between the 1970s and 2004. An investigating commission recommended each victim be compensated about $10,000, but the Czech government has not yet agreed. [2]

Today the Roma are Europe's most marginalized ethnic minority. Prejudices against them run deep. People often associate them with petty crime, making integration into the wider community extremely difficult.

"It's a vicious circle," says Hana Rihovsky, a Czech-German who lobbies on behalf of European railways. "People do not expect them to be honest so they won't give them a job. You hear stories — like about Roma burning down houses the government gave them — and don't know whether to believe them or not." For example, Czech Deputy Prime Minister Jiri Cunek said in April that to get state subsidies Czechs would have to "get a good suntan [an allusion to the Roma's darker skin tone], start trouble and light fires on town squares." Though Roma demonstrators took to the streets demanding his resignation for inciting racial hatred, Cunek has managed to keep his job. [3]

The EU has been pressuring governments to provide Roma with better healthcare, housing and family planning and to improve the linguistic skills of Roma children so they can have better access to higher education, vocational training and jobs.

New Europe's second-largest minority are the ethnic Hungarians, of whom 1.4 million live in Romania's

Transylvania province and 520,000 in Slovakia. They have ended up as minority communities because Hungary — which was on the losing side in World War I — lost much of its territory and population when Europe's borders were redrawn in 1920. Hungarians in Romania are fighting for the right to political representation, to use their own language and to run their own schools. For example, a bitter dispute is raging in Romania's largest university — Babes-Bolyai in the city of Cluj-Napoca — as ethnic Hungarians try to split the institution in two along ethnic lines.

Both the Roma and ethnic Hungarians have some strong supporters in the European Parliament. Günther Dauwen, director of the European Free Alliance Party (EFA), advocates on behalf of what he calls Europe's "stateless nations, regions and disadvantaged minorities." He accuses the Romanian authorities of making parties representing Hungarians illegal by forcing them to have members from across Romania even though they are concentrated in one region.

But Romania's chargé d'affaires in the United States, Daniela Gitman, insists Hungarians are well-treated. "We have an important political and social tradition for tolerance and diversity, of promoting minorities and respecting their rights," she says.

Less well known are Romania's 70,000 ethnic Germans. Once numbering about 700,000, they have dwindled dramatically in recent decades as many returned to Germany to claim citizenship. They began leaving in the 1970s, Gitman says, attracted by Germany's higher living standards and its government, which paid off Romania's communist-era leader Nicolae Ceausescu to secure their exit.

In tiny Latvia, Moscow has been demanding better treatment for the 500,000 Russian-speakers who arrived during the Soviet era and comprise nearly a third of the population. When Latvia won independence in 1991, the government revoked their citizenship. Some Latvians also accuse the Russians of marginalizing themselves by refusing to learn Latvian.

"There are a lot of intermarriages, but the Russians in Latvia are exposed to very different media influences, with their own newspapers, radio and television stations," says Dace Akule, a researcher for a Latvian think tank. "They do not want to go back to Russia. It was wrong to deprive them of citizenship." [4]

In Estonia, the Russians, Ukrainians and Belorusians account for more than a quarter of the 1.3 million inhabitants. Eva Maria Liimets, deputy chief of mission at the Estonian

Embassy in Washington, says the Russian minority supports the EU because it supports the rights of minorities. [5] Indeed, the EU is increasingly acting as a counterweight to nationalist tendencies.

In Bulgaria, 750,000 ethnic Turks have their own political party, which scored 20 percent in the country's European Parliament elections in May, much to the annoyance of far right nationalist groups like the Ataka party, which won 14 percent. Other minorities around the region include the Gagauz, a Turkic people in Romania and Bulgaria; the Vlachs, who speak a Romanian-type language and live in Bulgaria and Romania; and the Pomaks, ethnic Bulgarians who became Muslims during Ottoman rule.

The Macedonians in Bulgaria show just how contentious ethnic issues can be. The Bulgarian government says there are only 5,000 Macedonians living in Bulgaria, but in reality there are between 100,000 and 200,000, according to Metodija Koloski, a member of the Washington-based United Macedonian Diaspora advocacy group. The government also refuses to recognize the Macedonian language and prevents Macedonians from forming a political party or their own Orthodox Church, he contends. Unlike ethnic Hungarians, however, the Macedonians have no one defending them. The government of neighboring Macedonia does not want to alienate Bulgaria and Greece, according to Koloski, because it needs their support to join the EU and NATO.

In November 2006, when the European Parliament was voting on whether to accept Bulgaria into the EU, the EFA proposed demanding that Bulgaria allow ethnic Macedonians to register a political party. Bulgaria had banned the Macedonians' Umo Ilinden Pirin party because it did not have enough members.

"The amendment was rejected 303-141, but considering the fierce lobby from the Bulgarian government, 141 votes was quite a lot," says the EFA's Dauwen, noting that in 2006 the European Court of Human Rights ruled that Bulgaria had violated the Macedonians' right of freedom of association and that Sofia has been dragging its heels in implementing the judgment. [6]

But Bulgarian Ambassador to the United States Elena Poptodorova, who was born in Bulgaria's Macedonian region, insists "these people are not Macedonians. To recognize their language would be like saying Austrian is a different language from German." She feels the campaign is an effort by Macedonians to distance themselves from Bulgaria in order to establish their own identity.

Pavol Demes, a Slovak who is director of Central and Eastern Europe for the German Marshall Fund USA, points out that while tensions exist for ethnic minorities in New Europe, "the same is true in the U.K. with the Scots or in

Europe's most marginalized ethnic minority are the Roma — commonly known as gypsies — most of whom live in Central and Eastern Europe.

Spain with the Basques." But ethnic strife does not have "the capacity to destabilize the area."

For Hungarian journalist Laszlo Hofer, the solution is more economic than political. "If this region was stronger and wealthier, the minority question would be less painful," he says. [7]

---

[1] Kenneth Jost, "Democracy in Eastern Europe," *CQ Researcher*, Oct. 8, 1999, pp. 865-888.

[2] See Rosie Johnston, "Will the State Compensate Women Sterilized Against Their Will?" Radio Prague, July 24, 2007, www.romove.radio.cz/en/article/21568.

[3] See Daniela Lazarova, "Roma Demonstration Increases Pressure on PM," Radio Prague, April 12, 2007, www.romove.radio.cz/en/article/21432.

[4] Presentation at the School for Advanced International Studies (SAIS), Johns Hopkins University, Washington D.C., April 12-13, 2007.

[5] Discussion at Elliott School of International Affairs, The George Washington University, Washington D.C., March 21, 2007.

[6] Dauwen, *op cit.*

[7] Hofer, *op. cit.*

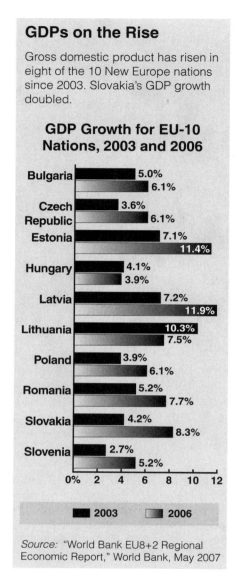

GDPs on the Rise

Gross domestic product has risen in eight of the 10 New Europe nations since 2003. Slovakia's GDP growth doubled.

GDP Growth for EU-10 Nations, 2003 and 2006

Country	2003	2006
Bulgaria	5.0%	6.1%
Czech Republic	3.6%	6.1%
Estonia	7.1%	11.4%
Hungary	4.1%	3.9%
Latvia	7.2%	11.9%
Lithuania	10.3%	7.5%
Poland	3.9%	6.1%
Romania	5.2%	7.7%
Slovakia	4.2%	8.3%
Slovenia	2.7%	5.2%

■ 2003   □ 2006

Source: "World Bank EU8+2 Regional Economic Report," World Bank, May 2007

The disparity in wage levels also has given low-wage EU-10 companies a competitive edge when bidding on contracts in the EU-15, which has caused conflicts. But the wage gap is beginning to narrow, primarily because of New Europe's economic success. [10] In Old Europe, the arrival of cheaper manual labor such as construction workers, general handymen, cleaning ladies, gardeners and fruit-pickers has imposed downward pressure on wages. Over the last 10 years, according to the European Commission, real wages increased only about 1 percent a year in the old member states while they jumped about 3.5 percent in the new states. [11]

In foreign policy, New Europe has been a close ally of the United States since the fall of the Soviet Union. But it must also adhere to the EU's common foreign and security policy, creating conflicting loyalties as it did in the run-up to the Iraq War. Europe was bitterly divided over the pending conflict, with France and Germany vigorously opposed to the war but with most new members providing military and political support to the United States. U.S. Defense Secretary Donald H. Rumsfeld memorably highlighted the split in January 2003, when he observed that "New Europe" was being helpful while "Old Europe" was being "a problem."

"You're thinking of Europe as Germany and France," Rumsfeld told journalists. "That's old Europe. If you look at the entire NATO Europe today, the center of gravity is shifting to the east." [12]

French environment minister Roselyne Bachelot angrily retorted that she would refrain from saying what she really felt like telling Rumsfeld because it would be "too offensive." [13]

"There is a lot of pressure on the new member states to be good Europeans, to look toward Brussels," Judith Garber, director of North-Central European Affairs at the State Department, said on April 3, 2007. "This is one of the largest threats to our alliance." Back in EU headquarters in Brussels, Belgium, countries with close U.S. ties like Poland are sometimes suspected of being Trojan horses promoting pro-U.S. positions inside the EU, says Karolina Pomorska, a lecturer in political science at the University of Maastricht in the Netherlands. [14]

In fact, New Europe has remained closer to the administration of President George W. Bush than most of Western Europe, and rejects the vision of some countries, like France, that advocate a world with multiple power centers. "We really are not involved in creating a united Europe as a certain counterbalance to the U.S.," declared Czech President Vaclav Klaus during President Bush's visit to Prague in June. And personal factors draw the Baltic States closer to Washington: The Estonian and Lithuanian presidents lived in the United States for much of their lives, and Latvia's ex-president lived in Canada.

New Europe's pro-American sympathies became even clearer in 2006 when the European Parliament investigated claims that the Central Intelligence Agency (CIA) had illegally abducted, transported, detained — and possibly condoned torturing — terror suspects in secret Central and Eastern European locations after the Sept. 11, 2001, terrorist attacks on the United States. EU-10 politicians of all political stripes were hostile to the inquiry; Polish members of the Parliament tried to sabotage it.

"The European Parliament does not have any power on these issues," Polish Sen. Franciszek Adamczyk said scathingly of the inquiry. "They speak without thinking." Besides, he shrugged, even if the Polish government knew about the secret sites, "they would not tell us because they are secret."

The Council of Europe, a human rights organization in Strasbourg, recently condemned Poland and Romania for hosting secret CIA prisons from 2002-2005. [15] The U.S. administration says the program is dormant.

However, New Europe's allegiance to the United States has been weakening since it achieved its twin foreign policy goals of joining the EU and the North Atlantic Treaty Organization (NATO). More domestic-oriented politicians are emerging, best embodied in the extraordinary rise to power of Lech and Jaroslaw Kaczynski. The identical twins and former child actors are now president and prime minister, respectively, of Poland.

"They have never been to the West," Eugeniusz Smolar, president of the Warsaw-based Center for International Relations, said in May. "They do not speak foreign languages." [16] (The twins visited the United States in July.)

Some observers say New Europe's support has slackened because its loyalty has not been rewarded by the United States. For example, Poland did not receive big construction contracts in Iraq, despite sending 6,000 troops, making Poland the third-largest contingent in Iraq after the United States and the U.K. 17 U.S. aid to New Europe also has decreased dramatically since the 1990s. EU-10 citizens are constantly reminded that it is Old Europe — known as the EU-15 — that is heavily subsidizing them now, underscored by the ubiquitous blue-and-gold-starred EU flags planted at new roads, bridges and buildings. [18] Some New Europe countries also resent the fact that the United States is building its own military bases in Poland, Romania and Bulgaria but has largely discountinued funding the militaries in those countries, which began after the fall of the Soviet Union.

Even so, New Europe is happy to have a U.S. presence to ward off its re-emergent Big Brother to the east — Russia. For its part, Moscow strongly opposes recent

Workers assemble Volkswagen Polo cars near Bratislava, Slovakia. Once dubbed by former U.S. Secretary of State Madeleine K. Albright "the black hole of Central Europe" because of its corruption and anti-democratic leanings, Slovakia since 1998 has embraced both democracy and capitalism and seen a dramatic drop in joblessness.

American plans to construct missile interceptors in Poland and a defense shield in the Czech Republic — and even some in New Europe are beginning to have second thoughts about it.

Meanwhile, the benefits of EU membership were made patently clear on July 24, when Libya released five Bulgarian nurses and a Palestinian doctor it had imprisoned for eight years and sentenced to death for allegedly deliberately infecting more than 400 Libyan children with the HIV virus. In return for release of the medics, the EU struck a deal with Tripoli that involved EU member countries paying more than $450 million for, among other things, compensating the victims' families. During nationwide jubilation after the nurses arrived in Sofia, Prime Minister Sergey Stanishev said the episode, "shows very clearly to Bulgarians what it means to be a member of the European Union." [19]

As the EU-10 and Old Europe seek common ground, here are some of the questions being asked:

Will New Europe continue to be pro-American?

While few expect a serious deterioration in the relationship, many expect New Europe's American loyalties to become somewhat more qualified. For one thing, observers point out, New Europe's support for the Iraq War likely was influenced by the fact that the U.S.

Unemployment on the Decline

Unemployment rates decreased in all of the EU-10 except Hungary and Romania. Significant declines for Lithuania and Poland are attributed to the migration of citizens to Old Europe for better-paid jobs.

Unemployment Rates for EU-10 Nations

* Joined EU in 2007

Source: "World Bank EU8+2 Regional Economic Report," World Bank, May 2007

Senate was considering their applications to join NATO when the war began.

"The only question Washington was asking then was 'Are they with us or against us,' " says Andres Kasekamp, a professor of politics at the Estonian Foreign Policy Institute.

Bulgaria's ambassador to the United States, Elena Poptodorova, puts the relationship in a similar historical context: "France and Germany already had relations with the U.S. We did not. We were looking for our new geopolitical positioning. Maybe we needed to go to the extreme before getting back to the center."

Romania's chargé d'affaires to the United States, Daniela Gitman, cites another factor in her country's case. "For us, Saddam equaled Ceausescu [Romania's brutal former communist dictator]. They were good friends," she says. "Our people wanted Iraq to be freed like we were.

"We are one of the strongest advocates of the transatlantic relationship," she adds. "It will be one of the key themes for the NATO summit in Bucharest in April 2008, which will be the biggest event that Romania has hosted."

Hungarian journalist Laszlo Hofer says that while "it is historically obvious" that the EU-10 were trying to cement their relationship with Western Europe and

America after the Soviet decades, he is convinced that "it will always be more important for them to belong to Europe than to be pro-American." He predicts their governments will remain pro-U.S. but the publics will be divided because of the Iraq War and missile defense. "At the same time, they cannot afford to be too anti-Russian because they cannot prosper without Russian oil."

But Pavol Demes, director of the German Marshall Fund USA's Central and Eastern Europe branch, thinks the Bush administration has seriously damaged relations with New Europe. "There is now a huge diversity in attitudes toward the U.S.," he says. "We will never see the homogeneity we had before. Our 'transatlantic trends' surveys provide empirical evidence of this. The Bush administration generally has not spent enough time on public diplomacy."

A recent Pew Research Center public opinion survey of non-Americans around the world found that support for the United States has fallen significantly in New Europe since 2000, but it is still higher than support levels in Old Europe. (*See poll, p. 352.*) [20]

Perhaps symbolic of that trend, Slovakia's new prime minister, Robert Fico, has taken a more critical stance toward the United States than his predecessors, probably responding to Slovakians' growing disenchantment with Bush's policies, according to Tim Haughton, a politics lecturer at the University of Birmingham in the U.K. [21]

And Svetlozar Andreev, a lecturer at Bulgaria's Sofia University, warns, "The U.S. should be careful about the rise of nationalists and populists who would prefer the foreign direct investment of nearby EU countries to a long-term strategic relationship with the U.S. or other faraway countries."

In Slovenia, initially favorable sentiment toward the United States was changed by the Iraq War, says Natasa Briski, a Slovenian broadcast journalist for the Pro Plus media company. But even before that Slovenia had been less pro-American than other parts of New Europe. In

2002 for example, it refused to bow to U.S. pressure to sign a bilateral agreement pledging not to hand over U.S. nationals to the nascent International Criminal Court (ICC). Slovenia's decision was heavily influenced by the EU, which opposed such bilateral accords on the grounds that they undermined the ICC's authority. [22] The more pro-U.S. Romania signed such an agreement but has not yet ratified it.

Bulgaria remains one of America's staunchest allies. It is permitting the United States to build a military base in Bulgaria and has 137 troops in Iraq. When President Bush visited Sofia on June 11, President Georgi Parvanov said relations were better than they had ever been, but he added: "I do hope we will have the support of President Bush and the United States in our effort to modernize our armed forces." [23]

On the security front, New Europe continues to look to NATO and the United States to protect it from serious military threats, since the EU's founding treaties prohibit it from launching a major military campaign. But viewing the United States primarily in security terms risks neglecting social, cultural and economic dimensions of the relationship. Polish Ambassador to the United States Janusz Reiter is acutely aware of this risk. "If we fail to develop the non-security side, we could end up with an empty shell," he says. [24]

Moreover, in the wake of the 9/11 terrorist attacks, even the security relationship is changing. America's security focus has shifted to Asia and the Middle East, making Central and Eastern Europe less of a priority than it was during the Cold War. In fact, according to the Center for International Relations' Smolar, Poles feel the United States is not paying enough attention to their security needs. [25] Since 2002, Polish support for NATO has fallen from 64 percent to 48 percent. [26]

Resentment also has developed over the United States' continuing visa requirements for New Europe, even though citizens of Old Europe (except Greece) can travel to the United States visa-free. President Bush said in November 2006 that he wanted to end the discriminatory treatment.

"I made it clear visa policy needs to be changed," Bush said during a joint press conference with Bulgaria's Parvanov on June 11. "I have laid out a way forward, and I'm committed to seeing it through."

On July 25 the U.S. Congress cleared legislation that makes it easier for EU-10 countries to qualify for the visa waiver program, but it is not expected to take effect for two to three years. Bush signed the measure into law on Aug. 3.

Is New Europe changing Old Europe?

EU membership is considered a two-way process in which new members "download" EU-wide policies — including up to 80,000 pages of law — and "upload" their own specific interests.

"Europe is Western Europe," notes Hungarian journalist Hofer. "The former communist countries joined the club. They were in no position to alter the statutes."

Now the new member states are starting to think about pressing the EU to embrace policies and issues they hold dear — such as enlarging the EU to include countries like Moldova, Ukraine, Croatia and Macedonia and pressing the EU to speak out against political repression in neighboring Belarus.

"The new member states do not think as strategically yet as old members like France," says Rihovsky, the European rail industry lobbyist. "They have not quite mastered the skill yet. But they will eventually learn."

New Europe states have received enormous cash injections from the EU, ranging in 2004 from 0.25 percent of Hungary's gross national income to 2.1 percent of Lithuania's. [27] Part of the payments are delivered in the form of farm subsidies, triggering a 70 percent rise in farm incomes since 1999. [28] Unlike most of Western Europe, agriculture is still important in New Europe, with farming the primary occupation for 25 percent of Bulgarians, 19 percent of Poles and 16 percent of Lithuanians.

But New Europe has done more than just accept subsidies. It's also been expanding its economy at a healthy rate: Growth in 2006 ranged from 4 percent in Hungary to 12 percent in Latvia. [29] The only Old Europe country with such consistently high growth rates is Ireland.

Seeing how well their economic model has worked, New Europe's leaders are aggressively pursuing free-market policies. Estonian Prime Minister Andrus Ansip has vowed to slash the country's flat-tax rate from 22 percent to 18 percent by 2011. [30] Slovakia and Romania also have adopted a flat tax. Western Europe is watching with interest, although no one has taken the plunge yet. The average corporate tax rate in New Europe stands at 19.2 percent compared to 31.4 percent in the EU-15. [31] By contrast, indirect taxes and social security contributions are higher in New Europe than Old Europe. [32]

CHRONOLOGY

1800s-1918 *Nationalism stirs in Austrian, Russian and Ottoman empires.*

1859 Principalities of Moldavia and Walachia merge to become Romania.

1867 Hungary becomes an equal half of the Austrian empire.

1878 Bulgaria shakes off five centuries of Ottoman rule to become autonomous principality.

1919-1945 *New nation-states get a flavor of liberal democracy before sliding into dictatorship and war.*

1919 Treaty of Versailles gives birth to Latvia, Lithuania, Estonia, Poland, Czechoslovakia, Hungary and Yugoslavia.

1934 Coups lead to dictatorships in Latvia and Estonia.

Aug. 23, 1939 Germany and Soviet Union sign Molotov-Ribbentrop Pact, carving up Central and Eastern Europe. World War II soon follows.

1945 The Soviet Union emerges victorious, having joined the Allies when Germany invaded the U.S.S.R. in 1941. The borders of Europe are redrawn at a conference in Yalta, leading to a U.S. sphere of influence in Western Europe and a Soviet one in the East.

1946-1988 *Soviet domination is omnipresent in Eastern Europe.*

1949 The Soviets establish Comecon, a trading block for Central and Eastern Europe intended to counterbalance U.S.-sponsored reconstruction program for Western Europe.

1955 The U.S.S.R., Poland, East Germany, Czechoslovakia, Bulgaria, Romania, Hungary and Albania sign the Warsaw Pact military alliance as counterweight to U.S.-dominated North Atlantic Treaty Organization (NATO).

1956 Moscow brutally suppresses revolt in Hungary. Workers' uprising in Poland is also crushed.

1961 Construction of the Berlin Wall begins, aimed at preventing East Germans fleeing westward.

1968 Warsaw Pact troops quell political liberalization movement in Czechoslovakia known as the "Prague Spring."

1980 First independent trade union in Eastern Europe — Solidarity — emerges in Poland, where an anti-communist strike by shipyard workers in Gdansk leads to imposition of martial law.

1985 Mikhail Gorbachev becomes leader of the Soviet Union and launches his glasnost and perestroika reforms.

1987 On June 12, U.S. President Ronald Reagan famously stands in front of the Berlin Wall and challenges Gorbachev to "tear down this wall."

1989-2008 *Democracy and capitalism spread to Central and Eastern Europe.*

1989 Pro-democracy demonstrations break out in former communist countries. Protesters begin tearing down the Berlin Wall on Nov. 9, heralding the end of communist era.

1991 Latvia, Lithuania, Estonia and Slovenia emerge as independent nations as the Soviet Union and Yugoslavia disintegrate.

1993 Czechoslovakia splits into two countries.

1999 Hungary, the Czech Republic and Poland join NATO.

2004 Latvia, Lithuania, Estonia, Slovakia, Slovenia, Romania and Bulgaria join NATO on March 29. Latvia, Lithuania, Estonia, Poland, Hungary, the Czech Republic, Slovakia and Slovenia join the European Union on May 1.

2007 Romania and Bulgaria join the EU on Jan. 1; Slovenia becomes the first of the EU-10 to introduce the euro as its currency.

Jan. 1, 2008 Slovenia is scheduled to assume the rotating presidency of the EU.

Despite the economic improvements, the large westward migration continues, especially to Britain and Ireland, largely because of the big divergence in wage levels between new and old member states. [33]

Bulgarian Ambassador Poptodorova points out that 900,000 Bulgarians have left since 1990 — 17 years before Bulgaria joined the EU. But unlike in Poland and Latvia, the Bulgarian exodus has decreased in recent years, she notes. Romanian diplomat Gitman says Romanian workers, with their Latin-based language, have migrated in large numbers to Mediterranean countries like Spain and Italy. Latvian policy researcher Dace Akule says 50,000 have left Latvia since it joined the EU. [34]

The difference in wage levels, however, gives companies from New Europe a competitive edge when bidding on projects in Old Europe, generating ill feelings and even lawsuits, illustrated by an ongoing legal spat between Swedish trade unions and the Latvian construction company Laval. The company refused to sign a wage agreement after posting workers to Sweden in May 2004. The unions retaliated by blockading the construction site, ultimately forcing the workers to go home to Latvia. Laval then sued the unions for the lost income. The case is pending before the EU Court of Justice. [35]

While many Westerners fear being swamped with EU-10 labor, the New European governments worry about losing their brightest and best. Akule says the exodus has been dubbed "the Irish problem" in Latvia because so many Latvians have immigrated to Ireland.

"They are well-educated people who take jobs below their skill level," says Akule. "We have economists working in Ireland as waitresses or strawberry-pickers. Back in Latvia, the queues in the supermarkets are like they were in Soviet times because there is not enough staff." In neighboring Estonia the new government raised medical staff salaries in an effort to retain workers. [36]

Yet Poland's former finance minister and deputy prime minister Leszek Balcerowicz is not so worried about the trend. "Not all emigration is harmful. Some return while others send money back home," he says. [37] In a similar vein, Lithuania's vice-minister for economics, Vytautas Nauduzas, points out the exodus has helped reduce unemployment in Lithuania from 12.4 percent in 2003 to 5.2 percent in 2007. And now, he adds, Lithuanian workers are beginning to return because new jobs are being created. [38]

Moreover, the wage gap is narrowing, in part because of New Europe's improving economies. In 2006, wages rose by 15.6 percent in Latvia, 14.7 percent in Lithuania. [39]

Are freedom and democracy at risk in New Europe?

While the general consensus has been that democracy is now firmly rooted in New Europe, a new study from Freedom House — which publishes "report cards" on the state of democracy and human rights around the world — is less upbeat.

"Reform fatigue and political polarization are contributing to an emerging governance crisis," the report warned, adding that the democratic consensus may be eroding as "populism and anti-liberal trends" gather strength and judicial independence comes under "increased pressure." [40]

Freedom House's democracy ratings for all the new member states fell in 2006, apart from Bulgaria and Romania, which kept their democratization efforts up because they were both seeking EU approval. The EU has no formal mechanism for encouraging democratization after a country joins, the report noted.

For instance, Freedom House complained that Poland has begun purging communist-era journalists, part of a controversial new "lustration" law that took effect on March 15, 2007. It requires 700,000 citizens to register with the Institute of National Memory, detailing links they had with the communist-era Polish Secret Service. Declarations will be cross-checked with communist archives, and if someone lies about his past, he can be banned from his profession for 10 years.

The law is deeply problematic, however, because some Poles were forced to pledge cooperation with the communists without ever actually informing on people. One high-profile victim of the anti-communist purge was Warsaw's Archbishop-designate Stanislaw Wielgus, forced to resign in January. The Romanian parliament is drafting its own lustration law. "It is similar to the Polish model but will only affect politicians, not ordinary citizens," says Gitman. While shedding light on what went on during the communist era can be healthy for democracy, if lustration laws are used to clamp down on political adversaries, the measures could have a chilling effect on democracy.

Critics of the EU would argue that the very act of joining the European Union is undemocratic because it cedes countries' regulatory powers to an unelected European Commission. In other words, New Europe's laws increas-

A Sliver of Russia Trapped in Europe

Kaliningrad residents feel isolated, abandoned

The 750-year-old Baltic Sea port city once known as Königsberg has much to be proud of. It was the birthplace of German philosopher Emmanuel Kant. And its seven bridges across the Preger River are revered as the inspiration for Swiss mathematician Leonhard Euler's graph theory.

But after World War II the city fell into Russian hands and was renamed Kaliningrad after former Soviet President Mikhail Kalinin. Today Russia's only ice-free European port brags it is the birthplace of Ludmila Putina, wife of Russian President Vladimir Putin.

"I witnessed evidence of this schizophrenic history in an antiques shop where Nazi-era china sets embossed with swastikas were displayed alongside busts of Lenin and Stalin," said BBC journalist Steven Paulikas, who visited in 2005. [1] The breakup of the Soviet Union in 1991 heralded a decade of neglect for the tiny Russian exclave of 1 million people, which is surrounded by Poland and Lithuania and accessible to Russia only by air or rail.

Traveling to and from Kaliningrad became even more difficult after Poland and Lithuania joined the European Union (EU) in May 2004, because area residents suddenly needed visas to pass through the EU en route to Mother Russia. "Kaliningrad is something of a regional court jester," according to Paulikas, "a dysfunctional bit of land so tragic it is actually comical in the eyes of its European neighbors." [2]

The city's most traumatic episode occurred during World War II, when on Jan. 30, 1945, just before they fled advancing Soviet troops, the Nazis rounded up the city's remaining 7,000 Jews, drove them to the beach in the coastal town of Yantarny — then called Palmnicken — and shot them, letting their bodies fall into the icy Baltic Sea. [3] When the Soviets came, they imprisoned or killed the residents who hadn't fled. By war's end, only 50,000 of the pre-war population of 316,000 had survived.

Olga Sezneva, a social sciences professor at the University of Chicago who grew up in Kaliningrad, says after the Soviet Union disintegrated in 1991 some Germans returned to visit but were very disappointed, she says. Only 12 percent of the buildings had survived the war. Ethnic Germans still living in Russia mostly chose to return to Germany where living standards were higher. But about 5,000 of them — unable to adapt to German culture, resettled in Kaliningrad, she says.

Today Kaliningrad is officially one of the poorest regions of Russia. "The little economic activity that exists in the rural regions looks post-apocalyptic," said the BBC's Paulikas. "I met men calling themselves 'fishermen' whose business consisted of pulling a few carp out of a nearby waterway and trading them for vodka." [4]

But Sezneva categorically rejects Paulikas' gloomy portrait. "A certain image and narrative of Kaliningrad has been formed in the Western media" she complains. "But the idea of Kaliningrad being in abject poverty does not make sense. The region has the highest immigration rate in [Russia]. Ownership of cars is the third-highest per capita nationwide, and the number of ethnic restaurants is incredible."

Official statistics support her more upbeat assessment. While Kaliningrad's economic decline in the 1990s was more pronounced than elsewhere in Russia, its economic recovery has been stronger, with annual economic growth from 1999-2005 averaging 10.5 percent, compared to 6.8 percent for Russia. Unemployment is 6 percent, down from 15 percent in 1998. [5] And while its $2,778 per capita GDP (in 2004) was below Russia and neighboring Poland and Lithuania, Sezneva says this does not include proceeds from the informal economy, thought to produce up to half of Kaliningrad's wealth. [6]

Kaliningrad has a similar image problem in the East, she

ingly are being debated and enacted in Brussels, Luxembourg and Strasbourg where the EU institutions are based — not in Warsaw, Prague or Bucharest. And even worse, critics say, the EU Council of Ministers — which has lawmaking powers comparable to the U.S. Senate — meets predominantly in secret. [41] "When our ministers journey to Brussels, they share with deputies in Pyongyang (North Korea) and Havana (Cuba) the dubious distinction of sitting in one of the only legislatures left passing laws in secret," said Graham Watson, leader of the Liberals and Democrats group in the European Parliament. [42]

says. "The Russian media depict it as a black hole of the economy — a parasite living off state subsidies that disappear into the private accounts of the business and political elite." Though she concedes corruption is a problem, "Kaliningrad is not a dying, collapsed place," she insists. "The problem for outsiders is that it just does not look like a typical East European city like Prague or Warsaw, nor does it look like Moscow."

While the fishing industry is in decline, she points out, the oil, peat and coal industries are doing well. The area also has about 90 percent of the world's amber reserves and produces 7.5 percent of Russia's furniture and most of its TVs and vacuum cleaners. [7] Real estate prices have begun to rise as wealthy Moscovites buy up coastal holiday homes. Three-quarters of the region's 365,000 tourists each year are Russian, largely because Kaliningrad retains an exotic aura for Russians. "Many think it is still German," Sezneva says. [8]

The EU provided Kaliningrad $68 million in subsidies from 2004-2006 to help clean up polluted waters, combat drug addiction and stop the spread of HIV-AIDS. [9] Life expectancy in Kaliningrad is lower than in the EU but higher than in Russia, Sezneva says, even though the public health-care system has collapsed.

Many of Kaliningrad's residents are ex-Soviet military personnel, while others are descendants of Russians the Nazis forced to work on farms in Belarus and Poland who migrated to Kaliningrad after the Germans fled. About 200,000 are undocumented, says Sezneva, primarily Uzbek and Tajik refugees from Central Asia.

Kaliningraders' isolation from Russia has had a negative psychological impact, according to Sezneva, and many travel to Europe more often than to Russia. "Thirty percent of youths have never been to Russia but go to Europe regularly," she says. "They feel looked down on by the EU and abandoned by Russia."

---

[1] Steven Paulikas, "Kaliningrad: The forgotten land," BBC News, March 26, 2005, http://news.bbc.co.uk/2/hi/programmes/from_our_own_correspondent/4382145.stm.

[2] *Ibid.*

Isolated Kaliningrad

The Russian province of Kaliningrad is surrounded by Poland and Lithuania and is two countries away from mainland Russia.

Source: *The World Factbook 2007*, Central Intelligence Agency, 2007

---

[3] For more information, see Federation of Jewish Communities of the Commonwealth of Independent States, www.fjc.ru/news/newsArticle.asp?AID=161287.

[4] Paulikas, *op. cit.*

[5] See Eugene Vinokurov, *The Economic Specialization of the Kaliningrad Oblast*, Kaliningrad State University, 2007.

[6] *Ibid.*

[7] Statistics cited by Sezneva from GosKomStat, Russia's official statistical agency.

[8] According to Alla Ivanova, EU Commission, Kaliningrad.

[9] European Commission, Directorate General for External Relations, http://ec.europa.eu/external_relations/north_dim/kalin/index.htm.

Czech President Klaus, for instance, says the EU should focus on economic rather than political integration. Klaus is a leading opponent of deeper EU integration in talks on redrafting the EU Constitution — necessitated because France and the Netherlands rejected it in referenda in 2005. "He is a bombastic, populist figure, but he does strike a chord with the people," says Carol Strong, a professor of comparative politics at Oklahoma State University. [43]

But Klaus' fears are not shared by all of New Europe. "In Slovenia, we had an open approach to EU membership talks, with high participation of parliament, business organizations and academics," says Manja Klemencic, a post-

EU Labor Market Still Blocks Bulgarians, Romanians

The free movement of labor is a cornerstone of the European Union (EU), but when the EU-10 joined, their access to Old Europe's labor markets was phased in over a seven-year period. Most restrictions have been lifted for the EU-8, which joined in 2004, but widespread limits still remain for the newest members, Romania and Bulgaria. All of the restrictions are to be lifted by 2014.

Labor Restrictions on Bulgarians, Romanians

EU-15
Austria
Belgium
Denmark
Finland
France
Germany
Greece
Ireland
Italy
Luxembourg
Netherlands
Portugal
Spain
Sweden
United Kingdom

restricted
partially restricted
free labor mobility

Source: "World Bank EU8+2 Regional Economic Report," World Bank, May 2007

Fragmentation of the political-party system has become problematic in Poland, with new parties and leaders springing up almost overnight. "There are constant changes of name and leadership," says Poland's Smolar. As a result, "the public comes to trust people more than parties." [44]

In Slovakia, notes the University of Birmingham's Haughton, parties do not have a strong ideological base and depend heavily on financial backers, making them more business-orientated. [45] Civil society and organized labor need to become stronger, he says. But he believes democracy is in no more danger in Central and Eastern Europe than it is in the West. For example, while new parties on the far right are springing up in New Europe, such as *Ataka* (Attack) in Bulgaria, the West is no stranger to the phenomenon. *Vlaams Belang* (Flemish Interest) in Belgium — an anti-immigrant, pro-Flemish independence party — and the equally anti-immigrant *Front National* in France have been attracting substantial support for decades.

Demes, of the U.S.-German Marshall Fund, is optimistic about the future. "The EU is the best democracy-promotion effort ever," he says. "There is no chance there will be backsliding."

Slovenian journalist Briski agrees, saying any slippage is "highly unlikely, even impossible," because of NATO and EU membership and because of people's memories of undemocratic regimes.

Sofia University's Andreev says the powers of executive branches of government are increasingly being challenged by parliaments across New Europe, but he adds, "I would not worry about this too much — it is probably a necessary transformation."

BACKGROUND

End of Empires

Europe's frontiers have been constantly changing due to wars and shifting alliances. The great Hapsburg, Romanov, Napoleonic and Ottoman empires paid little attention to ethnicity when drawing up borders, even erasing Poland from the map entirely between 1795 and 1918.

During the 19th century, however, awareness of ethnic identity sharpened. World War I was a major watershed, leading to the collapse of the German, Austro-Hungarian, Russian and Ottoman empires, whose ashes gave birth to a host of new nation-states

doctoral fellow in European studies at Harvard. "Today, the public is well-informed about the EU, and civil servants are trained in EU affairs."

based more on ethnic identity, including Hungary, Poland and Estonia.

Central and Eastern Europe got a taste of democracy during the interwar period, which proved invaluable in the 1990s when they were trying to re-establish it, says Bulgarian Ambassador Poptodorova. "We had representatives of these parties still living in 1989. This sets us apart from the Soviet Union, which was never really a democracy," she notes.

By 1938, however, many countries had lost their democratic credentials. A fascist regime was in place in Hungary, a military coup in Poland had installed a more authoritarian regime and royal dictatorships ruled in Bulgaria, Romania and Yugoslavia. [46]

When postwar leaders redrew the map of Europe at Versailles in 1919, they did not strictly adhere to ethnic frontiers. With many communities stuck on the "wrong" side of the border, it did not take long for nationalist tensions to flare up.

The presence of ethnic Germans in Czechoslovakia gave German Chancellor Adolf Hitler a pretext for occupying Czechoslovakia in 1939. Much of the remainder of Central Europe was carved up under the Molotov-Ribbentrop non-aggression pact signed by the Soviet Union and Germany on Aug. 24, 1939. [47] The secret protocol consigned Estonia, Latvia and half of Poland to the Soviet sphere and Lithuania, Romania and the rest of Poland to the German sphere.

World War II soon followed, decimating the region and leaving tens of millions massacred or exiled. The Baltic States were occupied first by

Breaking Away

Berliners begin tearing down the Berlin Wall on Nov. 9, 1989 (top), prompting many Eastern bloc countries to declare their independence from the Soviet Union. During Czechoslovakia's peaceful 18-day "Velvet Revolution," a demonstrator in Prague holds a bust of former Soviet leader Josef Stalin with a sign proclaiming "Nothing Lasts Forever" (center). In Vilnius, Lithuania, the toppled monument of Vladimir Lenin, the architect of Soviet communism, is loaded onto a truck on Aug. 23, 1991, after the Lithuanian parliament banned the Communist Party.

Reforms Embrace Democracy, Free Markets

Policies are beginning to bear fruit

Economic and political reforms implemented by the newly independent EU-10 countries following the Soviet Union's disintegration in 1991 embraced democratic and free-market principles. The changes — undertaken in part to qualify for admission to the European Union — included:

Political

- Shifting from one-party, authoritarian rule to multi-party democracy with free elections, sometimes triggering a parallel rise in populism and nationalism.
- Freeing police, judiciaries from political control and reducing corruption somewhat.
- Growing influence among a new business elite and new civil society/non-governmental organizations.
- Transferring considerable lawmaking powers to the EU's supranational institutions.
- Joining NATO and adopting pro-Western orientation.

Economic

- Switching from command-and-control economies to market economies.
- Privatizing telecommunications, financial services, electricity and transport.
- Adopting painful reforms, which in the 1990s caused price increases and job losses. Their economies are now the fastest-growing in Europe, with inflation relatively stable and unemployment falling.
- Liberalizing labor markets, triggering a westward exodus of workers to higher-wage Old Europe.
- Accepting large agricultural subsidies from the EU.
- Reducing communist-era welfare benefits such as pensions, subsidized transportation, rent controls and free health care.
- Reducing tax rates, including the introduction of a flat tax in some countries.
- Adopting EU guidelines on public spending, interest rates and inflation policy.

---

the Soviets, then by the Nazis and then by the Soviets again in 1944, paving the way for the annexation of Latvia, Lithuania and Estonia into the Soviet Union. The rest of Central and Eastern Europe alternated between Soviet and Nazi domination until Germany's defeat in 1945. Warsaw, Poland, suffered a particularly harrowing fate, with 200,000 Poles killed in an uprising against the Nazis in 1944. The Soviet army waited outside the capital until the slaughter subsided before occupying it themselves. [48]

The new map of Europe, charted at a victors' conference in Yalta, Ukraine, by U.S. President Franklin D. Roosevelt, British Prime Minister Winston Churchill and Soviet leader Josef Stalin, saw borders shifting westward at Stalin's insistence, causing 12 million Germans to flee Eastern and Central Europe. [49]

Iron Curtain Descends

Immediately after the war, communist regimes were installed throughout Central and Eastern Europe, usually with Soviet intervention or manipulation. The commu-nists' resistance to the Nazis and their pledge to end social inequalities, however, gave them some popular appeal.

For example, in Czechoslovakia communists won 38 percent of the vote in 1948. [50] That year, in response to the U.S. Marshall Plan for Western Europe, Comecon was established as a trading bloc for Central and Eastern Europe. [51] Some countries, notably Czechoslovakia and Poland, considered applying for Marshall aid but were pressured not to by Moscow. In the following decades, the Soviets provided Comecon nations with cheap oil, putting an increasing strain on the Soviet economy. [52]

In 1955, the Soviets, Poland, East Germany, Czechoslovakia, Hungary, Romania, Bulgaria and Albania signed a military alliance known as the Warsaw Pact in response to the emergence of the U.S.-dominated NATO alliance. Moscow kept a firm military grip on its satellites. Soviet troops entered Hungary in 1956 to suppress a rebellion against Soviet interference. In 1968 the Soviets moved into Czechoslovakia to halt the "Prague Spring" liberalizing reforms of leader Alexander Dubçek. [53]

Though the Soviets did not invade Poland, a strike at the Gdansk shipyard in 1980 by the Solidarity trade union movement led Poland's leader Gen. Wojciech Jaruzelski to impose martial law. Jaruzelski initiated some economic reforms in January 1988, causing a 40 percent rise in food prices and a doubling of energy costs. [54]

Hungary's leader Janos Kadar began easing state controls on agriculture and light industry in the 1970s and '80s, which helped push up living standards. Czechoslovakia gradually allowed more private enterprise in the 1980s. [55] Romania was ruled by Ceausescu and his wife Elena, who alienated the Kremlin by trying to make their country economically independent and occasionally criticizing Soviet actions. By contrast Bulgaria's Todor Zhivkov staunchly supported the Soviets. Slovenia was part of Yugoslavia, which though communist managed to distance itself from Moscow. Despite their differences, all regimes were characterized by single-party rule, socialist economic models and an oppressive state apparatus that stifled free expression.

AP Photo/Alik Keplicz

Poland's powerful Kaczynski twins, President Lech, left, and Prime Minister Jaroslaw, are leading a wave of social conservatism. Denis MacShane, a former U.K. minister for Europe, claims the Kaczynski brothers are "busy burying the democratic revolution that ousted communism."

Breaking Free

The seeds of revolution had been sown in 1980 with the emergence of the Solidarity movement in Poland — the first independent trade union in the Soviet bloc. A further milestone was reached in 1985 when Mikhail S. Gorbachev became leader of the Soviet Union and launched his glasnost and perestroika reforms promoting, respectively, greater openness and economic restructuring. Urging the Soviet president to make good on his reform promises, U.S. President Ronald Reagan famously stood in front of the Berlin Wall during a June 12, 1987, visit and challenged Gorbachev: "Open this gate" and "tear down this wall." [56] These stirrings of change culminated in a dramatic cascade of revolutions in 1989.

Poland elected a non-communist government in June that brought Solidarity leader Lech Walesa to power. On Nov. 9, Germans began tearing down the Berlin Wall — the ultimate symbol of a divided Europe — in what was the defining moment of the collapse of communism in the former Soviet satellites. On Nov. 10 Zhivkov resigned in Bulgaria. The removal of the Ceausescus from power in Romania — they were executed on Dec. 25 following a hastily convened trial — was a bloodier affair. [57]

Two years later, in June 1991, Slovenia seceded from Yugoslavia, triggering a 10-day, low-intensity war that ultimately confirmed its independence. The Delaware-size nation was mercifully spared the extreme violence and bloodshed that plagued much of the rest of ex-Yugoslavia in the 1990s. Latvia, Lithuania and Estonia gained full independence when the U.S.S.R. was dissolved on Dec. 31, 1991. [58]

"After 1989, it was briefly thought that the new member states would not relinquish their newfound freedom because of their Soviet experience," says Oklahoma State's Strong. "But it turned out they wanted to participate fully in the EU." [59] East Germany scored a fast-track route to EU membership by reunifying with West Germany in October 1990. For the rest, the first major step came in June 1993, when EU leaders meeting in Copenhagen agreed on the political, economic and administrative benchmarks — the "Copenhagen criteria" — that applicants would have to meet in order to join.

Czechoslovakia split into two nations in 1993. Slovakia was governed until October 1998 by the nationalist Vladimir Meciar. Dubbed by former U.S. Secretary of State Madeleine K. Albright "the black hole of Central Europe" because of Meciar's alleged anti-democratic leanings and corruption, Slovakia did not start EU accession talks until after Meciar's political demise. "This made Slovakia more obedient, because it wanted to catch up with Poland and Hungary," according to the University of Birmingham's Haughton. [60] Slovenia's path to membership was smoother, since it had had a democratic, stable, pro-EU government since 1992.

In December 1997, the EU approved membership talks for Poland, the Czechs, Estonia, Hungary and Slovenia. Two years later it did the same for Bulgaria, Romania, Latvia, Lithuania and Slovakia. Western Europe's reluctance to open its labor markets to workers from New Europe was a major stumbling block during the talks; in the end, the 2003 accession agreements allowed Old Europe to restrict access for up to seven years. Most countries in Old Europe have since lifted those restrictions.

The referenda on EU membership passed with varying degrees of support in the former communist countries. While 93 percent of Slovakians and 90 percent of Slovenians voted in favor, the Baltic States were more

> "The extent to which the EU is able to reverse its downward economic spiral may depend on the effort that Western European countries make to imitate the pro-business, pro-growth economic policies of Central Europe."
>
> — Center for European Policy and Analysis,
>
> May 6, 2006

circumspect, with some wondering why they were joining another union after struggling for decades to get out of one. Latvia and Estonia delayed their referenda until after the others, gambling correctly that strong Yes votes elsewhere would ratchet up the pressure. [61] The referenda passed in both countries with 67 percent of the vote.

On May 1, 2004, the Baltic States, Poland, the Czech Republic, Slovakia, Hungary and Slovenia entered the EU family. Bulgaria and Romania were forced to wait until Jan. 1, 2007, when the EU was satisfied with their efforts to tackle corruption and organized crime, among other things.

As for NATO, the Czech Republic, Hungary and Poland joined the Brussels-based Atlantic alliance on March 12, 1999. Bulgaria, Romania, Latvia, Lithuania, Estonia, Slovakia and Slovenia followed suit in 2004.

Once accession was accomplished, the debate shifted to what New Europe wanted from its EU membership. In Poland, divergent positions of former EU enthusiasts and euro-skeptics converged into one of "euro-realism," says Christine Normann, EU affairs lecturer at the University of Trier in Germany. [62]

For example, after EU farm subsidies began pouring in, the Polish peasant party Samoobrona (Self-defense) became less hostile to Brussels. And New Europe put Old Europe to shame by scoring a better record in implementing EU law. By the end of 2005, the new member states had transposed 98.8 percent of EU directives into national law on time, compared with 98.1 percent among old member states. [63]

Poland and Lithuania kept the plight of neighboring Belarus high on the agenda by pushing the EU to support fledgling Belarussian pro-democracy movements. The EU had severed relations with Minsk because it disapproved of the state of human rights and democracy in Belarus, which has been ruled since 1994 by autocratic President Alexander Lukashenko.

Bulgaria's EU enthusiasm was dampened in late 2006 when Brussels insisted that Bulgaria close down its nuclear power plant at Kozloduy due to safety concerns. Until then Sofia had been a major energy supplier to the region. Hungary had some setbacks, largely because its economy did not grow as strongly as some of its neighbors. And in the Baltic States, relations with ex-Big Brother Russia deteriorated.

CURRENT SITUATION

Wavering Allies?

The proposed U.S. missile defense program is fast becoming the new litmus test for European loyalty to the United States, just as the Iraq War was in 2003.

In recent months details have emerged about President Bush's plans to install 10 missile interceptors in Poland and tracking radar in the Czech Republic by 2013. Fears the program could reignite the Cold War have triggered growing opposition and weakened support for the United States among some EU-10 leaders.

Does joining the EU strengthen Central and Eastern Europe's transatlantic ties?

YES
Karen Donfried
Executive Vice President, The German Marshall Fund of the United States

Written for *CQ Researcher*, July 2007

At the end of the Cold War, a new map of Europe began to emerge from the rubble of the Berlin Wall. Successive U.S. administrations have sought to create a new Europe that was peaceful, democratic and undivided. To U.S. policymakers, membership in the European Union (EU) for the newly sovereign countries of Central and Eastern Europe was a critical means to that end. Thus, when the EU welcomed Poland, Hungary, the Czech Republic, Slovakia, Slovenia, Estonia, Latvia and Lithuania as full members in 2004 — and Romania and Bulgaria in 2007 — Washington stood on the sidelines, like a proud midwife.

Washington's high hopes for the new Europe — and for better transatlantic relations — have been largely realized. EU membership has brought profound changes both for the new member states and for the European Union. Poland, Romania and the Baltics today are among the most pro-American countries in the world. And it is virtually impossible to imagine the expanded, 27-member EU uniting in opposition to U.S. policy.

Missile defense is a case in point. In January, the Bush administration requested permission to place a radar base in the Czech Republic and 10 interceptor missiles in Poland as part of a global missile defense system. While the initial response from these two countries was positive, a huge and emotional debate unfurled across Europe. Russian President Putin strongly opposes putting the missile defense shield in Central Europe. The Bush administration just as forcefully insists the system is not aimed at Russia but is designed to protect Europe from missiles launched from a country such as Iran. Throughout this debate, Czech and Polish support has held firm.

Some Europeans say America should oppose EU enlargement because it will impede the deepening of EU-U.S. integration in areas like internal security or foreign policy. While a larger, more diverse EU probably will slow integration, EU expansion is more important to the United States than further deepening. The level of integration already achieved — from a single market to a single currency — is remarkable. And the basic goal of ensuring that member states will never go to war with one another has been achieved.

Now the top priority as far as U.S. interests are concerned is the EU's ability to spread prosperity, democracy and stability eastward. As recent experience shows, an expanded EU makes a better transatlantic partner for the United States.

NO
Sally McNamara
Senior Policy Analyst in European Affairs, The Heritage Foundation

Written for *CQ Researcher*, July 2007

Enlargement has been one of the European Union's few success stories in recent years. The symbolism of seeing Central and Eastern Europe fully integrated into the European community was indeed powerful. It is not difficult to see why these countries were lining up at Brussels' door. With vast agricultural subsidies and huge structural funds, the EU presented a heady economic package of incentives. Equally, the carrot of EU membership kept many countries on the reform path when the going got tough.

U.S. foreign policy has always supported the widening of the Euro-Atlantic community, both within the EU and in NATO. However, it is no longer clear whether a deepening of the EU is in America's interests.

The militarization of the EU through the European Security and Defense Policy (ESDP) centralizes critical elements of nation-states' power at the supranational level. The creation of duplicate and discriminatory military structures independent of the successful NATO Alliance marks one of the biggest geopolitical shifts in transatlantic alliance-making since the end of the Second World War. It is a political initiative that embodies the worst elements of European animosity toward the United States, and one that fundamentally undermines both NATO and the "Anglo-American Special Relationship."

In building global alliances, America must maximize its opportunities. Deeper European integration, however, especially toward a Common Foreign and Security Policy (CFSP), will limit America's options. The potential to destabilize transatlantic alliance-building has never been greater.

The U.S. alliance with the U.K. is one of the most successful in modern history, in part because both partners are willing to defend their shared values with force if necessary. Other countries clearly want to deepen their American ties. Poland and the Czech Republic are on track to enter into a special security relationship with the United States by hosting missile defense bases. Managing the fluidity and complexity of alliance-building can be achieved only if nations remain self-determining sovereign powers.

To maintain a working relationship with the United States that enables them to pursue an agenda in their national interest, Central and Eastern European countries must remain sovereign powers. They must resist pressure for deeper integration into EU structures such as the CFSP and the ESDP and must not be tempted to compromise on key elements of sovereignty during revived negotiations over the European Constitution this year.

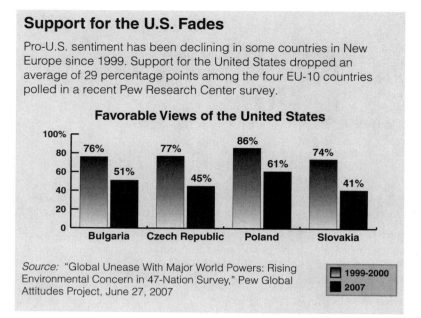

Support for the U.S. Fades

Pro-U.S. sentiment has been declining in some countries in New Europe since 1999. Support for the United States dropped an average of 29 percentage points among the four EU-10 countries polled in a recent Pew Research Center survey.

Favorable Views of the United States

Bulgaria: 76% (1999-2000), 51% (2007)
Czech Republic: 77% (1999-2000), 45% (2007)
Poland: 86% (1999-2000), 61% (2007)
Slovakia: 74% (1999-2000), 41% (2007)

Legend: 1999-2000, 2007

Source: "Global Unease With Major World Powers: Rising Environmental Concern in 47-Nation Survey," Pew Global Attitudes Project, June 27, 2007

"If we fail to change the perception that this is an ideological project, it could lead to new splits," warns Polish Ambassador Reiter, whose government broadly supports the plan. [64] Meanwhile, Russian President Vladimir Putin strongly opposes the missile defense program. The Czechs and Poles do not want to be told what to do by either the EU or Russia. "The Czech Republic will decide on this either through parliament or through a referendum . . . not someone in Brussels or Moscow," Czech Prime Minister Mirek Topolanek said on April 29. [65]

Support for the United States also is being sapped by New Europe's exclusion from the U.S. visa waiver program. "Poles do not know what a visa is until they try to go to the U.S." says Reiter. "Getting a visa is a very unpleasant procedure not understood by them. Our memories of President Reagan supporting the Solidarity movement are fading." [66]

Economically the picture is rosier. U.S. enterprises — including Philip Morris, Citibank, Procter & Gamble, Coca-Cola and General Motors — invested $2.6 billion in New Europe in 2004, more than ever before. [67]

Russian Shadow

On April 26, Estonia moved a Soviet-era Red Army war memorial from central Tallinn to a military cemetery outside the city. Russian Foreign Minister Sergei Ivanov angrily called it an act of vandalism and urged a boycott of Estonian products.

"Do not spend your holidays in Estonia but go to Kaliningrad instead," he urged his countrymen. [68]

Russian trains stopped delivering oil to Estonia, and Russian nationalists attacked Estonian diplomats outside the Estonian Embassy in Moscow. [69] Estonia suffered waves of cyber attacks, allegedly masterminded by the Kremlin, causing government Web sites to crash for several days. At the core of the dispute are divergent interpretations of history: Estonians see the Soviets' 1944 arrival as an occupation, Russians view it as liberation from the Nazis.

The European Parliament supports Estonia, passing a resolution on May 24 asserting Soviet occupation and annexation of the Baltic States "was never recognized as legal by Western democracies" and calling the dispute "a test case for EU solidarity." [70]

In any case, the spat exemplifies the poor state of relations between Russia and its former satellites. Arguably, Estonia has the most contentious relationship with Russia: The two countries have had no high-level visits, and no treaty establishes their common border.

The history question erupted again in April 2007, when EU Justice ministers were trying to agree on common criminal sanctions for racist offenses. The Baltic States, Slovenia and Poland wanted the sanctions to include denial of crimes committed under Stalin. But their EU colleagues rejected the notion, fearful that extending the law's scope would open a can of worms. The ministers decided instead to hold a public debate on totalitarian regimes, with EU legislation possibly to follow. [71]

New Europe's Soviet past is also being revisited via Poland's lustration law, which was partially invalidated on May 11, 2007. The constitutional court of Poland said the law, which seeks to shed light on Poles' collaboration with former communist authorities, could not be applied to non-public officials such as journalists, school principals and university rectors. [72]

"In its fight against the remnants of a totalitarian system, the state must respect the principle of the rule of law; otherwise the country is no better than a totalitarian regime," said Chief Justice Jerzy Stepien. The ruling was a vindication for Bronislaw Geremek, who had been threatened with the loss of his seat in the European Parliament for refusing to sign the required declaration. [73]

Russian President Putin's recent statements that the U.S. missile defense program could trigger a new arms race or even a nuclear war have not gone down well in New Europe either. [74] "We do not understand the criticism," says Eva-Marie Liimets, deputy chief of mission at the Estonian Embassy in Washington. "The program is not for defending us against Russia, but [against] Iran." [75]

Poland's Reiter agrees. "I do not see legitimate concerns from Russia. I see threats. I see Russian foreign policy as ad hoc. It wants to be a troubleshooter and troublemaker," he says. [76]

In the latest development, Russian Foreign Minister Ivanov went so far as to suggest that Russia might place missiles in Kaliningrad, its exclave wedged between Poland and Lithuania, if the Polish and Czech installations proceed. (*See sidebar, p. 344.*) [77] Putin also has proposed that the United States and Russia use a radar station in Azerbaijan instead of the Czech and Polish installations, adding somewhat menacingly that the Azeri plan would make it "unnecessary for us to place our offensive complexes along the borders with Europe." [78]

Anti-Russian feelings are tempered by the knowledge that New Europe — apart from Romania — relies heavily on Russian gas and oil imports. The EU is trying to reduce this dependency by subsidizing construction of a so-called Nabucco pipeline, which would transport natural gas from Turkey to Europe. In spring 2007 there were reports — denied by the Hungarian government — that Budapest was going to pull out of the project and do a separate deal with Russia. Hungary maintains economic ties with Russia because it buys oil or gas from Moscow. [79]

Hungary's possible defection is galvanizing others in New Europe, notably the Baltic States, to push for a common EU energy policy that could block Russia from picking off "good" partners like Hungary and penalizing "bad" ones like Estonia.

In yet another instance of conflict with Russia and the need for unified EU policy, Polish-Russian relations have remained strained since Moscow banned Polish meat exports in late 2005 on the gounds they did not meet

An Estonian Orthodox Church priest officiates at a reburying ceremony on July 3, 2007, for eight World War II-era Soviet soldiers. After their remains — and the statue of a Soviet soldier — were relocated from downtown Tallinn to a military cemetery outside of town, Moscow halted oil deliveries to Estonia. The spat exemplifies the strained relations between Russia and its former satellites.

food safety norms. The EU has shown solidarity with Poland by insisting Polish meat is safe and urging Moscow to end the ban. Russia must now confront not just one country but all 27 — underlining to New Europe the advantages of EU membership. By contrast, Russo-Bulgarian relations — close in the Soviet era — have remained good.

"The Russians liberated us from the Turks. We remember this," says Ambassador Poptodorova. Bulgarian President Parvanov said recently: "The Bulgarians must not choose between the U.S. and Russia. . . . [We] should and can maintain friendly relations with both." [80] Bulgaria also gets 100 percent of its natural gas from Russia.

Reform Fatigue

While the new member states' economies continue to grow strongly, a recent World Bank report warns that "reform momentum in the region has generally waned owing to post-accession reform fatigue, unstable political situations and weak administrative capacity." [81]

The report said governments were "not taking adequate advantage" of the current economic growth to improve their public finances." It also predicted a mild deceleration in growth in 2007 "towards more sustainable patterns . . . at least in the Baltic States and Romania." [82]

Unemployment rates remain slightly higher than in Old Europe, ranging from 4.7 percent in Estonia to 11.2 percent in Poland. [83] The overall employment rate in New Europe is 58.3 percent compared to 66 percent in Old Europe. [84] But New Europe remains poorer: Latvia's per capita GDP is only 43 percent of old member states' GDP, while Slovenia's is only 75 percent. [85] Life expectancy also is lower — just 65 years for Estonian and Latvian men, compared to the EU average of 75 years. [86]

The Baltic States have been the most effective in liberalizing their economies. In a setback to their economic model, however, the advocate general of the EU Court of Justice concluded on May 23 that Swedish trade unions were entitled to block the Latvian employees of Laval over the company's refusal to sign a wage agreement. But the full court has yet to deliver a definitive ruling. [87]

As living standards rise and business horizons expand, support for the EU among former euro-skeptic Estonia now stands at more than 70 percent. In this climate, the Baltic trio does not seem very worried about loss of national sovereignty to Brussels.

Poland is experiencing a wave of social conservatism, led by the powerful Kaczynski brothers. With church attendances in most European countries at historic lows, Poland is bucking the trend, ordaining 1,000 Catholic priests each year, notes European Parliament official O'Beara. Moreover, the church's influence is clearly permeating the political sphere: The government passed a bill to allow teachers to be fined, fired or even imprisoned for promoting "homosexual propaganda" in schools.

Denis MacShane, a former U.K. minister for Europe, laments the trend. "Poland should be a happy country," he said. "Its cities are booming with new skyscrapers, restaurants and one of the youngest populations in the old continent. But its politics are troubling." The Kaczynski brothers are "busy burying the democratic revolution that ousted communism." [88]

MacShane is particularly critical of the Kaczynskis' coalition partner, the League of Polish Families led by the father and son duo of Maciej and Roman Giertych. Roman, who is deputy prime minister and education minister, "won't talk to the BBC because it has reported on pedophile Catholic priests," MacShanes notes. "His father hated Solidarity and supported its suppression in 1981. In the European Parliament he praised [authoritarian Spanish leader Francisco] Franco and this year published a pamphlet saying that Jews were biologically different." [89]

Hungary's attempts to maintain generous Soviet-era welfare state benefits have necessitated higher taxes, thereby reducing its economic competitiveness. It is beginning to turn away from this model and to liberalize its economy.

Slovenia's per capita GDP — at 82 percent of the EU average — is highest among the new member states. On Jan. 1, 2007, it became the first country in New Europe to adopt the euro as its currency.

"We liked to think of ourselves as an Alpine or Mediterranean nation. But now, after years of turning our back on our Yugoslavia experience, we see how much of an asset this is to the EU in negotiating with the Balkan countries," says Klemencic, the Slovenian postdoctoral fellow at Harvard. [90]

Romania is experiencing a power struggle between President Traian Basescu and Prime Minister Calin Tariceanu. The parliament voted to impeach Basescu in April over claims he abused his authority in trying to fight corruption. However, a May 19 referendum reconfirmed Basescu until 2009 with 74 percent of the vote. European Commission President José Manuel Barroso said he hoped the result would allow judiciary reforms and anti-corruption efforts to proceed. The EU also is concerned about the dismissal of Romanian Justice Minister Monica Macovei — whom Brussels sees as the architect of Romanian judicial reform. [91]

In Bulgaria, Western Europeans are arriving in droves to buy holiday homes along the Black Sea coast, according to Ambassador Poptodorova. Sofia is also opening up its secret Soviet-era files. Only 28.6 percent turned out, however, for Bulgaria's European Parliament elections on May 20, and the country's ultranationalist Ataka Party made a relatively strong showing, at 14 percent. [92]

Ambassador Poptodorova likens Ataka to an "exotic weed" that is "anti-everything — the EU, NATO, minorities — they take the protest vote, the losers' vote."

OUTLOOK

Looking Back and Forward

New Europe has taken a hard look at its communist-era past, and now it is beginning to shine the spotlight of self-examination at another painful period — Nazi occupation.

Most of the 250,000 Jews living in the Baltic States were killed or forced to flee during World War II, with locals sometimes helping the Germans round up Jews for mass shootings and burials outside of towns. [93]

Estonia, for example, has set up two presidential commissions to explore the Nazi occupation. German-Polish relations also could be tested when Germans who were expelled from Poland after the war begin claiming property they lost when Europe's borders shifted.

With its high emigration levels and low birth rate, New Europe's aging population — ballooning even faster than in Old Europe — could be the next generation's biggest political challenge. The Czech Republic, for example, will be short 1.4 million workers by 2050 — one-third of its working population, according to the Dutch-based think-thank SEO Economic Research. [94] If tax returns suffer as a result, it could put upward pressure on public spending on healthcare and pensions, triggering public-debt problems.

That could make it more difficult for New Europe to adopt the euro because of the strict fiscal and monetary standards needed. However, the EU could show more flexibility on the standards to make it easier for them to join. Existing rules have been widely criticized for stifling economic growth.

The Brussels cash cow will continue to be milked, with EU subsidies rising to 3 percent of New Europe's gross national income for 2007-2013. [95] Whether New Europe economies continue growing at current rates will depend on how wisely they spend the aid money.

"If you build highways to nowhere, it won't help you," notes Poland's Balcerowicz, now chairman of the National Bank of Poland. [96]

In the ongoing effort to establish a new legal framework for the EU, New Europe likely will push for EU expansion rather than deeper political integration. Although Old Europe is much more skeptical of enlargement, New Europe backs the desires of Turkey, Ukraine and Moldova to join the EU, largely so they won't form a rival coalition with Russia. [97]

"We understand what it is like to be left aside and how beneficial it is to meet the EU standards," says Romanian diplomat Gitman. Bucharest wants its eastern neighbor Moldova to join at the same time the western Balkan countries of Serbia, Croatia, Bosnia-Herzegovina, Montenegro, Macedonia and Albania join. But Gitman says Moldova needs to become less dependent on Russia before this can happen.

On Jan. 1, 2008, Slovenia will become the first new member state to assume the EU presidency, allowing it to set the EU agenda for the next six months. "Our priority will be EU enlargement in the western Balkans," says Harvard's Klemencic, pointing out that 35 percent of Slovenia's trade goes there, and "the existence of border controls is very costly for us." [98]

Border controls between Old and New Europe and between the EU-10 countries themselves are due to be removed over the next two years as New Europe is integrated into the EU's "Schengen Area," the border-free zone named after the Luxembourg town where five Western European countries first agreed in 1985 to abolish border controls. There are widespread jitters that the enlargement of the Schengen Area will lead to more illegal immigration as Europe's borders expand and become more difficult to control.

With New Europe feeling increasingly threatened by Russia, observers question whether the EU-10 will look towards the EU, NATO or the United States for protection. Most likely they will continue to anchor themselves in all three, but problems could arise when the three disagree on how to deal with a specific threat. If that happens, New Europe may be forced to choose one vision over another.

After struggling for two decades to put the Cold War behind them, that is a scenario New Europe would like to avoid. As Hungarian journalist Hofer says, "the former communist states can no longer be viewed as a separate

'New Europe.' There is only one Europe. The ex-communist nations that have joined NATO and the EU — they have again become part of Europe."

NOTES

1. Eurostat, http://epp.eurostat.ec.europa.eu.

2. Wess Mitchell, "Tipping the Scales: Why Central Europe matters to the U.S.," Center for European Policy and Analysis (CEPA), May 6, 2006, p. 20, www.cepa.org.

3. *Ibid.*, p. 27.

4. *Ibid.*, p. 28.

5. *Ibid.*

6. *Ibid.*, p. 18.

7. For detailed U.K. figures, see "Accession Monitoring Report A8 countries May 2004-May 2007," U.K. Home Office, May 22, 2007, www.ind.homeoffice.gov.uk, p. 6.

8. *Ibid.*

9. Responding to recent U.K. government report on immigration, June 13, 2007, www.migrationwatchuk.org.

10. "EU8 + 2, Regular Economic Report, May 2007," World Bank, May 2007, p. 15, http://siteresources.worldbank.org/INTECA/Resources/EU8_2_RER_May_2007_Main_Report.pdf.

11. "Enlargement, two years after: an economic evaluation," *European Commission*, May 2006, p. 30, http://ec.europa.eu/economy_finance/index_en.htm. This report does not cover Romania and Bulgaria, which joined the EU on Jan. 1, 2007.

12. Rumsfeld was briefing journalists at the Foreign Press Center, U.S. Department of State, Washington D.C., Jan. 22, 2003, http://fpc.state.gov/fpc/16799.htm.

13. See "Outrage at 'old Europe' remarks," BBC, Jan. 23, 2003, http://news.bbc.co.uk/2/hi/europe/2687403.stm.

14. She was speaking at a conference on "Becoming Good Europeans? The New Member States in the European Union," School for Advanced International Studies (SAIS), Johns Hopkins University, Washington, D.C., April 12-13, 2007.

15. See Dick Marty, "Secret detentions and illegal transfers of detainees involving Council of Europe member states: Second report," approved by Council of Europe parliamentary assembly on June 27, 2007, www.assembly.coe.int/Main.asp?link=/Documents/AdoptedText/ta07/ERES1562.htm.

16. Smolar was speaking at a SAIS presentation on May 7, 2007.

17. Mitchell, *op. cit.*, p. 22.

18. See Sally McNamara, "The Polish American Relationship: Deepening and Strengthening the Alliance," The Heritage Foundation, Feb. 27, 2007, p. 4, www.heritage.org/Research/Europe/bg2010.cfm.

19. Quoted in Ivan Watson, "Bulgaria Celebrates Nurses' Release from Libya," "Morning Edition," National Public Radio, July 25, 2007.

20. Pew Research Center, "47-nation Pew Global Attitudes Survey," June 27, 2007, www.pewglobal.org.

21. Haughton was speaking at the SAIS conference, April 12-13, 2007, *op. cit.*

22. Discussion with Medlir Mema, Ph.D. candidate in political science at the Elliott School of International Affairs, The George Washington University, Washington, D.C., April 19, 2007. See also Coalition for the ICC, www.iccnow.org. For background, see Kenneth Jost, "International Law," *CQ Researcher*, Dec. 17, 2004, pp. 1049-1072.

23. Joint press conference with Presidents Parvanov and Bush, National Museum of History, Sofia, Bulgaria, June 11, 2007.

24. Reiter was speaking at the Woodrow Wilson Center for International Scholars, Washington, D.C., April 4, 2007.

25. Smolar, *op. cit.*

26. McNamara, *op. cit.*, p. 5.

27. European Commission, May 2006 report, *op. cit.*

28. *Ibid.*, p. 14.

29. World Bank, *op. cit.*, p. 5.

30. Article from EurActiv, April 6, 2007, www.euractiv.com.

31. Mitchell, *op. cit.*, p. 15.

32. European Commission, *op. cit.*, p. 92.

33. Mitchell, *op. cit.*, p. 18.

34. Akule was speaking at the SAIS conference, April 12-13, 2007, *op. cit.*

35. See Web site of EU Court of Justice, Luxembourg, for details, Case C-341/07, www.curia.europa.eu.

36. Discussion with Eva-Marie Liimets, deputy chief of the Estonian mission to the United States, Elliott School of International Affairs, The George Washington University, Washington DC, March 21, 2007.

37. Presentation at SAIS conference, April 12 and 13, 2007.

38. Nauduzas was speaking at The Heritage Foundation, Washington, D.C., June 14, 2007.

39. World Bank, *op. cit.*, p. 15.

40. "Nations in Transit 2007," Freedom House, June 14, 2007, www.freedomhouse.hu/index.php?option= com_content&task=view&id=84.

41. For background, see Kenneth Jost, "Future of the European Union," *CQ Researcher*, Oct. 28, 2005, pp. 909-932.

42. Speech to the Association of European Journalists, Oct. 14, 2005.

43. Strong was speaking at SAIS, April 12-13, 2007, *op. cit.*

44. Smolar, *op. cit.*

45. Haughton, *op. cit.*

46. For background, see Kenneth Jost, "Democracy in Eastern Europe," *CQ Researcher*, Oct. 8, 1999, pp. 865-888.

47. For background, see M. Packman, "Indirect Aggression," in *Editorial Research Reports, 1957* (Vol. I) and V. Pope, "Soviet Republics Rebel," *CQ Researcher*, July 12, 1991, pp. 465-488, both available at *CQ Researcher Plus Archive*, CQ Electronic Library; http://library.cqpress.com.

48. See Norman Davies, *Rising '44: The Battle for Warsaw* (2003).

49. For background, see "Founding of the United Nations and Emergence of the Cold War, 1945-1964," *Congress and the Nation Online Edition, 1945-1964*, available at http://library.cqpress.com.

50. See Davies, *ibid.*

51. For background, see Mary H. Cooper, "Communist Economies," *Editorial Research Reports*, Dec. 28, 1984, and H. Kellock, "Soviet Russia and the Border States," *Editorial Research Reports, 1943*, Vol. I and F. Van Schaick, "Conditions for American Aid," *Editorial Research Reports, 1947*, Vol. II, all available at *CQ Researcher Plus Archive*, http://library.cqpress.com.

52. Cooper, *ibid.*

53. For background, see W. Gerber and Richard Worsnop, "Czechoslovakia and European Security," *Editorial Research Reports, 1968*, Vol. II, available at *CQ Researcher Plus Archive*, http://library.cqpress.com.

54. See Jost, 1999, *op. cit.*

55. *Ibid.*

56. The Associated Press, " 'Mr. Gorbachev, Open This Gate, Tear Down This Wall'; President's Challenge in Berlin Talk," *Los Angeles Times*, June 12, 1987.

57. For background, see Hoyt Gimlin, "Balkanization of Eastern Europe (Again)," *Editorial Research Reports, 1989*, Vol. II, available at *CQ Researcher Plus Archive*, http://library.cqpress.com.

58. For background, see Pope, *op. cit.*

59. Strong, *op. cit.*

60. Haughton, *op. cit.*

61. Kasekamp, *op. cit.*

62. Presentation at SAIS conference, April 12 and 13, 2007, *op. cit.*

63. European Commission, *op. cit.*, p. 34.

64. Reiter, *op. cit.*

65. Quoted in "Czechs Will Not Bow to Pressure on Missile Defense," Agence France-Presse, April 29, 2007.

66. Reiter, *op. cit.*

67. Mitchell, *op. cit.*, p. 23.

68. EurActiv, *op cit.*

69. Tony Halpin, "Russia cuts off oil in battle over war statue," *The Times*, May 3, 2007, www.timesonline.co.uk/tol/news/world/europe/article1738813.ece.

70. See European Parliament Web site for text of resolution, www.europarl.europa.eu/sides/getDoc.do?pubRef=-//EP//TEXT+TA+P6-TA-2007-0215+0+DOC+XML+V0//EN&language=EN.

71. *EU Observer*, EU affairs subscription-only online news service, April 20, 2007, http://euobserver.com.

72. www.trybunal.gov.pl/eng/index.htm.

73. See Jan Cienski, "Judge curbs Polish informers law," *Financial Times*, May 11 2007, www.ft.com/cms/s/56ee999e-0004-11dc-8c98-000b5df10621,_i_rssPage=7c485a38-2f7a-11da-8b51-00000e2511c8.html.

74. See Bronwen Maddox, "Putin raises spectre of nuclear war in Europe," *The Times*, June 4, 2007, www.timesonline.co.uk/tol/news/world/europe/article1878730.ece.

75. Liimets, *op. cit.*

76. Reiter, *op. cit.*

77. Tony Halpin and Tom Baldwin, "Russian missile threat to Europe raises Cold War fear over US shield," *The Times*, July 7, 2007, www.timesonline.co.uk/tol/news/world/europe/article2028710.ece.

78. Press conference with President Bush at G-8 summit, Heiligendamm, Germany, June 7, 2007.

79. For background, see Peter Behr, "Energy Nationalism," *CQ Global Researcher*, July 2007, pp. 151-180.

80. G-8 press conference, *op. cit.*

81. World Bank, *op. cit.*, p. 2, http://siteresources.worldbank.org/INTECA/Resources/EU8_2_RER_May_2007_Main_Report.pdf.

82. *Ibid.*, p. 10.

83. Eurostat, April 2007, http://epp.eurostat.ec.europa.eu.

84. World Bank, *op. cit.*, p. 13.

85. European Commission, *op. cit.*, p. 50.

86. *Ibid.*, p. 117.

87. See EU Court of Justice press release, May 23, 2007, www.curia.europa.eu.

88. "We must help Poland to overcome its demons," *The Observer*, July 8, 2007, http://observer.guardian.co.uk/world/story/0,,2121281,00.html.

89. *Ibid.*

90. Klemencic was speaking at SAIS, April 12-13, 2007, *op. cit.*

91. See "Report of the Commission to the European Parliament and the Council on Romania's progress on accompanying measures following accession," European Commission, June 27, 2007, http://ec.europa.eu/dgs/secretariat_general/cvm/docs/romania_report_en.pdf.

92. See "Background note on the first-ever European elections in Bulgaria," May 20, 2007, www.europarl.europa.eu/news/expert/background_page/011-5401-140-05-20-902-20070418BKG05394-20-05-2007-2007-false/default_en.htm.

93. Presentation by Ina Navazelskis, U.S. Holocaust Memorial Museum, at Woodrow Wilson International Center for Scholars, Washington D.C., Feb. 9, 2007.

94. E. Berkhout, Christian Dustmann and Piet Emmer, "Mind the gap," SEO Economic Research, Feb. 2007, p. 53, www.seo.nl/en/index.html.

95. European Commission, *op. cit.*, p. 15.

96. Presentation at SAIS conference, April 12-13, 2007, *op. cit.*

97. Reiter, *op. cit.*

98. Klemencic, *op. cit.*

BIBLIOGRAPHY

Books

Hamilton, Daniel, and Joseph Quinlan, *The Transatlantic Economy 2006: Annual Survey of Jobs, Trade and Investment between the United States and Europe*, Center for Transatlantic Relations, 2007.
While political clashes between the United States and Europe have grabbed most of the headlines in recent years, economic cooperation has been strengthening, according to two leading researchers at the Johns Hopkins University's School of Advanced International Studies.

Articles

Andreev, Svetlozar A., "Bulgaria and Rumania in the EU: Game Over or Stumbling Blocks Ahead," Real Instituto Elcano, Dec. 15, 2006; www.epin.org/index.php.
A politics lecturer at the University of Sofia looks at Romania and Bulgaria's path to European Union (EU) membership, analyzing how prepared they really were on the eve of accession.

McNamara, Sally, "The Polish American Relationship: Deepening and Strengthening the Alliance," The Heritage Foundation, Feb. 27, 2007; www.heritage.org/Research/Europe/bg2010.cfm.

As Poland draws ever closer to the European Union since joining in 2004, a senior policy analyst at the conservative Heritage Foundation argues that Polish-American relations urgently need to be revitalized.

Reports and Studies

"Accession Monitoring Report, A8 Countries, May 2004 — May 2007," United Kingdom Home Office, May 22, 2007; www.ind.homeoffice.gov.uk.
This report charts the recent influx of workers from the New Europe member states to the United Kingdom, breaking them down by nationality and by the professional occupations they have gravitated toward.

"Enlargement, two years after: an economic evaluation," European Commission, May 2006; http://ec. europa.eu/economy_finance/index_en.htm.
The executive arm of the European Union assesses the economic performance of the 10 countries that joined the EU on May 1, 2004. The report does not cover Romania and Bulgaria, which joined on Jan. 1, 2007.

"EU8 + 2, Regular Economic Report, May 2007," World Bank, 2007; http://siteresources.worldbank. org/INTECA/Resources/EU8_2_RER_May_2007_Main _Report.pdf.
The momentum that spurred the new EU member states to grow faster than the old member states at the beginning of the decade is showing signs of fading, with reform fatigue setting in.

"Nations in Transit 2007: Governance Crisis in New Europe," Freedom House, 2007; www.freedom-house.hu/index.php?option=com_content&task=view &id=84.
A report card from Freedom House — a U.S.-based private organization that supports the expansion of democracy and human rights around the world — finds that reform fatigue and political polarization are contributing to an emerging governance crisis in Central Europe.

"Transatlantic Trends Survey 2006," German Marshall Fund of the United States, 2006; www.transatlantic-trends.org.

The fund's annual public opinion survey looks at American and European attitudes toward the transatlantic relationship.

Adamkus, Valdas, "Security and Insecurity in the EU Neighborhood and Beyond: In Search of Solutions," Woodrow Wilson International Center for Scholars, Feb. 9, 2007, www.wilsoncenter.org/index.cfm? topic_id=1422&fuseaction=topics.publications&gro up_id=7427#2007.
The president of Lithuania outlines how Europe and the United States can best work together to tackle today's major challenges to global security.

Berkhout, E., Christian Dustmann and Piet Emmer, "Mind the Gap," SEO Economic Research, Feb. 27, 2007; www.seo.nl/en/index.html.
A Dutch think tank predicts Europe's rapidly aging population — an especially acute problem in Central and Eastern Europe — will likely result in significant labor shortages in coming decades.

Bocka, Besian, Jasenka Jocic, Adrienn Petrovics and and Rossen Tsanov, "Security Threats and Responses in Central Europe," Center for Strategic and International Studies, April 23, 2007, www.csis.org/ component/option,com_csis_pubs/task,view/id,3847 /type,1/.
This report summarizes a two-day conference on transatlantic security issues such as the proposed missile defense sites in Poland and the Czech Republic, the transformation of NATO, conflicts in Eastern Europe and European energy security.

Mitchell, Wess, "Tipping the Scales: Why Central Europe Matters to the United States," Center for European Policy and Analysis (CEPA), May 6, 2006; www.cepa.org/file_download/CEPA_Tipping_the_ Scales.pdf.
A policy researcher at a Washington think tank examines the economic development of Central Europe in recent years, arguing that its enthusiastic adoption of free-market economic policies has made it more dynamic than most of its Western European neighbors.

For More Information

Business Europe, Avenue de Cortenbergh 168, B-1000 Brussels, Belgium; +32 (0)2 237-6511; www.businesseurope.eu. The umbrella body for national employers' federations in the European Union, representing 20 million businesses.

Center for European Policy Analysis (CEPA), 1155 15th St., N.W., Suite 550, Washington, DC 20005; (202) 551-9200; www.cepa.org. Independent, nonprofit, nonpartisan public policy research institute dedicated to the study of Central Europe.

Delegation of the European Commission to the United States, 2300 M St., N.W., Suite 300, Washington, DC 20037-1434; (202) 862-9500; www.eurunion.org. The representative office of the European Union's executive arm in the United States.

The Elliott School of International Affairs, The George Washington University, 1957 E St., N.W., Washington, DC 20052; (202) 994-6240; www.gwu.edu/~elliott. Includes the Institute of European, Russian and Eurasian Affairs.

European Centre of Enterprises with Public Participation and of Enterprises of General Economic Interest (CEEP), Rue de la Charité, 15 bte 12, B-1210 Brussels, Belgium; +32 (0)2 219-2798; www.ceep.org. Representative body at EU level for public-sector employers.

European Commission, Rue de la Loi 200, B-1040 Brussels, Belgium; +32 (0)2 299-1111; http://ec.europa.eu/index_en.htm. The executive arm of the European Union, which proposes EU legislation and oversees its implementation at the national level.

European Trade Union Confederation (ETUC), Blvd. du Roi Albert II, 5, B-1210 Brussels, Belgium; +32 (0)2 224-0411; www.etuc.org. The umbrella body for national trade union federations in the EU, representing 60 million workers.

The German Marshall Fund of the United States, 1744 R St., N.W., Washington, DC 20009; (202) 745-3950; www.gmfus.org. Nonpartisan American public policy and grant-making institution dedicated to promoting greater cooperation and understanding between the United States and Europe.

The Heritage Foundation, 214 Massachusetts Ave., N.E., Washington, DC 20002-4999; (202) 546-4400; www.heritage.org. Conservative think tank with experts in transatlantic relations in its Margaret Thatcher Center for Freedom, which stresses limited government, market economics, the rule of law and strong national defenses.

The Paul H. Nitze School of Advanced International Studies (SAIS), Johns Hopkins University, 1740 Massachusetts Ave., N.W., Washington, DC 20036; (202) 663-5600; www.sais-jhu.edu. One of the leading U.S. graduate schools devoted to the study of international relations.

Woodrow Wilson International Center for Scholars, One Woodrow Wilson Plaza, 1300 Pennsylvania Ave., N.W., Washington, DC 20004-3027; (202) 691-4000; www.wilsoncenter.org. Nonpartisan research forum with a particular strength in international affairs.

VOICES FROM ABROAD

Anton Niculescu

Secretary of State, Ministry of Foreign Affairs, Romania
Romania: Brain drain will hurt us
"How many will come to the U.K.? I doubt it will be a big change. Unfortunately, most of the people leaving are the skilled ones — it is a brain drain. Even if there is a significant rise it would not affect Britain as much as it would affect Romania."

— The Express *(United Kingdom), December 2006*

Olli Rehn

Commissioner for Enlargement, European Union
Our values extend beyond borders
"Every European country that respects values such as democracy, human rights and the rule of law can apply for membership. This does not mean that we have to accept every country. But it would be wrong to definitely close the door by drawing a line on the map that determines Europe's borders forever. With this, we would squander many strategic options."

— Die Welt *(Germany), April 2006*

Roman Kwiatkowski

President, Roma People's Association, Poland
Roma: We are no better off
"Accession of eight states of Central and Eastern Europe to the EU aroused great hope for improvement of the social, economic, educational and legal situation of Roma communities living in those states. Unfortunately . . . Roma must cope with the rising wave of discrimination, racism, xenophobia and ever more frequent acts of violence on racial grounds."

— PAP news agency *(Poland), December 2006*

Editorial

The West forgot the East
"We do not feel any real sense of ceremony here in Latvia with respect to the treaty of Rome. . . . [O]ur hearts are not happy about historical treaties in Western Europe which were concluded at a time when some of Europe rejoiced about a decade without war during which economies were being reborn, while the second part of Europe — Eastern Europe — was pretty much forgotten."

— Latvijas Avize *(Latvia), March 2007*

Valdas Adamkus

President, Lithuania
Solve conflicts now
" 'Frozen' conflicts [ethnic and territorial battles erupting after the collapse of the Soviet Union] are obvious threats, which raise fear and impede economic development in entire regions. It is necessary to find fast and peaceful solutions to those conflicts, because the union of law and democracy cannot coexist with conflicts and isolation."

— Speech, *"Common Vision for a Common Neighbourhood" conference in Vilnius, May 2006*

Editorial

New states pose no threat
"What real threats do the new EU states pose [to the United States]? . . . Protection against the threat of terrorism from Central Europe is . . . an absurd idea. . . . In other words, every sovereign state has a right to its own visa policy, only the reasons for it sometimes have feet of clay."

— Pravda *(Slovakia), May 2006*

Vladimir Spidla

Commissioner for Employment, Social Affairs & Equal Opportunities, European Union
Migration will enhance Europe
"The core of European integration is a country of people, not of things. A Europe where people cannot move is not a finished Europe."

— CTK news agency *(Czech Republic), November 2005*

Aigars Kalvitis

Prime Minister, Latvia
Membership has its rewards
"The EU's funds for economic and business development, education, agriculture, infrastructure and social issues are beginning to bear fruit, and this is serving to enhance the welfare of everyone in Latvia. We are one of the leaders among the new EU member states in making use of the EU's funds."

— Latvijas Vestnesis *(Latvia), May 2006*

José Manuel Barroso

President, European Commission
No more members anytime soon
"It would not be wise to proceed with any further enlargement before we have dealt with the constitutional issue. . . . It would be unwise to bring in other member states apart from Romania and Bulgaria."

— AP Worldstream, *September 2006*

Christo Komarnitski, Bulgaria

14

India Rising

Ken Moritsugu

New residential buildings rise above the slums of Mumbai, formerly known as Bombay. Increasing industrialization and foreign investment have helped create a new middle class in India, but a quarter of the 1.1 billion population still lives on less than $1 a day.

From *CQ Researcher,*
May 1, 2007.

A sea of slums greets passengers landing in teeming Mumbai, where thousands of tiny shacks squeeze right up to the airport fences.

The sprawling metropolis, formerly known as Bombay, is India's business capital. Fortunes are made on the city's soaring stock exchange, so-called Bollywood studios churn out more movies than Hollywood and film stars mingle with the young and wealthy at trendy clubs.

But the flashy goings-on are a world removed from the daily struggle to survive for most of Mumbai's 13 million residents, half of whom live in slums. Indeed, Asia's largest slum, Dharavi, home to 1 million people, sits smack in the middle of the city. Day laborers, who swarm from the impoverished countryside in search of work, sleep on the sidewalks, while others live in makeshift shacks with no electricity, running water or sewer system.

Mumbai epitomizes the two sides of India, one filled with a growing cadre of educated, latte-sipping, cell-phone carrying professionals, the other with often-illiterate workers barely touched by the country's recent economic boom.

"You have 50 percent who are tied into the global economy, and you have 50 percent who don't have hope of owning a house in their lifetime," says Kalpana Sharma, author of the book *Rediscovering Dharavi* and Mumbai bureau chief for *The Hindu,* India's leading liberal newspaper. "The new economy has not touched them."

One of the millions it has touched is Subramanian Pillai. Born and raised in Dharavi, he beckons a visitor up a narrow and steep staircase to a small second-floor room where the two Indias meet.

A Crowded Country in a Nuclear Neighborhood

India has 1.1 billion people — nearly four times as many as the United States — squeezed into a country one-third the size. Two of its neighbors — Pakistan on the west and China to the north — are nuclear powers, as is India. While economic growth has pulled many city-dwellers out of poverty, especially in technology centers like Bangalore, much of the rural population is still extremely poor.

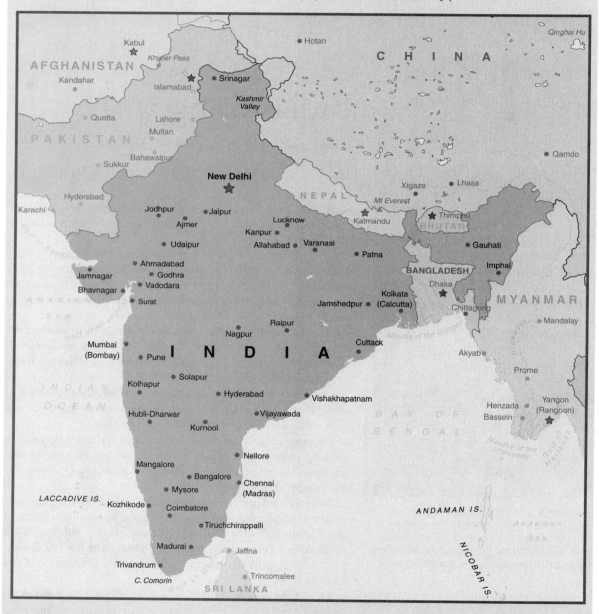

There, in a bare room with concrete walls and floor, Pillai sits doing graphic design on a desktop computer.

A friendly man in his mid-30s, Pillai studied printing technology and learned the trade in a shop. Then he bought a computer, on which he saves his designs — in this case graphics for a pet food box — on a compact disc that he dispatches to a printer. His dream: to be able to buy his own printing machinery and a home for his family outside the slum.

"Ten years back, nobody had a television in their house," he says of his neighborhood. "Now, the economy is growing. Money is coming to people at the bottom. Most people are getting a chance to do something."

Indeed, after two decades of unsteady growth, the economy appears to have shifted into sustained high gear. Gross domestic product (GDP) grew an estimated 9.2 percent for the fiscal year that ended March 31, following a 9 percent rise in the previous year. That puts growth over the last four years at a sizzling 8.6 percent. That's still behind China, which is growing about 10 percent annually. [1]

India has emerged as a global base for outsourcing, carrying out software development and "back office" functions — from call centers to processing health-insurance claims — for American and other overseas companies.

India at a Glance

Area: 3.3 million sq. km., slightly more than one-third the size of the United States.

Population: 1.13 billion (July 2007 est.)

Population growth: 1.6 percent per year

Infant mortality: 34.6 deaths per 1,000

Labor force: 509.3 million (2006 est.)

Unemployment rate: 7.8 percent (2006 est.)

Religion: Hindu 80.5 percent; Muslim 13.4 percent; Christian 2.3 percent; Sikh 1.9 percent; the remaining 1.9 percent includes Buddhists and Jains.

Languages: English is used for political and business communication. Hindi is the largest indigenous tongue, spoken by 30 percent of the population. Bengali, Urdu, Telugu and Tamil are among India's 32 other major languages.

Government: The most powerful political leader is the prime minister, who is elected by the lower house (Lok Sabha), which has 543 elected members serving five-year terms. All but 12 of the 250 members of the upper house — the Council of States — are elected by state and territorial legislatures. The remaining 12 are appointed by the president, who is elected by Parliament and state legislatures for a five-year term and has only limited power.

Economy: The economy ranges from subsistence farming and handicraft manufacturing to software and biotechnology industries. The country also has large service and manufacturing sectors, including textiles, chemicals and finance. The gross domestic product was $806 billion in 2005. About 25 percent of the population lived below the poverty line in 2002.

Communications hardware: There are 49.8 million land-line telephones, 69.2 million mobile phones and 1.5 million Internet hosts serving 60 million users.

Source: The World Factbook 2007, Central Intelligence Agency, 2007, and World Development Indicators 2007, World Bank

Unlike China, though, where exports power the nation's phenomenal growth, India's expansion has been largely driven by domestic market growth. For several decades, the Indian economy had been hampered by state controls. The loosening of those controls has unleashed an entrepreneurial and consumer boom.

With more than 6 million new connections a month, India surpassed China last year as the fastest-growing market for mobile phones. Auto sales are booming. Indian companies are going global, notably the venerable Tata Group, which gobbled up firms such as Tetley Tea and British steelmaker Corus. [2]

India's Soaring Economy

India's gross domestic product (GDP) — which is roughly equivalent to the nation's annual income — has more than tripled over the past two decades.

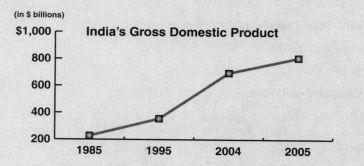

(in $ billions)

India's Gross Domestic Product

India's GDP Still Dwarfed by U.S., China

While India had the world's 10th-largest economy in 2005, its $806 billion GDP amounted to only 6.5 percent of the $12.4 trillion U.S. economy and about a third of China's $2.2 trillion GDP.

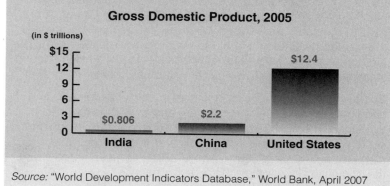

Gross Domestic Product, 2005

(in $ trillions)

Source: "World Development Indicators Database," World Bank, April 2007

That's a sea change compared to 2002, when growth was "only" 5.4 percent, and the future of India's economic expansion seemed at risk. The government desperately needed to "handle domestic political crises and deadly communal violence, while recharging India's faltering economy," wrote retired ambassador and State Department South Asia specialist Dennis Kux at the time. "Failure to balance these various challenges could . . . slow India's rise to great-power status." [3]

Today, such doubts have faded, both in India and beyond. "There is a new trust, there is a new confidence in India," said Commerce and Industry Minister Kamal Nath, who leads India's international trade negotiations. [4]

Still, the enthusiasm must be tempered by reality. India is growing rapidly, but from a relatively low base. According to the World Bank, while India had the world's 10th-largest economy in 2005, its $806 billion GDP amounted to only 6.5 percent of America's $12.4 trillion economy and about a third of China's $2.2 trillion GDP. [5]

At least for the moment, however, India appears squarely on the right path. Predictions of India emerging as a 21st-century world power — which once seemed fanciful — now appear possible.

In an oft-cited 2003 report, the Wall Street investment firm Goldman Sachs projected that the so-called BRIC nations (Brazil, Russia, India and China) would emerge as major economies over the next half-century, with China as the world's largest by 2050, the United States second and India third. [6]

Earlier this year, however, Goldman revised its findings based on India's improved economic performance. "India's influence on the world economy will be bigger and quicker than implied in our previously published BRICs research," Goldman analysts wrote, adding that India could surpass the U.S. economy by 2050. [7]

As India emerges economically, its foreign relations also are undergoing a transformation.

India came under intense international criticism after conducting successful nuclear tests in 1998 and declaring itself a nuclear weapons state. A United Nations Security Council resolution called on India and Pakistan, which had also conducted tests, to end their nuclear weapons programs. The United States imposed sanctions.

But with the rise of China, India is now being viewed through a different prism. As the United States, Japan and others in the Asia-Pacific region worry that China could become a threat to its neighbors, they increasingly see an economically strong and democratic India as a potential ally should China turn hostile.

That thinking led to a major shift in U.S. policy. The Bush administration, actively wooing India, held out a major carrot in 2005 when President George W. Bush agreed in principle to give India de facto recognition as a nuclear weapons state, something long sought by the Indians. The two countries are trying to hammer out a formal agreement needed under the U.S. Atomic Energy Act to turn that promise into a reality.

"The Bush administration was willing to treat India as a major power and give it a higher billing in the global strategic calculus," wrote C. Raja Mohan, a security analyst in India. "No wonder India found the Bush administration very congenial to its own national interests." [8]

India, which fought a border war with China in 1962, also has concerns about China as a potential threat. So while India continues to resist a formal alliance, it is nonetheless moving closer to the United States, conducting joint military exercises and initially supporting U.S. efforts to prevent Iran from obtaining nuclear weapons.

Even as India moves onto the world stage, however, most Indians remain abysmally poor and far removed from the basic comforts of the new India. "In a country where we talk of 5 million [new] cell phones per month, there are also 300 million people [living] on less than $1 a day," Nath said recently, using the World Bank's measure of extreme poverty.

"Here I [am] speaking to you about WTO," Nath told business leaders in New Delhi, referring to the World Trade Organization. "But when I go back to my own district, which has elected me for 27 years, it's a different world. We may be talking [here] about various formulas in the Doha trade talks, but how does that impact the life of those 300 million or 400 million people who still do not know that there is a thing called the WTO?"

Nevertheless, India has made a dent in its poverty. The percentage of its population living below the government's official poverty line dropped from 36 percent in 1993-94 to 27.5 percent in 2004-05 — or 22 percent according to an alternative survey method. [9] Either way, about 250 million people — a quarter of the population — are extremely poor. Moreover, the government's definition of poverty (anyone earning 43 cents a day or less) is even lower than the World Bank's standard of $1 a

IBM Chairman and CEO Samuel J. Palmisano (left) and Indian President A. P. J. Abdul Kalam preside over a company gathering in Bangalore — the center of India's high-tech industry — on June 6, 2006. Low labor costs and the burgeoning technology industry have enticed many U.S. companies to invest in India. With 53,000 employees in 14 cities, India is IBM's second-largest operational base, behind only the United States.

day. So many of those living above the official poverty line are still very poor.

Also troubling has been the slow or even negligible improvement in health, education and other measures of well-being. Malnutrition among young children, for example, remains higher than in sub-Saharan Africa. Forty-six percent of children under age 3 are underweight, according to the Health Ministry, vs. 35 percent in Africa.

A drive to get children to attend school — by such things as offering free lunch — has driven up elementary enrollment, but attendance drops off sharply for junior and senior high. Many poor parents must send older children to work to help feed the family.

And girls suffer disproportionately — even in the new economy — because boys are seen as the ones who will provide for their parents in old age. After girls marry they become beholden to their in-laws, so investing in their education and health is a secondary priority for their parents. Thus, boys get the lion's share of resources in poor families, whether it is receiving a larger portion at mealtime or being sent to school, which usually requires fees, uniforms and books. While 70.2 percent of males were literate in 2001, according to the decennial census, only 48.3 percent of women could read. [10]

Dalits Face Persecution Despite Ban

But some "untouchables" still find success

Fifteen-year-old Mamta Nayak, the first person from her rural Indian village to gain admission to high school, set off every day on her bicycle for the four-mile ride to class.

But there was a problem. She is a dalit, or an "untouchable" in the Hindu caste system. And by tradition, dalits were only allowed to pass on foot through Nanput, a village on her way to school, even though such discrimination has been outlawed for more than 50 years.

Nanput's elders demanded that she stop bicycling through their village, claiming that a dalit riding any vehicle through their village was an insult to them. "They warned me of dire consequences," her father, Ghanashyam Nayak, told an Indian newspaper. [1]

After intense media coverage, the government in the Indian state of Orissa finally intervened and provided police protection — in the form of a female officer on a motor scooter — to ensure that Nayak could bicycle to school. Still, the incident underscores the deep-rooted societal hurdles faced by India's 170 million dalits as they try to join India's economic boom.

India's 3,000-year-old caste system divides Hindus into four groups: priests, warriors, merchants and laborers. Dalits — which means the oppressed — are considered so low they do not even belong to a caste. Traditionally, they were relegated to menial jobs such as sweeping and carting away human excrement, and many still do such work.

After gaining independence in 1947, India outlawed discrimination against dalits and launched programs to improve their lives. But discrimination persists, particularly in rural India. Dalits who try to run for local political office have been threatened and beaten. Mobs have torched and looted entire Dalit villages over a perceived wrong, such as when dalit youths in the town of Gohana were accused of killing a non-dalit in an altercation. "The arson was . . . [their] way of teaching the dalits a lesson," said Vinod Kumar, a dalit whose house was among 54 that were burned. [2]

Just finding a dalit village can be a challenge. One small dalit village, a handful of mud-walled homes with thatched roofs, in the state of Tamil Nadu lies at the end of a sandy path, long after the paved roads have ended. Beyond the enclave lie only fields.

Only 44 percent of dalit households had electricity in 2001, compared to 56 percent in India overall. And while dalit literacy has risen from 37 percent in 1991 to 55 percent in 2001, it still trails the national rate of 65 percent for those age 7 and older. Only 42 percent of dalit females were literate. [3]

The government's biggest program to help dalits is a quota system that reserves 15 percent of government jobs and seats in publicly funded universities for dalits, approximately equal to their proportion of the population. Known as reservations, the quota system has enabled many dalits to move up the economic ladder.

Today, the children of those who entered government

Without adequate education, many migrants from rural areas seem stuck on the first rung of the economic ladder. Their only connection to the new India is that they are building it, brick by brick, often carried on their heads at construction sites in stacks four or five bricks high. "People come to earn money and feed themselves," says Jagjivan Ram, a 28-year-old man who lives alone in the Dharavi slum. "When I can feed myself, I like it here. In my village, there is nothing, so I have no other choice."

Ram cobbled together his windowless, dirt-floor shack with branches, scrap wood and corrugated metal sheets. Without electricity, it is pitch-black inside. He

and his neighbors walk on stones or planks to avoid the murky water that flows down narrow gutters in front of their huts.

In the face of these realities, "inclusive growth" has become the mantra of the current government. "Economic growth is not fully reflected in the quality of life of a large number of our people," Indian President A. P. J. Abdul Kalam said in March. "We are looking for inclusive growth for our 1 billion people." [11]

Against that daunting challenge, these are among the key questions being asked about India's economic and social future:

service through reservations are reaping the benefits. Dhanai Ram, the son of a farmer, joined the police force in the state of Uttar Pradesh under a quota. He ploughed his earnings into his children's education, not even buying his family a refrigerator. It paid off. Today, his son Yudhishthir Kumar is a computer network specialist in India's burgeoning high-tech industry.

"Reservation helped us a lot," Kumar says. "But we had determination, too, to do something and to prove that if we got an opportunity, we could do better than the upper castes."

But these success stories remain more the exception than the rule. India's economic liberalization has created a new challenge for dalit advancement. When the state dominated the economy, government jobs were regarded by many as the best careers, and the quota system ensured that dalits got a piece of that pie. In today's market economy, however, most new jobs are created in the private sector, prompting the government to propose quotas for private-sector jobs, too.

Fierce resistance from industry put the brakes on that plan. Rather than quotas, industry leaders want the government to improve education for dalits — and the poor generally. But given India's poor education system, that could be a lengthy process.

In the meantime, continuing discrimination against dalits like the bicycle-riding Nayak makes the task that much tougher.

---

[1] Arabinda Mishra, "Dalit Girl Crosses the Hurdle," *The Times of India*, Aug. 20, 2005, and "Girl Rides, With Cops," *The Telegraph*, Sept. 2, 2005.

[2] Basharat Peer, "D for Dalit, D for Defiance," *Tehelka*, Feb. 18, 2006.

[3] "Report of the Task Group on Development of Scheduled Castes and Scheduled Tribes," Government of India, Planning Commission, March 2005, pp. 22-23, 38. Literacy rates are for 2001.

Dalit Christian and Muslim women protest a ruling that reservations — or hiring and education quotas — for the so-called untouchables do not apply to those who converted to Christianity or Islam to avoid discrimination under India's 3,000-year-old Hindu caste system. India's 170 million dalits make up the lowest order in that Hindu system.

Can India match China's economic growth?

India grew in spurts in the 1990s, but never came close to China's torrid growth rates. While many economists believe official Chinese growth statistics were overstated in the early 1990s, they generally agree China expanded rapidly during the decade. [12] India is often described as an elephant, lumbering slowly forward, while China races ahead like a tiger.

Twice during the 1990s, the Indian economy surged, once after a series of economic reforms in the early part of the decade and later during the dot-com boom of the late '90s. Both times, hopes were raised and then dashed, as growth faltered.

Now, after four years of impressive growth, hope is back in fashion. India's four-year average growth rate of 8.6 percent annually represents the best performance since India gained independence from Great Britain in 1947.

Nevertheless, the government has vowed to reach 10 percent growth by the 2011-2012 fiscal year — something economist Surjit Bhalla, who runs the New Delhi asset-management firm Oxus Research and Investments, thinks is possible. [13]

"The likely trend rate of growth is around 9 percent," Bhalla wrote in an in-depth analysis of India's economy. "The inevitability of 10 percent growth is more likely now despite politics and populism." [14]

Poverty Level Drops Dramatically

In a little over a decade, the percentage of Indians living below the poverty line has dropped more than 8 points.

Percentage of Population Living in Poverty

Sources: "National Sample Survey," Government of India Planning Commission; "Poverty declines to 21.8 per cent: NSS," Press Trust of India, March 21, 2007

Economist Arvind Virmani, an adviser to the government's Planning Commission, is not as optimistic as Bhalla either. He puts India's growth in the 7.5 percent range — a rate he is "reasonably confident" can be sustained for the next decade or two "even if everything doesn't go right."

Over the long term, however, Shah sees reasons to hope for truly remarkable growth, but he prefers to use South Korea's impressive rise — rather than China's — as a benchmark for economic ascendancy. India has two advantages over South Korea, he says. As an English-speaking country, it does not face a language barrier when absorbing foreign technology or offering outsourced service jobs to the English-speaking world. Secondly, globalization has accelerated the pace of technological diffusion.

"So when we come out of being a miserable Third World country and are catching up and reaching the frontier, we can do in a generation what took South Korea two generations," says Shah. "India has an opportunity for extremely dramatic rates of growth."

"But that's an opportunity," he warns, "not a reality," and he cautions it's far from guaranteed. Much will depend on whether India can improve its education system and infrastructure. India had only a 61 percent adult literacy rate in 2004, compared to 91 percent in China. Roads and ports are improving but still lag behind China's, creating costly delays in getting goods to market. And perhaps most important, erratic power generation poses a huge hurdle. [16]

Frequent power outages force Indian companies to rely on their own back-up generators, adding to the cost of doing business. Legislation to overhaul the power system passed in 2003, but implementation by the states has been slow. The states own the power companies, and many vested interests benefit from the current system.

Business and political leaders constantly discuss what needs to be done to achieve China's double-digit growth rates. Many hope India can replicate China's success in manufacturing, creating jobs for less-educated workers in industries such as footwear production.

While manufacturing has begun to expand in India, the inadequate road, port and power infrastructure remains a major barrier. Fixing the educational system also is key; even blue-collar workers need a basic education, and manufacturing jobs today increasingly require technical training. Progress is being made in both these areas, but to business leaders, it is often frustratingly slow.

Such optimism, though, has been tempered by concerns that India's economy could be overheating. "Prices on Fire" screamed the March 5, 2007, cover of the weekly news magazine *India Today* after wholesale prices in early 2007 shot up 6.7 percent over the previous year. [15]

Others wonder whether India's recent growth represents a structural shift or simply the high end of a robust business cycle — bound to return to more earthly levels as the central bank hikes interest rates to tame inflation, which has reached worrisome levels.

Economist Ajay Shah, a former adviser to the Finance Ministry, attributes most of the recent growth to the business cycle. "I don't think that . . . from here on, for the next 20 years, we will get 9.2 percent GDP growth. That's not going to happen."

Some Indian commentators say that's the price of democracy. China, with a one-party dictatorship, is able to mandate quick policy shifts. In India, policies can get mired in political debate for years. But some say the democratic process may make India's reforms more durable.

"In 16 years, we had five prime ministers, six governments, but one economic policy," said Nath, the commerce minister. "It is this political consensus which is one of the bedrocks of our reform process. It's not a question of bulldozing reforms. You can bulldoze it through parliament if you have the majority, but how will you bulldoze it through the people?" [17]

Is India doing enough to help its poor?

With economic growth seemingly on autopilot, the government's new "inclusive growth" policy has become a political imperative for the ruling Indian National Congress, or Congress Party, which came to power at the head of a coalition government in 2004. Failure to spread the benefits of growth more widely could spell defeat at the polls in the next national elections, expected by May 2009.

But inclusive growth may be India's greatest social and political challenge. In luxury hotels in New Delhi, leading business groups devote day-long conferences to the subject, with businessmen in expensive suits discussing the future of some of the world's most impoverished people.

With 70 percent of India's population living in the countryside, business leaders realize the country's growth potential will be severely stunted if rural India is left behind. Moreover, an urban-rural divide can spark unrest. Already this year, pockets of farmers have risen up in protest against plans to acquire huge tracts of agricultural land for special economic zones and industrial or commercial development. They fear the developments will benefit corporations, not farmers and their families.

"I am very proud of the fact that we are no longer a sluggish economy," says G. S. Bhalla, an agricultural economist and emeritus professor at Jawaharlal Nehru University in New Delhi. "But growth that ignores a very large section of the people will not do in a democracy."

The growth of agricultural production has, in fact, slowed in the past decade, even as the rest of the economy has gathered steam. While economists have yet to pinpoint the reasons, Bhalla thinks inadequate government spending on agriculture has played a role.

The government has adopted ambitious goals to expand spending on education, health and rural infrastructure, projects applauded by A. K. Shiva Kumar, an economist and member of a council advising the government on development policy. The projects include the National Rural Health Mission, the National Rural Employment Guarantee Scheme and Bharat Nirman (which means "Build India") — a four-year plan to improve roads, telephone service, irrigation, water supply, housing and electricity in rural areas.

So far, though, spending in these areas has fallen short of the goals, Kumar says. India spends about 1 percent of GDP on health, despite a pledge to raise it to 3 percent. By comparison, China spends 2 percent of GDP on health and Brazil, 3.4 percent, while industrialized countries spend 7 to 9 percent. India today spends just over 4 percent of its GDP — about the same as Brazil — on education, even though in the 1960s it vowed to raise that to 6 percent. Industrialized countries, by comparison, spend between 5 and 8 percent of GDP on education. [18]

"India has just not invested adequately in these areas compared to other countries," says Kumar. "You have to increase the amount of spending on these areas. There's no doubt about it."

But, he adds, it's not just a matter of more money. Corruption siphons off significant amounts of government spending into the hands of local politicians and officials. Then-Prime Minister Rajiv Gandhi, whose widow Sonia Gandhi now heads the Congress Party, famously said in the mid-1980s that only 15 percent of government spending for the poor actually reaches the people. Still, India's corruption is not the highest in the world. India ranks 70th in Transparency International's annual index of most corrupt governments, tied with China and Brazil. [19]

Some voices are saying enough is enough. "Throwing money at the problem is not the solution," wrote Aroon Purie, the influential editor-in-chief of *India Today*, in his weekly letter to readers after the fiscal 2007-08 budget proposal was released. [20]

The government needs to monitor social spending to ensure positive results, Purie said. "For all the budgetary allocation on primary education, India still has amongst the lowest literacy rates in this part of the world," he said. "This budget once again caters to the slogan of inclusive growth but fails to address the core issue of how the inclusion will take place."

CHRONOLOGY

1947-1964 *A newly independent India pursues socialist economic policies and an idealistic, "nonaligned" foreign policy.*

Aug. 15, 1947 India gains independence from Great Britain. Jawaharlal Nehru becomes first prime minister.

1948 Mahatma Gandhi, the non-violent father of Indian independence, is assassinated by a Hindu extremist.

1951 Industries Act requires private companies to obtain permission to expand operations or launch new ones.

1962 China delivers humiliating defeat to India in brief border war along the disputed Tibet and Kashmir frontiers.

1964 Nehru dies in office.

1965-1990 *Indira Gandhi increases state control of the economy and brutally crushes political opponents.*

1966 Nehru's daughter Indira Gandhi becomes prime minister. Aided by the Ford Foundation, the government launches a "Green Revolution," using better seeds and irrigation that eventually enable India to become self-sufficient in grain production.

May 1974 India, which is not a signatory of the Nuclear Non-Proliferation Treaty, conducts its first successful nuclear test.

1975 Gandhi administration declares a "national emergency," leading to a brutal crackdown on political opponents and restrictions on the press.

1977 Voters reject Gandhi and the Congress Party.

1979 India achieves grain self-sufficiency.

1980 Gandhi is returned to office.

1984 Gandhi is assassinated by two of her Sikh bodyguards following her order to storm the Golden Temple, which results in the deaths of hundreds of Sikh pilgrims; her son, Rajiv, becomes prime minister and wins election for a new term.

1991-Present *India begins opening its economy to trade and competition, paving the way for economic growth and a larger international role.*

1991 India launches economic reforms in response to financial crisis.

1992 Hindu mob destroys the Babri Masjid mosque in Ayodhya. Thousands die in sectarian rioting that follows. The incident and ensuing violence are a political turning point, generating a new wave of support for Hindu nationalist parties.

1998 Hindu nationalist Bharatiya Janata Party (BJP) comes to power as head of a coalition government. . . . United States sanctions India and Pakistan after they conduct nuclear tests.

2001-2002 Attack on Indian parliament building leads to heightened India-Pakistan tensions and fears of a nuclear conflict.

May 2004 Indian National Congress party, led by Indira Gandhi's daughter-in-law Sonia Gandhi, unseats the BJP-led coalition in national elections. Former Finance Minister Manmohan Singh becomes prime minister of Congress-led coalition government.

July 2005 President Bush and Prime Minister Singh agree to a nuclear deal at the White House. Details announced during Bush visit to India in March 2006.

February 2006 National Rural Employment Guarantee Act provides 100 days of minimum-wage work each year for any rural household that requests it. Initially launched in 200 of India's 604 districts, it will be expanded nationwide by 2011.

March 2006 Multiple explosions in holy city of Varanasi kill 20; Pakistan-based terror group is primary suspect.

July 2006 Terrorist attacks on Mumbai commuter trains kill more than 200.

December 2006 U.S. Congress approves U.S.-India nuclear deal allowing India to purchase nuclear civilian technology without giving up its nuclear weapons.

March 2007 Economy grows 9.2 percent for the fiscal year ending March 31, the fourth year of high growth. . . . Study finds about one-quarter of Indians live below poverty line, compared to 36 percent in 1994.

A major World Bank review of India's development policies found that while India has set the right priorities and launched appropriate programs, often the programs are not carried out effectively on the ground due to the inefficiency of government agencies. "It is easy to be optimistic about India's economic prospects, but there is growing concern that the basic institutions, organizations, and structures for public sector action are failing — especially for those at the bottom," said the report. [21]

Among the problems, it said, were "corruption, absenteeism, low quality, excessive costs." The bank said "systemic reform," was needed, "not merely expansion of 'business as usual.' " [22]

Even with reform, no one suggests the task would be an easy one. More than 50 percent of Indians are farmers, but they produce only 20 percent of the nation's GDP. And while the rest of the economy races ahead at 9 percent growth rates, agriculture manages to grow at only about 2.5 percent. The only way to keep farmers from falling farther behind is to reduce the number of people in agriculture by shifting them to jobs in faster-growing economic sectors.

But two major obstacles stand in the way. First, with some 300 million workers in farming, creating new jobs for them will take decades. "There is tension between the structural necessity to get a large population out of agriculture and the reality that it's not going to happen for a long time," says Virmani, the government adviser.

Moreover, "a huge number of people have a very high degree of illiteracy" and have inadequate skills to do anything outside of agriculture, says Abhijit Sen, a professor of social sciences at Jawaharlal Nehru University who is on leave to serve on the government's Planning Commission advisory body. "So there is a problem in the short run in even thinking about taking these people into some other activity."

Given those obstacles, the government is following a two-pronged approach: It is trying to increase agriculture productivity to help people in the near future while investing more in educating the next generation of workers. On both fronts, with debt driving some Indian cotton farmers to suicide, progress is limited.

"These turning points in history have not anywhere in the world been easy times to go through," says Sen.

Should India conclude the nuclear deal with the United States?

For the much-trumpeted U.S.-India nuclear deal — announced on March 2, 2006, during a visit by Bush to New Delhi — the devil may be in the details.

The United States has agreed in principle to provide nuclear power technology and nuclear fuel to India while allowing it to retain its nuclear weapons. In return, India would open its civilian nuclear facilities for the first time to inspections by the International Atomic Energy Agency (IAEA), the international agency entrusted under the 1968 Non-Proliferation Treaty (NPT) with verifying that peaceful nuclear technology is not diverted for weapons use. [23]

Under the treaty, non-nuclear states agreed to refrain from developing nuclear weapons, and in return the five countries that already had tested nuclear weapons when the treaty was signed in 1968 — the United States, the Soviet Union, China, France and Great Britain — promised to share peaceful nuclear technology with nuclear "have-nots." The nuclear "haves" also agreed to reduce and eventually eliminate their own nuclear weapons, a commitment they have largely ignored.

India, which conducted its first nuclear test in 1974 and more advanced tests in 1998, never signed the NPT, which it viewed it as discriminatory since the treaty allowed no new members of the "nuclear club" outside the initial five members.

Critics of the U.S.-India nuclear deal argue that it could undermine the fundamental tenet of the NPT, which induced non-nuclear states to forgo nuclear weapons in return for access to peaceful nuclear technology.

In defending the deal, the Bush administration argued that the benefits of helping to give the South Asian giant energy security while bringing it into the global non-proliferation inspection framework would far outweigh the risks. Moreover, the administration points out, India has been scrupulous about preventing any of its nuclear technology from being transferred to other nations — something its neighbor Pakistan failed to do. [24]

IAEA Director Mohamed ElBaradei called the deal "an important step toward satisfying India's growing need for energy" and said it would "bring India closer as an important partner in the non-proliferation regime." [25]

The deal is also designed to foster closer U.S.-India ties, and is "intended to convey in one fell swoop the

New Middle Class Spends Freely

But only 6 percent earn more than $4,500

Kapil Khaneja had a typical middle-class upbringing in New Delhi. A cramped apartment, no family car and 30-hour train rides to vacation at India's tea plantations in Darjeeling.

What a difference a generation makes. Now a manager at an outsourcing firm, Khaneja, 29, bought a used car when he was 21. He upgraded to a new Hyundai a few years later and now is about to move up to a Honda. He sipped wine at Parisian cafes last October on vacation with an American friend. His office colleague, Kamani Sanan, does not think twice about dropping $50 to $100 on a night out. "We work and we spend," she says. "If I like something, I pick it up."

Economic growth is transforming the Indian way of life. Families that always ate at home dine at restaurants and buy Nike sneakers, digital cameras and the latest cellular phones. And as a half-dozen new discount airlines send fares plummeting, they are abandoning India's famously jam-packed trains. Although Khaneja lives with his mother, he inhabits an almost totally different world.

"I don't mind spending the extra buck because I have it," he says, relaxing in one of the Starbucks-like cafes that have sprung up in India's major cities. "Our parents were more driven by necessity than a want for luxuries. It's the difference between needs and desires."

Sanan points out, however, that she and Khaneja are far from average. The new middle class is mostly urban — in a country in which 70 percent of the population is rural — and represents just a sliver of India's total population.

Marketers talk about an Indian middle class of 300 million people, nearly a quarter of the total population of 1.1 billion, but that is widely considered to be inflated. A study by the National Council of Applied Economic Research in New Delhi classified about 6 percent of Indian households as middle class, earning more than $4,500 a year. [1]

Most of the 300 million are what the study called "aspirers." With annual household incomes in the $2,000-to-$4,500 range, they have started the upward climb. Few own a car or an air conditioner; only a third have a refrigerator and 40 percent a color television.

Still, they form part of a new group of consumers, albeit a small one. Companies have responded to their more limited affluence by shrinking product size — little packets of shampoo, for example, are available for the equivalent of a few cents. Cigarette vendors open packs

abiding American interest in crafting a full and productive partnership with India to advance our common goals in this century," said Ashley Tellis, a senior associate at the Carnegie Endowment for International Peace and a former State Department official who helped negotiate the agreement. [26]

But because the deal would set a new precedent within the NPT, some U.S. lawmakers — including leading Republicans — opposed it. Consequently, when Congress approved the deal last December it added conditions that have raised some hackles in India.

"The U.S. Congress, being always overbearing, passed a law called the Hyde Act, which is oppressive and has changed the public mood in India," says Brahma Chellaney, a professor of strategic studies at the Center for Policy Research in New Delhi.

The law exempts India from restrictions in the Atomic Energy Act on the sale of American nuclear materials, equipment and technology to other countries. But the new law allows the United States to nullify the deal if India conducts another nuclear weapons test and to demand return of any nuclear equipment and fuel already delivered to India. Other conditions limit India's ability to stockpile nuclear fuel and reprocess spent fuel. The law also requires the U.S. president to report to Congress on how India is helping to prevent Iran from obtaining nuclear weapons. [27]

"The Indo-U.S. nuclear deal is against India's national interest," former Indian Foreign Minister Yashwant Sinha wrote. "Through this deal, India shall mortgage in perpetuity, for all time to come, its freedom to develop its nuclear technology and the independence of its foreign policy." [28]

Indian proponents of the nuclear deal hope their country's objections will be addressed in ongoing negotiations on an accompanying technical pact. "There are

and sell individual cigarettes for three to five rupees (six to 11 cents).

"Companies that have been successful are the ones that have been able to deliver product to homes earning 5,000 to 7,000 rupees ($110 to $150) a month," said Ajit Balakrishnan, the co-founder of Rediff, an Indian Web portal. [2]

Indians' spending power should grow if the country's economy continues to enjoy rapid growth, as expected. Less than 1 percent of households qualify as "rich," with annual incomes above $45,000, but that has not stopped luxury-goods makers from betting on India's future. The first BMW rolled off an assembly line in India this spring. "We see significant sales potential," says Peter Kronschnabl, the executive leading the automaker's entry into India.

Further fueling the spending boom is the spread of consumer credit, a concept that barely existed in India a generation ago. For Khaneja and Sanan's parents, borrowing money is shameful. They look askance as their children pay the bill with a credit card.

"Our parents cannot agree with plastic money," Sanan says. "They still feel like it is borrowing money from someone and that that is not a good thing."

For their parents, buying a house involved borrowing quietly from relatives or private moneylenders who worked on trust, leaving no paper trail. Now, telemarketers besiege Indians on their cellular phones with offers of bank and auto loans.

Call center employees work the night shift in the small northern city of Mohali. India's emergence as a global base for call centers has helped create a rising middle class, but some researchers say only 6 percent of households have reached the middle class.

Khaneja's mother has grown accustomed to her son's credit card. "They've seen it, and they say, 'That's the way they do it,' " he says, "but they still don't approve of the fact that I do it."

---

[1] National Council of Applied Economic Research, *The Great Indian Middle Class* (2004).

[2] Ajit Balakrishnan, interview on "BT Big Thinkers Series," Oct. 3, 2006; www.networked.bt.com/bigthinkers_india.php.

some sticking points," acknowledges Ashok Mehta, a retired Indian Army general, which will "be negotiated and suitably couched in language to assuage each other's security concerns."

The talks, though, appeared to be stuck this spring on some of those very sticking points. If they fail — however unlikely that may seem given the importance both countries place on the deal — it could torpedo the entire agreement.

Opinions vary on how important the U.S. nuclear deal is to meeting India's future energy needs. India already faces power shortages, and the simultaneous rapid growth of the world's two Asian colossi — India and China — portends a squeeze on energy supplies and higher prices.

India must "be able to ensure some degree of energy security over the next two to three decades," says Uday Bhaskar, a retired Indian Navy commodore and an adviser to the government on security issues. "Clearly, you cannot do it without a stable nuclear base."

But others argue that nuclear energy is too expensive for India, which has sizable coal deposits. Even in the most optimistic scenarios, nuclear power would at best meet less than 10 percent of India's energy needs in 2020.

"The Americans are trying to induce India to accept a series of legally binding conditions to obtain this dubious right to import nuclear power reactors for generating electricity, which is a right India can do without," says Chellaney, who was an adviser to the government during the diplomatic brouhaha following India's 1998 nuclear tests.

Most analysts agree, however, that the nuclear deal is significant not only as a means of boosting India's nuclear power sector but also in elevating India's international stature and recognizing India's growing global role.

"[T]his nuclear agreement . . . brings you into the big league," Mehta says. "If this agreement falls through, obviously it dilutes that relationship."

Rural migrants, many illiterate, come to India's teeming cities seeking work but end up eking out a hardscrabble existence in slums filled with shacks made of scrap wood and corrugated metal, with dirt floors and no electricity or plumbing. The Congress Party has promised to help all Indians benefit from the economic boom, but spending on social programs has fallen short of goals.

BACKGROUND

Socialist Experiment

If India lives up to its promise and becomes one of the world's major economies, it wouldn't be for the first time.

In 1820, India accounted for 16 percent of global GDP, making it the second largest economy in the world, according to estimates by British-born economic historian Angus Maddison, an emeritus professor at the University of Groningen in the Netherlands. Indian cloth, which made up the vast bulk of the global trade in textiles and apparel, was prized throughout the world. [29]

But even then India was playing second fiddle to China, which accounted for 33 percent of the world economy. The fledgling U.S. economy represented a mere 1.8 percent of the world's GDP.

Then came the Industrial Revolution. While the West roared ahead, today's so-called developing world remained largely stagnant. By 1950, the United States produced 27 percent of global GDP. China's share had plummeted to 4.5 percent; India's, to 4.2 percent.

As Columbia University economist Jeffrey Sachs points out, before the Industrial Revolution "universal poverty" was the norm. [30] But the rise of factories, for all their worker abuses, enabled the Western masses eventually to climb out of poverty.

India, however, was still largely agrarian when it broke free from British colonial rule in 1947, with agriculture accounting for about half of its GDP, says Professor Sen of the Planning Commission. The country's first prime minister, Jawaharlal Nehru, decided the new nation would have to industrialize. Inspired in part by the Soviet model, he envisioned government playing a major role. Power generation was nationalized, and ambitious hydro-electric projects were launched. The government created the now famous Indian Institutes of Technology, inspired by the Massachusetts Institute of Technology.

In 1951 private companies were brought under government control through the Industries Act, which required companies to get official permission to expand production or set up a new business. The law — and subsequent measures — were designed to prevent corporate excesses and keep business working in the nation's interest. [31]

The pervasive regulation, however, had a stultifying effect on private enterprise. Permits and licenses were required at every turn. Critics of Nehru's socialist-leaning polices complained that the British Raj (rule by the British) had been replaced by the "license Raj."

Growth became sluggish, averaging 4.1 percent a year under Nehru, who died in office in 1964. [32] The economy fared even worse after his daughter, Indira Gandhi, became prime minister in 1966. She nationalized banks and further tightened government control of the economy. The two oil crises of the 1970s added to the economic woes. From 1965 to 1979, growth slumped to 2.9 percent a year.

Economist Shah calls Gandhi's rule "the terrible period of socialism, with all kinds of crazy laws, all kinds of crazy controls." By 1976, says Shah, India had "an incredibly repressive government that was interfering in every part of economic activity."

A bright spot during these tough times was the so-called Green Revolution, the development and introduction of new "high-yield" wheat, rice and other grain varieties, which swept across the developing world in the 1960s, from Mexico to India and eventually Southeast Asia and Africa, with support from the Ford and Rockefeller foundations. After back-to-back droughts led to severe grain shortages in 1965 and 1966, India accelerated efforts to introduce new high-yield grains, train farmers, expand irrigation and increase the use of fertilizers. By significantly improving the harvest per acre, India became self-sufficient in food grains by 1979.

Overall, though, the economy remained in the doldrums. From 1951 to 1980, India eked out only 3.5 percent average annual growth, a record that came to be known derisively as the "Hindu" growth rate.

Reform Era

In 1977, Gandhi and her Congress Party were unceremoniously dumped from office. The immediate reason was the "emergency" her government declared in 1975, during which tens of thousands of political opponents were rounded up and terrorized and the media muzzled — all in the name of law and order. [33]

The crackdown came amid growing labor unrest, coupled with declining popularity for Gandhi, who had brutally broken a nationwide strike by government railway workers the previous year. With an opposition political movement gaining strength, Congress' hold on power appeared vulnerable.

"If Indira Gandhi had thought she could win the 1976 elections, there would not have been an emergency," wrote Tariq Ali, a London-based social commentator. "Its purpose was basically twofold: to safeguard the Congress Party and her own political position while forcibly bringing to an end rural and urban unrest in many parts of the country." [34]

For the first time since independence, Congress was not the ruling party. But the new government quickly unraveled, and Gandhi led Congress back to victory in elections in 1980 and returned as prime minister. This time, she initiated modest economic reforms. After her assassination in 1984, her son, Rajiv Gandhi, succeeded her as prime minister and took India further down the reform path.

If the 1970s were an economic winter, the 1980s were a spring thaw. Growth accelerated to an average of 5.5 percent a year, better than at any time since independence.

Even India's long-struggling farmers were invited to the party, as the Green Revolution came to fruition. Annual growth in agricultural output, which had averaged only 2.3 percent a year from 1951 to 1980, jumped to 4.2 percent in the 1980s. [34]

Farmers traded in their bullock carts for tractors. Agricultural economist Bhalla calls the decade "a golden period" for Indian agriculture. "Farmers benefited immensely," he says. "I belong to a farming community, I was born in a village, I know people who sort of suddenly became rich — you know, tractors and all that. So it's a huge difference in lifestyle."

The 1990s began inauspiciously, however. Mounting government debt under Prime Minister Rajiv Gandhi, who succeeded his mother in 1984, and his successors sparked a financial crisis in 1991. [35] After Iraq invaded Kuwait in 1990, world oil prices soared, and India soon found itself rapidly running short of foreign reserves to buy oil.

Narasimha Rao, who had become prime minister in 1991, turned to respected economist Manmohan Singh, appointing him finance minister. Within a month, Singh had laid out the dire situation: The government had only enough foreign exchange for 13 more days of oil. "He explained the consequences to the Cabinet and he said this is what we have to do," Nath, now the commerce minister, recalled earlier this year. [36]

Rao and Singh took advantage of the crisis to brush aside vested interests and launch a fundamental shift in Indian economic policy. India would abandon Nehru's socialist principles, dismantle the hated license Raj, open the economy to foreign investment and embrace free-market economics.

Although many of the changes have been only partially carried out, they managed to boost India's growth rate in the 1990s to 6.1 percent, according to economist Virmani. "It's very clear now that the shift has happened," he says. "You can show that India is on a higher growth path."

Foreign Policy

As India gained its independence in 1947, the world was fracturing in two. British Prime Minister Winston Churchill had warned of growing Soviet dominance in Eastern Europe during his prescient "Iron Curtain" speech the previous year in Fulton, Mo. By 1949, Mao Zedong had led the communists to power in China.

Nehru, who was both foreign minister and prime minister, tried to set India on a pacifistic, "nonaligned" course that avoided taking sides in the nascent Cold War. He was a driving force behind a 1955 conference of Asian and African leaders in Bandung, Indonesia, that gave birth to the nonaligned movement. [37]

But Nehru's policy of non-alignment drove the United States to seek out and arm Pakistan, India's archrival, as a bulwark against communist expansion in the region. And his idealistic vision came crashing down after China seized disputed Himalayan territory in a brief and humiliating war along the India-China border in 1962.

Women spread red chilies to dry in Sertha, a village on the outskirts of Ahmedabad. Despite increasing industrialization, 60 percent of India's 509 million laborers work in agriculture.

"The invasion of '62 shattered India's pacifism in one stroke," says Chellaney, of the Center for Policy Research. "India had a military like a police force. It thought that if you seek peace, you will get peace. It did not understand the basic principle of national security: that to have peace, you should be able to defend peace. And therefore '62 was a big revolution in terms of changing Indian military planning and thinking."

Under Indira Gandhi, India moved away from Nehru's idealism toward a more hard-nosed foreign policy. [38] Feeling boxed in by China, Pakistan and the United States, India turned to the Soviet Union for everything from scientific exchanges to fighter aircraft.

Although India remained officially nonaligned, "it is impossible to characterize India's ties with the Soviet Union as anything other than an alliance-like relationship," said security expert Mohan. "India's 1971 peace and friendship treaty with Moscow, which consolidated this relationship, was a structural response to the emergence of what India saw as a U.S.-Pakistan-China axis in its neighborhood." [39]

In 1988 Prime Minister Rajiv Gandhi offered to forgo nuclear weapons if the five original nuclear club members made a long-term commitment to abide by the NPT's Article 6 and begin phasing out their nuclear arsenals. When the United States rejected the offer, the nuclear hawks in New Delhi gained ground. [40]

India upped the ante in May 1998 by conducting advanced nuclear tests and declaring itself a nuclear weapons state. Reaction was largely negative. The United States imposed sanctions, and a unanimous U.N. Security Council called on India and Pakistan — which conducted its own tests two weeks after India — to abandon their nuclear programs. "We're going to come down on those guys like a ton of bricks," said President Bill Clinton, who later that year called off a planned trip to India. [41]

But by 2000 Clinton's mood had changed; he visited India that March, and many of the sanctions were gradually lifted. Several fundamental changes triggered America's about-face: the end of the Cold War, the Internet-fueled globalization of the economy, India's economic emergence and its fresh approach to foreign policy.

India began to see that building relations with the United States and its economically vibrant neighbors in Southeast Asia would enhance India's future. And its economic emergence suggested to U.S. policymakers that India could play a bigger geopolitical role in Asia.

Although the 60-year-old dispute over Kashmir remains unresolved, the two countries have ratcheted down their warlike rhetoric and taken steps to ease tensions, re-establishing rail and air links, easing travel restrictions and starting a "comprehensive dialogue" on all issues, including Kashmir.

After President Bush took office in 2001, another key element fell into place. U.S. policymakers had long debated whether China was an opportunity or a threat. Clinton leaned toward opportunity; Bush, toward threat. In Bush's worldview, India gained heightened importance as a potential counterweight to Chinese influence in the region.

To entice India into its camp, the Bush administration offered to accept India as a nuclear power. For the Indian foreign-policy establishment, the July 2005 agreement was almost too good to be believed. Mohan called it a "gigantic reversal." [42]

"Within seven years of its nuclear tests, the international community led by the United States was now prepared to accept India's nuclear weapons program," he wrote. "The nuclear non-proliferation wheel had turned full circle." [43]

CURRENT SITUATION

Congress Party Returns

By 2004, the economy appeared to be back on track. "India Shining" was the campaign slogan of the ruling Bharatiya Janata Party (BJP) in parliamentary elections that spring. Re-election for Prime Minister Atal Bihari Vajpayee seemed assured.

In a stunning upset, the Congress Party returned to power under the leadership of Sonia Gandhi, Rajiv Gandhi's Italian-born widow. * But the party was far short of an outright majority, so it formed a government with the support of the communist and other leftist parties.

Financial markets panicked, fearing the new government would roll back or stall India's pro-market reforms. Calm was restored after Manmohan Singh, the finance minister who had launched India's pro-market reforms in 1991, was named prime minister.

However, while the Congress-led coalition has not gone back on reforms, it has made only slow progress in advancing them. And it has retreated often on planned steps in the face of vocal protests from its leftist allies.

Progress has come in dribs and drabs. After public protests, a proposal to allow foreign companies to own stores in India, which would have opened the doors to the likes of Wal-Mart, was watered down to allow only "single-brand" retailing — a Nike store or Starbucks, for example, but not a department store or supermarket.

India's record on helping the poor remains mixed. More children are attending school, but studies show that educational attainment remains low, says economist Kumar.

Early this year, the government proposed major increases in social spending for the upcoming fiscal year. "Faster economic growth has given us, once again, the opportunity to unfurl the sails and catch the wind," Finance Minister P. Chidambaram said in his annual budget speech to parliament. The government "will deliver on the promise of making growth more inclusive. I believe that, given the right mix of policies, the poor will benefit from growth." [44]

But Kumar says government spending is still far too

---

* Rajiv had been assassinated in 1991 by a Tamil extremist who opposed his government's support for the Sri Lankan government in its ongoing battle against Tamil separatists.

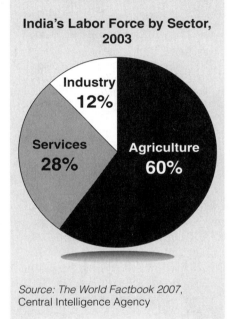

Majority of Indians Are Farmworkers

Despite rising industrialization, India remains largely agricultural: 60 percent of its 509 million labor force — mostly the rural poor — work in agriculture. More than one-quarter are in the service sector, many in call centers or other outsourced employment.

India's Labor Force by Sector, 2003

Industry 12%

Services 28%

Agriculture 60%

Source: The World Factbook 2007, Central Intelligence Agency

---

low. "We have really under-invested, and it [is evident] anywhere you go," he says. A quarter of schools in north India have only one teacher, handling perhaps 80 students in five grades. "It's a joke," he continues. "You have to increase the amount of spending on these areas."

Corruption remains the other over-arching issue. State governments control funding for most social programs, resulting in stark regional differences where officials and politicians siphon off government funds. Northern states such as Uttar Pradesh and Bihar are notably corrupt and lag both in economic growth and various measures of poverty, education and health. Much more progress has been made in the south and west where state governments tend to be less corrupt, more efficient and better at attracting private investment.

AP Photo/Gurinder Osan

Indian Communist Party activists burn an effigy of Wal-Mart Vice Chairmen Mike Duke during an anti-globalization protest in New Delhi on Feb. 22, 2007. Duke was in India to discuss setting up big-box stores across the country. Concerned about the potential loss of cultural identity, many Indians object to the growing presence of foreign retailers.

Neo-Nonalignment

While the nuclear deal with the United States grabbed headlines, India is actively trying to build relations with other powers as well — from China and Japan to Russia and Europe — in a multi-pronged approach that recognizes the U.S. role as the dominant global power.

This spring, for example, the Indian Navy sent five ships to participate in a naval exercise with the United States off Japan. Afterward, three of the Indian vessels made a "friendship" port call in Japan. The two others, described as "less formidable destroyers," headed for a "goodwill" port call in China.

"This aspect of the planning acquires importance as a possible message that India wants to stay engaged with China even while building new bridges with Japan," wrote P. S. Suryanarayana, a Singapore-based correspondent for *The Hindu*. [45]

The relationship with China may be the trickiest. The simultaneous emergence of the two big countries in the same region makes a degree of rivalry all but inevitable. Both need oil and other raw materials to fuel their booming economies, and both may end up competing for the same global resources.

"The size, the ambitions and the proximity make them natural competitors," says Chellaney at the Center for Policy Research. "These are two large states — huge — and both are coming into their own at the same time

in history. It's inevitable that you're going to be competing with each other."

Others concur. "Competition has a certain inevitability," says security adviser Bhaskar. "Whether it's friendly competition or prickly competition, we'll see how the two leaderships address it."

The budding U.S.-India relationship further complicates relations with China. No one is quite sure what China's ambitions are, but the United States sees India as a potential partner to contain China, should its ambitions threaten American interests in Asia. But that thinking apparently does not sit well in Beijing.

"The biggest challenge is going to be China," Bhaskar says. "If India-U.S. moves in a certain direction, it's causing some sort of anxiety in China. India needs to reassure China it's not an alliance or an India-U.S. combine."

Meanwhile, India harbors some of America's wariness toward China, which has concluded a series of agreements with many of India's neighbors that appear aimed at guaranteeing safe passage for energy supplies to China but could have potential military implications. The agreements include helping to finance and build ports in Pakistan, Myanmar, Sri Lanka and Bangladesh as well as a reported agreement to allow Chinese submarines to make port calls in the Maldives. It's a strategy Pentagon analysts call "a string of pearls."

"The Chinese, as part of their strategic and economic interests, are creating corridors on different flanks of India — east, west, north — which, even if they're not designed to contain India, do have strategic implications for India and, willingly or unwillingly, squeeze India strategically," Chellaney says.

"And on top of that, the Chinese are showing increasing interest in the Indian Ocean region," he adds, "where India has been the dominant power. And suddenly, China is appearing from nowhere and actually appearing in a very serious way. So, for Indians, this is a strategic reality that they have to confront."

Fundamentally, Chellaney says, India and China have differing visions of their role in the 21st century. The United States sees itself as the dominant world power, with power in Asia split between China and India. China wants a multipolar world but seeks to be the dominant power in Asia. India wants multipolarity both globally and in Asia.

In an editorial last year, *The Times of India* termed India's approach "neo-nonalignment." Under the earlier

Has globalization been good for India?

YES   Ajay Shah
Economist

Written for *CQ Researcher*, April 2007

In my view, globalization has been central to India's growth. In manufacturing, India engaged in substantial unilateral liberalization, removing quantitative restrictions, and brought down customs tariffs from 1991 onwards. Meanwhile, barriers to foreign direct investment (FDI) in almost all manufacturing were removed, and domestic entry barriers were eliminated. These initiatives came together to induce heightened competition in the goods market through new domestic start-ups, competition from foreign firms establishing operations in India and competition from imports.

Thousands of firms died as a consequence of the new levels of competition. From 1996 to 2001, these problems cast a pall over the economy: firms were going bust, profit rates were under attack, investment was sluggish and banks were nervous over non-performing assets. This "trial by fire" seems to have worked wonders for the economy, for the survivors have emerged as more efficient and innovative firms. Many of the winners of this period have gone on to turn themselves into global firms.

Over the last five years, manufacturing exports doubled and gross receipts on the current account tripled. GDP growth rates bounced back from a low of 4.4 percent to more than 8 percent. Globalization was central to these developments.

The next frontier for India lies in opening up the financial sector. Indian finance in 2007 is much like the non-finance sector in the early 1990s. There is a substantial presence of government-owned corporations; there is an elaborate regulatory system where all features of products are prohibited unless explicitly permitted; considerable entry barriers impede domestic start-ups; capital controls greatly impede imports of financial services; and there are barriers to FDI.

The Ministry of Finance recently set up an expert group to explore the possibility of Mumbai becoming an international financial center. This group has argued that India needs to do for finance what was done for the real non-financial economy. By opening up to competition, the Indian financial system will be brought up to world standards of efficiency. This matters disproportionately, because finance is the "brain" of the economy: A better financial sector will give better bang-for-the-buck in converting a 35 percent-of-GDP investment rate to more than 8 percent GDP growth. In addition, there is a significant opportunity for Mumbai to join the ranks of London and New York as one of the world's premiere global financial centers.

NO   Vandana Shiva, PhD
Author, Anti-Globalization Activist

Excerpted from "The Suicide Economy of Corporate Globalisation," www.countercurrents.org/glo-shiva050404.htm, February 2004

The Indian peasantry, the largest body of surviving small farmers in the world, today faces a crisis of extinction. . . . Two-thirds of India makes its living from the land. . . . However, as farming is de-linked from the Earth, the soil, the biodiversity and the climate and linked to global corporations and global markets, and the generosity of the Earth is replaced by the greed of corporations, the viability of small farmers and small farms is destroyed. . . .

Two factors have transformed the positive economy of agriculture into a negative economy for peasants — the rising costs of production and the falling prices of farm commodities. Both these factors are rooted in the policies of trade liberalization and corporate globalisation.

In 1998, the World Bank's structural-adjustment policies forced India to open up its seed sector to global corporations like Cargill, Monsanto and Syngenta. The global corporations changed the input economy overnight. Farm-saved seeds were replaced by corporate seeds [that] needed fertilizers and pesticides and could not be saved [from one harvest to the next]. . . . As seed saving is prevented by patents [and] the engineering of seeds with non-renewable traits, seed has to be bought for every planting season. . . . This increases poverty and leads to indebtedness. . . .

The second pressure Indian farmers are facing is the dramatic fall in prices of farm produce as a result of free-trade policies of the World Trade Organization. . . . They have allowed an increase in agribusiness subsidies while preventing countries from protecting their farmers from the dumping of artificially cheap produce. . . . Global prices have dropped . . . due to an increase in subsidies and an increase in market monopolies controlled by a handful of agribusiness corporations. . . . The rigged prices of globally traded agriculture commodities are stealing incomes from poor peasants of the south.

[U]nder globalisation, the farmer is losing her/his social, cultural [and] economic identity as a producer. A farmer is now a "consumer" of costly seeds and costly chemicals sold by powerful global corporations. . . . This combination is leading to corporate feudalism, the most . . . exploitative convergence of global corporate capitalism and local feudalism. . . .

It is necessary to stop this war against small farmers . . . rewrite the rules of trade in agriculture [and] change our paradigms of food production. Feeding humanity should not depend on the extinction of farmers and extinction of species.

Rising beside the Indian Ocean, bustling Mumbai is India's business capital and largest city, with more than 13 million residents. To continue its impressive economic growth, economists say India will have to continue infrastructure improvements, liberalize economic policies and fix its educational system.

definition, "India ploughed a lonely furrow, as it found itself factored out of everybody's security equation." By taking a neo-nonalignment stance, however, "New Delhi enters into security dialogue with everyone who has interests in South Asia." [46]

OUTLOOK

Full Speed Ahead?

Today it is all but impossible to find a pessimistic voice on India's economic potential. Healthy economic expansion seems assured for the foreseeable future; the only uncertainty is whether the rate of growth will be spectacular or merely steady.

To grow faster, most economists and business leaders say India will have to continue to make infrastructure improvements, liberalize economic policies and fix its education system. Given past experience, that's a tall order. Progress is being made in many areas, but it remains slow.

For example, New Delhi residents and businesses endure frequent power outages, particularly during the peak summer season and increasingly in winter. Even small shops must invest in generators — a costly and inefficient way to keep operations running.

"It's not a threat to basic growth," economist Virmani says. "But beyond a certain point, it's like somebody stepping down on the brakes while you're trying to accelerate."

Business leaders and politicians also engage in much hand-wringing over whether India's continued growth will help the country's poor — a problem for which no easy answer appears on the horizon. Yet signs indicate the notoriously slow Indian elephant may be lumbering toward tackling corruption, which has hindered the delivery of services to all Indians, most notably the poor.

"The nature of public vigilance has dramatically changed," says development adviser Kumar. Citizens have filed a flood of information requests under new right-to-information laws — akin to the U.S. Freedom of Information Act and state sunshine laws — demanding records showing how government money was spent, or misspent. While some requests have been frivolous, others have uncovered malfeasance or forced officials to do their jobs without demanding bribes.

The media, growing exponentially, are shining a new spotlight on official wrongdoing. Some of the new outlets — bordering on the sensational — are aggressive and competitive, often seeking scoops using hidden-camera "sting" operations.

And the Indian public is beginning to exercise a new-found pluck. After the acquittal of a well-connected defendant in a murder trial, protesters took to the streets, forcing authorities to re-open the case. Evidence was found of police complicity in destroying evidence incriminating the defendant. A new trial was held, and the man was convicted.

"That is the strength of our democracy, that these things happen," Virmani says. "They happen slowly, but they will happen because of public pressure."

Still, such instances remain more the exception than the norm. Many Indians continue to pay bribes with hardly a second thought; it's often the only way to get things done.

Virmani echoes other economists and business leaders who say reforming government holds the key to India's future. "The biggest challenge is not these individual things, one particular infrastructure or some other thing, it is governance," he says. "You cannot sustain high growth for several decades without improvements in governance."

NOTES

1. "Advance Estimates of National Income, 2006-07," Government of India press release, Feb. 7, 2007, and

"Quick Estimates of National Income, Consumption Expenditure, Saving and Capital Formation, 2005-06," Government of India press release, Jan. 31, 2007.

2. Dan Nystedt, "China Mobile Subscribers Top U.S. Population," IDG News Service, in *InfoWorld*, Jan. 22, 2007; www.infoworld.com/article/07/01/22/HNchinamobilesubscribers_1.html.

3. Dennis Kux, "India's Fine Balance," Foreign Affairs, May/June 2002. For an in-depth look at the 2002 communal violence, see David Masci, "Emerging India," *CQ Researcher*, April 19, 2002, pp. 329-360.

4. Kamal Nath, address to the 79th general meeting of the Federation of Indian Chambers of Commerce and Industry (FICCI), Jan. 9, 2007.

5. "World Development Indicators Database," World Bank, April 23, 2007; http://siteresources.world-bank.org/DATASTATISTICS/Resources/GDP.pdf.

6. Dominic Wilson and Roopa Purushothaman, "Dreaming with Brics: The Path to 2050," Goldman Sachs Global Economics Paper No. 99, Oct. 1, 2003.

7. Tushar Poddar and Eva Yi, "India's Rising Growth Potential," Goldman Sachs Global Economics Paper No. 152, Jan. 22, 2007.

8. C. Raja Mohan, *Impossible Allies: Nuclear India, United States and the Global Order* (2006), pp. 259-260.

9. Government of India press release, "Poverty Estimates for 2004-05," March 21, 2007; www.pib.nic.in/release/release.asp?relid=26316&kwd=poverty.

10. For background, see Masci, "For India's Women, a Hard Life," *op. cit.*, p. 338; and *World Factbook*, Central Intelligence Agency.

11. A. P. J. Abdul Kalam, address at the 81st Annual Day of Shri Ram College of Commerce, March 19, 2007. The office of president is largely ceremonial.

12. While China reported very high growth rates from 1992-1996 — ranging from 10 to 14 percent a year — the statistics were questioned; now some think China's current official estimates of 9 to 10 percent annual GDP growth may be understated. See Wayne M. Morrison, "China's Economic Conditions," Congressional Research Service, Foreign Affairs, Defense, and Trade Division, Jan. 12, 2006, p. CRS-3. Also see Vaclav Smil, "Podium: It Doesn't Add Up," *AsiaWeek*, Nov. 30, 2001.

13. Government of India Planning Commission, "Towards Faster Growth and More Inclusive Growth: An Approach to the 11th Five Year Plan," 2006. India's fiscal year begins April 1 and ends March 31 of the following year.

14. Surjit S. Bhalla, *Mid-Year Review of the Economy 2006-2007: India at a Structural Break* (2006), p. 84.

15. Shankar Aiyer and Puja Mehra, "Prices Out of Control," *India Today*, March 5, 2007, pp. 34-45.

16. *Human Development Report 2006*, United Nations Development Program (2006), pp. 284-285.

17. Nath, *op. cit.*

18. *Human Development Report 2006*, *op. cit.*, pp. 301-303 and pp. 319-321.

19. "Corruption Perceptions Index 2006," Transparency International (2006); www.transparency.org/policy_research/surveys_indices/cpi/2006.

20. Aroon Purie, "From the editor-in-chief," *India Today*, March 12, 2007.

21. *Overview of Indian Development Policy Review: Inclusive Growth and Service Delivery: Building on India's Success*, The World Bank (2006), p. 4.

22. *Ibid.*, pp. 6-7.

23. For background, see Roland Flamini, "Nuclear Proliferation," *CQ Global Researcher*, January 2007, pp. 1-26; also see Rodman D. Griffin, "Nuclear Proliferation," *CQ Researcher*, June 5, 1992, pp. 481-504.

24. With the apparent consent of the government in Islamabad, Pakistani nuclear scientist A. Q. Khan sold black market nuclear plans and materials to Libya, Iran and North Korea. For background, see Flamini, op. cit.

25. "IAEA Director Welcomes U.S. and India Nuclear Deal," International Atomic Energy Agency press release, March 2, 2002.

26. Ashley Tellis, "The U.S.-India 'Global Partnership': How Significant for American Interests?" testimony before U.S. House Committee on International Relations, Nov. 16. 2005.

27. For background, see Elaine Monaghan, "2006 Legislative Summary: U.S.-India Nuclear Pact," *CQ Weekly*, Dec. 18, 2006, p. 3350.

28. Yashwant Sinha, "Against National Interest," *India Today*, Dec. 25, 2006.

29. Jeffrey Sachs, *The End of Poverty* (2005), p. 173.

30. *Ibid.*, pp. 26-31.

31. Tariq Ali, *The Nehrus and the Gandhis: An Indian Dynasty* (2004), p. 87.

32. Arvind Virmani, *Propelling India from Socialist Stagnation to Global Power: Volume I* (2006), p. 43. This and subsequent growth figures come from Table 1.1, which breaks down India's growth from 1951 to 2002.

33. Ali, *op. cit.*, pp. 181-187.

34. Virmani, *op. cit.*, p. 56.

35. Gurcharan Das, *India Unbound: The Social and Economic Revolution from Independence to the Global Information Age* (2001), p. 214.

36. Nath, *op. cit.*

37. Ali, *op. cit.*, pp. 93-101.

38. Stephen P. Cohen, *India: Emerging Power* (2001), p. 41.

39. C. Raja Mohan, *Impossible Allies: Nuclear India, United States and the Global Order* (2006), p. 266.

40. See Selig S. Harrison, "How to Regulate Nuclear Weapons; The U.S. Deal with India Could Be a Good Starting Point," *The Washington Post*, April 23, 2006, p. B7.

41. Strobe Talbott, *Engaging India* (2004), p. 52.

42. Mohan, *op. cit.*, p. 15.

43. *Ibid.*, p . 7.

44. P. Chidambaram, speech to Parliament, Feb. 28, 2007.

45. P. S. Suryanarayana, "A Wave of Defence Diplomacy," *The Hindu*, March 10, 2007.

46. "Wooing Beijing," *The Times of India*, May 31, 2006.

BIBLIOGRAPHY

Books

Ali, Tariq, *The Nehrus and the Gandhis: An Indian Dynasty*, Picador, 2005.
A London-based author and commentator tells the story of one family's dominance of Indian politics.

Bhalla, Surjit S., *Mid-Year Review of the Economy 2006-2007: India at a Structural Break*, Shipra Publications, 2007.
A manager of a New Delhi-based investment fund and former World Bank economist makes the case for India having moved onto a higher growth plane.

Cohen, Stephen P., *India: Emerging Power*, Brookings Institution Press, 2001.
A veteran Indian scholar describes India's emergence as a strategic and military power in Asia and chronicles the course of U.S.-India relations.

Das, Gurcharan, *India Unbound: The Social and Economic Revolution from Independence to the Global Information Age*, Alfred A. Knopf, 2001.
The former CEO of Proctor & Gamble India provides an account laced with personal anecdotes of how India's economic policy and economy have evolved since Independence.

Luce, Edward, *In Spite of the Gods: The Strange Rise of Modern India*, Doubleday, 2007.
A former *Financial Times* South Asia bureau chief examines India's burgeoning growth amid mass poverty and illiteracy, institutional corruption and enduring religious traditions such as the Hindu caste system.

Mohan, C. Raja, *Impossible Allies: Nuclear India, United States and the Global Order*, India Research Press, 2006.
An Indian analyst and columnist for the Indian Express newspaper describes how India and the United States came to an agreement on a nuclear deal and his outlook for U.S.-India relations.

Sachs, Jeffrey, *The End of Poverty: How We Can Make it Happen in Our Lifetime*, Penguin Books, 2005.
The famed development economist offers his prescription for eradicating global poverty, based on his experiences in several countries including India.

Talbott, Strobe, *Engaging India: Diplomacy, Democracy and the Bomb*, Brookings Institution Press, 2004.
A former U.S. deputy secretary of State offers a firsthand account of the Clinton administration's negotiations with India after its 1998 nuclear tests.

Virmani, Arvind, *Propelling India from Socialist Stagnation to Global Power*, **Academic Foundation, 2006.**
An economist and adviser to the Indian government provides a comprehensive look at India's economic performance based heavily on his own pioneering econometric studies.

Articles

Chellaney, Brahma, "Don't Nuke the Facts," *The Times of India*, **Jan. 9, 2007.**
An Indian analyst says India needs to look closely at the details of the Hyde Act, passed recently by Congress, before agreeing to the U.S.-India nuclear deal.

Mohan, C. Raja, "India and the Balance of Power," *Foreign Affairs*, **July/August 2006, p. 17.**
A strategic-affairs expert explains India's outlook as it emerges as a more influential player in international affairs.

Reports and Studies

"Economic Survey 2006-2007," Government of India (Ministry of Finance), 2007.
This annual government review gives a detailed overview of the state of India's economy, government spending and receipts, financial and commodity markets and trade.

"Pursuit and Promotion of Science: The Indian Experience," Indian National Science Academy, 2001.
The chapter on agriculture describes how the Green Revolution transformed the production of wheat, rice and other agricultural products in India.

"Towards Faster and More Inclusive Growth," Government of India (Planning Commission), December 2006.
A government study describes India's current economic situation and the challenges it faces as it prepares a five-year development plan for 2007-2012.

Shukla, Rajesh K., S. K. Dwivedi and Asha Sharma, "The Great Indian Middle Class," National Council of Applied Economic Research, 2004.
A study of 300,000 Indian households finds that 6 percent have reached the middle class.

Tushar, Poddar, and Eva Yi, "India's Rising Growth Potential," Goldman Sachs Global Economics Paper No. 152, Jan. 22, 2007.
Financial analysts predict India's influence on the world economy will be bigger and quicker than previously thought.

For More Information

CARE, 27 Hauz Khas Village, New Delhi 110016; (91-11) 2656-6060; www.careindia.org. The Indian affiliate of the aid organization focuses on women and girls.

Carnegie Endowment for International Peace, 1779 Massachusetts Ave., N.W., Washington, DC 20036; (202) 483-7600; www.carnegieendowment.org. Its South Asia project tracks U.S.-India relations and the nuclear deal.

Centre for Policy Research, Dharma Marg, Chanakyapuri, New Delhi 110021; (91-11) 2611-5273; www.cprindia.org. Researches Indian public-policy issues.

Indian Council for Research on International Economic Relations, Core 6A, Fourth Floor, India Habitat Centre, Lodhi Road, New Delhi 110003; (91-11) 2464-5218; www.icrier.org. Conducts research and holds workshops.

The Institute for Defence Studies and Analyses, 1 Development Enclave, Delhi Cantt, New Delhi 110010; (91-11) 2671-7983; www.idsa.in. Conducts research.

Institute of Peace & Conflict Studies, B-7/3 Lower Ground Floor, Safdarjung Enclave, New Delhi 110029; (91-11) 4100-1900; www.ipcs.org. Studies security issues in South Asia.

National Council of Applied Economic Research, Parisila Bhawan, 11 Indraprastha Estate, New Delhi 110002; (91-11) 2337-9861; www.ncaer.org. Leading economic research institution that conducts surveys the Indian economy.

Observer Research Foundation, 20 Rouse Avenue Institutional Area, New Delhi 110002; (91-11) 4352-0020; www.observerindia.com. A public-policy research institute.

Research and Information System for Developing Countries, Zone IV-B, Fourth Floor, Indian Habitat Centre, Lodhi Road, New Delhi 110003; (91-11) 2468-2177; www.ris.org.in. A government-funded research institute.

V O I C E S   F R O M   A B R O A D

Rodrigo de Rato

Managing Director, International Monetary Fund
March 2005

Needed: 100 million jobs
    "India needs to continue to restructure its domestic economy, to allow it to reap the full benefits of globalization. It is sobering to think that India needs to generate in excess of 100 million jobs in the next decade simply to keep the unemployment rate from rising."

Bibek Debroy

Secretary General; Progress, Harmony and Development Chamber of Commerce and Industry (India)
January 2006

Government must facilitate growth
    "Though the target of single-digit income-poverty ratios in 2012 is a welcome target to have, this will not be possible unless the government creates a facilitating environment for growth and improves delivery of its anti-poverty programmes."

Mohamed ElBaradei

Director General, International Atomic Energy Agency
June 2006

No violation of nuclear pact
    "The U.S.-India deal . . . does not add to or detract from India's nuclear weapons program, nor does it confer any 'status,' legal or otherwise, on India as a possessor of nuclear weapons. India has never joined the NPT; it has therefore not violated any legal commitment, and it has never encouraged nuclear weapons proliferation."

Rahunath Mashelkar

President, Indian National Science Academy
February 2007

The brain drain is over
    "During the last three years, more than 30,000 top-class professionals — scientists and engineers — have come back to the country. . . . India is gradually becoming the land of opportunity. . . . The latest Intel chip is not being designed in the U.S. — it's being designed in Bangalore."

Kamal Nath

Commerce Minister of India
April 2006

Collaboration creates opportunities
    "It is only with a conscious multi-pronged, multi-dimensional effort that we can address the massive challenge of finding job opportunities for millions of our unemployed youth, and export-oriented production has a huge potential for generating jobs."

Haruhiko Kuroda

President, Asian Development Bank
November 2006

Inclusion must accompany growth
    "Infrastructure development has a crucial role to play if India is to sustain its high growth, which must become more inclusive as the country matures."

Arundhati Ghose

Former Indian Ambassador to the United Nations
February 2007

Just friends, not allies
    "India will never be an ally [of the United States]. . . . But we'll be a friend, which is different. In an alliance there is a leader, and what he says is carried out by the rest of the alliance. . . . [W]here we have common interests, we will work together. Where we disagree, we will continue to disagree."

A.P.J. Abdul Kalam

President of India
February 2007

Science and technology are top priorities
    "The growth of the economy is very important — and if the growth of the economy is important, so is science and technology, because it drives this growth. . . . As science transforms technology, it brings faster development to the nation. That's how, from 1947 onwards, science and technology became the top priority for all the governments."

Arundhati Roy

Author
June 2005

India joining war on terror
    "As a spokesperson for the jury of conscience, it would make me uneasy if I did not mention that the government of India is . . . positioning itself as an ally of the United States in its economic policies and the so-called War on Terror."

The International Herald Tribune/Patrick Chappatte

15

Emerging China

Peter Katel and Alan Greenblatt

Shanghai, China's financial capital and largest city, boasts 4,000 skyscrapers — twice as many as New York City. China's $1.6 trillion economic output is expected to triple in 15 years, overtaking the United States by 2039. Critics say low wages and unfair trade and currency policies are behind China's economic success as well as the loss of millions of jobs in the United States and other nations.

From *CQ Researcher,*
November 11, 2005 (updated October 2007).

Douglas Bartlett doesn't have any doubt why the Chicago-area firm his dad started in 1952 to make circuit boards has dropped from 140 employees to 68: Chinese manufacturers are stealing his customers.

"At a time when the U.S. government is rapidly and carelessly opening the U.S. market to any and all foreign competition, the Chinese government is . . . effectively destroying the [electronics manufacturing] industry in the United States," he testified last year. [1] Nationwide, he said, the industry's one-time payroll of 78,000 workers has dropped to half that number.

Other industries around the country share Bartlett's pain as they, too, try to cope with what *Business Week* calls "the three scariest words" in American industry — "the China price" — a price with which many U.S. manufacturers simply can't compete. [2]

The United States isn't alone in confronting the China price. In 2004, European Union (EU) members confiscated 75 million made-in-China sweaters, trousers and bras because they exceeded a new quota on Chinese textiles imposed by the federation after European manufacturers said a tidal wave of Chinese imports was killing them. The goods were released in September after the EU and China compromised on a new quota. Meanwhile, textile factories and workshops from Mexico to Africa and South Asia are shutting down in the face of competition from China and (to a lesser extent) India. [3]

More recently, Americans and Europeans have worried not only that China is undercutting domestic producers, but failing to insure the quality and safety of its exports. Throughout the spring and summer of 2007, U.S. agencies announced warnings and recalls due to problems with a range of imports from China, including haz-

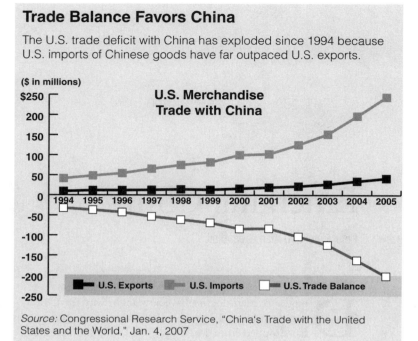

Trade Balance Favors China

The U.S. trade deficit with China has exploded since 1994 because U.S. imports of Chinese goods have far outpaced U.S. exports.

U.S. Merchandise Trade with China

($ in millions)

■ U.S. Exports　■ U.S. Imports　□ U.S. Trade Balance

Source: Congressional Research Service, "China's Trade with the United States and the World," Jan. 4, 2007

- China is the world's largest producer of coal, steel and cement, the second-largest consumer of energy and second-largest importer of oil, with its net imports of crude oil increasing by 18 percent during the first eight months of 2007. [7]
- China manufactures two-thirds of the world's copiers, microwave ovens, DVD players and shoes. [8]
- Starbucks has maintained an annual sales growth of about 30 percent in recent years in Beijing, with company founder Howard Schultz predicting that China will soon become the company's largest market outside the United States. [9]
- In the United States, 65,000 high-school students participated in Intel science and engineering fairs in 2004; in China, 6 million participated. [10]
- By 2010, China will produce more science and engineering doctorates than the United States. [11]

ardous tires, toys that contained lead paint, poisonous toothpaste and pet food and farm-raised fish that contained chemical residues.

Americans began worrying about China shortly after the new Asian powerhouse joined the World Trade Organization (WTO) in 2001. Indeed, China's accomplishments are enough to give pause to anyone who considers the United States to be far and away the world's most dynamic country:

- China is spending a record $40 billion on stadiums and airport and subway improvements in preparation for the Beijing Olympics, set to start on August 8, 2008, at 8:08 p.m. (Eight is a lucky number in China.) [4]
- China has grown about 10 percent a year for 30 years, the fastest growth rate for a major economy in recorded history. In that period it has moved 400 million people out of extreme poverty (defined as living on less than $1 a day) and quadrupled the average Chinese income. [5]
- China's exports to the United States soared from $41.4 billion to $243.5 billion from 1994 to 2005 — a 600 percent rise. [6]

The speed of China's economic takeoff has been stunning. In 1972, when President Richard M. Nixon traveled to Beijing to meet Chinese leader Mao Zedong, the world's most populous nation was effectively closed off to most of the world. The historic meeting eventually led to the reestablishment of diplomatic relations in 1979. Wal-Mart didn't even have a purchasing office in China until 2001. [12] Now 80 percent of the 6,000 factories in the retailer's worldwide network of suppliers are in China, and the world's biggest retailer buys $18 billion worth of Chinese products annually.

After 15 years in Beijing, James McGregor, author of a new book on doing business in China, knows the secret of China's success. "I'm from Duluth, Minn.," says the journalist-turned-businessman. "People there wake up in the morning and think of walleye fishing. People here get up and think about turning one dollar into three." [13]

But McGregor and other China hands urge Americans to remember that millions of Chinese remain desperately poor. China is still home to 18 percent of the world's poor, according to the World Bank, with 150 million Chinese living on less than $1 per day. And experts estimate that only 80 million Chinese are considered middle class by

American standards. "So there are still 1 billion to go," says David Lampton, director of the China Studies Program at Johns Hopkins University's School of Advanced International Studies.

The China of unmet needs bears little resemblance to China's impressive big-city skylines. And the public health-care system has all but collapsed. As a result, China, which in 2003 tried hiding a SARS (severe acute respiratory syndrome) epidemic, is among the likeliest starting points for a possible global pandemic of avian influenza or other global contagion. Joblessness grips more than a third of the rural population. The urban-rural imbalance in living conditions is largely responsible for making China the most unequal society in Asia, according to a recent United Nations (U.N.) assessment. [14]

The high unemployment — intensified by 10 million new workers entering the labor force annually — presents Chinese political and business leaders with an urgent task: "Every year, we have to find jobs for 24 million people," says a senior Chinese official who asked not to be identified. But fewer than half that many new jobs are created each year.

"People are talking about skyscrapers in Shanghai," the official says. "But over the past 27 years, it's only the people living in the eastern part of China who enjoy economic prosperity." The U.N. assessment found that the country's statistical measure of inequality — known as the "Gini Coefficient" — is past the point that's considered a threshold for social unrest. [15] According to the World Bank, China's income inequality has risen from 28 percent in 1981 to 41 percent today, as measured by the Gini index.

Indeed, as the government dismantles the old communist welfare state, protests have become commonplace throughout China. Police records show that in 2003 alone 3 million people participated in 58,000 protests; 87,000 protests were held in 2005, according to official records.

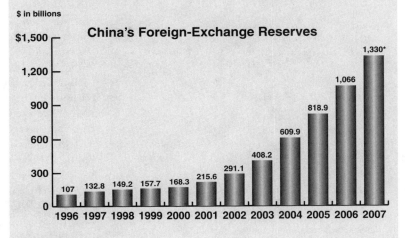

China's Bulging Bank Account

China has accumulated more than a half-trillion dollars in foreign-exchange reserves in the past 15 years, mostly in U.S. Treasury bills.

$ in billions

China's Foreign-Exchange Reserves

Year	$ in billions
1996	107
1997	132.8
1998	149.2
1999	157.7
2000	168.3
2001	215.6
2002	291.1
2003	408.2
2004	609.9
2005	818.9
2006	1,066
2007	1,330*

* As of June 2007

Source: Congressional Research Service, "China's Economic Conditions," July 13, 2007

"Disturbances derive most of their basic energy directly from dissatisfaction over the impact of economic reforms and market-based modernization," writes Albert Keidel, a former Treasury Department East Asia specialist and now a senior associate at the Carnegie Endowment for International Peace. Widespread corruption and malfeasance "supplement and greatly amplify" that dissatisfaction. [16]

For now, the government security apparatus quickly and often brutally nips protests in the bud, say experts. The potential spread of discontent "keeps the leadership awake at night," says Andrew Mertha, a Washington University political scientist who spent seven years in China.

Political repression and labor-rights violations remain a fact of life. The U.S. State Department notes that the only authorized labor union is the official union, controlled by the Chinese Communist Party. Workers, the report says, "are not free to organize or join unions of their own choosing." "Those who try to organize independent unions are arrested and sentenced to long prison terms," according to a former assistant secretary of state for human rights. [17] And New York-based Human

Some 90 million Chinese still live on less than $1 a day, mostly in rural areas where farming practices sometimes have not changed in hundreds of years. Much of China's stunning economic development has occurred in coastal cities.

Rights Watch reports that independent human-rights groups are prohibited from forming. [18]

Congress launched an investigation of Yahoo for revealing the identity of a Chinese journalist who used a Yahoo email account to send a copy of Chinese propaganda instructions to a pro-democracy Web site in New York. The journalist, Chi Tao, was sentenced to 10 years in prison. [19] China employs thousands of cybercensors who monitor blogs and other Internet activity. The Chinese government shut down 18,000 blogs ahead of the 17th Communist Party Congress in October 2007. "They really control your mind, constantly reminding the Internet users that you are constantly being watched," says Xiao Qiang, director of the Berkeley China Internet Project and professor of journalism at UC Berkeley.

China's authoritarianism, communist ideology and trade practices have strained U.S.-China relations in recent years. For instance, businessmen like Bartlett say the unbeatable China price is due not only to low labor costs but also to unethical trade practices. U.S. manufacturers argue that China keeps the value of its currency artificially low, making Chinese exports cheaper.

"They are not playing by the rules," says Carolyn Bartholomew, chair of the U.S.-China Economic and Security Review Commission, echoing the view that China's suppressed currency is a form of government subsidy prohibited under WTO rules. Several pieces of legislation are pending in Congress in what has become a perennial issue. The bills would pressure China to allow the *yuan* to "float" in world currency markets, letting free-market forces establish its value, or increase tariffs on Chinese goods if federal agencies determined the currency was being manipulated.

But critics of the "currency-manipulation" thesis say revamping China's currency system would not automatically raise the China price. "Show me where they're cheating," says Keidel. "I don't think the case holds up."

U.S. concern about Chinese trade tactics triggered a political firestorm in August 2005 when the state-controlled Chinese National Overseas Oil Corp. (CNOOC) announced plans to buy Unocal Corp., a major U.S. oil producer. CNOOC pulled out of the deal amid a barrage of overheated rhetoric. At one point Virginia Republican Rep. Frank Wolf all but accused CNOOC's Washington lobbyists — the prominent firm of Akin Gump Strauss Hauer & Feld — of betraying U.S. ideals. Akin Gump was representing a client, Wolf said, that "poses a growing national security threat and blatantly disrespects free-trade norms, human rights, religious freedom and political dissent." [20]

Politics aside, the aborted deal focused global attention on another fact of economic life: China's entry into the global competition for Earth's limited energy supplies. Until the mid-1990s, China produced all the petroleum it needed. Now, however, it's the world's second-biggest oil consumer and second-biggest importer. As China has intensified the competition for limited energy supplies, it also has driven up prices on the world market. [21]

China's growing energy use raises another issue that affects U.S. business — and planetary health. China's growth has heightened concerns about the difficulty of curbing greenhouse gas emissions, and the possible futility of curbs on energy use in the United States as China and India contribute heavily to global warming. China was expected to overtake the United States as the leading producer of greenhouse gases by the end of 2007. [22]

China's position, however, is that rich nations have caused most of the global warming problem and should not seek to stymie its growth. "China should not be blamed just because of its development," said Yu Jie, an

AFP/Getty Images/Liu Jin

environmental advocate from China, at a White House conference on global warming. "[What] they will follow is the European Union and the United States lead." [23]

Still, already as much as one-quarter of the pollution haze over Los Angeles originates in China, according to the U.S. Environmental Protection Agency. The World Bank reports that 20 of the world's 30 most polluted cities are in China, with 300 million people living in rural areas with unsafe drinking water. According to one estimate, environmental damage costs the country $226 billion each year. [24]

One indication that China's environmental-damage problem looms so large is that local officials ignore pollution-control requirements on factories that are making vital tax payments. That record of allegedly lax environmental enforcement crops up in the political debate over China's economic policies.

"Failure to enforce internationally recognized labor and environmental standards is another source of competitive advantage," the U.S.-China commission argues. In other words, American manufacturers are forced to adhere to environmental regulations that their Chinese competitors can flout. [25]

Critics of China's business practices have also attacked labor conditions in China's mines and factories. "There is significant evidence that China is playing by its own unfair rules that allow the systematic violation of workers' human rights to illegitimately skew the commercial 'playing field' in its favor," Human Rights Watch and Amnesty International said in a joint letter to the U.S. Trade Representative. They noted, among other violations, that China prohibits independent unions. [26]

Given the pressure to produce millions of new jobs each year and tamp down civil unrest, China's need to keep its economic engine humming looms far larger than foreign complaints about competition for energy supplies or unfair trade practices. Indeed, the United States wants the Chinese government to crack down on production and sales of counterfeit DVDs of Hollywood movies, but for Chinese citizens and their government, selling DVDs in the underground economy beats no job at all.

Despite disputes over China's currency and trade tactics, most foreign-policy experts are rooting for China to successfully get a handle on unemployment and to keep political instability at bay. "The real threat is a failing China," says Clyde Prestowitz, a corporate executive-turned-counselor to the secretary of Commerce during

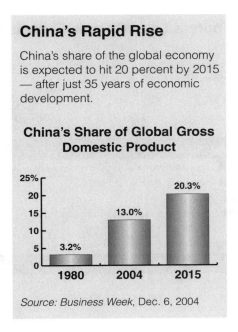

China's Rapid Rise

China's share of the global economy is expected to hit 20 percent by 2015 — after just 35 years of economic development.

China's Share of Global Gross Domestic Product

1980: 3.2%
2004: 13.0%
2015: 20.3%

Source: Business Week, Dec. 6, 2004

the Reagan administration and now the president of the Economic Strategy Institute. "Imagine a billion-and-a-half people all running away and spawning who knows what kinds of diseases — and the country has nuclear weapons."

But Bartlett and his fellow small-scale manufacturers have more immediate concerns. They focus more on keeping American workers employed than on the prospects of China's jobless millions. "This is an issue for Washington leaders," he says. "They don't know what the heck's going on. Washington should just say, 'We're going to lock our borders to a country that cheats.' "

China's emerging economic and political presence is prompting far-reaching debates concerning both U.S. and Chinese policy. Among the most hotly debated questions are:

Does China threaten U.S. global economic dominance?

American anxiety about China stems from more than worries about lost jobs. Its recently created semi-capitalist system has been booming to the tune of an average GDP growth of 9 percent a year for the past 10 years [27] — almost triple the U.S. economy's 3.3 percent GDP growth rate during the same period. [28]

Computers Lead China's Exports to U.S.

U.S. consumers purchased $40 billion worth of Chinese computer equipment in 2006. By comparison, the U.S. shipped just $6.8 billion in electronic components to China.

	2006 ($ in billions)	Percentage change 2005-2006
Top Five U.S. Exports to China		
Semiconductors and other electronic components	$6.8	70.1%
Oilseeds and grains (mainly soybeans)	2.6	10.9
Waste and scrap	6.1	65.4
Aerospace products and parts (mainly aircraft)	6.3	39.1
Basic chemicals	2.5	19.8
All commodities	**$55.2**	**32.1%**
Top Five U.S. Imports From China		
Computer equipment	$40.0	12.9%
Miscellaneous manufactured commodities (e.g. toys, games)	28.9	9.2
Audio and video equipment	18.8	22.9
Communications equipment	18.0	27.3
Apparel	19.2	17.5
All commodities	**$287.8**	**18.2%**

Source: Congressional Research Service, China-U.S. Trade Issues, July 11, 2007

But no one should panic, says Washington University's Mertha, asking rhetorically, "Is U.S. global economic dominance necessarily a good thing? China does now what the U.S. can no longer do — produce manufactured goods at prices that the market is willing to bear."

Still, China today accounts for 13 percent of global GDP, while the U.S. share is about 21 percent. And if China keeps growing at its current rate, its share of global GDP is expected to reach 20.3 percent in 10 years, cutting into the U.S. share. [29]

Those figures generate more advice not to panic, this time from former Commerce consultant Prestowitz. "That doesn't mean our national income will fall," he says. Translated from economists' shorthand, the comment means that Americans can earn as much as they do now, even if their earnings account for a smaller slice of the world's economic pie.

Until now China's growth has been based on exporting products made by its abundant supply of low-wage, low-skilled workers. But now the Chinese are moving into the "knowledge economy" — that is, jobs based on science and technology — the very sector that politicians and free-traders promised would be the salvation of American workers whose low-skilled jobs migrated to low-wage countries as a result of globalization. [30] The Chinese would focus on manufacturing that its legions of low-skilled workers could do and would only slowly adopt advanced science and technology, the argument went.

However, electronic goods now make up a third of Chinese exports — negating those earlier predictions, according to Michael Pillsbury, an influential China-policy consultant to the Pentagon. [31] "A systematic underestimation has occurred," he noted in a report for the U.S.-China Economic and Security Review Commission earlier this year. "Without a new assessment, U.S. policymakers will likely be further surprised in the decade ahead, as China gradually surpasses the U.S. in technology exports." [32]

Some of those who say America is unfairly losing out to Chinese competition focus on China's currency system. Unlike other big trading countries, China does not allow its currency to "float" on the world currency market, but sets a fixed rate — now valued at 7.5 *yuan* per $1. The practice keeps the value of the *yuan* artificially low compared to other currencies, critics say, making Chinese products relatively cheap for those paying with foreign currencies.

"In China . . . a mid-size American car costs $2,000 more — just because of currency manipulation — and their [cars] cost $2,000 less," Sen. Debbie Stabenow, D-Mich., told the Senate Finance Committee. She introduced a bill that would clamp a 27.5 percent duty on all Chinese imports to compensate for alleged currency manipulation. It would also require the administration to open talks with China on changing its currency system. Related bills have been introduced by other members of Congress.

As proof that China's currency is overvalued, critics cite the $1.3 trillion in foreign currency piling up in China's central bank. [33]

That cash wealth combined with China's remarkable economic growth ought to make China's *yuan* worth more than its present rate, China's critics argue. They might or might not be proved right, if the *yuan* were traded on the world's currency markets as is, for example, the U.S. dollar.

But China isn't a completely capitalist country. The government doesn't allow the market to determine the value of the *yuan* relative to other currencies. What critics like Stabenow are arguing is that the Chinese government has set the rate low in order to make China's goods unbeatably priced to foreign buyers. "The undervaluation of the Chinese *yuan* has contributed to the trade deficit with China and has hurt U.S. manufacturing," the U.S.-China Economic and Security Review Commission concluded in a report to Congress. [34]

But some experts disagree. "Evidence on whether the *renminbi* [another term for the *yuan*] is substantially undervalued . . . is far from conclusive," wrote three International Monetary Fund economists. For one thing, they cited studies showing that much of the foreign capital pouring into China is speculative, not aimed at long-term investment. For that reason, they argue, it can't be considered a sustained contributor to the Chinese economy. The bottom line is that if Chinese currency were traded on the open market, traders wouldn't consider those speculative funds a reason to set a high value on the *yuan*. [35]

In 2005, China finally responded to growing American political pressure by allowing the *yuan* to move slightly upward in value, from 8.3 to 8.1 *yuan* against the dollar. The government also said it would reset the currency's value daily in relation to a group of other currencies, but that this "float" wouldn't exceed 0.3 percent in either direction, measured against the dollar. The financial effects of the move were small, but it was taken as a signal that China was ready to begin loosening control of the *yuan*. [36]

But others point out that the rising tide of Chinese exports flooding U.S. and world markets isn't all bad. Consumers worldwide have enjoyed a higher standard of living in recent years, thanks to cheap Chinese prices for everything from underwear to televisions. And China has been plowing its billions of dollars in export receipts into U.S. Treasury bonds, helping to stabilize the U.S. money supply and keep the lid on inflation and interest rates. [37]

"I can have my worries" about China's trade surplus, says Lampton of Johns Hopkins, "but ask the American home-buyer how he likes the [low interest] rates."

Lampton was talking about the approximately $400.2 billion in U.S. Treasury securities that China holds. By keeping demand high for these securities, China has been keeping the repayment interest rate low, which in turn has been helping maintain relatively low interest rates for U.S. consumers. [38]

But China critics see danger lurking. "The People's Bank of China might choose to . . . shift out of U.S. bonds. If this shift were large and sudden, it could cause a spike in U.S. interest rates," the U.S.-China commission argued in its report to Congress, adding that "financial turmoil" could result. "This is a dangerous economic vulnerability for the United States," the commission concluded. [39]

The root cause, the commission and other critics argue, is the trade deficit, which has provided China with the profits that it has poured into the U.S. Treasury securities market. Hence, the criticism circles back to the value of China's currency, which keeps its exports irresistibly priced. [40]

Lampton and other supporters of the U.S.-China economic relationship acknowledge that the United States must pay back China's investment in U.S. bonds. But that doesn't make the Chinese villains for selling cheap goods and buying American debt, he says. "Is it China's moral responsibility to protect us from our own consumption patterns?"

Some critics of the current U.S.-China trade system say Americans haven't acted in their own interest. "Maybe it's to your short-term advantage to get subsidized goods, but it's sacrificing the long-term interests of the country and its future," says Patrick Mulloy, a former Clinton administration secretary of Commerce who served on the U.S.-China commission until 2006. "High-tech jobs are moving out of this country, and this reliance on imports helps spur that."

But some China experts argue that the sheer size of China and the speed of its economic reforms have led to overblown judgments about China's capabilities. Only 10 percent of Chinese engineering graduates possess the skills for international employment, points out Minxin Pei, director of the Carnegie Endowment's China Program, citing a recent McKinsey Global Institute study. Pei adds, "The United States is decades ahead of China in scientific infrastructure and in the quality of researchers. Their system is a rotten system, very bureaucratic." [41]

Other China-watchers say America's biggest challenge is at home, not in Asia. "America threatens its own economic dominance" by being "totally economically irresponsible," says Prestowitz. "Our budget is out of control; we're not investing in education, in infrastructure — and we have a trade deficit with everyone in the world, not just China."

Does China threaten U.S. energy supplies?

The emerging middle class in China is becoming a driving class, and many Chinese factories run on petroleum, helping to make China the world's second-biggest oil consumer and the third-biggest oil importer. China's oil consumption was 7.16 million barrels a day in 2006 — still just roughly a third as much as the United States uses. But China's consumption is growing by 6 percent annually and Deutsche Bank estimates that China's demand will grow to 10 million barrels a day by 2015. [42]

"The U.S. will have to make room for China," said Youssef M. Ibrahim, managing director of the Strategic Energy Investment Group of Dubai, United Arab Emirates. "If it doesn't . . . China will take the room." [43]

In fact, China is already making deals with suppliers throughout the world's oil belt. In recent months, China has bought $1.4 billion worth of oil and pipeline assets in Ecuador, spent $4.2 billion for oil resources in Kazakhstan and agreed to purchase oil assets in Canada for an undisclosed sum. [44]

China also has been courting oil from countries that are considered international outcasts — or at least nations that are out of favor with the United States. Venezuela — whose president, Hugo Chávez, has become one of Washington's loudest critics — pledged to sell China 100,000 barrels of oil a day, plus 3 million metric tons of fuel oil a year; the starting date of this arrangement hasn't been reported. The deal is estimated to cost $6 billion, possibly partly offset by China agreeing to build 10,000 dwellings for a Venezuelan government-housing program.

Petroleos de Venezuela, the state-owned oil company, and China National Petroleum will invest more than $10 billion in a heavy-oil venture in Venezuela's Faja del Orinoco region. The venture is intended to produce up to 1 million barrels a day. It is the biggest oil deal announced since ConocoPhillips and Exxon Mobil left the country in June. [45]

But despite efforts at diversity, more dependence on the Middle East — the source of 58 percent of China's oil now — will grow to 70 percent by 2015, according to the Institute for the Analysis of Global Security.

China has sunk more than $8 billion into the oil industry in Sudan, whose record of human-rights violations has put it off-limits to Western oil companies. Plainclothes Chinese security forces now protect Sudanese oil facilities, which provide 7 percent of China's oil supply. And China has invested more than $70 billion in Iran's petroleum industry, which supplies 11 percent of China's energy needs. Experts worry that because of the two countries' energy link China — which has veto power in the U.N. Security Council — will intercede on Iran's behalf in Iran's dispute with the United Nations over whether it is developing nuclear weapons. [46]

China National Petroleum Corp. has sought to elbow into position to win a share of oil exports from Iraq. The company also announced a joint venture in Chad to build the first refinery in that country, which has been producing oil in 13 fields since 2003.

"They are getting a double bang for their buck," says U.S.-China commission member Bartholomew, "getting access to energy resources and positioning themselves as an alternative. Where the U.S. and other countries are raising concerns about human-rights abuses, the Chinese government says, 'We're not concerned about that.' " Bartholomew argues that China's unconditional energy purchases undermine U.S. efforts to pressure oil-rich countries — particularly Muslim nations where authoritarian governments are thought to be spawning anti-U.S. terrorists — to improve their human-rights practices. [47]

Others point out, however, that Saudi Arabia — America's No. 3 oil supplier — is no model of respect for human rights. "Where do you want to put the Saudis on an ethical plane?" asks Lampton of Johns Hopkins.

Lampton also argues that U.S. political opposition in 2005 to CNOOC purchasing Unocal reinforced China's efforts to make deals with oil-rich countries rather than buying petroleum on the world market. "Congress said no, and drove [the Chinese] back to rogue regimes," he says.

But putting aside questions of whose oil suppliers are more oppressive, consumers want to know whether China will elbow the United States out of the purchasing line for the world's diminishing petroleum supplies.

"They're a threat to our easy, inexpensive access to energy that relies on excluding others that compete for it," says former Commerce Department official Prestowitz.

However, he welcomes that outcome. "If you're going to have something that pollutes the world and is in short supply, the fairest and most decent way to control it is to let the price go up," he says. Rising prices will force energy conservation, which Prestowitz and others favor for environmental-protection reasons.

Though China and the United States both thirst for more of a resource that won't last forever, some China-watchers say the United States won't be adversely affected by China's rising oil consumption, in part because U.S. companies have long-term supply contracts. "China has the potential to challenge the world's energy supply, not necessarily the United States' supplies," says David Finkelstein, director of the Asian Security Studies Center at CNA Corp., an Alexandria, Va., think tank whose main clients are U.S. government agencies. China's dependence on coal for electricity generation is a bigger challenge to all countries, Finkelstein says, because it is a major source of global air pollution.

Others say China's influence on the global energy supply and also on United States' energy access is overstated. "The Chinese are latecomers to the game and playing with a weak hand," says Kenneth Lieberthal, former senior director for Asia on the National Security Council in the Clinton administration. "In Sudan, Iran, Venezuela they're doing just fine — but those governments don't have great records on sticking to contracts."

Moreover, Lieberthal says America's major energy threat is Americans themselves. "Our lack of an energy policy is startling," he says, adding that the Bush administration's policy of accelerating production, rather than a search for better conservation methods, "is something most sane people would question." [48]

Is China a military threat to the United States or its Southeast Asian allies?

No single question divides China-watchers more than whether China poses a military challenge to the United States or its allies in Southeast Asia. Of the latter, the biggest question mark is Taiwan, the island nation founded in 1949 by anti-communists who fled the Chinese revolution. China still considers Taiwan as Chinese territory.

The United States, which ended formal diplomatic relations with Taiwan in 1979, recognizes the "One-China" policy. In April 2001, President George W. Bush said the United States would defend Taiwan if it were attacked by mainland China. [49] But following the 9/11 attacks, the Bush administration moved to a warmer — though not cozy — relationship with the Asian giant. [50]

In 2005, China turned up on the heat on Taiwan, adopting a law in March authorizing the use of force in response to any move toward formal independence by the island. As many as 1 million Taiwanese took to the streets to protest the action, which was seen as harming China's international image. In addition, the European Union held back on lifting the arms embargo it imposed on China after military repression of pro-democracy demonstrators in 1989. [51]

The Defense Department has noted that China's president has called the defense of sea lanes for Chinese oil imports a vital national security issue. These routes run from the Arabian Sea through Southeast Asian waters. [52]

Chinese officials insist their country harbors no hostile plans. "China's defense expenditure, per capita or total, is much lower than any of the other major countries in the world," Chinese ambassador to the United States Zhou Wenzhong told a packed auditorium at Georgetown University in Washington in 2005. For instance, he said, China only spent $27.5 billion on defense in 2004 — less than 6 percent of what the United States spent on defense that year. China's defense spending has since spiked sharply upward, rising 18 percent to $45 billion in 2007. [53]

In a February 2007 speech in Australia, Vice President Dick Cheney expressed concern about "China's continued fast-paced military buildup," saying it was not constructive and "not consistent with China's stated goal of a 'peaceful rise.' " [54]

But the Carnegie Endowment's Pei says Chinese military modernization looks more impressive on paper than in real life. "In the quality of their personnel, they're catching up, but the U.S. lead is huge," he says. "Military hardware-wise, [the United States is] probably two decades ahead, and let's not even talk about discipline, training, morale."

Pei maintains that Chinese weapons systems — which include items that are both domestically produced and bought from Russia, Israel and a few other countries — are nowhere near as effective as their U.S. equivalents. [55] Those of the "threat" school of thought are overestimating China's military preparedness, he suggests, just as many analysts did concerning Iraq's military, which was reputed to be lethal and loyal but which quickly collapsed after a U.S.-led coalition invaded in 2003. [56]

CHRONOLOGY

1800s *Chinese empire opens country to the West.*

1842 Following military defeat by opium-exporting Britain, China opens ports to Western traders.

1899 Boxers United in Righteousness, a powerful secret society, rises up against the foreigners.

Early 1900s *Chinese nationalism grows, leading to the collapse of the Qing Dynasty.*

1912 After mutinies by anti-monarchists in the military, the dynasty collapses, ending 2,000 years of imperial rule.

1920-21 Chinese Communist Party is founded in Shanghai; historians disagree on the year.

1927 Former communist ally Gen. Chiang Kai-shek, leader of the nationalist army, crushes a communist-led insurrection in Shanghai.

1934 Communists break out of Shanghai, beginning the "Long March"; Mao Zedong is one of the leaders.

1949 Facing certain defeat by communist forces, Chiang and other nationalists flee to Taiwan; Mao declares the founding of the Peoples' Republic of China, unifying China for the first time since the imperial dynasties.

1950s-1960s *Mao's Great Leap Forward triggers a rural famine that kills 20 million people.*

1959 Beginning of Great Leap Forward, Mao's industrialization campaign.

1966 Cultural Revolution exiles millions of intellectuals and professionals.

1970s-1980s *China establishes diplomatic and trade ties with the West.*

1972 President Richard M. Nixon journeys to China to begin building ties between the two countries.

1976 Mao dies.

1979 Deng Xiaoping launches wide-ranging, non-ideological economic reforms. China and the United States open relations.

1989 Student democracy activists occupying Beijing's Tienanmen Square are crushed by the army.

1990s *Chinese leaders expand economic freedoms, attracting Western businesses.*

1992 Retired leader Deng triggers a foreign-investor stampede when he says China's only hope lies in deeper economic changes.

1994 U.S. business executives in Beijing warn that U.S. pressure for human-rights reform in China could doom business prospects in China.

1997 Britain returns Hong Kong to China, ending the era of Western-run ports.

2000s *China joins World Trade Organization (WTO).*

Sept. 20, 2000 U.S. Senate approves normal trade relations with China after a bruising political battle, ending annual reviews of China's trade status.

Nov. 10, 2001 China enters WTO, committing itself to play by "fair" global trade rules.

2003 China becomes world's second-largest oil consumer and third-largest importer.

2004 Wal-Mart imports about $18 billion in Chinese products.

2005 *June-Oct.:* Defense Secretary Donald H. Rumsfeld voices suspicion of China's military spending, prompting its reiteration of peaceful intentions. *Sept.:* Top U.S. officials visit China, including Rumsfeld and Federal Reserve Chairman Alan Greenspan. *April:* A protester infiltrates a joint White House news conference held by President Bush and Chinese President Hu Jintao, disrupting their summit meeting.

2007 *Jan:* China destroys one of its own satellites with a missile, the first such test of military might in space by any nation in more than two decades. *July:* The former commissioner of the State Food and Drug Administration is executed for accepting bribes from drug companies seeking quick product approval.

August 2008 China hosts the Summer Olympics in Beijing.

The Iraq analogy is apt at least in one respect. The 1991 Gulf War — which ended in almost-immediate defeat for Saddam Hussein's forces — hit the Chinese brass like a thunderbolt, says CNA's Finkelstein, a Chinese-speaking West Point graduate and retired U.S. Army colonel. "It showed the leadership of the Chinese military that they were already 20 years behind most developed militaries and would remain so if they didn't do something about it."

Whatever the scale and effectiveness of military modernization, there is no danger of a Chinese attack on the United States, Finkelstein says, conceding that China "certainly poses a threat to Taiwan."

But no one has publicly hypothesized how immediate that threat might be. And even those who view China as a military threat of some kind differ on how and where China might act aggressively. The Pentagon report refers briefly to China's relatively scanty recent history of armed conflict with nearby countries. China fought a 29-day war with Vietnam over territory and other issues in 1979, for instance. Fighting ended in what is widely considered a defeat for the more numerous Chinese forces. [57] China's present leadership may have that past outcome in mind as it upgrades the military, the Pentagon report suggests. "As China's military power grows, China's leaders may be tempted to resort to force or coercion more quickly to press diplomatic advantage, advance security interests or resolve disputes." [58]

Pentagon consultant Pillsbury observes that a consensus exists in Chinese military circles that relative U.S. global power is declining, with some strategists arguing that the decline is fairly rapid. Pillsbury has edited a 456-page book of writings by Chinese military thinkers and authored a 420-page book on veiled debates within Chinese and political circles concerning China's geopolitical and military place in the world over the next several decades. [59] He writes in the latter book that Chinese officials' often-voiced statements that China will always be a force for peace and stability are merely "platitudes." [60]

Chinese strategists remain wedded to Marxist notions that war is the outcome of a struggle for resources, Pillsbury writes. The dominant American view that wars occur because of "miscalculations and misperceptions" has no place in Chinese military thinking. Seen in this light, Chinese plans for conflict must be taken more seriously than American contingency plans, which assume that only accidents or errors cause wars. [61]

But Thomas P. M. Barnett, a noted geopolitical strategist, ridicules Pillsbury's views, likening the China-threat model to past overestimates of Soviet strength and capabilities. [62] "[Pillsbury has] spent decades perusing Chinese military writing, which he finds — gasp! — fixated on U.S. military power. Can you believe it? Chinese military leaders are strongly anti-American! I am stunned. And they [have] dreams of future high-tech war against us. And we read those documents, and we take their statements of aspiration and treat it as gospel truth," Barnett writes in his blog. [63]

Bartholomew of the U.S.-China commission echoes Pillsbury in arguing that there is no reason to assume that the Chinese government has benign intentions. For one thing, as it steps up its diplomatic activity around the world, China is, in effect, exploiting resentment about the U.S. role as lone superpower, she says. "We don't want to wake up one day and find out they weren't this friendly country that we wanted them to be."

But Lieberthal, the former National Security Council official, argues that Chinese leaders aren't bent on war. Instead, debate within China's ruling circles grows out of a consensus that favors a "peaceful and secure environment for decades to come." Economic growth remains the main goal, he says, not throwing the United States out of Asia. But the low level of trust between the two countries is in itself hazardous because it reinforces the views of hard-liners on both sides.

Lieberthal maintains that those who see China as a threat enjoy a built-in advantage in the policy debate over how to engage with China: "If people listen to them, what they prophesy will come true."

BACKGROUND

Foreign Domination

China's history goes back some 4,000 years, but it was only about 300 years ago that Westerners first arrived seeking Chinese goods. From China's standpoint, foreign interference and territory grabbing, backed by troops and warships, have marked relations with the West. [64]

Western aggressiveness in China was all the more resented because it followed centuries in which China all but shut out the rest of the world. Indeed, when Confucius, China's revered moral philosopher, was teaching in the 5th century B.C., other countries were

Trying to Do Business in China

To media baron Rupert Murdoch, the opportunity to do business in China — with its millions of eager workers, low costs and capitalism-infatuated government — must have seemed like an entrepreneur's dream back in 1993. His News Corp. spent nearly $1 billion to buy a startup Hong Kong-based satellite network, Star TV.

But when he tried to expand its offerings to mainland China — where the communist government controls media content — the government said no. [1]

In August 2005 police raided an affiliate of Murdoch's company for allegedly selling TV signal decoders that would give buyers unauthorized access to satellite broadcasts. Shortly after that, Murdoch said he had hit a "brick wall in China." The government is "quite paranoid about what [content] gets through." [2] More recently, China censors have patrolled user comments on the social-networking site MySpace China, which Murdoch launched in 2007 (putting his wife in charge of the delicate assignment). [3]

Murdoch's ordeal doesn't surprise Beijing-based journalist-turned-businessman James McGregor, author of a book on doing business in China. "The government of China has one overall objective — to hold the country together as tightly as it can as long as it can, in order to make the country wealthy and comfortable," McGregor says. "They have absolute intolerance for anything [like outside news] that could splinter society."

In 2006, Time Warner, which had been planning a major expansion in movie houses there, said it would close shop in the country instead, noting a policy change that no longer allowed foreign companies to control domestic theaters in most locations. [4] Chinese censors reportedly caught sensitive Google and Microsoft queries as they exited the country en route to servers elsewhere, blocking results (an effect that's been dubbed "the Great Firewall of China"). In 2007, eBay announced that it would close its Web site in China due to its problems with Chinese regulations that put limits on financial transactions conducted by foreign companies.

In addition to these pressures on foreigners, doing business in China is tough simply by the fact that there is so much internal competition. "You have a dog-eat-dog society here," McGregor says. "It's all about individual competition — at school, you compete against the kid at the next desk; if you go to a better college, you get a better job. There are 1.3 billion people competing for resources — and no safety net."

In addition, McGregor points out that Western businessmen's dependence on signed agreements puts them at a disadvantage. "Contracts are not a guarantee of anything" in China, he warns. [5]

The Paris-based Organization for Economic Cooperation and Development — a think tank on governance — warns, "trained judges are short in supply" in China, and there is "judicial ignorance of the law, corruption within the judicial system, pressures on judges from local government and [Communist Party] officials and inability of courts to enforce their own decisions." [6]

Chinese officials acknowledge their legal system isn't yet up to international standards. "China is a developing country undergoing profound transformation," a high official says, asking not to be named. "People outside of China just take it for granted that China should do an equally good job on every front. It takes time to train a lawyer; it takes time to train a good judge."

Despite the problems, the American Chambers of Commerce in Shanghai and Beijing count some 2,000

deemed insignificant. As late as the 18th century, businessman McGregor notes in his 2005 book, Chinese maps depicted China as vast, with Africa, Europe and the United States little more than flyspecks.

Despite China's efforts to bar outsiders, European and American consumers — clamoring for Chinese tea, silk and porcelain — would not be denied. At the same time, Western manufacturers wanted access to China's vast market. By the early 19th century, the British Empire was buying quantities of Chinese products, but China wasn't purchasing enough British products to satisfy London. The British devised a coldly calculated solution — export opium to China wholesale from India, which was then a British colony. Opium (the raw material of heroin) is addictive, so steady sales were virtually guaranteed.

China caught on immediately to the British marketing strategy. As early as 1839, the Chinese emperor ordered the opium trade in southern China wiped out. His officials destroyed a big quantity of the drug, lead-

members. Meanwhile, Chinese red tape is infuriating, according to E. Anthony Wayne, assistant secretary of state for economic and business affairs, who says the bureaucracy can be "molasses slow." [7]

Perhaps in part because of that, U.S. direct investment in Chinese business operations in 2004 — $15.4 billion — amounted to only about 20 percent of the $80.2 billion that U.S. companies have invested in Japan. In other words, a Commerce Department economist says, most of China's $196.7 billion in exports to the United States last year were generated by sales contracts or by investments in China made by businesses from other countries. [8]

Sometimes business disputes can be personally hazardous. David Ji, the Chinese-American president of a Los Angeles electronics wholesaler, Apex Digital, was jailed on Oct. 23, 2004, over payments allegedly owed by Apex to its main supplier of DVD players and TV sets, state-owned Sichuan Changhong Electronic. Changhong claims the Apex debt stands at $470 million; Apex says it owes $150 million.

"Your only way out [of jail] is to do what Changhong tells you to do," a company official told Ji. "If I decide today I want you to die, you will be dead tomorrow." Ji was conditionally released in August 2005. [9]

In addition, quality control is a relatively new concept for Chinese factories operated by domestic firms, says Washington, D.C., trade lawyer Matthew McConkey, who has lived in Beijing for the past 16 months. Items produced for the Chinese domestic market are substantially inferior to those produced for China's export trade, says McConkey, who represents Chinese firms accused of "dumping" products in the United States — that is, selling below cost to gain competitive advantage.

"When you get to any kind of precision electronics, anything that really requires an eye for detail, an eye for qual-ity, there are lots of areas where they lag," McConkey says. "When we go home once a year, everything we buy is made in China, and Chinese people [back here] are amazed because it's so good. Consumers here still don't know how to demand quality."

But as Murdoch discovered, officials have no trouble making demands of the tycoons who want to do business in China. Murdoch's problems were compounded, according to *The Wall Street Journal*, when a high-level government official who had been his champion suddenly was shuffled into another job. [10]

"You depend on your personal relationships," McGregor says. "That's the network who supports you. The system is never trustworthy, and the system has never been fair."

[1] "Publishing in Asia; paper chase," *The Economist*, Sept. 11, 1993, p. 62; James McGregor, *One Billion Customers: Lessons from the Front Lines of Doing Business in China* (2005), pp. 190-208.

[2] "Murdoch Says News Corp. Has Hit a 'Brick Wall' in China," Bloomberg, Sept. 19, 2005.

[3] Joseph Menn, "New Corp.'s China Moves a Worry in U.S.," *Los Angeles Times*, June 25, 2007, p. C1.

[4] Ariana Eunjung Cha, "China Gets Cold Feet for Foreign Investments," *The Washington Post*, Feb. 2, 2007, p. D1.

[5] McGregor, *op. cit.*, p. 57.

[6] Organization for Economic Cooperation and Development, "Governance in China," 2005, p. 26.

[7] Remarks before Executives' Club of Chicago, May 25, 2005.

[8] Wayne M. Morrison, "China-U.S. Trade Issues," Congressional Research Service, updated July 1, 2005; www.fas.org/sgp/crs/row/IB91121.pdf; Department of Commerce, "U.S. Direct Investment Abroad: Balance of Payments and Direct Investment Position Data — Detailed annual country by industry tables," www.bea.doc.gov/bea/di/di1usdbal.htm.

[9] Quoted in Joseph Kahn, "Dispute Leaves U.S. Executive in Chinese Legal Netherworld," *The New York Times*, Nov. 1, 2005, p. A1.

[10] Geoffrey A. Fowler and Kathy Chen, "China Blocks News Corp. Plan for TV Channel," *The Wall Street Journal*, Aug. 25, 2005, p. B1.

ing the British to demand compensation. After British and Chinese warships began trading shots, the Opium Wars began.

The wars ended badly for China in 1842. For the first time — but not the last — China was forced to cede territory to Britain, which took Hong Kong as a colony and set up commercial enclaves in five other port cities. These were also opened to other nations, including the United States. American citizens and other foreigners were exempted from Chinese law. In addition, China was pressured into paying $21 million for the destroyed opium and Britain's war costs.

A new round of fighting that began in 1858 ended in more concessions by China, which had been unable to prevent the British from taking Beijing and burning the enormous Summer Palace to the ground. Following that demonstration of imperial might, the Chinese allowed the virtual legalization of opium sales and foreign access to — and, in effect, control of — 10 new ports. China's humiliating defeats during the Opium Wars have colored its foreign policy ever since, many experts say.

The foreign penetration continued over the ensuing decades. In 1898-99, Germany responded to an attack on German missionaries by taking over a port city, then claiming mining and railway rights in the surrounding territory. During the same period, Britain forced China to grant it a 99-year lease on farmland north of Hong Kong, and the Russians and French expanded their footprints in Manchuria and the Indochina border areas, respectively.

Rise of Communism

Britain and the other foreign powers nibbling away at China didn't grasp the magnitude of the anti-imperialist response they were provoking. A nationalist movement known as the Boxers United in Righteousness began building in Shandong Province, south of Beijing, drawing in small, secret societies whose members practiced martial arts. Its first target was Chinese Christian converts.

In 1900, the Boxers converged on Beijing, harassing and killing Christians and some foreigners. When Western powers sent 2,000 troops to the rescue, the Boxers repulsed them. As the movement gathered strength, the Empress Dowager Cixi declared war against the foreign powers, lauding the "brave followers of the Boxers" for "burning churches and killing Christians."

But China's military and provincial governors didn't join the Boxers, and the United States, Russia, Britain and Japan crushed the Boxer Rebellion, leading to a peace treaty in 1901.

The empress' failure to support the Boxers signaled a trend that accompanied the nationalist surge: the deterioration of central authority. As the Qing (pronounced "Ching") Dynasty — which had ruled since 1636 — weakened, young people formed groups seeking to modernize China. The new organizations tended to be either nationalist or socialist. Sun Yat-sen — considered the father of Chinese independence — occupied more or less a middle position between those camps.

By 1911, anti-monarchists had infiltrated the military, and when rebellion finally broke out in November 1911 among civilians near Wuhan, southwest of Shanghai, military units joined in. As other mutinies followed, 44 top army commanders urged the founding of a republic. On Feb. 12, 1912, the monarchy dissolved itself.

For the next 37 years, China functioned without a central government. Regional warlords and armed political parties took its place.

The 1917 Bolshevik Revolution in Russia, replacing the czarist state with communism, electrified Chinese students, intellectuals and political activists as much as it did their counterparts elsewhere in the world. The Chinese Communist Party (CCP), founded in the early 1920s, joined forces with Sun's Guomindang (Nationalist) Party. [65]

After Sun died in 1924, Chiang Kai-shek, a top Guomindang military leader, filled the leadership vacuum. But after consolidating power, he turned on the communists. In 1927, backed by businessmen and gangsters, he halted a communist insurrection in Shanghai, massacring and executing participants. But the CCP retreated to the countryside and thrived.

Chiang Kai-shek's troops eventually blockaded the communists, who escaped from encirclement in October 1934 and began a 6,000-mile retreat toward Shaanxi Province, nearer Beijing. During constant fighting on the 370-day "Long March," a young officer rose in the ranks — Mao Zedong.

Communist Conquest

Meanwhile, the rise of Japanese militarism in the 1930s brought to power a political class that aimed to dominate Asia. In 1937, Japanese troops in Manchuria began expanding southward into China. When Chiang's forces confronted the advancing Japanese, Japan sent additional forces to north and central China. The horrific takeover of historic Nanjing is known as the "Rape of Nanjing."

World War II postponed the settling of accounts between Chiang's nationalists and the communists, now led by Mao. By war's end, the communists boasted 1.2 million members and an army of 900,000. Chiang had 2.7 million troops and U.S. support.

But Chiang's economic management was disastrous. He eventually lost the allegiance of the professionals, intellectuals, students and workers. In 1949, Mao's forces crushed the Guomindang army, whose leaders fled to Taiwan, and declared China unified as the People's Republic of China.

In 1950, only a year into the People's Republic's history, China invaded Tibet, which has been occupied ever since. The Dalai Lama, the dynastic Buddhist ruler, fled into exile nine years later. A 1989 Nobel Peace laureate, he has been calling for Tibetan autonomy under Chinese sovereignty. [66]

Mao remade China — and the country paid a bloody price for his work. Millions died as a result of Mao's agricultural collectivization, industrialization, ideological purges and foreign policy. During the "Great Leap Forward" in 1959-62, for instance, famine claimed at least 20 million people as collective farms were forced to turn over more and more of their harvests, partly to pay for heavy machinery imports from the Soviet Union.

But the disastrous "Leap" did not slow Mao's drive to transform China. In 1966 he launched the "Cultural Revolution," a mass movement by students and workers that channeled popular discontent with the system into a campaign against so-called "conservatives," who included intellectuals, professionals, and party and government officials. Millions of them were beaten to death, publicly humiliated or exiled to the countryside to be "re-educated" by doing manual labor.

Reform and Repression

By the early 1970s the Cultural Revolution had burned itself out. Even as it decayed, China's top leaders, including Premier Zhou Enlai, were holding secret talks with Nixon's national security adviser, Henry A. Kissinger. The negotiations burst into the open in 1972, when Nixon traveled to China to meet with Mao. After that, China began importing high-tech goods from the United States, Japan, Britain and West Germany.

Mao died in 1976, and party veteran Deng Xiaoping maneuvered his way into the supreme leadership, widening the opening to the West. The United States and China opened diplomatic and trade relations in 1979.

Deng launched a new phase in Chinese communism. As 1978 ended, the party decreed that managers of successful state-owned enterprises could reap some of the companies' profits. As a new party slogan declared: "To get rich is glorious." [67] Deng later explained his abandonment of Marxist economic doctrine by saying: "It doesn't matter whether a cat is black or white, as long as it catches mice." [68]

By the late 1980s, restrictions on free expression of views began to loosen, and people began demanding even more freedoms. On April 17, 1989, discontented students rallied in Beijing's huge Tiananmen Square. By May a million protesters had gathered.

They refused to leave. On June 3, 1989, a tough army unit sealed off the square and gunned down or arrested hundreds of students and their supporters as they tried to leave. On June 9, after an international outcry, Deng said he had had no alternative but to crush the "counter-revolutionary rebellion." But he insisted that economic change would proceed.

Eight years later, political, economic and historical trends merged when Britain's lease on Hong Kong expired in 1997 and the city-state reverted to Chinese control. China pledged to respect Hong Kong's Western-style political and economic system. Although human-rights campaigners say civil liberties are eroding and Hong Kong does not have a democratic political system, many note that Hong Kong continues to thrive — and China has imitated rather than quashed one of its main economic engines. "In many ways, the last 10 years have been a testament to how much China has changed and Hong Kong has stayed the same," concluded the *Los Angeles Times*. [69]

As the new millennium approached, Deng's long campaign to make China part of the global trading system was beginning to pay off. In the United States, a knock-down-drag-out fight over granting "normal trade status" to China opened the debate that continues today over U.S. policy in regard to Chinese business, labor and human-rights practices.

Normal trade status would eliminate annual congressional reviews of China's human-rights record, a condition for its eligibility to trade with the United States. The new arrangement would open the United States to low-tariff Chinese imports, lower Chinese tariffs on U.S. goods and further open the Chinese market. President Bill Clinton lobbied hard for the trade bill, which passed the House 237-197. The 83-15 Senate vote came on Sept. 20, 2000. [70]

Enactment of the U.S. legislation was a prelude to WTO membership, which was granted on Nov. 10, 2001 — four years after Deng's death. As a WTO member, China agreed to international arbitration of trade disputes and elimination of some trade tariffs and protectionist practices. [71]

With those actions, China's export trade skyrocketed. On the American side of the equation, the trade deficit with China nearly tripled, from $83.8 billion in 2000, to $162 billion in 2004. Wal-Mart helped lead the trend, accounting for 12 percent of the entire inventory of China imports in 2004. [72]

The political outcry from small-scale American manufacturers, and the labor movement, now centers on China's currency system, which critics maintain is designed to keep China's exports unbeatably priced.

What's Behind China's Space Program?

When two Chinese astronauts safely floated back to Earth on Oct. 17, 2005, after five days in orbit, China reaffirmed its status as a major player in space exploration. Two years earlier — after launching its first manned space probe — China had joined the United States and Russia to become one of only three countries that have sent men into space.

The successful flight of *Shenzhou-6* ended the first phase of China's space program. The next phase includes a robotic lunar probe by 2010, an orbiting space laboratory and a moon landing by 2020.

Some U.S. space experts say economic gain and national pride are behind China's space exploration efforts and even suggest collaborating with the Chinese. But others worry that military ambitions motivate China's space program — noting that it is run by the People's Liberation Army (PLA).

China is now seeking to position itself as a space leader in the developing world. Most prominently, in May 2007 China launched a $300 million communications satellite for Nigeria, a major oil producer. "They want to play a leadership role for developing countries that want to get into space," said Joan Johnson-Freese, chair of the National Security Studies Department at the U.S. Naval War College. "It's just such a win-win for them. They are making political connections, it helps them with oil deals, and they bring in hard currency to feed back into their own program to make them even more commercially competitive." [1]

Chinese officials insist the program's goals are scientific and economic. "China's space mission is solely based on peaceful purposes," said President Hu Jintao at the launch of *Shenzhou-6*. [2] China plans to build a Mars probe, con-duct its first spacewalk and send astronauts to the moon. At a March 2007 congressional hearing, NASA administrator Michael D. Griffin testified that China could "easily" put humans on the moon before U.S. astronauts would return there under the agency's proposed Moon-Mars Project. [3]

Dean Chang, a senior analyst at the CNA Corp., a research firm in Alexandria, Va., says that "the economic aspect is the top priority for China's space program [and has been] for most of the past 20 years."

In the 1970s, he notes, China's leaders, led by Deng Xiaoping, decided to focus on national economic growth and met with the nation's top scientists to develop a plan. The scientists advised the government to utilize science and technology to produce economic growth and suggested aerospace as a key focus.

Johnson-Freese says China's manned-space program will spur the creation of technical jobs and encourage foreign investment. "It shows China as a technically developed country, not just [able to make] cheap party favors but ready for the more high-growth type industries they really want to get," she says.

But Peter Brookes, a senior fellow at the Heritage Foundation's Asian Studies Center, says that while China supports the space program to improve its international standing, it also has a military facet. In January 2007, China conducted an antisatellite test in January, firing a missile that destroyed one of its own orbiting satellites — the first such successful test by any country in more than 20 years. "This is the first real escalation in the weaponization of space that we've seen in 20 years," said Jonathan MacDowell, a Harvard astronomer who tracks space activity. "It ends a long period of restraint." [4]

CURRENT SITUATION

Product Safety

In March 2007, the U.S. Food and Drug Administration issued warnings and recalls on pet foods that had caused sickness and death in many animals. Two months later, the FDA warned that some Chinese toothpaste (some of which turned out to be counterfeit) contained poisonous chemicals.

In June the Consumer Product Safety Commission announced the first of what proved to be a series of recalls involving Chinese-made toys that contained lead paint. That same month, the National Highway Safety Traffic Safety Commission announced a voluntary recall of Chinese tires that had a major safety defect. Also in June, the FDA announced import controls on various types of farm-raised fish from China that were found to contain chemical residues. [73]

These scandals were soon followed by revelations of

The Chinese "don't want to be looked at as a backward sort of country," Brookes says. But he also believes the large sums being spent on the space program indicate its military importance. "All of these technical capabilities that China's spending a lot of money on — I mean a space program isn't cheap — have military applications," he says.

Likewise, Richard Fisher, Jr., vice president of the International Assessment and Strategy Center, a U.S. think tank that focuses on security issues, believes China's space program is designed for military purposes. The first five of the six *Shenzhou* missions since November 1999 — four unmanned launches and the first manned mission in 2003 — were used for military research, he points out. "What more compelling evidence do we need?" he asks.

Chang also believes the program has a military component, which is at least partially defensive in nature. In analyzing recent wars the Chinese have seen that the United States uses space-based sensors, communication systems and navigation systems, Chang points out. "[The Chinese] say, 'to fight the kinds of wars that Americans fight we need to be able to cope with that,' " he says.

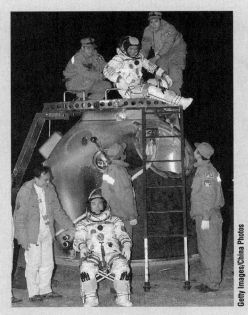

A Chinese astronaut climbs out of the *Shenzhou-6* re-entry capsule on Oct. 17, 2005, after he and a fellow astronaut orbited Earth for five days.

The military importance of space technology is also increasing, he says, because of Beijing's security concerns, particularly its ongoing conflict with Taiwan. China has threatened to attack Taiwan if it declares independence, and the United States might be compelled to intervene on Taiwan's behalf. "China understands that if you can damage the American military space constellation, you can also delay and possibly prevent American military forces from rescuing Taiwan," Fisher says.

But Johnson-Freese isn't worried about China's intentions, noting that China won't have better luck than the United States and Russia, which so far have not yet succeeded in finding a military use for space platforms.

"I'm not sure what the angst [over China's military intentions] is all about, except that it sounds good," she says.

— *Melissa J. Hipolit*

[1] Jim Yardley, "Snubbed by U.S., China Finds New Space Partners," *The New York Times*, May 24, 2007, p. A1.

[2] Howard W. French, "On Live Television, 2 Chinese Astronauts Begin 5 Days in Low Orbit on Earth," *The New York Times*, Oct. 12, 2005, p. A9.

[3] Guy Gugliotta, "New Challengers Emerge, Threatening to Take the Lead," *The New York Times*, Sept. 25, 2007, p. F11.

[4] William J. Broad and David E. Sanger, "Flexing Muscle, China Destroys Satellite in Test," *The New York Times*, Jan. 19, 2007, p. A1.

even more serious problems involving food and other products meant for domestic consumption in China. In July 2007, the Xinhua News Agency reported on an extensive government survey of 7,200 different products that concluded that nearly 20 percent of the products made in China for domestic consumption in the first half of 2007 were substandard. (This represented a slight improvement over the figure for 2006.)

Clearly, the lack of regulatory controls over domestic products was causing problems with China's exports.

Sen. Charles E. Schumer, D-N.Y., called for the creation of a new Commerce Department "import czar" to improve regulatory defenses.

Chinese regulators are notorious for corruption. In July 2007, China executed the former commissioner of the State Food and Drug Administration for accepting about $850,000 from eight drug companies looking for quick approval of their products. The country also entered into negotiations with the U.S. Consumer Product Safety Commission, with the head of China's product-quality agency publicly acknowledging the scope of the problems. In August 2007, China committed to state inspections of all food-related exports leaving Chinese ports. [74]

Nevertheless, some critics complained that China had not done nearly enough. Many in the United States were shocked that a high-ranking Mattel executive appeared with Chinese government officials in September 2007 to apologize for having to recall more than 19 million Chinese-made toys due to lead paint and dangerous markets. "China should be apologizing as well to consumers around the world for exporting shoddy products and dangerous food," Schumer complained. [75]

"Look at China's reaction to the food, toy and toothpaste scandals, created by shoddy products," writes John Pomfret, a former Washington Post Beijing bureau chief. "Instead of acknowledging the concerns of Western consumers, the Chinese Communist Party's propaganda organs have gone into attack mode, branding these worries as a campaign to isolate and weaken China." [76]

Most Chinese food producers are small operations with fewer than 10 employees and generally lack any real understanding of safety standards. "Sometimes it's a shock to discover how poor the quality processes are," said Sebastien Breteau, head of a Hong Kong company that audits Chinese factories for 158 U.S. companies. [77]

Despite the complaints, Chinese exports continued to soar. The country exported $878 billion worth of goods during the first nine months of 2007, up 27 percent from the same period in 2006 (which had set a record). Even the specific types of products that had caused trouble continued to sell well. China's food and agriculture exports to the United States were up by 27 percent, while global exports of Chinese-made toys rose 18 percent, despite the recalls. [78]

China's pricing advantages continued to work strongly in its favor. But the country was hoping to increase its profits by moving into higher-end manufacturing, such as computer equipment and automobiles. Although tech products represent a growing share of Chinese exports, by total value, China has wanted for innovation. It can make and sell products developed elsewhere cheaply, but it hasn't come up with impressive products of its own.

China now spends more on research and development than Japan, according to the Organization for Economic Cooperation and Development (OECD), but has comparatively little to show for it. Telecommunications equip-

ment, electronics and computers accounted for 43 percent of China's 2005 exports by value, but *China Economic Quarterly* noted that these high-tech products were still mostly assembled from foreign parts and components. [79]

"China is spinning its wheels," said Zhu Jian-Gang, director of Carnegie Mellon University's electrical engineering department and an advisor to China's national optical lab. He fears that institutions are more concerned about turning technology into products than making new breakthroughs. They also base promotions on seniority and connections rather than merit. "They do a lot of research, but it isn't important," he said. [80]

Exporting Soft Power

China has emerged as a leading diplomatic force around the world, its economic interests helping it gain influence and respect in many countries. The country's top leaders have traveled abroad much more often than their predecessors.

In some cases, China's new diplomatic ties serve mainly to forward its economic needs, such as access to raw materials including oil. But China has also swayed some countries into dropping their formal recognition of Taiwan. And China's positions have sometimes been at odds with the United States when it comes to protecting regimes that abuse human rights, as in Myanmar.

China has been an ally to the United States in helping to curb North Korea's nuclear ambitions. China has also won praise for sending a special envoy to Sudan who helped persuade Khartoum to approve a hybrid African Union — United Nations peacekeeping force to patrol the troubled Darfur region.

For the most part, of course, China pursues its own interests — which often center on access to commodities. China is building and fixing railroads in oil-exporting countries such as Angola and Nigeria and has major exploration contracts in Congo and Guinea. China has been active in large-scale agricultural efforts as well. "In mineral-rich countries that had been all but abandoned by foreign investors because of unrest and corruption," reports *The New York Times*, "Chinese companies are reviving output of cobalt and bauxite." [81]

China is building roads in Africa, as well as cell-phone networks, water pipelines and hospitals. Two-way trade between China and Africa surged 40 percent to $55.5 billion in 2006, up more than 500 percent since 2000. [82] China has built textile factories in several countries, as well as uranium and iron mines.

Some African leaders, including South African President Thabo Mbeki, have complained that China could be reenacting the destructive tendencies of past colonizers, exploiting the continent for its raw materials without building wealth on the ground. China is exporting huge amounts of finished goods, including clothing, flashlights and radios, which some say is hampering African nations' ability to build up their own manufacturing sectors and diversify beyond commodity production. "They are not here to develop Zambia, they're here to develop China," Zambian legislator Guy Scott has complained.

China has pledged to devote $20 billion to trade and infrastructure in Africa over the next three years, including $800 million for Zambia alone. "There is no doubt China has been good for Zambia," said Felix Mutati, Zambia's finance minister. "They are bringing investment, world-class technology, jobs, value addition. What more can you ask for?" [83]

China is also seeking new investment opportunities in the United States and other rich nations. The Chinese government has established a $200 billion overseas investment fund and encourages Chinese companies to buy foreign businesses with valuable technology. More than 500 Chinese companies now have offices or operations in California. [84]

China, which had long encouraged foreign investment to fuel its growth, has begun to clamp down. In 2007, the country set new limits on foreign acquisitions, based on national security grounds. Even a French purchase of a Chinese cookware company was delayed for a national security review. [85]

Destination Beijing

The Bush administration has clashed occasionally with China, but for the most part relations between the countries have improved, with both sides recognizing their mutual economic dependence. Treasury Secretary Henry M. Paulson has inaugurated a biannual set of meetings between top officials of the two nations and Defense Department reports on China have mostly softened in their tone and conclusions about China's activities in recent years.

China and the United States have conflicts as each tries to assert its influence in Asia and elsewhere, but the two countries have found common ground on certain issues. China organized and hosted six-nation talks in 2005 aimed at getting North Korea to dismantle its nuclear weapons program. The first round of negotiations ended with North Korea agreeing in principle to give up its nuclear weapons. [86] The talks bore real fruit in 2007, when North Korea agreed to abandon its nuclear programs. North Korea agreed to disclose and disable all facilities by the end of the year in exchange for 950,000 metric tons of fuel oil or its equivalent in economic aid. [87]

China has considerable leverage over impoverished North Korea as one of its few trading partners and food donors. [88] "China has become the first stop for any American diplomacy," said Christopher R. Hill, the lead American negotiator in the North Korea talks. [89]

China's initiative reflects the advantages it sees in pushing a new power arrangement in the Koreas, some analysts say. For instance, a reunified Korea with closer ties to China "could tilt the balance of power vis-à-vis Japan and China, while reducing the influence of the United States," according to You Ji, a political scientist at Australia's University of New South Wales. [90]

"Old Wine, New Bottle"

Although foreign leaders consistently urge China to begin political and social reforms, China's leadership insists the Communist Party's political monopoly will remain intact.

"China's socialist democratic politics embody distinctive Chinese characteristics," said one of the authors of an official, new white paper on Chinese democracy. [91] Translated from political jargon, the 23,000-word policy statement means China has no intention of loosening political control, say Western China-watchers and Chinese democracy activists.

"It is old wine in a new bottle," said Liu Xiaobo, a Chinese dissident. "At the least, the hypocritical government realizes it needs democracy to decorate its corrupt bureaucracy." [92]

The document's release followed an increase in criticism from Western and international leaders about the pace of political reform in China. "Closed politics cannot be a permanent feature of Chinese society," Zoellick said. "Some in China believe they can secure the Communist Party's monopoly on power through emphasizing economic growth and heightened nationalism. This is risky and mistaken." [93]

And only days before the white paper was released, World Bank president Paul Wolfowitz said on a visit to China, "The development process tends to bring along political development." But, he added, "There is still a long way to go."

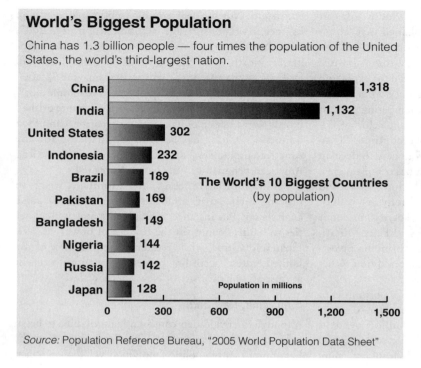

World's Biggest Population

China has 1.3 billion people — four times the population of the United States, the world's third-largest nation.

The World's 10 Biggest Countries
(by population)

Country	Population in millions
China	1,318
India	1,132
United States	302
Indonesia	232
Brazil	189
Pakistan	169
Bangladesh	149
Nigeria	144
Russia	142
Japan	128

Source: Population Reference Bureau, "2005 World Population Data Sheet"

At one point, Wolfowitz joined members of China's Muslim minority in prayer in impoverished Western China, where the government harshly represses both peaceful activists and violent terrorists seeking regional autonomy, says Human Rights Watch. [94]

The white paper, written by more than 100 specialists, did not refer to specific instances of dissent. [95] But it clearly rejected Western models of democracy. "There is no one, single and absolute democratic mode in the world that is universally applicable," the document says. [96]

Outside criticism isn't the only explanation for the document's publication, according to some Western experts. "There is a great deal of repressed demand [in China] for political expression," said Richard Baum, director of the Center for Chinese Studies at the University of California, Los Angeles. However, he added, the government's view on democratic activism is that "if you give an inch, they will take a mile." [97]

"Raw Capitalism"

The epic transformations that have made China a global economic power almost overnight are bound to con-

tinue. Chinese leaders clearly realize they must spread the wealth that only a minority of citizens in coastal cities enjoy. Hence, China's fierce drive — some call it ruthlessness — will likely remain a defining characteristic of Chinese interaction with the rest of the world.

"All we have is our aggression," said Yin Tongyao, president of Chery, a state-owned Chinese car manufacturer. "We have no brand name, no recognition, nothing. We are simply aggressive." [98] Chery Automobile announced plans in 2007 to export small cars to the United States in partnership with DaimlerChrysler. Earlier deals to break into the U.S. market fell apart, however. [99]

"China is [simultaneously] undergoing the raw capitalism of [the United States'] Robber Baron era of the late 1800s; the speculative financial mania of the 1920s; the rural-to-urban migration of the 1930s; the emergence of the first-car, first-home, first-fashionable-clothes, first-college education, first-family vacation, middle-class consumer of the 1950s and even aspects of social upheaval similar to the 1960s," writes businessman McGregor. [100]

Geopolitics strategist Barnett echoes McGregor's view. "The Chinese mirror-image us like you wouldn't believe . . . spanning a lot of different time periods from our own past," he writes. "Give them 40 or 50 years, and we'll see a China amazingly addicted to a middle-class lifestyle, with Disney vacations and all." [101]

An obstacle to that vision becoming reality is a possible social crisis arising from a glaring shortage of women. "You're going to have all these 20-year-old boys having difficulty getting good jobs and women," says an American lawyer living in Beijing. China now produces 116.8 boys for every 100 girls — much higher than global norms. China's infamous "one-child" policy, which led to abortions or sterilizations of tens of millions of women, is a major contributing factor, though the policy is no longer in force nationwide. Another cause for the imbalance is a cultural preference for boys, especially in the countryside, where female infanticide still

Does China present a technological challenge to the U.S.?

YES Michael Pillsbury
Associate Fellow, Institute For National Strategic Studies, National Defense University

From testimony presented to U.S.-China Economic and Security Review Commission, April 21, 2005

The Chinese say: The primary source of economic growth and national strength is science-and-technology policy. Now, when a Communist Party chairman says to a country of 1.3 billion, "This is our new national strategy," pardon my saying this: It's not like a member of the House of Representatives making a speech back home during recess.

It is not easy to [develop] cloning technology to produce a live buffalo; the Chinese just did it. It's not easy to have a super-computer that operates at one teraflop — 1 trillion calculations per second. The Chinese now claim they can scale up the new [supercomputer] that they've just begun operating in Shanghai to 50 [teraflops], and perhaps higher to 64. We have one at about 36. My friends in the computer community say, "We never imagined China would do this 20 years ago."

There's something called "pebble-bed reactor technology." It means to have your nuclear fuel inside a graphite ball so there cannot be a meltdown. It can change nuclear reactor design so that nuclear power becomes feasible once again. We haven't built one reactor in America for 35 years. The Chinese just announced that they want to build 40 reactors, and the implication is [they will do it] using this technology, which is being developed in a military area just outside of Tsinghua University.

The image of China we've had for 30 years under what I call the old paradigm is: They are poor, they are backward. Sometimes it eases into racism: They're not very bright. Yes, they can learn if we show them how and we — nice white boys — go over there and teach them something, but they really can't ever innovate on their own.

The old paradigm also has a national security angle to it, which is that China is our friend. More than our friend, our quasi-ally.

In the 1980s Ronald Reagan, who we all know is seen as a conservative against communism, approved six weapons systems for sale to China. I would submit to you we may be getting into a period where there's another paradigm beginning to take shape. We're hearing about it from Silicon Valley and from the Japanese and from the Indians.

[But] we Americans, generally speaking, especially our China-expert community, are still stuck in the old paradigm, and therefore any discussions of improving our own science education programs, improving the [National Science Foundation] budget, most American China experts would think, "What's that got to do with China? They're not a challenge."

NO Richard P. Suttmeier
Professor Of Political Science, University of Oregon

From testimony presented to U.S.-China Economic and Security Review Commission, April 21, 2005

We should not become excessively alarmed by facile accounts of China as a rising technological superpower. It is instructive to recall the many voices in the 1980s warning of a rising East Asian techno-nationalist power and of a coming Japanese technological domination [and] to ask why so many of these voices were wrong in such important ways and why so many of us seemed to want to believe their message.

We made lots of misjudgments because we didn't look as carefully as we might have at underlying vulnerabilities.

Clearly, there are ample indications that Chinese scientific and technological capabilities are improving, and in some cases improving rapidly. In spite of the progress, China finds itself struggling to escape from a series of enduring conditions, which have long frustrated its hopes for indigenous technological progress. China's patenting activity is disappointing, and it is rare that Chinese products incorporate indigenous intellectual property.

Instead, China's remarkable growth as a center of manufacturing and its emergence as a significant exporter of high-technology goods have involved a dependence on foreign technologies that seemingly has deepened. There is a growing sense of frustration in the Chinese technical community that so much of what China produces doesn't incorporate Chinese innovations.

The creation of this demand might be expected to stimulate China's domestic R&D system and lead to expanded industrial research. While there have been changes in this direction, problems remain. Chinese enterprises have long tended to regard technology originating from the domestic research system as immature and, when available, have preferred foreign technology. In a number of industries, therefore, Chinese firms wind up paying substantial license fees for this know-how, payments that cut into already slim profit margins. At the same time, this bias towards foreign technology does nothing to stimulate the domestic research system.

Unfortunately, U.S. public policy has at times reflected a serious misinterpretation of this "new world in the making" and China's role in it. As a result, we may be seeing a worrisome, growing divergence between a public policy shaped by those in Congress, the administration and certain advocacy groups who have a deep distrust of China and [as well as a distrust of] the increasingly intimate relations with China in science and technology being pursued by U.S. firms, institutions of higher education, and government technical agencies that have identified China's role in this new world as critical for their own futures.

occurs. Now many parents are using ultrasound exams to detect a fetus' sex, and aborting female fetuses. A law prohibiting that use of ultrasound is not widely enforced, according to the U.S. State Department. [102]

But Bartholomew of the U.S.-China Commission and many other critics question whether agreements reached with repressive regimes can be trusted. "We do want a peaceful future with China, but people forget it is still an authoritarian government, a government that represses its own people. If it were a democratic government, some of these concerns would be allayed."

China's determination to maintain the present political system suggests that changes in U.S.-China relations likely will come from the American side. Critics predict the United States will take a tougher attitude toward China's trade and economic policies, given the economic disruption Americans are experiencing.

"In the past, we had people in the factory who were working 48-to-50-hour weeks, and they could provide a single-family home and educate their kids with the hope of sending them on to college," says Illinois manufacturer Bartlett. "Nowadays, that is impossible." Those bleak prospects could drive Americans to demand a government crackdown on what they see as China's unfair trade practices.

Apart from potential congressional demands for high-powered investigations of trade practices, the government could force action on the currency issue by hauling China before the WTO, which prohibits currency manipulation as a competitive maneuver. The United States could also call in the WTO on the intellectual property rights issue. For that matter, the United States could demand that China's entrance in the WTO be renegotiated, on the ground that it's no longer entitled to some of the market protections it received on joining. [103]

Meanwhile, deep uncertainties exist concerning China's ability to improve the lot of the hundreds of millions of "losers" who haven't benefited from the economic takeoff, says CNA's Finkelstein.

It is especially difficult to predict China's future, he observes, because modern China is a rarity in human affairs: an exceptional country that is creating economic success while under communist rule.

"I've been doing China for over 20 years," he says, "and I have never been as unsure of what I think I understand about China as I am today."

OUTLOOK

The mixed emotions aroused by China's rise in the United States were exemplified by a debate late in 2007 in Pasadena, Calif. China planned to enter a float in the annual Tournament of Roses Parade to honor the upcoming Beijing Olympics, which drew protests from human rights groups and Chinese activists who objected due to the country's human rights record. "For an elected official that worries about potholes and planning, this international diplomacy is a little heady," said Mayor Bill Bogaard. [104]

Despite occasional grumbles, China has grown closer to the United States in recent years under President Hu Jintao. The 17th Party Congress, held in October 2007, unsurprisingly brought Hu in power for a second five-year term, but the meeting was not considered a complete success for him. Hu was unable to install an heir apparent of his own choosing. In a second term, Hu will want to pursue policies that put more of an emphasis on environmental protection and income equality. Indeed, the Congress enshrined in the Chinese constitution Hu's concept of "scientific development," referring to policies pursuing more balanced and sustainable development.

"Until now, the Chinese have promoted growth at any cost. It is a very perverse incentive that destroys any social or environmental limitations," said Krzysztof Michalak, an OECD researcher. "Now, at the state level, there is an appreciation that the environment can be a limitation on economic growth." [105]

Hu has strengthened his country's ties to the United States; he has also traveled far more than previous Chinese premiers in seeking influence with Africa and other trading and military partners. His regime helped persuade North Korea to halt its nuclear weapons development program. But he hasn't notably softened China's record on human rights or spread power outside the one-party communist system.

"Of course, such widening [economic] disparity has some conflicts with our government's policy of building a harmonious society," said Ma Fei, general manager of Realize Human Resource Consulting Co. in Beijing. [106]

Just before the Party Congress, China promoted several senior military officers with experience in planning for war over Taiwan as part of its continuing effort to block the self-governing island from declaring independence. China has also increased the number of warheads it has positioned along the Taiwan Strait. China is not expected to make any overt moves against Taiwan ahead of the Beijing Olympics in August 2008, however.

But the moves are part of a military buildup in which China has engaged. Although U.S. military planners are wary of China as a potential rival, China's strategy seems more focused on strengthening its position within Asia than in directly challenging the global superpower.

Walter Russell Read, a senior fellow at the Council on Foreign Relations, argues that China's rise is part of a larger story about the emergence of Asia as a force on the world stage. China may not even dominate Asia, he argues, much less emerge as a dominant superpower. "With the U.S. also prepared to defend the balance of power in Asia [between China, India and Japan], it seems unlikely that China, or any other nation, will waste time and money to overturn it," he says. [107]

China has, however, used its power to limit the United States' role in Asia. In 2005, China quietly helped turn Uzbekistan against the United States after Washington had criticized the country for a crackdown on activists. That year, Uzbekistan revoked U.S. access to its military bases. [108]

If China has no immediate plans to challenge the United States on the field of battle, though, the country has already taken bold steps to increase its "soft power" and diplomatic influence around the globe, pursuing trade deals and influence in countries across Asia, Africa and Latin America.

China's rise has been based on its ability to act as workshop to the world, manufacturing a vast array of products at a price that other countries could not beat. But, despite enormous investments in research and development, Chinese companies have come up with few breakthrough products. China's hope is that it can take the lead not just in making but designing high-end products, from computer equipment to cars.

Susan Shirk argues in a recent book that although "China may be an emerging superpower . . . it is a fragile one." The reasons she states pretty well sum up the challenges that China faces looking ahead, including a rapidly aging population, health-threatening pollution, mounting unemployment and a growing gap between rich and poor. "All around them, the leaders see new social forces unleashed by economic reforms that could subvert the regime." [109]

China's consumer inflation reached its highest rates in a decade in 2007, and many economists predict that its stock market, where share prices rose 400 percent between 2005 and 2007, may soon be overvalued. The nation's working-age population will reach its peak in 2015 and then begin to decline, although the World Bank argues that the nation — with 60 percent of its population still living in rural areas — is years away from facing any labor shortage.

In a July 2007 cover story, *Business Week* suggested that China might be "broken," unable to move its economy to a more sophisticated level. "The party has talked for decades about building a social safety net, yet as the working population ages the government isn't investing nearly enough to head off looming crises in health care, education and pensions," the magazine concluded. "In its pursuit of growth at all costs, China skimped on investments needed to provide basic affordable health care and the regulatory machinery that can enforce environmental, safety and corporate governance regulations nationwide." [110]

But China's leaders have proven highly adaptable, coming up with new ways of controlling the country's population despite the spread of technology and the rapid rise of a semi-capitalistic economy.

For all its increasingly apparent problems, China has become a beacon of economic progress, if not of liberty, to nations throughout the world. China will soon surpass Germany as the world's third-largest economy, behind the United States and Japan. The country holds enormous investments in the Unites States and its engagement in U.S. business continues to grow.

The country's need for raw materials has also led the nation's leaders to skillfully position China as a trading partner and ally to nations Western industrialized countries find abhorrent. In that regard, while the United States finds itself bogged down in the Middle East, China has become an alternative power in places such as Africa and Latin American and an important influence in powder kegs such as Sudan, Myanmar and North Korea.

China's awe-inspiring growth may not be sustainable, but there is no indication that the country will soon slip back, either in terms of its newly central place in the global economy or back into its historic isolation. China has become one of the world's great powers.

NOTES

1. Testimony in Akron, Ohio, Sept. 23, 2004; www.uscc.gov/hearings/hearingarchive.htm#hearings2004.

2. Pete Engardio, *et al.*, "Special Report — The China Price," *Business Week*, Dec. 6, 2004, p. 102.

3. For coverage, see Christopher Buckley, "Europe and China Seek Solution to Textile Backup," *The New York Times*, Aug. 26, 2005, p. C5; Graham Bowley, "Europe: Agreement Reached on Chinese Textiles," *The New York Times*, Sept. 8, 2005, p. C12; Evelyn Iritani, *et al.*, "A World Unravels; When Fear Follows Fabric Along the Assembly Line," *Los Angeles Times*, Jan. 17, 2005, p. A1.

4. Calum MacLeod and Paul Wiseman, "Whatever It Takes, China Aims for Dazzling Games," *USA Today*, Aug. 6, 2007, p. 1A.

5. Fareed Zakaria, "Special Report: Does the Future Belong to China?" *Newsweek*, May 9, 2005, p. 26.

6. Thomas Lum and Dick K. Nanto, "China's Trade With the United States and the World," Congressional Research Service, Jan. 4, 2007, p. 46.

7. William Spain, "China Oil Imports Soar," MarketWatch, Oct. 7, 2007, www.marketwatch.com/news/story/china-says-oil-imports-soar/story.aspx?guid=%7bEFEC3C0F-BADB-493E-B726-9168305BFC40%7d&print=true&dist=printTop.

8. Zakaria, *op. cit.*

9. Elisabeth Malkin, "Founder Sees Lots of Room for Lots More Starbucks," *The New York Times*, Sept. 22, 2007, p. C2.

10. Zakaria, *op. cit.*

11. National Academy of Sciences, "Rising Above the Gathering Storm: Energizing and Employing America for a Brighter Economic Future," 2005, p. 9-9.

12. Gary Hamilton, University of Washington, Seattle, testimony before U.S.-China Economic and Security Review Commission, May 19-20, 2005. For background, see Brian Hansen, "Big Box Stores," *CQ Researcher*, Sept. 10, 2004, pp. 733-756.

13. James McGregor, *One Billion Customers: Lessons from the Front Lines of Doing Business in China* (2005).

14. U.N. Country Team China, "Common Courtesy Assessment 2004," [undated], www.uchina.org; see also Melinda Liu, "The Flimsy Wall of China," *Newsweek*, Oct. 21, 2005, p. 41.

15. *Ibid.*

16. Albert Keidel, "The Economic Basis for Social Unrest in China," conference paper, May 26, 2005, p. 1; carnegieendowment.org/publications/index.cfm?fa=view&id=16993. See also, Mark Magnier, "China Defends Its 'Socialist' Democracy," *Los Angeles Times*, Oct. 20, 2005, p. A5.

17. "China's Hard Line on Free Unions," *The New York Times*, July 13, 2007, p. A18.

18. Philip P. Pan, "Internal Times Memo Key to China's Case," *The Washington Post*, Oct. 5, 2005, p. A18; Human Rights Watch, "Country Summary, China," January 2005.

19. Keith Bradsher, "China Cracks Down on News Media as Party Congress Nears," *The New York Times*, Aug. 16, 2007, p. A3.

20. Matt Pottinger, *et al.*, "Cnooc Drops Offer for Unocal, Exposing U.S.-Chinese Tensions," *The Wall Street Journal*, Aug. 3, 2005, p. A1; Keith Bradsher and Christopher Pala, "China Ups the Ante In Its Bid for Oil," *The New York Times*, Aug. 23, 2005, p. C1.

21. Office of the Secretary of Defense, "Annual Report to Congress: The Military Power of the People's Republic of China, 2005," p. 2. See also, Mark Magnier, "China Stakes a Claim for Major Access to Oil Around the World," *Los Angeles Times*, July 17, 2005, p. A1.

22. Joseph Kahn and Jim Yardley, "As China Roars, Pollution Reaches Deadly Extremes," *The New York Times*, Aug. 26, 2007, p. A1.

23. John M. Broder, "At Its Session on Warming, U.S. Is Seen to Stand Apart," *The New York Times*, Sept. 27, 2007, p. A10.

24. Wayne M. Morrison, "China's Economic Conditions," Congressional Research Service, July 13, 2007, p. 22.

25. Jim Yardley, "China's Next Big Boom Could Be Foul Air," *The New York Times*, Oct. 30, 2005, Sect. 4, p. 3; U.S.-China Economic and Security Review Commission, "2004 Report to Congress," p. 49; www.uscc.gov.

26. "Joint HRW-AI USA Letter to United States Trade Representative Robert B. Zoellick," April 13, 2004.

27. Wayne M. Morrison, "China's Economic Conditions," Congressional Research Service, updated July 1, 2005, p. 2; www.fas.org/sgp/crs/row/IB98014.pdf.

28. Department of Commerce, news release, "Gross Domestic Product," Oct. 28, 2005.

29. Morris Goldstein, "What Might the Next Emerging-Market Financial Crisis Look Like," Working Paper, International Institute of Economics, July, 2005, p. 11, www.iie.com/publications/wp/wp05-7.pdf. See also, Michael J. Mandel, "Does It Matter if China Catches Up to the U.S.?" *Business Week*, Dec. 6, 2004, p. 122.

30. For background, see Mary H. Cooper, "Exporting Jobs," *CQ Researcher*, Feb. 20, 2004, pp. 149-172.

31. Neil King Jr., "Secret Weapon: Inside Pentagon, A Scholar Shapes Views of China," *The Wall Street Journal*, Sept. 8, 2005, p. A1.

32. Michael Pillsbury, "China's Progress in Technological Competitiveness: The Need For a New Assessment," report for the U.S.-China Economic and Security Review Commission, April 21, 2005, pp. 3-4; www.uscc.gov.

33. Morrison, *op. cit.*, p. 10.

34. "U.S.-China Economic and Security Review Commission," *op. cit.*, p. 36.

35. Eswar Prasad, *et al.*, "Putting the Cart Before the Horse? Capital Account Liberalization and Exchange Rate Flexibility in China," IMF Policy Discussion Paper, January 2005.

36. Tim Annett and David A. Gaffen, "FAQ: China's Yuan Revaluation," *The Wall Street Journal*, July 22, 2005.

37. Steve Lohr, "Who's Afraid of China Inc.?" *The New York Times*, Sect. 3, p. 1. See also John Cranford, "For China, a Buying Buffet," *CQ Weekly*, June 27, 2005, p. 1691.

38. Wayne M. Morrison, "China-U.S. Trade Issues," Updated July 1, 2005, Congressional Research Service, p. 10; www.fas.org/sgp/crs/row/IB91121.pdf.

39. "2004 Report to Congress," p. 49.

40. *Ibid.*

41. McKinsey Global Institute, "The Emerging Global Labor Market," June 2005, p. 7; www.mckinsey.com/mgi/publications/emerginggloballabormarket/index.asp.

42. Jad Mouawad, "Oil Prices Continue to Rise, With a Close Above $78," *The New York Times*, Aug. 1, 2007.

43. Magnier, *op. cit.*, July 17, 2005.

44. Ben Dummett, Dow Jones Newswires, "Chinese Petroleum Companies Buy Interests in Ecuador," *The Washington Post*, Sept. 14, 2005, p. D6; "China Country Analysis Brief," Energy Information Administration, August 2005; www.eia.doe.gov/emeu/cabs/china.html.

45. Keith Bradsher and Jad Mouawad, "China Oil Giants Crave Respectability and Power," *The New York Times*, July 9, 2005, p. C1.

46. Jonathan Broder, "Balancing Fuel and Freedom," *CQ Weekly*, Sept. 12, 2005, p. 2384.

47. *Ibid.*

48. For background, see Jennifer Weeks, "Domestic Energy Production," *CQ Researcher*, Sept. 30, 2005, pp. 809-832.

49. John Pomfret, "China Growing Uneasy About U.S. Relations," *The Washington Post*, June 22, 2001, p. A1.

50. Richard W. Stevenson, "In Unocal Bid, U.S. Struggles With China Policies," *The New York Times*, June 26, 2005, p. A1.

51. Mark Magnier, "Anti-China Protesters Inundate Taipei," *Los Angeles Times*, March 27, 2005, p. A3; Ching-Ching Ni, "China Gives Gift of Friendship, But Big-Ticket Orders Help," *Los Angeles Times*, May 16, 2005, p. A3.

52. Office of the Secretary of Defense, *op. cit.*

53. Edward Cody, "China Boosts Military Spending," *The Washington Post*, March 5, 2007, p. A12.

54. Reuters, "Cheney Wary of China's Military and North Korea's Credibility," *The New York Times*, Feb. 24, 2007, p. A3.

55. Office of the Secretary of Defense, *op. cit.*

56. For background, see the following *CQ Researcher* reports: Pamela Prah, "War in Iraq," Oct. 21, 2005, pp. 881-908; David Masci, "Confronting Iraq," Oct. 4, 2002, pp. 793-816; and David Masci, "Rebuilding Iraq," July 25, 2003, pp. 625-648.

57. "Chinese Invasion of Vietnam, 1979," globalsecurity.org; www.globalsecurity.org/military/world/war/prc-vietnam.htm.

58. Office of the Secretary of Defense, *op. cit.*

59. Michael Pillsbury, ed., *Chinese Views of Future Warfare* (1998).

60. Michael Pillsbury, *China Debates the Future Security Environment* (2000), pp. xxi-xxxiii.

61. *Ibid.*

62. Ann Scott Tyson, "A Brain Pentagon Wants to Pick," *The Washington Post*, Oct. 19, 2005, p. A19. Barnett's *The Pentagon's New Map: War and Peace in the Twenty-First Century* (2004) was a bestseller; he is a former professor at the U.S. Naval War College in Newport, R.I.

63. www.thomaspmbarnett.com/weblog/, Sept. 8, 2005.

64. Unless otherwise specified, material in this section is drawn from Jonathan Spence, *The Search for Modern China* (1990).

65. See Nicholas Kristoff, " 'Mao': The Real Mao," *The New York Times Book Review*, Oct. 23, 2005, p. 1, review of June Chang and Jon Halliday, *Mao: The Unknown Story* (2005).

66. Stephanie Ho, "Dalai Lama Heading to Washington," Voice of America, Nov. 6, 2005, www.voanews.com/english/2005-11-06-voa35.cfm.

67. Daniel Southerland, "China's Reforms Yield Profits," *The Washington Post*, Oct. 31, 1987, p. A1.

68. Seth Faison, "China After Deng: The Overview," *The New York Times*, Feb. 20, 1997, A1.

69. Ching-Ching Ni, "Hong Kong Thrives Under China," *Los Angeles Times*, July 1, 2007, p. A10.

70. Matthew Vita and Juliet Eilperin, "House Passes China Trade Bill," *The Washington Post*, May 25, 2000, p. A1; David E. Sanger, "Opening to China," *The New York Times*, Sept. 20, 2000, p. A1.

71. Joseph Kahn, "World Trade Organization Admits China, Amid Doubts," *The New York Times*, Nov. 11, 2001, p. A16; Mark Landler, "International Business: New Game, New Rules," *The New York Times*, Nov. 17, 2001, p. C1.

72. *Op. cit.*, "China Trade Issues,' p. 2; John Cochran, "Unions See Battle Moving to China," *CQ Weekly*, Nov. 7, 2005, p. 2976.

73. Morrison, *op. cit.*, p. 10.

74. Edward S. Steinfeld, "The Rogue That Plays by the Rules," *The Washington Post*, Sept. 2, 2007, p. B3.

75. Abigail Goodman, "Mattel Plays Diplomat in China," *Los Angeles Times*, Sept. 22, 2007, p. C1.

76. John Pomfret, "A Country on the Edge," *The Washington Post*, Sept. 30, 2007, p. BW5.

77. David J. Lynch, "Suspect Imports Raise Questions About the Real Value of Getting Lowest Price," *USA Today*, July 3, 2007, p. 1B.

78. David Barboza, "Big Recalls Don't Slow Exports From China," *The New York Times*, Oct. 13, 2007, p. C1.

79. "The Export Juggernaut," *The Economist*, March 31, 2007.

80. Pete Engardio, Dexter Roberts, Frederik Balfour, and Bruce Einhorn, "Broken China," *Business Week*, July 23, 2007, p. 38

81. Howard W. French and Lydia Polgreen, "China, Filling a Void, Drills for Riches in Chad," *The New York Times*, Aug. 13, 2007, p. A1.

82. Heidi Vogt, "China's Influence on the Rise in Africa," The Associated Press, Sept. 9, 2007.

83. Lydia Polgree and Howard W. French, "China's Trade With Africa Carries a Price Tag," *The New York Times*, Aug. 21, 2007, p. A1.

84. James Flanigan, "China Seeking Presence in States," *Chicago Tribune*, Aug. 20, 2007, p. 3.

85. Keith Bradsher, "Beijing Seeks New Scrutiny of Investments by Outsiders," *The New York Times*, Aug. 28, 2007, p. C3.

86. Glen Kessler and Edward Cody, "N. Korea, U.S. Gave Ground to Make Deal," *The Washington Post*, Sept. 20, 2005, p. A1. For background, see Mary H. Cooper, "North Korean Crisis," *CQ Researcher*, April 11, 2003, pp. 321-344.

87. Helene Cooper, "North Koreans in Nuclear Pact," *The New York Times*, Oct. 4, 2007, p. A1.

88. State Department, Bureau of East Asian and Pacific Affairs, "Background Note: North Korea," August 2005; www.state.gov/r/pa/ei/bgn/2792.htm.

89. Steven Lee Myers, "Look Who's Mr. Fix-It for a Fraught Age," *The New York Times*, Oct. 7, 2007, p. 4:1.

90. You Ji, "Understanding China's North Korea Policy," *China Brief, Vol. IV*, Issue 5, March 3, 2004; www.jamestown.org/images/pdf/cb_004_005.pdf.

91. "Official interviewed on China's white paper on democratic politics," BBC Monitoring Asia Pacific — Political; Xinhua news agency domestic service, Beijing, Oct. 20, 2005.

92. Minne Chan and Kristine Kwok, "White paper just a big lie: activists; even government realises report is a sham, says writer," *South China Morning Post*, Oct. 20, 2005, p. 9.

93. Glenn Kessler, "Zoellick Details Discussions with China on Future of the Korean Peninsula," *The Washington Post*, Sept. 7, 2005, p. A22.

94. Richard McGregor, "Bank president defends loans for China," *Financial Times* (London), Oct. 18, 2005, p. 10; Human Rights Watch, "World Report 2005: China," January 2005.

95. BBC, *op. cit.*

96. Frank Ching, "Not amused by those 'colour revolutions,' " *New Straits Times* (Malaysia), Oct. 27, 2005, p. 19.

97. Quoted in Jim Yardley, "Report Calls Communist Party Rule Essential to Democracy in China," *The New York Times*, Oct. 20, 2005, p. A5.

98. Quoted in Peter Hessler, "Car Town: An upstart automaker targets the American market," *The New Yorker*, Sept. 26, 2005.

99. Sholnn Freeman, "Made in China, Driven in USA," *The Washington Post*, July 4, 2007, p. D1.

100. James McGregor, *op. cit.*, p. 3.

101. Barnett, *op. cit.*

102. U.S. State Department, "Country Reports on Human Rights Practices — 2004," Feb. 28, 2005; www.state.gov/g/drl/rls/hrrpt/2004/41640.htm; U.N. Country Team China, *op. cit.*, pp. 10-12.

103. Paul Magnusson, "Commentary: How to Level the Playing Field," *Business Week*, Dec. 6, 2004, p. 114.

104. David Pierson, "A Thorn for Rose Parade," *Los Angeles Times*, Oct. 6, 2007, p. A1.

105. David Greising, "China Takes Aim at Its Smoggy Skies," *Chicago Tribune*, Sept. 24, 2007, p. 1.

106. Don Lee, "In China, Disparity Takes a Great Leap," *Los Angeles Times*, June 10, 2007, p. C1.

107. Walter Russell Mead, "China Doesn't Own the Future," *Los Angeles Times*, Oct. 14, 2007, p. M5.

108. Joshua Kurlantzick, "China's Latest Export: Soft Power," *Los Angeles Times*, Sept. 2, 2007, p. M9.

109. John Pomfret, "A Country on the Edge," *The Washington Post*, Sept. 30, 2007, p. BW5.

110. Engardio, *op. cit.*

BIBLIOGRAPHY

Books

Chang, Jung, and Jon Halliday, *Mao: The Unknown Story*, Rough Cut, 2005.
This new biography is making waves among China scholars with its claims that accounts of Mao's military prowess are fabrications and that Mao ranks with Hitler and Stalin in the pantheon of world villains. Chang, born in China, wrote a well-regarded family memoir; Halliday, her husband, is a historian.

Fishman, Ted C., *China Inc.: How the Rise of the Next Superpower Challenges America and the World*, Scribner, 2005.
A former trader on the Chicago Mercantile Exchange offers a businessman's view of the U.S.-China competition.

Kristof, Nicholas D., and Sheryl Wudun, *China Wakes: The Struggle for the Soul of a Rising Power*, Vintage, 1995.
Husband-and-wife *New York Times* reporters describe China's economic transformation and moves toward a freer society after the Tiananmen Square events, which they both witnessed. The book anticipates many of the changes Chinese society later underwent.

McGregor, James, *One Billion Customers: Lessons from the Front Lines of Doing Business in China*, Free Press, 2005.
An American entrepreneur in China who started there as a journalist offers stories — and plenty of advice — about foreigners and Chinese alike who have tried to cash in on the emerging economic giant.

Pillsbury, Michael, *China Debates the Future Security Environment*, Institute for National Strategic Studies, 2000.
A Defense Department consultant examines a semi-public debate among senior Chinese military strategists about China's security concerns.

Spence, Jonathan D., *The Search for Modern China*, W. W. Norton, 1990.
A Yale University professor fortifies this old-fashioned narrative with details about China's complicated and violent past. Many China specialists recommend it as the best beginning to an education about China.

Articles

"China's New Revolution: Remaking our world, one deal at a time," *Time*, June 27, 2005, p. 24.
The magazine offers a people-centered view of the big issues, including conditions in the countryside, human rights and the growing ties between the United States and China.

Engardio, Pete Dexter Roberts, Frederik Balfour and Bruce Einhorn, "Broken China," *Business Week*, July 23, 2007, p. 38.
The business magazine concludes that China's remarkable growth may not last since the country has stinted on education and health care for its citizens and regulatory and safety infrastructure for its economy.

French, Howard W. and Lydia Polgreen, "China, Filling a Void, Drills for Riches in Chad," *The New York Times*, Aug. 13, 2007, p. A1.
China has increased its influence in African countries that are rich in mineral and oil production, extracting commodities helpful to industry back home.

Gross, Daniel, "Attack of the Tentacle Lady: At last, a business the Chinese can't dominate," *Slate*, posted Sept. 21, 2005.
A funny account of dealings with Chinese salespeople at an international trade fair argues persuasively that China has a long way to go in training salespeople in how to sell.

Kahn, Joseph, and Jim Yardley, "Amid China's Boom, No Helping Hand for Young QingMing," *The New York Times*, Aug. 1, 2004, p. A1.
The life and death of an 18-year-old rural youth tells the larger story of those who aren't benefiting from China's leap forward.

Kahn, Joseph and Jim Yardley, "As China Roars, Pollution Reaches Deadly Extremes," *The New York Times*, Aug. 26, 2007, p. A1.
Pollution has made cancer China's leading cause of death, and the country was set to overtake the United States as the leading producer of greenhouse gases.

Kaplan, Robert D., "How We Would Fight China," *The Atlantic*, June 2005, p. 49.
Despite the headline, Kaplan writes mainly about how not to fight China — by mounting a naval-based strategic presence in the Pacific that would help defuse the possibility of any catastrophic conflict with the "rising behemoth."

Lynch, David J., "Suspect Imports Raise Questions About the Real Value of Getting Lowest Price," *USA Today*, July 3, 2007, p. 1B.
Given the problems with Chinese pet food, fish, tires, toothpastes and toys, the "Made in China" label is starting to sound like a warning.

Ramstad, Evan, and Gary McWilliams, "Computer Savvy: For Dell, Success in China Tells Tale of Maturing Market," *The Wall Street Journal*, July 5, 2005, p. A1.
To the astonishment of some industry-watchers, Dell is selling computers online and by phone in China — helped by the fact that some of its parts suppliers are local.

Reports and Studies

Morrison, Wayne M., "China's Economic Conditions," Congressional Research Service, updated July 1, 2005; available at www.fas.org/sgp/crs/row/IB98014.pdf.
A dispassionate overview of the much-debated Chinese economy provides a solid introduction to the main issues.

Organisation for Economic Cooperation and Development, "Governance in China," September 2005.
OECD experts examine some of the toughest problems facing modernizing China, including government corruption, theft of intellectual property and environmental protection.

U.N. Country Team China, "Common Country Assessment 2004."
A group of United Nations experts assesses socioeconomic conditions throughout China, including health, rural-urban inequalities and environmental degradation and the prospects for their improvement.

U.S.-China Economic and Security Review Commission, "2004 Report to Congress," June 2004.
A congressionally established commission tends to be critical of the Chinese government in an annual in-depth look at the issues that dominate relations between the two countries.

For More Information

Carnegie Endowment for International Peace, China Program, 1779 Massachusetts Ave., N.W., Washington, DC 20036; (202) 483-7600; www.carnegieendowment.org/programs/china/. The think tank's Web site has extensive data on China.

China View, www.chinaview.cn. Covers domestic and international developments involving China; operated by China's state-owned news agency, Xinhua.

Commonwealth Institute, Project on Defense Alternatives, P.O. Box 398105, Inman Square Post Office, Cambridge, MA 02139; (617) 547-4474; www.comw.org/cmp. A vast, constantly updated online library.

Heritage Foundation, Asian Studies Center, 214 Massachusetts Ave., N.E., Washington, DC 20002; (202) 546-4400; www.heritage.org. Conservative think tank; features analysts' congressional testimony on China, policy memoranda and documents.

Human Rights in China, 350 5th Ave., New York, NY 10118; (212) 239-4495; www.hrichina.org. Maintains contacts with reform activists in China and monitors political and civil rights, trade and working conditions.

United Nations in China, c/o United Nations Development Programme (UNDP), 2 Liangmahe Nanlu Beijing, PR China 100600; (8610) 8532-0800; www.unchina.org/. Offers information on U.N. agencies active in China.

U.S.-China Business Council, 1818 N St., N.W., Suite 200, Washington, DC 20036; (202) 429-0340; www.uschina.org. Represents firms doing business in China.

U.S.-China Economic and Security Review Commission, 444 N. Capitol St., N.W., Suite 602, Washington, DC 20001; (202) 624-1407; www.uscc.gov/index.html. Bipartisan commission established by Congress in 2000 to study the evolving relationship between the two world powers.

16

Fair Trade Labeling

Sarah Glazer

Starbucks is one of several big U.S. chains that sells fair trade coffee and other products. The fair trade label signifies that farmers in the developing world received a fair price for their crops. Only 20 percent of coffee-drinking Americans are familiar with the fair trade label, compared to more than half of British consumers.

From *CQ Researcher,*
May 18, 2007.

At the upscale London supermarket chain Waitrose, the smiling faces of small farmers from Africa and Latin America lend a human touch to coffee packages bearing a distinctive green and blue "Fairtrade" label. [1]

In testimonials, the farmers say the fair trade company they deal with, Cafédirect, pays them better than competing coffee buyers and helps them preserve the environment. But Cafédirect coffee costs more than the competing brand, posing a dilemma for shoppers: Is it worth the extra cost, and do the farmers really benefit?

The answer for many British shoppers is apparently yes, judging from galloping sales of fair trade products, which have doubled every two years since 2002. [2]

The Fairtrade label, which signifies that farmers in the developing world received a fair price for their crops, now covers some 2,500 retail and catering lines in Britain, including fresh fruit, tea, chocolate and baby food. [3] Sainsbury's, a supermarket chain, sells fair trade bananas exclusively. Marks & Spencer, a major department store, touts its commitment to fair trade cotton T-shirts and underwear with full-page newspaper ads.

Britons now spend about five times more per capita on fair trade items than Americans. But U.S. sales of fair trade items have also grown rapidly — averaging an estimated 50 percent annually since 2001 — and some experts predict the United States could soon overtake Britain in per capita spending on fair trade products. [4] Coffee represents the lion's share of fair trade products, and U.S. fair trade coffee consumption alone already dwarfs any other nations' total retail spending on fair trade. (*See graph, p. 420.*)

Fair Trade Imports by U.S. Increase

U.S. importation of fair trade-certified coffee, tea and cocoa has risen significantly in recent years. Coffee imports alone have increased by over 850 times since 1998.

Imports of Fair Trade-Certified Products, 1998-2006
(in pounds)

Year	Coffee	Tea	Cocoa
1998	76,059	N/A	N/A
1999	2,052,242	N/A	N/A
2000	4,249,534	N/A	N/A
2001	6,669,308	65,261	N/A
2002	9,747,571	86,706	14,050
2003	19,239,017	95,669	178,888
2004	32,974,400	180,310	727,576
2005	44,585,323	517,500	1,036,696
2006	64,774,431	629,985	1,814,391

Source: "Fair Trade Almanac 1998-2006," TransFair USA

At the same time, awareness of fair trade products is far lower in the United States than in Europe. Only 20 percent of coffee-drinking Americans are familiar with the fair trade label, compared to more than half of British consumers. [5] The U.S. selection of fair trade items is also more limited — the most common items are coffee, chocolate, tea and bananas — and they often are available only in health food or gourmet stores.

Fair trade brands hope to raise their profile by gunning for the market niche known as "conscious consumers" — those who care about the environment, health and fair-labor standards. Big chains like Wal-Mart, Dunkin' Donuts, Starbucks and McDonald's have begun offering fair trade coffee and other items.

Sam Magona, a Ugandan coffee farmer, says his revenues have more than tripled since he started selling under the fair trade banner in 1998. Until farmers organized into cooperatives — a requirement of fair trade certification — exploitative middlemen were taking "most of the profits," says Magona, chairman of the Gumutindo cooperative union, which represents about 3,000 small farmers in Uganda.

Many families in his village could not afford to send their children to school and needed them to work in the fields. And when the world price of coffee dropped precipitously in 2001-2004, coffee farmers who sold on the open market could not even cover their costs, Magona recalls. By contrast, selling fair trade products guarantees a minimum price, insuring farmers against disaster when the price of coffee, traded on international markets, drops.

Now, children in the Gumutindo community are attending school. "People have a roof instead of grass thatch," Magona says, and "they eat more meat now after selling the coffee." But when Magona factors in how much it would cost to pay the family members who donate their labor for free, he says he is just "nearly breaking even."

Experts say this is the reality of subsistence farming in developing countries — farmers live on the margins, fair trade or not. At the same time, the fair trade system often pays up to one-third more than farmers would get on the open market, according to Christopher Himes, chief financial officer of TransFair USA, the leading labeling organization that certifies fair trade goods sold in the United States.

But some consumers may be disturbed to learn that as little as 10 percent of the extra price they pay for a fair trade cup of coffee goes to the grower, according to some estimates. That's because wholesalers, processors, branders and retailers each take a little of the extra price for themselves. TransFair has no control over those extra dips into the profit chain, Himes responds; it merely guarantees that a fair price was paid to the grower.

Some critics say fair trade's guarantee of a good return — no matter what the market price — sends the wrong economic signal to farmers. When the price of a commodity like coffee, which is traded on world markets, tumbles in response to global oversupply, overcompensated fair trade farmers will remain in an uneconomic sector long after they should have switched to some other livelihood, free-market economists argue.

"If there's an artificial inducement — like fair trade — to stay in the market, then that retards the exit process [of farmers] needed to rebalance supply and demand," and encourages more farmers to enter the market, driving down the world price for everyone else, says Brink Lindsey, vice president for research at the conservative Cato Institute in Washington, D.C.

And, critics add, fair trade doesn't help the very poorest farmers, those who don't own land or aren't members of a growers' co-op, because the movement aims primarily to help small land-owning farmers. Large coffee plantations and their workers are barred from certification. "The cooperative system can end up discriminating against people who uphold the values of the fair trade movement but who happen to be part of bigger farms, or just don't want to join a cooperative," according to Lawrence Solomon, director of the Energy Probe Research Foundation, a Toronto firm that analyzes trade and consumer issues. [6]

Responding to free-marketers, other analysts say fair trade is sending an accurate market signal: Some consumers are willing to pay more for a product when they know the producer is paid fairly. The movement has been savvy enough to focus on the fastest-growing slice of the coffee market — the gourmet sector — and recently has been winning awards at international tasting competitions.

When Britain's Twin Trading Ltd. first started marketing fair trade coffee, the product had a reputation for poor quality, and "everyone laughed at us," says Communication Manager Simon Billing. "Now everyone's talking about its chocolaty, velvety flavors," he says at the firm's London headquarters, as a white-coated quality-control taster swishes samples of Peruvian coffees in his mouth and spits them into a bowl.

"If you talk to gourmet coffee or chocolate companies, they will say there's not enough good-quality coffee or chocolate out there," says sociologist Laura T. Raynolds, co-director of Colorado State University's

How Fair Trade Guarantees Safety Net

Fair trade certification guarantees coffee farmers a minimum price of $1.26 per pound — $1.21 per pound plus a five-cent "social premium" to fund community projects (dotted line). When the world market price of coffee plummets, as in 2001-2002, the fair trade price remains stable and can be twice the market price. If the market price rises above $1.21, as it did last January, the fair trade minimum meets it, plus pays the social premium.*

Fair Trade Price vs. Market Price, Arabica Beans, 1997-Present

(Price in $)

Market price
Fair trade price

Jan. 1997 / Jan. 98 / Jan. 99 / Jan. 2000 / Jan. 01 / Jan. 02 / Jan. 03 / Jan. 04 / Jan. 05 / Jan. 06 / Jan. 07

* Under new rules starting June 1, 2007, the social premium rises to 10 cents per pound.

Source: TransFair; Market prices are from New York Board of Trade for Arabica beans, the type imported to the United States under fair trade

Center for Fair and Alternative Trade Studies. "Fair trade is bolstering the capacity of producers to enter into this stronger specialty market." Indeed, as fair trade growers continue to improve their coffee beans, gourmet brands could lure them away with even higher prices than fair trade buyers offer.

Since 1997, the fair trade movement has been overseen by Fairtrade Labelling Organizations International (FLO), a Bonn, Germany-based association of 20 national labeling organizations like TransFair. FLO sets minimum prices and standards and monitors sites wherever fair trade products are grown and produced. Organizations like TransFair USA — the national labeling organization for North America — license and certify the actual buying and selling of fair trade products bearing their black-and-white label.

Most experts prefer the FLO system, with its independent inspectors, over efforts by corporate growers to create their own "fair trade" labels. Yet the *Financial Times* last year found seasonal workers for fair trade growers in Peru were paid below minimum wage and

U.S. Leads in Fair Trade Sales

With $499 million worth of Fair Trade Certified coffee alone in 2005, the United States leads the world in the retail value of Fair Trade Certified products. The United Kingdom is second, with a value of $351 million.

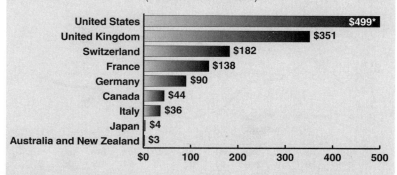

Retail Value of Fair Trade-Certified Products, 2005
(in millions of dollars)

United States	$499*
United Kingdom	$351
Switzerland	$182
France	$138
Germany	$90
Canada	$44
Italy	$36
Japan	$4
Australia and New Zealand	$3

$0   100   200   300   400   500

* Only includes Fair Trade Certified coffee. Figures for other countries also include other products such as tea, cocoa, rice, sugar and fruit.

Source: Fair Trade Almanac 1998-2006, TransFair USA

questioned whether the inspection system could keep up with growing demand for fair trade products. [7] (*See sidebar, p. 421.*)

Fair trade's roots can be traced in part to the broader "trade justice" movement, which seeks to reform world trading rules seen as discriminating against poor countries. Massive demonstrations at World Trade Organization meetings have been among the most widely publicized protests against the current "free trade" regime, which critics say favors wealthy countries' markets at the expense of developing countries.

For Americans who are not likely to protest arcane trade rules, fair trade products are another way of reaching them, says Laura Rusu, a spokeswoman for Oxfam America, a leader in the trade justice movement. Her organization is currently lobbying to reduce the billions of dollars in federal agricultural subsidies coming up for a vote later this year in the U.S. farm bill. Government subsidies to American farmers encourage overproduction of products like cotton, driving down the world price and putting farmers in Africa out of business, Oxfam charges.

"If we look at only one thing to achieve change for most farmers — it's definitely through changing the rigged rules at the international level," says Rusu. Fair trade certification is "something in the meantime where we can make a change."

Yet with multilateral trade talks at a stalemate and wealthy countries reluctant to give up their subsidies and trade protections, some academics agree with activists that fair trade labeling may be a faster way to achieve some of those goals. The labeling scheme "is essentially an end-run around the government; it doesn't rely on policy makers making politically risky decisions," says Michael J. Hiscox, a political economist at Harvard University. Ironically, even though the labeling initiative grew out of a left-leaning movement hostile to free-market ideology, it has turned out to be a "market-based solution that relies on good information," he observes.

When it comes to international trade talks, "we're not holding our breath," confirms Himes of TransFair USA. "We're taking an approach that allows us to assist growers right now and raise society's awareness as we do that."

As the market for fair trade products continues to grow, here are some of the questions being debated among consumers, activists and the international community:

Does fair trade certification improve life significantly for small farmers in developing countries?

The face of Nicaraguan coffee farmer Melba Estrada darkens when she recalls 2001, the "sad and difficult" year when the world coffee price fell to a historic low of 49 cents a pound. After Estrada had paid the half-dozen seasonal workers who helped harvest the coffee on her three-acre family farm, "there was not enough money for our own food," recalls the widowed mother of six.

The major standard-setting body for fair trade, FLO, aims to keep small farmers like Estrada afloat during those difficult times by setting a floor price calculated to cover the farmer's costs and provide a decent standard of living.

Is Fair Trade Monitoring Adequate?

Financial Times *uncovers problems in Peru*

Some critics have suggested the monitoring system run by Fairtrade Labelling Organizations International, or FLO, may be inadequate, or even weakened by corruption. A *Financial Times* reporter wrote last year that four out of five fair trade-certified farms he visited in Peru paid summer coffee pickers below minimum wage, despite FLO standards requiring payments in line with minimum-wage laws. [1]

"Our standards for small-farmer co-ops don't cover their payments to seasonal workers," responds Ian Bretman, vice chairman of the Fairtrade Foundation, Britain's labeling organization, partly because it's "nearly impossible to verify" at every farm.

Bretman stresses that monitoring is aimed primarily at verifying the price paid to small growers — the main group the movement is trying to help. While small farmers are encouraged to pay decent wages, they're not subject to the rigorous inspections carried out at larger plantations with many full-time workers, according to Bretman.

Officers with the labeling organizations also point out that the farmworkers interviewed by the *Financial Times* were still being paid more than the prevailing local wage. "Certification isn't a guarantee that nothing bad ever happens; it's a guarantee there are repercussions when bad things happen," says Christopher Himes, chief financial officer of TransFair USA, the leading labeling organization that certifies fair trade goods sold in the United States. "The *Financial Times* article was interviewing groups we were in the process of decertifying."

While FLO does annual inspections of cooperatives when they're first certified, its visits become more infrequent once a co-op is established after several years. In a cooperative of 1,000 farmers, only 10-15 of the farms might be visited, according to Bretman, so certifiers won't necessarily catch every violation.

In a written response to the *Times*, the Fairtrade Foundation said that of the Peruvian cooperatives mentioned in the article, one group sold only 10 percent of their beans on fair trade terms; another 15 percent. "This means they remain heavily at the mercy of the conventional market, often forced to sell for less than the cost of production" and "are often still very poor themselves." [2]

The *Times* reporter also quoted industry insiders saying non-certified coffee was being falsely exported under a fair trade label. The Fairtrade Foundation responded that FLO audits "had already identified irregularities in the supply chain in Peru" and had scheduled an inspection for the week following the appearance of the article.

Nevertheless, industry observers have questioned the ability of certifiers to keep up with growing demand for ethically grown coffee — possibly creating an incentive to misleadingly export non-certified coffee. Some also questioned the independence of the certifiers. FLO answers that inspections are conducted by FLO-CERT, a company owned by FLO but operated independently.

---

[1] Hal Weitzman, "The Bitter Cost of 'Fair Trade' Coffee," *Financial Times*, Sept. 8, 2006, at www.ft.com.

[2] "Fairtrade Foundation Briefing on *Financial Times* Article," at www.fairtrade.org.uk.

Currently, the basic minimum price FLO guarantees for coffee from Central America, Africa and Asia is $1.21 per pound, plus a five-cent "social premium" for community projects the growers' cooperative chooses, such as schools or clinics. If the world coffee price rises above the minimum, the fair trade price rises to meet it, and the fair trade importer must pay that price plus the social premium.

For example, on Jan. 4, the world price was $1.25 per pound. [8] So the lowest an importer could have paid for fair trade coffee was $1.30 (the world price plus the social premium).

While the five-cent premium may not seem like much when the coffee price is high, as it is now, fair trade farmers say the guarantee can mean having enough to eat in lean years when the price drops precipitously, as it did between 2001 and 2004. (*See graph, p. 419.*) During those years, fair trade farmers could sell their coffee at more than double the street price paid by local "coyotes" — or middlemen. [9]

Indeed, while small coffee farmers around the world received an additional $17 million in income last year as a result of U.S. fair trade sales, they received an even bigger premium of $26 million in 2004, when world prices

Fair Trade Coffee Sales Rise

Since 2000, the retail value of fair trade coffee sales in the United States has increased dramatically (left). As a percentage of all U.S. coffee sales, the market share of fair trade coffee rose from 0.20 percent in 2000 to 3.31 percent in 2006 (right).

Retail Value of U.S. Fair Trade Coffee Sales

(in millions of dollars)

Fair Trade Market Share of All Coffee

(percentage)

Source: Fair Trade Almanac 1998-2006, TransFair USA

were at a low point, even though they exported half as many beans. [10]

But how much does that improve individual farmers' lives? Estrada, who started selling to fair trade six years ago, says the extra income allowed her to convert her dirt-floor adobe hut into a cement home and make investments on her farm to improve the quality of her coffee.

Fair trade provides credit in cash-poor seasons, better information about current world prices and bargaining power, advocates say, especially for farmers like Estrada who live in remote areas and used to sell to exploitative itinerant buyers.

"We were fairly impressed by the range of benefits," says Douglas L. Murray, co-director of the Center for Fair and Alternative Trade Studies, who directed a two-year study of fair trade's impact on farmers in Mexico and Central America. "But," he adds, "our conclusion was most of the benefits were beyond income."

Murray found that fair trade cooperatives gave growers technical skills to convert to more profitable organic coffee, developed marketing strategies to enter the gourmet market and helped farmers diversify into other products they could sell in slack seasons. "The social premium in some cases resulted in some fairly nice ben-

efits, from health clinics and schools," he adds.

Yet those benefits only reach a minority of farmers and farmworkers. Only about 30 percent of the world's small-scale coffee producers are linked to fair trade networks. [11]

In addition, fair trade growers generally receive only a small fraction of the extra margin consumers pay. Take the fair trade cup of coffee sold at Costa, a London coffee bar. For several years, Costa charged an extra 20 cents a cup. But when *Financial Times* writer Tim Harford analyzed the costs, he found that more than 90 percent of that premium did not reach the farmer. The extra cost to Costa of buying free trade coffee beans should have translated to a cost increase of only 2 cents a cup, Harford calculated, since it only takes a quarter-ounce of coffee to make a cappuccino. The other 90 percent, he figured, went to Costa's bottom line.

"The truth is that fair trade coffee wholesalers could pay two, three or sometimes four times the market price for coffee in the developing world without adding anything noticeable to the production cost of a cappuccino, because coffee beans make up such a small proportion of the cost," Harford writes in his new book, *The Undercover Economist*. So why was Costa charging so much more? Harford's answer: fair trade coffee "allowed Costa to find customers who are willing to pay a bit more if given a reason to do so." [12]

Even analysts sympathetic to fair trade estimate that only five cents of an additional 20 cents the shopper pays for a pound of fair trade bananas would go to the farmers, largely because wholesalers and retailers all ratchet up their mark-ups. [13] Fair trade labeling organizations also charge fees to co-ops and wholesalers for their services — like inspecting farms — which are reflected in the price.

Defenders of fair trade say this is the way the free enterprise system works, and fair trade is no different. "This is a business, not a charity," says Billing, at Twin Trading in London. "We have no way of controlling the margins beyond what we're paying growers."

Even Harford acknowledged that at the time of his Costa study, the extra 80 cents-$1.10 a pound that fair trade was paying farmers could still nearly double the income of a farmer in Guatemala, where the average income is less that $2,000 a year. [14]

Still, some critics consider fair trade pricing deceptive for the consumer who thinks the extra cost is going entirely to the farmer. "It may be more efficient to provide that help by supporting a charity than it is to pay 40 pence (80 cents) more for your coffee when you don't know what happens to the 40 pence," says Philip Booth, editorial and program director at the Institute of Economic Affairs, a conservative London think tank.

"Only a very small percent of all the people who buy fair trade coffee would ever write a check to [a charity like] Oxfam," TransFair USA's Himes retorts. "For all the people who don't have writing a check to farmers on their top 10 list of things to do today, what we're talking about here is millions of consumers in tens of thousands of outlets."

Moreover, the money farmers get is helping them develop a business; a charity check is merely a handout, Himes adds.

The extra cost of fair trade products can also reflect the fees fair trade labeling organizations like TransFair charge to farmers and wholesalers, which Booth criticizes as excessive. But if consumers want the fair trade label to be trustworthy, Murray notes, labeling organizations need to conduct inspections, and charge fees to cover the cost.

Some critics question the fair trade premise that farmers should stay on the soil, where they're only earning a few pennies more — rather than improving their lot through education and city jobs. "Fair trade is about Western feelgood rather than transforming people's lives," says Ceri Dingle of WORLDwrite, a London cultural exchange organization. The fair trade movement's encouragement of organic methods means farmers are doing more weeding by hand and don't have access to modern agricultural methods, she charges, encouraging manual toil.

Indeed, free-market economists like Booth argue that fair trade doesn't work as a large-scale development strategy; usually it takes urbanization and industrialization to accomplish that. For farmers like Estrada, the most dramatic change from fair trade may occur in the next generation, when children leave the farm. Her eldest daughter is studying medicine — the first in her community to attend college — under a scholarship funded by fair trade social premiums.

Ugandan coffee farmer Sam Magona proudly holds a bag of Mt. Elgon coffee produced by his cooperative of 3,000 farms on fair trade terms. Magona was visiting the London office of Twin Trading Ltd., which buys his coffee beans for Cafédirect, a fair trade company.

Surprisingly, some leaders of the movement agree their effect on people's lives is modest. Ian Bretman, vice chairman of the Fairtrade Foundation, Britain's labeling organization, calls the experience of Uganda's Magona "very typical" for subsistence farmers. "They're barely getting by," he concedes. "It's almost utopian to think we can transform that position in such a short period of time." With fair trade, he says, "We hope people don't fall below the level where they can sustain a decent lifestyle."

Does fair trade certification distort markets, ultimately hurting some small producers?

Some free-market economists have suggested that the fair trade approach could ultimately hurt most farmers, especially those not fortunate enough or savvy enough to join co-ops that sell to higher-paying fair trade buyers.

In a widely quoted report last December, the weekly British newsmagazine *The Economist* took up that argument. "By propping up the price, the Fairtrade system encourages farmers to produce more of these commodities rather than diversifying into other crops and so depresses prices — thus achieving, for most farmers, exactly the opposite of what the initiative is intended to do," the magazine editorialized. [15]

In the case of coffee, the propped-up price encourages more producers to enter the market and drives down the price of non-fair trade coffee even further, "making non-Fairtrade farmers poorer," the magazine said. [16]

But fair trade coffee is still such a small part of the U.S. market — less than 4 percent — that the idea it could sway world prices is almost laughable to those active in the movement. [17]

"If we did get to that [influential] level of market share, fair trade is flexible enough that we can change the standards," says Charlotte Opal, chair of FLO's Standards Committee, which sets minimum prices.

And some economists say fair trade coffee beans are essentially a different market from the world commodity market, which determines pricing for run-of-the-mill blends for consumers looking for the lowest-cost product.

"They're two different products and have a different demand-and-supply curve. To the extent that the signal is, 'Consumers want more fair trade coffee,' the effect should be to get more producers to grow fair trade coffee," says Harvard political economist Hiscox. "And that is the correct signal."

Studies by Hiscox and others have shown that consumers of fair trade products are willing to pay a higher price for the assurance that growers are paid fairly. (*See sidebar, p. 432.*)

Yet skeptics like Booth at the Institute of Economic Affairs doubt consumers would be willing to keep paying a premium if the world coffee price sends competitive brands plummeting. Could wholesalers sell enough fair trade coffee to keep farmers afloat in a glutted supply market? he asks.

"Absolutely, we'll be able to sell," responds Rick Peyser, director of social advocacy and coffee-community outreach at Green Mountain Coffee Roasters in Waterbury, Vt., a wholesaler of fair trade and other specialty coffees. That situation "already happened in 2001," he says, when world coffee prices hit bottom. "That's when our fair trade sales started to skyrocket," as customers' sympathies were roused by news stories about the thousands of poor coffee farmers being driven out of business.

Some critics say fair trade unfairly creates insiders — those inside the fair trade co-ops who get superior prices — and outsiders, who are still beholden to market prices. "Whether it brings significant net benefits to the poor in general is questionable," the Institute of Economic Affairs' Booth concludes in an upcoming article. [18]

The poorest farmers are the least likely to benefit from fair trade, co-author Booth says, because they're not organized in co-ops and can't afford the certification fees charged to co-ops by labeling organizations.

"My concern is that the improvement for a small number of growers comes at a price — in particular restricting the corporate forms of the organizations involved by requiring them to be cooperatives," says Booth. He argues that co-ops are prone to corruption and mismanagement because there are no clear lines of authority.

Supporting that concern, a recent study of Latin American coffee cooperatives at Colorado State University found rather than democratically choosing a community project to fund from the five-cent-per-pound social premium, cooperative leaders have at times "made the unilateral decision to use the premium to cover operational costs." [19]

So why are co-ops a requirement? They provide the kind of central management crucial to checking that fair trade standards are actually being met, explains TransFair's Himes, and he says fair trade pricing provides incentives for small farmers to join them. "Dealing with the absolutely poorest unaffiliated farmer — that's not what fair trade does right now," he acknowledges.

Although cooperatives don't always live up to the vision of democratic institutions, Murray at the Center for Fair and Alternative Trade Studies says companies are equally prone to flaws in how management decisions are made.

Opal maintains that even farmers who don't sell to fair trade can benefit from a fair trade cooperative in their community. "We see prices for non-fair trade coffee going up" in those localities, she says, because "there's more information, and farmers in the village know what they should be earning." And projects funded by fair trade's social premiums, such as new roads, schools, clinics and wells, often benefit everyone in the village, she notes.

In the long run, the *Financial Times'* Harford speaks for many free-market believers when he concludes that "fair trade cannot fix the basic problem: Too much coffee is being produced." As long as growing coffee looks economically attractive, he argues, "it will always be swamped with desperate people who have no alternative." [20]

But it's hard to expect a coffee farmer, who must wait four years for trees to bear and who may farm on soil unsuitable for anything else, to turn on a dime in response to dropping world prices. "A coffee farmer who loses his land won't become a software engineer," observes Himes. More likely he'll join the illegal immigrants seeking work in some North American city, suggests Billing at Twin Trading.

Meanwhile, and somewhat contrary to classical economics, the gourmet retailers who buy from Green Mountain are willing to pay more in low-priced cycles to tide over farmers of specialty beans so they can ensure a continuing supply of high-quality coffee, Peyser says.

Would trade reforms help small farmers more than fair trade certification?

If buying fair trade cappuccino at your local Starbucks is not the answer to addressing poverty, in the eyes of free-market economists, what is? It's something that's "less fun than shopping," suggests *The Economist* in a widely cited editorial.

"Real change will require action by governments," the editors wrote, including "reform of the world trade system and the abolition of agricultural tariffs and subsidies, notably Europe's monstrous common agricultural policy, which coddles rich farmers and prices those in the poor world out of the European market." [21]

Similar U.S. government subsidies for crops like cotton and rice have been assailed by economists for encouraging overproduction of unprofitable crops, driving their prices so low that poor rice farmers in Ghana, for example, have been forced out of business.

Although they may disagree on the precise solutions — free-marketers want to remove all trade barriers, liberals generally want to keep some for poor countries — some prominent liberal economists agree that the current world-trade regime benefits rich countries at the expense of poor countries.

Since World War II, writes Nobel Prize-winning economist Joseph E. Stiglitz in his book *Fair Trade for All*, developed countries like the United States have been "somewhat duplicitous" in advocating that other nations reduce their tariffs and subsidies for goods in which the rich nations have a comparative advantage. At the same time, rich countries have been reluctant to open up their own consumer markets when it comes to goods where developing countries have an advantage. [22]

If governments really want to "make poverty history," as some British Labor Party leaders have pledged, they would change the way that world trade currently contributes to poverty, Stiglitz wrote in the *London Daily Telegraph*. Rich nations currently cost developing countries three times as much with their protectionist trade policies as they give them in aid each year, he estimated. A mere 1 percent increase in Africa's share of world trade would bring it some $60 billion, he calculated. [23]

In light of these huge monetary inequities, the relatively small fair trade movement may be a distraction from efforts to make trade agreements more equitable between rich and poor countries, some liberal economists worry. [24]

Oxfam America, which is lobbying to reduce some $4 billion in cotton subsidies to American farmers, calculates such a reform could increase the world price of cotton by as much as 20 percent. "When you look at a farmer earning a little over $100 a year on his farm in West Africa, an extra 20 dollars a year could mean his or her daughter going to school or a successful village effort at getting a well," says Oxfam America spokeswoman Rusu.

Recent multilateral trade rounds have continued to give the advantage to developed countries, which keep their protectionist trade barriers while persuading developing countries to drop theirs, according to Stiglitz. [25] The 2003 trade meeting in Cancun, Mexico, for example, ended in a walkout after many participants accused the United States and Europe of reneging on their promises over agricultural reform.

But even some advocates of trade reform doubt there's any life left in multilateral trade talks. "The Doha Round is in a coma right now, and it's unknown whether it will ever revive," says the Cato Institute's Lindsey, an advocate for reductions in U.S. tariffs. * "The outlook isn't promising for putting real discipline on our subsidies," either, he predicts.

That gloomy political outlook is one reason Harvard's Hiscox has become enthusiastic about fair trade as an alternative to trying to insert labor standards in trade agreements — for manufacturing as well as farming. Historically, poor countries have opposed such standards for fear they'll lose their cheap-labor advantage when it comes to exporting goods. And inserting economic penalties for countries that violate labor standards could ultimately hurt poor farmers in those countries and stifle economic growth, he points out.

On the other hand, if higher fair trade prices actually compensated firms for their higher labor costs, "everyone

---

* The so-called Doha Round in Doha, Qatar, in 2002 launched a new round of multilateral trade talks focusing on aiding poor countries.

CHRONOLOGY

1940s-1960s *Churches and philanthropies sell Third World handicrafts, returning profits directly to craftsmen. Post-World War II attempts to liberalize trade begin.*

1948 U.N.'s General Agreement on Tariffs and Trade (GATT) is set up, begins "rounds" of negotiations to reduce trade barriers.

1965 British humanitarian organization Oxfam starts "helping by selling" program, leading to sales of Third World crafts.

1980s *World coffee prices plunge, impoverishing thousands of small farmers; early fair trade labeling efforts start to pick up steam.*

1986 Equal Exchange, a worker-owned cooperative in the United States, begins importing and roasting only "fairly traded" coffee.

1988 The Max Havelaar Foundation in the Netherlands begins marketing coffee under its own label, certifying that a guaranteed minimum price is being paid to the farmers.

1990s *Fair trade labeling efforts start in England and United States; international umbrella group formed to set fair prices and inspect farms; EU expresses support; coffee becomes dominant product.*

1992 Oxfam and other philanthropic groups in England establish the Fairtrade Foundation, Britain's third-party auditor of fair trade practices.

1997 Fairtrade Foundation and labeling groups in other countries form Fairtrade Labelling Organizations International (FLO), to set prices.

1998 TransFair USA, the lead certifying organization in the United States, is founded.

1999 TransFair begins serious labeling effort; fair trade coffee sales begin average annual growth of 79 percent.

2000s *Major U.S. chains start selling fair trade coffee and other items; U.S. fair trade sales average 50 percent growth annually; activists demonstrate at international trade talks.*

2000 Starbucks introduces fair trade coffee.

2001 Demonstrators charging that trade rules hurt poor countries stall World Trade Organization (WTO) talks in Seattle.

2002 WTO launches new trade talks in Doha, Qatar, known as the "Doha Round," focusing on development of poor countries.

September 2003 Trade talks in Cancun, Mexico, end as walkouts charge rich countries reneged on reducing farm subsidies; first fair trade fair held at talks. . . . Green Mountain Coffee Roasters in Waterbury, Vt., begins producing fair trade coffee for supermarket chains.

2004 Fair trade organizations from 30 countries sign declaration at Conference on Trade and Development in Sao Paulo, Brazil, calling for fair prices for small farmers. . . . Wal-Mart begins selling fair trade coffee. . . . Starbucks quadruples purchases of fair trade coffee over 2001.

2005 McDonald's begins serving fair trade coffee blend in New England, Albany, N.Y.

2006 European Parliament calls for European Union to support the fair trade movement . . . The number of certified fair trade producer organizations reaches 586 by year's end in 58 nations in Africa, Asia and Latin America. . . . Awareness of fair trade label among U.S. coffee drinkers rises to 20 percent from 7 percent in 2003.

Feb. 14, 2007 On Valentine's Day Divine Chocolate, a U.S. fair trade chocolate, is launched.

March 2007 Whole Foods Market chain announces it will sell TransFair-labeled products, with 10-year goal of making half of imported foods from the developing world fair trade. . . . TransFair announces more than 600 U.S. businesses carry fair trade products in about 40,000 retail outlets. . . . Fair trade coffee, fastest-growing segment of U.S. specialty market, sells $730 million retail in 2006.

could win," he writes, and "it could be possible to improve working conditions without adversely affecting investment and growth in developing countries." [26]

Trade justice activists, as advocates for reform of international trade rules are known, are reluctant to admit to internal tension within their movement caused by fair trade activists, but there are some differences. "You can admit fair trade is part of a solution to a much bigger problem — one way of addressing poverty, but it's not a panacea and will not fix the problem overall," says Amy Barry, trade spokeswoman for Oxfam International, a leader in the trade justice movement and a founder of Fairtrade International, the British fair trade labeling organization.

Leaders of the fair trade movement in both Britain and America say they're linked in principle to the goals of the larger trade justice movement. But they say fair trade offers a market solution right now while the prospects for trade reform look dim. And, Oxfam's Rusu agrees, "given that it will take some time to get to a fair international-trading system, fair trade-certified products encourage consumers to use their dollar to choose products that are more fair."

The big question, according to Colorado State sociologist Raynolds, is: "Does an initiative like fair trade heighten awareness of inequalities in our current trade system so we can start to get the consensus and effort to get some significant reforms?"

BACKGROUND

Rise of Fair Trade

The roots of fair trade can be traced to projects initiated by churches in North America and Europe in the late 1940s to provide relief to refugees and other poverty-stricken communities by selling their handicrafts to wealthier markets.

In Western Europe, just after World War II, charities began to import handicrafts from impoverished Eastern Europe to promote economic development. [27] In the United States, around the same time, the Mennonite Central Committee began to develop a market for embroidery from Puerto Rico by creating a crafts-selling organization that would become known as Ten Thousand Villages.

By the 1960s, these initiatives had evolved into "world shops," marketing goods from the developing world. Their goal was to eliminate middlemen and return more of the profits to Third World craftsmen. Oxfam led this effort with its "helping by selling" program in 1965, marketing imported handicrafts in its charity shops in England. [28]

The first independent fair trade labeling initiative began in the Netherlands in 1988, when world coffee prices started to plunge. The Max Havelaar Foundation began marketing coffee under its own label, certifying that a guaranteed minimum price was being paid to the farmers.

Oxfam followed in 1992, joining with four other British philanthropic groups to establish the Fairtrade Foundation, Britain's third-party auditor of fair trade practices. Today, affiliated fair trade certifying organizations are active in Europe, Australia, New Zealand, Canada, Japan, Mexico and the United States.

In 1997, the Fairtrade Foundation joined with other national initiatives to form the umbrella Fairtrade Labelling Organizations International (FLO), to pool certification and marketing efforts. The FLO subsequently established detailed standards for certified commodities governing pricing and labor standards. It monitors producer and trader groups to ensure compliance and may de-certify groups for failing to meet the criteria. [29]

To ensure fair prices, producers must receive a guaranteed minimum price and an additional "social premium" for community projects, set separately for each product by FLO.

FLO has developed specific standards for coffee, tea, cocoa, quinoa, bananas, cane sugar, rice, cotton, wine grapes, nuts and oil seeds, dried fruit, fresh fruit and vegetables, fruit juices, herbs and spices, flowers and plants. Until the recent introduction of fair trade cotton goods, sports balls were the only manufactured item certified by FLO.

For coffee, the main fair trade product, FLO requires that producers be small, family-based growers organized into politically independent democratic organizations — cooperatives — and that they limit the use of environmentally harmful chemicals. FLO has developed separate standards for operations employing large numbers of workers, such as farms growing tea, bananas and other fruit.

Importers of fair trade products must comply with another set of FLO standards aimed at giving cash-poor farmers, often beholden to extortionate money-lenders, credit at reasonable rates: Buyers must agree to long-term purchasing agreements (beyond one year) and provide advance financing to farmers.

Fair Trade Towns Boost Consumer Awareness

Business picks up too in British, Pennsylvania towns

Outside Bar 19 in England's Avon River Valley, a chalkboard proudly proclaims the "Fair Trade" menu. Inside, lunchtime tables filled with parents and children on Easter break testify to the restaurant's successful transformation from a seedy bar to popular — and socially conscious — family spot.

In 2003, when Richard Smith reopened the café with blond wood paneling in the picturesque town of Keynsham, he advertised it as an "alternative" venue featuring organic and local products and the first smoke-free dining environment in town. But he was reluctant to load the menu with fair trade items, fearing customers would think "they're overpaying for poor quality foods."

Confidence replaced reluctance a year later, when Keynsham, nestled in an agricultural river valley between Bath and Bristol, started a campaign to become a "fair trade town." The town council passed a unanimous resolution pledging to serve fair trade tea and coffee at town functions, encourage businesses to sell fair trade products and promote the concept of fair trade in the schools and local media. To qualify, the town of 15,000 residents had to satisfy the Fairtrade Foundation, Britain's lead fair trade labeling and certifying organization.

The proliferation of fair trade towns — at last count 262 in the U.K. — helps explain the rapid growth in British consumption of fair trade goods, some activists believe. The movement started in 2000 when Garstang, a small market town in Northern England, declared itself

Richard Smith finds that patrons willingly accept fair trade products at his Bar 19 in Keynsham, in England's Avon River Valley.

CQ Press/Sarah Glazer

"fair trade." A year later, 71 percent of the town's residents recognized the "Fairtrade" label, compared to about 20 percent nationally. Today, more than half of adults in Britain recognize the label. [1]

Keynsham's campaign made it possible for Smith to do "a lot less advertising" to convince customers fair trade foods could be good quality and well-priced. Smith started promoting fair trade wines from South Africa and rum from Paraguay, which he features in the café's rum cake. (The tea, coffee and even pineapple juice are fair trade, too.) If anything, fair trade helped his business grow, he says.

"This is a good example of where fair trade has added to the business and is part of its identity," says Rachel Ward, a Keynsham official who kick-started the campaign. "Fair trade is a way of telling people this is a place worth shopping." Local officials hope fair trade status will help revive the main shopping street of the historic market town and even draw some of the tourists who flock to nearby Bath.

Across the "pond," attracting visitors and shoppers also figured in support for turning Media, Pa. into the first — and so far the only — fair trade town in the United States. When Media resident Elizabeth Killough pitched the idea to the local business association, she says, "They got it right away" as a way to attract "conscious consumers" — the well-heeled niche that goes for organic and fair trade products. Though Media has only 5,000 residents, restaurants and shops on its quaint Main Street compete for a daytime population of around 25,000 who converge on the county seat.

The idea was the brainchild of local tour magnate Hal Taussig, whose Untours Foundation makes low-interest loans abroad to create jobs and support fair trade products. "My own interest is to get all the merchants in Media to sell fair trade goods so when you walk down the street and ask people, 'What is Fair Trade?' they'll know what it is," says Taussig who donates the profits of his tour company to the foundation.

Media's town fathers decided to adopt the same criteria used in Britain after they learned how Garstang had pioneered the concept.

"As far as bringing people to Media, anything we can do to promote our town in a positive way is a bonus. And we're getting recognition around the country from other towns," says Media Borough Councilwoman Monica Simpson.

Media's restaurants were surprisingly resistant to serving fair trade coffee, because they usually rely on a single distributor for pre-measured coffee and urns, says Killough, associate director of the Untours Foundation. A supplier was finally located who had started offering fair trade coffee to compete for contracts at college campuses, where students demanded it.

Similarly, when Keynsham approached its largest employer, Cadbury Chocolate, about serving fair trade products in its employee canteen, the company resisted on the grounds its food supplier didn't offer them, town officials say. It's no small irony that the work force at the chocolate plant has been decimated as Cadbury jobs have migrated overseas to low-wage countries.

The chocolate giant does not carry the fair trade label on most of its products although it says on its Web site that it pays its growers a fair return.[2] But local employees still decided to put in a vending machine featuring fair trade hot drinks at the social club on the plant's campus.

In Garstang, the inspiration for fair trade germinated in 1999, when veterinarian Bruce Crowther attended workshops by the British charity Oxfam on Third World poverty, which condemned unfair trade practices. "They drew my attention to the realization that a child is dying somewhere in the world every two to three seconds because of poverty," he recalls. "That statistic totally horrified me."

Crowther draws a direct line from his activism as coordinator of Britain's fair trade towns initiative to 19th-century abolitionists, who campaigned against the slavery on sugar plantations with brochures asking, "What price is your sugar?"

Local official Rachel Ward, right, helped turn Keynsham into one of Great Britain's 262 fair trade towns.

"It's absolutely the same argument today," Crowther says, for products that rich countries can buy cheaply because they pay Third World farmers so poorly. "It's morally unacceptable that people should suffer in order for us to get sugar for a cheap price," he declares.

Garstang is mirroring the slave triangle of more than 200 years ago — but in a reverse, fair trade image. In the 1800s, the triangle connected neighboring Lancaster, Britain's fourth-largest slave-trading port; Ghana, the source of the slaves; and the former American colonies where slaves were shipped. Since 2002, Garstang has forged a cultural exchange with a town in Ghana, New Koforidua, home to cocoa farmers selling to fair trade. In March, Garstang also accepted an invitation to become a twin town with Media, once an important stop for runaway slaves on the Underground Railroad.

---

[1] Elisa Arond, "The Fairtrade Towns Initiative: Lessons from across the Ocean," May 2006, Oxfam America, pp. 15, 40.

[2] "Fairtrade is not the only way to ensure farmers receive a fair return for their crops," the Web site notes, since many farmers are not in cooperatives as required by the Fairtrade Foundation. See www.cadburyschweppes.com/EN/EnvironmentSociety/EthicalTrading/fair_trade.htm.

By the end of 2006, there were 586 certified fair trade producer organizations in 58 developing nations in Africa, Asia and Latin America. [30]

U.S. Enters Market

As the fair trade market picked up steam through the 1980s, coffee quickly became the dominant product. [31] In the United States, the pioneer in the market was Equal Exchange, a worker-owned cooperative in West Bridgewater, Mass., which began importing and roasting only "fairly traded" coffee in 1986.

TransFair USA, the lead American certifying organization, opened in 1998 and began a serious labeling effort the following year. Since then, fair trade coffee sales have grown an average of 79 percent annually, according to TransFair, and coffee remains the dominant crop.

In addition to coffee, TransFair introduced fair trade-certified tea and cocoa to the U.S. market. Sugar, rice and vanilla recently came under its label. Flowers, wine and nuts are new products on the horizon, according to Chief Financial Officer Himes.

Total U.S. sales of fair trade-certified products grew by 350 percent between 2001 and 2005 and by 60 percent between 2004 and 2005, estimates Harvard's Hiscox. [32] Today, more than 600 U.S. businesses carry fair trade products in about 40,000 retail outlets, according to TransFair USA. (For a list of stores, go to www.transfairusa.org.)

Much of the rapid U.S. growth is due to the "mainstreaming" of fair trade beginning in 2000, when Starbucks introduced fair trade coffee. In 2003, Green Mountain Coffee Roasters began producing fair trade coffees for large supermarket chains, and in 2004, Wal-Mart began selling it. Starbucks quadrupled its purchases of fair trade coffee between 2001 and 2004. [33]

In 2005, McDonald's introduced a fair trade coffee blend created for it by Green Mountain and Newman's Own Organics, which the chain now serves in 650 restaurants in New England and Albany, N.Y. But McDonald's doesn't tell customers the coffee — the only kind served in those restaurants — is fair trade. Indeed fair trade was not the main reason behind McDonald's choice. According to McDonald's USA spokeswoman Danya Proud, the "main impetus" was that "Green Mountain is a name well-known in that part of the country, and the quality of the coffee is high."

The United States currently accounts for almost a third of global fair trade sales, and Europe almost two-thirds. [34] The enormous scale of the American consumer market, especially for coffee, makes the United States the largest single consumer of fair trade goods. But as individuals, European consumers spend far more per person than the average American. Swiss consumers spend about 20 times more on fair trade and Britons almost five times more than the average American. [35] In 2003, the average Swiss spent 19 Euros ($26), the Briton $7, and the average American $1.60 on fair trade products.

Awareness of fair trade labels among American consumers remains far behind their European counterparts, although it is rising. A recent survey of the nation's coffee consumers — those most likely to have seen fair trade coffee in coffee bars — showed awareness grew from 7 percent in 2003 to 20 percent in 2006. [36] By contrast, more than half of British consumers recognize the label.

Fair trade became well-known in the United Kingdom partly because nonprofits like Oxfam, with hundreds of thousands of subscribers, had been conducting campaigns about injustices they perceived in the world trading system some 25 years before they started the labeling system.

"By doing that work for so long, you have quite a lot of the population that knows something about it in quite a detailed way," says Sophie Tranchell, managing director of Divine Chocolate Ltd., a fair trade company in England. The development of fair trade brands like Divine Chocolate and Cafédirect, exclusively for fair trade coffee, and their growing presence in British supermarkets also contributed to rapid sales growth.

Trade Justice Movement

The growth of the fair trade movement coincided with growing concern and activism over trade inequities for poorer countries amid expanding globalization. Widespread attempts to liberalize world trade and bring the benefits of trade to all countries began after World War II. In 1948, the General Agreement on Tariffs and Trade (GATT), set up under the auspices of the newly formed United Nations, attempted to arbitrate international trade disputes through a series of "rounds" of negotiations designed to eliminate trade barriers between countries.

Since those initial efforts, the world has been moving toward reduced tariffs and restrictions on trade. For example, between 1960 and 1980, lending by the International Monetary Fund and the World Bank was often tied to requirements that developing countries drop their trade barriers. [37]

GATT and its successor, the World Trade Organization (WTO), succeeded in generating more free trade; total trade in 2000 was 22 times that in 1950. "Global inequality has also grown," however, note two advocates of fair trade, citing figures showing that the share of the world's income among the poorest 10 percent fell during this period, while the richest 10 percent got wealthier. [38]

As developing countries continued to liberalize their trade barriers, wealthy nations like the United States were increasingly reluctant to drop their protections for products for which developing countries had an advantage, writes economist Stiglitz. "As a result, we now have an international trade regime which, in many ways, is disadvantageous to the developing countries," he concludes. [39]

These tensions came to a head in September 2003, when a series of multilateral meetings in Cancun, Mexico, ended abruptly without any agreement on the major issues. The meetings were intended to follow up on a declaration made at the WTO's meeting in Doha, Qatar, in 2002. The so-called Doha Round launched a new round of multilateral trade talks focusing on aiding poor countries. But the Cancun talks fell apart in large measure because many participants felt the United States had reneged on its promises, particularly pledges to reduce its own agricultural subsidies. [40]

Philanthropic groups focusing on Third World poverty, like Oxfam, have become increasingly convinced over the last decade that "trade not aid" is the best route to alleviating poverty in the developing world. [41]

Meanwhile, college-student activists concerned about overseas sweatshops and child labor have at times merged with anti-globalization activists, whose sentiments culminated in violent demonstrations at the WTO talks in Seattle in 2001. [42]

Supporting a wider campaign for global trade reform and trade justice is one of three aims of the fair trade movement — in addition to alleviating poverty and empowering small farmers — write fair trade activists Charlotte Opal and Alex Nicholls in their book *Fair Trade*. "Fair Trade began as a campaigning issue driven by activists and maintains a powerful international network of lobbyists," they write. [43]

The movement's growing political impact, the authors claim, could be seen in 2004 at the U.N. Conference on Trade and Development in Sao Paulo, Brazil, which generated a declaration signed by more than 90 fair trade organizations from 30 countries call-

TransFair USA is the leading third-party certifier of Fair Trade products in the United States (left). Fairtrade Labelling Organizations International (FLO) is the worldwide fair trade standard-setting and certification organization (right).

ing for greater trade price stability and fair prices for small farmers in developing countries. [44]

An evaluation by researchers at the London School of Economics found no "direct impacts" on WTO rules could be attributed to the fair trade movement but noted its increasing lobbying presence at international meetings, including a trade fair at the Cancun meeting. [45]

Poverty activists' increased interest in fair trade has been sparked by the perception that international aid, the main alternative to the fair trade movement, "often seems to have had little long-term effect," note Nicholls and Opal. While aid can alleviate sudden world crises like famines, they argue, it "often fails to offer a developmental path for the poor out of poverty and dependence on outside support." [46]

CURRENT SITUATION

Government Support

Governments and political leaders in the United Kingdom and throughout Europe and have given the fair trade movement considerably more support than it has received in the United States, where politicians are more likely to scratch their heads over the meaning of the term.

In 2006, the European Parliament, in a largely symbolic move, unanimously adopted a resolution that called for a European Union-wide approach to support-

Consumers *Say* They Will Support Fair Trade

But what do they do at the mall?

A majority of American consumers say in surveys they would pay more for clothes and other products if they knew they weren't made in sweatshops. But do they?

In a 2002 experiment, University of Michigan sociologists placed two groups of identical athletic socks in a department store, labeling only one group as being made under "Good Working Conditions." [1]

About a quarter of the consumers were willing to pay more for the labeled items — far fewer than the 70-80 percent who tell survey takers they will pay extra. [2]

More recently, a Harvard study at ABC Carpet in New York City found that more consumers bought towels and candles promising "fair labor conditions" than similarly priced products without the label. Intriguingly, when researchers raised prices of the fair trade products 10 percent above the competition, sales rose even more. When they raised prices 20 percent, they rose higher yet.

"It was more believable that standards were higher if the price was higher," suggests Harvard political economist Michael J. Hiscox, whose team created the label, "Fair and Square," and presented it as ABC's own for the experiment. His tentative conclusion: Retailers could increase their sales and their profits by charging 10-20 percent more for fair trade-labeled goods. (Another possibility is that consumers think there's some hidden quality advantage in a higher-priced item. Hiscox is designing new experiments to tease out that question.)

But Hiscox cautions that shoppers with less money are less likely to behave like ABC's customers, who are generally "well-to-do New Yorkers with a taste for contributing to social causes."

Hiscox has become an enthusiast for fair trade labeling because he thinks it might be able to achieve what the World Trade Organization has not — better labor standards abroad. Unions and activists have lobbied for including such standards in international trade agreements, but developing countries like China and India have resisted for fear they'd lose their cheap-labor advantage in their exported goods.

So far, sports balls are the only manufactured item certified by TransFair USA, the lead fair trade labeling organization in the U.S., which focuses on paying small farmers fairly. Cotton goods are the newest product to win fair trade labeling in Britain, but the label only guarantees that a fair price is paid to cotton growers in poor countries, not to makers of the garment.

No cotton goods are certified fair trade in the U.S. because of TransFair's concerns that it can't guarantee workers' conditions all the way up the manufacturing chain — from sewers to zipper makers. "Although African cotton farmers have a compelling story, that's not where the concern is in the U.S.," says Christopher Himes, chief financial officer of TransFair. "The sweatshop issue is very important to us. We want to make that the core mission of fair trade cotton garments in the U.S. We think we will do fair trade garments eventually, but we're not there yet."

Whether factory-made goods can be included in the existing fair trade labeling scheme — and inspected and certified in a way that's credible to consumers — is "the big enchilada," Hiscox says, if fair trade goods are to become a major player in this country's retail market and ultimately affect working conditions on a large scale.

"There are a lot of consumers that would like to advance [fair labor] causes while they're shopping," he says, "but we don't know how big a [group] that is and how much they're willing to pay extra."

---

[1] The study, by Howard Kimeldorf, *et al.*, is cited in Michael Hiscox and Nicholas F.B. Smyth, "Is There Consumer Demand for Improved Labor Standards? Evidence from Field Experiments in Social Labeling."

[2] A study by Marymount University Center for Ethical Concerns found 86 percent of those surveyed in a 1999 poll said they would be willing pay $4 more for a $20 garment made under good conditions. A 1999 poll by the National Bureau of Economic Research found about 80 percent of those surveyed would be willing to pay more. See *ibid.*, p. 8.

ing the movement. In previous resolutions in 1997 and 1998, it called on the European Commission to support importers of fair trade bananas and other goods.

The commission issued a declaration of support for fair trade with developing nations in 1994. And the 2000 Cotonou trade agreement between the European Union and African, Caribbean and Pacific nations called for the promotion of fair trade initiatives. [47] Several European governments also provide grants to cover the costs of certification for producers in developing countries. [48]

Is fair trade the best way to help poor farmers?

YES
Charlotte Opal
Chair, Standards Committee, Fairtrade Labelling Organizations (FLO)
Co-author, Fair Trade: Market-driven Ethical Consumption

Written for *CQ Researcher*, May 2007

To many poor farmers in developing countries, the free market is a distant dream. There are no roads connecting their farms to market, so they are dependent on middlemen to come to their farm and buy their crops. They do not have access to price information, so they don't know how much the middlemen should be paying them. They can't take out loans to improve the quality of their products, build roads to access more buyers or switch to a more profitable crop.

Fair trade turns this reality on its head by ensuring farmers the income and organization they need to make the market work for them. In the fair trade system, small farmers are organized into cooperatives that pool their income to buy their own trucks to deliver product to the market, apply for low-interest loans or hire experts to help them diversify their crops. Individual small farmers living hand to mouth cannot access these free-market instruments — but once they are earning enough to live on and are organized into a cooperative, the benefits of a properly functioning free market are finally available to them.

Guaranteeing that the extra money consumers pay for fair trade-certified products actually goes to the farms with the best living and working conditions requires audits and inspections, some of which are paid for by companies, and some by the farmers themselves. Companies that carry the Fair Trade Certified label must pay a nominal fee for auditing to a nonprofit certifier. In the United States, this certifier is TransFair USA, and each $1 of its budget guarantees an extra $7 in income to fair trade farmers and workers — quite a strong return on a social investment.

Farms must also pay an inspection fee, although it is much lower than the fees they pay for organic, food safety and other certifications. As fair trade is the only system that guarantees farmers more money, it is no wonder that more than 1 million farming families are willing to pay for these inspections to gain access to the fair trade market.

If we believe the free market is the best way to relieve poverty for the rural poor, fair trade is the only mechanism consumers have for making sure the free market actually reaches small farmers. American families who buy coffee, tea, bananas, vanilla, and other tropical products every day want to know that their purchases are empowering, not impoverishing, farmers and workers. Fair trade certification gives them that guarantee.

NO
Philip Booth
Editorial and Program Director, Institute of Economic Affairs, London

Written for *CQ Researcher*, May 2007

The best way to improve the lives of the poor is to ensure that the necessary preconditions for development exist. These include good governance, a favorable business climate and free trade. These three conditions are mutually reinforcing. One of the biggest sources of corruption in developing countries is the regulation of trade. The fair trade movement in Europe has the potential to do considerable harm through its campaigning for the restoration of trade regulation in the coffee market, though its position on the regulation of the cotton trade is more sensible.

The movement should stick to its basic business principles, the application of which can help some farmers in particular conditions. Fair trade can help farmers by providing credit facilities, contracts with price guarantees and business facilities and information sharing in unsophisticated markets.

But fair trade has its downsides, too. There is considerable reliance on inefficient and unaccountable cooperative structures. The fair trade price promise is not quite what it seems to well-meaning and possibly naïve Western consumers. The various fair trade organizations do not promise to buy the farmers' produce at the price. They buy at a fixed price only what the market demands. In poor market conditions, there is a risk of "insider/outsider" markets where those who are able to sell at the price do very well at the expense of others.

Western consumers are probably also not aware that organizations charge wholesalers for the use of the fair trade label and that a huge proportion of this charge, in the U.K. at least, goes simply into marketing the brand. It is no wonder we only hear good things about fair trade! I doubt, too, that consumers know organizations charge producers to join up and that the fee is about 10 times the annual income of the average Kenyan.

Different business models have different disadvantages. There are, of course, costs and benefits of all ways of doing business, so the above points are not intrinsic criticisms of fair trade. In international development policy, we are used to important people campaigning for politicians to pull big levers. The reality is that once certain preconditions for development are in place, prosperity comes as a result of lots of people doing small things in the business economy. The fair trade organizations can help this process. But they should be modest in their economic claims and very cautious regarding their ethical claims.

© 2003 Fairtrade Foundation

Fair trade bananas are grown at the Juliana Jaramillo Cooperative in the Dominican Republic. Big banana growers are permitted to take part in the fair trade scheme, but big coffee growers and other large operations currently are not included.

In 2000, government agencies in several European nations began purchasing fair trade-certified coffee and tea to serve in government offices, including the European Parliament building. The European Commission has co-financed a project securing commitments from policy-makers to include fair trade criteria in public-procurement legislation.

Serving fair trade coffee, tea and biscuits in government offices can have a big ripple effect, says Divine Chocolate's Tranchell. "It's difficult for small fair trade product companies to get on the list of big catering companies," she says. "So if key accounts like government departments start to ask for products, then they're on the menu and other people can buy them too."

In Britain, the government has provided loan guarantees to help fair trade start-up companies like Divine Chocolate and has made grants to educate schoolchildren about how fair trade products help Third World families.

As Tranchell explains, the lure of chocolate "gives us an in" with kids. Divine Chocolate has used grant money it received with a nonprofit partner to set up a Web site named after its "Dubble" chocolate bar, where 50,000 young people have signed up as "a Dubble agent" to change the world "chunk by chunk." Another Web site provides teaching materials teachers can download.

More than 260 towns in the U.K. have passed resolutions declaring themselves Fair Trade Towns, a designation that requires the town's governing body to commit to serve fair trade products at town functions and to encourage local business to sell the products. Some activists think the designation helps explain the movement's rapid growth and high level of public recognition. Inspired by the British example, Media, Pa., dubbed itself the first U.S. Fair Trade Town. (*See sidebar, p. 428.*)

On Valentine's Day, Divine Chocolate introduced its brand to the United States. It set up headquarters in Washington, D.C., because "Divine Chocolate's mission is to be a highly visible and vocal advocate for better conditions in the chocolate industry," according to Erin Gorman, U.S. CEO. At a briefing on Capitol Hill, "there was clear interest on the part of Hill staffers about how the U.S. government might follow the example of the U.K. in supporting fair trade companies such as Divine," Gorman says.

However, some leaders of the movement say they're leery of government involvement, particularly since, in their view, interest-group lobbying has watered down the organic food standards set by the U.S. Agriculture Department. "I don't think we would look for legislation or even necessarily standardization," says TransFair's Himes. "It introduces complexity and politicking."

Coming in for criticism was a recent $8.6 million grant from the U.S. Agency for International Development (AID) to the Rainforest Alliance, an international environmental group based in New York, to certify products from more than 300,000 acres of forest and farmland as well-managed environmentally. The Rainforest Alliance label, which also pledges good working conditions, would apply to 90 million boxes of certified bananas and 30,000 tons of certified coffee through partners including Chiquita and Kraft Foods.

But the certification project could lead to an "undermining" of fair trade standards, according to Colorado State University researchers, because the Rainforest label is focused primarily on environmental management, and brings fewer benefits to small farmers and less reliability in monitoring them than TransFair's certification. [49]

Proliferating Labels

Competition from the Rainforest Alliance and other labels pledging good working conditions poses a challenge to the fair trade movement. Some advocates worry proliferating labels could lead to consumer confusion or distrust, especially if they dilute the TransFair standards. The Rainforest label, for example, avoids Transfair's fees since the organization doesn't have to pay for such extensive monitoring, critics say.

But some proponents of alternative labels say TransFair doesn't have a moral monopoly on judging labor standards. The Organic Consumers Association has campaigned against Starbucks, charging that by buying only a small percentage of its coffee from farmers certified by TransFair, the company has not made a good-faith effort to help farmers in developing nations. According to Starbucks' annual report, 6 percent of the coffee beans it purchased in 2006, some 18 million pounds, were certified by TransFair. [50]

Cooperative Coffees, a group of 21 small coffee companies committed to selling only fair trade beans, uses a different label — the insignia of the Fair Trade Federation — to distinguish themselves from competitors that sell only a minority of fair trade coffee. "Many companies use a few token Fair Trade items as a marketing tool to give the impression of being a fair trade company," says the group on its Web site. By contrast, each of the 21 companies claims to sell 100 percent fair-traded coffee, although not all of it has been certified by FLO. [51]

"The argument of the '100 percenters' is that someone like Green Mountain Coffee Roasters takes your customer account away by offering cheaper prices. And the reason they can do that is that most of their purchases are much cheaper coffee, because they're not paying the fair trade price on 100 percent of their products," says Organic Consumers Association National Director Ronnie Cummins. Fair trade products are about one-quarter of Green Mountain's total sales.

In an e-mail, TransFair's Himes responds that for growers, Starbucks' purchase of 18 million pounds at fair trade prices is "extremely significant." TransFair just certifies the product being sold, not the company, he stressed. "If we took the company-certification approach," he adds, "we'd have very few partners, and very few people would have heard of or been able to buy fair trade products."

Some activists also have expressed impatience with the slowness of TransFair to certify manufactured goods like organic cotton clothing, a market that is booming. TransFair has decided not to certify cotton now because

it is not yet capable of ensuring no sweatshops are involved in production, according to Himes.

The Organic Consumers Association has joined some 80 groups and companies participating in the Domestic Fair Trade Working Group, which is developing a new label that would certify products as both organic and fair trade.

"If we want consumers to be able to tell that the garment was not made in an exploitative factory, we need a label," says Cummins. "And we can't wait around for TransFair to decide it's a priority." Although TransFair encourages its growers to farm organically and guarantees a premium for organically grown products, not all of its products have government-certified organic status.

As for the proliferation of labels, some observers see it as a positive sign — that the marketplace is increasingly recognizing consumer demand for fair working conditions.

OUTLOOK

Growth Potential

How much further can the fair trade market grow? The American fair trade market is now only about one-fortieth the size of the organic market, which attracts similar consumers. If fair trade sales continue growing at their current rate, by 2012 they should match today's $15 billion-plus organic market, predicts Harvard political economist Hiscox. [52]

A major factor in determining how big the market grows will be whether large coffee farms, some owned by multinationals, will be allowed to enter the fair trade scheme. It currently bars them from FLO certification on grounds that the movement is trying to help the most disadvantaged growers. But some observers think big producers eventually will be included, as banana growers already are.

Market growth could also be held back by limited demand for fair trade products. Fair trade cocoa producers in Ghana, for example, could sell only 8 percent of their crop to fair trade, and fair trade coffee producers in Tanzania sold only 10 percent, one study found. [53]

By emphasizing high-quality products, however, the market will have a better chance of attracting new consumers, some observers believe. Fair trade-certified coffee is now the fastest-growing segment of the $11 billion U.S. specialty coffee market. [54] Yet as small farmers grow savvier about the market, they may take different avenues to capturing more of the final retail value of their gourmet coffees and chocolates.

Ugandan coffee farmer Magona says his cooperative would like to capture more of the profit margin taken by wholesalers and retailers for his prized high-altitude Mt. Elgon coffee — by processing the beans in Uganda instead of abroad. The Ethiopian government, meanwhile, has been trying to obtain trademark status from the U.S. Patent Office for three specialty coffees, an alternative approach that would allow Ethiopian farmers to keep more of the profit margin now charged by Starbucks, says Oxfam's Rusu.

But trade barriers blocking the importation of processed goods, opposition by established companies in consuming countries and the practical difficulties of developing a new industry in a poor country could hinder those kinds of efforts. If fair trade makes consumers more aware of trading inequities between countries, it might increase pressure for more equitable trading agreements, removing barriers to growers' efforts to do more of the processing and branding themselves.

As fair trade grows, another challenge for certifying organizations will be keeping up with the need to monitor more farms. Reports last year in Peru of some farmers selling non-fair-trade beans at fair trade prices might be a sign of the movement's growing pains. [55]

If fair trade is to make a major dent in the consumer market, some observers say, it will have to start including manufactured products, like cotton clothing, as Britain has already done. But experts inside and outside the movement agree it will be much harder to monitor sweatshops in the apparel industry, which often employs numerous subcontractors in a variety of countries before finishing a garment.

As savvy growers learn more about the value of their products, they may be lured into selling to high-end companies that aren't necessarily part of the fair trade system.

Would that necessarily be a bad thing? It might be if those companies abandoned growers during cycles of excess supply and plummeting prices — just the time fair trade helps them most.

On the other hand, some advocates say, the ultimate goal for the fair trade movement is to put itself out of business: When all products become fairly traded.

NOTES

1. In Britain, the label promoted by the lead certifying organization, The Fairtrade Foundation, spells the term as one word. In the United States the equivalent label, with a black-and-white symbol, approved by TransFair, is two words: "fair trade."

2. Fairtrade Foundation press release, "Boost for Farmers," Feb. 26, 2007; www.fairtrade.org.uk.

3. *Ibid.* The full range of Fairtrade products is: coffee, tea, chocolate, cocoa, sugar, bananas, pineapples, mangoes, oranges, satsumas, clementines, lemons, avocados, lychees, grapes, apples, pears, plums, fruit juices, smoothies, quinoa, peppers, green beans, coconuts, dried fruit (apricots, mango, raisins, dates), herbal teas, rooibos tea, green tea, ice-cream, cakes, biscuits, honey, muesli, cereal bars, jams, chutney, sauces, herbs, spices (vanilla pods, cinnamon sticks, ground ginger, ground turmeric, black pepper, cloves, nutmeg), nuts (brazils, cashews, peanuts), nut oil, wine, beer, rum, rice, yoghurt, baby food, flowers, sports balls, sugar body scrub, cotton wool and other cotton products.

4. Michael J. Hiscox, "Fair Trade as an Approach to Managing Globalization," memo prepared for the Conference on Europe and the Management of Globalization, Princeton University, Feb. 23, 2007, p. 7. Between 2001 and 2005, the average annual growth rate was around 50 percent; between 2005 and 2006 the market grew by over 60 percent.

5. More than 50 percent of adults in the U.K. recognize the Fairtrade mark. See Elisa Arond, "The Fairtrade Towns Initiative: Lessons From Across the Ocean," Oxfam America, May 2006, p. 40. Twenty percent in the U.S. recognized the Fair Trade Certified label in 2006. See Transfair USA, *Fair Trade Almanac*, 1998-2006, p. 18.

6. Sam Kornell, "The Pros and Cons of Fair Trade Coffee: Bean Counting," *Santa Barbara Independent*, April 5, 2007.

7. Hal Weitzman, "The Bitter Cost of 'Fair Trade' Coffee," *Financial Times*, Sept. 8, 2006; www.ft.com.

8. This is the world price for Arabica, the type of beans TransFair USA imports to the United States. The $1.21 fair trade floor price is for Arabica.

9. Douglas L. Murray, *et al.*, "The Future of Fair Trade Coffee: Dilemmas Facing Latin America's Small-Scale Producers," *Development in Practice*, April 2006, pp. 179-192.

10. TransFair USA, *op. cit.*, pp. 4, 7.

11. Murray, *et al.*, *op. cit.*, p. 182.

12. Tim Harford, *The Undercover Economist* (2007), pp. 33-34. At the end of 2004, following Harford's questioning, Costa began to offer fair trade coffee for no extra cost. The 40 British pence additional cost reported by Harford has been converted to U.S. currency using current exchange rates.

13. Hiscox, *op. cit.*, p. 5.

14. Harford, *op. cit.*, p. 33.

15. "Good Food? Ethical Food," *The Economist*, Dec. 9, 2006.

16. "Special Report: Voting with Your Trolley-Food Politics," *The Economist*, Dec. 9, 2006.

17. In 2006, fair trade coffee accounted for 3.31 percent of all coffee sold in the United States. See TransFair USA, *op. cit.*, p. 15.

18. Philip Booth and Linda Whetstone, "Half a Cheer for Fair Trade," *Economic Affairs* (forthcoming) June 2007.

19. Murray, *et al.*, *op. cit.*, p. 188.

20. Harford, *op. cit.*, p. 232.

21. "Good Food? Ethical Food," *op. cit.*

22. Joseph E. Stiglitz and Andrew Charlton, *Fair Trade for All: How Trade Can Promote Development* (2005), p. 12.

23. Joseph Stiglitz and Andrew Charlton, "The Way to Help Ourselves by Helping Others," *Daily Telegraph* (London), Dec. 12, 2005, p. 8. The estimate of $60 billion for Africa is an approximate equivalent of the 30 billion British pounds cited in this article. For background see Peter Katel, "Ending Poverty," *CQ Researcher*, Sept. 9, 2005, pp. 733-760.

24. Hiscox, *op. cit.*, p. 10. Hiscox cites economist Dani Rodrik.

25. Stiglitz and Charlton, *op. cit.*, Dec. 12, 2003, p. 6.

26. Michael J. Hiscox and Nicholas F.B. Smyth, "Is there Consumer Demand for Improved Labor Standards? Evidence from Field Experiments in Social Labeling," (unpublished paper), p. 2.

27. Alex Nicholls and Charlotte Opal, *Fair Trade: Market-Driven Ethical Consumption* (2005), p. 21.

28. Hiscox, *op. cit.*, p. 8.

29. See www.fairtrade.net.

30. Hiscox, *op. cit.*, p. 4.

31. Murray, *et al.*, *op. cit.*, p. 181.

32. Hiscox, *op. cit.*, p. 8. Total U.S. retail sales figures for 2006 were not available at press time, but according to TransFair, total U.S. fair trade coffee sales reached $730 million in 2006.

33. Hiscox, *op. cit.*, p. 8.

34. *Ibid.*

35. *Ibid.*

36. TransFair USA, *op. cit.*, p. 18. Statistics are from National Coffee Association.

37. Nicholls and Opal, *op. cit.*, p. 17.

38. *Ibid.*, p. 18.

39. Stiglitz and Charlton, *Fair Trade for All*, *op. cit.*, p. 13.

40. *Ibid.*, p. 4.

41. Nicholls and Opal, *op. cit.*, p. 22.

42. For background, see Brian Hansen, "Globalization Backlash," *CQ Researcher*, Sept. 28, 2001, pp. 761-784.

43. Nicholls and Opal, *op. cit.*, p. 22.

44. *Ibid.*, pp. 26-28.

45. Philip Riedel, *et al.*, "Impacts of Fair Trade," Trade and Market Linkages; Proceedings of the 18th International Symposium of the International Farming Symposium, Oct. 31-Nov. 3, 2005, p. 15; www.fao.org/farmingsystems/pdf/IFSA/Theme2_Trade_and_Markets.pdf.

46. Nicholls and Opal, *op. cit.*, p. 30.

47. Hiscox, *op. cit.*, p. 9.

48. *Ibid.*

49. Murray, *et al.*, *op. cit.*, p. 187.

50. Starbucks Corporation, "Social Responsibility-Fiscal 2006 Annual Report," p. 4; www.starbucks.com/aboutus/csrannualreport.pdf.

51. See "Frequently Asked Questions," www.coopcoffees.com.

52. Hiscox, *op. cit.*, p. 7.

53. Riedal, *et al.*, *op. cit.*, p. 7.

54. Fair trade-certified coffee grew an average of nearly 80 percent every year since 1999, according to TransFair.
55. Weitzman, *op. cit.*

BIBLIOGRAPHY

Books

Harford, Tim, *The Undercover Economist*, Abacus, 2006.
Financial Times columnist Harford downplays benefits of fair trade and says only a small fraction of the extra price consumers pay for fair trade coffee reaches small farmers.

Nicholls, Alex, and Charlotte Opal, *Fair Trade: Market-Driven Ethical Consumption*, Sage Publications, 2005.
Two fair trade advocates take a comprehensive look at fair trade's history, inner workings and impact on the market.

Raynolds, Laura, *et al.*, *Fair Trade: The Challenges of Transforming Globalization*, Routledge, 2007.
Researchers from Colorado State University explore the rapid growth of fair trade and future challenges, emphasizing the tensions of a movement working both in and against the market.

Stiglitz, Joseph E., and Andrew Charlton, *Fair Trade for All: How Trade Can Promote Development*, Oxford University Press, 2005.
Nobel Prize-winning economist Stiglitz and Charlton, a scholar at the London School of Economics, trace how international trade rules have disadvantaged poor countries and lay out their program for fairer trade rules.

Articles

"Good Food? Ethical Food," *The Economist*, Dec. 9, 2006.
A widely cited editorial charges the fair trade system could depress prices and leave farmers worse off by encouraging them to grow too much coffee and other crops.

"Voting with Your Trolley-Food Politics," *The Economist*, Dec. 9, 2006.
A special report lays out economists' arguments against fair trade.

Baggini, Julian, "Free Doesn't Mean Unfair," *The Guardian* (London), March 5, 2007, p. 9.
This editorial response by the editor of *Philosophers' Magazine* to *The Economist*'s criticism of fair trade (see above) argues that "fair trade is a triumph of the free market."

Booth, Philip, and Linda Whetstone, "Half a Cheer for Fair Trade," *Economic Affairs* (forthcoming, June); www.iea.org.uk.
The authors criticize fair trade from a free-market and moral perspective; Booth is editorial and program director at the Institute of Economic Affairs, a conservative London think tank.

Hiscox, Michael J., and Nicholas F.B. Smyth, "Is there Consumer Demand for Improved Labor Standards? Evidence from Field Experiments in Social Labeling"; www.people.fas.harvard.edu/%7Ehiscox/papers.html.
Harvard political economist Hiscox finds sales rise when prices of fair trade goods go up.

Ickle, Louise, "Graduate: Fairtrade for Fashionistas," *The Guardian* (London), March 3, 2007, p. 28.
Fair trade cotton clothing, which is certified in Britain, has attracted major department stores as buyers.

Murray, Douglas L., Laura T. Raynolds and Peter L. Taylor, "The Future of Fair Trade Coffee: Dilemmas Facing Latin America's Small-Scale Producers," *Development in Practice*, April 2006, pp. 179-192; www.colostate.edu/Depts/Sociology/cfats/research.html.
After two years of researching Mexican and Central American farmers growing coffee for the fair trade market, Colorado State University sociologists lay out the challenges they see for future successful growth of the fair trade movement.

Taylor, Jerome, "Café Society: The Rise of Consumers with a Conscience," *The Independent*, Feb. 12, 2007; www.independent.co.uk.
A journalist reports on how fair trade has changed the lives of Nicaraguan coffee farmers.

Weitzman, Hal, "The Bitter Cost of 'Fair Trade' Coffee," *Financial Times*, Sept. 8, 2006; www.ft.com.
A reporter finds fair trade farms in Peru paying below minimum wage and coffee beans falsely sold as fair trade.

A response by the Fairtrade Foundation is at www.fairtrade.org.uk.

Reports and Studies

Arond, Elisa, "The Fairtrade Towns Initiative: Lessons from Across the Ocean," Oxfam America, May 2006.
A report looks at the British fair trade towns movement, its role in raising awareness of fair trade and how it might be duplicated in the United States.

Quigley, Maureen, and Charlotte Opal, "Fair Trade Garment Standards: Feasibility Study," prepared for TransFair USA, July 2006; www.transfairusa.org/pdfs/FT%20Garment%20Standards%20Feasibility%20Study.pdf.
The authors conclude the complexity of the garment-supply chain means "much more work needs to be done" to decide if a stringent fair trade garment standard is feasible to develop in the United States.

TransFair USA, "TransFair Almanac 1998-2006"; www.transfairusa.org/pdfs/2007FairTradeAlmanac.pdf.
The lead fair trade-labeling group in the United States presents the latest statistics about the fair trade market.

For More Information

Center for Fair and Alternative Trade Studies, Department of Sociology, Colorado State University, B258 Clark Building, Fort Collins, CO 80523-1784; (970) 491-6044; www.colostate.edu/Depts/Sociology/cfats/index.html. A research group at Colorado State University that studies fair trade.

Cooperative Coffees, 302 W. Lamar St., Suite C, Americus, GA 31709; (229) 924-3035; http://coopcoffees.com. A group of 20 small U.S. and Canadian coffee roasters committed to selling 100 percent of their coffee fair trade.

Fairtrade Foundation, Room 204, 16 Baldwin's Gardens, London EC1N 7RJ, United Kingdom; +44-(0)20-7405-5942; www.fairtrade.org.uk. The leading labeler of fair trade goods in the United Kingdom.

Fairtrade Labelling Organizations International, Bonner Talweg 177, 53129 Bonn, Germany; +49-228-949230; www.fairtrade.net. FLO is an umbrella organization for 20 fair trade-labeling organizations around the world that sets prices and monitors transactions for fair trade-certified products.

Institute of Economic Affairs, 2 Lord North St., Westminster, London SW1P 3LB, United Kingdom; +44-(0)20 7799 8900; www.iea.org.uk. A free-market think tank that has been critical of the fair trade movement.

Organic Consumers Association, 6771 South Silver Hill Dr., Finland, MN 55603; (218) 226-4164; www.organic-consumers.org. A consumer association that has been critical of Starbucks' level of commitment to fair trade coffee.

Starbucks, 2401 Utah Ave. South, S-NV1, Seattle, WA 98134; 1-800-235-2883; www.starbucks.com. Perhaps the largest purchaser of fair trade coffee, although it has been criticized for its level of commitment.

TransFair USA, 1500 Broadway Ave., Suite 400, Oakland, CA 94612; (510) 663-5260; www.transfairusa.org. The lead labeling group in the United States for fair trade goods certified by FLO (see above).